1985

University of St. Francis

D0148615

THE PAPERS OF

WOODROW WILSON

VOLUME 48

MAY 13–JULY 17, 1918

SPONSORED BY THE WOODROW WILSON
FOUNDATION
AND PRINCETON UNIVERSITY

THE PAPERS OF

WOODROW WILSON

ARTHUR S. LINK, *EDITOR*

DAVID W. HIRST, *SENIOR ASSOCIATE EDITOR*

JOHN E. LITTLE, *ASSOCIATE EDITOR*

FREDRICK AANDAHL, *ASSOCIATE EDITOR*

MANFRED F. BOEMEKE, *ASSISTANT EDITOR*

PHYLLIS MARCHAND AND MARGARET D. LINK,
EDITORIAL ASSISTANTS

Volume 48

May 13–July 17, 1918

PRINCETON, NEW JERSEY
PRINCETON UNIVERSITY PRESS
1985

LIBRARY
College of St. Francis
JOLIET, ILL.

Copyright © 1985 by Princeton University Press
All Rights Reserved
L.C. Card 66-10880
I.S.B.N. 0-691-04708-1

Note to scholars: Princeton University Press subscribes to the Resolution on Permissions of the Association of American University Presses, defining what
we regard as "fair use" of copyrighted works. This
Resolution, intended to encourage scholarly use of
university press publications and to avoid unnecessary
applications for permission, is obtainable from the Press
or from the A.A.U.P. central office. Note, however, that
the scholarly apparatus, transcripts of shorthand, and
the texts of Wilson documents as they appear in this
volume are copyrighted, and the usual rules about the
use of copyrighted materials apply.

Publication of this book has been aided by a grant
from the National Historical Publications and Records
Commission.

Printed in the United States of America
by Princeton University Press
Princeton, New Jersey

921
W754b
48

EDITORIAL ADVISORY COMMITTEE

KATHARINE E. BRAND, *EMERITUS*

HENRY STEELE COMMAGER, *EMERITUS*

JOHN MILTON COOPER, JR.

WILLIAM H. HARBAUGH

AUGUST HECKSCHER

RICHARD W. LEOPOLD

ARTHUR M. SCHLESINGER, JR.

BETTY MILLER UNTERBERGER

113013

INTRODUCTION

As this volume opens, in mid-May 1918, Wilson is under increasingly heavy pressure from the Allied governments and his Ambassador and consuls in Russia to participate in a joint Allied-Japanese-American intervention in Siberia. Fighting has just broken out in Cheliabinsk between Bolshevik forces and Austro-Hungarian prisoners of war of Czech nationality, who by now are organized into what has been called the Czech Legion. Indeed, that legion will soon declare that, although its main desire is to fight on the western front, it is willing, should the Allies so determine, to remain in Siberia and, in cooperation with White Russian groups which are springing up, to take control of Siberia all the way to the Ural Mountains in order either to defend Siberia against German control or to pave the way for the reestablishment of the eastern front.

On June 3, the Supreme War Council, in Joint Note No. 31, proposes that the United States and the Allies send troops to Murmansk and Archangel to defend military supplies against the advancing Germans and Finns. Joint Note No. 31 also advises support of the Czech forces in Siberia, since they might become a nucleus of a new eastern front. Wilson is still extremely reluctant to take any action which, as he believes, would throw the Russians into the arms of the Germans. However, thinking that Trotzky has approved such action, Wilson agrees in principle to send a limited number of troops to the northern ports, but only if General Foch sanctions this diversion of personnel and shipping.

Wilson's hand is forced in Siberia by a series of events. On June 29, the Czechs seize control of Vladivostok, announce their determination to go to the rescue of a large body of their compatriots at Irkutsk, far to the west, and report renewed and serious attacks upon Czech forces all along the Trans-Siberian Railway by former German and Hungarian prisoners of war under German-Bolshevik command. While demands on Wilson to join the Japanese in a major effort to "rescue" the Czech Legion now intensify, he thrashes about for alternatives. One is the dispatch of a relief mission to Russia. The British and French encourage this idea, since they are convinced that it would also necessitate the sending of a large military guard. However, the pressure for a purely military intervention continues, and Wilson opens negotiations with the Japanese government looking toward the sending of 7,000 troops by each government to Vladivostok. The Japanese agree to cooperate but make it clear that they might be compelled to send a larger force. Hence, Wilson, in an aide-mémoire which he completes on

July 17, announces to the Associated Powers that the United States is prepared to "send the few troops it can spare" to Siberia, but "only to help the Checho-Slovaks to consolidate their forces and to get into successful cooperation with their Slavic kinsmen and to steady any efforts at self-government and self-defence in which the Russians themselves may be willing to accept assistance." In the same statement, Wilson makes absolutely clear his deep conviction that the war has to be fought and won on the western front and that any American action in Russia is in no way to be considered as "military intervention." What Wilson does not say in his aide-mémoire is that he is deeply suspicious of Japanese imperialistic ambitions in Manchuria and Siberia.

Meanwhile, the German *Friedensoffensive* to win the war in the West is in its first stages, and British and French leaders redouble their efforts to persuade Wilson to send virtually raw American recruits to be brigaded with British and French forces. As this volume ends, the issue of the titanic struggle on the western front is still in doubt; in fact, the Germans are still maintaining the momentum of their drive toward Paris.

On the home front, war production is now in high gear, and Wilson can turn his attention to other matters: takeover of the telephone and telegraph lines in order to avert a nationwide strike, the need for new revenue legislation, an investigation of the meat-packing industry by the Federal Trade Commission, and the problem of fixing the prices of wheat and steel. In addition, Wilson continues to work assiduously for approval by the Senate of the woman-suffrage amendment. In the immediate future loom the congressional and senatorial elections. Wilson writes a platform for the Indiana Democratic party, but, by the end of this volume, he has refused to become involved in various Democratic primary contests or to endorse individual candidates.

"VERBATIM ET LITERATIM"

In earlier volumes of this series, we have said something like the following: "All documents are reproduced *verbatim et literatim*, with typographical and spelling errors corrected in square brackets only when necessary for clarity and ease of reading." The following essay explains our textual methods and review procedures.

We have never printed and do not intend to print critical, or corrected, versions of documents. We print them exactly as they are, with a few exceptions which we always note. We never use the word *sic* except to denote the repetition of words in a document; in fact, we think that a succession of *sics* defaces a page.

We usually repair words in square brackets when letters are missing. As we have said, we also repair words in square brackets for clarity and ease of reading. Our general rule is to do this when we, ourselves, cannot read the word without having to stop to puzzle out its meaning. Jumbled words and names misspelled beyond recognition of course have to be repaired. We correct the misspelling of a name in a document in the footnote identifying the person.

However, when an old man writes to Wilson saying that he is glad to hear that Wilson is "comming" to Newark, or a semiliterate farmer from Texas writes phonetically, we see no reason to correct spellings in square brackets when the words are perfectly understandable. We do not correct Wilson's misspellings unless they are unreadable, except to supply in square brackets letters missing in words. For example, he consistently spelled "belligerent" as "belligerant." Nothing would be gained by correcting "belligerant" in square brackets.

We think that it is very important for several reasons to follow the rule of *verbatim et literatim*. Most important, a document has its own integrity and power, particularly when it is not written in perfect literary form. There is something very moving in seeing a Texas dirt farmer struggling to express his feelings in words, or a semiliterate former slave doing the same thing. Second, in Wilson's case it is crucially important to reproduce his errors in letters which he typed himself, since he usually typed badly when he was in an agitated state. Third, since style is the essence of the person, we would never correct grammar or make tenses consistent, as one correspondent has urged us to do. Fourth, we think that it is very important that we print exact transcripts of Charles L. Swem's copies of Wilson's letters. Swem made many mistakes (we correct them in footnotes from a reading of his shorthand books), and Wilson let them pass. We thus have to assume that Wilson did not read his letters before signing them, and this, we think, is a significant fact. Finally, printing typed letters and documents *verbatim et literatim* tells us a great deal about the educational level of the stenographic profession in the United States during Wilson's time.

We think that our series would be worthless if we produced unreliable texts, and we go to considerable effort to make certain that the texts are authentic.

Our typists are highly skilled and proofread their transcripts carefully as soon as they have typed them. The Editor sight proofreads documents once he has assembled a volume and is setting its annotation. The Editors who write the notes read through documents several times and are careful to check any anomalies. Then, once the manuscript volume has been completed and all notes checked, the Editor and Senior Associate Editor orally proofread the documents against the copy. They read every comma, dash, and character. They note every absence of punctuation. They study every nearly illegible word in written documents.

Once this process of "establishing the text" is completed, the manuscript volume goes to our editor at Princeton University Press, who checks the volume carefully and sends it to the printing plant. The galley proofs are read against copy in the proofroom at the Press. And we must say that the proofreaders there are extraordinarily skilled. Some years ago, before we found a way to ease their burden, they queried every misspelled word, absence of punctuation, or other such anomalies. Now we write "O.K." above such words or spaces on the copy.

We read the galley proofs at least three times. Our copyeditor gives them a sight reading against the manuscript copy to look for remaining typographical errors and to make sure that no line has been dropped. The Editor and Senior Associate Editor sight read them against documents and copy. We then get the page proofs, which have been corrected at the Press. We check all the changes three times. In addition, we get *revised* pages and check them twice.

This is not the end. The Editor, Senior Associate Editor, and Assistant Editor give a final reading to headings, description-location lines, and notes. Finally, our indexer of course reads the pages word by word. Before we return the pages to the Press, she comes in with a list of queries, all of which are answered by reference to the documents.

Our rule in the Wilson Papers is that our tolerance of error is zero. No system and no person can be perfect. There may be errors in our volumes. However, we believe that we have done everything humanly possible to avoid error; the chance is remote that what looks at first glance like a typographical error is indeed an error.

Readers will please note that Abbott Lawrence Lowell was misnamed "Amos Lawrence Lowell" on page 513 of Volume 43 and on page 12 of Volume 44. The name of this colleague and friend of Wilson was and will ever be Abbott Lawrence Lowell!

We thank our editor at Princeton University Press, Alice Calaprice, for her help in the preparation of this volume. We are grateful to Professors John Milton Cooper, Jr., William H. Harbaugh, Richard W. Leopold, and Betty Miller Unterberger—all members of our Editorial Advisory Committee—for reading the manuscript of this volume and for being, as before, constructively critical.

Once again, we thank Dr. Mary Giunta and Anne Harris Henry

of the staff of the National Historical Publications and Records Commission for their unflagging and always cheerful help to us in the search for documents.

THE EDITORS

Princeton, New Jersey
July 11, 1984

CONTENTS

CONTENTS   XV

Collateral Materials

ILLUSTRATIONS

Following page 358

Speaking at Mount Vernon, July 4, 1918. Mrs. Wilson at Wilson's left.
Library of Congress

David Rowland Francis
Missouri Historical Society

Etching by Bernhardt Wall
Princeton University Library

DeWitt Clinton Poole, Jr.
National Archives

John Kenneth Caldwell
National Archives

Austin Melvin Knight
Princeton University Library

Thomas Garrigue Masaryk
Princeton University Library

U.S.S. Brooklyn arriving in Golden Horn Bay, Vladivostok. H.M.S. Suffolk in the foreground.
National Archives

ABBREVIATIONS

ALI	autograph letter initialed
ALS	autograph letter signed
CC	carbon copy
CCL	carbon copy of letter
CLS	Charles Lee Swem
CLSsh	Charles Lee Swem shorthand
DFH	David Franklin Houston
EMH	Edward Mandell House
FKL	Franklin Knight Lane
FLP	Frank Lyon Polk
FR	*Papers Relating to the Foreign Relations of the United States*
FR 1918, Russia	*Papers Relating to the Foreign Relations of the United States, 1918, Russia*
FR-WWS 1918	*Papers Relating to the Foreign Relations of the United States, 1918, Supplement, The World War*
HCH	Herbert Clark Hoover
Hw, hw	handwritten, handwriting
JD	Josephus Daniels
JPT	Joseph Patrick Tumulty
JRT	Jack Romagna typed
MS, MSS	manuscript, manuscripts
NDB	Newton Diehl Baker
RG	record group
RL	Robert Lansing
T	typed
TC	typed copy
TCL	typed copy of letter
TI	typed initialed
TL	typed letter
TLS	typed letter signed
TS	typed signed
TWG	Thomas Watt Gregory
WBW	William Bauchop Wilson
WCR	William Cox Redfield
WGM	William Gibbs McAdoo
WHP	Walter Hines Page
WW	Woodrow Wilson
WWhw	Woodrow Wilson handwriting, handwritten
WWhwL	Woodrow Wilson handwritten letter
WWsh	Woodrow Wilson shorthand
WWT	Woodrow Wilson typed
WWTL	Woodrow Wilson typed letter
WWTLI	Woodrow Wilson typed letter initialed
WWTLS	Woodrow Wilson typed letter signed

ABBREVIATIONS FOR COLLECTIONS
AND REPOSITORIES

Following the National Union Catalog of the Library of Congress

CSt-H	Hoover Institution on War, Revolution and Peace
CtY	Yale University
DARC	American National Red Cross
DeU	University of Delaware
DLC	Library of Congress
DNA	National Archives
FFM-Ar	French Foreign Ministry Archives
FMD-Ar	French Ministry of Defense Archives
FO	British Foreign Office
InU	Indiana University
IOR	India Office Library and Records
JDR	Justice Department Records
KyU	University of Kentucky
LDR	Labor Department Records
MH-Ar	Harvard University Archives
NcD	Duke University
NDR	Navy Department Records
NjP	Princeton University
PMA	Allegheny College
PRO	Public Record Office
RSB Coll., DLC	Ray Stannard Baker Collection of Wilsoniana, Library of Congress
SDR	State Department Records
TxU	University of Texas
WC, NjP	Woodrow Wilson Collection, Princeton University
WDR	War Department Records
WP, DLC	Woodrow Wilson Papers, Library of Congress

SYMBOLS

[June 15, 1918]	publication date of published writing; also date of document when date is not part of text
[*June 26, 1918*]	composition date when publication date differs
[[May 18, 1918]]	delivery date of speech if publication date differs
**** ***	text deleted by author of document

THE PAPERS OF

WOODROW WILSON

VOLUME 48

MAY 13–JULY 17, 1918

THE PAPERS OF
WOODROW WILSON

To Charles Evans Hughes

My dear Judge Hughes: The White House 13 May, 1918

You have doubtless noticed that very serious charges of dishonesty have been made in connection with the production of aircraft.

Because of the capital importance of this branch of the military service, I feel that these charges should be thoroughly investigated and with as little delay as possible, in order that the guilty, if there be any such, may be promptly and vigorously prosecuted and that the reputations of those whose actions have been attacked may be protected in case the charges are groundless.

I requested the Department of Justice to use every instrumentality at its disposal to investigate these charges, and, with the approval of the Attorney General, I am writing to beg that you will act with him in making this investigation. I feel that this is a matter of the very greatest importance, and I sincerely hope that you will feel that it is possible to contribute your very valuable services in studying and passing upon the questions involved.

      Cordially and sincerely yours,   Woodrow Wilson

TLS (C. E. Hughes Papers, DLC).

To Newton Diehl Baker, with Enclosure

My dear Mr. Secretary: [The White House] 13 May, 1918

A few days ago you will remember I sent you certain charges against the Governor of Porto Rico which had been lodged with me by Mr. Gompers, acting for the labor organization in Porto Rico.[1]

I take pleasure in enclosing now a letter from the Honorable Felix Cordova Davila, the Resident Commissioner from Porto Rico in the House of Representatives, to which I have replied as follows:

"Your letter of May tenth gratifies me very much. My long acquaintance with Governor Yager convinces me that you are right in believing that the charges made against him are without sufficient foundation. Those charges are now in the hands of the Secretary of War, to whom I sent them immediately upon receiving them and I have no doubt that the Secretary would be

perfectly willing to let you see them and would welcome your
advice in the matter."[2]

Cordially and faithfully yours,   Woodrow Wilson

TLS (Letterpress Books, WP, DLC).
    [1] See S. Gompers to WW, May 6, 1918, and WW to NDB, May 9, 1918, both in Vol.
47.
    [2] WW to F. Cordova Davila, May 13, 1918, TLS (Letterpress Books, WP, DLC).

ENCLOSURE

From Felix Cordova Davila

Mr. President: Washington, D. C. May 10th, 1918.

I see by the public press of this morning that President Gompers
of the American Federation of Labor has requested the removal of
Governor Yager of Porto Rico on the ground that he is incompetent
and inimical to the best interests of the laboring element on the
Island.

I am extremely anxious to avoid the appearance of partisanship
in matter[s] affecting labor and I especially recognize the consideration that is due a communication from such high authority.

At the same time I am sure that this accusation will be received
with great surprise by the people of Porto Rico including a large
proportion of the labor element. While not wishing to appear as
rushing to the defense of Governor Yager, as I realize that he is
fully capable of meeting such charges, yet, inasmuch as the matter
has been given publicity and the charges against the Governor are
vested with a public character, may I ask, if entirely consistent and
agreeable, that I be furnished with a copy of the same. And should
you desire any further information regarding labor conditions in
general upon the island, which have culminated in these charges,
may I have the honor of being permitted to call in person and explain
the same.   Very respectfully yours,   Felix Cordova Davila

TLS (WP, DLC).

To Newton Diehl Baker

Dear Baker   The White House. 13 May AM [1918].

Will you not read these enclosures[1] as soon as you can. We should
discuss them at the earliest available time.   W.W.

ALI (N. D. Baker Papers, DLC).
    [1] Most probably the enclosures with EMH to WW, May 12, 1918, Vol. 47, one of
which is printed.

To Newton Diehl Baker, with Enclosure

CONFIDENTIAL.

My dear Mr. Secretary: The White House 13 May, 1918

I entirely agree with your conclusions about the enclosed matter, for they are founded upon unanswerable considerations.

Cordially and sincerely yours, Woodrow Wilson

TLS (N. D. Baker Papers, DLC).

E N C L O S U R E

From Newton Diehl Baker

Dear Mr. President: Washington. May 11, 1918.

General Pershing, as the Commanding General of the Army in the Field, now has authority by virtue of the provisions of Article 48, paragraph D, of the Articles of War, to execute sentences of death in the cases of persons convicted in time of war of murder, rape, mutiny, desertion, or as spies, without referring such cases to the War Department for revision or to you for approval. By a cablegram recently received from him he points out that General Haig and General Petain are each entrusted with a much larger authority in the enforcement of the death penalty, and suggests that an amendment be made in the 48th Article of War enlarging his power in the premises. The other offenses for which the death penalty are permissible are attempted desertion, advising or aiding another to desert, misbehavior before the enemy, subordinates compelling commander to surrender, improper use of countersign, forcing a safeguard, corresponding with or aiding the enemy, misbehavior of sentinel, assaulting or wilfully disobeying superior officer, failure to suppress mutiny or sedition.

You will understand that the death penalty is permitted in the last enumerated cases but may not be executed by the Commanding General of the Army in the Field without reference to the War Department and to you. My own judgment is that the power of the Commanding General ought not be enlarged in this regard, and I am not disposed to ask Congress to amend the Articles of War as suggested by General Pershing. My reasons are three: In the first place, the gravest offenses against military discipline are already included in the narrower class of cases in which he may so execute the law; second, American public opinion would, in my judgment, be less patient with summary execution than that of the other countries to which General Pershing refers—it will always be a safeguard to be able to assure people in this country that except in the gravest cases a careful review by the Judge Advocate General and by you must precede execution; third, there has been a good deal of agitation for increased severity in dealing with disloyal persons in this country, and I am afraid there would be some disposition to believe that the soldiers in our Army were being subjected to harsher and more summary discipline than disloyal and enemy civilians here at home.

If you do not concur in my judgment in this matter I will be glad to lay General Pershing's request before the appropriate committees, but I do not desire to take that course unless such regulations, if passed by Congress, would be in accordance with your judgment in the case.   Respectfully yours,   Newton D. Baker

TLS (N. D. Baker Papers, DLC).

To Jesse Holman Jones

My dear Mr. Jones: The White House 13 May, 1918

I would if I could give you immediately my definite promise that I will be in New York on Saturday evening to speak for the Red Cross, but I dare not.[1] I can only say that my present hope and intention are to be there, but I must frankly say that I cannot speak at the Hippodrome. I know by many years experience my limitations in such matters and I ought not undertake to speak in any auditorium larger than the Carnegie Institute[2] or some one of the larger theatres.

Confidentially, I would much prefer Mr. Cleveland Dodge as a presiding officer.

In haste   Sincerely yours,   Woodrow Wilson

TLS (J. H. Jones Papers, TxU).
  [1] Wilson was replying to J. H. Jones to WW, May 11, 1918, Vol. 47.
  [2] He of course meant Carnegie Hall.

To Jessie Woodrow Wilson Sayre

My dear little Girl: [The White House] 13 May, 1918

Here is the Secretary of War's letter about the Y.W.C.A. in France.[1] I am afraid it will disappoint you, but I must say that there seems to me a great deal of force in the position the Secretary takes, and I am sure that he means what he says in the last paragraph by asking whether there is any further consideration you would like to have him give the subject.

We are all well. My hand is practically well again, though I have to put ointment on it every morning and wear a glove during the day. I am now playing golf with two hands, though not very well.

Margaret is slowly working her way towards home through the camps, and we are of course very eager to see her.

Our days go as usual and there is really nothing to report, and it will be no news to you that we all love you tenderly and dearly.

Lovingly yours, ⟨W⟩ Father

TLS (Letterpress Books, WP, DLC).
[1] That is, NDB to WW, May 11, 1918 (second letter of that date), Vol. 47.

From Herbert Clark Hoover, with Enclosure

Dear Mr. President: Washington 13 May 1918

I enclose herewith the report on the packing house industry formulated by the committee appointed by you in response to my letter of the 26th March.[1] The report has been approved by Messrs. Secretary Houston, Secretary Wilson, Doctor Taussig of the Federal Tariff Commission, by Governor Fort of the Federal Trade Commission and myself for the Food Administration. I wish to add that two members of the Federal Trade Commission are not fully in accord and are of the opinion that there is no solution to the problem short of government operation.[2]

I should be glad to know if the course laid down in this memorandum meets with your approval.

Yours faithfully,   Herbert Hoover

TLS (WP, DLC).
[1] HCH to WW, March 26, 1918, Vol. 47.
[2] But see J. F. Fort to W. B. Colver, May 16, 1918.

E N C L O S U R E

11 May, 1918.

Having examined the suggestions of the Sub-Committee, we make the following recommendations to the President with regard to meat policies:

REGULATION

1. We recommend the continuation of regulation of the meat packing industry by the Food Administration and do not favour governmental operation of the industry unless it should be found impossible to enforce regulatory measures.

2. The auditing of the packers' bi-monthly profit returns to the Food Administration and the installation of uniform bases of accounts by the Federal Trade Commission should proceed as already settled between the Federal Trade Commission and the Food Administration. The present regulation by the Food Administration as to maximum profits should be continued to July 1st. In the meantime the Federal Trade Commission should report upon the reasonableness of these maximums. If found reasonable they should continue in effect until further notice. If found unreasonable such maximums should be made effective as facts warrant.

3. The packers should be required to report wholesale prices received for meat products and the transfer value of the principal by-products from their meat departments should be furnished by the packers to the Department of Agriculture for publication in their market reports as the Department may require.

4. The reports showing the wholesale prices of food dealers, now being made to the Food Administration, which includes the wholesale prices made by packers' branch houses, should be given local publicity to consumers.

5. The stockyards should be placed under license and regulation by the Department of Agriculture which should also establish a governmental system of animal grading under suitable regulations and methods of price reporting of actual transactions. Daily reports should be made on distribution and destinations of livestock, meats and other products from principal packing points.

GOVERNMENT AND ALLIED PURCHASES

1. The Food Purchase Board established last November by the Food Administrator, and the Secretaries of War and Navy, with the approval of the President, for the co-ordination of policies in purchases of official governmental agencies of certain food commodities, should extend its activities to the co-ordination of the purchase of packing house products by all official agencies.

2. It must be recognized that the meat purchases thus co-ordinated through the Food Purchase Board during periods of sparse marketing or during periods of extreme production broadly influence market levels in meat and in animals and, at such times as they do influence prices, they should be made in accordance with economic conditions as they affect both producers and consumers and at prices on one hand sufficiently stimulative to ensure production at a point necessary to furnish supplies of meat during the war period, and, on the other hand, at such ranges as will prevent extortionate prices to the consumer. The packers' profits should be controlled so as to prevent excessive charges and so that the policy

already declared by the President in cases where war buying dominates the market, that "We must make the prices to the public the same as the prices to the Government," may be effectuated. Any changes in prices the Food Purchase Board proposes to pay from month to month should be referred to the price committee of the War Industries Board for review and any substantial representatives of producers or consumers should be heard by them thereon. The advice of the Agricultural Advisory Committee, for the producers, through its Committee on Livestock, and the Department of Labour, representing the consumers, should be sought in event any substantial changes are contemplated.

GENERAL

1. The Food Act gives no regulatory powers with regard to retailers. It is desirable, however, that an investigation should be made of the conditions of the retail trade with view to determination of some constructive effort that may be made in retail distribution and it is recommended that a committee should be created for thorough investigation of, and recommendation upon, the subject.
2. The privately-owned cars of the packing industry should continue to be controlled by the Director General of Railroads.[1]

T MS (WP, DLC).
[1] About the publication of this statement, see WW to HCH, May 28, 1918, n. 1.

From Joseph Taylor Robinson

Dear Mr. President: [Washington] May 13, 1918.

I have just received your letter of the 11th instant calling my attention to an item proposed to the District of Columbia appropriation bill relating to the establishment and maintenance of a Bureau of Child Welfare.[1] As usual, I find myself in hearty accord with you, and it will afford me very great pleasure to present the item to the sub-committee, and, in the event it is rejected, to offer the necessary amendment on the floor of the Senate.

With expressions of sincere regard, I am
                    Yours very truly,   Jos. T. Robinson.

TLS (WP, DLC).
[1] WW to J. T. Robinson, May 11, 1918, Vol. 47.

From Gutzon Borglum

Stamford, Conn., May 13, 1917 [1918]

Statement in papers yesterday that I might publish any letters sent to me by you is untrue. I am incapable of that sort of business, nor shall I permit a controversy that is patriotic in purpose and in fact be diverted to any improper use by anybody on either side in any way that I can possibly control, nor shall I allow in any way any unfair reflections on the Executive that comes to my knowledge. I want you to know this and I want you to believe it.

Gutzon Borglum.

T telegram (WP, DLC).

To Thomas Staples Martin

My dear Senator: The White House, May 14, 1918.

I am sincerely obliged to you for calling my attention to Senate Resolution 241,[1] which in effect proposes to constitute the Military Affairs Committee of the Senate a committee on the conduct of the war.

I deem it my duty to say that I should regard the passage of this resolution as a direct vote of want of confidence in the Administration. The purpose which it undoubtedly expresses has been expressed again and again in various forms during the present session and has always seemed to originate in a rooted distrust of those who are at present in charge of the executive functions of the Government. Those executive functions are very clearly understood. They have been defined both by the Constitution and by long experience, and no one can doubt where the responsibility for them lies or what the methods are by which those who are responsible can be held to their duty.

Such activities on the part of a particular committee of the Senate as this resolution would look forward to would constitute nothing less than an attempt to take over the conduct of the war, or, at the least so superintend and direct and participate in the executive conduct of it as to interfere in the most serious way with the action of the constituted Executive.

I protest most earnestly against the adoption of any such action and shall hope that every Senator who intends to support the present Administration in the conduct of the war will vote against it. These are serious times, and it is absolutely necessary that the lines should be clearly drawn between friends and opponents.

Cordially and sincerely yours,   Woodrow Wilson

Printed in the *New York Times*, May 16, 1918.
  ¹ Introduced by Senator Chamberlain on May 9. It authorized the Committee on Military Affairs, or any subcommittee thereof, to inquire into and report to the Senate upon the progress of aircraft production or "any other matters relating to the conduct of the war, by or through the War Department." *Cong. Record*, 65th Cong., 2d sess., p. 6238.

To Franklin Knight Lane

My dear Lane: [The White House] 14 May, 1918

Of course, I am greatly interested in any plans to eliminate adult illiteracy in the country,¹ but I am very much afraid that under my present pledges to the leaders of the two Houses I am not at liberty to urge any legislation which has not some immediate connection with the conduct of the war. I shall be glad to help at any time that it is possible for me to do so.

Cordially and faithfully yours,   Woodrow Wilson

TLS (Letterpress Books, WP, DLC).
  ¹ Wilson was replying to FKL to WW, May 11, 1918, Vol. 47.

From George B. LaBarre¹

The President: Trenton, New Jersey May 14th, 1918.

Is George Creel a damn fool or just a plain nut? He is quoted in the New York Evening Sun of the 13th instant (clipping enclosed) as follows:

" 'What is meant by a loyal heart? was one of the questions put to him. Do you think every Republican and every Democrat in the Senate and House has a loyal heart?' "

" 'I don't like slumming; so I won't explore the heart of Congress for you,' replied Mr. Creel."²

It would be uncharitable to assume that an official appointee of the President having full control of his mental faculties would deliberately insult members of the legislative branch of our national government.

The word "slumming" has by common use been accepted as the act of visiting a low quarter of a city or town or visiting a place where debauchers or criminal persons live or resort. It is particularly offensive in the connection used by Mr. Creel.

If an employee of either branch of Congress were to wantonly insult the President of the United States, his dismissal would be demanded by a justly indignant public.

As a red blooded American citizen, I protest against the retention in office of an official who thus outrages the public sense of decency, increases the distrust of our national representatives and thereby promotes the growth of Bolshevikisa in the United States.

Very respectfully yours,   G. B. LaBarre

TLS (WP, DLC).
[1] Member of the City Commission and Director of the Department of Public Safety of Trenton, N. J.
[2] Creel spoke on May 12 at a public forum at the Church of the Ascension in New York. While not all of the New York newspapers saw fit to mention this particular question and answer, the *New York Herald*, the *New York Tribune*, and the New York *World*, although they differed in the exact wording, all agreed that Creel responded essentially as quoted in the text above. For Creel's explanation of his remark, see n. 1 to the extract from the Diary of Josephus Daniels printed at May 16, 1918.

From William Gibbs McAdoo

Dear Governor,   [Washington] May 14/18

I wish you would read the enclosed copy of a letter I have sent Baker.[1]

I dont think we are doing the intelligent thing in crippling the Railroads by drafting their skilled men. We are deliberately inviting certain disaster if the policy is continued.

Affectionately   WGM

ALI (WP, DLC).
[1] WGM to NDB, May 13, 1918, TCL (WP, DLC).

From Thomas Watt Gregory

My dear Mr. President: Washington, D. C. May 14th, 1918.

I am in receipt of the letter addressed to me by your Secretary under date of May 10th transmitting the Bill H.R. 8753 commonly known as the amendment to the Espionage Act,[1] with the request that I advise you whether I know of any objection to its approval.

With the exception of the last paragraph of Section 2, I know of no proper objection to this Bill. The provisions of Section 1, defining what are criminal violations, while very broad are not more broad than present exigencies require. With the use of a reasonable amount of discretion and caution on the part of law officers there should be no abuse of the powers conferred. The same observation is true of the first paragraph of Section 2, which extends the powers of the Post Office Department to exclude from the mails all postal matter which in itself violates any portion of the Espionage Act.

I respectfully call your attention however to the last paragraph of Section 2, which grants to the Postmaster General something more than the right to exclude objectionable matter from the mails and which reads as follows:

"Title XII of the said Act of June fifteenth, nineteen hundred and seventeen, be, and the same is hereby, amended by adding thereto the following section: Sec. 4. When the United States is at war, the Postmaster General may, upon evidence satisfactory to him that any person or concern is using the mails in violation of any of the provisions of this Act, instruct the Postmaster at any post office at which mail is received addressed to such person or concern to return to the postmaster at the office at which they were originally mailed all letters or other matter so addressed, with the words 'Mail to this address undeliverable under Espionage Act' plainly written or stamped upon the outside thereof, etc."

The enactment of this section involves questions of policy rather than questions of law, but in view of your request that I inform you of any objections to the Bill I deem it my duty to call your attention critically to the very sweeping grant [of] power here made. You will observe that under the language of this section, the Postmaster General would have power to deprive an individual or corporation of all right to receive any incoming mail *of any description* and by the exercise of this power could inflict upon such a party a penalty worse than a money fine and one which in some cases might conceivably destroy a whole enterprise. The power is in its last analysis more far reaching than the power of censorship whose effect ordinarily is confined to particular mail matter. This provision would also have an indirect but far reaching inhibitory effect upon the right of free public discussion the exact character of which effect it is not possible at this time to foresee.

It is true that the Postmaster General has heretofore exercised somewhat similar powers under the Fraud Order Section and the Lottery Section of the Revised Statutes, but in those classes of cases he has been passing in reality upon the intrinsic character of alleged fraudulent schemes and he has been guided by more or less definite standards. He has also exercised under Title XII of the Espionage Act power to declare certain specific mail matter non-mailable. The power granted him under this paragraph acquires its extraordinary range and potency from the fact that the standards defined in Section 1 are in themselves so vague and broad. They are necessarily made thus broad because they deal with the one subject most difficult to define, namely, the legitimate limits of free speech.

For example Section 1, makes punishable whoever

"Shall utter * * * any *disloyal*, profane, scurrilous or abusive language about the form of government, etc., or Shall wilfully advocate, teach, *defend, or suggest* the doing of any of the acts or things in this Section enumerated, and whoever shall by word or act support or favor the cause of any country with which the

United States is at war or by word or act oppose the cause of the
United States therein."
Taking Section 1 by itself, such language is not too broad; because,
upon a charge of its violation, the accused will have the full protection of his constitutional privileges and must be convicted by
proof beyond a reasonable doubt, to the satisfaction of a court and
jury. But under this paragraph of Section 2, power is granted to an
administrative official to practically determine this same question
of guilt or innocence, and inflict punishment without regard to
whether the same man could be legally tried and convicted under
Section 1. It is a power in the highest sense judicial in character
carrying with it the right to impose serious penalties, yet it would
be wielded by an administrative official.

In my opinion it is probable that the courts would review in proper
cases the exercise of the authority here sought to be conferred; but
because of the vagueness of definition and the broad category of
acts proscribed in the first section, it would be difficult for the courts
to interfere seriously with the exercise of discretion on the part of
the Postmaster General. Although some previous decisions of the
Courts indicate that this section may be constitutional, I am not
prepared to express the opinion that its constitutionality can be
successfully maintained. I take this view chiefly because of the
grant of power to the Postmaster General to refuse delivery of *all
letters* or other mail matter addressed to a person who in his opinion
has used the mail in a single instance in violation of Section 1.[2]

Respectfully,   T. W. Gregory

TLS (WP, DLC).
    [1] The Sedition bill, which the Senate and House had approved on May 4 and May
7, respectively, and about which see J. L. O'Brian to TWG, April 18, 1918, n. 4, Vol.
47.
    [2] Wilson signed the Sedition bill on May 16.

From the Diary of Josephus Daniels

May Tuesday 14 1918
WW referred to new plan of Senate Military Com. to sit in recess
and investigate & go to all places of war activity and virtually to try
to take over the conduct of war. W.W. had told Martin he wished
a record vote.

Should ministers be sent to England & English preachers come
here? Pres. spoke of how most English preachers came here and
regarded this as the mother country & that was not pleasing. Some
were condescending. Might do more harm than good

Bound diary (J. Daniels Papers, DLC).

From Charles Evans Hughes

My dear Mr. President: [New York] May 15, 1918.

I beg to acknowledge receipt of your letter of May 13th. Appreciating fully the gravity of the matter, I shall be glad to cooperate with the Attorney General in making a prompt and thorough investigation of the charges of dishonesty in connection with aircraft production. You may be assured that nothing would give me greater pleasure than to render any assistance within my power. I assume that the Attorney General will advise me as to his wishes for a conference with a view to the making of definite and adequate plans for the investigation and I shall endeavor to arrange my affairs so that these plans may be carried out with as little delay as possible.

I remain, with great respect,
                    Very sincerely yours,   Charles E. Hughes

TLS (WP, DLC).

From Newton Diehl Baker

My dear Mr. President: Washington. May 15, 1918.

I am unable to see that any useful purpose would be served by sending a commission to Porto Rico as suggested by Mr. Gompers and urged by Mr. Iglesias, to go into the matters that are the subjects of Mr. Iglesias' attack on the Governor.

That the accusations that the Governor has lacked interest in the war activities of the government are without basis is shown by the records of the Department.

Such a commission would find the condition of the great mass of the agricultural laborers in Porto Rico, if anything, worse than it is reported by Mr. Iglesias. The commission would find that even the poorly paid laborers in the sugar fields were in fact among the more fortunate of the agricultural laborers. The commission would find that the question of the days wage would be relatively unimportant, in view of the fact that so many people in Porto Rico can not get a day's work at any wage, except occasional[l]y. This condition is unfortunately chronic in Porto Rico and has been frequently reported by Governor Yager as well as his predecessors. From no official source has it been brought in question. As to agricultural conditions the commission would, therefore, have no divergent views to compose. Fortunately, these evils have not been intensified by the war.

There would remain then for the commission but the question of veracity which Mr. Iglesias raises between himself and the Gov-

ernor as to the extent of the recent strikes and as to the legality of
the methods used to maintain order.

The Governor's statements on these matters are abundantly cor-
roborated from independent sources.

Very sincerely,   Newton D. Baker

TLS (WP, DLC).

From Jesse Holman Jones

My dear Mr. President: Washington, D. C. May 15, 1918.

The meeting in New York will be under the auspices of the
National War Fund Finance Committee, Cleveland H. Dodge,
Chairman, at 8:15, Metropolitan Opera House, Saturday evening,
May 18th, Mr. Dodge presiding.

The plan is to have music by a good orchestra, and national airs
sung by a large chorus. We expect that Mr. Davison will return
from France about Thursday of this week, and after your speech,
the plan is to have a short talk by him. This will complete the
evening programme.

The reviewing stand for the parade will be at 23rd Street and
Fifth Avenue. The parade will start from downtown at 2 o'clock
and reach the reviewing stand at 2:40. Governor Whitman and
Mayor Hylan have also been asked to review the parade.

Reservations will be made in the reviewing stand and boxes at
the Metropolitan for any of your friends that you might like to have.
Any part of this programme that does not meet with your entire
approval, can be changed, if you will let me have the suggestions.

In order to complete arrangements for the meeting, the Committee is anxious to announce in tomorrow's papers that you will
open the national campaign for the Second Red Cross War Fund,
at the Metropolitan Opera House, Saturday evening. No mention
need be made of anything except the Saturday evening meeting.
May we not give them permission to make the announcement to
that extent?   Sincerely yours,   Jesse H Jones

TLS (WP, DLC).

From Arthur W. Ricker

Mr. President: New York May 15th, 1918.

I think you will be interested in the enclosed clipping.[1]

A number of us, widely scattered over the United States, have entered upon a determined campaign to change the policy and attitude of the Socialist Party.

Sincerely yours,   A. W. Ricker

TLS (WP, DLC).
[1] "Urges Socialist Party to Back President Wilson: A. W. Ricker Says Executive is Hope of Liberals—Wants St. Louis Platform, Condemning War, Amended," New York *Globe and Commercial Advertiser*, undated clipping (WP, DLC). The title and subtitle of the article summarize its content—a description of a recent speech by Ricker to a group of leaders of the Socialist party.

From Edmond A. Whittier[1]

Dear Mr. President: New York, May 15, 1918.

In view of the public controversy concerning alleged indiscretions of Mr. George Creel I conceive I would be derelict in duty if I did not inform you concerning a statement Mr. Creel was reported to me as having made in conference about a week ago.

A personal friend of mine—a man whose word is absolutely good— in conversation with Mr. Creel mentioned Senator Watson's[2] proposal to investigate him. Mr. Creel replied quickly, in effect, "we need not worry about that. The President has assured me that if they start to investigate me he will go to the capitol as my attorney."[3]

For obvious reasons it is unwise to mention in a letter the name of my friend, who, as one of those present, casually related the incident to me but, of course, I stand ready to make it known to you in any way which would not involve him in unpleasant notoriety.

If my informant were not absolutely reliable I would not venture to trespass upon your time in the matter of an utterance of such astounding and almost incredible indiscretion, regardless of its truth or falsity.   Yours faithfully,   Edmond A. Whittier

TLS (WP, DLC).
[1] Secretary-treasurer of the American Fair Trade League.
[2] That is, Senator James Eli Watson, Republican of Indiana.
[3] See the extract from the Diary of Josephus Daniels printed at April 12, 1918, Vol. 47.

From Peter Joseph Hamilton

My dear Mr. President: San Juan, P. R., May 15, 1918.

A cable published in the newspapers here is to the effect that Mr. Gompers has requested you to remove Governor Yager. Without conferring with Yager, or his knowing of my writing, let me say that any such course would be an injustice to the Governor and a misfortune to the Island. I purposely keep out of everything political here, but cannot help being much interested in Porto Rico and am sure I am devoted to its best interests.

The alleged ground is that Governor Yager has not done anything for the working man. I am afraid that Mr. Gompers, for whom I have a high respect, is misled by a labor agitator here, who is Socialist and everything un-American. It is said that he was run out of Cuba, but he has become influential here among the ignorant classes and has been elected a member of the local senate. Labor problems here are closely connected with race problems and should be handled very carefully. The working men do not class at all with those in the States, either in love or work or in mental acquirements. They are largely Socialists and their symbol is the red flag, carried openly in parades on all occasions, sometimes with and sometimes without the American flag.

Whether the police (of whom they complain) have acted correctly with them I do not personally know, but at least no laboring man has come into the Federal Court asking to have any of his constitutional rights protected. They seem to prefer appealing to the executive.

Porto Rico certainly owes a debt of gratitude to Governor Yager for his efforts in securing local self-government. Some of our best citizens think that he has not managed the subsequent situation tactfully, for he has let the politicians run over him in the way of certain important test appointments. One admirable official, whom you originally had appointed, was turned down because he did not belong to the dominant Unionist Party.[1] I am afraid Yager has made the mistake of trying to do right without regard to the political axiom that one must help his friends and fight his enemies. The result is that neither class is satisfied. However, he has acted from the best motives, and has to my knowledge aimed at the highest good of Porto Rico in general and the working men in particular.

Moreover, if this effort is yielded to, it will encourage all the worst elements here. They will think that they are in charge, and infinite harm be done. Congress has made these people Americans in name, but it will be one or more generations before they lose the Latin-American spirit. There can be no revolutions under the American flag, but there can be and are here many strikes and similar movements. Yager needs to take a page out of your notebook as to handling politicians with firmness, but I think anything less than standing squarely behind him at this time would do a great deal of harm.

Very sincerely,   P. J. Hamilton

TLS (WP, DLC).
[1] The party which advocated greater autonomy for Porto Rico and eventual inde-

pendence, about which see Truman R. Clark, *Puerto Rico and the United States, 1917-1933* (Pittsburgh, Pa., 1975), *passim.*

From Cordell Hull

My dear Mr. President: Washington, D. C. May 15, 1918.

I would not presume to offer my individual views, even briefly, with respect to the state of our revenues and finances, present and prospective, except for the reported divergent attitudes of the Treasury and some of the leading members of the two Houses of Congress.

The controlling question for determination at this time, I think, is whether it is deemed wise and necessary to make an additional tax levy on profits arising during the calendar year 1918. If so, it is manifest that Congress should take action during the present rather than the short session next winter. A bill offered next winter would not become a law before near the 4th of March, 1919, whereas tax returns under such measure would be due on the first of March preceding, and besides the treasury would be obliged to consume several weeks in the preparation of regulations. The loud cry of "retroactive legislation" would be promptly offered after the turn of the year, as it has been effectively offered in similar circumstances heretofore. The general demand would be that the law should only apply to profits of the calendar year 1919. In making immense war tax levies, running into the billions, business should be given as nearly a year's notice as possible, in view of the fact that most large business concerns adopt plans and contract financial obligations several months in advance of their fulfillment. I think that most business people would prefer that if an additional tax levy is to be made with respect to the calendar year 1918, it should be made during this session so as to avoid the confusion, apprehension, and protracted suspense that would occur during next winter and spring under the effects of similar legislation at the short session.

The necessity for an additional levy on this year's profits is, in my judgment, manifest. The English government, realizing that it will be confronted by an annual tax levy of about $3,500,000,000 after the war, prepared in its recent budget to increase revenues $550,000,000 for each full year in the future, making a total aggregate of $4,500,000,000 of tax revenue. This action has proceeded with the general approval of the public and the press, on the ground of war necessity.

The United States will probably find itself carrying a debt of not less than $40,000,000,000 at the close of the war. If the amount we are loaning and shall loan to the Allies, together with the interest they are expected to pay on it, should be treated as a sinking fund, the government would then pay 4¼% interest on a total debt of $40,000,000,000 during the years following the war. Pensions and similar compensation to soldiers and sailors will then doubtless exceed $500,000,000. The amount of our pre-war expenditures for material, supplies, etc., will on account of the increase in prices be considerably augmented after the war. New expenditures growing out of the war, such as those for reconstruction work and the maintenance of new agencies created during the war which cannot be discontinued, at least for some time, will involve several hundred millions additional. These sums added to our normal pre-war expenditure of a little over $1,000,000,000 will make the total annual expenditures after the war not less than $4,000,000,000, in my judgment.

If we can only levy $4,000,000,000 taxes during the war when war profits are swollen and when the people are disposed to accept forms of taxation they will not accept in times of peace, how can we expect in a satisfactory way to raise $4,000,000,000 from taxation after the war, when profits have largely declined and there is demand for repeal of more or less war taxation? It is true, furthermore, that the great war expenditures contracted in inflated prices of about 100% should be met as fully as possible in similar inflated values, otherwise a much larger amount of commodity values would be required to pay off a given amount of bonded debt some years after the war than at present. The principle now recognized as sound finance by every country at war is that the maximum amount of taxation which can be levied during the war without material injury to business should be imposed. Another point worthy of note is that under war conditions when government control is very general, taxation will not injuriously affect business except when imposed to a point where business concerns have not left an adequate amount for reserves and necessary additions to capital. Fortunately, our business concerns were able prior to our entry into the war to pay off floating and much other indebtedness and fully to fill up their reserves. In another respect heavy war taxation is a great benefit in keeping down inflation, because it operates greatly to diminish useless private expenditures.

It is agreed that every employe should have reasonable compensation for his services and every producer a reasonable profit on his products, in the light of all the conditions and circumstances.

A glance at the income tax returns of corporations and of from 300,000 to 429,000 individuals for the years 1915-16-17 shows that those subject to the income tax alone derived an aggregate net profit of substantially $30,000,000,000 for these three years, whereas the amount of taxes imposed by the federal government on these

taxpayers under the income and excess profits tax laws is below
$3,500,000,000. This reveals a net profit of $26,500,000,000. The
net income returned by these classes for the calendar year 1916
was $13,000,000,000. It is probably $14,000,000,000 or more for
the calendar year 1917. This would indicate a total net income for
the entire population of an amount in the neighborhood of
$18,000,000,000.

England had handled her excess profits law with the minimum
of complaint by giving the Treasury the fullest latitude a statute
can give to deal with individual cases of hardship according to the
special circumstances and to make such allowances, deductions,
etc., in computing both "capital invested" and taxable profits as
would most nearly insure to each taxpayer a good and reasonable
profit from his business, in view of the amount of capital invested
and the nature, hazards, etc. of the business. After thus satisfying
each taxpayer, the government takes 80% of the remainder, which
is surrendered much more cheerfully than under our law which
does not permit the same full and liberal computation in many
cases and which imposes an average tax of some 30% on a larger
excess of taxable profit. To illustrate, the English returns, I believe,
only indicate excess profits of $1,500,000,000, but the government
takes $1,200,000,000 of this, whereas our law shows some
$6,000,000,000 excess profits on account of the lower capital per-
centage and denial of specific allowances when meritorious, and
on which amount we levy an average of near 30%, as best I can
estimate it.

Congress could without protracted delay combine all income and
excess profits tax rates, exemptions, etc., into one set of rates and
exemptions and eliminate such features of the present revenue laws
as are inequitable, and such action would materially off-set any
dissatisfaction arising from the increased tax levy.

I agree that our revenue situation presents a serious problem,
but am of opinion that a prompt dealing with such problem and a
consequent readiness to meet the great responsibility involved would
be approved by the people generally. When the full facts as to the
necessities of the government are presented to the American people,
they will be ready in a patriotic spirit, just as the people in other
countries at war, to meet without complaint such further burdens
as an additional tax levy may impose. To make our tax laws equitable in their operation is the controlling consideration with the
taxpayer.

Asking pardon for having elaborated to a far greater extent than
I intended, I am,   Very sincerely,   Cordell Hull

TLS (WP, DLC).

From Harry Augustus Garfield, with Enclosure

Dear Mr. President: Washington, D. C. May 15, 1918

I am sorry to learn that you are not feeling well today.

In response to your inquiry made through Mr. I. H. Hoover whether it seems to me necessary for us to meet before next Wednesday, I beg to submit the enclosed memorandum prepared for today's meeting. In my judgment, the settlement of the railroad fuel question[1] ought not to be further postponed and, inasmuch as it involves the industries represented by most of the gentlemen attending the Wednesday meetings, I venture to urge that we be called together at the earliest moment possible.

Cordially and faithfully yours,   H. A. Garfield.

TLS (WP, DLC).
[1] About this problem, see John Skelton Williams to WW, April 23, 1918, and its Enclosure, and J. S. Williams to WW, April 24, 1918, all in Vol. 47.

E N C L O S U R E

Washington, D. C., May 15, 1918.

MEMORANDUM PREPARED BY THE FUEL ADMINISTRATOR,
FOR THE PRESIDENT.
EFFECT UPON GENERAL FUEL SITUATION OF THE DELAY
IN SETTLING RAILROAD FUEL QUESTION.

By long custom the coal year in the United States runs from April 1 for twelve months, ending the succeeding March 31. Delayed settlement of the locomotive fuel question has already seriously impaired the bituminous coal supply for the current year. Every day of further delay adds to this impairment. Unless immediately ended it renders likely, and perhaps unavoidable, a fuel crisis before next April.

It is possible to pursue a hand-to-mouth policy so far as supplying the railroads is concerned. This policy has kept the railroads supplied now for seven weeks. The railroads have not suffered, but the entire coal program for the country as a whole, is today 52 days late in starting. Indeed the determination of a definite and final method of supplying locomotive fuel was first taken up with the railroads about March 1st. This loss of time is irreparable. At this season, when coal is easily produced and transported, the process of storage for the winter season should be in full swing.

The probable coal shortage makes it imperative that every consuming need should be supplied from the nearest available source, regardless of price and all other considerations, except that coal specially suitable for certain uses should not be diverted to other

uses for which other coal is equally satisfactory. To assist in effecting this result the zoning system was adopted. Perhaps un-
wisely, the railroads have been excepted from the application of the
zoning system. To that extent the governing necessity of the principle just mentioned has been relaxed. As much the largest coal
consuming industry, taking from one-fourth to one-third of the total
bituminous output, the omission of the railroads from the principle
which should govern the coal program must obviously greatly affect
the success of the program itself. At present and for 52 days the
railroads have been thus omitted. The various coal fields are dotted
over with old and still continuing railroad fuel contracts, to which
have been added many others of recent execution. Substantially all
these contracts have been placed having regard chiefly to low cost
of fuel. Many of them were secured through assurances of preferential car supply. Little regard appears to have been given to the
need of the output of the contract mines for gas, by-product coke,
bunkering, or other special uses. Higher priced coal nearer the
distributing points for railroad consumption, or capable of easier
and quicker transportation to such points, has been passed by for
less accessible coal procurable at lower prices. A hand-to-mouth
policy permits no improvement in this situation. At best it leaves
the Fuel Administration free to apply the principle of its program
merely to such deficiency in the railroad requirements as exists
above their contract tonnage. Even within this limited field, the
Fuel Administration, so long as price is considered an element, can
fully apply the principle of supplying coal from the most available
sources only at the risk of accusations of hostility to the railroads.

The zoning system has been arranged and coal prices have been
fixed in entire disregard of the effect upon the cost of fuel to any
particular individual, class of industries, or section of the country.
Applications from the state administrators and from individual consumers are filled in like disregard of prices. The Fuel Administration
has named a price deemed to be fair and not excessive for the
production at each field. Its main duty, and most difficult one, is
to procure, so far as possible, an adequate supply of coal for domestic
consumers and essential industries, including among the latter, the
railroads. The accomplishment of this duty necessitates a maximum production from each field. This result has not been accomplished since April 1, nor can it be accomplished until the status
of the largest consuming industry has been fixed. It cannot be
accomplished at all unless that status is fixed upon the same basis
as that of all other essential industries. Consequently, a hand-to-
mouth policy for the railroads involves a marking-time policy for
the Fuel Administration.

The country is engaged in a most fateful war. Time is of the essence of success in war. By the President's action in fixing coal prices a billion dollars has been saved to the American people. Those prices must be regarded in their aggregate result, not in their minor differences, nor in the effect of those differences upon individual consumers. The people as a whole need more coal than the country as a whole, under present restricted transportation facilities, can produce, consequently someone must pay the fixed price for every ton of coal that can be produced and transported. Even then there will not be enough. Every day's delay in adopting and applying such a distribution plan as will insure the maximum production increases the ultimate deficiency. The Administration will be judged by the ultimate amount of deficiency in production, and by the effect of that deficiency upon the successful prosecution of the war. Every patriotic American would rather see the railroad fuel bill for this year doubled, than to witness a repetition of last winter's curtailment of essential productions due to a deficiency in the supply of coal caused by the inability of the carriers promptly to move it from the mines to the consumers. So long as the railroads are placed on an equality with other industries as regards price, and are given a preference over other industries only in the reliability of their supply, every citizen will be satisfied with the result.

The Fuel Administration is confronted with other problems besides that of locomotive fuel. The question of a sufficient fuel-oil supply is most serious and pressing. If fuel oil is to be restricted, because of a limited supply, to its most essential uses, its place for less essential uses must be taken by coal. How and from what source this coal is to be obtained, depends largely upon the solution of the locomotive fuel question. An increased supply of fuel oil is dependent upon the possibility of an increased supply of certain steel products and machinery. This latter increased supply is dependent upon a maximum coal production, which again is dependent upon the settlement of the locomotive fuel question. Thus it will be found at almost every turn that this troublesome question lies at the foundation of the settlement of other fuel questions.

T MS (WP, DLC).

To Joseph Patrick Tumulty, with Enclosure

Dear Tumulty: [The White House, c. May 16, 1918]

Please say to Mrs. Catt[1] that I have examined the enclosed with a great deal of interest and will keep the suggestion in mind. Whether I can wisely act on it just now or not, I cannot say offhand.

The President.

TL (WP, DLC).

[1] Carrie C. L. C. Catt to JPT, May 14, 1918, TLS (WP, DLC):

"I enclose herewith translation of appeal sent to the President from the women of Great Britain, France, Italy, Belgium and Portugal.

"We venture to suggest that the President might use this appeal as the peg on which to hang a message to the women of the world similar to that given last autumn to the women of New York. In view of the fact that the Germans and some Americans profess to believe that America is not sincere in her war aims, the President might also find in this address the opportunity to give to the world one of his immortal expressions upon democracy.

"It is clear to many of us that we are fighting to make the men of the world free from militarism, from autocracy, from the government of kaisers and emperors, and to replace these autocratic institutions by the newer ones of democracy. Our war aims indirectly pledge individual liberty to men, but no promise is given to women who have also given their all.

"There is no other mind in all the world which possesses the clear, well analyzed conception of democracy as that of the President, and a pronouncement upon that subject which will *include all the people* will ring round the world and bring new hope and courage to men and women in all nations.

"If the President is willing to do this, we will, if it pleases him, come with a small deputation, present the French address, and receive the response; or if he prefers, it can be accomplished in some other way."

E N C L O S U R E[1]

UNION FRANCAISE POUR LE SUFFRAGE DES FEMMES

Paris, February 1, 1918.

In the historic message which announced to the world the entry into the struggle of American force and thought, you declared unforgettable formulae upon which your great Republic awaits a victory—the right of peoples to self determination and a durable peace for generations to come.

The French suffragists and those of the allied countries have heard your beautiful and strong words and they unite in prayer to you for the accomplishment of the following resolution:

"Considering that from this war there has come a new international right founded upon the right of peoples to self determination,

"That nothing can be claimed to speak authoritatively in the name of the people which excludes women from the life of nations,

"Considering moreover that women during the actual conflict have shown the value of the social work which they are capable of performing,

"Considering that the participation of wives and mothers in the suffrage would be the greatest guarantee of the peace to come, the need that the belligerent countries have of their help in the present conflict, the sufferings, moral as well as physical, which this war has cost them, have given definite proof that no longer, without iniquity and imprudence, can one refuse to give them through their vote an influence in the undertakings which decide peace and war,

"The women of the allied countries express the wish: that Pres-

LIBRARY
College of St. Francis
JOLIET, ILL.

113013

ident Wilson in one of his future messages will proclaim the principle of woman suffrage one of the fundamental rights of the future."

We have read with emotion in the Woman Citizen, Mr. President, the very profound words which you have spoken in response to the delegation of women from New York.[2] If we recite them here it is because they are the same words that we would ask you to address to all humanity in one of your declarations which resound throughout the world:

"It is a struggle which goes deeper and touches more of the foundation of the organized life of men than any struggle that has ever taken place before, and no settlement of the questions that lie on the surface can satisfy a situation which requires that the questions which lie underneath and at the foundation should also be settled and settled right. I am free to say that I think the question of woman suffrage is one of those questions which lie at the foundation."

I beg you to accept, Mr. President, the expression of our great appreciation of our American sisters and our profound admiration for the high moral tone of the declarations which you have uttered in her name. It is this which encourages us to ask your aid, which will be a powerful influence for woman suffrage in the entire world.

For the Committee of the Union Francaise pour le Suffrage des Femmes, and in the name of other National Committees of which the list is joined hereto:

President, de Witt Schlumberger,[3]

Vice-president de l'Alliance Internationale du

Suffrage des Femmes:

Vice-president,	Jane Misme
Vice-president,	Marie Louise LeVerrier
Secretary,	Cecile L. Brunschvieg
Treasurer,	Marguerite Desavis
Secretary,	Marguerite Pichon Landry
Secretary,	Suzanne Grinberg

Owing to the difficulties of communication due to the war several of our allies have not written to reply, but we do not wish to wait longer to send you this address. The list of the allied countries the National Woman's Suffrage Associations of which have been consulted are as follows:

Great Britain	Belgium,
France	Portugal
Italy	The United States

All of these have expressed their earnest desire that the President of the United States shall send the message to the nations of the

world. The suffrage associations of the following countries have
been addressed and no replies have been received:

Russia	Africa
Australia	Serbia
Canada	Roumania

T MS (WP, DLC).
   [1] The TLS of the following letter, in French, is in WP, DLC.
   [2] Printed at October 25, 1917, Vol. 44.
   [3] Marguerite de Witt (Mme. Paul de) Schlumberger, president of the Union Française
pour le Suffrage des Femmes.

To Cordell Hull

My dear Mr. Hull: [The White House] 16 May, 1918

   Your letter of yesterday, which I have just read, embodies a very
weighty argument indeed for immediate action upon taxation. I am
waiting for the release of the Secretary of the Treasury from the
sick room to which he has been confined since his return from his
Liberty Loan campaign, and am very glad indeed to have my mind
furnished with the considerations which you urge with so much
clearness and so much force.

                    Cordially and sincerely yours,   Woodrow Wilson

TLS (Letterpress Books, WP, DLC).

To Robert Lansing

My dear Mr. Secretary,   The White House. 16 May, 1918.

   I am of course willing to accept this honour,[1]—who would not
be? I beg that in conveying to Ambassador Sharp this message you
will be kind enough to ask him to express also my deep appreciation
of the high honour that is thus conferred upon me and my great
satisfaction in being associated with so distinguished a body.

                    Faithfully Yours,   W.W.

WWTLI (SDR, RG 59, 811.001 W69/364, DNA).
   [1] That is, election as an Associé étranger of the Académie des Sciences Morales et
Politiques of the Institut de France. Wilson's acceptance was sent as RL to W. G. Sharp,
May 17, 1918, T telegram (SDR, RG 59, 811.001 W69/364, DNA). The formal election
took place on June 15.

To Anna Howard Shaw, with Enclosure

My dear Doctor Shaw: [The White House] 16 May, 1918

The enclosed beautiful and touching letter will speak for itself. My present judgment is that it would not be wise for me to make any public utterance in this delicate matter, because I would inevitably seem to be conveying a warning that mourning might presently become universal amongst us. It has occurred to me, therefore, that your own committee[1] might think it timely and wise to give some advice to the women of the country with regard to mourning. My own judgment is that the English are treating it more wisely than the French. It may be that service badges, upon which the white stars might upon the occurrence of a death be changed into stars of gold, would be a very beautiful and significant substitute for mourning. What do you think? Can your committee wisely act in the matter?

Cordially and sincerely yours,   Woodrow Wilson

P.S. I will be very much obliged if you would be kind enough to return the enclosed letter.   W.W.

TLS (Letterpress Books, WP, DLC).
[1] Dr. Shaw was chairperson of the "Woman's Committee" of the Council of National Defense.

E N C L O S U R E

From Caroline Seaman Read[1]

My dear Mr. President,   New York, May 3rd, 1918.

Mrs. Henry P. Davison tells me that you fear this is not the right moment to open the discussion as whether the women of America are to meet the inevitable death roll of our heroic defenders of Liberty as a matter of glory, honor, and pride, or as a matter of prostrating grief and mourning.

One of my four Naval Aviator sons has recently been killed on active service at Dunkirk, so I know the costliness of such supreme glory and sacrifice, and weighing both the selfish temptation to hide our pain behind a mourning that would hold off intrusion, and the inspiration and stimulation of keeping up to my gallant son's expectation that I should regard his death as a happy promotion into higher service, I must urgently beg of you, Mr. President, to speak *now* to the tense American motherhood your personal message of courage and understanding that patriotism means such exalted living that dying is not the harder part.

Could we have awarded by our President, Commander in Chief of our men in Army, Navy, Air and all service, a badge of honor to wear, showing only the gold star with the rank and branch of service of our man, gladly dedicated to his country's service in this Great Cause, we should not *dare* to *mourn*, lest those seeing our insignia and knowing of that supreme sacrifice, might think we felt it a precious life thrown away.

Not one of us who have been in touch with the magnificent spirit which takes these finest of our country's young manhood unfalteringly to face the New Death, renouncing without complaint or bitterness life at its most beautiful moment, can feel that we are rightly bearing the glory they bestow upon their families unless we keep the flame of their high devotion clear burning until the accomplishment of the Victory they died to hasten, and not one of us could fail with such an emblem of our country's gratitude and trust in our unfaltering patriotism.

In every home in this wide land is now a service flag, or explanations for the embar[r]assing lack of one, and nothing could so unite our nation now as the President's word of understanding that our forces are composed of individuals each the central object of intense love, pride, and high hope and costly sacrifice.

The sublime loyalty to you, Mr. President, of all these magnificent men, in spite of the heartbreaking delays and wastage of officialdom, is a possession I long to make known to you as you are the only one who never hears their fine voices, excluded from official reports.

With high respect,

Faithfully yours   (Mrs. Wm. A. Read.) Caroline S. Read.

ALS (WP, DLC).
  [1] Mrs. William Augustus Read, widow of a New York banker.

To Charles Raymond Macauley

My dear Mr. Macauley: [The White House] 16 May, 1918

I am very much interested in what you tell me of the interest which is being shown in the approaching meeting of the League to Enforce Peace,[1] but I must beg that you will be very careful not to confuse my very warm support of the idea of a league of nations to preserve and insure the peace of the world with an endorsement of any particular plan or programme. You will notice that I have carefully refrained from any such endorsement. It would be most imprudent and I do not think that this is the time to discuss a constitution and executive action of such a league, as I have explained to representatives of the League who were gracious enough to call upon me for my advice and whose judgment I took to be the same as my own in that matter.

Cordially and sincerely yours,   Woodrow Wilson

TLS (Letterpress Books, WP, DLC).
  [1] Wilson was replying to C. R. Macauley to WW, May 14, 1918, enclosing Herbert S. Houston to WW, May 14, 1918, both TLS (WP, DLC). Houston, the chairman of the Committee on Information of the League to Enforce Peace, stated that, in a speech before the convention of the league to be held in Philadelphia on May 16 and 17, he intended to urge the immediate creation of a league of nations, to be composed initially of the countries at war with Germany. Houston said that in so doing he would only be following Wilson's lead. Macauley, chairman of the Organization Committee of the League to Enforce Peace, in his covering letter urged Wilson to send a message to the convention in support of the immediate establishment of a league of nations.
  Despite Wilson's caveat in his letter, Houston did make a speech at the convention which included essentially what he had outlined in his letter, although he did not spell out the precise form which his proposed league of nations might take. Herbert S. Houston, "Commerce and the Mailed Fist," *Win the War for Permanent Peace: Addresses made at the National Convention of the League to Enforce Peace, in the City of Philadelphia, May 16th and 17th, 1918* (New York, n.d.), pp. 143-48.

To Newton Diehl Baker

My dear Baker: [The White House] 16 May, 1918

I value very highly your gift of "The Frontiers of Freedom,"[1] and shall look forward with genuine pleasure to reading the addresses contained in the volume.

And may I not say that I am particularly grateful to you for the inscription which the fly-leaf bears?[2] I value your friendship and approval more highly than you realize, and am deeply complimented that you should feel that I have contributed in any respect to a new understanding of the spirit of liberty.

Cordially and faithfully yours,   Woodrow Wilson

TLS (Letterpress Books, WP, DLC).
  [1] Newton D. Baker, *Frontiers of Freedom* (New York, 1918).
  [2] "My dear Mr President: I hope these imperfect reproductions of very imperfect addresses about the War will still be found to have caught and represent some of the spirit of Liberty which you have taught us all to revere with a new understanding Respectfully Newton D. Baker" ALS in the copy in the Wilson Library, DLC.

To John Hollis Bankhead, Jr.

My dear Mr. Bankhead: [The White House] 16 May, 1918

I did not reply to your telegram of May sixth[1] by wire because I wished you to know my feeling more fully than I could express it in a telegram.

I am sure I may count upon you to put the proper interpretation upon my words when I say that in every contest between Democrats of equal loyalty to the Government I have felt that I did not have the right to do anything that would indicate my personal preference. I have no right to press my personal preferences upon the voters of any constituency.

Senator Bankhead needs no certificate from me as to what his attitude has been or as to the course he has pursued. The record is there plainly written, and nothing that I could say would enhance or alter it.

I fully understand the purpose and spirit of your telegram, and I am sure you will justly assess the spirit and purpose of this letter.

Sincerely yours,   Woodrow Wilson

TLS (Letterpress Books, WP, DLC).
¹ It is missing.

To Harry Augustus Garfield

My dear Garfield: The White House 16 May, 1918

I am greatly impressed by what you say about the effect of the delay in settling the general fuel situation, and I greatly deplore the fact that the settlement has been delayed by Secretary McAdoo's illness. I have felt in duty bound not to press the matter with him until he could get his strength back, but I will do so at the earliest possible moment, you may be sure. I believe that McAdoo can attend the conference early next week.

Cordially and sincerely yours,   Woodrow Wilson

TLS (H. A. Garfield Papers, DLC).

To Maurice Francis Egan

My dear Mr. Minister: [The White House] 16 May, 1918

Your letter of yesterday¹ was entirely welcome and I want to assure you that the subject matter of it has been a good deal in my mind of late. I must say that I have not yet been able to determine the wisest and most serviceable course, but I will canvass the matter in all its aspects very thoroughly.

Cordially and sincerely yours,   Woodrow Wilson

TLS (Letterpress Books, WP, DLC).
¹ M. F. Egan to WW, May 15, 1918, ALS (WP, DLC). Egan, then on medical leave in Washington, suggested that there should be some representative at the Vatican who could explain "the American ideas." He did not think that this person should be a formal diplomatic representative; but, he continued, "some kind of a representative,—not a Bishop or a priest, but a Catholic not 'entangled' with foreign ideas,—would be very useful at Rome."

From Joseph Patrick Tumulty

Dear Governor: The White House. May 16, 1918.

I am advised that the District Commissioners have decided in favor of Sunday baseball in order that some recreation should be afforded the thousands of war workers who have come into the District of Columbia. I believe that the action of the Commissioners is quite generally approved.   J.P.T.

The President is very sorry the Commissioners took this action, since he personally does not approve of it at all.   C.L.S.

TL (WP, DLC).

From Newton Diehl Baker, with Enclosure

[Washington, c. May 16, 1918]

Cen Pershings reply to my cable asking a sympathetic attitude should General Foch reopen the subject

Baker

ALS (WP, DLC).

E   N   C   L   O   S   U   R   E

From GHQAEF May 15th.   CONFIDENTIAL.

Number 1124 Rush. Chief of Staff and Secretary of War.

Paragraph 1. Reference cable 1297.[1] The original recommendations by the Military Representative[s] on the Supreme War Council of an exclusive infantry program for troop shipments from America[2] was evidently made without considering the serious effect upon our plan, although it was explained to them that certain classes of troops and service of rear organizations would be necessary not only to carry out our purpose of building an army but to meet present requirements. However, the Abbeville conference[3] took little note of the original recommendations as the sole request made was that the London agreement[4] be extended to include June and July. I stated in substance that our program had been already materially reduced and that the extension of an infantry program for three months would defer the shipment of artillery and other troops and make it impossible with the shipping then in sight to catch up for several months and the organization of American divisions would be indefinitely postponed and our service of the rear would be unable to function sufficiently to meet our increasing demands for supplies, and urged that we could meet the situation later if the crisis seemed to demand it. After full discussion in committee, Mr. Lloyd George said: "I agree that you should form American Divisions and I think we shall be able to bring over all the infantry we want and also bring over the extra troops you want." He then guaranteed the extra shipping mentioned in the agreement, and we agreed to include June in the infantry program leaving July to be reviewed later. This was declared entirely satisfactory by all concerned. Lord Milner came to me afterwards and said: "I wish you to know that I have been no party to this as I was entirely satisfied with the London agreement." General Foch afterwards said in the most friendly manner: "We are in thorough accord as always, I am very satisfied." His Chief of Staff sent word that General Foch was very much pleased. Although the British War Office was quite satisfied with the London agreement, it is understood that Lord Reading took Lord Milner severely to task for accepting the London program.

Subparagraph A. The aid we shall furnish with shipping promised during May and June will be first, the 240,000 infantry and machine gun units, and, according to British estimates, possibly about 50,000 more in June; second, practically 5 divisions in line, two in Picardy, or on the way, and three in Lorraine, including the 32nd now moving into line; the third and 5th divisions, which will be hurried as much as possible and will replace French divisions within a short time. This will make about 175,000 men in divisions plus 240,000 men in infantry units, with possibly 50,000 additional in the battle or preparing to go in, besides 4 regiments of colored troops, and several batteries of heavy artillery already with the French and British, not to mention the divisional artillery that follows the infantry in May and June—approximately half a million men.

Subparagraph B. If we include July in the program, the troops will not be ready to take their places in line until some time in August. But even the British state that in August they will have 400,000 to 500,000 drafts and the French 1919 class, about 200,000, will also be coming in then. The main reason for our hurrying infantry units for service with the Allies is to help out until the Allied drafts are available. Notwithstanding Allied demands for infantry alone, a recent request comes from the British for 10,000 artillery men. While appreciating that we should give every early assistance possible to meet an emergency, I am strongly of the opinion that we must form our own divisions and corps as rapidly as possible and use them as such for the additional moral effect such an army would have. Many French officers of high rank hold this view and want entire divisions. General Sir Douglas Haig said he would like to have our divisions placed beside the British divisions as soon as possible. Our own officers and men are constantly asking whether newspaper reports are true that they are to be amalgamated with French and British units, and are unanimous in their desire to fight under our own flag. It is not impossible that we shall find Irishmen refusing to fight under the British. We can not ignore what our own soldiers and our people will think and should not keep units too long with either Ally. The Germans are now saying that Americans are inefficient and that French and British do not trust them and so are absorbing them in Allied divisions.

Subparagraph C. In conclusion, I think we have fully and fairly met the situation. We have given the Supreme War Council all it asked at Abbeville. The statement in your cable places a limit upon further concessions which had really been about reached in the Abbeville agreement. It is believed that the action at Abbeville should be considered as the deliberate expression of the Supreme War Council's latest views and that the flanking operations be regarded as definitely settled as to May and June, otherwise as long as there is the slightest hope of getting further concessions, there will be a continual clamor regardless of how it affects us. I have fully set forth the above to present the matter as it appears to me.

Subparagraph D. Judging from what occurred at Abbeville and from the expressions of approval by General Foch, I think he can not consistently reopen the subject until the question of July needs arises. But above all, I wish to be understood as having every desire to meet this question in the broadest way possible and do everything to aid in this emergency, and both the President and the Secretary of War may be fully assured that I shall approach any future discussion in the spirit suggested by the Secretary of War.

Pershing.

T telegram (WP, DLC).
    [1] That is, H. P. McCain to J. J. Pershing, May 11, 1918, Vol. 47.
    [2] See NDB to WW, March 28, 1918; WW to NDB, March 29, 1918; NDB to WW, April 19, 1918; and Lord Reading to D. Lloyd George, April 21, 1918, all in Vol. 47.
    [3] See the memorandum by F. Foch printed at May 2, 1918; J. J. Pershing to H. P. McCain, May 3, 1918, printed as an Enclosure with NDB to WW, May 4, 1918 (first letter of that date); and J. J. Pershing to H. P. McCain, May 7, 1918, printed as an Enclosure with NDB to WW, May 8, 1918 (second letter of that date), all in Vol. 47.
    [4] J. J. Pershing to H. P. McCain, April 25, 1918, printed as an Enclosure with NDB to WW, April 29, 1918 (first letter of that date), Vol. 47. For a helpful summary of the complex negotiations from November 1917 to June 1918 about the composition and disposition of American forces in Europe, see Daniel R. Beaver, *Newton D. Baker and the American War Effort, 1917-1919* (Lincoln, Neb., 1966), pp. 110-50.

From Newton Diehl Baker, with Enclosure

My dear Mr. President: Washington. May 16, 1918.

I enclose a memorandum made by General McIntyre upon the papers submitted to you by Mr. Gompers, which I herewith return. I also return the letter of Mr. Davila which you enclosed to me on the 13th of May.

General McIntyre's acquaintance with conditions in Porto Rico is so intimate that I feel disposed to recommend your reliance upon his judgment in the matter; particularly because Mr. Iglesias would be greatly magnified should his charges be deemed worthy of such an inquiry as the one suggested by Mr. Gompers; and also because apparently the Governor's action in several of the matters as to which Mr. Iglesias complains was manifestly beyond criticism.

I enclose a more formal letter on this subject which might be forwarded to Mr. Gompers for comment by him.[1] Indeed, perhaps the wisest course would be for you to submit my formal letter to Mr. Gompers and suggest his taking the whole matter up with me for conference. I would be glad to invite General McIntyre to such a conference, and try to arrive at a just course of action, if any is needed, to be recommended to you.

Respectfully yours,   Newton D. Baker

TLS (WP, DLC).
[1] It is missing, but see WW to S. Gompers, May 20, 1918.

ENCLOSURE

Washington. May 15, 1918.

MEMORANDUM for the Secretary of War.

I believe it would be extremely unwise to act upon Mr. Gompers' suggestion and send a commission of inquiry to Porto Rico to go into all of the matters brought up by Mr. Iglesias' letter of complaint.

Mr. Iglesias is a socialist Senator of Porto Rico. He is the President of the Free Federation of Labor of Porto Rico, and is the editor of a weekly paper in Porto Rico, La Justicia. The sending of a commission could have no result other than that of advertising Mr. Iglesias and emphasizing in Porto Rico his importance in the United States.

It could develop no fact that is not now entirely known.

Mr. Iglesias complains that the Governor did not give timely assistance to the American Red Cross in Porto Rico, was slow in naming a Committee of National Defense in Porto Rico and that he lacked interest in the Liberty Loans in Porto Rico. This is manifestly trivial. The Red Cross has but recently sent a representative to Porto Rico and he has returned to the United States and any facts desired could be obtained from him. In fact I have talked to this representative both before he went to Porto Rico and since, and the American Red Cross has no such complaint as this. The Governor was deeply interested in the success of the several Liberty Loans, a fact which can be verified from the records of the War Department and from the Treasury Department. The Governor was deeply interested in a matter of much more importance to Porto Rico in the war, that is, the training of the troops there and the appointment of a Food Commission, which has done immense good. In fact he appointed the Food Commission in advance of the legislation in the United States for the appointment of a Food Administrator.

The unfortunate conditions of the agricultural workers in Porto Rico and of the much more numerous and more unfortunate agricultural people in Porto Rico, who can not work, because the work is not there for them, has been officially set forth in the reports of the Governors of Porto Rico, in the hearings before Congress, since the report of the first Military Governor on American occupation of Porto Rico. The facts which would be developed by an inquiry would show conditions much worse than they are painted by Mr. Iglesias, for the reason that Mr. Iglesias' present interest is in the sugar workers, who even at the low wages they are receiving are of the relatively fortunate class in Porto Rico.

The Governor of Porto Rico must be interested not only in the sugar workers, but in the great number of people who can not obtain work, or can obtain work only occasionally. Governor Yager has set this forth with clearness on several occasions, notably at the Mohawk Conference in 1915, in which he emphasized that the labor situation could be relieved only by the emigration of a great many of the people from Porto Rico.[1]

The statements of Governor Yager bearing on the extent of the recent strike in Porto Rico is [are] born out in every detail by independent testimony from many sources. I attach a clipping from the San Juan Times, a paper which is uniformly unfriendly to Governor Yager on this subject.[2] I have received from the office of the Alien Property Custodian an oral report from the representative which that office sent to Porto Rico to take over the sugar properties in Porto Rico belonging to alien enemies. I should regard these two as being rather free from prejudice in the matter. On the other hand, I have received statements of those who would be interested in the controversy and all bear out the complete accuracy of the reports which Governor Yager has made on this subject.

Mr. Iglesias, in his La Justicia and in public speech, is constantly abusing the freedom of the press and the freedom of speech accorded in Porto Rico. His conduct towards authority in Porto Rico is overbearing and abusive. He is both by speech and publication a constant provocation to disorder. Were his influence greater, or were the miserably poor people of Porto Rico at all disposed to disorder, he would have made the island one of the most disorderly places under the American flag. He abuses the confidence of Mr. Gompers, on whom he depends for his power in Porto Rico and takes advantage of the charity of Governor Yager, who endures his abuse as a part of the days work. To appoint a committee at his suggestion, which committee was without power to punish him, would be to give him that advertisement and help in exploiting himself, which he has constantly sought.

Frank McIntyre.

TS MS (WP, DLC).
    [1] Arthur Yager, "Fundamental Social and Political Problems of Porto Rico," *Report of the 33rd Annual Lake Mohonk Conference on the Indian and Other Dependent Peoples* (1915), pp. 145-53.
    [2] "A Rapid Fire Gun of Rot," San Juan *Times*, May 8, 1918. This article branded Santiago Iglesias as a socialist agitator who had repeatedly incited the laborers of Porto Rico to acts of violence and destruction of property. It defended Yager for his efforts to preserve the peace and declared that he had always insisted upon better wages for the sugar-cane workers.

From Robert Lansing, with Enclosures

My dear Mr. President: Washington May 16, 1918.

I have had another seance with Lord Reading on the question of intervention in Russia, during which he read to me the enclosed memoranda. These I agreed to submit to you.

In a previous interview I pointed out to him that the proposed intervention in Russia had become divided into two problems, the Siberian and the Murmansk, and that they seemed to me to require separate treatment; that the question of intervention in Siberia depended upon the certainty of military benefit which as yet was not evident; and that intervention by way of Murmansk was different since it was a question of ability to land a sufficient military force.

The British Ambassador, acting under instructions from his Government, persists in seeking to have us unite with Great Britain and France in the endeavor to obtain from Trotsky a request that we intervene on the condition that we obtain from Japan a declaration that the territory occupied would be restored to Russia without conditions after the war.

I pointed out to Reading that this confusion of the two problems was unfortunate, that I did not perceive how the conditional entry into Siberia by a Japanese force had anything to do with the occupation of Murmansk and the railway south, and that while intervention through the port of Murmansk might be desirable, intervention through Vladivostok or Harbin was very questionable in view of the inexpediency, if not the impossibility, of a Japanese force advancing farther west than Irkutsk.

Lord Reading said that he had already advised his Government as to my statement that the two problems were distinct and should be treated separately, but that he had not had a reply.

I told him that I could see no objection to securing a request from Trotsky that we should intervene via Murmansk, but that I was not at all sure we would gain anything by a request as to a conditional Japanese intervention in Siberia since to act upon such a request would array us against Semenoff and the elements antagonistic to the Soviets. I said that if we took hold of either one or the other horns of the dilemma we probably would find ourselves in hot water.

In view of the present situation do you think it wise to advise Francis to unite through unofficial channels in obtaining from Trotsky a request for us to intervene by way of Murmansk? I do not feel that we should go further than at the present time and I am not sure that this is expedient in view of the uncertainty of Trotsky's power. To bring Japan into the question seems to me to be unwise at the present time.

Will you please give me your opinion as to the course which should be taken?

Since writing the foregoing I have received the enclosed telegram from Ambassador Sharp.[1] Probably you have also received a copy.

Faithfully yours,   Robert Lansing.

TLS (SDR, RG 59, 861.00/1894½, DNA).
    [1] W. G. Sharp to RL, May 12, 1918, No. 3871, T telegram (SDR, RG 59, 763.72/9967, DNA). Sharp described a conversation which he had just had with Gen. Henri Albert Niessel, former chief of the French military mission in Russia. Niessel characterized Trotsky as "a man of ability and cunning, but so lacking in political sense and able judgment as to render impossible anything like a constructive work, such as all Russia now needs most." He noted the economic and political chaos then pervading Russia and warned that many Russians were in such despair that they would prefer the domination of Germany to that of the Bolsheviks. Niessel concluded that Japanese intervention was necessary if Russia was to be kept out of German control. Sharp added that many prominent French political and military leaders believed that "immediate Japanese intervention on as effective a scale as possible" was the only way to prevent German domination of Russia and the East.

Handed me by Lord Reading
May 15/18 RL.

PARAPHRASE OF A TELEGRAM FROM MR. LOCKHART.
April 23rd, 1918.

VERY CONFIDENTIAL

I give below a summary of the views held by Lenine. His one ambition is to provide at any cost for the protection of the system of Soviet organization, a form of Government which he thinks will be adopted in the future by the whole of Europe.

He understands quite clearly the extent of the danger to Russia from Germany and, if it were possible, he would wish that the Allies could be in a position to resist attacks by Germany until his own organization had been completed and until Russia had recovered strength sufficiently to enable her again to intervene in the war. The interests of Russia are his only consideration and it would agree with his policy if both Germany and the Allied powers were to be weakened to such an extent that Russia would be left in a more powerful position in comparison with the other countries of Europe than she now holds.

Lenine realizes that this policy may not be practicable and he acknowledges that the interests of Russia and the Allied countries are similar as long as they are faced by the German danger. He is, however, afraid of intervention by the Allies because he believes that their real purpose is the destruction of the system of Soviet Government. In support of this attitude, he cites the fact that, although the Soviet Government is now the only one in Russia, the Allied and Japanese Consuls at Vladivostok[1] are in negotiation with the Mayor and with the Zemstvo.

As regards the position in the Far East, Lenine attaches too much weight to the suspicions of Japan entertained by America, and he considers it certain that the United States will prevent forcible intervention in the Far East by Japan.

If the Allies could assure Lenine that they would not make any endeavour to upset the Soviet form of Government, but would, on the other hand, work with the Soviet Government and would offer guarantees to protect the inviolability and independence of Russian territory, there are good grounds for the opinion that he would probably not decline any reasonable offer which the Allies might make. It would mean a great deal to him if the present Government were to be recognized.

It will be understood from the above that, in dealing with the question of intervention in the Far East, Lenine is a factor of great importance.

In reply to the above telegram a communication was sent to Mr. Lockhart, dated May 11th, pointing out that His Majesty's Government had done their best to make it quite plain that they had no wish to interfere in the internal affairs of Russia. Mr. Lockhart was also instructed that he had full authority to make a statement to this effect to the Bolshevist Government.

BRITISH EMBASSY, WASHINGTON,
May 14, 1918.

[1] The American and British Consuls were John Kenneth Caldwell and Robert MacLeod Hodgson, respectively. The Japanese Consul General was Giro Kikuchi. The French Consul was Louis Blanchet.

E N C L O S U R E   I I

Handed me by Lord Reading
May 15/18 RL.

PARAPHRASE OF A TELEGRAM
FROM THE BRITISH REPRESENTATIVE AT MOSCOW.
May 8, 1918.

To-day I had an interview with Mr. Karachan and the Minister of Foreign Affairs.[1] The former is one of the most important figures in the Foreign Office, the others being Radek[2] and Chicherin.

The Minister again mentioned the problem of Murman and said that the enemy had threatened in their communication to occupy Petrograd in case British troops were not withdrawn from Murmansk. We may therefore expect to receive a protest very shortly from the Russian Government. The Russian authorities are not clear as to the action which they desire us to take, and are endeavouring to develop some scheme which would prevent their suffering directly from the consequences of Allied co-operation at Murmansk.

The Minister said that his Government recognized the fact that Russia would eventually be the battlefield for two imperialistic groups. It was perfectly obvious that Russia could not now seriously resist Germany, and that the Allied Powers could not come to their help in time, and it was therefore in the interest of the Bolshevists to defer as long as possible the moment at which this contest would start. The Russian Government quite realized that it would be obliged to fight, and was attempting to reconstitute its forces as rapidly as was possible: it was important in the interest of the Allies themselves that Russia should be given some time at any rate for this reorganization.

The Minister added, however, that the departure of the German Minister[3] was possible at any time, and that if, as appears possible, a counter-revolutionary party were to be formed in the Ukraine under German guidance, the Russians would be obliged to fight whether they were prepared or not. I answered that the Allied Governments naturally desired the strengthening of the Russian Army, but that they wanted to feel convinced that this Army would be employed against the Central Powers.

The Minister then told me that his Government was quite prepared for an understanding with the Allied Powers on the general principles indicated by you. The question of time was the principal difficulty and he was sorry that the Allies seemed to have taken no steps to put forward their views in an explicit form, although several weeks had passed since this question first came up.

It is true that there has been this delay, and it is clearer daily that the Government are fully aware that they will eventually find themselves obliged to fight. From their standpoint it is also plain that it is important to defer as far as possible the moment at which they will have to fight, and they will therefore not agree to Allied intervention until they realize that it cannot be avoided. They cannot take the side of Germany and, when the moment arrives, they will not decline to receive our co-operation, subject to the provision that Russia is properly safeguarded from any annexationist views in Japan.

I do not wish to defend the Bolshevist authorities, though I must again point out that it is foolish to believe that Trotsky and Lenine are German agents. Both of them are disliked by an important section of the public and it is probable that this unpopularity is increasing. There is not, however, any party now in Russia which is in any way likely to get rid of them for a considerable time. For this reason it is important for us to obtain their agreement to intervention. It would be possible to obtain their consent on the basis of the suggestions you have made, if only the Allied Governments could agree among themselves and put concrete proposals before the Russian Government.

Whatever policy may be decided upon, it is possible that continued indecision and hesitation by the Allied Governments may result in our losing not only the Bolshevists but also all other parties in Russia.

BRITISH EMBASSY WASHINGTON.
May 14th, 1918.

T MSS (SDR, RG 59, 861.00/1894½, DNA).
    ¹ Lev Mikhailovich Karakhan and Georgii V. Chicherin.
    ² Karl Radek.
    ³ Wilhelm, Count von Mirbach-Harff.

From Scott Ferris

My dear Mr. President: Washington, D. C. May 16th, 1918.

You have been so good and generous to me in helping me with all of my Public Lands Committee matters that I am daring to intrude on you with a matter outside of my strictly Congressional work.

As you are aware, the conferees on the Agricultural Appropriations bill are in a deadlock. Each of the two branches of Congress have their jaws set. The House has instructed their conferees against the $2.50 Wheat Amendment.¹ The Senate on the other hand has instructed their conferees to insist upon the $2.50 Wheat Amendment. In each case this has been done by a positive vote of the respective bodies. This apparently leaves them in a hopeless deadlock, which of course ties up the Agricultural Appropriation bill.

As you know, the wheat farmers of the west are very earnestly hopeful that you may come to their rescue and help them out. They feel sincerely and very earnestly that as compared with the prices of other products they have been somewhat discriminated against. I do not personally desire to lay too great stress upon this contention of theirs. I do, however, feel that it would be unfortunate to create a feeling among the wheat farmers of the west that they were being discriminated against, as I believe it would result in decreasing rather than increasing the production of wheat. I feel sure this would be traveling in the wrong direction rather than in the right direction, and I also feel sure would result in getting less wheat rather than more wheat.

The west have and are following you Mr. President, irrespective of party lines, as I believe they ought to do. I think they will continue to follow you to the end. They did do it in the last election, and as a result of communications recently carried on with more than 1100 County Chairmen in that number of Counties, I am confident that they will continue to do so. However, it would please me very much, it would please them very much, if you would say the word "relent," and allow the differences to be arbitrated by cutting them squarely in two and fixing the price half way between the two extremes.

This would, I believe, cement the differences and get the matter disposed of altogether.

With great respect and friendship, I am

                    Very sincerely yours,   Scott Ferris

TLS (WP, DLC).
[1] Senator Thomas P. Gore, on March 21, had introduced an amendment to the agricultural appropriations bill (H.R. 9054) which raised the *minimum* price for No. 2 northern spring wheat from the level of $2.00 per bushel set in the Food and Fuel Act of August 10, 1917, to $2.50. The Senate adopted the amendment that same day. *Cong. Record*, 65th Cong., 2d sess., pp. 3830-32. When the bill went to a conference committee in early April, the House conferees refused to accept the Gore amendment. By this time, as Ferris indicates above, both houses had reaffirmed their stands on the amendment and sent the bill back to conference.

From William Bauchop Wilson

My dear Mr. President: Washington May 16, 1918.

I am in receipt of your letter of the 8th instant,[1] expressing a wish that at least Mr. Matthew Hale and Mr. Henry Ford could be substituted for two of the gentlemen in the list submitted to you.

Mr. Ford's generous treatment of his employees and Mr. Hale's broad and sympathetic grasp of economic problems are widely known. From this standpoint their selection would be admirable. These umpires are to be selected by lot unless the Board makes a unanimous choice, and as these men are both large employers of labor, I feared that even their generosity might be construed as making them not altogether disinterested.

Upon further consideration I am of the opinion that their well known characteristics will outweigh any claims of interest that may be set up. I suggest therefore the elimination of Messrs. Rowland B. Mahany and Hywel Davies from the list I submitted to you and the substitution of Messrs. Hale and Ford.

I am inclosing herewith draft of a letter addressed to the National War Labor Board naming the umpires.[2]

Faithfully yours, W B Wilson

TLS (WP, DLC).
[1] WW to WBW, May 8, 1918, Vol. 47.
[2] [WW] to W. H. Taft and F. P. Walsh, n.d., T MS (WP, DLC). This draft was misplaced in the White House files. White House Staff to WW, July 12, 1918, TL (WP, DLC). It was finally sent as WW to W. H. Taft and F. P. Walsh, July 12, 1918, TLS (Letterpress Books, WP, DLC), and is printed in the *Official Bulletin*, II (July 15, 1918), 1. Hale and Ford were among the ten nominees.

From Park Trammell

Personal.

Dear Mr. President: Washington, D. C. May 16th, 1918.

Your recent letter regarding the Suffrage Amendment received,[1] and I wish to thank you for the same and also to assure you of my keen appreciation and high regard for your views upon this as well as all other subjects.

Prior to an expression of your views upon this question, I had made public announcement, in opposition to adopting the Federal Suffrage Amendment, and the people of Florida naturally expect me to vote accordingly. I very much regret that I am not now in a position to harmonize my attitude with your wishes in this matter.

With assurance of high esteem, I am,

Very respectfully,   Park Trammell

TLS (WP, DLC).
[1] It was probably a WWTLS or a WWhwL, which is missing.

John Franklin Fort to William Byron Colver

My dear Mr. Colver: Washington May 16, 1918.

Your memorandum, in relation to the letter that was written to the President in the Meat matter, and signed by Mr. Hoover, is before me.

That statement I fear was made by Mr. Hoover from what I said to him, and if it in any way was unfortunate enough to misrepresent your views it was probably in part my fault, although of course, not intended.

I think, in view of your fear that it may give a wrong view to the President of your mind on this question, that your statement which you send me in your letter of May 16 of your views should go to the President.[1]

Mr. Hoover wrote his letter to the President in my presence, and rather hastily, and put the following statement in his letter, "I wish to add that two members of the Federal Trade Commission are not fully in accord, and are of the opinion that there is no solution to the problem short of Government ownership." This was put in because I did not want to have it appear that I was representing, by my views, the views of all the Commissioners. I knew that Mr. Murdock held the view as stated by Mr. Hoover, and I was under the impression that you did.

I think the only fair way now is to send the statement which you gave to me when I went to the conference with the rest of the Committee, and which you had presented to our Commission; to the President in connection with that report. I should want my views to appear before him if I had any doubt about the correctness of what I believed to have been stated in any statement that was presented to him.

I am, therefore, taking the liberty of sending this correspondence to the President in order that you may be absolutely set right in your position before him on the Meat proposition.

Very truly yours,   John Franklin Fort

TLS (WP, DLC).
[1] Colver's letter and memorandum are printed as Enclosures with WW to HCH, May 20, 1918.

From Eleanor Foster Lansing

My dear Mr. President   [Washington] May 16th [1918]

I am a Captain of one of the Red Cross teams in the present campaign, and I find your name is at the head of the list that has been handed me, from whom we are to ask for subscriptions.

I feel some delicacy about doing this, but you will understand I really have no option in the matter. In view of the influence of your name, I hope that you will be willing to make your contribution in this way, and also do so in time for me to announce the fact on Monday, the 20th.

I will be most grateful if you and Mrs. Wilson will make your contributions to the Red Cross through my team.

Very sincerely yours   Eleanor Lansing

ALS (WP, DLC).

From the Diary of Josephus Daniels

May Thursday 16 1918

Pres. called me up & asked to see G.C. about his statement about Congress. Asked in a meeting in New York what he had to say about Congress, Creel answered "I haven't time to go slumming." Resolution in Congress. Creel will write a letter[1]

[1] Allen Towner Treadway, a Republican congressman from Massachusetts, had introduced a resolution (H. Res. 347) on May 14 which directed the House Rules Committee to investigate certain "statements alleged to have been made by George Creel," that is, the speech containing the remark about "slumming." *Cong. Record,* 65th Cong., 2d sess., pp. 6525-27. Creel wrote a letter on or about May 17 to Representative Pou, chairman of the Rules Committee, in which he expressed his belief in the integrity of Congress. Concerning his by then notorious remark, he wrote as follows: "At the Church of the Ascension I had spoken for an hour and for more than an hour answered questions bearing upon every phase of public misunderstanding. The question under discussion seemed so utterly silly and its silliness was so well understood by the audience, that I made a quick and thoughtless answer that left itself open to exaggeration and distortion. I admit the indiscretion and regret it deeply." *New York Times,* May 18, 1918. Nothing further came of the congressional investigation.

To Charles Evans Hughes

My dear Judge Hughes: En Route, 17 May, 1918

I warmly appreciate your action in consenting to cooperate with the Attorney General in making a thorough investigation of the charges of dishonesty in connection with the aircraft production, and I am sure that the Attorney General looks forward with as much pleasure as I do to acting with you in this important matter.

With warm appreciation,

Sincerely yours,   Woodrow Wilson

TLS (C. E. Hughes Papers, DLC).

To Caroline Seaman Read

My dear Mrs. Read: En Route 17 May, 1918

Your very beautiful and touching letter of May third moved me very deeply and I have not replied to it sooner only because it concerned a subject upon which I have had no confident judgment. I do not mean that I am not confident in my judgment that it would be a mistake and inconsistent with the heroism of our men under arms for those who are dear to them at home to wear mourning when they are gone, but only that I am not clear in my judgment as to what symbol of loss it would be best to use, and I hope you will indulge me in a little further consideration of the subject.

I have taken the liberty of consulting in this matter the committee of women which is associated with the Council of National Defense. I would very much like to have their judgment in the matter.

A further question in my mind is this: If I were myself publicly to make a recommendation in this matter, it might cause premature uneasiness by creating the impression that I was expecting large losses of life among our troops in the near future. I would not like so to disturb the hearts of the mothers of the country unless it were necessary to do so.

With great respect and admiration and profound sympathy,

Cordially and sincerely yours,   [Woodrow Wilson]

CCL (WP, DLC).

From Herbert Clark Hoover, with Enclosure

Dear Mr. President: Washington 17 May 1918

Please find attached hereto copy of a telegram I have sent to Mr. Poland,[1] who is Director of the Belgian Relief in Europe. I have seen Mr. Hurley this morning and he has given directions that such ships as can be diverted from the Cuban sugar trade shall be assigned to the Belgian Relief, as we shall have to justify this further shortage in sugar supplies on the basis of a contribution of the American people to saving life in Belgium.

I am in hopes that Mr. Lloyd George will see to it that the British authorities provide at least an equal amount of tonnage to that which will be supplied by these and other means on this side. I feel sure that we have an issue here that transcends in its moral and, therefore, in its eventual military significance the earlier despatch of soldiers to France and I am confident that on a definite consideration of the problem by Premiers Clemenceau and Lloyd George they will again adhere to this conclusion which has had to be debated in each crisis of the Relief so often in the past.

Yours faithfully,   Herbert Hoover

TLS (WP, DLC).
    [1] William Babcock Poland, who before the war had been a civil engineer specializing in railway construction.

ENCLOSURE

Washington, D. C.
16 May, 1918.

Would like you to present the following with the British National Committee to Mr. Lloyd George as from me as head of the Relief, not as a government official. Quote. As Chairman of the Belgian Relief I wish to again ask your personal intervention upon behalf of these suffering people. Three years ago upon my personal appeal you intervened to save the Relief and established it firmly as an unparalleled enterprise in humanity with the full sympathy and generous financial support of the British peoples. That action, which cost much in sacrifice to the British people by its demonstration of their true and broad humane objectives in the war, became one of the most potent forces in the conviction of the American people of the Allies' just cause. At our adherence to the Allied cause our government considered its obligations included a participation in the maintenance of these people who have suffered first and continue to suffer most from barbarism and in so doing we have not only taken our share of a burden and humane duty but we have all of us in the midst of the freezing flood of war contributed to keep alive in the hearts of our peoples its higher aims. The problem today is ships. Our people have stripped to the bone to furnish transport of supplies and men for Allied support. We can furnish no tonnage unless sacrifice is made somewhere in these directions. The tonnage required is so pitiable either in transport of men or supplies in the vast totals as to seem to justify the risk. Today to consign the Belgian people to starvation after three and one half years of almost unendurable suffering and steadfast loyalty and service in the Allied cause is indeed a terrible fate and it will destroy an invisible but great spiritual force among our two peoples worse than the loss of a great battle. I feel that without Your Excellency's intervention and positive instruction the Relief cannot be saved and a direction from yourself to your authorities and a communication of your approval of necessary diversions to our President would yield solution by our joint shipping authorities.

Herbert Hoover.

TC telegram (WP, DLC).

From Peter Joseph Hamilton

My dear Mr. President: San Juan, P. R., May 17, 1918.

In writing you the other day about Mr. Gompers' letter as to removal of Governor Yager, I tried to show how impolitic that act would be, but find that I neglected adding something of importance.

The particular accusation against Yager is that he has not advanced the condition of the working men in Porto Rico. I am afraid the facts have not been presented by creditable or reputable representatives, but nevertheless they should of course receive careful consideration.

I think you are going to take a place in history alongside the Gracchi and other great men who have tried to equalize social injustice, which generally assumes the form of oppression of the poor by the rich, and in our day of labor by capital. All hail to you in that noble work. It should apply of course to Porto Rico as well as to any other part of the United States, but conditions here require very careful handling, because of the difference of race, language and climate. The real difficulty here, as I take it, is not unlike that down South. The claim of the employers is that the laborers as a rule have no ambition and aim to make only enough to live on, with the result that they will work two or three days and be idle the rest of the week.

I am afraid there is a good deal of truth in this, if I can judge from domestic servants. It is in the climate.

Will raising wages change conditions, or will it result in more spendthrift habits to laborers and a fatal falling off in the production of sugar, coffee and tobacco, the island's great products? If so, there is no gain to labor and a great loss to capital.

But nevertheless Porto Rico could not be left out of the readjustment of social conditions. The real American way is to appoint a commission to investigate any question, and that would be one method, which, however, has not commended itself to Governor Yager because of the danger to industrial conditions among these ignorant and excitable people. Four out of five of the population are what they call peons, people who cannot read or write, have little religion, and have no idea of the English language or American institutions. Spanish language and customs are universal.

It occurs to me that an investigation which will get at all the facts could be managed through the custodian of alien property, Mr. Palmer. Two or three sugar factories, centrals as they call them here, as well as some other industries, have been seized by him, and I should think that quietly his agents or some impartial commission for him could make all necessary investigation and make a repirt [report] which would put the facts in their true light for governmental use. This could be as expeditious as the case will admit. The sugar men are unquestionably making a great deal of money and labor should share in it, but it seems to me that the public have an interest as well as labor. Labor should get more returns if the present are inadequate, but there must be some method of compelling labor to keep at work, or the whole thing would amount to putting the bottom rail on top without doing good to any one. It may be that a solution somewhat as has been managed in the Southern States will be the best way out. There is a great deal of negro blood in the laboring class here, but it may be, on the other hand, that conditions would not admit of the extension to a new country of the Southern solution.

Pardon my writing at length, but the problem is important and I am sure you would like to have first-hand impressions. Whatever plan is adopted could readily be enforced, as Porto Rico is an island and absolutely under American regulation. On the other hand, any mistake here may react upon American relations throughout Latin-America.

With all good wishes,

Very sincerely yours,   Peter J. Hamilton

P.S. I have asked the publishers to send you with my compliments vol. 9 of the P.R. Federal Reports, the decisions I had the honor to render during the past season and now just out.

TLS (WP, DLC).

From Newton Diehl Baker

Dear Mr President: Washington. May 16 [17], 1918

From this you will see that the entire German air-service is only slightly over 3000 planes.[1] You will be glad, too, to see that we are actively in the air fighting and are increasing our contribution. I hope to be able to report, in a day or two actual shipments of American made bombing planes to France. Some have gone already but I have not yet learned how many

Respectfully,   Newton D. Baker

ALS (WP, DLC).
[1] J. J. Pershing to H. P. McCain, received May 17, 1918, TC telegram (WP, DLC). In the course of his daily communiqué, Pershing gave a detailed listing of German aircraft believed to be in service on various portions of the western front. The actual total of aircraft given was 3,570 on all fronts. Pershing mentioned that the United States now had three pursuit and two observation squadrons of eighteen planes each at the front and that plans called for a further increase of four pursuit, seven observation, and one bombing squadrons within a month. He also noted a recent incident in which an American aviator had shot down two German planes within the space of one minute.

From the Diary of Colonel House

[New York] May 17, 1918.

I have been busy all morning since my return with the President's visit to New York. Loulie and I went to the station to meet the 3.18 train. While no one knew until the last minute that the President was to arrive, there was a large crowd gathered at the entrance of the station, and they cheered him lustily as we drove by. I had a half hour's conference with him at the Waldorf and then he, Mrs. Wilson and I motored for two hours or more along Riverside Drive and the Park. We had a good opportunity to talk and we covered both domestic and foreign affairs.

I told the President that a friend of mine happened to be present when the news of Hughes' appointment to investigate the aircraft charges was announced and some of the Members were very angry. They declared that Hughes was nothing but a "damned piker" to accept, for he must have known that it would blanket the Senate Inquiry.[1] The President said he had been complimented over Hughes' selection, but that he had told everyone that the suggestion was not his own. The newspapers this morning, without exception, praise him for the appointment.

The President expressed a lack of confidence in the present British Government. He said he did not trust them; that they did not "stand put." He told of a cable which had come from General Bliss in reference to an interview he had with Lord Milner in which Milner presented him a memorandum preparing to repudiate any

[1] The Senate, on May 22, adopted a watered-down version of S. Res. 241 (about which see WW to T. S. Martin, May 14, 1918, n. 1) which allowed the Committee on Military Affairs to carry on investigations under an existing Senate resolution. *Cong. Record,* 65th Cong., 2d sess., pp. 6641-43, 6885-86. With this authorization, a subcommittee of the Committee on Military Affairs carried on an investigation of aircraft production parallel to that of the Hughes committee and issued its report in August 1918. Seward W. Livermore, *Politics Is Adjourned: Woodrow Wilson and the War Congress, 1916-1918* (Middletown, Conn., 1966), pp. 129-34.

understanding we had regarding military affairs, if it suited their convenience to do so.[2] The President had Lansing send it to the British Ambassador for his edification and information.

Mrs. Wilson said that Tumulty had talked to her nearly all the way from Washington about Harry P. Davison and his evident intention of running for the republican nomination for President. My reply was that instead of being incensed, Tumulty should do everything to encourage it. If a member of the firm of Morgan & Company can be elected President of the United States, my political sagacity has been tremendously over-rated.

I believe the New York crowds have cheered the President with more enthusiasm on this trip than at any time before. However, he evidently feels it is hostile territory. I tried to get him to differentiate between the great mass of people here and the selfish few.

In discussing the Senate he expressed his profound contempt for most of them, naming Reed, Hoke Smith, Chamberlain, and Hitchcock, without going into the republican ranks, most of whom he thoroughly despises. I nearly always ask him if he is still committed to Reed as the worst of the lot, and he invariably replies that he is.

I asked if Hitchcock knew that he, the President, had tried to depose him from the Chairmanship of the Foreign Relations Committee. He replied that Hitchcock not only knew it, but probably also knew what he had told Senator Martin and other Senators, that is, that he, Hitchcock might be Chairman, but he, the President, would not consult with him about anything because he would not trust him with any information. Pinning the President down, I found that there was no one else on the democratic side, or even the republican side of the Foreign Relations Committee, that he would have chosen for Chairman. He considers them all "a rum lot."

The President and Mrs. Wilson dined with us at seven. There was no one else present. After dinner we had a few minutes of intensified conversation. He wanted my advice about George Creel. He said Congress would not give him any money if Creel continued as head of the Bureau of Public Information. He liked Creel and thought, in the main, his work was being well done and in a spirit quite in harmony with his, the President's, views. Therefore, he did not wish to do him an injustice or injure his future. I suggested he might send him abroad in some capacity, and to this he agreed if it could be done. He wondered if Frank Cobb would undertake the work. I believed that he would.

We went from Creel to McAdoo. McAdoo has not yet presented

---

[2] Wilson may have referred to T. H. Bliss to RL *et al.*, No. 103, May 3, 1918, Vol. 47.

his protest against the coal arrangement which Garfield and the others are contemplating. I told him that McAdoo intended to take it up with him next Monday and that I foresaw a stormy interview. He asked if I meant by this that he would threaten to resign. I thought that he would. He replied "he may resign if he wants to but I am determined that he shall not have his way because he is wrong in this instance." He said, too, that McAdoo had gotten so arbitrary that he presumed that, sooner or later, it would have to come to a crisis between them. He complained that McAdoo drew up revenue bills and other important papers without even consulting him. He said "son-in-law or no son-in-law, if he wants to resign he can do so." "The country will probably blame me, but I am ready to stand it." On the contrary, I thought the country would blame McAdoo. I consider it a perfectly intolerable position for McAdoo to place the President in. He might differ and he might argue, but it is the President after all upon whom the responsibility lies, and who must make the final decisions.

The President wondered what we would do in the event McAdoo should resign. My first suggestion was to segregate McAdoo's activities under different heads. I thought there was nobody else except McAdoo who would wish to be both Secretary of the Treasury and Director General of the Railroads, besides directing the Federal Reserve Bank System, to say nothing of War Insurance and a half dozen other things. The President wondered whether Houston could do the Treasury end. I thought he could, though he would not be my selection. It is in my mind to get McAdoo over our private telephone tomorrow and try and talk him out of his position.

It seems that McAdoo has been indiscreet enough to tell Grayson of his intention to resign in the event the President did not yield. Grayson thinks thinks [sic] the adulation which McAdoo has been getting throughout the country on his Liberty Loan campaigns has turned his head. I gave Grayson a comprehensive lecture on this subject and told him it was the most difficult matter in the world for a man to keep his balance under such circumstances, and that no one ever seemed to profit by the experience of others, no matter how recent the example set. I called attention to Secretary Garrison, and how completely he went under, disappearing not only from public view, but from public memory.

We went to see Fred Stone in "Kack-o-Lantern" at the Globe Theater.[3] There was a large audience and the President seemed to

---

[3] *Jack O'Lantern*, a musical variety show with book and lyrics by Anne Caldwell and R. H. Burnside and music by Ivan Caryll, featuring the song-and-dance actor, Fred Andrew Stone. For a review of the show, see the *New York Times*, Oct. 17, 1917.

enjoy the performance thoroughly. The audience was warm in its reception and between the acts applauded so vociferously that it was necessary for him to say a few words. He merely told them they were mistaken in believing that they saw the President of the United States; they merely saw a very tired man trying to enjoy himself. The President insisted upon driving us home before going to his hotel.

T MS (E. M. House Papers, CtY).

An Address in New York on Behalf of the American Red Cross[1]

[[May 18, 1918]]

Mr. Chairman and fellow countrymen: I should be very sorry to think that Mr. Davison in any degree curtailed his exceedingly interesting speech for fear that he was postponing mine, because I am sure you listened with the same intent and intimate interest with which I listened to the extraordinarily vivid account he gave of the things which he had realized because he had come in contact with them on the other side of the water. We compass them with our imagination. He compassed them in his personal experience.

And I am not come here tonight to review for you the work of the Red Cross. I am not competent to do so, because I have not had the time or the opportunity to follow it in detail. I have come here simply to say a few words to you as to what it all seems to me to mean.

And it means a great deal. There are two duties with which we are face to face. The first duty is to win the war. And the second duty, that goes hand in hand with it, is to win it greatly and worthily, showing the real quality of our power, not only, but the real quality of our purpose and of ourselves. Of course, the first duty, the duty that we must keep in the foreground of our thought until it is accomplished, is to win the war. I have heard gentlemen recently say that we must get five million men ready. Why limit it to five million? I have asked the Congress of the United States to name no limit, because the Congress intends, I am sure, as we all intend,

[1] Wilson spoke in the evening at the Metropolitan Opera House before an audience composed largely of volunteer workers for the Red Cross, most of whom had made special donations to the organization in return for their tickets. Cleveland H. Dodge introduced Wilson, and Henry P. Davison also spoke. Pierre Monteux led the Metropolitan Opera Orchestra in a brief program of musical selections and in the national anthems of France, Great Britain, Italy, and the United States.

Wilson's speech climaxed a day in which he had surprised almost everyone by marching some two miles down Fifth Avenue at the head of a huge parade in honor of the Red Cross. *New York Times* and New York *World*, May 19, 1918.

that every ship that can carry men or supplies shall go laden upon every voyage with every man and every supply she can carry.

And we are not to be diverted from the grim purpose of winning the war by any insincere approaches upon the subject of peace. I can say with a clear conscience that I have tested those intimations and have found them insincere. I now recognize them for what they are, an opportunity to have a free hand, particularly in the East, to carry out purposes of conquest and exploitation. Every proposal with regard to accommodation in the West involves a reservation with regard to the East. Now, so far as I am concerned, I intend to stand by Russia as well as France. ("God bless you!" shouted someone.) The helpless and the friendless are the very ones that need friends and succor, and, if any man in Germany thinks we are going to sacrifice anybody for our own sake, I tell them now they are mistaken. For the glory of this war, my fellow citizens, so far as we are concerned, is that it is, perhaps for the first time in history, an unselfish war. I could not be proud to fight for a selfish purpose, but I can be proud to fight for mankind. If they wish peace, let them come forward through accredited representatives and lay their terms on the table. We have laid ours, and they know what they are.

But behind all this grim purpose, my friends, lies the opportunity to demonstrate not only force, which will be demonstrated to the utmost, but the opportunity to demonstrate character, and it is that opportunity that we have most conspicuously in the work of the Red Cross. Not that our men in arms do not represent our character, for they do, and it is a character which those who see and realize appreciate and admire, but their duty is the duty of force. The duty of the Red Cross is the duty of mercy and succor and friendship.

Have you formed a picture in your imagination of what this war is doing for us and for the world? In my own mind I am convinced that not a hundred years of peace could have knitted this nation together as this single year of war has knitted it together; and, better even than that, if possible, it is knitting the world together. Look at the picture! In the center of the scene, four nations engaged against the world, and at every point of vantage, showing that they are seeking selfish aggrandizement; and against them, twenty-three governments, representing the greater part of the population of the world, drawn together into a new sense of community of interest, a new sense of community of purpose, a new sense of unity of life. The Secretary of War told me an interesting incident the other day. He said when he was in Italy a member of the Italian government was explaining to him the many reasons why Italy felt near to the United States. He said, "If you want to try an interesting experiment, go up to any one of these troop trains and ask in English how many of them have been in America, and see what happens." He tried the experiment. He went up to a troop train and he said, "How many of you boys have been in America," and he said it seemed to him as if half of them sprang up: "Me from San Francisco," "Me from New York,"—all over. There was part of the heart of America in the Italian army—people that had been knitted to us by association, who knew us, who had lived amongst us, who had worked shoulder to shoulder with us, and now, friends of America, were fighting for their native Italy.

Friendship is the only cement that will ever hold the world together. And this intimate contact of the great Red Cross with the peoples who are suffering the terrors and deprivations of this war is going to be one of the greatest instrumentalities of friendship that the world ever knew; and the center of the heart of it all, if we sustain it properly, will be this land that we so dearly love.

My friends, a great day of duty has come, and duty finds a man's soul as no kind of work can ever find it. May I say this: the duty that faces us all now is to serve one another, and no man can afford to make a fortune out of this war. There are men amongst us who have forgotten that, if they ever saw it. Some of you are old enough— I am old enough—to remember men who made fortunes out of the Civil War, and you know how they were regarded by their fellow citizens. That was a war to save one country. This is a war to save the world. And your relation to the Red Cross is one of the relations which will relieve you of the stigma. You can't give anything to the Government of the United States. It won't accept it. There is a law of Congress against accepting even services without pay. The only thing that the government will accept is a loan and duties performed, but it is a great deal better to give than to lend or to pay, and your great channel for giving is the American Red Cross. Down in your hearts you can't take very much satisfaction, in the last analysis, in lending money to the Government of the United States, because the interest which you draw will burn your pockets. It is a commercial transaction; and some men have even dared to cavil at the rate of interest, not knowing the incidental commentary that that constitutes upon their attitude.

But when you give, something of your heart, something of your soul, something of yourself goes with the gift, particularly when it is given in such form that it never can come back by way of direct benefit to yourself. You know, there is the old cynical definition of gratitude as "the lively expectation of favors to come." Well, there is no expectation of favors to come in this kind of giving. These things are bestowed in order that the world may be a fitter place to live in, that men may be succored, that homes may be restored, that suffering may be relieved, that the face of the earth may have the blight of destruction taken away from it, and that, wherever force goes, there shall go mercy and helpfulness.

And when you give, give absolutely all that you can spare, and don't consider yourself liberal in the giving. If you give with self-adulation, you are not giving at all, you are giving to your own vanity, but if you give until it hurts, then your heartblood goes into it.

And think what we have here! We call it the American Red Cross, but it is merely a branch of a great international organization which is not only recognized by the statutes of each of the civilized governments of the world, but which is recognized by international agreement and treaty as the recognized and accepted instrumentality of mercy and succor. And one of the deepest stains that rests upon the reputation of the German army is that they have not respected the Red Cross. That goes to the root of the matter. They have not respected the instrumentality they themselves participated in setting up as the thing which no man was to touch because it was the expression of common humanity. We are members, by being members of the American Red Cross, of a great fraternity and comradeship which extends all over the world. And this cross which these ladies bore today is an emblem of Christianity itself.

It fills my imagination, ladies and gentlemen, to think of the women all over this country who are busy tonight, and are busy every night and every day, doing the work of the Red Cross, busy with a great eagerness to find out the most serviceable thing to do, busy with a forgetfulness of all the old frivolities of their social relationships, ready to curtail the duties of the household in order that they may contribute to this common work that all their hearts are engaged in and in doing which their hearts become acquainted with each other. When you think of this, you realize how the people of the United States are being drawn together into a great intimate family whose heart is being used for the service of the soldiers, not only, but for the service of civilians where they suffer and are lost in a maze of distresses and distractions.

And you have, then, this noble picture of justice and mercy as the two servants of liberty. For only where men are free do they think the thoughts of comradeship, only where they are free do they think the thoughts of sympathy, only where they are free are they mutually helpful, only where they are free do they realize their dependence upon one another and their comradeship in a common interest and common necessity.

I heard a story the other day that was ridiculous, but it is worth repeating, because it contains the germ of truth. An Indian was enlisted in the army. He returned to the reservation on a furlough. He was asked what he thought of it. He said: "No much good; too much salute; not much shoot." Then he was asked: "Are you going back?" "Yes." "Well, do you know what you are fighting for?" "Yes, me know; fight to make whole damn world Democratic party." He had evidently misunderstood some innocent sentence of my own. But after all, although there is no party purpose in it, he got it right as far as the word 'party,' to make the whole world democratic in the sense of community of interest and of purpose.[2]

And if you ladies and gentlemen could read some of the touching dispatches which come through official channels—for even through those channels there come voices of humanity that are infinitely pathetic; if you could catch some of those voices that speak the utter longing of oppressed and helpless peoples all over the world to hear something like "The Battle Hymn of the Republic," to hear the feet of the great hosts of liberty going to set them free, to set their minds free, set their lives free, set their children free; you would know what comes into the heart of those who are trying to contribute all the brains and power they have to this great enterprise of liberty. I summon you to the comradeship. I summon you in this next week to say how much and how sincerely and how unanimously you sustain the heart of the world.[3]

Printed in *Address of President Wilson . . . May 18, 1918* (Washington, 1918); with corrections and additions from the text in the New York *World*, May 19, 1918, and from a reading of the CLSsh notes in the C. L. Swem Coll., NjP.

[2] This paragraph omitted in the official text.

[3] There are two WWT outlines, one dated May 18, 1918, and a WWhw outline of this address in WP, DLC.

From Ida Minerva Tarbell

My dear Mr. President: [Washington] May 18, 1918

The Woman's Committee of the Council of National Defense is sending you a formal, though very heartfelt expression of gratitude for the generous way in which you treated our recent conference.[1] I want to add a personal word. It is not anything that needs an answer, only something that I feel I should like to say to you, if it were right or proper for me to ask a conference.

When this committee undertook its work, I had an unexpressed but real doubt about our success. As you of course know the great woman's organizations of this country are fairly jealous groups. There has grown up among them something that approximates a caste system. They divide, in many communities in something the way churches did thirty or forty years ago, and do still, I fear, in some parts of the country. There have been times when I have felt that this growing separation of groups might become a real danger. When the Woman's Committee asked these organizations to come together in what might be called a federation of organizations, and to establish in each community a clearing house for women's war efforts, I must confess that while I thought it was a beautiful idea I feared it impractical. The wonderful way in which the women have answered to the suggestion of unifying their powers in order to serve to the best advantage in the winning of this war, has been an amazement and a joy to me. There is enormous potentiality in this merger. I never felt this so strongly as I did at this recent conference.

Of course we go to the women with the government requests and they work together but the response is voluntary on their part and if they respond it means in the case of hundreds of thousands of them the sinking of some special interest or association which they have always put before anything else in their public and social activities. I know you will agree with me that this is a wholesome thing for the women and that the more completely they do it, the better for the future.

Our first year's experience shows that if we are to carry this out as effectively as we should, we ought to have a little more general recognition to call your attention to the fact that if this great co-operative force which is voluntarily gathering in this country is to go on to full completion, the time may come that we shall ask of you a little more definite recognition than as yet has been wise.

You see, my dear Mr. President, this is to put an idea into your mind about this Woman's Committee. As a woman, I have never worked in organizations. I have been, I fear, very individualistic in my activities. I come with a new eye and a fresh outlook. I have rarely in my life been stirred more deeply than by the response that the women all over this land have made to the suggestion of the Council of National Defense that they coordinate their undertakings. It will not only be a wonderful thing for the Government, but a most wonderful thing for the women in the future if this movement can be fostered.

I have taken the liberty of writing this to you, not in my capacity as a member of this committee, but as an outsider—I really believe I am both! I have ventured to do it because of the exceeding kindness with which you have always treated any communication of mine.   Most sincerely and faithfully   [Ida M. Tarbell]

CHAIRMAN: NEWS DEPARTMENT

CCL (Ida M. Tarbell Coll., PMA).
[1] The Woman's Committee of the Council of National Defense held its first conference of state and local representatives in Washington from May 13 to 15, 1918. The conference reviewed the work of the committee during the past year and discussed plans for more efficient and active service in the future. For Wilson's letter of greetings to the delegates, see WW to Ida M. Tarbell, May 1, 1918, Vol. 47.
Wilson and Mrs. Wilson received 227 delegates at the White House at 2 p.m. on May 14, 1918. No record of Wilson's remarks on this occasion has survived.

From Jesse Holman Jones

My Dear Mr President   New York. May 18th, 1918

Permit me to express in a small degree my appreciation of your visit and all it has meant. Your speech was the strongest and best utterance that could have been made and the world needed just such a message from you at this time. Your marching in the parade and your letting the people see you as you did was just the big good man that you are.

I appreciate the tax upon your strength but it is energy well spent and rewarded.

Gratefully and sincerely yours,   Jesse H. Jones

ALS (WP, DLC).

From Upton Beall Sinclair

My Dear President Wilson: Pasadena California May 18th 18

I write this lying on my back after an operation for appendicitis, so I can only write a few words. I feel that this matter[1] should have your consideration. The Attorney's view point is the narrow legal one.[2] There is a broader. These men are ready to give real support to your policies, & they have a large & very active following. It seems to me a tragic blunder to drive them into irritated opposition. Your personal intervention would be honored by them, I know.

Sincerely Upton Sinclair

ALS (WP, DLC).
[1] U. B. Sinclair to Francis Gordon Caffey, United States district attorney for the Southern District of New York, May 3, 1918, TCL (WP, DLC). Sinclair argued that the fact that there had been a hung jury in the trial of the editors of The Masses on April 27, 1918 (about which see A. R. E. Pinchot to WW, May 24, 1918, n. 1) provided an opportunity for a compromise settlement with the defendants. Their opposition to the American war effort had been motivated solely by humanitarian motives and, in any case, they had more recently come to the support of the administration. Sinclair urged Caffey to bear in mind that these men would be "of use to the administration out of jail, while sending them to jail would put an end to their work and would still further embitter those whom they may influence."
[2] F. G. Caffey to U. B. Sinclair, May 10, 1918, TCL (WP, DLC). Caffey declared that the motives of the editors of The Masses did not matter. What did matter was that,

subsequent to June 15, 1917, the date upon which the Espionage Act took effect, the editors had attempted, both in print and in speech, to obstruct the raising of an army. He said that their seeming change of heart and consequent support of the government were motivated solely by their present belief that "the cause of the international proletariat" would best be served by the defeat of Germany. If this belief changed, they would not hesitate again to obstruct prosecution of the war. Caffey wrote that he would be more inclined to accept Sinclair's argument that the defendants would be of more use to the administration outside of jail if, at their trial, they had admitted their error and pledged themselves to obey the law. Instead, they had posed as martyrs to the cause of free speech. "It was and is the Government's contention," Caffey concluded, "that no right of free speech as such is involved in their case, but merely the question whether under cloak of that right, persons may wilfully obstruct the raising of an army to wage a war which has been declared by Congress."

From Margaret Woodrow Wilson

Precious, darling Father,   Asheville, N. C. May 18th 1918

The more I hear about that hand of yours the more dreadful it seems to me that such an accident should have happened to you.[1] When I first heard about it I was driving through the Desert along the Mexican border. Or rather we were having lunch in a tent at an out-post on the border. The Colonel[2] was called to the telephone where he was told that the latest bulletin was that you had hurt your hand *slightly*, having *touched* something hot on a tank. It didn't sound bad and the next day the papers I read did not even mention your hand, so I dismissed the idea of telephoning you from my mind. Then when I saw people, much later, who had seen you, and learned how you had been suffering I was distressed beyond words for you and to think that I had taken your hurt so casually— a hurt to beloved you! It does seem too hard that you had to have that nervous strain added to everything else. I do hope it has stopped hurting—your precious hand.

Several persons have told me that they saw you get out of the tank and never disclosed anything had happened to you—that you didn't flinch even, for they were watching you closely! I don't see how you could have helped jumping sky high!

Mrs David and I are here with Mee-Mee and Marjorie taking a four days rest before our last lap. I'll be home by the ninth of June, if not before. I may "do" Meade and Quantico from there—in that case I'll be home by the fifth.

The tide water District set up such a howl when we planned to go to Camp Hill and not to them, that we felt compelled to add another week to our tour, to include them.

Oh it will be good to be home again! I love you and adore you. I don't believe that your most enthusiastic admirers know as well as I do how wonderful you are.

Good night, darling Father. Give my dear love to blessed Edith
and tell her I think she was a darling to write to me.

Your devoted daughter,   Margaret.

ALS (WP, DLC).
  [1] See WW to H. B. Fine, April 20, 1918, Vol. 47.
  [2] Probably the local commander.

A Memorandum

(*Strictly Confidential*)   Handed me by Japanese
                                              Amb. May 18/18 RL.

SUBSTANCE OF THE NOTE EXCHANGED BETWEEN THE JAPANESE
AND CHINESE GOVERNMENTS ON THE 25TH OF MARCH, 1918.

The German influence steadily penetrating into the Russian territories and threatening the general peace and security in the Far
East, the two Governments will consider in common what measure
should be taken in order to meet the situation and to do their part
in the allied cause.

The co-operation between the two armed forces in the joint defensive movements against the enemy will be arranged by the competent Authorities of the two Governments who will from time to
time consult freely upon all questions of mutual interest. The Arrangement reached by the said competent Authorities will be put
into operation only at such time as the two governments may eventually decide.

T MS (SDR, RG 59, 861.00/1865½, DNA).

David Lloyd George to Lord Reading

[London, May 18, 1918]

Following from Prime Minister begins.

I think it is of the utmost importance House should come over
for the next Supreme War Council. It will be a very important
meeting at which vital decisions will be taken especially in regard
to use of United States troops.

I do not think it is possible to come to satisfactory conclusions
unless a political authority representing U. S. Government is present with whom we can deal on equal terms and who can come to
a decision on the spot.

Even if we follow the course you suggest recommendations will have to be cabled to Washington which is sure to mean more discussion before action follows.

Delay and indecision entailed by negotiations by telegraph are most injurious. Monsieur Clemenceau has now pressed for the next meeting on June 1st and Foch and he are very anxious we should come to final decisions without delay.

We entirely agree as to urgency of meeting. This date of course would barely give House time to arrive before the opening session even if he started early next week. If however House can come I would ask postponement for a few days though I should deeply regret delay so great is the importance I attach to House's presence. Will you urge these considerations upon the President and if he agrees try to induce House to sail as soon as he can. Please apologise to him for the short notice. I know how embarrasing these sudden journeys are; unfortunately Germany waits for no man. I asked Wiseman to warn him by cable some days ago. Reply at once as I must answer M. Clemenceau without delay.

T telegram (Reading Papers, FO 800/223, PRO).

From the Diary of Colonel House

May 18, 1918.

Herman Kohlsaat came this morning to talk about the interview I have arranged for him and Victor Lawson with the President at six o'clock this afternoon.[1]

B. M. Baruch was with me two hours going over the different phases of his activities, especially as to the Ordnance Department and its proposed reorganization, and the controversy between McAdoo and Garfield as to coal. Baruch almost wholly disagrees with McAdoo and believes he is making a mistake in creating so much trouble over a matter about which he is largely wrong.

I went to the Waldorf a few minutes before six to take Kohlsaat and Lawson up to the President's room. I left them without sitting down, because I had much to do and because I preferred them to do their talking alone. I cautioned Kohlsaat not to remain longer than fifteen minutes, but he telephoned me later to say that the President did most of the talking and they stayed a half hour. He was delighted with the interview.

The President, Mrs. Wilson, Admiral Grayson and Tumulty dined with us. After dinner the President went to my study where he remained about ten minutes looking over some hastily made notes for his speech tonight. He is determined to speak extemporaneously. I am always fearful of such efforts and discourage them when possible.

We drove to the Metropolitan Opera House, he going on the stage and Mrs. Wilson, Loulie and I going with some invited guests to Boxes 33, 34 and 35 which had been reserved for our party. The Opera House was beautifully decorated with flags and was crowded to the roof with a great and enthusiastic audience. The President's speech was cheered to the echo and he received a notable reception.

Our guests were Mrs. Marshall Field of Chicago, Mrs. Charles Marshall, Mr. and Mrs. Adrian Iselin, Mrs. Jas. W. Gerard, Mr. and Mrs. Charles Dana Gibson, David Miller and Sidney and Nancy.[2] After the meeting the President drove us to 115 East 53rd Street. The crowds cheered him repeatedly on his way out. I regard this as a great triumph for the President because the audience was composed almost wholly of those who, eighteen months ago, thoroughly detested him.

[1] Herman Henry Kohlsaat, former editor and proprietor of several Chicago newspapers, and Victor Freemont Lawson, proprietor and editor of the Chicago *Daily News*.

[2] Those persons not heretofore identified in this series were Evelyn Marshall Field, wife of Marshall Field III; Josephine Banks (Mrs. Charles Henry) Marshall, mother of Evelyn Marshall Field; and Adrian Iselin, a banker of New York, and Sara Gracie King Bronson Iselin. "David Miller" and "Sidney" were David Hunter Miller and Sidney E. Mezes. "Nancy" was Annie Olive (Mrs. S. E.) Mezes.

From Robert Lansing, with Enclosure

My dear Mr. President: Washington May 19, 1918.

The enclosed papers are translations of decoded German messages relating to the Sinn Feiners' intercourse with the German Government through Sinn Fein agents in this country prior and subsequent to the rebellious outbreak at Dublin at Easter time in 1916.[1] These arrived from London on Friday after you had departed for New York.

Before the documents reached us we had been importuned by the British Government through Ambassador Page to make them public. (See enclosed yellow telegrams.) I assume that they are anxious to have this done so that they can employ them as evidence against the conspirators now operating in Ireland, some of whom have already been arrested as announced in the morning papers. By employing copies obtained from this Government the British Government would not be subject to embarrassing questions as to the authenticity of the documents and the nature of the German code. Our certification would be sufficient.

I replied to Page yesterday that I would submit the documents to you on your return to the city, and would then send him an instruction, so I hope that you will read them at once since a decision should be reached without delay. I would recommend a careful reading because I found them most enlightening.

My impression is, although I cannot say that it is a settled judgment, that it would be impolitic at the present time for us to assume the responsibility for the publication of these papers. The Irish situation is very delicate and anything which we might do to aid either side in the controversy would, I fear, involve us in all sorts of difficulties with the Irish in this country. Of course last September we made public in the Official Bulletin some communications bearing on this subject (I enclose a marked copy) which mentioned Judge Cohalan and John Devoy,[2] so that probably no new American names would be brought out. Nevertheless publishing these papers at this time would be construed as a direct assistance to Great Britain in the matter of conscription in Ireland.

While I am not unmindful of the usefulness of the publication to the British Government in their endeavors to discredit the Sinn Fein movement, which is undoubtedly in the interest of Germany and, therefore, hostile to us as well as to Great Britain, I am loath to involve this country in the quarrel unless convinced that the reason is really vital and necessary.

Without denying that the fundamental idea of the Sinn Feiners has merit, their present willingness to cooperate with the Germans shows a blindness to the great issues to the war and a willingness to sacrifice democracy to their own selfish ends which seems utterly unpardonable. Of course I feel that we should do everything within reason to suppress the movement as long as it aids the enemy or weakens Great Britain, but I am doubtful as to whether the proposed assistance would be sufficiently valuable to warrant the trouble it would probably cause over here.

I hope that you can give me, as soon as possible, your opinion as to the answer we should make as to publication, as the British Government are very anxious and Page is very insistent, though I can well understand the reason for that.

Faithfully yours,   Robert Lansing.

TLS (SDR, RG 59, Office of the Counselor, Confidential Files of Chief Special Agent, No. 137—German Interest in Irish Matters, DNA).
  [1] These documents, thirty-two in number, consist of decoded telegrams, cipher letters, and one wireless message which passed between the German embassy in Washington and the Foreign Office in Berlin from September 25, 1914, to January 18, 1917. Many of the telegrams were sent by the Swedish Minister in Washington and the Foreign Ministry in Stockholm, some directly and some via Buenos Aires.
  Hitherto unknown to historians, these documents add vital information to what is already known about the activities of Bernstorff and particularly of the Irish-American nationalists, John Devoy, Daniel F. Cohalan, and Joseph McGarrity, in fomenting, financing, and coordinating acts contrary to the security of a nation in friendly relations

with the United States, all in gross violation of the neutrality laws of the United States. The documents, together with covering documents, are all filed in a group in SDR, RG 59, Office of the Counselor, Confidential Files of Chief Special Agent, No. 137—German Interest in Irish Matters, DNA. About this subject, see Reinhard R. Doerries, "Die Mission Sir Roger Casements im Deutschen Reich, 1914-1916," *Historische Zeitschrift*, CCXXII (1976), 578-625.

² *Official Bulletin*, I (Sept. 27, 1917), 7. Lansing also enclosed L. Harrison to RL, May 18, 1918, TL, in the file cited above, which reviewed the contents of the more important documents.

E N C L O S U R E

London. May 10, 1918.

Urgent. 9969. Most secret. My 9570, April 18, 3 P.M.¹ Confidential pouch number two now in transit on steamer PHILADELPHIA contains letter dated April 29th² enclosing decodes and translations of thirty-two important communications exchanged between Bernstorff and his Government in the years nineteen fourteen to nineteen seventeen inclusive establishing connection between Sinn Feiners and German Government and showing conclusively that the latter was involved both in the insurrection of Easter, nineteen sixteen, and in a similar outbreak planned for February last year and later postponed.

These documents I obtained from Admiral Hall and I have myself compared the copies with the originals. The Prime Minister who knows of the existence of the information but does not know its form now wishes it to be made public in the interests of the Allied cause and consequently this will be done at an early date. In order to give the appearance of consistency in respect of previous disclosures of German telegrams all of which have been made by our Government Hall would, in communicating the documents to higher authority for publication, have to intimate that after interchanging information with the American Secret Service for a period of over a year he is now in a position to decipher German messages himself. He greatly regrets that owing to superior orders he may be obliged to publish before copies of documents reach the President which will not be for another week, but if he can hold back publication until after that date he will do so in order that the President may if he desires make the contents public himself or authorize their publication as coming from our authorities. One of the papers is a cipher wireless message to Bernstorff which shows he had a receiving station in the United States which handled such messages unknown to our authorities as late as December 1916, while three messages from Bernstorff were appended without our Government's knowledge to cipher telegrams sent for him by the Department of State.

Please acquaint me with the President's views or suggestions at the earliest possible moment.   Page.

T telegram (SDR, RG 59, Office of the Counselor, Confidential Files of Chief Special Agent, No. 137, DNA).
¹ WHP to RL, April 18, 1918, No. 9570, T telegram (SDR, RG 59, 841.00/77, DNA). Page reported that the Germans were trying once again to arrange with the Sinn Feiners for an "outbreak" in Ireland.
² WHP to RL, April 29, 1918; also E. P. Bell to L. Harrison, April 30, 1918, both TLS (SDR, RG 59, Office of the Counselor, Confidential Files of Chief Special Agent, No. 137, DNA). The document referred to in n. 1 above is also in this file.

From Edward Wright Sheldon

My dear Mr. President: [New York] May 19th, 1918.

It was a great pleasure to see you marching down Fifth Avenue yesterday afternoon looking so well, and to sit a few feet behind you last evening, feeling your immediate presence and drinking in your uplifting and memorable words. It would have been a lasting satisfaction also to have spoken a word of greeting to you, but naturally that privilege had to be cheerfully forgone. And dear old Cleve, what a joy it must have all been to him!

So we have another historic occasion to link with your name. By what you said and were to that great audience, you have put the cause of the Red Cross and of mankind still more deeply in your debt, and its ever widening influence will move the world.

Believe me, with warmest regards,
                        Sincerely yours,   Edward W. Sheldon.

ALS (WP, DLC).

Henry Noble Hall to Lord Reading, with Enclosure

                                        Washington, D. C.
My dear Mr. Ambassador   Sunday [c. May 19, 1918]

I am taking the liberty of sending you a copy of a despatch which I sent to The Times last night. It reflects President Wilsons views very closely, almost in his own words: but in order to avoid trouble with the American Censor I have said "America believes" where I might truthfully have said "President Wilson believes"
                        Yours very respectfully   Henry N Hall

ALS (Reading Papers, FO 800/222, PRO).

ENCLOSURE

Times, London.[1]

French's[2] proclamation announcing the discovery of a German plot in Ireland and calling on all loyal Irishmen to defeat the conspiracy[3] is given great prominence in all the American newspapers. Further details are anxiously awaited[4] and pending their receipt there is an evident disposition in official circles to refrain from comment. But if proof is forthcoming that the Sinn Fein leaders have been guilty of treasonable communications with the German enemy no one in America will have the slightest sympathy for them. On the contrary their summary execution as soon as their guilt is established is looked upon here as a foregone conclusion.

American opinion towards Ireland has recently undergone a very radical change. The United States is heart and soul for the war, and sentiment against Germany is growing stronger every day. Sympathy for Ireland has rapidly dwindled ever since open opposition to conscription was declared. President Wilson's message to France in which he says that this is "a war in which every man who loves the right ought to be proud to take part" exactly mirrors public feeling in this country and Americans cannot understand Ireland's refusal to fight in the cause of liberty and justice which Irish-Americans consider good enough to fight for and die for.

America is unswerving in its belief that conscription is the only fair and truly democratic method of raising armies and Irish opposition to conscription estranged American sympathy overnight. If now any real evidence can be adduced showing recent dealings between Irish leaders and Germany, if proofs exist that the Sinn Fein has appealed to the Kaiser for support, American opinion will become as violently hostile to the Sinn Fein as it is hostile to Germany. No disloyal Irishman will have any standing at the bar of American public opinion.

But too great importance cannot be attached to the immediate publication of the proof on which the charges against the men arrested in Ireland are based, because Irish-Americans have already raised the cry that this is a new English campaign of terrorism against Ireland and is designed to cloak the military suppression of Irish aspirations for self-government. Outside of professional Irishmen the presumption of the average American will be in favor of England which at no time since the beginning of the war has stood so high in the estimation of the American people as now. The splendid stand made by the British army fighting "with their backs to the wall" to stem the tide of German invasion, and bearing the brunt of the great struggle on the Western front has won the admiration of the whole American people and created a strong pro-British sentiment.

When the present German-Irish plot has been dealt with, however, the question of self-government for Ireland will remain, and Americans will not visit upon the whole of Ireland the sins of the Sinn Fein traitors. Every American of every party and of every class is in favor of self-government for Ireland and believes that the whole Irish problem has been messed. The prospect of the coercion of Ireland is most distressing and most distasteful to Americans especially as the adjournment of the House of Commons without even the introduction of a bill for the self-government of Ireland so definitely promised by Mr. Lloyd George seems to indicate that the hope of setting up an Irish parliament before the enforcement of conscription is receeding, if indeed it has not been abandoned altogether. And Americans do not believe that Field-Marshal French's proclamation will bring voluntary enlistments in the present state of Irish feeling.

Despite America's admiration for Mr. Lloyd George and its confidence in his leadership there exists a striking unanimity of opinion that his handling of the Irish situation has been crude and uninspiring, that he blundered in coupling conscription with self-government putting the cart before the horse. America is convinced that no real progress can be made in the settlement of the Irish problem until the British Government is guided by fundamental principles instead of by expediency.

America believes that if British statesmen will look critically upon the existing system of government applied to Ireland they will see that the old familiar form which seemed so natural has altered its aspect and when examined with fresh and awakened minds reveals itself as sinister and repugnant to democratic ideals. America believes that autonomy for Ireland looked upon frankly by men willing to comprehend its true character will assume the aspect of things long believed in, of rights long cherished by Englishmen themselves.

The most enlightened opinion in America would not hesitate to apply to Ireland the principles laid down in the Virginia Bill of Rights which Americans look upon as the very cornerstone of government by consent of the governed, and which is the landmark whereby the policy of the United States towards the self-determination of small nations is guided. There is no responsible thought in America of separating Ireland from the British Empire any more than of separating one of the forty eight States from the American Union, but America undoubtedly favors a most generous recognition of nationalist, not separatist, aspirations.

Hope is expressed here that the German plot which has been discovered in Ireland involves only a small number of extremist agitators without the support of any such large section of the population as would render it impossible to proceed with the promised plans for the self-government of Ireland.

Saturday midnight.

T MS (Reading Papers, FO 800/222, PRO).
  [1] Only the first four paragraphs of the following dispatch appeared under the heading "Disloyalty Not Tolerated in America," London *Times*, May 20, 1918. The final sentence of the first paragraph and the first sentence of the fourth paragraph were also omitted.
  [2] That is, Field Marshal John Denton Pinkstone French, Viscount French of Ypres and of High Lake, who had been appointed Lord Lieutenant of Ireland on May 5.
  [3] "Firm Rule in Ireland. An Intrigue with Germany. Many Arrests," London *Times*, May 18, 1918. This article, dated May 17, discussed briefly French's proclamation, to be issued on May 18, in regard to "certain of the King's subjects in Ireland" who had "entered into a treasonable communication with the German enemy." A late bulletin, dated May 18, 3 a.m., printed immediately below the article, stated that thirteen of the alleged Irish conspirators, including Eamon de Valera and Arthur Griffith, had been arrested on May 17. More detailed analyses of the plot appeared in *ibid.*, May 20-22, 1918.
  [4] An official British statement, which summarized the evidence in the government's possession of intrigues between Germany and Irish revolutionary leaders, appeared as "German Plots in Ireland," *ibid.*, May 25, 1918.

From the Diary of Colonel House

May 19, 1918.

The President and Mrs. Wilson called for us around noon and we motored to Cleveland Dodge's Riverdale home. The weather was exquisite, and we sat on the open veranda overlooking the Hudson enjoying the beauties of Spring. After lunch we drove through Bronx Park to the Pelham Bay Naval Training School. We did not return until around 5.30. On the drive the President and I sat together on the small front seats and discussed many pending questions of interest. I suggested, in the event McAdoo persisted in his determination to have his way about the coal order or resigned, that he, the President, reorganize the Cabinet in the following way:

Let Lane become Director General of Railroads; put Houston in the Treasury; make Vance McCormick Secretary of Agriculture. I thought Lane's appointment would be applauded by the public because of his long experience on the Interstate Commerce Commission, and because of the belief that he had the ability to maintain himself in such a position. I suggested that his appointment would be a good one because he was not elegible for the Presidency[1] and therefore could not play politics which was a great temptation to anyone in that position. I thought if Lane was made Director General of Railroads, he ought to relinquish the Interior. The President thought so too, but wondered if Lane would consider it a demotion. We thought McAdoo would not make the issue, but he was determined in the event he did make it to accept his resignation without argument. The President said he would never again try to persuade any man to remain in service when he wanted to retire. He thought McAdoo's retirement would make him, the President, unpopular for the moment. I felt otherwise for the people would applaud his standing up against his son-in-law in a matter of this kind, and accepting his resignation rather than yield where he considered the public service involved.

We both thought McAdoo's resignation would ruin his chances for the democratic nomination for President, but the President said this was the most comforting thought in the whole situation for he did not believe it was good public policy to take members of the same family in succession for President. He wondered whether people would not think he had forced McAdoo to resign merely to gratify his own ambition to become President for a third term. This I considered possible but of no particular moment.

We discussed the question of declaring war against Bulgaria and Turkey. He was more inclined to declare war against Bulgaria than Turkey, giving as his reason that the Turks would massacre the entire Christian population. I considered the best reason for not declaring war on Bulgaria was that there were no Bulgarian soldiers on the Western Front, and as long as they refused to help the Germans there, we might well refuse to declare war on them.

We took up the pending tax measures in Congress. He frankly confessed ignorance as to them, and very dryly remarked that McAdoo seemed to think that was his particular province. He wondered if McAdoo could make a living should he go out. I thought that he could and that he need not concern himself about that feature. He was somewhat sceptical himself. He also wondered whether it would not be disagreeable for Eleanor, his daughter, because of the strained relations between her father and husband. I did not consider strained relations a necessary corollary. I advised doing the whole disagreeable business pleasantly and without any trace of heat. I also advised talking to McAdoo as kindly as if he were giving him some new and great reward. He might thank him for all he had done, and express regret that his high sense of public duty would not permit him to go along further in the service.

We dined with the President and Mrs. Wilson at the Waldorf. There was no one else present excepting Admiral Grayson. After dinner and [sic] the President complained of rather acute indigestion. There were a few pending matters and a few papers which I placed in his hands for attention. He promised to come to Magnolia during the summer if it were at all feasible.

We left early and Dr. Grayson walked home with me. I told Grayson to see McAdoo the first thing tomorrow and to tell him that in my opinion he would make a grave mistake to go into any argument with the President regarding the coal controversy; that what he should do was to tell the President that he thoroughly disagreed with the whole business, but since the President had decided otherwise, he, as a good soldier, would go ahead and not give it another thought.

Grayson thinks McAdoo is in a highly nervous condition and doubts whether he will be able to make him see reason.

I was surprised at the indiscretion of the President and Mrs. Wilson talking before the waiters while we were at dinner about people and things which if repeated would cause no end of trouble.

Grayson is to report to Gordon[2] tomorrow morning just as soon as he has had his interview with McAdoo, and Gordon is to telephone me.

[1] Because he had been born in Canada.
[2] That is, Gordon Auchincloss.

To Robert Lansing

My dear Mr. Secretary,   The White House. 20 May, 1918.

I am going to keep the Sinn Fein documents a little while to study them, but I have clear judgment with regard to our publishing them. It is the judgment you yourself indicate. I do not think that the British Government ought to use us to facilitate their fight for conscription in Ireland. I believe that the difficulties that would be created for them as well as for us by the publication in this country, by official release, would be greater than any of the alleged advantages; and I hope that you will reply to Page in that sense.[1]

Faithfully Yours,   W.W.

WWTLI (SDR, RG 59, Office of the Counselor, Confidential Files of Chief Special Agent, No. 137, DNA).
[1] RL to WHP, May 20, 1918 (SDR, RG 59, Office of the Counselor, Confidential Files of Chief Special Agent, No. 137, DNA):
"The President believes that the difficulties that would be created for the British Government as well as for this Government by the publication of these documents in this country, by official release, would be greater than any of the advantages to be gained thereby in the light of the information now before us.

"You may so inform the British Government and say that this Government is not prepared to publish these documents at this time and is not willing publicly to sanction their release."

To Robert Lansing, with Enclosure

My dear Mr. Secretary,   The White House. 20 May, 1918.

I would be very much obliged if you would let me have your comments and judgment on the suggestion with which this despatch from Reinsch closes.   Faithfully Yours,   W.W.

WWTLI (WP, DLC).

ENCLOSURE

Peking, May 16, 1918.

Semenoff advance continues. He announces policy not to interrupt Siberian railway traffic, Allied passengers and freight under special permit are to pass. He is ready to turn over operation of railway to American Commission.

Charles H. Smith, formerly aid to Oustrogoff,[1] reports Siberian railway men anxious to have American assistance believes coalition of forces in Siberia possible. Offers his services to investigate, speaks Russian.

My telegram of May 14, noon.[2] Horvath disclaims intention to publish government proclamation. Japanese and Russian ministers recently informed the Chinese Government that the transfer of the Harbin Changchuen section to Japan was agreed to by Kerensky Government and will be consummated when stable government established in Russia. This gave rise to loan rumor.

Situation in Siberia seems more favorable than ever for effective joint action of Allies and American initiative. A commission authorized to command moderate financial support would be able to reconstruct at least Siberia as an Allied factor. Should America remain inactive longer friendly feeling is likely to fail.

Reinsch.

T telegram (WP, DLC).

[1] Charles Hadden Smith, a civil engineer, at this time associated with the Advisory Commission of Railway Experts headed by John F. Stevens. "Oustrogoff" was L. A. Ustrugov, identified in Vol. 47 of this series.

[2] P. S. Reinsch to RL, May 14, 1918, T telegram (SDR, RG 59, 861.00/1789, DNA). The relevant sentence reads as follows: "The Chinese government is greatly concerned because of reports from Harbin that General Horvath has issued a government proclamation and that he has concluded a loan with a Japanese bank secured on the Harbin-Chinese Eastern Railway, the proceeds to be used in recruiting troops." By a "government proclamation," Reinsch meant a proposed proclamation by Horvath of an independent government in Siberia. On this point, see James William Morley, *The Japanese Thrust into Siberia, 1918* (New York, 1957), pp. 189-91.

To Robert Lansing

My dear Mr. Secretary,   The White House. 20 May, 1918.

I do not know what to say by way of comment on these papers[1] that I have not already said repeatedly. The two parts of this question (as you properly discriminate them) must not and cannot be confused and discussed together. Semenov is changing the situation in Siberia very rapidly, apparently; and General March and the Staff are clear and decided in their opinion that (1) no strong enough force to amount to anything can be sent to Murmansk without subtracting just that much shipping and man power from the western front, and (2) that such a subtraction at the present crisis would be most unwise.

They believe, moreover, that there is no sufficient military force, in Japan or elsewhere, to do anything effective in Siberia.

Please follow very attentively what Semenov is accomplishing and whether there is any legitimate way in which we can assist.

Faithfully Yours,   W.W.

WWTLI (SDR, RG 59, 861.00/1895½, DNA).
[1] That is, the Enclosures printed with RL to WW, May 16, 1918.

To Newton Diehl Baker, with Enclosure

Dear Baker,   The White House. 20 May, '18

I sign this with great satisfaction. Thank you for preparing it so carefully   Woodrow Wilson

ALS (N. D. Baker Papers, DLC).

E   N   C   L   O   S   U   R   E

From Newton Diehl Baker

My dear Mr. President: Washington. May 17, 1918.

I beg to hand you herewith a proposed executive order.[1] It is prepared on the assumption that you have approved the Overman Bill[2] and desire immediately to accomplish a separation of military aeronautics and aircraft production from the Signal Corps.

The effect of this order is to restrict the Signal Corps to communications to establish a division of Military Aeronautics as an entirely independent division under General Kenly,[3] whose nomination to Major General was promptly recommended for confirmation by the Military Affairs Committee of the Senate and confirmed. It further establishes a Bureau of Production under Mr. Ryan and separates the property of the Signal Corps appropriately to this new distribution of functions, and also separates the funds appropriated so that they can be expended directly under the authority of General Kenly in the training and military use of aircraft, and by Mr. Ryan in the matters of production.

I have gone over this order very carefully with General March, General Crowder and Mr. Ryan, and I respectfully recommend its approval and promulgation. The provisions of the order will, I feel quite sure, convince everybody that the old order in this matter is terminated and that the reorganization is complete.

Respectfully yours,   Newton D. Baker

TLS (N. D. Baker Papers, DLC).
[1] CC MS (WP, DLC). Baker describes it below. Wilson signed it on May 20, and it is printed in the *Official Bulletin*, II (May 21, 1918), 1-3.
[2] About which see WW to L. S. Overman, March 21, 1918, n. 1, and J. Betancourt to WW, May 8, 1918, n. 1, both in Vol. 47.
[3] William Lacy Kenly, formerly chief of the Air Service of the A.E.F., most recently commander of the 2d Field Artillery Brigade in France.

To Scott Ferris

My dear Ferris: [The White House] 20 May, 1918

It is hard to differ from you in any matter, because our minds generally come together so easily, but I cannot believe that it is right to yield in the matter of the $2.50 wheat amendment, because I believe that the legislative fixing of prices is a mistake. If $2.50 is a fair price, it ought to be ascertained to be by such means as we have already been employing, such means as we did employ in establishing the $2.20 price. Rigidity in such a matter would break into and destroy the whole method by which we are dealing with the industries of the country. I feel this so strongly that I could not assent to the method which is indicated by a legislative fixing. I have discussed this matter with others and in my own mind so often and so seriously that my conviction is clear in the matter and my only doubt arises from the fact that you disagree with me.

Cordially and faithfully yours,   Woodrow Wilson

TLS (Letterpress Books, WP, DLC).

To Samuel Gompers

My dear Mr. Gompers: [The White House] 20 May, 1918

As you know, I believe, I took up the matter of the representations against Governor Yager of Porto Rico which are contained in the papers sent you by Mr. Iglesias, and I now have a memorandum from General McIntyre[1] which satisfies me that the charges are not well founded. But I want you to be satisfied and at the suggestion of the Secretary of War himself I am writing to ask if you would not be kind enough, after reading the enclosed letter of the Secretary of War to me,[2] to take the whole matter up yourself with the Secretary for conference. He would be glad to invite General McIntyre to such a conference and try to arrive at a just course of action, if any is needed, and I think that this is much the best way to bring our minds together.

Cordially and sincerely yours,   Woodrow Wilson

TLS (Letterpress Books, WP, DLC).
[1] That is, the Enclosure printed with NDB to WW, May 16, 1918 (second letter of that date).
[2] NDB to WW, May 15, 1918.

To Herbert Clark Hoover, with Enclosures

My dear Mr. Hoover: The White House 20 May, 1918

I have examined the enclosed report[1] and before forming a judgment on it I would be very much obliged if you would read the letter from Mr. Colver which I also enclose. It struck me as containing some unusually interesting suggestions. Do you think that the half-way course he proposes is not feasible or advisable?

Cordially and sincerely yours,   Woodrow Wilson

TLS (Hoover Archives, CSt-H).
[1] That is, the Enclosure printed with H. C. Hoover to WW, May 13, 1918.

E N C L O S U R E   I

William Byron Colver to John Franklin Fort

My dear Governor: Washington May 16, 1918

You have handed me a copy of the letter written to the President by Mr. Hoover under date of May 13th. In this letter Mr. Hoover says:

> I wish to add that two members of the Federal Trade Commission are not fully in accord and are of the opinion that there is no solution to the problem short of Government operation.

This is unintentional and unfortunate but a complete mis-statement of my beliefs and I am sorry that the President should have it fixed in his mind as being my mind.

As you know, I have taken no part in the Packing Commission's deliberations but I did write to the Federal Trade Commission as a matter of record, suggesting a solution which I thought and still think, occupies a middle ground between the majority and minority views.

I am enclosing you copy of my memorandum and if you deem it fair and wise, I should appreciate it if I could be set straight.

Yours very truly,   William B. Colver.

TLS (WP, DLC).

ENCLOSURE   I I

MEMORANDUM
for the
COMMISSION

TO THE COMMISSION:

There seem to be two schools of thought with respect to the packing situation.

One group believes that Government operation is necessary because the packers are too big to submit to discipline or to be coerced by penalties.

Another group holds that the packers should remain in private operation under public regulation because they are too big to be publicly operated.

On various other points all seem to be agreed and still other points are actively urged by some and not actively opposed.

It would seem that there must be a common ground which all can occupy.

It is not the purpose of this memorandum to attempt to cover all the points raised in all the plans, but to cover a few of the essential ones and ones which if agreed upon, may lead to a complete and unanimous program.

FIRST: Treat stockyards as freight houses and turn them, with all belt lines and marketing facilities over to the Railroad Administration.

SECOND: Establish standard grades of quality in meat animals with appeal to a small board of arbitrators whose decision on price and grade as between buyer and seller, shall be final. Determine at the beginning of the feeding season a reasonable price for a standard feed animal as a basis for all grades; prices to be fixed on this basis, plus feed and feeding as determined by the average costs of primary feeds.

THIRD: Control flow of stock by (a) a system of Government

reports on prices and market conditions; (b) a system of country buying; (c) Government advice and information that will prevent a heavy proportion of stock from being entered upon feed at the same time and especially early in the season; (d) local publicity of wholesale prices.

FOURTH: The private car lines being instruments of transportation in Interstate Commerce, should, naturally, remain in the hands of the Railroad Administration.

FIFTH: Take over, under the Lever Law, Wilson & Co. and have it operated by Thomas Wilson, Mr. Boyden of the Food Administration (or W. C. Boyden of Chicago) and Mr. Wallace of Des Moines.[1]

SIXTH: Use the experience gained in the operation of Wilson & Co. to enforce uniform accounting, measure reasonable profits and as a general standard for comparisons as against the remaining members of the Big Five.

Wilson & Co. may best be taken over for several reasons—(1) it is a comparatively recent concern, less complicated in its relation to subsidiaries; (2) to all intents and purposes, Wilson & Co. is jointly owned by the other four, so that in taking it over, the Government lays its hand upon all five; (3) aside from Ogden Armour, Wilson is the brains of the outfit and would bring to the Government operation, the acme of packing talent; (4) Boyden and Wallace give the public interest control and veto power in the executive board and both could be usefully employed in the actual operation aside from their primary duty as sentinels; (5) as a matter of magnitude of task, taking over Wilson & Company is infinitely simple as compared to taking over all five; and (6) through the actual operation of one company coupled with the control of marketing facilities, of public and private car lines, the Government should be sufficiently armed to cope successfully with the Big Four.

In conclusion, it may be that with the foregoing as a ground work, details as to price regulation, uniform accounts, auditing, control of retail prices, etc., might be simple to work out.

If an advisory committee is used under any plan, it is suggested that such advisory committee have a continual and official standing and active duties so that it would be in during operations instead of merely coming in to appear in cases which go to adjustment or arbitration.   Respectfully submitted,   William B. Colver.

TS MS (WP, DLC).
   [1] Thomas Edward Wilson, president of Wilson & Co., meat packers of Chicago; Roland William Boyden, head of the legal enforcement division of the Food Administration; William Cowper Boyden, lawyer of Chicago; and Henry Cantwell Wallace, editor and proprietor of *Wallace's Farmer*.

To Alexander Theodore Vogelsang[1]

My dear Mr. Secretary: [The White House] 20 May, 1918

Before signing the enclosed,[2] I would like to have an expression of your personal judgment as to whether it is pressingly necessary, because I have felt a good deal of misgiving about the too general relaxation of the eight-hour rule with regard to government work and I would like to be very clear as to the pressing necessity for each case before signing the order. Probably you have considered the matter from this point of view, but I should like to be assured by you that you have.

Cordially and sincerely yours,   Woodrow Wilson

TLS (Letterpress Books, WP, DLC).
[1] First Assistant Secretary of the Interior; at this time Acting Secretary of the Interior.
[2] A. T. Vogelsang to WW, May 18, 1918, TLS (WP, DLC). Vogelsang enclosed a proposed Executive Order which suspended the provision of the law limiting workers to an eight-hour day on federal projects for the specific purpose of speeding construction of an addition to St. Elizabeths Hospital in the District of Columbia. The new buildings, Vogelsang explained in his covering letter, would house military veterans with mental-health problems.

To Edwin Augustus Woods

My dear Mr. Woods: [The White House] 20 May, 1918

What you tell me[1] of what Ralph Harbison[2] reports is indeed very delightful to hear, though I must say that the feeling which the people in Europe apparently have for me and the expectations they apparently entertain fill me with misgiving as much as anything else, because I realize only too well how little of their expectation I can in all probability fulfill. I need not say that I will do my best.

With warm appreciation,
Cordially and sincerely yours,   Woodrow Wilson

TLS (Letterpress Books, WP, DLC).
[1] Woods' letter is missing.
[2] About Harbison, see n. 2 to the address to the Pittsburgh Y.M.C.A. printed at Oct. 24, 1914, Vol. 31. Harbison had been in France for several months investigating the work of the Y.M.C.A. among the American forces there. *Princeton Alumni Weekly*, XVIII (March 13, 1918), 504, and Ralph W. Harbison, "In the Front Line Trenches," *Missionary Review of the World*, XLI (Aug. 1918), 605-606.

To Eleanor Foster Lansing

My dear Mrs. Lansing: [The White House] 20 May, 1918

It is a pleasure to contribute through you to the Red Cross Fund, and I am enclosing my check for $1,000.

Cordially and sincerely yours,   [Woodrow Wilson]

CCL (WP, DLC).

From Edward Mandell House

Dear Governor: New York. May 20, 1918.

Reading took breakfast with me this morning. He is just back from Ottawa. He had a cable from the Prime Minister instructing him to see you and request that you send me, or someone else, to represent the civil end of our Government at the next meeting of the Supreme War Council.

This meeting is scheduled to meet Saturday, but he thinks it could be postponed for a few days if I could leave within the next day or two. Reading confessed to me that he thought it would be a mistake for me to go, or for you to send anyone, because it is so evident that what Lloyd George wants is someone to over-rule Pershing. They probably intend to bring up the same old question, and they will try to go back to the understanding which you, Baker and Reading had and which they amended.

We both believe that whatever is contemplated at this next meeting can rest long enough to get a cable directly from you in the event it is necessary to decide any difference which may arise between them and Pershing. Please be assured that I am perfectly willing to go now or at any time when in your judgment I should go. We think, however, that it would be much better for me to go later, probably in September or October, if you think it wise for me to go at all.

Reading indicated, and the newspaper despatches from Washington this morning bear him out, that the British Government wish this Government to pretend that we have found some of the treasonable matter concerning Ireland. If I were you I would caution Lansing about this. The British have made several attempts in this direction before as you will remember.

Affectionately yours,   E. M. House

I wish you could know how much I have enjoyed the past three days with dear Mrs. Wilson and you.

TLS (WP, DLC).

From Robert Lansing

My dear Mr. President: Washington May 20, 1918.

Enclosed is the reply of the British Foreign Office to our inquiry as to the advisability of declaring war on Turkey and Bulgaria.[1]

This makes the situation as follows: The British, French and Italian Governments agree in advocating a state of war with both countries, while the Supreme War Council favors war against Turkey at once and probably war against Bulgaria later in the event of the latter not being affected by a declaration against Turkey.

From the political point of view the Council's advice seems to me unwise. As to the united opinion of the Allied Governments I think careful consideration should be given. I feel, however, that a decision cannot be much longer delayed.

Faithfully yours,   Robert Lansing

TLS (WP, DLC).
¹ W. H. Page to RL, May 17, 1918, T telegram (WP, DLC). Page quoted a note from the Foreign Office which stated that the British government favored an American declaration of war against Turkey and Bulgaria on the grounds that this action would discourage those nations; give heart to the Greeks, Serbs, and Armenians; and assure a significant role for the United States at the peace table in regard to the settlements to be reached concerning the Near East and Middle East.

From Herbert Clark Hoover

Dear Mr. President: Washington 20 *May 1918*

I am informed that my cable, which I dispatched to Lloyd George and of which you have a copy, was delivered to him on the 17th. I am also informed that he considers that the Belgian Relief should have priority over other war needs and in any event the British Government has acted at once by offering to find one-half of the tonnage necessary to support the Belgian Relief and has assigned already, for immediate loading, four ships. This is contingent upon the United States Shipping Board's assigning one-half the necessary tonnage *pari passu* with the British. Our Shipping Board has been directly advised of these arrangements.

I am happy to state that this apparently reverses the attitude of mind expressed from the inquiry sent through the various departments here to various departments in England and I am sincerely in hopes that you can see your way to complete the matter by giving positive directions to the Shipping Board that they should at once undertake to comply with this arrangement in preference to other war measures.   Yours faithfully,   Herbert Hoover

TLS (WP, DLC).

From William Gibbs McAdoo, with Enclosure

Dear Governor,   [Washington] May 20/18

I hope you may find time to read the enclosed letter before I see you Tuesday.

I am sorry it is so long but I could not give you the railroad picture

and the relation of the coal question to it, in a briefer communication.   Affectionately yours   W G McAdoo

ALS (WP, DLC).

ENCLOSURE

From William Gibbs McAdoo

Dear Mr. President: Washington May 20, 1918.

The Fuel Administration has urged you to require the railroads
to pay to the mine operators of the United States the maximum
price for coal fixed by the Fuel Administration, instead of the railroads contracting as heretofore with mine owners for their coal at
the best procurable price within the maximum.

If you comply with this request, it will mean that the Director
General will have to pay approximately $60,000,000 more for rail-
road fuel in the year 1918 than if he is allowed to contract for it on
reasonable terms as has been the long standing practice. Since the
railroads are now in the possession and control of the Government
and are being operated for public account, the $60,000,000 extra
cost for railroad coal, as urged by the Fuel Administration, will be
taken out of the pockets of the people of the United States and
turned into the pockets of the rich coal operators who are already
making profits on coal, which, in my opinion, cannot be justified
upon any reasonable ground.

The Government, as you know, is obligated for a certain return
or rental for the use of the railroads while they are under public
control. As things now stand, it is impossible for the Government
to earn this year from the railroads as much as the guaranteed
rental. Every dollar of unnecessary cost, therefore, imposed upon
the railroads must be made good out of the public treasury, or by
an increase of freight and passenger rates. The Railroad Wage
Commission has just recommended to me that the wages of
employees be increased for the year 1918 by a sum estimated
at.. $300,000,000
To this must be added:

  (a) Increased wages made in 1917 which
      will be reflected in operating
      expenses for 1918, estimated at........................ 75,000,000
  (b) Increased cost of coal and other fuel
      for 1918 over 1917 (excluding the
      additional $60,000,000 which the Fuel

        Administration wishes to impose on the
        railroads) estimated at.................................... 167,000,000
  (c) Increased cost of all kinds of railroad
        supplies for 1918, estimated at 190,000,000
  (d) Miscellaneous increases in expenses on
        account of taxes, further readjustments
        of wages, abnormal shifting of labor,
        abnormal handling of traffic under war
        conditions, etc. estimated at............................ 100,000,000
                                                Total.............. $832,000,000

This unavoidable increase in cost of railroad operation for 1918 will unhappily impose a great burden on the public. This should be met, I think, by increase in freight and passenger rates instead of by general taxation, as the railroads ought to be made self-sustaining. Such rate increases must in the nature of things be very heavy. In the tentative schedule submitted to me (which does not take into consideration the proposed extra payment of $60,000,000 for railroad coal), I find that an increase of 30 cents per ton on coal is suggested. This of itself, if adopted, will impose a heavy load on the American people through a largely increased charge for coal to the consumer.

If to this $832,000,000 we add unnecessarily $60,000,000 by taking it from the railroads, and, therefore, from the people, and transferring it to the already over-enriched coal operators, the people will have to stand a greater increase in the transportation rate on coal than thirty cents per ton; the increase will have to be forty-five cents per ton of coal to cover this extra $60,000,000 payment. The difficulty about all freight rate increases is that by the time they reach the consumer they are multiplied several times, and those least able to bear the load are required to take the most of it.

To really reduce the public's burdens instead of increasing them should be our first thought. With this end in view I have already made drastic cuts in railroad operating costs in numerous directions; many more are in contemplation and will be made effective as soon as possible. This is a painful process, involving discharge of thousands of men whose lives have been spent in railroad work, as well as reduction in railroad service involving in many cases genuine inconveniences to the public. These economies and sacrifices will be negatived in large measure if $60,000,000 at one stroke should be added unnecessarily to operating costs. It would seem almost sardonic if these economies and sacrifices should be translated into a $60,000,000 reward for over-prosperous coal operators who have no just claim for such recognition.

Every reasonable consideration, therefore, argues in favor of preventing avoidable and unnecessary increases in the cost of operating the railroads. This consideration becomes in fact an imperative duty of Government at this time when such increases must be paid by the people, when the cost of living is steadily mounting higher and when the cost of coal is already one of the heaviest burdens the public has to bear.

In an effort to meet these objections the Fuel Administration has suggested that a horizontal reduction of ten cents per ton might be made in the price of coal at the mines, if the operators should be allowed to charge the maximum price for railroad coal. This sounds plausible but it will not bear analysis. It would profit nobody except the mine operators; the public would not benefit. By this plan the mine operators would get $45,000,000 extra from the railroads and the general public would secure an apparent saving of $45,000,000 in the cost of coal. But this "saving" is wholly illusory because the railroads are now operated for public account and the $45,000,000 payment to the operators for railroad coal would create a deficit of a like amount in railroad earnings which the public would have to pay through increased taxation or increased railroad rates. As a matter of fact, I believe that the general public would never get the benefit of the suggested reduction of ten cents per ton at the mine even if it did not create the railroad deficit to which I have referred. Such reduction would doubtless be absorbed by the wholesale and retail coal dealers before it ever reached the consumer. The only way in which such a reduction in the price of coal could be made to benefit the consumer is to have the Government take the entire output of coal at the mines and distribute it at reasonable prices to the American people as hereinafter suggested.

The claim of the coal operators and the Fuel Administration that this added pecuniary burden on the public is needed in order to get a properly distributed car supply is almost wholly imaginary because the difference between the car distribution under the Fuel Administration's proposal and under a properly coordinated system of contracts for railroad coal will be negligible. In its essence the difference between the two plans is that under the Fuel Administration plan the railroads will obtain their coal from all available mines in a given district, whereas under the Railroad Administration plan the railroads will obtain their coal from all mines in a given district which are willing to make contracts to supply that coal. The Railroad Administration plan will involve just as wide a placement of railroad orders as will the Fuel Administration plan, except to the extent that the operators are unwilling to make contracts with the railroads on a reasonable basis and insist on selling all their coal at the maximum prices, notwithstanding the inevitable and marked advantages they gain from supplying coal for railroad purposes. It may be that under *private* management in some districts railroads by preference concentrated their entire contracts upon a few mines, but such will not be the policy of the Railroad Administration, and if any available mine fails to get its share of the railroad contracts it will be because of the unwillingness of that mine to sell a portion of its coal at a reasonable price fairly reflecting the advantages which the mine will derive from the opportunity to supply railroad coal.

Once the present uncertainty is ended, it is believed that railroad contracts will be so widely and equitably placed that the difference between that situation and the situation which would arise under the Fuel Administration's plan will be entirely negligible from the standpoint of car supply; and if any mine is put at a disadvantage it will be because of its own greedy policy.

The coal operators were willing to cooperate with the railroads for a wider distribution of railroad orders at reasonable prices until the Fuel Administration insisted that the railroads should pay the maximum price, whereupon the operators promptly refused to cooperate in bringing about this desirable result. This is not unnatural in view of the fact that the coal operators will profit by the Fuel Administration's attitude, if sustained, to the extent of an extra $60,000,000 in the year 1918.

The question of an equal car supply or distribution does not arise except in time of car shortage. If there is car shortage it cannot affect the railroads, since they must have, as they have always had, a preference in coal deliveries. This is necessary because all industries, and, in fact, the life of the people, depend upon the uninterrupted operation of the railroads. The priority of the railroads' claim for fuel is, for this reason recognized everywhere as inherent in the situation and as operating not adversely but beneficially to the public interest. In time of car shortage, therefore, the railroad needs must first be supplied and the remaining available cars should be distributed as equitably as possible among all the mines. If there is no car shortage, then no issue arises, because everybody will get an equal car supply. This situation is not affected in the slightest degree by the price the railroads pay for coal.

As I understand it, the principal argument advanced by the Fuel Administration is that fundamentally there ought to be an equal car supply and that the railroads ought not to take advantage for their benefit of an unequal car supply. Of course, if it were possible always to have sufficient railroad facilities and cars, there would be no problem. But in the nature of things this cannot always be the case. At times there will be car shortages for which even the railroads are not responsible, and when they do occur, there cannot be any such thing as an equal car supply, because cars must first be furnished for the coal needed to keep the railroads going. Under such conditions the fact that coal must first be loaded for railroad use is not a matter of railroad volition but of the necessities of the case. This fact is one of a number of legitimate considerations which ought to determine the price of railroad coal.

The mine operators have taken advantage of the conditions prevailing last winter (which were not due wholly to car shortage or to failure of transportation, but in great part to weather conditions, to orders of the Fuel Administration for preferential car placements, and to other causes, which seriously impeded the efficient operation of the railroads) to frighten the public and make it believe:

First, that priority of railroad coal operated prejudicially to the public in the distribution of coal; and,

Second, that there will of necessity be a repetition of these conditions next winter unless the railroads pay the maximum price for coal.

The policy of the operators to exaggerate conditions and alarm the public is illustrated by their publishing with great elaboration erroneous figures issued by the Geological Survey which indicate a heavy current shortage in coal cars. Inquiry develops that these theoretical car shortages rest upon estimates of coal capacity which assume a normal annual coal production of nearly 850,000,000 tons, whereas the total production last year was less than 550,000,000 tons, and no one can seriously contend that more than 650,000,000 tons will be consumed this year under the most favorable imaginable circumstances. Yet on the basis of these theoretical and erroneous figures, the coal operators have tried to alarm the public with the notion that there is at present a serious car shortage—all this being a part of their program to increase their grossly excessive profits. Of course, the figures issued by the Geological Survey are not intentionally erroneous and no doubt we shall have the cooperation of that Bureau and of the Department of the Interior in correcting this manifest error. I have already drawn it to the attention of Secretary Lane.

There is, in my judgment, no adequate ground for the claims of the coal operators. As to the *first*: The railroads are now under Government control and will be operated primarily in the public interest. No private interest will be permitted to interfere with their operation in the public interest. This of itself assures a more equitable distribution of car supply among all the mines of the United States in the future regardless of the price the railroads pay for coal or the necessary priority of railroad coal. This means that there should be a very much wider distribution and a larger movement of coal throughout the country than in the year 1917. This is already being realized. The railroads transported in April, 1918, approximately 88,000 cars, or 4,400,000 tons more than in April, 1917. In fact, the railroads are now handling more coal than consumers can unload in many cases, and individual embargoes may have to be applied. As to the *second*: Conditions of last winter are not likely to be repeated if, among other things, the Shipping Board furnishes promised shipping so that the New England situation (which was thrown upon the railroads last winter because coastwise tonnage was taken by the Navy and the Army for overseas service, reducing the amount of coal ordinarily transported by water from Hampton Roads to New England) will not have to be carried by the railroads to the same extent as in the winter of 1917-1918; if also there is no undue interference in the matter of preferential car placements and the proper operation of the railroads. The price paid for railroad coal has no bearing on these matters.

To prevent, if possible, a repetition of the misfortunes of last winter, the Director General of Railroads has ordered 100,000 freight cars, of which 45,000 are coal cars. The locomotive builders have orders on their books for more than 3500 locomotives for railroad account, which absorbs their entire capacity for the remainder of 1918. It is expected that most of this equipment will be delivered before next winter. It will certainly be delivered if the requirements of the Army and Navy and Shipping Board for steel and other products are not permitted to deprive the railroads of essential motive power and equipment to enable them to perform their proper functions to the American people.

With this large increase in cars and motive power, with the repair of existing locomotives and cars, now proceeding with unusual diligence, all of the equipment (motive power and cars) should be in infinitely better condition for service next winter. The Director General has also ordered large improvements in railroad facilities. The completion of these improvements which are now in progress and the general reorganization of the Federalized railroads should be so perfected before next winter that the railroads should be able, in the absence of extraordinary weather, to render much better service to the public than in the winter of 1917-18.

Of course, this depends in very considerable measure upon ships for the New England trade, which have been promised to the Railroad Administration by the Shipping Board; upon the delivery of necessary raw materials for cars, locomotives, supplies, etc., as promised by the War Industries Board; upon the ability of the railroads to get sufficient labor to maintain tracks and equipment in proper condition; and upon the policy of the War Department with respect to drafting railroad employees.

If the War Department continues to take from the railroads skilled labor and essential man power which cannot be replaced, a serious and perhaps irreparable injury will be done not only to the conduct of all war operations in the United States, but to war operations in Europe as well, because they are dependent in large part upon what we do in the United States.

The point I wish to impress is that the payment by the people of the United States to the mine owners of $60,000,000 extra for coal in the year 1918 will not assure or promote an equal car supply; that it is not a remedy for any of the conditions complained of; that it will not make the railroads or mines function better; that it will not produce ships for the New England coal trade; that it will not influence deliveries of locomotives and cars, nor increase essential railroad facilities; that it will not supply needed railroad labor nor affect the policy of the War Department with respect to railroad employees. This $60,000,000 has nothing to do with the case and would be, in effect, merely a gift to the mine owners without any compensating advantage to the public, and, in my opinion, could neither be justified nor defended.

The claim has been advanced by the mine owners that unless they are paid the maximum price for railroad coal, there will be strikes and production will be diminished. I do not believe it. I have no doubt the mine owners have played upon the mine workers to a very considerable extent by the skillful propaganda in which they have engaged and that many mine workers have been made to believe that the difficulty about car supply is due to the lower price the railroads have been accustomed to pay for coal. It is, of course, true that when there is car shortage, due to insuperable weather conditions or other causes, mines are shut down, labor is idle and the mine worker suffers; but to increase the profits of the mine operator is not a remedy.

I believe it to be the fact that the greatest cause of discontent among the miners is the fabulous profits the coal operators are making without an equitable participation by the miners in these profits. The greater you make the profits of the coal operators, the greater the incentive to the mine workers to strike in order to get their share. My sympathies are with the mine workers and I do not blame them for this. I believe that if the coal operators were today limited to reasonable profits instead of being permitted to take exhorbitant profits, the mine workers would be more contented and that the chances of labor disturbances would be greatly diminished.

I am going to make every conceivable effort to keep the mines supplied with cars in order that there shall be as little interruption of the miners' work as it is possible to bring about. With more locomotives and cars and reasonable cooperation on the part of those whose cooperation is essential, this can be accomplished without paying the coal operators the extra $60,000,000 as proposed by the Fuel Administration. This great sum could be expended far more advantageously to the public and to the mine workers for additional railroad equipment and enlarged railroad facilities.

The Fuel Administration also argues that where the Government fixes a maximum price for an article, every Government agency should pay the maximum price equally with the general public, and that as the railroads are now under Government control, they should pay the maximum price for coal. This argument has no proper relation to railroad coal. When we entered this war, the Government at once became a consumer on an abnormal scale of many important products, particularly iron and steel. The excessive Government demands inevitably reduced the available supply of these products for normal and general consumption.

If the Government, while absorbing such a large part of the supply of these things, had taken them at a comparatively low price and at the same time had left all other consumers to scramble for the greatly reduced remainder at whatever prices the manufacturers chose to exact, it is evident that the manufacturers would promptly have made up, out of the private consumers thus placed at their mercy, whatever concessions in prices they had been forced to make to the Government. Obviously, therefore, it was proper policy in such cases to protect the general public by establishing reasonable prices applicable equally to all.

But the coal situation is wholly different. The railroad demand for coal is not an abnormal war demand but a normal peace time demand. To satisfy the railroad demand does not decrease the normal supply available for the general public, but on the contrary, conserves it, because the more effectively the railroads operate, the more satisfactorily the production of the mines will be maintained and increased. The supplying of railroad coal does not involve any sudden and disrupting change in the relative quantity of coal available for private consumers, as is the case where the Government suddenly absorbs the larger part of the steel production of the country and leaves a relatively small amount available for general consumption.

For thirty or forty years the whole commercial situation, so far as coal is concerned, has adjusted itself to the relative needs of the railroads and the rest of the public and to the relative price paid by the railroads and the rest of the public. The Government is not called upon to adopt a new policy in order to protect the public so far as railroad fuel is concerned. The fact is that the Fuel Administration is trying to get the Government to adopt a new policy with respect to railroad fuel which will inure solely to the private profit of the coal operators without any compensating benefits to the public. Such a policy will, in fact, be a discrimination against the railroads and, therefore, a discrimination against the public because the railroads are now operated for public account.

If the prices fixed for coal by the Government are reasonable, no valid objection can be raised to the principle that all shall pay the same price—the railroads as well as the general public. For my part, I am willing that the mine operators shall have not only reasonable, but liberal profits. The present Government coal prices are not reasonable; they are more than liberal; they are excessive and, to my mind, unjustifiable. They are giving the coal operators fabulous profits and building up enormous private fortunes at the expense of the general public. This is demonstrated by the sworn reports of thousands of coal companies to the Bureau of Internal Revenue showing their net earnings for the year 1917. The profits of the coal operators as disclosed by these reports are amazing and almost incredible. The following taken at random from these reports show the net earnings (without deduction for Federal taxes) on their capital stocks of a number of coal companies in West Virginia, Ohio, Pennsylvania, Kentucky, Indiana, Illinois and other States:

2,344.40 %	669.41 %
200.55 %	575.41 %
208.16 %	372.38 %
121.13 %	334.21 %
102.79 %	297.76 %
875.10 %	846.18 %
214.81 %	146.85 %
149.75 %	137.08 %
2,133.72 %	203.00 %
2,337.12 %	7,856.42 %
404.29 %	484.60 %
563.64 %	1,223.10 %
509.58 %	472.01 %
398.52 %	301.92 %
1,248.79 %	2,360.40 %
470.00 %	104.23 %
126.45 %	57.57 %
130.07 %	222.07 %
134.70 %	388.21 %

561.67 %	701.10 %
208.54 %	1,321.34 %
86.86 %	796.81 %
244.83 %	231.87 %
1,361.90 %	139.31 %
2,574.89 %	1,802.11 %
4,731.25 %	90.69 %
2,779.44 %	518.24 %
146.09 %	4,218.16 %
285.91 %	311.49 %
147.47 %	122.21 %
193.40 %	346.18 %
119.96 %	1,393.34 %

I could continue at length with similar examples, but it is unnecessary. Of course, all coal companies have not earned such huge profits, but the reports show that net earnings ranging from 30% to 200% and 300% on capital stock are quite general. Income and excess profits taxes will reduce these net earnings, but even then the remaining profits are abnormal.

I respectfully suggest that you permit me to make public the reports of the coal companies, as the law gives you authority to do. These reports are most illuminating and offer a proper basis for the formation of just and accurate public opinion. I think this is particularly necessary in view of the fact that the propaganda actively carried on by the coal operators has misrepresented the facts to the American people. The effective way to combat this is to make the reports of the coal companies public.

The burden imposed upon the American people by excessive coal prices will become increasingly difficult to bear. The inequality in the profits of the coal operators also shows that the most efficiently conducted and most fortunately placed mines are unduly favored by the high prices fixed by the Fuel Administration, and that even the inefficiently operated and less fortunately placed mines are making profits. I presume that the Fuel Administration proceeded upon the theory that a high price for coal would bring all classes of mines into production, and that sound economics and equitable distribution of profits should, therefore, be disregarded.

But to accomplish this, the American people are forced to endure excessive prices for every necessity as a result of the abnormal prices fixed by the Fuel Administration for a basic commodity which enters into the production of everything essential to the National life.

What is the remedy? It is in your hands absolutely. It is to commandeer the entire output of all the coal mines of the United States

at cost plus a reasonable profit per ton of coal delivered at the mouth
of the mines. By averaging the cost the Government could furnish
coal and coke to consumers throughout the United States at a
reasonable price, give a just and fair return to the coal operators,
save millions of dollars to the American people, and assure at all
times fair wages to labor.

Already the Congress has put this power in your hands, and I
know that the American people would appreciate your handling of
this coal problem with your characteristic courage and vision, just
as they have appreciated from one end of the land to the other your
courage and vision in taking control of the railroads in the interest
of the people. In fact, the commandeering and distribution by the
Government of the entire coal and coke output is simplified now
that the Government controls the railroads. Transportation can be
made to reciprocate completely with the distribution of coal and
coke, now that it is under Government control.

The time to take this step is now. It may have been too late to
consider it in 1917, but certainly it is not too late to do it for 1918.
If the Nation is to successfully grapple with the coal problem and
is to exercise a restraining influence upon the mounting prices of
all the essentials of life, it must take control of the Nation's fuel
and see that the discriminations against the people, which are inherent in the present plan, are transformed into a discrimination
in favor of the people through the agency of Government control.
I think the time is ripe for this important step, and that it is absolutely necessary for the adequate protection of the public. The
coal situation cries out for a thorough remedy which will protect
the public, tranquilize labor, and strike at the very root of the profiteering which now constitutes one of the gravest menaces to the
country.

The present experiment in dealing with coal prices has not worked
satisfactorily. It has created great social injustice and unrest. To
commandeer the entire coal production of the United States, as the
Act of Congress approved August 10, 1917, gives you full power to
do, is, I think, the true solution of the problem. Reasonable prices
could then be fixed for everybody, including the railroads.

If, however, you reach the conclusion that the present high prices
for coal shall continue and that the right of the Director General
to contract for coal on reasonable terms shall be denied, then some
way should be found to make the coal operators and not the coal
consumers of the country pay the extra cost. Through the power
the law gives you to fix railroad rates, you could fix a car placement
rate or charge of 25 cents per ton on all coal, to be paid by the
operators out of the present established price and not by the con-

sumers. It would then be unnecessary to increase the existing transportation rates on coal by more than a small amount, and the general public would, therefore, have to absorb that small increase only.

The chief weakness in this plan is that it may take all or nearly all of the profits of those relatively few mines whose operating costs are high and whose profits are small. If this is true, however, it merely demonstrates the fact which cannot be escaped that the only way to deal with the situation without gross injustice to the public is to abandon entirely the plan which gives operators with low costs preposterous profits in order that operators with high costs may continue production and to adopt, instead, the plan of commandeering all the coal at cost plus a reasonable profit, and selling to the public at a reasonable average price. Even the car placement charge, however, has the virtue of transferring a large part of the burden of increased railroad rates to the over-prosperous coal operators who are fully able to bear it and of taking it off the general public which has suffered already too much from excessive prices for coal.

I earnestly hope that you will exercise immediately the power conferred upon you by the Act of August 10, 1917 (copy attached as Exhibit A),[1] take the entire coal and coke product of the United States and distribute it to the public at reasonable prices, and thus put an end to a situation which is highly prejudicial to the public interest, and which will, in my judgment, soon become intolerable.

I need not assure you of the genuine pleasure it will give me to see that the railroads cooperate to the utmost limit in the execution of such a plan.

To recapitulate:

1. It is not necessary to give the coal operators $60,000,000 more per annum at public expense to secure more equal car distribution among the mines.

2. The railroads are now a part of the public. They will be operated solely in the public interest, which means that such discriminations between mines, if any, as were practiced under private control will be abolished without giving the coal operators an unjustifiable price for railroad coal.

3. There will be a larger and more equal car supply under public control, not only because of public control, but also because of new equipment ordered by the Director General.

4. The suggested reduction of 10 cents per ton at the mine on condition that the coal operators may get a corresponding amount from the railroads and hence from the public will benefit the coal operators only. It will not advantage the public.

5. The present Government prices for coal are excessive and are giving the coal operators unjustifiable and unconscionable profits, as shown by reports of coal companies to the Bureau of Internal Revenue.

6. The remedy: The Government to take the entire output of the mines at cost plus a reasonable profit and sell it to the American people at a fair average price. This will reduce cost of coal to everybody, prevent discriminations and save millions of dollars to the American people. The law gives you full power to do this.

7. If you are unwilling to take this course, then

   (a) The Director General should be left free to contract for railroad coal on reasonable terms; or

   (b) If this is denied, then a car placement charge of 25 cents (or if this is too much, then a reasonable amount) per ton at the mines should be imposed on the coal operators to be paid by them and not transferred to the general public.

Cordially yours,   W G McAdoo

TLS (WP, DLC).
¹ Not printed.

From William Kent

Dear Mr. President: [Washington] May 20, 1918.

After having sat in with Max Eastman, I feel sure that it is a great mistake to continue the prosecution in court and to maintain a boycott against The Liberator¹ from the mails, when, as near as I can understand, there are no specific charges against the issues that are refused second class privileges. I believe that Eastman has a realizing sense of the need of cooperative work in defining the terms of productive and non-destructive democracy, and that he, like Clarence Darrow, would be an agency for good. I think you will find a sympathetic tendency in Solicitor General Davis, who is wise and clear-headed, and who has met Eastman. Fred Howe is deeply interested.

As far as resistance to the idea of going into the war is concerned, there are many of us who must say *peccavi*. The ends and objects of the struggle have at length become clear, and I am sure that Eastman clearly and loyally recognizes the situation, and that henceforth he will be an asset and not a liability, if given the opportunity.   Yours truly,   [William Kent]

CCL (W. Kent Papers, CtY).
¹ The name of *The Masses* since March 1918.

From Cleveland Hoadley Dodge

My dear President   New York May 20th 1918
Now that your visit to New York is history (and I thank God that no harm came to you) I want to thank you from the bottom of my heart for the great service you have rendered in our Red Cross venture. You have touched the hearts & pockets of not only this big city, but of the whole country, as nothing else could have done, and have given us all new cheer and encouragement.
It was a great joy to have you at Riverdale & Mrs Dodge & I appreciate your coming to us more than we can tell you. You evidently made a hit at Pelham & I am glad you went there.
Trusting that your visit has not tired you, I am as always
                    Your's devotedly & affly   Cleveland H Dodge

ALS (WP, DLC).

From Eleanor Foster Lansing

My dear Mr. President   [Washington] May 20th [1918]
I am deeply grateful to you for sending your very generous check to the Red Cross through me. It is a great encouragement to my team.   Cordially yours   Eleanor Lansing

ALS (WP, DLC).

From the Diary of Colonel House

                                        May 20, 1918.
Lord Reading telephoned from Ottawa yesterday asking if he could see me this morning as early as eight o'clock. I invited him to breakfast and he arrived promptly at that hour. We had breakfast together and went over the letters and cables which he had received from his Government. The main cable he wished to discuss was one from the Prime Minister asking that he see the President immediately and point out the necessity of my coming to the next meeting of the Supreme War Council. This has been set for June 1st, but the Prime Minister said if I would leave at once it would be deferred until I could reach there. I told Reading it was impossible for me to go now and to my surprise he agreed with me.
What Lloyd George wants is for me to supercede General Pershing and to dominate our military action over there. He knows my views and intimated in the cable that I was the only one who would be able to act with authority. He said there was no use sending

someone who would have to refer matters back to Washington, and that I was the only one who would be able to make immediate decisions.

Reading said the cable was of such a peremptory nature that it would be necessary for him to ask for an immediate interview with the President so as to present it to him. I asked him not to argue the matter with the President but merely present it. It is my purpose to write the President and "beat Reading to it" by a lap or two. Reading promised to send me a copy of the cable and it will be attached to the diary.

We decided it would be best for me to go to Europe late in August or early in September, and he wishes to go at the same time. He did not agree to remain here longer than six months, and if he is to stay longer, he wishes to have the agreement directly with the Government and not through cables.

I advised him again to give up the office of Lord Chief Justice and to do the bigger work he was doing here as Ambassador, and later enter the political arena and try to become Prime Minister. It is a pity he is not Prime Minister today. It is not his ability that places him to the fore at this time, but it is the fact that he is on good terms with both the Liberals and Conservatives and he has a good level head for both business and politics.

Gordon has just telephoned that Grayson has been with McAdoo for three and a half hours. He found him in an excitable condition. McAdoo had written a long argument in favor of his position and Grayson persuaded him to eliminate such portions as indicated an intention to resign in the event his wishes were not met. Grayson said that McAdoo charges that Garfield will make an additional profit of $25,000. this year in his own coal properties, which he would not make if the President follows McAdoo's advice. This looks as if McAdoo was in an ugly mood, and he has considerable ability as a "scrapper."

To Thomas W. Brahany

Dear Mr. Brahany: [The White House, c. May 21, 1918]

Please say that I do not feel that it would be wise for me to do this,[1] because coming from me it might seem like something more than an endorsement and put a sort of moral compulsion on the employees, which I should not like to exercise.

The President.

TL (WP, DLC).
[1] Wilson was responding to William John Eynon to T. W. Brahany, May 16, 1918, TLS (WP, DLC). Eynon, chairman of the Special Committee on Governmental Organ-

izations of the District of Columbia chapter of the American Red Cross, had asked Brahany to persuade Wilson to write a public letter urging governmental employees in Washington to contribute generously to the Red Cross War Fund.

Three Letters from Robert Lansing

My dear Mr. President: Washington May 21, 1918.

Allow me to bring to your attention a much delayed telegram[1] from the late Consul General at Moscow, Mr. Summers,[2] which, although dated May 1st, has just been received together with a report from the Military Attaché at Vologda, dated May 11th.[3] These telegrams together indicate that the rapid progress of economic conditions from bad to worse is affecting the following of the Bolsheviki.   Faithfully yours,   Robert Lansing.

TLS (WP, DLC).

[1] M. Summers to RL, May 1, 1918, T telegram (WP, DLC). Summers reported upon two divergent trends in Russia. On the one hand, German "agents" were taking control of Russian factories, banks, and other business enterprises, as well as land and governmental securities. On the other hand, the continuing "anarchy" in both political and economic affairs was greatly hurting Germans and Russians alike.

[2] Maddin Summers had died in Moscow on May 4. Although he, himself, during his illness of only one day, apparently believed that he might have been poisoned by the Germans, his assistant, Consul DeWitt Clinton Poole, Jr., after a thorough discussion with the attending physicians, was satisfied that Summers' death was due to a brain hemorrhage, probably induced by overwork and worry. See George F. Kennan, *The Decision to Intervene* (Princeton, N. J., 1958), pp. 186-87.

[3] Col. James A. Ruggles to Milstaff, Washington, May 11, 1918, T telegram (WP, DLC). Ruggles summed up his view of the present situation in Russia in his first sentence: "Although still very desirable consent of bolshevik government to Allied intervention not now considered of vital importance due to increasing opposition of workmen[,] peasants amongst whom great dissatisfaction with present political and economic conditions is becoming daily more manifest." In support of this contention, he asserted that no workingmen had participated in the May Day demonstration in Petrograd and that meetings of workingmen "in all large manufacturing establishments" in Petrograd had adopted resolutions demanding increased food rations, the immediate convening of a "constitutional assembly," immediate cessation of civil war, and the immediate election of a responsible person to rectify "bolshevik financial inefficiency." In Ruggles' opinion, a majority of the Russian people would welcome Allied intervention, especially if the United States participated. He insisted that the food situation was becoming "more and more desperate." "From Moscow," he added, "all reports agree that bolshevik[s] are losing in influence and power and that their relations with Germany becoming more strained daily."

My dear Mr. President: Washington May 21, 1918.

I presume that you read the meaning of this telegram from Page at Rome (No. 1635, May 18)[1] as I do. To me it indicates that Italy is very willing to weaken Austria by exciting the Czecho-Slovaks with the hope of independence or at least of self-determination, but is unwilling to encourage the Jugo-Slavs because of their relations with the Serbs whose ambitions and claims over-lap those of Italy along the Adriatic.

The claim that the Serbs and Jugo-Slavs will fall under Austrian influence seems to me a very flimsy argument put forward to disguise the real motive of the Italian objection to giving encouragement to the political aspirations of the Jugo-Slavs. It is all after a piece with the selfish policy which wrecked the Balkan situation early in the war.

Should we, or should we not, listen to Italy, knowing her motive, and give no encouragement to the Slavs of the south? Will the possible dissensions aroused in the Austrian Empire by awaking in those peoples the hope of an autonomous nationality be worth while even though it may not be in accord with the ambitious expectations of Italy as to the eastern shores of the Adriatic?

It seems to me that the Jugo-Slavs are a sufficiently defined nationality to be entitled to self-determination and to have their desire recognized, unless policy prevents.

It all comes down to the expediency of listening to Italy or of recognizing the justness of the Jugo-Slav desire for nationality disregarding the extreme claims of Italy to territory now occupied by Jugo-Slavs.

From the standpoint of principle I think that the Jugo-Slavs and Serbs are entitled to support, but from the standpoint of winning the war a decision is more difficult. Nevertheless, I feel that a decision should be speedily reached, because, if the suppressed nationalities of Austria-Hungary are to be aroused, now seems to be the time.   Faithfully yours,   Robert Lansing.

TLS (WP, DLC).
[1] T. N. Page to RL, May 18, 1918, T telegram (WP, DLC).

My dear Mr. President: Washington May 21, 1918.

On March 15th I ventured to inquire as to your wishes regarding relief measures for Poland and Turkey and suggested that, in view of changed conditions, it might be advisable to reduce the amount of relief which had hitherto been forwarded. In your reply of March 16th you concurred in these recommendations and left to my judgment the amount of relief which should be allowed.[1] Copies of my letter and of your reply are enclosed herewith.

I accordingly fixed $175,000 as the maximum monthly amount for Turkey and $300,000 as the maximum monthly amount for Poland. Furthermore, because of recent political and military developments in occupied Russia, the territory to which relief could be sent was limited to Poland and excluded Lithuania and Courland.

The interested Jewish relief societies have felt constrained to protest against the reduction of the amount of relief and of the area benefitting from the remittances. As I stated in my letter of the 11th instant, in reply to yours of the 8th instant, transmitting a copy of this protest,[2] I have instituted further inquiries regarding the advisability of extending the relief measures to Lithuania and Courland. Replies have been received from the Legations at Copenhagen and Stockholm, copies of which are enclosed herewith,[3] strongly advising against such a step and, indeed, seriously arguing against the continuation of relief for any portion of occupied Russia. I must confess that, in spite of the many humanitarian arguments which may be advanced in favor of the relief measures for Lithuania and Courland, I am convinced that it is unwise to extend the relief beyond Poland proper. Unless you disapprove, therefore, relief will continue to be restricted to Poland only, and after June 1st will exclude Grovno, Vilna and Kovno.

I also beg to submit whether, in view of the developments in the Russian provinces which have taken place since your memorandum of March 16th,[4] it may not be advisable to consider reducing still further the amount of relief allowed even for Poland. I fear that under existing conditions the political effect of the relief remittances is largely lost.

There have recently passed through my hands copies of a report from a Dr. van Raalte,[5] a Dutch subject who has recently completed a journey through these provinces to investigate conditions on behalf of the Jewish relief societies. From this report it appears that the educated upper-class Jews have almost entirely disappeared and that the relief is received and distributed by uneducated persons of little if any political sense who cannot in the nature of things appreciate the significance of American assistance. Furthermore, postal and banking facilities are so inadequate that several districts not far from large centers have received no funds at all.

More serious than this is the danger that because of these conditions the German authorities will be able to turn American charity to their own advantage by holding forth that they are the ones who are bringing relief by admitting these funds, or even by alleging that these are German moneys. This is the easier in that the funds are necessarily forwarded through German as well as neutral agencies, that all correspondence is in German, and that the receipt forms in many instances do not bear any reference to American funds.

Dr. van Raalte bears this out in his report when he states that he "was informed in Lodz that quite a short time previous to the arrival of Dr. Magnes[6] the Committee did not know that the monies, sent by the Hilfsverein, originated from the American Jews, so that it appears the elimination of the Hilfsverein was really necessary."

I am, my dear Mr. President,

Faithfully yours,   Robert Lansing

TLS (SDR, RG 59, 861.48/596, DNA).
¹ See WW to RL, March 16, 1918, and its Enclosure, both printed in Vol. 47.
² See RL to WW, May 11, 1918 (second letter of that date), and WW to RL, May 8, 1918, and its Enclosure, all printed in Vol. 47.
³ U. Grant-Smith to RL, May 15, 1918, and I. N. Morris to RL, May 15, 1918, both T telegrams (SDR, RG 59, 861.48/596, DNA).
⁴ That is, the letter cited in n. 1 above.
⁵ Albert van Raalte, Dutch chemist and Zionist leader.
⁶ Judah Leon Magnes, Zionist leader, chairman of the Kehillah of New York, and active in the American-Jewish Joint Distribution Committee, a leading Jewish agency for overseas relief.

From Robert Lansing, with Enclosures

My dear Mr. President: Washington May 21, 1918.

Lord Reading handed me, this noon, the two enclosed papers which are paraphrases of telegrams received from London in relation to intervention in Russia.

I do not see that either of them present facts or arguments sufficient to warrant a change in our present policy. Of course I realize that inaction causes concern both in Great Britain and France and yet, for my own part, I do not see what action can be taken which will materially improve the situation. I so informed Lord Reading during our interview and I trust that I represented your views in the matter.   Faithfully yours,   Robert Lansing.

TLS (WP, DLC).

E N C L O S U R E   I

Handed me by Lord
Reading May 21/18 RL

PARAPHRASE OF A TELEGRAM FROM MR. BALFOUR TO LORD READING.
Dated May 15, 1918.

It will probably be useful to send you the following summary of points from recent correspondence, all of which seem to indicate a disposition on the part of the Bolshevist authorities to accept the assistance of the Allies, although, in view of the risk of an advance being made immediately by the Germans, they are unable formally to invite our intervention.

On April 3 our representative at Moscow already reported that Trotsky personally favoured armed assistance on the part of the Allies and would give his support to this policy. The help given must, however, not be under the control of Japan nor of a predominantly Japanese character. Five days later Lockhart reported that these questions had been under discussion for two days between the Bolshevist leaders and Mr. Tokomatt,[1] the head of the Finnish Socialist Government. The latter stated his conviction that military help from the Allies would be accepted by the Bolshevists if the scheme was proposed to them in a reasonable manner, since, however much they might be pressed by the Allies, they recognized that they could hope for nothing from the enemy. Lockhart said that this opinion was identical with his own view, but that for intervention to be a success the consent of the Bolshevists must be secured. It should be noted that to secure their consent is by no means the same thing as securing a formal invitation from them. On the 13th April a conversation, which Lockhart reported as being very satisfactory, took place between him and Trotsky on the question of intervention, and in the course of this conversation Trotsky made a statement as follows:

"As he recognizes that sooner or later Russia will be obliged to fight Germany for the purpose of liberating herself from the bonds of an unfair peace, and that the help of the Allies would in this situation be most valuable, he invites the Allied Powers to submit as soon as possible a complete and proper statement of the support which they are in a position to offer and of the guarantees which could be given by them. If satisfactory conditions are reached, he thinks that it would be both necessary and desirable to come to an agreement."

Trotsky also requests our help and advice on the reorganization of the Fleet in the Black Sea, he requested the services of Colonel Boyle[2] for the purpose of placing the Russian Railroads under his control and he also asked for the services of a British Officer, who should participate in and furnish a report on the work of the Russian Commission at Archangel. The action of the Bolshevist authorities in this matter, when we consider the situation in which Trotsky is, appears to be as near an approach to a direct invitation as can be expected. In a report dated April 28th relative to the request made by the Bolshevists for the recall of the French Ambassador[3] by his Government, Mr. Lockhart stated that he had received assurances that this matter was solely a personal one and that a better understanding with the Allies was desired by the Bolshevist Government. The Government was being driven to despair by the action of Germany and did not wish to break with the Allies and he felt convinced that a favourable settlement of the question of intervention could be reached if only there were quick and united action on our part.

An interview took place on May 8th between Lockhart, Trotsky and other leading members of the Russian Foreign Office, at which the position at Murmansk was discussed. Trotsky's endeavour was to extricate himself from the difficulty of retaining the co-operation of the British force at Murmansk, which he was desirous of doing, and at the same time of avoiding the occupation of Petrograd by the enemy, a step which had been threatened unless the British Force were removed from Murmansk. During this discussion Trotsky said that his Government was quite prepared to reach an arrangement with the Allies on the general lines which had already been indicated by myself, and he said that he regretted that the views of the Allies had apparently not yet been presented in a more concrete shape, although some weeks had passed since the question first came up. In his report Mr. Lockhart added that it was daily clearer that the Bolshevists perfectly recognized that they would be fighting sooner or later, but that our intervention would not be accepted by them until it became inevitable, that they could not take the side of Germany and that, when the moment came they would not decline to receive our co-operation subject to the provision that Russia was properly safeguarded from any annexationist views in Japan.

As regards Murmansk, a report from Lockhart dated May 6th stated that he had discussed the matter on several occasions with Mr. Tokomatt. On Mr. Lockhart's observing that the Bolshevists would not permit us to take action in Russia to stop penetration by the enemy, even if we desired to do so, Tokomatt replied that whether or not the Bolshevists fought Germany they would not join her against the Allies, nor would they take any serious step to hinder the Allies. He added that he had been told by Lenine that he was ready to wink at any steps which might be taken by Great Britain at Murmansk with the object of assisting the Finns. Mr. Lockhart on May 9th, in dealing with the same question of the position at Murmansk, reported that an immediate decision by the Allies on the question of intervention was imperative, that he considered that such intervention would not be declined if properly presented and that although he thought that the Bolshevists were in communication with Germany, the latter felt certain that there was a secret agreement between the Bolshevists and ourselves and for this reason were determined on their destruction before we could take any steps in their support.

On April 23rd Mr. Lockhart telegraphed a summary of Lenine's views. He reported that if we could assure Lenine that no endeavour would be made by the Allies to injure the Soviet form of Government, that we would honestly co-operate with this Government and would give proper guarantees that Russian territory should remain inviolable and independent, there were good grounds for thinking that Lenine would not decline any reasonable offer which the Allies might make. In view of the mentality of Lenine this point is an important one.

The whole trend of recent events seems to indicate that, although the Bolshevist Government cannot extend a formal invitation to the Allies, they are nevertheless ready to accept our intervention, while, if there is much further hesitation on the part of the Allies, Germany will have strengthened her position to such an extent that our intervention will not only be useless but will be opposed by large numbers of Russians who now support it. Germany will impose a condition of law and order, and this regime will be received, if not with gratitude, at least with satisfaction: and there will be few people in Russia who will be ready to give up immediate peace in favour of a distant prospect of expelling Germany from their country.   BRITISH EMBASSY

WASHINGTON.

May 16th, 1918.

[1] Antti Oskari Tokoi, who had been Premier of the first semi-independent government of Finland from March to August 1917. More recently he had been Minister for Food in the socialist or "Red" government which seized power in January 1918. Following the defeat of the Reds by the bourgeois, or "White," forces in the Finnish civil war, he and other members of the former socialist government had fled to Russia in late April.
[2] Joseph Whiteside Boyle, Canadian mining engineer and adventurer. He had gone to Russia in July 1917 to aid in the rehabilitation of the railway system. More recently, he had spent much time in Rumania, where he carried out various relief activities and quasidiplomatic missions on behalf of the Rumanian government. See William Rodney, *Joe Boyle: King of the Klondike* (Toronto, 1974), pp. 118-97 *passim*.
[3] That is, Joseph Noulens.

E N C L O S U R E   I I

Handed to me by Lord
Reading May 21/18 RL

FOLLOWING RECEIVED FROM H. M. REPRESENTATIVE AT MOSCOW
RECEIVED via LONDON—May 15.

The seriousness of the situation cannot be exaggerated. Owing to the military weakness of Russia the Germans are able to do what they like and relations between the Bolshevist Government and Germany are extremely strained. The sympathies of the large majority of the Russian Bourgeoisie and aristocracy will turn to Germany owing to their action in setting up a Bourgeois Government in the Ukraine.[1] The new Ukrainian Government, it is clear, will serve rather as a rallying point for a counter-revolution in Russia itself than as a Ukrainian Government. Many influential Russians, it is probable, will now go to Kieff and although they are unable by themselves to overthrow the Bolshevists, yet they may become a serious menace if they receive German assistance.

Unless I am supported by the other Allies in my attempt to obtain from the Bolshevists an invitation for Allied intervention it is practically impossible for me as an unofficial agent to do so alone. Unless the Allies are prepared to take action it is practically of no use reaching an agreement of this kind. The following points have always been insisted upon at our frequent meetings with the military representatives of the Allies:

(a) If possible intervention should be obtained by invitation, but failing that, without.

(b) Military preparations should be pushed forward as rapidly as possible. This is essential. Intervention will not be refused when it is plain that Allies are agreed and that intervention is inevitable.

The Bolshevists see plainly as does everyone that if they agree to a joint intervention their rule is over. But it is impossible for them to expect to come to terms with the Germans and from them they have still more to fear. Thus the Bolshevists are doing all in their power to delay a decision until the last possible moment.

The German position is fortified and that of the Allies weakened by each day's delay and the greatest danger now is that the Germans, before the Allies are prepared to take action, may force the hands of the Bolshevists. I am convinced that the only assistance to be obtained from Russia herself will be that which we may be able to focus round our own forces.

From statements of the U. S. Ambassador, who is now in Moscow, it is clear that no agreement has been come to by the Allies and that no definite decision has been arrived at respecting intervention in particular by America.

This afternoon I shall see him alone and I shall then do all in my power to convince him of the dangers which threaten us if the Allies hesitate and delay any longer.

I strongly recommend for political reasons simultaneous action in the Far East, at Murmansk and at Archangel. If anything is to be saved from the Russian wreck immediate action must be taken.

Directly an agreement has been reached by us on this point the representatives of the Allies here should be given authority to consult the Bolshevists in order to gain their concurrence. For the commencement of our action, at any rate, this is important. The conduct of these negotiations should be such that when we are ready to strike, our proposals may be handed in in the form of an ultimatum. Our actions should be as imposing and rapid as possible. This is highly important for political reasons.

BRITISH EMBASSY,

WASHINGTON,

May 16, 1918.

T MSS (WP, DLC).

[1] That is, the puppet government headed by Lt. Gen. Pavlo Petrovich Skoropadski, which was placed in power by the German army on April 28-29, 1918. Following the Bolshevik seizure of Kiev on February 8 and the peace treaty between Germany and the Ukrainian Central Rada on February 9 (about both of which see D. R. Francis to RL, Feb. 13, 1918, n. 4, Vol. 46), the Germans had overrun much of the Ukraine, including Kiev. At first they chose to rule through the temporarily revived Rada, but when that body proved unable to secure and protect grain shipments to the Central Powers, the Germans turned to Skoropadski. His Ukrainian "bourgeois" support, such as it was, consisted primarily of large landholders. He took the ancient monarchical title of "Hetman." In theory, his government was an absolute monarchy; in practice, a petty dictatorship supported by German arms. See John S. Reshetar, Jr., *The Ukrainian Revolution, 1917-1920: A Study in Nationalism* (Princeton, N. J., 1952), pp. 114-53, and Richard Pipes, *The Formation of the Soviet Union: Communism and Nationalism, 1917-1923*, rev. edn. (Cambridge, Mass., 1964), pp. 130-34.

From Robert Lansing, with Enclosure

My dear Mr. President: Washington May 21, 1918.

Replying to your letter of the 20th asking for my comments and judgment on the suggestion made by Mr. Reinsch in the enclosed telegram,[1] I do not feel that the time is opportune for adopting his suggestion as to intervention in Siberia. For your information I am enclosing a memorandum prepared by our Russian Division dealing with the Semenoff movement and also the general situation in Eastern Siberia.   Faithfully yours,   Robert Lansing

TLS (WP, DLC).

[1] That is, P. S. Reinsch to RL, May 16, 1918, printed as an Enclosure with WW to RL, May 20, 1918 (second letter of that date).

E N C L O S U R E

Washington May 21, 1918.

MEMORANDUM FOR THE SECRETARY OF STATE

The Military Advance of Semenoff

Semenoff's military movement was begun in the early part of this year as a rather unpromising experiment. The latest reports dated May 16th, show that his success has exceeded all expectations. He was defeated about six weeks ago on the Russian frontier, but his force, instead of withering in the face of reverses—as in the case of the military movements led by Kaledine and Korniloff—

seems to have gained strength. Where he previously had seven hundred men he now has about twenty-five hundred, and apparently has seized the junction of the Amur and Trans-Siberian railways at Karymskaya and menaces, if he has not already occupied, Chita. At least one observer, with this force very recently, was much impressed with the serious purpose of Semenoff himself and his officers and men.

At present the principal Russian individuals at Harbin are reported to be receiving for the assistance of Semenoff, money from both the British and French Governments, arms from Japan and contributions from the peasant Cooperative Societies in Siberia.

Semenoff's policy is to keep the Siberian Railway open and overthrow the Bolsheviki. He is variously reported as a liberal and as a reactionary; the former appears to be nearer the fact. The local Buryiats[1] in the Trans-Baikal are said to be flocking to him, sending deputations and offering voluntary subscriptions for his Red Cross and voluntary labor for road repairing.

Altogether his movement is now reported to represent the strongest, most law-abiding, popular and hopeful force active in Siberia against Germany.

The Horwath faction appear to have backed Semenoff with a view to riding in on the wave of his success, but without committing themselves so far that, if he fails, they cannot back another effort. A telegram of March 1st from the Consul at Harbin[2] indicated that the original plan of the Horwath faction was for Semenoff to advance to Irkutsk and there await the support of the Japanese, whose money and troops at that time had been promised. Now it would seem that Semenoff has been for a time at outs with Horwath and Pleshkoff[3] (the latter was appointed by Horwath as Commander-in-Chief of all troops in the military zone of the Chinese Eastern Railway) as not wholly amenable to their control and as being in unnecessarily close relations with the Amur Zemstvo and Amur-Cossacks. This very jealousy and desire to secure exclusive control of Semenoff on the part of the Horwath faction, if true, would seem an encouraging indication that perhaps all groups are bidding for his support and that consequently his further success may offer the prospect of forcing an amalgamation of all the different elements seeking reconstruction in Siberia.

Any open support of Semenoff should be prepared to face the prospect of a definite break with the Bolsheviki, resulting in civil war and, not unlikely, the consequent abandonment of European Russia for the time to Germany. When the Bolshevik authorities discovered the alleged activities of the foreign consuls in Siberia in encouraging anti-Bolshevik movements, they demanded the recall of the consuls and withdrew code privileges from them. When the French Ambassador, in an interview, for which Mr. Francis reports he saw no occasion, discussed openly the subject of intervention, the Soviet demanded his recall.

In spite of the great pressure urging a policy to deal officially with the Bolsheviki, it is difficult to see how this, or any liberal government, can become too closely associated with political leaders whose creed involves the destruction of all democratic Governments.

On May 9th, the Department telegraphed the Ambassador at Vologda, en clair, repudiating the charges that American representatives had assisted in any movements affecting the internal welfare of Russia and stating that the friendly purpose of the United States toward the Russian people will remain unaltered so long as Russia does not willingly accept the domination of the Central Powers.[4] Reports from Vologda and Moscow over the recall of the French Ambassador indicate that the Bolshevik leaders are rapidly tending to create a situation which will justify this Government in assuming that they accept German domination.

If it be decided to support Semenoff the suggestion has been made that the Czecho-Slovak troops organized by Professor Masaryk would be most useful. Six thousand are at Vladivostok; forty thousand preparing to go to Archangel; an additional fifty thousand in process of organization. Some of them might be taken over by this Government and assisted by American officers.

Colonel Emerson[5] and three assistants left Vladivostok for Vologda May 19th, to confer with Mr. Francis as to whether anything can be done for the Railways in European Russia. Mr. Stevens with one hundred engineers are working on the Chinese Eastern Railway; the balance of the Corps of American Railway engineers—about eighty men—are at Nagasaki awaiting developments.

Basil Miles

TS MS (WP, DLC).

[1] Members of an ethnic group, most of whom lived in the area around Lake Baikal. The Buryats and Kalmyks are the two principal groups of Mongols in the present Soviet Union.

[2] That is, Charles K. Moser.

[3] Gen. Mikhail Mikhailovich Pleshkov.

[4] "The Department has received your 127 and 128, also telegrams from Vologda, Vladivostok and Moscow reporting refusal to receive messages for code. In reply, you are informed that American representatives have not assisted in any movements affecting the internal situation of Russia, as alleged in the statements sent you. The friendly purpose of the United States towards Russia was made clear in the President's address to Congress January eighth and in his message to the Russian people through the Soviet. It will not be modified by charges of the character reported nor by any withdrawal of the diplomatic courtesies and privileges recognized universally among nations. Paragraph.

"This Government has received appeals for support from several groups who claim a purpose to establish a new government in Siberia; it has answered none of these appeals.

As you were informed by the Department's telegram of May first, when Colonel Semenoff was reported requesting assistance of Russian Railway Service Corps, a body of American engineers organized to assist the railway Administration of Russia, instructions were issued that the work of these engineers should not be diverted to support any movement partaking of civil war nor to facilitate the military operations of Semenoff, and if this could be avoided only by their withdrawal then they were to be withdrawn. At the same time you were notified that Colonel Emerson and some of his assistants were proceeding to Vologda to confer with you as to how these engineers could be used in helping the Russian people in European Russia and assisting in strengthening their resistance to the aggressions of the Central Powers. Colonel Emerson and three assistants left Harbin for Vologda May third. Paragraph.

"The purpose of the United States is clear and disguised by no measures of secret diplomacy. The United States is at war with the Central Powers for the purpose of overthrowing German militarism, thus making it possible for the peoples of the world to live in peace free from the menace of autocratic domination. Paragraph.

"The Government of the United States thoroughly understands the desires for repose of the Russian people exhausted after heroic sacrifices of war, and shares their hopes for a lasting peace based on the principles of liberty and justice. The United States now sees Russia over-run by German and Austrian troops. Where Russians in peaceable centres will not conform at once to the decrees of German commanders, Soviet reports show that they are brutally set aside or shot, and the military machine of Germany rolls on over the prostrate body of the Russian people. In spite of the fact that the people of many regions of Russia already suffer hunger and the prospect of a general famine in northern Russia, the Central Powers insist on the letter of their bond and are removing from the Ukraine, food supplies which the rest of Russia requires and must have, if it is to live. The Department does not understand how such conditions can continue without arousing the Russian people to the dangers which threaten the liberties won by their revolution. Nevertheless, the Department desires you to reflect the friendly purpose of United States towards Russia, a purpose which will remain unaltered so long as Russia does not willingly accept the autocratic domination of the Central Powers."
RL to D. R. Francis, May 8, 1918, T telegram (SDR, RG 59, 861.00/1729, DNA).

The telegrams numbered 127 and 128, referred to above, were D. R. Francis to RL, April 26, 1918, T telegram (SDR, RG 59, 861.00/1728, DNA), and D. R. Francis to RL, April 27, 1918, T telegram (SDR, RG 59, 861.00/1729, DNA). They are printed in *FR 1918, Russia*, II, 139, 142-43. In his first telegram, Francis repeated a note from Chicherin, the Commissar for Foreign Affairs, to the effect that the American, British, and French Consuls at Vladivostok had participated in a conspiracy with counterrevolutionary elements to overthrow the Soviets in Siberia. Chicherin also demanded the recall of the American Consul, a public investigation of his activities by the American government, and a definite, unequivocal declaration by the United States of its policy toward the Soviet government and toward all attempts by American diplomatic representatives to interfere in the internal affairs of Russia. In his second telegram, Francis gave summaries of documents presented by the Soviet government as evidence of the alleged conspiracy of the Consuls and counterrevolutionaries at Vladivostok.

[5] George H. Emerson, general manager of the Great Northern Railway, at this time chief of the Railway Service Corps in Russia.

From Herbert Clark Hoover, with Enclosure

Dear Mr. President: Washington *21 May 1918*

I enclose herewith a memorandum mentioning some of the objections to Mr. Colver's proposed experimental Government operation of one of the packing plants.

I have consulted Mr. Houston on this matter and he is strongly of my opinion that Mr. Colver's suggestion is directed more towards a determination of some permanent remedy of the faults of the packing industry than to meeting war emergencies.

Whatever our opinions may be as to the method for rectifying the packing industry, I am strongly of the view that we will have less interruption and disturbance to our present difficult economic situation through regulation of the packers than through any form of Government operation and that the permanent solution of this matter is one for legislation and not for experimental work under emergency powers.

I return herewith the report of the committee and I would be glad to discuss the subject at our next meeting.

Yours faithfully,   Herbert Hoover.

TLS (WP, DLC).

E N C L O S U R E

MEMO

Mr. Colver's interesting suggestion was before the Committee at the time the report was settled. The members of the Committee were in full agreement that the situation at the present time did not warrant any Government operation and that a determination should be made as to whether the war objectives of the Government could be attained by regulation without the necessity of Government operation.

There are two principal points of departure from the committee's report. First, a proposal of limited and experimental operation by the Government, and, second, regulations impigning [impinging] upon the producer.

As to the first, it must be recognized that this is one of the most complex and speculative industries in the country, due to the fundamental variations in every individual animal, the perishable character of products and the daily changing demands of the consuming public and from abroad. The Government, in operation of all five of the big plants, or even of one of them, would at once become the target of pressure on the part of both producers and consumers, and for an extended fixing of all factors entering into production and consumption. We should amass around ourselves an amount of political pressure and the ultimate definition of political issues between producer and consumer that would be most confusing and embarrassing during the period of the war.

To operate one packing concern, or all five large ones, means that the Government comes into competition with some hundred other packing houses in the country and is of course subject to the same methods of competition as exist between members of the trade. If the Government were to operate Wilson and Company's business alone and retain its volume of business—and it would be necessary to hold it if it is to become an experimental situation of any value—it must be prepared to take all of the risks of competition with the others and this competition drives into the price determination of every single animal bought and practically every commodity sold. There would seem to be serious danger that the other packers, if they were willing to sacrifice the money, could put the Government out of action in a month. We could not say to the people that they must consume Government meat at larger prices than private enterprise. Wilson and Company, roughly, do about ten per cent of the total business of the five big packers. This situation would be somewhat different if we took over all five packing plants, because we should have such a dominant part of the purchases as to fix prices even as against the other hundred packers. But if the Government forced them from business by competition the difficulties would be considerable.

Another factor in this matter that must not be overlooked is that the packers are engaged in many other avenues of activity than meat, such as fertilizers, leather, groceries and canned goods of all sorts, which they either pack themselves or buy under contract from other packers, and we should be entering competitive business upon all these lines.

Mr. Colver's plan also involves the control of the flow of animals to the markets and government advice to stockraisers in the country as to marketing. It also involves the determination of prices for standard fed animals as a basis of all purchases, with an advance fixation of animal prices on the basis of the cost of feed. Aside from the fact that no government has the power to assure consumption at such prices, this would constitute an interference in the daily life of the producers that they would resent and carries price fixing to a degree hitherto not contemplated. One instance will illustrate a minor phase of difficulty. The price of corn in Illinois today is $1., whereas in Kansas it is $1.50. If the Government attempted to fix the price of animals from Illinois for fifty per cent less than Kansas a situation would arise in Washington overnight.

Whatever the sins of the packers have been, the general fact that they have more than doubled the whole of their export business and at the same time cared for domestic consumption during the past few months, should be credited to them as an endeavour on their part to assist in the war situation. We are not satisfied that we need to despair in the control of their profits. It does seem that if the intelligence does not exist by which the profits of the packers can be controlled, it certainly does not exist by which the packing houses can be operated. To solve the whole problem of the packing monopoly would seem to be a matter for a permanent legislation, not for experiment under emergency legislation.

We are in intimate contact with the great majority of livestock associations in the country and, with the exception of one or two individuals out of many thousands of such representative men with whom we have been in contact, from no single association has there been any expression in favour of taking over and operating the packing houses for the Government. The only thing wanted is the proper operation of the packing houses to war ends and that there shall be a "square deal" to both producer and consumer.

T MS (WP, DLC).

From Lee Slater Overman

My dear Mr. President: Washington, D. C. May 21, 1918.

I beg to acknowledge receipt of your highly esteemed favor[1] and to say in reply that I have looked at the question of woman suffrage from every angle. Besides having firm convictions in the matter, the people of my state are overwhelmingly against it as shown by the action of our State Convention which went on record practically unanimously as opposing it. I, therefore, consider it my conscientious duty to vote against the proposed Federal Suffrage Amendment.

Also I have committed myself as being unalterably opposed to this Amendment and I am sure it will be exceedingly unwise at this time, from a political standpoint, for a North Carolina Senator to favor the passage of this measure, as our people believe it might result in a very dangerous inroad into our social condition, if adopted, and would give us a great deal of trouble in the future.

Regretting, my dear Mr. President, that I cannot comply with your request in this matter, I am, with great respect,

                    Very sincerely yours,   Lee S. Overman

TLS (WP, DLC).
[1] No copy found.

From Elizabeth Merrill Bass

My dear Mr. President: Washington, D. C. May 21st, 1918.

The women of the country are growing daily more disturbed over the situation in the Senate in regard to the Federal Amendment. The fact that we are failing to pick up the necessary two votes, although there were half a dozen possibilities from among which to gather them in, is creating the impression that we are not really trying for them. The so-called Woman's Party are engaged in active propaganda to discredit us, and especially just now among the women of New York, who are going to register for the coming Congressional election, and who have to take a party ballot.

I believe Mrs. Catt, for the National American Suffrage Association, has made a suggestion to you in regard to some foreign communications in the matter of suffrage, and I have another practical suggestion to make which I hope you will find it convenient to listen to during the next few days. I have to begin an active campaign among the women voters of the western states in order to keep our control of Congress, and really feel the responsibility tremendously.   Respectfully yours,   Elizabeth Bass.

TLS (WP, DLC).

From Anna Howard Shaw

My dear Mr. President: Washington May 21 1918

Upon my return to Washington on Monday morning, I found your letter of May 16, enclosing one from Mrs. William A. Read, of New York, concerning a badge of loyalty and remembrance as a substitute for mourning for those who have given up their lives in the service of their country.

As the Woman's Committee is meeting in executive session this week, I submitted the matter at yesterday's conference, with the result that the Committee voted to recommend a three-inch black band, upon which a gilt star may be placed for each member of the family whose life is lost in the service, and that the band shall be worn on the left arm.

We have had numerous letters and discussions on this subject, and it is quite evident that the time has come for some definite understanding.

Trusting, my dear Mr. President, that our Committee's action in this matter will receive your approval, I am
                    Faithfully   Anna Howard Shaw.

TLS (WP, DLC).

From Robert Bridges

Dear Mr. President: [New York] May 21, 1918

It is a great disappointment to me that I missed your call at my office on Saturday morning. I had gone to Princeton with Charles

& Arthur Scribner, but I got back in time to hear your speech in the evening. Cleve sent me a good seat, and I had a great evening. You have put yourself ahead a year in this town by your visit. I do not mean this selfishly—but I do mean that all the difficult things you have to do will be seen more easily by the glimpse the people got of your personality. I have felt this so keenly, and have resented the misinterpretations of a man who has always seemed to me intensely human.

It was a great day's work, and I step higher for having witnessed the triumph.

With my love, as always,

Faithfully Yours   Robert Bridges

ALS (WP, DLC).

Basil Miles to Robert Lansing, with Enclosure

The Secretary of State: [Washington] May 21, 1918

The attached telegram from Mr. Francis at Vologda, dated May 11 shows much keen insight and contains valuable comment bearing on the position of the Bolshevik Government. It has just been received.   Basil Miles

TLS (WP, DLC).

E N C L O S U R E

Vologda. May 11, 1918.

160. Had conference with Lockhart ninth. He is only diplomatic representative his country has here if may be so called; showed me in strict confidence copy of cable from Balfour to Reading in Washington concerning allied intervention which was sent from London to Washington April 25th, and to Lockhart April 28th for his information.[1] Main object of cable was to persuade President to consent to Allied intervention. Meantime Italian Embassy Vologda received cable stating Reading has informed Italian Ambassador Washington that President unalterably opposed to allied intervention unless desired by Russian people. Lockhart strongly favors allied intervention with or without Soviet Government approval but says approval desirable if, to which I agree but if securable only by promise to sustain even secretly Bolshevik domination I think cost would be too dear as Lockhart says he is officially informed that Germany has made imperative demand of Soviet Government to require allies to evacuate Murman. Robins of whom I made the

same inquiry says no such ultimatum issued. I think report is correct.

Monarchial sentiment growing also opposition to Bolshevik domination increasing throughout. Confidentially, had a consultation with Sadoul[2] French Captain in close relations with Soviet Government, commissioned in French army after a defeat as radical socialist candidate for chamber of deputies. French Ambassador socialist also but Bolshevik dislike socialists who disagree with them more than they dislike non socialists while moderate socialists bitterly denounce Bolshevik for delaying by their policies the triumph of socialism for half a century or more. Sadoul says Bolshevism is dead, and only way to prevent restoration of monarchy is assisting in coalition of socialistic democratic and anti-monarchical governments for formation of extremely liberal republic. When asked if Lenin hitherto Bolshevik dictator would compromise his radical policies the affirmative reply was so prompt that suggestion rose in my mind whether Sadoul was not Soviet agent to sound me on the subject. I replied the suggestion was new and very interesting. Sadoul said Lenin contemplates denationalizing banks, and revoking decree repudiating loans. In my opinion Soviet Government realizes its unsatisfied condition and is playing for time. Checcherin telegrams to me direct, one expressing regret if prohibition cipher messages had inconvenienced me, another expressing condolence concerning Summers (*)[3] together with request to participate in funeral ceremonial which I granted, all indicate desire to establish friendly relations with us. Such desire augmented by information imported by me through consulate that Emerson and seven engineers coming to assist in transportation betterment. I am not discouraging such advances because wish De facto Government to side with Allies when steady Allied intervention unavoidable, or when compelled to decide between Germany and Allies. I think that Soviet Government when replying to German ultimatum concerning Murman will make evasive statement to gain time.

Had four extremely full days in Moscow but consider profitable. Retaining consulate-General under consul will justify my returning soon and often as I contemplate. Hope the Department will not send as consul-General one unacquainted with prevailing conditions; I think Harris[4] best qualified for place but his services and judgment required for present on Siberian situation which growing extremely interesting; Poole is quick capable and untiring. Furthermore, chief Far Eastern division Soviet Foreign Office,[5] and representative of Soviet Government at funeral, whom I granted audience tenth after much insistence, asked why I did not engage house Moscow and move from Vologda, and when I replied Allied

Missions had joined me in Vologda and we thought safer from German interference, he remarked German Ambassador in Moscow, and my rejoinder was: he is treated much more considerately than Allied representatives.

Meantime, I trust sincerely we have been making all possible preparations for Allied intervention as I have recommended for months past, and that active negotiations have begun among Allies therefore, as urged in my number 140 of May 2, 6 p.m.[6]

Francis.

T telegram (WP, DLC).
[1] Actually, A. J. Balfour to Lord Reading, April 18, 1918, Vol. 47.
[2] Jacques Sadoul, a member of the French Military Mission in Russia.
[3] Chicherin's telegram of condolence is summarized in Kennan, *Decision to Intervene*, p. 188n41.
[4] Ernest Lloyd Harris, who had been appointed Consul General at Irkutsk on May 14.
[5] Arsenii Nikolaevich Voznesenskii.
[6] D. R. Francis to RL, May 2, 1918, T telegram (SDR, RG 59, 861.00/1955, DNA); it is printed in *FR 1918, Russia*, I, 519-21.

Arthur James Balfour to Lord Reading

[London] 21 May 1918.

Personal and Secret.

Your telegram of May 17th to Drummond. Father Fay[1] has already sailed for U. S. For your own confidential information. Policy of trying to detach Austria from Germany at present time seems to us both inopportune and impracticable. Recent meeting of Emperors obviously led to bonds between two Empires being tightened.[2] We think best plan is to give all possible support to oppressed nationalities in Austria in their struggle against German magyar domination * * * * Austria may thus be reduced to a reasonable frame of mind. American advances to Austria in present circumstances will only afford encouragement to Central Powers and may give rise to misconceptions and misunderstandings between the Allies.

It may be advisable for you to speak in this sense privately to Colonel House.

T telegram (Reading Papers, FO 800/222, PRO).
[1] Msgr. Cyril Sigourney Webster Fay, an American priest who was a friend of Balfour and had recently been involved in negotiations to expunge from the Treaty of London of 1915 the clause which would exclude the Holy See from an eventual peace conference. About this provision of the Treaty of London, see T. N. Page to WW, Jan. 29, 1918, n. 3, Vol. 46.
[2] In the wake of the public revelation of the Sixtus letter (about which see RL to WW, May 10, 1918 [first letter of that date], n. 1, Vol. 47), Charles and his chief advisers felt obliged to undertake a political fence-mending trip to Germany. Charles met William II and his principal policy-makers at the German military headquarters at Spa from May 12 to 14. For contrasting views of the significance of this meeting, see Arthur J. May, *The Passing of the Hapsburg Monarchy, 1914-1918* (2 vols., Philadelphia, 1966), II, 722-24, and Fritz Fischer, *Griff nach der Weltmacht: Die Kriegszielpolitik des kaiserlichen Deutschland, 1914/18* (Düsseldorf, 1961), pp. 698-701.

To Joseph Patrick Tumulty

Dear Tumulty: [The White House, c. May 22, 1918]

Of course, I am taking no part one way or the other in this fight
and do not intend to take any.¹ The disturbing rumor has reached
me that Senator Reed's friends, probably without Governor Folk's
knowledge, are backing up his candidacy.² I wonder if you could
find out in any way whether that is true or not?

The President.

TL (WP, DLC).

¹ Wilson was responding to Ewing Young Mitchell to Francis P. Walsh, c. May 22,
1918, T telegram (WP, DLC). Mitchell, a lawyer of Springfield, Mo., and manager of
Joseph W. Folk's senatorial campaign, reported a rumor circulating in St. Louis to the
effect that an effort would be made to "induce" President Wilson to give out a "general
letter" to be used by Xenophon Pierce Wilfley in his primary campaign against Folk.
Wilfley had been appointed to fill the seat vacated by the death of William J. Stone until
a new senator could be nominated and elected. He then became the state Democratic
organization's candidate in the primary. Walsh forwarded Mitchell's telegram to Tumulty
with a note praising Mitchell's wisdom and party loyalty and predicting that Folk would
"beat the life" out of Wilfley in the primary.

² It seems highly unlikely that "Senator Reed's friends" were supporting Folk for the
nomination. Although Folk and Reed had on several occasions worked together for
reasons of political expediency, they were usually in opposition to each other within the
Democratic party in Missouri. Reed was notoriously unpredictable, but he usually supported conservative, city-machine candidates, whereas Folk usually spoke for the progressive wing of the Missouri Democracy. Moreover, Folk based much of his primary
and election campaigns on his loyalty to the Wilson administration and explicitly attacked
Reed during the postprimary campaign. See the index references to James A. Reed in
Louis G. Geiger, *Joseph W. Folk of Missouri* (Columbia, Mo., 1953). For a brief discussion
of the Missouri senatorial primary and election campaigns in 1918, see *ibid.*, pp. 165-
68, 173-74.

To Newton Diehl Baker

My dear Mr. Secretary: The White House 22 May, 1918

I write to ask if you will not be kind enough to give a little further
thought to the matter of putting all men who are necessary in the
running of the railroads into a deferred class in the matter of the
draft. I do not mean, of course, the unskilled laborers, but those
who have become qualified for some task which requires experience
and who are very difficult to replace. The railroads are so manifestly
part of our present military and industrial machinery that this seems
to me a matter almost of necessary, and of rather pressing necessity.
Does it not seem so to you?

Cordially and faithfully yours,   Woodrow Wilson

TLS (N. D. Baker Papers, DLC).

To Elizabeth Merrill Bass

My dear Mrs. Bass: [The White House] 22 May, 1918

It was supposed, as you say in your letter of May twenty-first, that there were "half a dozen possibilities" in the Senate from whom we might draw sufficient support to put the federal amendment through, but as a matter of fact I have done my best to draw from that half-dozen and have utterly failed. We have left nothing undone that I can think of which could have been wisely or sufficiently done.

If you will be kind enough to come to the Executive Office on Friday at 2:30, I will be very glad to talk the matter over with you, as you suggest.   Sincerely yours,   Woodrow Wilson

TLS (Letterpress Books, WP, DLC).

To Jesse Holman Jones

My dear Mr. Jones: The White House 22 May, 1918

It was generous of you to write me your note of May eighteenth. You may be sure that I enjoyed rendering such little service as I rendered the Red Cross in New York so much as more than to compensate me for the effort and inconvenience I was put to. I hope most sincerely that your hopes will be realized to the utmost in the present drive.

Cordially and sincerely yours,   Woodrow Wilson

TLS (RSB Coll., DLC).

To William Kent

My dear Kent: The White House 22 May, 1918

I have your letter of May twentieth about Max Eastman. You may be sure the matter has been giving me a great deal of thought, and troubled thought at that, but I have not yet been able to come to a conclusion that satisfies me.

Cordially and sincerely yours,   Woodrow Wilson

TLS (W. Kent Papers, CtY).

To Anna Howard Shaw

My dear Doctor Shaw: [The White House] 22 May, 1918
    Thank you for your letter of yesterday. I do entirely approve of
the action taken by the Woman's Committee in executive session,
namely, that instead of the usual mourning a three-inch black band
should be worn upon which a gilt star may be placed for each
member of the family whose life is lost in the service, and that the
band shall be worn on the left arm. I hope and believe that thoughtful people everywhere will approve of this action, and I hope that
you will be kind enough to make the suggestion of the Committee
public with the statement that it has my cordial endorsement.
                Cordially and sincerely yours,   Woodrow Wilson

TLS (Letterpress Books, WP, DLC).

To Various Ethnic Societies

                                        [May 23, 1918]
    I have read with great sympathy the petition addressed to me by
your representative bodies regarding your proposed celebration of
Independence Day;[1] and I wish to convey to you, in reply, my heartfelt appreciation for its expressions of loyalty and good will. Nothing
in this war has been more gratifying than the manner in which
our foreign-born fellow citizens and the sons and daughters of the
foreign-born, have risen to this greatest of all national emergencies.
You have shown where you stand not only by your frequent profes-
sions of loyalty to the cause for which we fight, but by your eager
response to calls for patriotic service, including the supreme service
of offering life itself in the battle for justice, freedom and democracy.
Before such devotion as you have shown, all distinctions of race
vanish; and we feel ourselves citizens in a republic of free spirits.
    I therefore take pleasure in calling your petition, with my hearty
commendation, to the attention of all my fellow countrymen, and
I ask that they unite with you in making the Independence Day of
this, the year when all the principles to which we stand pledged
are on trial, the most significant in our national history.
    As July 4, 1776, was the dawn of democracy for this nation, let
us on July 4, 1918, celebrate the birth of a new and greater spirit
of democracy, by whose influence, we hope and believe, what the
signers of the Declaration of Independence dreamed of for themselves and their fellow countrymen shall be fulfilled for all mankind.
    I have asked the Committee on Public Information to cooperate
with you in any arrangements you may wish to make for this celebration.
                                    Woodrow Wilson[2]

TS MS (Letterpress Books, WP, DLC).
    [1] Miran Sevasly *et al.* to WW, n.d., printed with Wilson's message in the *Official Bulletin*, II (May 25, 1918), 1, 7.
    [2] Creel's typed draft of this message, heavily emended by Wilson, is in WP, DLC.

To Joseph Patrick Tumulty

Dear Tumulty: [The White House, c. May 23, 1918]

Here is a letter which it seems to me dangerous for me to answer.[1] You have a true instinct in such matters. How would you advise that I handle it?   The President

TL (WP, DLC).
    [1] Marguerite Maginnis to WW, May 21, 1918, ALS (WP, DLC). Frankly describing herself as a " 'Sinn Fein' admirer," the writer asked Wilson, whom she addressed in flattering terms, to "do something for my people, the Irish." "My America," she asserted, "demands an open and hasty trial for the Sinn Fein prisoners."

From Joseph Patrick Tumulty

Dear Governor: [The White House] 23 May 1918.

At the Sinn Fein meeting held in New York this week at which speeches of the most seditious character were made, one of the orators of the evening was a man named Maginnis.[1] I would not be surprised if this girl were in some way related to this individual. I suspect that the hand of some able Sinn Feiner is back of this letter and that an attempt is being made to draw you out. I do not think you ought to recognize it in any way or that you should personally acknowledge it. I think the way to handle this is to allow me personally to acknowledge it and to say that it will be brought to your attention at the earliest possible moment.

                              Sincerely yours,   Tumulty

Okeh W.W.

TLS (WP, DLC).
    [1] The Friends of Irish Freedom sponsored the "Second Irish Race Convention" at the Central Opera House in New York on May 18 and 19. The convention adopted resolutions urging Wilson to support self-determination for the people of Ireland. There were also some inflammatory speeches. The Very Rev. Peter Elias Magennis, an Irish-born member of the Order of Carmelite Fathers, did not attend any of the sessions, although he was elected president of the Friends of Irish Freedom for the ensuing year. He had, however, presided at recent similar meetings in New York and had just been admonished by John Cardinal Farley, Archbishop of New York, not to participate in further political meetings. There is no evidence that Father Magennis was related to Marguerite Maginnis. See the *New York Times*, May 19-22, 1918; Charles Callan Tansill, *America and the Fight for Irish Freedom, 1866-1922* (New York, 1957), pp. 270-73; and Francis M. Carroll, *American Opinion and the Irish Question, 1910-23: A Study in Opinion and Policy* (Dublin and New York, 1978), pp. 113-14.

To Joseph Patrick Tumulty

Dear Tumulty: [The White House, c. May 23, 1918]

Won't you say gently to Mr. White that I am very sorry but I don't like Sunday meetings and would feel very ill at ease at one?[1]

The President.

TL (WP, DLC).
[1] Wilson was responding to Henry White to WW, May 23, 1918, ALS (WP, DLC). White invited Wilson to attend a mass meeting sponsored by the District of Columbia Committee of the American Red Cross War Fund of 1918 to be held in the National Theatre on May 26. White noted that he was aware that Wilson made it a rule not to appear in public on Sundays but hoped that he would make an exception in this case, since it was the only date upon which Henry P. Davison could be present to speak.

To Henry Thomas Rainey

My dear Mr. Rainey: [The White House] 23 May, 1918

Thank you for your letter of yesterday, enclosing a copy of your letter of May twenty-first to the Secretary of the Treasury.[1] I realize the difficulties and embarrassments of the whole situation and am looking forward with a great deal of interest to a conference this afternoon with Mr. Kitchin and Senator Simmons and Senator Martin and others, at which we shall try to come to a conclusion.[2]

Cordially and sincerely yours,   Woodrow Wilson

TLS (Letterpress Books, WP, DLC).
[1] Both Rainey's letter and its enclosure are missing.
[2] This conference was necessitated by McAdoo's demand for legislation during the current session of Congress to raise additional revenue to meet the rapidly rising costs of the war effort. Wilson met for almost two hours on May 23 with Furnifold M. Simmons, chairman of the Senate Finance Committee; Thomas S. Martin, chairman of the Senate Appropriations Committee; Claude Kitchin, chairman of the House Ways and Means Committee; J. Swagar Sherley, chairman of the House Committee on Appropriations; and John N. Garner, a member of the House Ways and Means Committee. The congressional conferees were all strongly opposed to additional revenue legislation before the proposed adjournment of Congress for the summer on July 1. They argued that sufficient revenue was available, or could be secured under existing legislation, to carry the government until March 1919. They also said that they thought that McAdoo's estimates of funds needed were much too high. They observed as well that a good revenue bill could not be framed in so short a time and that, if drawn up on the eve of an election, was bound to be partisan and hence unsatisfactory both to the public and to the administration. They promised that the House Ways and Means Committee would hold extensive hearings and prepare a bill during the congressional recess and have it ready for consideration by December. They also undoubtedly raised strong objections to any extension of the present session past July 1 on the ground of the need of most members of Congress to return home to campaign. The newspaper accounts of the meeting agree that Wilson was swayed by the arguments of the delegation and agreed to forego immediate revenue legislation, provided only that McAdoo could be persuaded to agree to this. The congressional conferees saw McAdoo immediately after the White House conference and restated their arguments to him. He promised to reconsider the matter and give them an answer as soon as possible. However, as following documents will soon reveal, McAdoo in fact had not altered his stand at all and soon convinced Wilson of the need for new legislation at once. See the *New York Times*, *New York Herald*, and *Washington Post*, all of May 24, 1918, and the New York *World*, May 25, 1918.

To George Creel

My dear Creel: [The White House] 23 May, 1918

Of course I will waive my interests in the History of the American People on behalf of the Italian-American Union in order that they may publish the volumes for the good of the cause for which our armies are fighting, and I do so with a great deal of pleasure.[1] I have written to this effect to Mr. Briggs of Harper & Brothers.[2]

In haste   Faithfully yours,   Woodrow Wilson

TLS (Letterpress Books, WP, DLC).
[1] Wilson had discussed this matter in a conference with Creel at the White House on May 22.
[2] WW to W. H. Briggs, May 23, 1918, TLS (Letterpress Books, WP, DLC).

To Ida Minerva Tarbell

My dear Miss Tarbell: The White House 23 May, 1918

Your letter of the eighteenth has interested me in a very unusual degree. It apprises me of things that are happening which I was not in a position to realize, and I rejoice as much as you do that they should be happening. If there is any way in which I can help, please do not hesitate to call on me because you think me over-burdened, because I know you would not call upon me to do any-thing except what was thoroughly worth while.

With the warmest appreciation,
                    Cordially and sincerely yours,   Woodrow Wilson

TLS (Ida M. Tarbell Coll., PMA).

To Edward Wright Sheldon

My dear Sheldon: The White House 23 May, 1918

I don't know when a letter has given me more genuine pleasure or has touched me more than yours has done about the meeting Saturday night. It would have been a genuine pleasure to have a grasp of your hand and a word with you if I had only been fortunate enough to see you at the meeting, and knowing you as I do, I know how to value your singularly generous words about the speech itself and about the influence which you think I am exercising. The older one gets, I think, the more delightful and reassuring and invigo-rating it becomes to have the support and approval of tested friends, and I thank you with all my heart.
                    Cordially and sincerely yours,   Woodrow Wilson

TLS (photostat in RSB Coll., DLC).

To Cleveland Hoadley Dodge

My dear Cleve: The White House 23 May, 1918

Thank you with all my heart for your letter of the twentieth. A very great part of the pleasure I derived from being in New York I derived from being with you. Your whole attitude at the meeting and everything that you said was admirable and delightful, and our little talks afterwards I enjoyed to the utmost. Your faith in me and your generosity are a constant support to me.

Mrs. Wilson joins me in the warmest regards to you all.

Faithfully yours, Woodrow Wilson

TLS (WC, NjP).

Two Letters from William Gibbs McAdoo

Dear Mr. President: Washington May 23, 1918.

It is with the greatest reluctance that I have been forced to the conclusion that new revenue legislation must be enacted at the present session of Congress if the needs of the Government for the fiscal year 1919 are to be met.

At the present rate of expenditure the Treasury will actually have to disburse during the fiscal year ending June 30, 1919, approximately $24,000,000,000. This estimate is not based merely upon appropriations, nor merely upon estimates made by other Departments as to their probable expenditures, although they have been obtained and considered; they are based upon the actual experience of the Treasury during the past year, which has shown that actual expenditures have increased at the average rate of $100,000,000 per month since March, 1917. You will observe from the enclosed statement (Exhibit A)[1] that in March 1917, the expenditures were in round figures $100,000,000. In May, 1918 (partly estimated) they will be $1,585,500,000. If there should be no further increase during the coming fiscal year, the cash expenditures upon the May basis would be more than $18,000,000,000. If, as seems inevitable, the increase in expenditures should increase at the rate of $100,000,000 per month for the next six months, or until December, 1918, and if thereafter the monthly expenditures should remain stationary until the 30th of June, 1919, the Treasury would have to finance expenditures aggregating $24,000,000,000 during the fiscal year ending June 30, 1919.

In the fiscal year ending June 30, 1918, our cash disbursements

[1] "Statement Showing Classified Disbursements by Months from March, 1917 to June, 1918, as Published in Daily Treasury Statement (May and June [1918] Estimated)," T MS (WP, DLC).

will amount to between $12,500,000,000 and $13,000,000,000. Of this amount, roughly one-third will have been raised by taxes and two-thirds by loans, all of which will be represented by long-time obligations, that is, bonds of the First, Second and Third Liberty Loans and War Savings Certificates. We shall thus have completed fifteen months of the war with a financial record unequalled, I believe, by that of any other nation.

We cannot wisely contemplate nearly doubling our cash disbursements in the fiscal year 1918 without providing additional revenue. We cannot afford to rely upon $4,000,000,000 only from taxation because we shall then have to rely on raising $20,000,000,000 by loans. This would be a surrender to the policy of high interest rates and inflation, with all the evil consequences which would flow inevitably therefrom, and which would, I firmly believe, bring ultimate destruction upon the country. We cannot afford to base our future financing upon the quicksands of inflation or unhealthy credit expansion. If we are to preserve the financial strength of the Nation, we must do the sound and safe things, no matter whether they hurt our pockets or involve sacrifices—sacrifices of a relatively insignificant sort as compared with the sacrifices our soldiers and sailors are making to save the life of the Nation. The sound thing to do is unquestionably to increase taxation and the increases should be determined upon promptly and made effective at the earliest possible moment.

I doubt seriously if the Government can be financed with only $4,000,000,000 derived from taxation because sufficient economies will not be enforced upon the people of America with so small a tax bill as this, and without such economies I see no way in which the great financial operations of the Government can be safely conducted.

On the basis of the present revenue laws, we should have to raise in the fiscal year 1919 $20,000,000,000 by the sale of Liberty Bonds or by loans of one sort or another. Personally, I do not believe that it can be done. I believe that if we are to preserve the soundness and stability of our financial structure, we must raise not less than one-third of our expenditures by taxation. Not merely should $8,000,000,000 be assessed in taxes, but these taxes should be made available in cash to the Treasury during the fiscal year 1919, so that the amount to be secured by loans during that fiscal year shall not be more than $16,000,000,000.

The existing war revenue act was approved by you on October 3, 1917, yet there has been a strong demand among taxpayers for legislation authorizing the deferred payment of these taxes. This demand is not without basis in justice. The income and excess profits taxes imposed by that law covered the entire calendar year 1917, so that the business of the country had been conducted for nine months of the year without certain knowledge as to what the basis of taxation was to be, and all individuals subject to the income tax had expended their incomes during the nine months without knowledge of the Government's tax requirements. This was most unfair to the business of the country and to the taxpayers generally. They ought to know in advance of each calendar year the basis upon which individual expenditures may be made. This is particularly true of salaried men who have fixed incomes and, therefore, are put at a great disadvantage when they are taxed retroactively and after they have expended their incomes. Even if a tax measure is passed at this session of the Congress, the business of the country will have been conducted upon the old tax basis for more than one-half of the calendar year 1918, to which the new tax measure must be applicable. Notwithstanding the fact that the present taxpayers have had less than nine months since the enactment of the law of October 3, 1917, to prepare for the payment of their taxes, I have been obliged to refuse to recommend to Congress legislation permitting deferred payment of taxes, because the necessities of the Treasury are so imperative as to absolutely forbid it.

If the consideration of new revenue legislation by Congress were deferred until the short session in December, or even until a special session called, as has been proposed, as early as possible after election day in November, no one thinks that legislation could be had before February or March. If that happened the payment of income and excess profits taxes for the fiscal year 1919 would have to be postponed until the fiscal year 1920. This would mean that the whole amount of $24,000,000,000 less say $1,500,000,000 miscellaneous revenue, would have to be raised by loans during the fiscal year 1919; a sum equal to about the amount of the First Liberty Loan ($2,000,000,000) would have to be borrowed each month.

It has been said that income and excess profits taxes are not due until June and that to defer legislation until February or March to increase these taxes would not increase the amount of cash available to the Treasury. But we have borrowed $1,500,000,000 on Treasury certificates of indebtedness issued in anticipation of the payment of income and excess profits taxes and sold to taxpayers during the current fiscal year, nearly half of it before January 1, 1918. The prompt enactment of a law providing for heavily increased taxes will not only serve to give notice to the community to prepare for these taxes, but will place the Treasury in funds through the sale of Treasury Certificates of Indebtedness maturing on tax day in June, 1919. I am afraid we could sell only a negligible amount of such certificates if the tax legislation were left undisposed of until February or March. A propaganda for the deferred payment of taxes would receive an inevitable further impetus from that fact and would be irresistible.

It would be impossible to administer a new tax law covering the fiscal year 1919 if it were enacted as late as February or March, 1919. The new forms for tax returns and the new regulations under the new law involve a tremendous amount of work requiring ample time, and the distribution of the forms for returns and the making of the returns themselves take months of time and effort. Therefore, no revenue would be available from taxes during the fiscal year 1919, and every dollar of the $24,000,000,000 of expenditures would have to be raised by temporary loans and Liberty Loans. We could not even sell Certificates of Indebtedness in anticipation of tax payments because there would be no tax payments available in the fiscal year 1919. It is simply impossible to finance the Government for the fiscal year 1919 upon the basis of borrowed money only.

At the risk of repetition, I desire to say that the community is entitled to be informed, and informed promptly, if increased taxes are to be levied. To raise $8,000,000,000 by taxation is no light matter. To levy taxes such as these on incomes and profits, after those incomes and profits have been expended, is unjust, unsafe and unsound. The tax due in June, 1919, will be based upon incomes and profits accruing during the calendar year ending December 31, 1918. If new taxes are not provided until two or three months after that date, the people will be misled and the whole situation gravely imperiled. One of the most important objects of heavy taxes in war time is to curtail wasteful and unnecessary expenditure. To allow the people to continue to make wasteful and unnecessary expenditures and then, after the incomes and profits upon which the tax is based have been invested or dissipated, to tax them, is wrong.

I have indicated the reasons why I think the immediate enactment of a law to produce additional revenue is necessary. There are also certain general considerations bearing upon the problem of taxation and the character of legislation which should be enacted to which I wish to draw your attention.

The existing excess profits tax does not always reach *war* profits. The rates of taxation are graduated and the maximum rate is 60%. In Great Britain there is a flat rate of 80% on all *war* profits. The War Department and other disbursing departments of the Government, under great pressure as they are to get necessary war materials and supplies with the utmost expedition, cannot in the nature of things fix their prices nor guard their contracts in such a way as to avoid the possibility of profiteering. The one sure way is to tax away the profits when they have been realized. I do not say this in a spirit of criticism towards the corporations or business men of the country who have for the most part loyally supported the Government. In entering into war contracts they take grave risks. They are called upon to make vast expenditures of capital for purposes which may prove unproductive after the war. They are not to be blamed in these circumstances for asking for prices and terms which cover these risks. On the other hand, when the risk has been liquidated by proper allowances, and the contract has proved profitable, the Government should take the great bulk of the profits back in taxes. Under the existing law that does not happen because the rates are not high enough and could not safely be made high enough since the test now is not how much of the profits are due to the war, but what relation the profits bear to the capital invested. A company with a swollen capital and huge war profits escapes. The laboring men of the country, the great mass of the people of the country, will not rest content while corporations engaged in war industries pay huge dividends from Government war contracts or Government price fixing. The people are impatient, and rightly impatient, of war profiteering. They are impatient of the financial slacker, whether he be rich or poor.

This brings me to another consideration of great moment in the Government's financial plans. I hope and expect to prevent further increase in the interest rate on Government bonds. The 17,000,000 people who have bought Liberty Bonds are impatient of those who have not. I have had urged upon me varying plans for forcing the people to buy Liberty Bonds. The man of small means who buys a $100 bond wants his neighbor to do so too. There is a popular demand for high taxes upon war profits. There is also a popular demand that all the people, rich and poor, should contribute to financing the war. There should, therefore, be an important increase in the normal income tax rate and a higher tax should be levied upon *un*earned than on *earned* incomes. Income derived from Liberty Bonds would be exempt from this taxation and the millions of holders of bonds would benefit by this exemption. The relation between the income derived from Liberty Bonds and from other securities would be readjusted without an increase in the rate of interest, and this relation would subsequently be restored after the war. It would not tax the holders of Liberty Bonds on their holdings. It would weigh heavily upon the shirkers who have not bought them. It would make the return from Liberty Bonds compare favorably with the return from other securities. It would give the

Government's bonds a great advantage over those of corporate borrowers and would very greatly decrease the relative advantage which State and municipal bonds now enjoy through the total exemption which they carry. It would produce a gradual readjustment of the situation in the investment markets instead of an abrupt one, as would be the case if the Government's interest rate were increased. A normal tax falls upon all alike. Therefore, as I pointed out to Congress last summer, there is not the same objection to the exemption from normal income taxes as there was to the exemption from surtaxes. A great and, if necessary, repeated increase in the normal income tax is the one sound, sure way of stabilizing the price of the Government's bonds. If we have to increase the interest rate on the Government's bonds, the interest rate so created will continue for thirty years and some of the bonds which we have issued will go to great premiums not long after the war is over. If we make the bonds at the present rate more attractive by increasing the normal tax then the decrease in taxation which will follow the close of the war will automatically adjust the situation. I believe that to stab[i]lize the price of the Government's bonds by first increasing and subsequently reducing the normal income taxes, from which the holders of these bonds are exempt, is sound finance and sound economics.

There is another feature deserving of your consideration. We are asking the people to finance this war and we are offering them an investment paying 4¼% interest. The people have responded wonderfully to this appeal in the last Liberty Loan campaign—17,000,000 approximately having subscribed. They naturally feel that the rich people of the country, especially those who are making vast profits out of the war, are not doing their part. It is, in fact, true that many rich people are investing in bonds and stocks, especially in war industries or those profiting by the war such as iron and steel companies and coal companies, which pay huge dividends, instead of buying Government bonds paying 4¼% interest. It is a natural feeling among the masses of the people that taxation upon incomes and upon war profits should be so high as to bring the return from corporate investments of this character more nearly on a parity with the Government's bonds; that the Government should not be forced to compete for credit with war industries which are profiting abnormally and which, unless restrained by the exercise of sound and just taxation, will constantly add to the difficulties of the people of the United States in their effort to supply the Government at reasonable interest rates with the credit it needs to fight successfully this war for liberty.

To summarize the main features of the tax legislation which I recommend:

(1) Such legislation should be calculated to provide in cash during the fiscal year ending June 30, 1919, not less than one-third of the cash expenditures to be made during that year. According to my estimates, $8,000,000,000 should be raised in taxes payable in cash into the Treasury during that year.

(2) A real war profits tax at a high rate should be levied upon all war profits. This tax should be super-imposed upon the existing war profits tax in such a way that the taxpayer would pay whichever tax were the greater, and the existing excess profits tax should be amended in certain important particulars so as to remove inequalities.

(3) There should be an important increase in the amount of normal income tax upon unearned incomes. Under existing law earned incomes above certain exemptions are taxed 4% as an income tax and 8% under the name of an excess profits tax, making a total of 12%, while unearned incomes, derived from securities, etc., are taxed only 4%. The 8% tax should be recognized as an income tax and the rate of 12% retained in respect to earned incomes, while a higher rate than 12% should be imposed on unearned incomes.

(4) A heavy tax should be imposed upon all luxuries.

The only reasons which have been urged upon me against revenue legislation at this time are political. Many have expressed the fear that it would cause the loss of the next House of Representatives to the Democrats. I do not know whether this be true or not. It seems to me that the fear is ill-founded, because I am sure that the people of the United States will have much more respect for and confidence in those who are willing to tell them before they are asked to vote just what their position is about taxation upon profiteering and upon incomes than in those who dodge the issue. But whether such legislation does or does not affect the political complexion of the next Congress, how can we allow any political consideration to stand in the way of our doing the things which are manifestly demanded to save the life of the Nation? I believe that these political fears are unjustified and I further believe that if you should present this important matter to the Congress in a strong message, it would result in prompt and adequate legislation to meet what is without exaggeration a genuine war emergency.

Cordially yours,   W G McAdoo

TLS (WP, DLC).

Dear "Governor":   Washington May 23, 1918.

For a man who is ordered not to talk, I have been very voluble, I fear, in my letter on taxation which I sent you today!

Since sending that letter, Mr. Fordney[1] called to see me, and suggests that he thinks it would be possible to get an understanding with his Republican colleagues, both in the House and Senate, for prompt action on a revenue bill if it were deferred until a special session to be convened in November next shortly after the election. He also thinks that it would be possible to get an understanding among the leaders of both Houses that they would support new taxation upon some basis to be agreed upon if a similar understanding could be arrived at with the Democratic leaders. He says that it could then be announced unofficially that increases in taxation would be made at the next session, and that this would put business and the country generally on notice; that it could be announced that the Ways and Means Committee of the House was considering the measure now with a view to having a bill in readiness for prompt consideration at the November session.

Mr. Fordney seemed to think that if this was done, it might satisfy the immediate situation and that it would result in expediting very much the passage of a revenue measure at the next session.

I thought this information might be of value in the discussion you are to have this evening. Perhaps it would be wise for you to hear what the Democratic leaders have to say and to take the matter under advisement without committing yourself this evening.

Cordially yours,   W G McAdoo

P.S. I shall then see what, if any thing can be done, in the way of an arrangement altho. nothing at the moment seems possible.

TLS (WP, DLC).
[1] Joseph Warren Fordney of Michigan, ranking Republican member of the Ways and Means Committee.

From Joseph Patrick Tumulty

Dear Governor: [The White House] 23 May 1918.

I do not know how you will decide the question of revenue legislation which Mr. McAdoo faces and which the Senate and House are opposing. From what I have heard put forward by the Senate and House, I am inclined to believe that their attitude toward this legislation is based upon politics and their desire to get back to their districts as soon as possible. If you intend to take sides with Mr. McAdoo in this matter, I would suggest that you write a letter either to Martin or Simmons, saying that the Treasury Department and those in charge of the finances of the country feel that this legislation is absolutely necessary; that you are bound to be influenced by their advice in the matter and that to ignore it would be fraught with the greatest danger. And then say that many of the arguments against it have taken on circumstances of a political character, circumstances which you are bound to ignore, and that regardless of what the political effect of it may be, you feel it your duty to urge it and to ask for the united support of both Houses in the passage of this legislation. If you will write a letter of this kind, it will put the whole country back of you and make it impossible for the gentlemen on the Hill to oppose this measure with any hope of success.   Sincerely yours,   Tumulty

TCL (W. G. McAdoo Papers, DLC).

From Alexander Theodore Vogelsang

My dear Mr. President: Washington May 23, 1918.

Replying to your note of 20th instant upon the subject of suspension of the eight-hour law in the completion of new buildings at St. Elizabeths Hospital, I beg to say that I carefully read the reports and papers accompanying the request, which, with my general knowledge of conditions at the Hospital, convinced me that there was real and pressing necessity for the relaxation requested.

Since your letter was received, I have had a conference with Dr. White,[1] Superintendent, and with those of our Department in charge of hospital affairs, the result of which confirms my conclusion that this suspension should be granted if we are to have these buildings completed on time.

A special appropriation of $200,000 was made in the last Urgent Deficiency Act for the construction of new wards for the accommodation of soldiers and sailors abroad who may become mentally deranged. I attach hereto the testimony of Dr. White upon this subject before the Committee.[2] The plans for the buildings were expeditiously completed and contract entered into on the 7th day of this month with the Oscawana Building Company of New York, the work to be completed by August 1, 1918.

The contractor claims that it is almost impossible to obtain laborers or mechanics to work on any other basis than that of a ten-hour day, which means full wages for eight hours and time and a half for the remaining two hours of each day, for the reason that practically all labor now performed for the Government in the erection of buildings for the War, Navy, and Treasury Departments, and others, is upon this basis, and that the workmen demand this arrangement. See copies of two letters attached.[3]

There are now more than 3,300 patients in the institution with only a narrow margin of space to provide for current admissions. The early completion of the additional wards is essential to the end that we be prepared to receive and care for those mentally impaired soldiers and sailors who are soon to reach us from over-seas.

We firmly believe the attached order should be signed.[4]

Cordially and faithfully yours,   Alexander T. Vogelsang

TLS (WP, DLC).
  [1] William Alanson White.
  [2] "Statement of Dr. William A. White . . . July 20, 1917," T MS (WP, DLC).
  [3] F. W. Wocher to E. J. Ayers, May 7, 1918, and A. J. Van Suetendael to [A. T. Vogelsang], May 22, 1918, both TCL (WP, DLC).
  [4] Wilson signed the Executive Order on May 24, 1918.

From Samuel Gompers

Sir: Washington, D. C. May 23, 1918.

Your letter of May 20th with the enclosed letters from Secretary of War Baker and the memorandum to him from General McIntyre relating to my communication to you regarding Governor Yager of Porto Rico, reaches me just a few hours prior to leaving the city to fulfill a number of important engagements. Mr. Iglesias is also out of the city and will not be able to return for several weeks as he has been assigned to a very important mission. On June 5th, I shall have left for St. Paul, Minnesota, to attend the Convention of the American Federation of Labor. It is hardly probable that I will be able to return to Washington before the 27th or 28th of June at best. After I get back from St. Paul and Mr. Iglesias shall have returned to Washington I shall then be very glad to comply with your suggestion for a conference with Secretary Baker in which General McIntyre could participate, and when I should of course desire Mr. Iglesias to be present.

I return to you herewith the enclosures as you requested but have taken the liberty of having copies made for my records.

                              Respectfully,   Saml. Gompers.

TLS (WP, DLC).

William Graves Sharp to Robert Lansing

Paris May 23, 1918.

3966. Referring to my number 3871, May 12, 3 p.m.[1] in which General Nies[s]el, Chief of the French Military Mission to Russia, was quoted, as to the situation in that country and the problems of Japanese intervention. I have since had placed in my hands a written statement of the General, elaborating his views on those questions. A statement was first submitted to Monsieur Clemenceau and then transmitted by the Premier in a letter to me. The views therein contained undoubtedly have the approval of the French Government. I shall in the outgoing mail to-day transmit the text in full but deem it advisable to telegraph its salient features. The document impresses me as very carefully thought out by one who had most favorable opportunities to study the situation.

The General states in brief, that there is a universal desire for the restoration [of] order and would welcome intervention in Siberia conditional to its assuming an Inter-Allied character. Declarations should first be made of the intention to respect the integrity of Russian territory. All Russians agree that social order cannot be restored without help from outside. Undoubtedly the Central Powers will offer such help at a propitious moment. There is no reason to believe that the Bolsheviks could win over Russian public opinion against Japanese intervention, because their own wickedness has exasperated the whole population which has lost confidence in them.

The General does not believe that the Japanese would encounter any check in the way of resistance in their operations in Siberia. The time of transportation would be considerably shortened on account of using a base afforded by Manchuria, where the railroad is in the hands of the Allies as far as the Trans-Baikal frontier. Irkutsk would be the first important objective. Siberia is not and can not be Bolshevik inasmuch as individual property is there the general rule. Irkutsk and Vladivostok, on account of their working classes, constitute the only Bolshevik centers, all the other representative classes of Siberia during the last winter clamored for Allied intervention. General Niesel thenceforth goes on to point out the immediate advantage of the occupation of Occidental Siberia in being able to seize the reserve food stuffs to which the Central Powers must soon look, as they have been disappointed in Ukrania, and in greater Russia. Imperative that action should be taken soon so as not to allow time for the Austro-German prisoners in Siberia to be armed and organized by Germany, to oppose the seizure of the Trans-Siberian by the Allies. During the last winter while the

General was in Russia the Germans made offers tending to restore order in Russia. The orderly elements however were afraid of the overbearing qualities of the Germans and hoped only for Inter-Allied intervention. Belief is expressed that the Japanese people would be proud to take part in events of world-wide importance; that the Allies should cooperate with Japanese army to direct and keep it within bounds and while utilizing Russian port preserve its disinterested character in regard to Russia. In relation to the expediency of intervening in the Caucasus particularly to prevent the massacre of the Armenians any action in that region, inasmuch as it could only start from Mesopotamia, would have to overcome very great obstacles on account of the distance, the nature of it, and the difficulty of transportation similar to the action in the objective ports largely rests with the seizure of the food reserve which is at this moment the main endeavor of the Central Powers. General Niesel concludes his statement by observing that, in view of all the above considerations, intervention in Siberia appears to be the most efficacious action in the shape of helping the Russian nation by restoring social order and safeguarding it and which is, however, mastery of the Central Powers. He adds that it is high time now to pass on to deeds. Whether the Bolshevik party is consenting or not these deeds are looked for by all the orderly element of Russia.

Sharp.

T telegram (SDR, RG 59, 861.00/1852, DNA).
  [1] See RL to WW, May 16, 1918, n. 1.

Three Telegrams from Lord Reading to Arthur James Balfour

Washington. 23rd May, 1918.

Following for Sir E. Drummond.

Personal and Secret.

Your personal tel. of May 18.[1]

At a long interview I had yesterday with the President I suggested that he should send a confidential agent to the Vatican. This was the only possible plan which could be put to him of the three alternatives and from my knowledge of his view I fully expected the answer he made which was that the state of opinion in the U. S. would not permit him to accede to the proposal. It would be impossible for him to send a confidential agent for it would be bound to be known that he had sent some representative to the Vatican. You who know the U. S. can well understand that the fact would get out. The President was sorry he could not accede to the suggestion but his knowledge of the sentiment of the U. S. convinced him that in the end the proposed course would be disadvantageous both to us and to the United States. In addition, the powerful body of Irish opinion would particularly resent such action by him.

I did not think it wise to press the matter hard as I am sure I should not have succeeded for we had well discussed the advantages that might ensue. He obviously had not any intention of accepting the suggestion.

T telegram (Reading Papers, FO 800/224, PRO).
  [1] A. J. Balfour to Lord Reading, May 18, 1918, T telegram (FO 800/385, Miscellaneous Papers, p. 141, PRO).

Washington. May 23rd, 1918

No. 2338 At my interview with the President yesterday I again represented your views on intervention in Russia. As I expected, I found the President quite decided in the opinion that the moment was inopportune, in other words that he did not think the circumstances sufficiently warranted the proposed action. He expressed himself anxious that you should not think he was stubborn in this matter but he was not alone in his opinion (and he had the support of his military advisers) (a) that the total force available would not be sufficient to cause any diversion of German troops from the West or retention of them in the East. According to his reports the line would become so thin owing to the length of communications and difficulty of supply that it would be useless as a fighting force in opposition to Germans. It was evident that the reports of his military advisers support his view previously expressed that no military advantage would be gained by intervention, and (b) that the proposed operations would be resented by the Russians. The confusion caused by varying reports from Russia and Siberia is never ending but American and Japanese reports substantially agree as to the effect upon Russians of Japanese & Allied & American armed intervention. President thinks Trotsky and his Govt. may be amenable at one moment and may be prepared to give an invitation or an assent or a promise not to object but President regards him as absolutely untrustworthy and is convinced that any action Trotsky or his Government may take would be simply and solely for his or their own ends. The President's expression was that the only certainty in dealing with such a man was that he would deceive you.

The President was further of opinion that Trotsky's invitation would be of no avail in Siberia where his authority was not recognized. He referred to the Seminov movement which according to U. S. reports was gaining strength and might prove a powerful factor.

I asked the President whether in the present circumstances he was of opinion that no action should be taken or whether he proposed any other operation. His answer was that he much regretted it but saw no alternative at the moment other than an anxious watching of the situation. I suggested that without committing his Govt. preparations and arrangements might be made so that the U. S. Govt. and Allies would be ready to act promptly should circumstances change. The President said that he was not averse from making enquiries and preparations of a character which would not prematurely disclose an intention to intervene but that these must be of a very tentative character. Otherwise reports would be published of military preparations which would have almost the effect of a declared policy of armed intervention. President said that as result of inquiries the U.S.G. had troops in Phillipines which could be made available in case of need (these represent the greater part of a regiment). The difficulty would occur however in the transport of men and supplies as U.S.G. had no shipping for this purpose without subtracting from its aid for transport to France.

Generally I can only confirm what I have now repeatedly told you which is that the President sees no advantage to be gained by intervention in Siberia.

The President's statement in his last speech that the U. S. would stand by Russia is the subject of much discussion in Press and by the public. It is now quite freely and openly stated that the U. S. will not take part in armed intervention in Siberia. There is much speculation in Press as to how the U.S.G. proposes to help Russia but I do not believe that any definite scheme has yet been arrived at. The public is quite ready to endorse any action which will prove the wish of America to benefit Russia.

The President drew the distinction between intervention in Siberia and intervention to protect Murmansk and Archangel. As I was not yet in position to state what could be done as regards Murmansk protection I did not pursue the subject.

T telegram (FO 115/2446, pp. 338-40, PRO).

Washington. 23rd May 1918.

No. 2347. Your telegram No. 2788.[1] Mexico.

I took the opportunity yesterday of discussing this question with the President. He said that they were carefully watching events in Mexico and especially in regard to (a) possible attempts by Carranza to bring about a war between U. S. and Mexico and (b) interruption of supply of oil for allied fleets. The President desired me to convey to you that according to all the information of the U. S. Government the situation in Mexico was not so threatening or acute as it had been. The U. S. Government was doing everything possible to cultivate better relations in Mexico and he thought their efforts were meeting with some success. The President fully appreciated the importance of a continuance of the supply of oil from Mexico. His view is that Carranza will not take any definite step in support of the German cause unless events prove that Germany has won the war and Carranza will be very careful not to commit himself.

The President is evidently determined not to be provoked into hostilities with Mexico unless these become imperative. Naturally he sees the advantage to Germany of a war between Mexico and the United States but he is determined not to be drawn into it unless he cannot possibly avoid it.

The President's general view is that the situation has somewhat improved.[2]

T telegram (FO 115/2413, pp. 419-20, PRO).
  [1] A. J. Balfour to Lord Reading, May 7, 1918, Vol. 47.
  [2] Another copy of this telegram is Lord Reading to A. J. Balfour, No. 2347, T telegram (FO 371/3244, p. 186, PRO).

From the Diary of Colonel House

May 23, 1918.

Gordon telephoned last night and again this morning concerning the British Ambassador's interview with the President regarding Lloyd George's request that I come abroad at once. Reading in making the request at first did not commit the diplomatic blunder of mentioning my name, because it is an unusual thing for one government to request that a particular person be sent. He asked permission of the President to be entirely candid and upon receiving it, he told the President that his Government and French desired me.

The President replied that if he sent anyone he would send me, for I was the only one who knew his mind and whom he would be willing to have speak for him. However, he entirely agreed with me as to the inadvisability of my going at this time, and asked Reading what he personally thought. Reading confessed that he was of the same opinion.

Reading told Gordon that it was the most satisfactory interview he had had with the President since he had been in America, and that it lasted for an hour and a quarter.

To Newton Diehl Baker

My dear Mr. Secretary: [The White House] 24 May, 1918

I always doubt my judgment when I find myself disagreeing with you and therefore I am glad to ask for a further word from you about the case of Major Henry R. Freeman, 337th Field Artillery.[1]

I have received such unusual and striking testimony as to his character and ability as a soldier,[2] and there seems in the evidence to be so much ground for believing that it was not really what he drank but the doubtful character of it that led to his condition, that I am writing to ask if you think it would be demoralizing to the service for me to sign the commuted form of sentence with a change. I can see how demoralizing it might be to confine him within camp limits where he now is. Is there no method of suspension under restraint elsewhere which could be adopted? I know you will be perfectly frank with me as always about the possibility and advisability of this.

Cordially and sincerely yours,   Woodrow Wilson

P.S. Do not trouble to return the report   W.W.

TLS (Letterpress Books, WP, DLC).
[1] Wilson was replying to NDB to WW, May 18, 1918, CCL (N. D. Baker Papers, DLC). Baker commented upon the trial by court-martial at Camp Dodge, Iowa, on April 3, 1918, of Major Freeman, who had been charged with violating the 95th Article of War "under a specification alleging that at Des Moines, Iowa, on the 5th of March, 1918, he was so drunk in uniform in a hotel in the presence and hearing of several persons as to disgrace the military service." The court had found Freeman guilty of the charge, which carried the penalty of dismissal from the service, but seven of the nine members of the court recommended clemency in view of Freeman's previous excellent record and his present usefulness to the service. The Judge Advocate General, Enoch H. Crowder, after reviewing the case, recommended that the sentence of dismissal be commuted to confinement for six months to the limits of his post or camp when not engaged in official duties, forfeiture of $100 per month for the same period, and a reprimand by the commanding general of his division. Baker dissented from Crowder's recommendation on the ground that, as a person who had always abstained from drink, Freeman should have been all the more aware of the consequences, both physical and legal, of that act. He also argued that, if Freeman was merely confined to base while performing his regular duties, it would set a bad example to officers and men alike. He recommended to Wilson that the original sentence of dismissal be carried out. However, he enclosed two forms of order from which Wilson could choose, one to carry out the sentence, the other to commute it as recommended by Crowder.
[2] Knute Nelson to WW, May 24, 1918, TLS (WP, DLC).

To Robert Lansing

My dear Mr. Secretary: The White House 24 May, 1918

I have your letter of May twenty-first about relief in Poland and Turkey. I should not like to see the relief in Turkey curtailed in the least, because it is more desperately needed there now perhaps than ever before, but I realize the weight of what you say with regard to Poland and the impossibility of making it evident even in Poland where the relief comes from. I would be very much obliged if you would have someone in your department who is in touch with these matters consult with the most sensible representatives of Poland in this country and see if they have any means to suggest by which we could control this matter a little bit without absolutely cutting it off.

Cordially and faithfully yours, Woodrow Wilson

TLS (SDR, RG 59, 861.48/596, DNA).

To Joseph Swagar Sherley

My dear Mr. Sherley: [The White House] 24 May, 1918

I take the liberty of writing to call your attention to an appropriation which seems to me of capital importance in connection with the effective conduct of the war. I refer to the sum for National Security and Defense which has been placed at my disposal during the past fiscal year. I think that it is of the utmost importance that a similar fund should be put at my disposal for the next fiscal year, though in my judgment it need not be so large as the last appropriation for that purpose. I think that a sum of half the amount, namely, $50,000,000, would be abundant.

I believe that you and your colleagues on the Committee on Appropriations are familiar with the objects for which I have used the appropriation, but perhaps you will permit me to summarize them and to append an outline of the actual expenditures.[1]

I have used considerable sums for the maintenance of the Food Administration, the Fuel Administration, and the War Trade Board, and for the maintenance of the proper agencies for the allocation of labor, a matter of very great consequence and of no little difficulty just now when there is so general a dislocation of labor throughout the country. For these objects it seems probable that the fund is no longer necessary, inasmuch as their administration has now been quite thoroughly organized and is susceptible of being maintained by definite appropriations assigned to their use in the usual manner. Of course, this method of appropriation is preferable to any other.

Besides these objects, I have spent very large sums for the repair of ships owned by alien enemies which we took possession of immediately after our entrance into the war and which, as you know, had been deliberately damaged in the most serious way by their own crews; for the providing of temporary accommodations for the newly-created services connected with the war; for advances to the regular departments for services appropriated for in the usual way when it seemed unwise in the circumstances to wait until appropriations, which could certainly be counted upon, could be acted upon by the Congress; to provide additional facilities for the Civil Service Commission in order that it might more nearly meet the exceptional demands of the time for clerical aid; for miscellaneous expenses connected with the very serviceable action of the Council of National Defense; and for labor matters of many sorts, investigation, mediation, the settlement of strikes, and many objects arising from time to time and impossible to foresee or calculate for beforehand. Most of these matters may also now, fortunately, be taken care of in the regular way, though similar occasions for the immediate expenditure of money may no doubt arise on a smaller scale than before. Some of these objects, as for example the repair of ships, have now been, I assume, entirely covered.

There remain the uses for such a fund which I may perhaps characterize as continuing but incalculable. I refer to the conduct of many necessary investigations, for example, in connection with the determination of the prices which the Government is to pay and which the governments associated with us in the war are to pay;

To indispensable secret service and to confidential uses abroad;

To the very large necessities of record and information;

To the maintenance of the instrumentalities, both on this side of the water and on the other, which are doing admirable work in informing public opinion both here and there of the real aims of America, of the progress she is making in the conduct of the war, and of the real facts with regard to all the larger aspects of our policy;

And to the service and guidance to all sorts of patriotic movements in the United States which appeal to the Government for its assistance and for materials wherewith to conduct their work.

Besides these things which can now be stated, the experience of the past year convinces me that there are many occasions which will arise which I cannot now even conjecture, but which will make it necessary that I should have a free fund at my disposal.

May I not take the liberty of saying a word of special emphasis with regard to the work which the Committee on Public Information has been doing? I have had very close personal connections with the work of that committee and have watched its development and its activities with particular care and interest, feeling a special responsibility. The work of the Committee has, on the whole, been admirably done, and I think it very likely that nobody, not even those intimately connected with the Government, is aware of the extent, the variety and the usefulness of that work or of the really unusually economical manner in which it has been accomplished, so far as the expenditure of money is concerned. I should feel personally crippled if any obstacle of any kind were put in the way of that work.

It is probable that it will now be possible to a considerable extent to submit estimates of the usual sort to take care of the work of the committee, and I hope that in connection with those estimates at least some of the members of the Committee on Appropriations may have an opportunity to know more particularly what it has been doing.

Cordially and sincerely yours,   Woodrow Wilson

TLS (Letterpress Books, WP, DLC).
  ¹ This enclosure is missing.

Two Letters to Bernard Mannes Baruch

My dear Baruch: The White House 24 May, 1918

Do you think that it would be practicable to effect some kind of organization through which we could have a sort of picture or conspectus of all the present war activities of the Government and upon that base a periodical checking up of the actual operations and results? I think a good deal of loose talk and perhaps a good deal of loose action might be avoided if we could have such a basis of judgment and such a periodical checking up.

Cordially and sincerely yours,   Woodrow Wilson

TLS (B. M. Baruch Papers, NjP).

My dear Baruch: [The White House] 24 May, 1918

In a conversation I had yesterday with Mr. Sherley, the Chairman of the Committee on Appropriations in the House of Representatives, he suggested that it would clarify a great many matters and render our tasks easier if the committee could be supplied with estimates of the necessary expenditures in connection with the administration of the Board in all particulars which are calculable beforehand, and I think myself that that would bring about a more satisfactory relationship to Mr. Sherley's committee. I am, therefore, writing to ask if you think that it will be possible within a short time to submit such estimates?

Cordially and faithfully yours,   Woodrow Wilson

TLS (Letterpress Books, WP, DLC).

To Edward Nash Hurley

My dear Hurley: [The White House] 24 May, 1918

In a talk the other day with Mr. Sherley, the Chairman of the House Committee on Appropriations, he suggested the desirability of having a proper audit system worked out between the Emergency Fleet Corporation and the Treasury Department to cover the expenditures of the Corporation. Of course, the Corporation is using its own auditors now, and I dare say is exercising the proper and prudent care in these matters, but it would assist the Committee on Appropriations and, I think, strengthen the whole business with them if the system of audit could be coordinated with that of the Treasury, or at least conducted under the Treasury's direction. What do you think?[1]

Cordially and faithfully yours,   Woodrow Wilson

TLS (Letterpress Books, WP, DLC).
  [1] As E. N. Hurley to WW, May 25, 1918, TLS, enclosing E. N. Hurley to WGM, May 23, 1918, TCL, both in WP, DLC, reveal, Hurley had already requested the Treasury Department to make a special audit of the Emergency Fleet Corporation.

To George Creel

My dear Creel: The White House 24 May, 1918

In a conversation I had yesterday with Mr. Sherley, the Chairman of the Committee on Appropriations in the House of Representatives, he suggested that it would clarify a great many matters and render our tasks easier if the committee could be supplied with estimates of the necessary expenditures in connection with the administration of your Committee in all particulars which are calculable beforehand, and I think myself that that would bring about a more satisfactory relationship to Mr. Sherley's committee. I am, therefore, writing to ask if you think that it will be possible within a short time to submit such estimates?

This would afford you the same opportunity that others have of laying before the Committee on Appropriations the real facts with regard to what you are doing and how you are doing it, because they would in all likelihood wish to have a sub-committee do the very thing that we want them to do, namely, go into the matter until they comprehend it.

Cordially and faithfully yours,   Woodrow Wilson

TLS (G. Creel Papers, DLC).

To Robert Bridges

My dear Bobby: The White House 24 May, 1918

It was a great disappointment not to find you at your office, but your delightful note is part compensation for what I missed, and I thank you for it with all my heart. Your affection and confidence mean a vast deal to me.

In unavoidable haste,

Affectionately yours,   Woodrow Wilson

TLS (WC, NjP).

From Robert Lansing, with Enclosure

My dear Mr. President: Washington May 24, 1918.

While this message from Ambassador Francis has been sent to you it may have escaped your notice. I am, therefore, calling it directly to your attention.

Faithfully yours,   Robert Lansing

TLS (WP, DLC).

E N C L O S U R E

Vologda May 16, 1918

173. Robins passed [through][1] Vologda yesterday in Red Cross car attached to Siberian express en route Vladivostok thence America, saying departure in compliance with your 22 of the 7th signed Davison, Lansing,[2] which was received Moscow 10th through Consulate General and was seen by me before delivery. Robins construed this cable as definite recall and when asked by me if Davison returned [ordered return] replied no but said message was from State Department. Robins had intended remaining in the hope that Thompson would influence Department to recognize Soviet Government. He planned to leave Moscow second instant but telegraphed me that departure delayed by cables from Paris and Washington. I saw in Moscow a telegram from Thatcher[3] stating received Robins cable and had told Davison and others of Robins' good work and thought effective. Also saw cable from Davison saying had received Robins' cables and had seen Thatcher and understood situation but could do nothing before reaching Washington and advising Robins to remain until further instructions. Consequently recall surprised Robins. When asked to what he attributed same replied: Summers' suggestion. He stated yesterday he had received

cable from Thatcher dated tenth instant stating that he had been Washington and thought had made impression. I do not know whether Robins can reach Vladivostok as Harbin route closed and Amur route reported cut by Semenoff but Robins said latter reported untrue as Soviet Government unadvised thereof. Robins was accompanied by Hardy Goniberg and Browne[4] representative of CHICAGO NEWS.

ASSOCIATED PRESS representative here and Groves[5] after talking to Robins at the station understand that he had definite proposition to the United States from the Soviet Government and was hastening to America in expectation of receiving favorable reply and definitely stated expected to return promptly if Soviet Government survi[v]ed,[6] but Robins with whom I talked fully made no mention of such mission nor of returning.

Have instructed Consuls along Trans-Siberian Railway to assist Robins if possible and advise me of his progress; also to transmit through Embassy or Consulate General all messages "on matters of political policy" whether cipher or enclair (see your 78 April 21, 5 p.m.)[7] as Robins said has procured order of Soviet Government directing acceptance of cipher messages signed by himself through Consuls.

Some three months ago Robins after repeated effort to convert me to the support of Soviet Government upon asking if I had recommended recognition, when I replied, "no," he said would inform Government and tell them I would not. I replied assenting first proposition but requested him not to advise Government as to my future course which would depend upon resistance offered to Germany. Robins as I have cabled Department [has] been earnestly advocating recognition and has persuaded several well meaning Americans that such policy wise, notably ASSOCIATED PRESS representatives, Red Cross members and Jerome Davis, the latter I am informed cabled Mott recommending support of recognition. Thatcher when at Murman awaiting vessel for London, participated in meetings and advocated evacuation of Murman by Allies not with standing Marrill[8] advised him that my policy contrary thereto.

I do not understand Robins' failure to inform me of his plans as he has continuously since *breaches* with Ridsdag [Thompson's departure] expressed friendliness and admiration of my course. I regret forgetting to tell him yesterday contents of your 78 April 21, 5 p.m. and that would instruct Consuls accordingly.

Of course have no fear of Department recognizing Soviet Government if it should [last] until Robins arrival Washington which I doubt. Bolshevik Press states Robins going to America and will return soon while opposition press claims his recall final.

May I suggest advising Red Cross and Christian Association to instruct their representatives to confine their activities strictly to the line of their work? Permit me most (#) [earnestly] to say that if the Department would refuse Russian passport issued to Socialist fanatics and sensational news mongers it could diminish difficulties and lessen embarrassments of this Embassy. Striking examples *of a satisfactory* [unsatisfactory] class are Alberto Rees Williams, Louis Edgar Browne of CHICAGO NEWS, Minor[9] PHILADELPHIA LEDGER, first two of whom are now en route America; Browne boasted yesterday would return after acquainting America of POSTS policies here. Williams returning to propagate Bolshevism.[10]

Francis.

(#) Apparent omission

T telegram (WP, DLC).
  [1] Corrections from the text in *FR 1918, Russia*, I, 530-31.
  [2] RL to D. C. Poole, Jr., May 7, 1918, *ibid.*, pp. 523-24.
  [3] That is, Thomas D. Thacher, who had recently returned to the United States from Russia. William Kent, Thacher's uncle-in-law, had written to Wilson on May 22 urging him to see Thacher to get the benefit of his first-hand knowledge of the Russian situation. Kent also noted that Thacher believed "that the present soviet government is representative of the people and that it is the only hope against a reaction manipulated by Germany." Wilson replied on May 23 that he did not have the time for a "real talk" with Thacher but intended to suggest to Lansing that he should see Thacher if he had the time for such an interview. Lansing did make an appointment to see Thacher on May 28. W. Kent to WW, May 22, 1918, and WW to RL, May 23, 1918, both TLS (R. Lansing Papers, DLC), and WW to W. Kent, May 23, 1918, TLS (Letterpress Books, WP, DLC).
  [4] Capt. D. Heywood Hardy, a member of the American Red Cross mission to Russia; Alexander Gumberg; and Louis Edgar Browne.
  [5] The Associated Press representative may have been Charles Stephenson Smith, at that time head of the Russian service of the A.P. "Groves" was J. Philip Groves, a clerk at the American embassy.
  [6] Robins was carrying on his person a lengthy plan for the resumption and expansion of Russian-American commercial relations which had been sent to him by Lenin himself on May 14. The plan, together with Lenin's covering note, is printed in C. K. Cumming and Walter W. Pettit, eds., *Russian-American Relations, March, 1917-March, 1920: Documents and Papers* (New York, 1920), pp. 204-12. For a summary of its contents and a discussion of its background and significance, see Kennan, *Decision to Intervene*, pp. 217-25.
  [7] RL to D. R. Francis, April 23 [not 21], 1918, T telegram (SDR, RG 59, 811.142/3200, DNA); printed in *FR 1918, Russia*, I, 503.
  [8] He meant Lt. Hugh Street Martin, at this time Assistant Military Attaché in Russia. About this incident, see Kennan, pp. 37-38.
  [9] Albert Rhys Williams, correspondent for the New York *Evening Post*, and Robert Minor, political cartoonist and reporter, later a leading figure in the American Communist party.
  [10] While Williams never joined the Communist party, he was strongly pro-Soviet both then and for the rest of his long life.

From Edward Mandell House, with Enclosure

Dear Governor: New York. May 24, 1918.

I am sending you a postfolio [portfolio] of Nast Cartoons. Harper & Brothers fished the best of them from their files. I hope you may enjoy them.

Tumulty writes me that he has suggested Hugh Wallace for

Denmark in Egan's place. I do not believe Wallace would consider it. Why not give it to Norman Hapgood? He is a staunch friend, very capable, and is eager to serve in that country.

I do not believe you can realize what a success your last trip to New York has been. Everyone is talking about it, and I heard a prominent and well informed man say that in his opinion no President ever had such a reception and no President was ever so popular in New York as you are today.

I am leaving tomorrow for Magnolia, stopping for a few days at Chestnut Hill with Mona.

With deep affection, I am,

Your devoted,   E. M. House

I shall think of you with sympathy at lunch time tomorrow.[1] I met the Prince today.

TLS (WP, DLC).
[1] Wilson entertained Prince Arthur of Connaught at luncheon on May 25.

E N C L O S U R E

William Christian Bullitt to Edward Mandell House

Dear Colonel House: Washington. May 20, 1918.

The appended memorandum has just been written for me by Jack Reed[1] who served for a time as Director of Revolutionary Propaganda for the Bolshiviki, and returned to this country a few weeks ago. Reed knows Lenine and Trotzky so intimately that his recommendations, which you will find on page 14 of this memorandum, may be regarded, I think, as the recommendations they would make themselves.

I wish I could see Russia with as single an eye as Reed. I am unable to win through the welter of conflicting reports about the Bolshiviki to anything like solid conviction. After all, isn't indecision the keynote of our Russian policy just now? It is the keynote of England's policy—so Lord Eustace Percy writes me from London, and adds, "One wonders whether in any allied country there is not perhaps some man of sufficient imaginative stature to go to Russia as a Commissioner for the Allies and *lead*. Such a man might disentangle from the present confusion the real democratic movement and launch it on the landlords of the Ukraine and Poland, on the Baltic barons and all the other aristocratic and capitalist protegés of Germany from the Black Sea to the Baltic." I doubt that any man from a foreign country could lead Russia today.[2]

But as I started to say, we must get away from our present indecision. As nearly as I can discover we have plenty of observers in Russia, but their work is not intelligently directed and the information they furnish is not properly digested. Russia today is a problem not only for the State Department but for the War Department, the Navy Department, the Treasury Department, the Department of Commerce, the Shipping Board, the War Trade Board and the War Industries Board. It is a problem of huge complexity. At present Basil Miles is vaguely responsible for our general policy. Miles is an excellent diplomatist, really excellent, but he is not an expert on military, economic and financial matters. And one man with two stenographers can not handle the problem presented by Russia.

I feel that the President should create at once a Russian Board, to consist of representatives of the Departments and Boards enumerated above, with a Chairman in whom the President could have complete confidence. The Chairman of this Board would not be subservient to any Department. He would deal personally with the President. It would be his business to gather all the information in regard to Russia received by any Department and to plan our Russian policy,—political, commercial, military.

In Russia there should be another Board, organized on similar lines, to carry out the orders of the Chairman of the Russian Board in Washington and to act on its own responsibility in commercial matters when the delay incident to using the cable would be fatal to a desirable transaction. It occurs to me that Mr. Justice Brandeis would be particularly well fitted to head such an organization. Basil Miles might be the representative of the State Department on the Board. Legge[3] might represent the War Industries Board, Chadbourne[4] the War Trade Board,—and so on.

Such an organization should be able to end our indecision very soon. It should be able to furnish a really well-considered opinion on any phase of Russian policy. It should be able to end the wobbling of ourselves and the Allies.

Very sincerely yours,   William C. Bullitt.

This is Bullitt's view of the Russian situation.   E.M.H.

TCL (WP, DLC).
  [1] The Editors have been unable to find this memorandum in the House, Bullitt, and Reed collections, or in any other collection. John Reed, "The Case for the Bolsheviki," *The Independent*, XCV (July 13, 1918), 55, 72, was probably a compacted version of Reed's memorandum, but it contained no recommendations concerning policies toward the Bolsheviks.
  [2] At this point the next sentence was omitted: "Certainly the only man who would have any chance to handle the job would be yourself, and that I suppose is not to be considered." W. C. Bullitt to EMH, May 20, 1918, TLS (E. M. House Papers, CtY).
  [3] Alexander Legge, vice-president and general manager of the International Harvester Co.; at this time, vice-chairman of the War Industries Board, head of its requirements division, and manager of the Allied Purchasing Commission.
  [4] That is, Thomas Lincoln Chadbourne, Jr., at this time counselor of the War Trade Board.

From Amos Richards Eno Pinchot

My dear Mr. Wilson: New York May 24, 1918

It is hard for me to write impartially about the second trial of The Masses editors.[1] Three of the defendants accused of conspiracy are my close personal friends. And my judgment, as to the general wisdom of continuing such a prosecution, cannot but be affected by the horror I feel at the possibility of seeing these men broken and embittered by a conviction of a crime, of which I know they are neither technically nor morally guilty.

Others have spoken to you of the doubtful wisdom of pushing these prosecutions, of their effect on liberal people and policies—and of the fact that, if rights like that of common counsel are taken from the public in an emergency, they can never be restored as *rights*. They have become revocable permissions.

On these matters, important as they are, I will not waste your time or mine. But I want you to think of a side of the case far removed from questions of war policies or political expediency. Max Eastman, Art Young, John Reed and the others are not guilty. I listened to most of the trial myself and read a good deal of the record; and I know, as a lawyer who has tried many criminal cases, that evidence proving the charges of the indictment was quite lacking. After both sides had summed up, a distinguished professor of law, who sat in the court room throughout the entire trial, said to me that there was not a shred of evidence to substantiate the conspiracy charge. Aside from this, I know, as a friend of Eastman, Young and Reed, that there was no conspiracy or any intent to block the policy of the government. Whatever criticism of the war and conscription appeared, they uttered as individuals and without desire to prevent the operation of the law.

While the jury was out, I had a talk with Marshal McCarthy,[2] whom I knew when he was Jimmy Gerard's secretary. I told him that, in my opinion, a conviction was impossible, in view of the lack of evidence showing conspiracy. He replied that evidence didn't matter in such cases; that now juries convict anybody who is indicted[3]—and that he had little doubt at all as to the outcome of the case.

To me, this sort of thing—the attempt by the government to convict innocent men of crimes as a part of the routine of carrying on a war for justice—is infinitely horrible. When you consider that especially Eastman, Young and Reed (the others I do not know as well) are men of the finest social feeling, who, though endowed with unusual and highly marketable artistic and literary power, have chosen to live a hand-to-mouth existence, rather than compromise with their consciences and sell out the cause of democracy in which they have fought so loyally, it seems the more incredible that the government of the United States has taken this mistaken stand.

You may remember that when you were running for re-election, John Reed was on the staff of the Metropolitan Magazine drawing a big salary. He antagonized his employers, and took his future in his hands by campaigning for you. By his articles on Rockefeller absolutism at Bayonne[4] and other places, he lost power to sell his stuff to magazines and metropolitan papers; and last year, in spite of the fact that he is perhaps the most brilliant of all magazine reportorial correspondents, he became a hack reporter, covering prize-fights, etc. for an evening paper, until he worked himself up again through sheer talent and determination.

Max Eastman, though a Socialist Party member, editing a socialist magazine, was almost thrown out of his party because, during the campaign, he pointed out the reasons why socialists should vote for you.

You know Young's work yourself. Lately he resigned from the Metropolitan Magazine, partly on account of his indictment, and partly because he would not preach the kind of camouflage parlor socialism that Whigham and Hovey[5] demanded. No one can know Art Young without feeling the unselfishness and nobility of his character.

These are the men whom the government is following up as if they were the most hardened criminals. They are being put on trial again on an indictment unsustained by evidence, and with, as the mainstay of conviction, the atmosphere of fear and hysteria which envelopes every jury that in war time is called upon to deal with those accused of disloyalty. And yet, in spite of such an atmosphere, the last jury disagreed. At least three men told the judge that they would sit in the jury room forever, if necessary, rather than vote to convict without evidence.

I believe Mr. President that, in view of the circumstances of this case, the prosecution should be dropped. Not to drop it is unjust not only to the defendants, but to the integrity of the government. It could be called off without publicity by a series of postponements, ending at length in a dismissal.

Very sincerely yours,   Amos Pinchot.

TLS (WP, DLC).
[1] The first trial of Max Eastman, Arthur Young, and two other persons associated with *The Masses* on charges of violating the Espionage Act, held in the federal district court in New York from April 15 to 27, 1918, had ended in a hung jury, reportedly with ten in favor of conviction and two opposed. Assistant United States District Attorney Earl B. Barnes had immediately announced that the defendants would be retried. John

Reed, also indicted, was not present for the trial but returned to the United States on April 28 to face the charges. The indictment of one other defendant was dropped, and the whereabouts of another defendant were unknown to federal officials. *New York Times*, April 15-30, 1918.

² Thomas D. McCarthy, United States marshal for the Southern District of New York.

³ In the two fiscal years ending June 30, 1918, 2,089 persons were brought to trial under the Espionage and Sedition Acts. Of the 1,804 cases terminated by the latter date, 973 resulted in convictions, while the remaining 831 were either discontinued, quashed, dismissed, or resulted in acquittals. Harry N. Scheiber, *The Wilson Administration and Civil Liberties, 1917-1921* (Ithaca, N. Y., 1960), p. 63.

⁴ "A City of Violence," *New York Tribune*, Oct. 29, 1916, and "Industrial Violence in Bayonne," *Metropolitan Magazine*, XLV (Jan. 1917), 12-13, 63 ff.

⁵ That is, Henry James Whigham. Carl Hovey was the managing editor of *Metropolitan Magazine*.

From William Gibbs McAdoo

Dear Governor,   [Washington] May 24/18

Dr. Garfield has just gone to Norfolk after agreeing with me on the enclosed statement.¹ I thought you might like to see it & have a chance to revise it before it goes out. He wants to give it to the press tonight. Could you send it to me at 1312, 16th St. so I may send it to Dr. Garfield's Secretary?   Affy Yours   WGM

If you have no suggestions to offer, let Hoover² telephone me & I will notify Dr. Garfield's Secretary.³

ALI (WP, DLC).

¹ Press release, May 24, 1918, T MS (WP, DLC). The release announced that Garfield had ordered an immediate reduction in the price of bituminous coal of ten cents per short ton. This represented an average reduction of "nearly five per cent" and was estimated to mean an annual saving to consumers of $60,000,000. The press release also announced that Wilson had directed the railroads to pay the government price for coal. The newly fixed price meant that the railroads would pay some $45,000,000 more per year for coal. Wilson had also decided that the railroads should henceforth furnish cars to all coal mines alike, without discrimination except as dictated by the prior requirements of the railroads for operating purposes and the needs of domestic consumers and of the war effort.

² That is, Irwin H. Hoover.

³ Wilson approved the press release, and an expanded version of it was printed in the *Official Bulletin*, II (May 25, 1918), 6.

From Franklin Potts Glass

My dear Friend: Washington, D. C., May 24, 1918.

As you may know, I have undertaken at Mr. Creel's request to form a committee of representative newspaper men¹ for the purpose of carrying out his desire for a thorough investigation of the work of the Committee on Public Information.

I have had this undertaking in hand over two weeks by letter and by wire, and a large majority of those I have approached on the subject declined to act. I have not been able to get a committee of the men I desire, whose record and prominence would give authority to a report.

There is a general indisposition to investigate Mr. Creel. The enclosed letters from Mr. Charles H. Taylor, Jr., of the Boston Globe and Mr. Frank Cobb of the New York World are types.[2] These are for your personal information.

I have this day made a suggestion to Mr. Creel and with his approval I am submitting it to you.

It is that you should write me as President of the American Newspaper Publishers Association such a letter as you may think wise, asking the appointment of a committee of say seven or ten men who shall undertake a *general consideration of the entire publicity question*, to the end that a more effective use of means of co-operation between the Government and the people be brought about. This letter should make no specific mention of Mr. Creel. When the committee should come to work, it would unavoidably discover the many good things he is doing and would help him supplement them in every expedient way.

I would enclose a copy of your letter to me with my notice of appointment to each man, and this would be tantamount to a summons by you to a patriotic service, and no newspaper man would fail to respond.

Upon gathering, this committee could first visit you, if you chose, and get from you a broad inspiration as to its opportunities for investigation and service. Its members would be experts in publicity and in the psychology of reaching public opinion in strategic ways. They could clarify the present confusion, and would suggest means of coordination between all sources of news and the agencies for its diffusion.

In my judgment this program will be a sure and prompt means to the important end desired by all of us.

I plan to remain here for some days in connection with this and other matters, and will be pleased to discuss any further details that may occur to you, in person, if you so desire, and to cooperate in any expedient program you may suggest.

Sincerely yours,   Frank P. Glass

TLS (WP, DLC).
[1] Through the American Newspaper Publishers' Association, of which Glass was president. Glass was vice-president and editor of the *Birmingham News*.
[2] Charles Henry Taylor, Jr., to F. P. Glass, May 13, 1918, and F. I. Cobb to F. P. Glass, May 13, 1918, both TLS (WP, DLC).

From William Bauchop Wilson

My dear Mr. President: Washington May 24, 1918.

I would like to talk with you at your convenience about the policies to be pursued in the Housing Administration. Now that the Committee on Appropriations is about to report a bill to carry into effect the authorizations contained in the measure approved by you on May 16th,[1] there are certain alternative policies that should be finally determined.

First: Is it your desire that the Department of Labor shall continue to handle the housing program?

Second: Should the buildings erected be of a temporary or permanent character?

Third: Should the Government build, own, control and rent the houses until after the war, writing off from the houses of a permanent character the additional cost due to war conditions before disposing of them to private owners?

Fourth: Should we supplement local capital by loans up to seventy or eighty per cent of the cost under contracts that would provide for proper security, interest, amortization, control of types of houses, sanitation, rentals, etc.?

Fifth: If loans are advanced as suggested in paragraph four, should it be through the Housing Administration direct, or through a general corporation, or through the establishment of a local corporation created for the purpose, in which the local capital and the Housing Administration should have representation on the directorate?

Sixth: What should be the annual rate and the length of time of amortization, and should the minimum rate of interest (five per cent) provided in the law be the rate required?

Seventh: Should arrangements be made to sell houses to workmen during the period of the war, or should we refuse to sell until normal conditions had determined proper valuations? It is suggested that houses might be sold to workmen with an agreement that the excess war cost of building be written off at some date after the war.

Eighth: Should policies in these matters be general or should they be variable as local conditions may make advisable?

Ninth: Should the housing to be erected in the District of Columbia be permanent or temporary?

Tenth: Should the Housing Administration operate them as dormitories with dining rooms attached?

Eleventh: We have an offer from the Young Men's Christian Association of this city to erect a ten-story building on G Street adjacent to their present building which would accommodate not less than 950 men, with a total investment of $860,000.00, on conditions that we loan eighty per cent of the cost to be amortized in fifteen annual payments on principal and interest, this to be a permanent building. The cost is somewhat higher per individual to be housed than the estimates made for temporary housing. It however assures the ultimate payment to the Government of every cent invested. Should propositions of this kind be accepted?

While there is of course a mass of detail, these items of policy cover the principle points that should be immediately determined. May I ask an early interview on the subject?

Faithfully yours,   W B Wilson

TLS (WP, DLC).
[1] This Act empowered the President to acquire and dispose of existing housing and land and to erect housing for governmental employees in the District of Columbia and for workers engaged in vital war industries in other areas. He was authorized to spend up to $60,000,000 for these purposes, $10,000,000 of this amount being reserved for housing in the District of Columbia. 40 *Statutes at Large* 550.

To Albert, King of the Belgians

The White House May 25, 1918.

Your Majesty's generous message[1] has been read with deep pleasure and appreciation and I beg to assure you that nothing that the American Red Cross or the body of my fellow citizens have done has been done more truly from the heart than the aid, all too little, which they have been able to render the gallant and suffering people of Belgium. We feel our common dependence with them upon the full vindication of the cause of freedom.

Woodrow Wilson.

T telegram (Letterpress Books, WP, DLC).
[1] Albert to WW, c. May 20, 1918, CC MS (WP, DLC).

From Newton Diehl Baker

Dear Mr. President: Washington. May 25, 1918.

I have received your letter of the 22d with regard to a deferred classification for railroad employes.

In a letter addressed to me on May 13, the Director General of Railroads requested general instructions to draft boards directing them to observe more uniformly the existing regulations whereby skilled railroad operatives are put in a deferred class. An investigation of the actual situation discloses that very few skilled men, if any, are being included by the draft boards. I enclose a copy of my reply to the Director General's letter, which I think fairly states the case.[1]

I hope it will not seem even for a moment that I have any pride of opinion or obstinacy in the matter; I not only want to do what you want done, but whatever is necessary to help the Director General.   Respectfully yours,   Newton D. Baker

TLS (WP, DLC).
    [1] NDB to WGM, May 16, 1918, TCL (WP, DLC). Baker wrote that most skilled railroad employees were already exempt from the draft under existing regulations. He pointed out, however, that some skilled persons would have to be called to military service to run railroads in Europe. However, Baker devoted most of his letter to a discussion of his basic problem of creating a large army in the face of demands of representatives of many industries, such as agriculture, mining, and the production of steel and munitions, that their workers be exempted from the draft because of their indispensability to the war effort. Baker argued that the only solution to the problem lay in creating rules which would exempt all who were truly indispensable but would, so far as possible, spread the inconvenience caused by the drafting of less skilled individuals evenly to all industries.

From Edward Mandell House, with Enclosure

Dear Governor: New York. May 25, 1918.

Sir William Wiseman arrived today. He has a story of absorbing interest which you ought to hear. He will be in Washington tomorrow and until Tuesday afternoon.

You can reach him either at the Embassy or through Gordon. It would be better, I think, to do it through Gordon as no one at the Embassy ever knows that he sees you.

Sir William has opportunities for getting the entire picture, and this is what no one else has. I have asked him to talk as frankly to you as he has to me which he will do if you indicate your desire that he should.

I could not get away today but I am leaving early tomorrow. Gordon can always reach me, as I keep him informed of my movements.   Affectionately yours,   E. M. House

P.S. Edwards[1] wrote me the enclosed letter and learning from Martin[2] that Lowell was in town, I asked Martin to let him read the letter. The penciled comments are Lowell's. I merely send it to indicate what you already know, and that is, how very few can be trusted.

TLS (WP, DLC).
    [1] Charles Jerome Edwards, manager of the Equitable Life Assurance Society of the United States, 120 Broadway, New York.
    [2] Probably Edward S. Martin.

ENCLOSURE

Charles Jerome Edwards to Edward Mandell House

My dear Colonel House: Brooklyn, May 21, 1918.

It may be indecent for me to repeat this, as it is to a certain extent a breach of trust to pass it on to you; but I believe it is my reasonable duty, as a friend of The President, to see that he gets it.

It is in effect, that President Lowell makes the statement that he was told directly by the President that if Germany would make satisfactory terms about Belgium and Alsace Lor[r]aine, he (the President) was inclined to give Germany a free hand in the East.   *This is not true[1]*

President Lowell, in being questioned as to the authenticity of the statement, and asked to deny it, by some of his friends, stated, "I am sorry I cannot deny it because it is substantially true"; and further that the President had said to him that he did not agree with Lloyd George in thinking we could beat Germany on the Western Front. Also, that after this drive was over, the President ⟨felt sure⟩ thought[2] that peace terms would be put forward by Germany and that he would give them serious consideration.   *This is true and it disturbed me very much A.L.L.*

I hesitate to mention any further names in connection with this, but I understand that President Lowell was so "disturbed" by what the President had said, that he at once took the matter up with Roosevelt.

I am sending this to you for your consideration and entirely apart from any desire to know if it is so or not; or to secure any satisfaction to myself. It seems to me important that the President should "know" where, or how some stories get afloat, and how somewhat confidential information gets out.

With cordial regards as always.

                    Very truly yours,   Chas Jerome Edwards

TLS (WP, DLC).
    [1] Marginal comments by A. Lawrence Lowell. About Lowell's most recent interview with Wilson, see the memorandum by William Howard Taft printed at March 29, 1918, Vol. 47.
    [2] Lowell's deletion and substitution.

From Furnifold McLendel Simmons

My dear Mr. President: [Washington] May 25, 1918.

I regret very much that on account of the sudden change of front on the part of our Republican friends in the Senate I am unable to give you the assurances which you suggested in our interview of last night and which were embraced in the memorandum you gave me.[1]

I earnestly hope that this failure may not entirely foreclose the question of the postponement of the revenue legislation. I cannot escape the conviction that it would be unfortunate to undertake to finally deal with this question at this session under conditions which will inevitably confront us in our efforts to frame a wise and just revenue law.

I have talked with Mr. Kitchin and Senator Martin this afternoon and they both concur with me in the hope and view expressed above.   Very truly yours,   F M Simmons

TLS (WP, DLC).
    [1] It is missing both in WP, DLC, and the F. M. Simmons Papers, NcD, but see the extract from the Daniels Diary printed at May 27, 1918.

From Prince Arthur of Connaught

My dear Mr. President,   Washington, D. C. May 25. 1918.

Before leaving Washington I beg to express to you the real pleasure which I have felt at being privileged to visit the capital of the United States, at a time when our two countries are so closely bound together in the common cause.

May I thank you most sincerely for the cordial hospitality extended to me in this country. My only regret is that my visit on this occasion is through force of circumstances but a short one. I venture however to hope that at some future time my duties may permit me to make a more intimate acquaintance with this great country. Meanwhile I carry away with me the most pleasant impressions of my short stay in Washington.

In conclusion,   I remain Yours Very Sincerely Arthur.

ALS (WP, DLC).

A Memorandum

Washington, D. C., May 25, 1918.

MEMORANDA CONCERNING THE NEGRO AND THE PRESENT
POLITICAL SITUATION IN THE U. S.
SUBMITTED FOR THE CONSIDERATION OF THE PRESIDENT
AT THE SUGGESTION OF SECRETARY TUMULTY
by J. Milton Waldron and John MacMurray[1]

THE IMPORTANCE OF THE CONGRESSIONAL ELECTION THIS FALL.

The Congressional election this Fall will be exceedingly important, for President Wilson must have a working majority in both
the House and the Senate who will carry out his wishes or he will
find it next to impossible to carry on the war against Germany and
her allies as he thinks it must be carried on to win.

President Wilson and his party are, we believe, neglecting a fertile
field, and a field, if carefully cultivated, that will yield sufficient
votes this Fall to enable the Administration to remain in control of
Congress even though some other factors in the coming election
fail to stand heartily by the President. That neglected field is the
Negro (or colored) vote in the North and West.

THE PRESENT STRENGTH OF THE COLORED VOTE IN THE NORTH AND WEST.

In 1915 there were in the North and West between three hundred
and five hundred thousand Negro citizens of voting age. During
the past three or four years this number has increased to about
600,000 voters; (a) by the enfranchisement in New York and in
several Western states of the women (b) by the young men who
have reached their majority during this period, (c) and by the large
number of Negro citizens who have gone from the South, South-
west and the border states into the North and West recently and
who have been in their new home sufficiently long to entitle them
to vote in the Fall election this year.

THE NEGRO VOTERS IN NORTH AND WEST NOT WEDDED TO ANY ONE PARTY AS A CLASS.

(a) The colored voters who had lived in the North and West for
any considerable time prior to 1912 have frequently shown in many
places a disposition to break away from old party alliances and vote
as Independents, or remain away from the polls rather than vote
for Republican candidates whom they regarded as inimical to their

---

[1] The Rev. John MacMurray, pastor of the Union Methodist Episcopal Church in
Washington.

own interests and those of their Race. (b) The young Negro men in the North and West who have reached their majority within the past four or six years and the Negro women who have been recently enfranchised and the young Negroes from the South who have moved into the North and West have no special love for the Republican party and are not attached to that party as their fathers were. (c) The present Negro vote in the North and West is intelligent and has already seen the necessity of using the ballot for its protection. (d) The Negro citizens in the North and West are better organized to-day than ever before, and this work of organization is being rapidly and effectively carried forward by leaders of the Race and by numerous white friends of the Negro, and he is awaking as never before to the power there is in organized numbers. (e) While the Negroes in the North and West are not controlled by any one leader they are all dominated by the one idea, viz. the necessity of using their ballot to secure for themselves and their Race everywhere in this Country the protection, rights and privileges guaranteed them by the Constitution. (f) In one or more Congressional districts in each one of ten Northern and Western states the Negro vote is sufficiently large to become the determining factor in the election this Fall.

THE NEGRO CITIZENS DISSATISFIED WITH THE ADMINISTRATION.

The Negro citizens everywhere in America are much dissatisfied at the treatment the Race has received at the hands of the present Administration and unless something substantial is done between now and November next to remove this dissatisfaction many Democratic Congressmen and several Senators in the North and West will fail to secure the necessary number of colored votes which they must have to win the election.

THE NEGRO VOTE CAN BE PLACATED.

The Administration can, if it wills and thinks it worth while to do it, placate the Negro vote in the North and West by removing the following grievances of which colored citizens everywhere are now complaining:

I. THE NEGRO SOLDIERS NOT RECEIVING A SQUARE DEAL.

President Wilson, out of a sense of fairness and justice and as Commander-in-Chief of the United States Army and Navy, assured the Negro citizens of the Country through Secretary of War Baker (and through other sources) that at least one Fighting Division of the Army to be sent to the front in France would be made up entirely of Negro soldiers and officered as far as possible by colored Lieutenants and Captains, and that the said Negro Division would be equipped both as to men and material and the various branches of the army exactly like the fighting divisions composed of white soldiers, and that the Negro Division would be allowed to fight as a unit whenever it is possible to do so. The Negroes of the Country believe President Wilson meant what he said, and they are deeply grieved that the President's intentions are not being carried out and that the Negro soldiers are not receiving a square deal.

While the Negro Division[2] has been formed it has not been "assembled," and it has not been properly equipped with the necessary branches of the Service, and it seems that everything possible is being done to make the Negro Fighting Division a failure. (a) The Commanding General of the Division[3] is, seemingly, not convinced that President Wilson really intends to have in the trenches in France a Negro Fighting Division, and he lacks the "punch," tact, and enthusiasm in his work, and the confidence and esteem of his officers and men so necessary to make any fighting organization a success. (b) The personnel of the artillery regiments in the Negro Division has been manipulated so as to insure the failure of these organizations and thus have it said (with some show of truthfulness) that Negroes are incapable of becoming artillery fighters; (1) instead of placing into the Negro artillery regiments the volunteers and draftees who are graduates from high schools, colleges, and technical institutions, these men were put into the Stevedore regiments, and the men from the rice swamps of South Carolina, the cane-brakes of Florida, the bayous of Missi[ssi]ppi and Louis[i]ana, and the backwoods of Georgia and Texas—men without education and many of whom are unable to write their names—were put into the Negro artillery regiments. (2) The colored Lieutenants and Captains placed in those artillery regiments were without artillery training and those in command refused to detail sufficient artillery instructors to train these colored officers. (3) One or more white officers in these Negro artillery regiments have assiduously and constantly criticised and belittled colored commissioned officers in the presence of the privates and otherwise striven to destroy the respect and obedience due these officers by the enlisted men.[4]

With such conditions prevailing in the Negro artillery regiments

[2] It was the 92d Division, the only full-strength division of black draftees in the United States Army during the First World War. A second, incomplete, black division, the 93d, composed primarily of former National Guard units, was already in service in France.
[3] The commander of the 92d Division was Maj. Gen. Charles Clarendon Ballou, an officer of long experience, including combat duty in the Philippines and, more recently, the commander of the Officers' Training Camp for blacks in Des Moines, Ia.
[4] For a lengthy, critical evaluation of these and many other problems associated with the experience of the 92d Division, both at home and abroad, see Arthur E. Barbeau and Florette Henri, *The Unknown Soldiers: Black American Troops in World War I* (Philadelphia, 1974), pp. 81-88, 136-63.

it is not to be expected that anything but failure would result, and that most of the white commissioned officers in these regiments would become discouraged.

If President Wilson will let everybody in the Army, from the Chief of Staff down, know that his order forming a Negro Fighting Division, with all arms of the service that go with a Fighting Division, must be carried out to the letter and that the Division must be "assembled" in France without further delay it will be done and the Negro Fighting Division will uphold the best traditions of the United States Army and will sustain the well-earned reputation of the Negro American Soldier for loyalty, bravery and courage in the most trying positions and for the winning of victory in the most stubbornly contested battles.

The unjust, cruel and insolent treatment being accorded certain Negro companies, (and here and there whole regiments) in camps in Virginia, Georgia, and Texas, and in some Northern and Western cantonments, is destroying the morale of these soldiers and breeding a spirit of discontent and resentment that will result disastrously unless this evil treatment ceases at once. In many instances colored commissioned officers are placed on the inactive list when there seems to be no just cause for it, while others are railroaded out of the service altogether and denied the redress allowed commissioned officers under the rules of the Army. Some of the white officers in charge of colored soldiers are totally unfit in every way for their positions; they are not in sympathy with their men, they don't believe in Negro soldiers and deal with them as though they were slaves instead of soldiers in the United States Army.

A little investigation into these things by the President in his own way would, we believe, soon convince him of the truthfulness of these statements and lead him to see the necessity of seeing to it that the Negro officers and men in the Army receive a square deal.

II. INJUSTICES PRACTICED BY THE ADMINISTRATION AGAINST NEGRO GOVERNMENT EMPLOYEES.

Clerical positions and employment in the skilled occupations are denied, in most cases, to colored men and women even when they have passed the required Civil Service examinations. There seems to be everywhere in the Government departments an organized and determined effort to confine Negro citizens to menial work and to those positions that pay very small wages and require little or no skill.

Instances are frequent where colored young women and men living in places outside of Washington pass the Civil Service examinations for clerkships and skilled occupations and are appointed and ordered to report for service in this and other cities, and when they present themselves at the departments to take the positions and it is discovered that they are colored they are told that "some mistake has been made" and they are not allowed to take the positions to which they had been appointed.[5]

If the President will take a hand in this matter and put an end to this injustice, and let it be known that clerical and skilled positions in the Government as well as other occupations connected with the war are open here and elsewhere in the Country to colored men and women on exactly the same terms and conditions as to other citizens, he can secure at once a thousand or more loyal, competent, and enthusiastic colored clerks and skilled workers who will come to Washington and do their part in helping the Country to win the war. And what is more, their coming will not aggravate the Housing situation here, for these clerks and skilled workers will be able to find good homes readily and at reasonable rates in respectable colored families in this city.

III. DISCRIMINATION AGAINST NEGRO CITIZENS AND WAR WORKERS IN THE EXECUTION OF THE EMERGENCY HOUSING PROVISION.

The $60,000,000 Emergency Housing Bill recently enacted into law places the expenditure of this money and the execution of the law in the hands of the President, and contains this provision: "Provided further, That the expenditure in the District of Columbia shall be made with a view to caring for the alley population of the District when the war is over, so far as it can be done without interfering with war housing purposes." This bill is designed to provide housing for war workers—and also for "employees of the United States whose duties require them to reside in the District of Columbia and whose services are essential to war needs, and their families," this bill, no doubt, applies to Negro war-workers and their families as well as white-war workers and their families who have been called, or shall be called, to Washington and who are in need of housing. But it seems that those who are in immediate charge of the execution of this law are deliberately planning to ignore both of the provisions referred to above.

If the President will give his subordinates in charge of the execution of this bill to understand that all the provisions of the Emergency Housing Bill must be carried out, the despicable alley conditions in Washington which are a standing menace to the health and morals of Washington will be partially removed and two thou-

---

[5] This charge, though obviously difficult to verify, was often made at this time. See Charles Flint Kellogg, *NAACP: A History of the National Association for the Advancement of Colored People, Vol. I, 1909-1920* (Baltimore, 1967), p. 181.

sand or more Negro war-workers will be provided with homes and kept out of the alleys.

IV. JIM CROW-CAR LAWS ARE BEING SANCTIONED AND ENFORCED BY THE NATIONAL GOVERNMENT.

The National Government has taken over, as a war measure, the railroads of the entire Country, and the Administration is responsible for the management and operation of the same and is putting into the up-keep and equipment of these railways hundreds of millions of money collected from *all* the people and justice demands that the National Government shall not engage in the despicable and unjust business of discriminating against its citizens on account of race or color when they travel on Government operated and supported railroads. The Administration should give railroad officials everywhere to understand that they will not be allowed to outrage and humiliate Negro Army officers by forcing them out of sleeping cars and imprisoning them as was done recently in Oklahoma,[6] and that no soldier of the United States Army shall be forced to ride in a "Jim crow car." Now that the Administration has the authority and power to abolish the iniquitous "Jim Crow car" system, it will bring down upon its head the condemnation of all justice loving and fair-minded men and nations if it allows the railroads it controls and supports to continue to discriminate against and rob loyal and patroitic [patriotic] citizens who travel over these roads because they are black, brown, or yellow.

V. LYNCHINGS AND BURNINGS OF NEGRO CITIZENS.

And finally, the 12,000,000 Negro citizens of America and the many millions of white citizens who believe in law, order, and justice for all feel that the lawlessness, lynching and burning of human beings so prevalent in the United States is the strongest ally the Germans can have in helping them to defeat our Country; the Kaiser and his allies are exploiting the lynchings and burnings of Negroes in this Country before the darker races of the world in order to make them fear and distrust America. And the blood of ten thousand colored people lynched and burned in this Country during the last forty-five years is crying out to God against this nation, and unless it is stopped and confessed it will stand between America and victory in the war with Germany. As a war measure, if on no other ground, the Administration has power to suppress

---

[6] The Editors have found no information on this specific incident. However, Barbeau and Henri, p. 63, note that the twenty-four black artillery officer candidates who trained at Fort Sill, Oklahoma, "had a rough time," and that the four black men admitted to the Fort Sill aviation school were "treated with extreme discourtesy." While these comments refer primarily to their treatment on the base, they may also refer to events off base.

everywhere in this Country with an iron hand lawlessness, murder, lynchings, and the burnings of human beings.

If the Administration will set to work at once and in earnest to afford the Negro citizens relief among all of the above mentioned five lines it will win the hearty support of the Negro vote in the North and West and the votes of the white friends of the Race throughout the Country, and in this way will make sure of a working majority in the Senate and House this Fall, and insure victory in the war of Democracy against Autocracy and German Militarism.

TS MS (WP, DLC).

From Morris Sheppard

My dear Mr. President: [Washington] May 26, 1918.

Some weeks ago I submitted to you a draft of a war time prohibition measure which I had thought of introducing. You replied that you did not think it opportune for such a measure to be enacted at this session, largely because you thought it would disturb the labor situation as related to the war.[1] Yielding to your judgment I did not introduce the bill.

You have doubtless noted the action of the House in adding the Randall amendment to the bill further encouraging agriculture.[2] The Randall amendment is a limitation on the appropriations carried in the bill. It will doubtless be supplanted in the Senate by an amendment prohibiting the making of food stuffs into intoxicating liquors during the war, and in this form the issue will in all probability be presented to the Senate.

I shall be very glad to be advised if your views have undergone any change on this subject, and to know what your judgment now is as to the advisability of its enactment. It is needless to say that I shall be glad to continue to cooperate with you in every way in bringing about what you believe to be essential to the proper conduct of the war.

Please give me such a reply as I can show to both prohibition and anti-prohibition Senators in the endeavor to reach the solution you may consider desirable.

                    Yours very sincerely,   Morris Sheppard

TLS (WP, DLC).
[1] M. Sheppard to WW, March 20, 1918, and WW to M. Sheppard, March 22, 1918, both in Vol. 47.
[2] Charles Hiram Randall of California, reelected in 1916 as the candidate of the Prohibition, Democratic, Republican, and Progressive parties, had, on May 21, introduced an amendment to H.R. 11945, an agricultural appropriation bill, which had the effect of withholding from use a part of the appropriation, amounting to $6,100,000,

until President Wilson should have issued a proclamation prohibiting the use of food-stuffs in the production of wine and beer for the duration of the war, as he had been authorized to do by the Food Control Act of August 10, 1917. The House adopted the amendment that same day. *Cong. Record*, 65th Cong., 2d sess., pp. 6868-72; *New York Times*, May 22, 1918.

An Address to a Joint Session of Congress[1]

Copy used in delivery 27 May 1918[2]

Gentlemen of the Congress: It is with unaffected reluctance that I come to ask you to prolong your session long enough to provide more adequate resources for the Treasury for the conduct of the war. I have reason to appreciate as fully as you do how arduous the session has been. Your labours have been severe and protracted. You have passed a long series of measures which required the debate of many doubtful questions of judgment and many exceedingly difficult questions of principle as well as of practice. The summer is upon us in which labour and counsel are twice arduous and are constantly apt to be impaired by lassitude and fatigue. The elections are at hand and we ought as soon as possible to go and render an intimate account of our trusteeship to the people who delegated us to act for them in the weighty and anxious matters that crowd upon us in these days of critical choice and action. But we dare not go to the elections until we have done our duty to the full. These are days when duty stands stark and naked and even with closed eyes we know it is there. Excuses are unavailing. We have either done our duty or we have not. The fact will be as gross and plain as the duty itself. In such a case lassitude and fatigue seem negligible enough. The facts are tonic and suffice to freshen the labour.

And the facts are these: Additional revenues must manifestly be provided for. It would be a most unsound policy to raise too large a proportion of them by loan, and it is evident that the four billions now provided for by taxation will not of themselves sustain the greatly enlarged budget to which we must immediately look forward. We cannot in fairness wait until the end of the fiscal year is at hand to apprise our people of the taxes they must pay on their earnings of the present calendar year, whose accountings and expenditures will then be closed. We cannot get increased taxes unless the country knows what they are to be and practices the necessary economy to make them available. Definiteness, early definiteness, as to what its tasks are to be is absolutely necessary

[1] Wilson spoke in the House chamber at 1 p.m. For details of the event, see the *New York Times*, May 28, 1918.
[2] WWhw.

for the successful administration of the Treasury: it cannot frame fair and workable regulations in haste: and it must frame its regulations in haste if it is not to know its exact task until the very eve of its performance. The present tax laws are marred, moreover, by the inequities which ought to be remedied. Indisputable facts, every one; and we cannot alter or blink them. To state them is argument enough.

And yet perhaps you will permit me to dwell for a moment upon the situation they disclose. Enormous loans freely spent in the stimulation of industry of almost every sort produce inflations and extravagances which presently make the whole economic structure questionable and insecure and the very basis of credit is cut away. Only fair, equitably distributed taxation, of the widest incidence and drawing chiefly from the sources which would be likely to demoralize credit by their very abundance, can prevent inflation and keep our industrial system free of speculation and waste. We shall naturally turn, therefore, I suppose, to war profits and incomes and luxuries for the additional taxes. But the war profits and incomes upon which the increased taxes will be levied will be the profits and incomes of the calendar year 1918. It would be manifestly unfair to wait until the early months of 1919 to say what they are to be. It might be difficult, I should imagine, to run the mill with water that had already gone over the wheel.

Moreover, taxes of that sort will not be paid until the June of next year, and the Treasury must anticipate them. It must use the money they are to produce before it is due. It must sell short time certificates of indebtedness. In the autumn a much larger sale of long time bonds must be effected than has yet been attempted. What are the bankers to think of the certificates if they do not certainly know where the money is to come from which is to take them up? And how are investors to approach the purchase of bonds with any sort of confidence or knowledge of their own affairs if they do not know what taxes they are to pay and what economies and adjustments of their business they must effect? I cannot assure the country of a successful administration of the Treasury in 1918 if the question of further taxation is to be left undecided until 1919.

The consideration that dominates every other now, and makes every other seem trivial and negligible, is the winning of the war. We are not only in the midst of the war, we are at the very peak and crisis of it. Hundreds of thousands of our men, carrying our hearts with them and our fortunes, are in the field, and ships are crowding faster and faster to the ports of France and England with regiment after regiment, thousand after thousand, to join them until the enemy shall be beaten and brought to a reckoning with

mankind. There can be no pause or intermission. The great enterprise must, on the contrary, be pushed with greater and greater
energy. The volume of our might must steadily and rapidly be
augmented until there can be no question of resisting it. If that is
to be accomplished, gentlemen, money must sustain it to the utmost. Our financial programme must no more be left in doubt or
suffered to lag than our ordnance programme or our ship programme or our munitions programme or our programme for making
millions of men ready. These others are not programmes, indeed,
but mere plans upon paper, unless there is to be an unquestionable
supply of money.

That is the situation, and it is the situation which creates the
duty, no choice or preference of ours. There is only one way to
meet that duty. We must meet it without selfishness or fear of
consequences. Politics is adjourned. The elections will go to those
who think least of it; to those who go to the constituencies without
explanations or excuses, with a plain record of duty faithfully and
disinterestedly performed. I, for one, am always confident that the
people of this country will give a just verdict upon the service of
the men who act for them when the facts are such that no man
can disguise or conceal them. There is no danger of deceit now.
An intense and pitiless light beats upon every man and every action
in this tragic plot of war that is now upon the stage. If lobbyists
hurry to Washington to attempt to turn what you do in the matter
of taxation to their protection or advantage, the light will beat also
upon them. There is abundant fuel for the light in the records of
the Treasury with regard to profits of every sort. The profiteering
that cannot be got at by the restraints of conscience and love of
country can be got at by taxation. There is much profiteering now
and the information with regard to it is available and indisputable.

I am advising you to act upon this matter of taxation now, gentlemen, not because I do not know that you can see and interpret the
facts and the duty they impose just as well and with as clear a
perception of the obligations involved as I can, but because there
is a certain solemn satisfaction in sharing with you the responsibilities of such a time. The world never stood in such case before.
Men never before had so clear or so moving a vision of duty. I know
that you will begrudge the work to be done here by us no more
than the men begrudge us theirs who lie in the trenches and sally
forth to their death. There is a stimulating comradeship knitting
us all together. And this task to which I invite your immediate
consideration will be performed under favourable influences if we
will look to what the country is thinking and expecting and care
nothing at all for what is being said and believed in the lobbies of

Washington hotels, where the atmosphere seems to make it possible to believe what is believed nowhere else.

Have you not felt the spirit of the nation rise and its thought become a single and common thought since these eventful days came in which we have been sending our boys to the other side? I think you must read that thought, as I do, to mean this, that the people of this country are not only united in the resolute purpose to win this war but are ready and willing to bear any burden and undergo any sacrifice that it may be necessary for them to bear in order to win it. We need not be afraid to tax them, if we lay taxes justly. They know that the war must be paid for and that it is they who must pay for it, and if the burden is justly distributed and the sacrifice made a common sacrifice from which none escapes who can bear it at all, they will carry it cheerfully and with a sort of solemn pride. I have always been proud to be an American, and was never more proud than now, when all that we have said and all that we have foreseen about our people is coming true. The great days have come when the only thing that they ask for or admire is duty greatly and adequately done; when their only wish for America is that she may share the freedom she enjoys; when a great, compelling sympathy wells up in their hearts for men everywhere who suffer and are oppressed; and when they see at the last high uses for which their wealth had been piled up and their mighty power accumulated and, counting neither blood nor treasure now that their final day of opportunity has come, rejoice to spend and to be spent through a long night of suffering and terror in order that they and men everywhere may see the dawn of a day of righteousness and justice and peace. Shall we grow weary when they bid us act?

May I add this word, gentlemen? Just as I was leaving the White House I was told that the expected drive on the western front had apparently begun. You can realize how that solemnized my feeling as I came to you, and how it seemed to strengthen the purpose which I have tried to express in these lines.

I have admired the work of this session. The way in which the two Houses of the Congress have cooperated with the Executive has been generous and admirable, and it is not in any spirit of suggesting duty neglected, but only to remind you of the common cause and the common obligation that I have ventured to come to you to-day.[3]

Printed reading copy (WP, DLC), last two paragraphs from the text in *Cong. Record*, 65th Cong., 2d sess., p. 7115.

[3] There is a WWsh outline and a WWT draft (the one which Wilson sent to the Public Printer), with one emendation by Tumulty, in WP, DLC.

To Joseph Patrick Tumulty, with Enclosures

Dear Tumulty: The White House [c. May 27, 1918].
    I think this ought to be reserved until it is necessary to give some reason why I cannot approve of the action of the House the other day in this matter. Mr. Hoover is entirely right about it, but probably it isn't necessary to fire this off just now.   The President.

TL (WP, DLC).

E N C L O S U R E   I

Herbert Clark Hoover to Joseph Patrick Tumulty

My dear Tumulty: Washington 27 *May 1918*
    With regard to the action of the House in stipulating for closing down the breweries, it seems to me that the time has arrived when some sort of statement on the subject might well be made from the White House.
    I have drafted a short memorandum on the reasons for the action hitherto taken by the Administration in this matter and I am wondering if you would see if the President thinks it desirable to make such a statement; if so, whether you would issue it from the White House with all the authority of that quarter behind it?
                        Yours faithfully,   Herbert Hoover

TLS (WP, DLC).

E N C L O S U R E   I I

MEMO

27 May, 1918.
    As to the provision attached to the Food Production Bill in the House, stipulating that the appropriations shall only be available if the use of grain in brewing in the country shall be stopped under the provisions of the Food Bill.—The reasons why the Administration has not exercised the discretionary powers in the Food Bill to close the breweries are very simple.
    All distillation of whiskey, brandy and other distilled spirits was stopped under the Food Bill in September, 1917, but there are stocks of these liquors in the country sufficient to last for a very long period. The brewers' products, on the other hand, are not durable and if brewing were stopped, there can be no stocks of consequence and brewed drinks would practically cease to exist at

once. The effect would be to place the country entirely on a whiskey basis. The Food Act does not provide for closing the saloons and if brewing were stopped they would remain open and be compelled to sell whisky and heavy alcohol drinks only. The Food Administration has, under the direction of the President, reduced the alcohol content of beer to a maximum of 2¾% and the amount of grain used in brewing by 30% and the closing of the breweries has not been considered to be a real temperance measure under these circumstances for it has been felt that the moral effect of throwing the drinking class in the country entirely on a whiskey basis would be intensely demoralizing and would constitute a constructive monopoly of the most deleterious of all the drinks.

If Congress wishes that the country should go dry it will require an entirely new act prohibiting the sale. The course proposed in the House would have a conservation value in saving the use of grain by the breweries and no one is so sympathetic with the saving of all grain as the government, but the moral issues involved of stimulating the worst form of drinking, have deterred any such action hitherto. ⟨The Administration is in no way opposed to any constructive prohibition measures.⟩[1]

T MS (WP, DLC).
[1] Excision probably by Tumulty.

To Furnifold McLendel Simmons

My dear Senator,   The White House. 27 May, 1918

Because of some oversight at the Executive Office and the fact that Sunday generally draws my attention away to other things, I did not see your letter of Saturday until a few minutes ago. I beg your pardon for the delay in replying.

In the absence of definite assurances such as I suggested, my dear Senator, I dare not agree to postpone financial legislation. The problems with which the Treasury is confronted are too big and too pressing and too difficult at best to make delay in such circumstances anything but extra hazardous, and I dare not take the responsibility of risking a breakdown in the very foundations of every part of our programme. I hope that you do not need to be assured that I would not differ from your judgment willingly or without what seem to me compelling reason[s].

With warmest regard,
Faithfully Yours,   Woodrow Wilson

WWTLS (F. M. Simmons Papers, NcD).

Two Letters from William Gibbs McAdoo

Dear Mr. President: Washington May 27, 1918.

In our discussion a few days ago about the coal question, I promised to inform you as to whether or not there is any available fund which you could use as a revolving fund or as working capital, if you should determine to take over the output of the mines and sell them for Government account, as you are authorized to do by the Act of August 10, 1917. The Act in question provides for a revolving fund of $150,000,000 which is placed at your disposal for this and other purposes. I find that $50,000,000 has been turned over to the Food Administration and that there is available $100,000,000 for the coal operation if you should decide to enter upon it. This, I believe, would be more than sufficient for your purposes. You can also, to the extent that you may desire to do so, make use of your War Emergency Fund, or such part of it as you may be able to spare.   Cordially yours,   W G McAdoo

Dear "Governor":   Washington May 27, 1918.

Dr. Healy[1] and Admiral Grayson both tell me that it is imperative that I should rest my voice absolutely for a week. The important conferences and discussions in which I was forced to engage last week have brought about a recurrence of the trouble with my throat, so I fear that I shall have to surrender to the doctors' advice. I purpose leaving tonight. If I do not go, they tell me I may lose my voice completely for a month or more.

Meanwhile, the Treasury Department is so organized on the revenue question that the preliminary work before the Ways and Means Committee can proceed in my absence without delay, if you should decide that a revenue measure should be passed at this session.

I am deeply distressed to have to be absent, but I suppose it is the short cut to my return to active duty.

Affectionately yours,   W G McAdoo

TLS (WP, DLC).
    [1] Charles B. Healy, M.D., whose office was at 1726 M Street, N.W., Washington.

From Furnifold McLendel Simmons

To the President: [Washington] May 27, 1918.

Some of our friends in the Senate and of the newspaper fraternity think that it is advi[s]able to print the memorandum which you prepared and handed to me at our conference last Friday night.[1]

I am advised that various misrepresentations are being made as to the contents of this memorandum and that it is being alleged that your message of today is inconsistent with the memorandum.

I think it would be well to have these misrepresentations corrected before they gain general currency and I am sure that the publication of the memorandum will show that your message is entirely consistent with it.

While the memorandum was shown freely to members of the Committee it has not, so far as I am concerned, been made public and I do not feel free to do so without your consent. Please advise me whether I am authorized to furnish a copy of it to the press.[2] That you may have the document before you, I am sending you herewith the original.   Very truly yours,   F M Simmons

TLS (WP, DLC).
  [1] Simmons and other congressional leaders had met with Wilson on May 23 (see WW to H. T. Rainey, May 23, 1918, n. 2), and Simmons also came to the White House on the evening of May 24. The memorandum which Wilson prepared and gave to him at that time is missing.
  [2] "Dear Governor: I would like to talk to you on the telephone about this matter before you act on it. J.P.T." JPT to WW, May 27, 1918, TL (WP, DLC).

From Herbert Clark Hoover

Dear Mr. President: Washington 27 *May 1918*

I have now consulted the members of the committee on the packing industry and they are in entire accord with your suggestion as to the elimination of the War Industries' Price Fixing Board from the machinery proposed and I am sending you the report as amended.

I am extremely anxious that it should be issued to the public at the earliest moment as some indications as to its content have leaked out and it is a matter of great interest to a considerable portion of the public. If it now meets with your approval, in its present form, would you be so kind as to instruct that it should be issued to the Press?   Yours faithfully,   Herbert Hoover

TLS (WP, DLC).

From Anna Howard Shaw, with Enclosure

                                              Washington
My dear Mr. President and Mrs. Wilson: May 27/1918

The enclosed resolution, unanimously adopted at the recent conference of the Woman's Committee of the Council of National Defense, speaks for itself.

Personally, I feel that the courtesies shown us by you during the week of the conference have had a profound effect upon the women of this country, even those who were unable to be in Washington at the time, but who were represented by delegates from the various states. I am sure that they have returned to their home communities more fully determined than ever to measure up to the standard expected of American womanhood at this turning point in the world's history, resolved to keep before the people the high and exalted purpose and object of the war, and to cheerfully sacrifice all that they must, knowing that the stake for which we are fighting demands the patriotic loyalty of men and women alike.

Again thanking you, believe me,

Faithfully   Anna Howard Shaw

TLS (WP, DLC).

E N C L O S U R E

RESOLUTION

Washington May 15, 1918

WHEREAS, the President of the United States, engrossed and burdened with national and international responsibilities, has, in face of insistent demands upon his head and heart, given time, effort, and a gracious welcome to our officers and delegates; Therefore Be It

RESOLVED, that we, the Woman's Committee of the Council of National Defense, in convention assembled, extend our sincere appreciation of and gratitude to

THE PRESIDENT AND MRS. WILSON

for the unusual attention they have conferred upon us; and we further pledge our loyal support and coöperation to

THE PRESIDENT OF THE UNITED STATES

in all the duties he may assign to us for performance.

T MS (WP, DLC).

From Scott Ferris

My dear Mr. President: Washington, D. C. May 27, 1918.

It pleases me to advise you that we have at last succeeded in passing through the House of Representatives, without a dissenting vote, the General Oil Leasing Bill, in the form desired by you, and as presented to you at my recent conference.

I am perfectly sure this could never have been accomplished but for your steadfastness in sticking to me while I was temporarily at loggerheads with my committee over this oil relief provision.

The real truth is, every member of my committee now feel kindly toward me and have full respect for me. The oil men, while claiming we did less than scant justice to them, are at least keeping up good diplomatic relations with us, and I think will come out all right.

Of course we shall expect quite a long pull with the Senate conferees, but I shall try to work it out and maintain your every suggestion in it without troubling you more about the matter.

I fully understand how tired you must be of this matter, but as it deals with both coal and oil, two of the more important resources of the west, I hope your patience and tolerance with us will not be in vain.

With great respect, I am   Sincerely yours,   Scott Ferris

TLS (WP, DLC).

From Paul Moritz Warburg

Dear Mr. President: Washington May 27, 1918.

On August ninth my four year term of office as a member of the Federal Reserve Board will expire. I do not know whether or not, under the constant burden of grave and pressing decisions, you have reached the point where you wish to deal with the question of naming my successor, or whether or not you contemplate to have me continue in this work. Nor would I presume to broach this question were it not that I felt that, in consequence of recent occurrences, it has become one of policy rather than of personalities.

Certain persons have started an agitation to the effect that a naturalized citizen of German birth, having near relatives prominent in German public life, should not be permitted to hold a position of great trust in the service of the United States. (I have two brothers in Germany who are bankers. They naturally now serve their country to the utmost of their ability, as I serve mine.)

I believe that the number of men who urge this point of view is small at this time. They probably have not a proper appreciation of the sanctity of the oath of allegiance or of the oath of office. As for myself, I did not take them lightly. I waited ten years before determining upon my action, and I did not swear that "I absolutely and entirely renounce and abjure all allegiance and fidelity to any foreign potentate, and particularly to Wilhelm II, Emperor of Germany," etc., until I was quite certain that I was willing and anxious to cast my lot unqualifiedly and without reserve with the country of my adoption and to defend its aims and its ideals.

These are sad times. For all of us they bring sad duties, doubly hard indeed for men of my extraction. But, though, as in the Civil War, brother must fight brother, each must follow the straight path of duty, and in this spirit I have endeavored to serve during the four years that it has been my privilege to be a member of the Federal Reserve Board.

I have no doubt that all fair-minded and reasonable men would consider it nothing short of a national disgrace if this country, of all countries, should condone or endorse the attitude of those who would permit the American of German birth to give his all, but would not trust him as unreservedly and as wholeheartedly as he, for his part, serves the country of his adoption. Unfortunately, however, in times of war, we may not always count upon fair reasoning. It is only too natural that, as our casualty lists grow, bitterness and undiscriminating suspicion will assert themselves in the hearts of increasing numbers—even though these lists will continue to show their full proportion of German names.

Much to my regret, Mr. President, it has become increasingly evident that should you choose to renominate me this might precipitate a harmful fight which, in the interest of the country, I wish to do anything in my power to avoid and which, even though resulting in my confirmation, would be likely to leave an element of irritation in the minds of many whose anxieties and sufferings may justify their intense feelings. On the other hand, if for reasons of your own, you should decide not to renominate me it is likely to be construed by many as an acceptance by you of a point of view which I am certain you would not wish to sanction. In these circumstances, I deem it my duty to state to you myself that it is my firm belief that the interests of the country will best be served if my name be not considered by you in this connection.

I am frank to admit that I have reached this conclusion with the deepest regret both on account of its cause and its effect. I have considered it the greatest privilege to serve my country at this time, and I do not abandon lightly a work, half done, in which I am deeply and genuinely interested. But my continuation in office under present conditions might make the Board a target of constant attack by unscrupulous or unreasoning people, and my concern to save any embarrassment to you and to the Board in the accomplishment of its work would make it difficult for me to conserve that independence of mind and freedom of action without which nobody can do justice to himself or his office.

In writing you this letter, I have been prompted solely by my sincere conviction that the national welfare must be our only concern. Whatever you may decide to be best for the country will determine my future course. We are at war, and I remain at your orders.

May your patience and courage be rewarded and may it be given to you to lead our country to victory and peace!

Respectfully and faithfully yours,   Paul M Warburg[1]

TLS (WP, DLC).
[1] Wilson's reply is WW to P. M. Warburg, Aug. 9, 1918.

From the Viscount of Alte[1]

My dear Mr President: Washington, May 27th, 1918

Pray allow me to thank you most sincerely for your kind inquiries during my recent illness and for the beautiful flowers that you were good enough to send

I am also deeply obliged to Mrs. Wilson for the interest she was graciously pleased to show in my condition. I am, my dear Mr President,   very cordially your's   Alte

ALS (WP, DLC).
[1] José Francisco da Horta Machado da Franca, Visconde de Alte, Portuguese Minister to the United States.

From the Diary of Josephus Daniels

1918 Monday 27 May

Returned late from Goldsboro.

Went to capitol to hear President Wilson. He urged a tax bill.

Talked to Kitchin who early in the year wished tax bill to reach profiteers but McAdoo thought best to wait. Now wished to postpone, but would accede to wishes of President. WW proposed to Kitchin, Simmons & others to postpone bill now if Reprs. would agree to come back Nov. 10th & pass bill before Dec. 15 & put 40% of cost of war on excess profits, incomes and luxuries. Reps. refused & Pres. delivd message.

An Unpublished Statement

[c. May 28, 1918]

I am sorry that General Wood, by protesting his orders,[1] should have made it necessary for me to say publicly why I cannot send him to France. General Wood is a very able man and can be made

serviceable to the army in many ways; but he is by temperament—
and I dare say by conviction—an agitator. He boldly contests and
attempts to discourage the decisions of his superiors in command.
Such contests can do little harm here at home: they can be taken
care of by public opinion; but in the face of the enemy they would
be fatal. I cannot permit them in France, where our officers must
be single-minded and devote every thought to doing a single thing.

T transcript of WWsh MS (WP, DLC).
  ¹ In early May, General Leonard Wood had received orders informing him that the
89th Division, then in training under his command at the Fort Riley Military Reservation
in Kansas, would sail for France before the end of the month. Since the orders did not
state otherwise, Wood assumed that he would continue in command and go with the
division to Europe. Wood departed for New York on May 23 to prepare for the embarkation. There, on May 24 or 25, he received a telegram from the Adjutant General which
ordered him to go to San Francisco to assume command of the Western Department
as soon as the last units of the 89th Division had left Fort Riley. Wood went to see
Colonel House about the matter on May 26. House advised him to go to Washington
and see Baker and Wilson, if possible. Wood went to Washington and had an acrimonious
interview with Baker on May 27. Baker repeatedly told Wood that Pershing did not want
him in Europe, that he (Baker) considered him to be insubordinate, and that the decision
to keep him in the United States would not be altered. Baker did agree, however, to
consider permitting Wood to continue to train troops in Kansas, rather than take over
the purely administrative post in San Francisco, and to arrange an immediate interview
for the General with Wilson.
  As the extract from the Diary of Josephus Daniels, printed at May 28, 1918, reveals,
Wilson drafted the above statement in anticipation of his interview with Wood, which
took place at the White House at 5 p.m. on that date. Wilson apparently assumed that
Wood would be insubordinate to his face. News of Wood's new assignment had appeared
in the press that day, e.g., the New York Times, May 28, 1918.
  As it turned out, the forty-five-minute interview between Wilson and Wood seems to
have been perfectly correct, if rather frigid. According to Wood's notes—the only extant
record of the meeting—he first presented his case for being sent to Europe, or, barring
that, for playing an active role in the war effort in the United States. Following this, he
and Wilson engaged in a wide-ranging discussion of American military policy. Although
polite, Wilson clearly made no concessions or commitments.
  Over the next few weeks, the Wood affair led to much comment in the press. Many
writers questioned the wisdom and/or the alleged political motivation of the War Department's decision to keep Wood at home; almost all condemned the manner and the
timing of the implementation of the decision.
  Hermann Hagedorn, Leonard Wood: A Biography (2 vols., New York and London,
1931), II, 282-302, is the fullest account of the incident and has extensive summaries
and quotations from Wood's notes of the interviews with Baker and Wilson and from
press comment on the affair. See also Jack C. Lane, Armed Progressive: General Leonard
Wood (San Rafael, Cal., 1978), pp. 224-28, and Beaver, Newton D. Baker and the
American War Effort, pp. 152-56.

To Anna Howard Shaw

My dear Doctor Shaw: [The White House] 28 May, 1918
  I am deeply gratified by the generous resolution unanimously
adopted at the recent conference of the Woman's Committee of the
Council of National Defense. Mrs. Wilson and I did nothing for
which we deserved any thanks. We merely followed the dictates
of our own hearts and our own interest in the work the women are

doing. But it is none the less delightful to have the members of the Woman's Committee feel as they do about us.

Cordially and sincerely yours,   Woodrow Wilson

TLS (Letterpress Books, WP, DLC).

To Morris Sheppard

My dear Senator: The White House 28 May, 1918

Thank you very much for your letter of the twenty-sixth.

Frankly, I was very much distressed by the action of the House. I do not think that it is wise or fair to attempt to put such compulsion on the Executive in a matter in which he has already acted almost to the limit of his authority. What is almost entirely overlooked is that there are, as I am informed, very large stocks of whiskey in this country, and it seems to me quite certain that if the brewing of beer were prevented entirely, along with all the other drinks many of them harmless, which are derived from food or feed stuffs, the consumption of whiskey would be stimulated and increased to a very considerable extent.

My own judgment is that it is wise and statesmanlike to let the situation stand as it is for the present, until at any rate I shall be apprised by the Food Administration that it is necessary in the way suggested still further to conserve the supply of food and feed stuffs. The Food Administration has not thought it necessary to go any further than we have in that matter already gone.

I thank you most cordially, Senator, for your kindness in consulting me in this matter, which is of very considerable importance and has a very direct bearing upon many collateral questions.

Cordially and sincerely yours,   Woodrow Wilson

TLS (TxU).

To Furnifold McLendel Simmons

My dear Senator: The White House 28 May, 1918

It was friendly and kind of you to tell me about the misrepresentations which are being attempted in connection with the suggestions I made with regard to promises as to what might be done in a special session after the elections, and I have thought about the matter a good deal since receiving your note of yesterday.

My conclusion is that perhaps we had best just let the thing take its own course. There will be misrepresentations made in any case, no matter whether my memorandum to you is published or not, and I think it would only be giving opportunity to those who wish to make mischief to pay any attention to it. That has been the way in which I have generally treated misrepresentations and so far it has "worked."

Cordially and sincerely yours,   Woodrow Wilson

TLS (F. M. Simmons Papers, NcD).

To Bernard Mannes Baruch, with Enclosure

My dear Baruch: The White House 28 May, 1918

Thank you for your letter of the twenty-fourth,[1] which I was slow in getting to. I have taken pleasure in signing the order which you were kind enough to have drafted and send you herewith a signed copy, together with my approval of the letter to the Secretary of the Treasury with regard to the transmission of the request for appropriation.[2]

Cordially and faithfully yours,   Woodrow Wilson

TLS (B. M. Baruch Papers, NjP).
 [1] B. M. Baruch to WW, May 24, 1918, TLS (WP, DLC). Baruch asked Wilson to sign the proposed Executive Order and a formal request for an appropriation of $1,500,000 for the W.I.B. in fiscal year 1919.
 [2] [WW] to WGM [May 28, 1918], TCL (B. M. Baruch Papers, NjP).

E N C L O S U R E

The White House, 28 May, 1918.
EXECUTIVE ORDER

I hereby establish the War Industries Board as a separate administrative agency to act for me and under my direction. This is the Board which was originally formed by, and subsidiary to, the Council of National Defense under the provisions of "An Act Making Appropriations for the Support of the Army for the Fiscal Year Ending June 30, 1917, and for other purposes," approved August 29, 1916.

The functions, duties and powers of the War Industries Board, as outlined in my letter of March 4, 1918, to Bernard M. Baruch, Esquire, its Chairman,[1] shall be and hereby are continued in full force and effect.   Woodrow Wilson

TS MS (B. M. Baruch Papers, NjP).
 [1] Printed at that date in Vol. 46.

To Newton Diehl Baker

My dear Baker: The White House 28 May, 1918

Thank you warmly for the enclosed letter.[1] I am taking pleasure in signing the commuted sentence.

Cordially and faithfully yours,   Woodrow Wilson

TLS (N. D. Baker Papers, DLC).
[1] NDB to WW, May 25, 1918, TLS (WP, DLC). Baker informed Wilson that he had changed his mind about the case of Maj. Henry R. Freeman (about which see WW to NDB, May 24, 1918, and n. 1 thereto) and now wished to have Freeman's sentence commuted as recommended by the Judge Advocate General.

To Scott Ferris

My dear Ferris: [The White House] 28 May, 1918

Thank you for your letter of yesterday. I am heartily glad to hear of the fine vote by which the General Oil Leasing Bill went through. You need not be afraid that I will get tired of the business. I am ready to help at any time, and congratulate you on the way in which you have handled it.

Cordially and sincerely yours,   Woodrow Wilson

TLS (Letterpress Books, WP, DLC).

To Franklin Potts Glass

My dear Glass: [The White House] 28 May, 1918

I need not tell you, I am sure, how warmly I appreciate your desire to help in the matter of doing Creel the justice he deserves, or how disappointed I am at the attitude the members of the News-paper Publishers Association have taken in response to your request for a committee of investigation; but I must frankly say that my judgment is that it would not be wise to take the alternative course which you propose in your letter of May twenty-fourth.

You know the attitude of many of the Eastern newspaper men towards Creel has from the first been most hostile and, in my judgment, most unjust, and I personally have very little doubt that if they were asked to give comprehensive advice with regard to how the whole matter of publicity ought to be handled, they would wish to see the thing changed *de novo*, and my expectation would be that they would make recommendations which I could not accept and that the new situation created by my failure to accept them would be more unpleasant than the present situation.

If you could get even two or three members of the Association whose judgment would not be doubted to come down here and really go into this matter of the way in which Creel has been doing his work, I for one would be very glad, because Creel thoroughly deserves entire vindication.

Cordially and sincerely yours,   Woodrow Wilson

TLS (Letterpress Books, WP, DLC).

To Ferdinand Foch

My dear General Foch,   [The White House] 28 May, 1918

I appreciate most sincerely your thoughtful kindness in having the map prepared for me which I have just received.[1] It is of the greatest interest, and will be most serviceable to me.

May I not take this occasion to express my personal regards and my great confidence in you as our Commander-in-Chief.

With sincere regard,

Faithfully yours,   Woodrow Wilson

TCL (Letterpress Books, WP, DLC).
[1] Foch had sent Wilson an autographed copy of a map which hung in his own office at his headquarters. The map depicted the advances made by the German army since the beginning of its offensive on the western front on March 21. NDB to WW, May 24, 1918, TLS (WP, DLC).

To Herbert Clark Hoover

My dear Mr. Hoover: The While House 28 May, 1918

I have your letter of yesterday containing the revised report of the members of the Committee on the Packing Industry and take pleasure in approving the conclusions of that report,[1] which I herewith return.

Cordially and sincerely yours,   Woodrow Wilson

TLS (Hoover Archives, CSt-H).
[1] It was published in the *Official Bulletin*, II (May 31, 1918), 1, 4. The published text is identical to that of the Enclosure printed with HCH to WW, May 13, 1918, except that the last two sentences of paragraph 2 under the heading "Government and Allied Purchases" were deleted.

From Newton Diehl Baker, with Enclosures

Dear Mr. President   [Washington, c. May 28, 1918]

You may care to have the full text of Gen Bliss' message and the reply   Respectfully,   Newton D Baker

ALS (WP, DLC).

ENCLOSURE I

Versailles May 26th [1918]

Rush Number 115 Secret.

Paragraph 1. For the Secretary of War. At the instance of the French Representative and probably under direction of his government the question of intervention in Siberia will again come up for discussion on May thirtieth. I think it important that I receive if practicable some instructions from our government to guide my action. The form in which the French submit the subject is as follows:

Subparagraph A. "The permanent Military Representatives believe it their duty to again invite the attention of their governments to the urgency for finding a solution to this question, because events are hastening in Russia and the situation may soon become unfavorable to the Allies. The details to be considered are the following.

Subparagraph 1. The danger of the complete isolation of Russia by the Central Powers is increasing: the Northern ports and Petrograd are threatened with attack, the Turks are continuing their advance in the direction of the Caspian Sea; German propaganda in Russia is growing stronger each day.

Subparagraph 2. The organization of the German prisoners in Russia is confirmed and may soon become a serious danger.

Subparagraph 3. German infiltration into Russia, if we do not rapidly oppose it, would leave to the Germans the disposition of the resources of all kinds which would not only permit them to prolong the war but also would assure them after the war the economic domination of Asia and the extreme east.

Subparagraph 4. The establishment of German submarine bases on the coast of eastern Russia would be a very serious danger for navigation of the Pacific.

Subparagraph 5. Finally, if Japanese interests should be some day directly menaced, Japan would not hesitate to act alone in Russia and might then brush aside all allied cooperation.

Subparagraph B. On the other hand there are certain signs which warrant the assumption that circumstances are daily becoming more favorable and that military intervention in Russia would not encounter throughout the country the opposition which it would have met a few months ago because

Subparagraph 1. The mass of the Russian people feels the German yoke weighing heavily on it and all opposition parties are unanimous in demanding foreign action against Germany;

Subparagraph 2. The Bolshevik government, which has promised peace at any price, is doubtlessly unable to declare itself openly in favor of such action, but it will see to admitting that the resumption of war with Germany is inevitable and that it will then need the aid of the Allies.

Subparagraph C. As a result of the foregoing the Military Representatives are of opinion that the Entente Powers have the greatest interest in agreeing as soon as possible upon the principles of an effective military intervention in Russia which if allowed will be able to reform an Eastern Front against the Central Empires. The method of this intervention remains as defined by Joint Note Number Two Naught of the Military Representatives."[1]

Subparagraph D. In my very Confidential Number Three Two dated February 19th I transmitted the text of Joint Note Number one six on the subject of Japanese intervention in Russia.[2] The intervention then contemplated was relatively slight and subsequent action was to be guided by the effects which this limited intervention would have produced on the Russian people. Paragraph five of my Number Three Two gives the reason why I joined with my colleagues in Joint Note Number One Six notwithstanding the personal views expressed in same telegram. In reply to my number Three Two I received a telegram from War Department saying that this subject was a matter for diplomatic negotiations and expressing the hope that the Military Representatives would not press it further.[3] Joint Note Number Two Naught (see paragraph three of my Number Eight Five dated April 12th)[4] on same subject of intervention in Russia was not signed by me. My reason for this was given on page eight of my personal letter to the Secretary of War dated April Two Naught.[5] Joint Note Number Two Naught was before the Supreme War Council at its session on May Two at Abbeville. The Prime Minister took no action on it but simply noted it. You will observe that the proposition which the French desire to have discussed on May Three Naught states that "The method of this intervention remains as defined in Joint Note Number Two Naught of the Military Representatives." Joint Note Two Naught provided for Japanese intervention in Russia which "should extend as far west as possible, at least to Omsk or Cheliabinsk, submitted proposition preferably as far as Samara." For further details see Joint Note Number Two Naught. The original draft of Joint Note Number Two Naught provided for territorial compensation to Japan in Asia. This was stricken out on objections made by me but it is generally accepted here that such compensation will be necessary.

Subparagraph E. Perhaps French interest in the Russian debt partly accounts for their unanimity in favoring Japanese intervention. It is generally conceded here that the United States must finance the Japanese Military operations. In my opinion the only thing that will prevent the proposed intervention from proving an ultimate disaster for the Entente Allies will be its cordial welcome by the Russian people. The Germans are the most skilful propagandists in Europe. If the coming of the Japanese re-arouses a warlike spirit among the Russians adverse to the Japanese, the Germans may consolidate the sentiment in their own favor. The result may be a great immoderate force dominated by the Germans and able at the same time to block the Japanese advance and to help the Germans on the West. If the Japanese become committed to a costly policy and then find that it will probably fail it will reinforce the possibility of a division of sphere of influence between them and the Germans. In other words, we may find the east combining with middle Europe against the West. Therefore it is of importance first to learn whether the Russian Government and the people will welcome this intervention. I distrust everything I hear on this subject here. I hear only denunciation of the Bolshevik and everything they stand for. Would like to see something like the old regime restored. It is from the old Russian regime that come declarations in favor of intervention. Members of that regime will listen to any one who favors its restoration. But when the time is ripe for listening to them the Germans can help them more quickly than can the Allies. My present disposition is to consent only to a recommendation that the allied governments ascertain beyond shadow of doubt what the real attitude of the Russian people will be toward this intervention. But it must be that these governments have been trying to do this for months past and are not yet satisfied. But I do not want to continue in an attitude which may not be supported by our government. On important politico-military questions like this one the other military representatives are advised by their governments of the general attitude which they must take. Can I be advised as to whether our government desires me to continue in the attitude that the Military Representatives, having already submitted this question to their Governments, must await their decision without saying anything further? If not what general policy is it desired that I follow on this subject? In another Joint Note to be discussed on May three naught the British French and Italian will probably agree to an occupation of the Ports of Murmansk and Archangel by British Navy and a land force of not more than four or six battalions of British French and possibly Americans. In view of pressing danger to these ports I propose to agree with my colleagues unless instructed to the contrary.

Paragraph 2. For the Chief of Staff. Heartiest congratulations on your appointment as Chief of Staff.[6] Nothing could be better.

Bliss.

¹ It is printed as an Enclosure with NDB to WW, April 25, 1918, Vol. 47.
² T. H. Bliss to H. P. McCain, Feb. 19, 1918, Vol. 46.
³ H. P. McCain to T. H. Bliss, No. 25, Feb. 22, 1918. It is quoted in full in n. 1 to T. H. Bliss to H. P. McCain, Feb. 25, 1918, printed as an Enclosure with NDB to WW, Feb. 26, 1918, Vol. 46.
⁴ T. H. Bliss to H. P. McCain, April 12, 1918, Vol. 47.
⁵ It is missing in all known collections and repositories.
⁶ Peyton Conway March had been promoted to General and appointed Chief of Staff on May 20, 1918.

E N C L O S U R E   I I

Washington. May 28, 1918.

MEMORANDUM for the Adjutant General:

Please cable the following to General Bliss at Versailles:

"[No. 59] Secretary of War has presented your Number 115, May 26, to the President. The President's attitude is that Russia's misfortune imposes upon us at this time the obligation of unswerving fidelity to the principle of Russian territorial integrity and political independence. Intervention via Vladivostok is deemed impracticable because of the vast distances involved, the size of the force necessary to be effective, and financing such an expedition would mean a burden which the United States at this time ought not assume. In order to be effective, either to create a military situation on the eastern front which would relieve the pressure on the western front, or to prevent the Central Powers from exploiting the agricultural and other resources of Russia, such an intervening expedition would have to penetrate into European Russia and, however such an expedition were safeguarded by the approval and concurrence of the Allies, its appearance would be such that German propagandists would be able to persuade the Russian people that compensation at their expense and out of their territory was ultimately to be exacted. In this way and others Germany would be able to arouse Russian patriotic feeling and thus secure military and other aid from the Russians far outweighing any foreseeable advantage from so difficult an intervention.

The idea of compensating Japan by territory in Asiatic Russia is inadmissible. The President is heartily in sympathy with any practical military effort which can be made at and from Murmansk or Archangel, but such efforts should proceed, if at all, upon the sure sympathy of the Russian people and should not have as their ultimate object any restoration of the ancient regime or any other interference with the political liberty of the Russian people. March."

T telegrams (WP, DLC).

From Robert Lansing, with Enclosure

Dear Mr. President,   [Washington] 5/28/18

This letter from George Kennan[1] is well worth reading.

Will you be good enough to return it to me after you have finished with it?   Faithfully yours   Robert Lansing

ALS (R. Lansing Papers, NjP).
   [1] (1845-1924) explorer and journalist, best known for his studies of Russia.

E N C L O S U R E

George Kennan to Robert Lansing

Dear Mr Secretary: New York City, May 26 1918

I enclose herewith a copy of an article that I have recently written for The Outlook, entitled "Can We Help Russia?"[1] and also a letter, a pamphlet and two or three clippings on the Russian situation which seem to me deserving of attention.[2]

My own opinions with regard to the matter, which, of course, you will take for what they seem to be worth, are as follows:

First: Under no circumstances should the United States recognize the Bolsheviki as constituting either a *de jure* or *de facto* government in what there is left of the old Empire. They are usurpers pure and simple; their authority is not recognized by anything like a majority of the Russian people; they obtained what power they have by criminal violence, and they are retaining it by a system of terrorism which prevents the majority of the nation from giving expression to its will.

Second: We should not cooperate with the Bolsheviki, or give them assistance, even if they make a show of fighting the Germans:

a. because they never can unite the people against the invader, on account of the general distrust of them, or hatred for them;

b. because they are wholly lacking in military capacity, as well as in constructive and administrative ability; and

c. because their political and economic opinions and theories constitute a disrupting and destructive force which would demoralize any people and ruin any country.

Third: We can probably do little, if anything, to improve the state of affairs in European Russia while the Bolsheviki retain power:

   [1] G. Kennan, "Can We Help Russia?" *The Outlook*, CXIX (May 22, 1918), 141, clipping, R. Lansing Papers, NjP.
   [2] Arcady Joseph Sack, director of the Russian Information Bureau, New York, to G. Kennan, May 21, 1918, TLS (R. Lansing Papers, NjP). The pamphlet is missing. The only other clipping found with Kennan's letter is G. Kennan, "Russia's Dual Government," *The Outlook*, CXVI (May 23, 1917), 138.

a. because our agents would have to cooperate more or less with them and act more or less under their control. This would be infinitely worse than cooperating with, or taking the orders of, Huerta or Villa in Mexico;

b. because it is impracticable, under existing conditions, to send any considerable amount of goods there to meet the needs, or relieve the sufferings of the great masses of people whom the war and the economic policy of the Bolsheviki have reduced to complete destitution.

Fourth: The Bolsheviki are almost as great enemies of the Allies as are the Germans:

a. because they regard the governments of France, Great Britain and the United States as "capitalistic" governments which ought to be overthrown (see Lenin's recent statements);

b. because they number in their ranks hundreds of pro-Germans and German agents. A Petrograd newspaper—the "Dyello"—published some months ago a list of the real names and the assumed names of one hundred and fifty nine German agents who were working with the Bolsheviki and whose identities had been ascertained. How could Lenin and Trotzky fight the Germans successfully, or even effectively, when among their associates and followers there are more German spies and German agents than there ever were in the old government under Sukhomlinof, Sturmer and Protopopof?[3] It is not a conceivable proposition. Besides that, there is no good reason for believing in the sincerity of the Bolsheviki when they assume an anti-German attitude. Certain it is that, in one way or another, they have been playing into the hands of the Germans ever since they acquired power.

Fifth: the real friends of the Allies, and the only people capable of setting up anything like a strong or stable government, are the so-called "intelligentsia," that is, the university men and teachers; the merchants, bankers, and business men of all classes; the liberal nobility; the Constitutional Democrats, Octobrists and Progressives; the right wing of the Social Revolutionists; the members of the old zemstvos; the Cossacks, and last but not least the peasant cooperative societies, which numbered a year ago more than 40.000, which had an adult male membership of 15.000.000. and which represented a total population of perhaps 60.000.000. All of these

[3] Vladimir Aleksandrovich Sukhomlinov, former Minister of War (1909-1915), who had been sentenced to life imprisonment for treason by the Provisional Government but was released by the Bolsheviks in May 1918 and emigrated to Germany; Boris Vladimirovich Stürmer, former Prime Minister (February-November 1916) and Minister of Foreign Affairs (July-November 1916), who had been arrested after the Bolshevik takeover and had died in prison; Aleksandr Dmitrievich Protopopov, former Minister of Internal Affairs (September 1916-March 1917) and one of Nicholas II's closest advisers, who had been executed by the Bolsheviks.

classes are practically unrepresented in the Bolshevik government; all are hostile to it, and most of them are in favor of continued resistance to the Germans.

Sixth: From the Bolsheviki we can expect nothing, either in the shape of help, or of constructive work. They are bound to be over-thrown eventually (I regard this as an absolute certainty) and the sooner their downfall comes the better it will be for Russia, for the Allied cause, and for the whole civilized world. From the anti-Bolsheviki, on the other hand, that is, from an overwhelming ma-jority of the nation including all of its brains, we might reasonably expect the restoration of order, and as much resistance to the Ger-mans as it would be possible for a liberated and encouraged majority to make.

If these judgments are trustworthy, and they are the judgments of all the men who know Russia best, we should not hesitate to take sides against the Bolsheviki, no matter what they may do, and no matter what may be their resultant attitude toward us. It is not a case of taking the side of one "faction" against another faction, it is a case of taking the side of a majority of the Russian people against a minority of criminal usurpers who have almost ruined them and who are not willing or not able to resist German en-croachment. We should therefore treat the Bolsheviki either as open enemies who are cooperating with the Germans, or as weak neutrals who are unwilling or unable to prevent the Germans from using the resources of Russia and Siberia against us.

The danger that Germany will acquire economic domination in Siberia—the richest part of the old Empire that is still left intact—seems to me very great. What are we going to do about it? Prudence, if not the imperative demand of self-protection, would seem to re-quire that an Allied expeditionary force, consisting of Americans, Japanese, Canadians perhaps, and patriotic Russians and Poles recruited in the United States and the Far East, be sent to eastern Siberia, not to take possession, or to rule, but to help the Russians of the trans-Baikal to throw off the Bolshevik yoke and to set up an independent, anti-Bolshevik and anti-German government of their own. The Japanese, of course, would have to do most of the work, and one of their best generals should, I think, be in command of the Allied force. If we don't do this, the Japanese and Chinese, in the not distant future, may be forced to do it for their own self-protection, and that would be much less desirable.

Such action would involve at least one near-certainty, and one strong probability. The near-certainty is that the Allies, including the patriotic Russians and the small but capable Cossack army of General Semeonof, would take and hold all of the trans-Baikal as far west as Irkutsk. The Russians, under Allied supervision, would then set up their own government, and would intern all the German prisoners of war, as well as the Bolsheviki and their sympathizers. A large part of Siberia, including the rich Amur valley, two railroads, the mines of the trans-Baikal, and probably Kamchatka with its fisheries and its untouched mineral resources, would thus be saved for the Russians and for the Allies.

The strong probability is that the people of western Siberia, including many hundreds of peasant cooperative societies, would be so encouraged by the successful establishment of an independent Russian republic in the trans-Baikal that they, with such help as we and the Japanese could give them in the shape of arms and ammunition, would also throw off the Bolshevik yoke, and would also establish an independent, anti-Bolshevik and anti-German government. Then, with all Siberia safe, there would be some hope even for European Russia.

The Siberian people have always had a strong separatist tendency. Many years ago, when the old government was still dominant, many prominent Siberians said to me: "Oh! If we could only get free from European Russia, set up a government of our own, and invite you, Americans, to come here and show us how to develope our resources, we would become more prosperous and more powerful, in a few generations, than all the rest of the Empire."

Of course, intervention in eastern Siberia might compel all the Allied powers to sever such diplomatic relations as they have with the Bolsheviki and withdraw their ambassadors. But I should not regard that as a calamity. What have our ambassadors been able to do in the way of influencing Lenin and Trotzky? Little or nothing. They could not prevent the latter from making a treacherous and shameful peace. They could not prevent them from destroying their own armies, disastrous as that was for us all. They could not prevent them from attacking Finland and the Ukraine, although it was perfectly evident that such action would throw those countries into the hands of the Germans. In what respect should we be worse off now if we had made a protest and withdrawn our ambassadors four or five months ago? In no respect whatever that I can see. Why, then, should we be afraid of breaking with the Bolsheviki?

It is said that intervention in Siberia might unite the Bolsheviki and the Germans against us. It possibly might, but what if it should? I doubt whether they could have done us more harm than they have done if they had united against us three months ago. The Bolsheviki are not Russia, nor could they swing all Russia against us. A majority of the people would still be anti-Bolshevik and anti-German, and there would still be the same internal fighting that there is now. As Harold Williams[4] justly says in the special cable despatch that I enclose: "They (the Bolsheviki) are the enemies of the cause we are fighting for." Why not then force them into the open and deal with them as enemies?

The best part of European Russia is already lost, so far as we are concerned. Why not save Siberia? With the aid of the Japanese, and the sane and patriotic Russians, we could certainly hold eastern Siberia, and probably western Siberia, against Bolsheviki and Germans combined. And they are worth holding, apart from the influence that their union with us would exert on the population of European Russia. The revolt of all Siberia, or even eastern Siberia, against the rule of Lenin and Trotzky might bring about the overthrow of the Bolsheviki everywhere, and then the Germans would soon have to hustle troops back from the western front.

I don't often make unsolicited suggestions with regard to governmental matters; but in this case I am, to some extent, an expert. I have lived three years in eastern Siberia, I have been three times across the Empire from the Baltic to the Pacific, and I know the Russian people—and particularly the people of Siberia—as well as any foreigner. I believe it to be my duty, therefore, to lay before you my view of the extremely critical state of affairs in Russia, for your own information and that of the President if you see fit to bring my letter to his attention. If Germany succeeds in getting military, or even economic domination in what remains of the old Empire, I shall at least have the satisfaction of knowing that I did what little I could, by argument, to prevent it.

In your crowded life, Mr Secretary, you cannot have the time that I have to select and read books. May I not therefore venture to call your attention to one that has attracted little or no attention in this country, but that ought to be—if it is not already—in the State Department library. It is "Russia's Agony," by Robert Wilton,[5] an Englishman who has spent half his life in Russia and who has been for years correspondent of the London Times in Petrograd. The title is not one that I should have chosen, but the book contains the best and most trustworthy account of the Russian revolution and its consequences that has yet appeared. It was published in the early part of this year by Longmans Green & Co. London.

With sincere regard and esteem I am

Faithfully yours   George Kennan

TLS (R. Lansing Papers, NjP).

[4] Harold Eugene Williams, a correspondent for the American News Co. His dispatch is missing.

[5] Robert Wilton, *Russia's Agony* (London and New York, 1918). There is a copy of this book in the Wilson Library, DLC.

Two Letters from Bernard Mannes Baruch

My dear Mr. President: Washington May 28, 1918.

I have given careful consideration to the question you raise in your letter to me of May 24th, concerning the creation of an organization through which all the war activities of the Government may be reported periodically as a basis for checking up actual operations and results, and I heartily agree with you that a good deal of loose talk, and perhaps a good deal of loose action, might be avoided if we could have such a basis of judgment and such a periodical checking up.

Your letter of March 4th appointing me Chairman of the War Industries Board stated that, "the Chairman should be constantly and systematically informed of all contracts, purchases, and deliveries, in order that he may have always before him the schematized analysis of the progress of business in the several supply divisions of the Government in all departments." I have already arranged to be informed continually of such progress of business in the several divisions of all departments.

This, as yet, comprises only information in regard to contracts, purchases and deliveries, but it seems to me that your suggestion could easily be carried out by enlarging the scope of this work which is already under way. If it were clearly understood by all departments that the requisite information should be furnished periodically and as promptly as possible, I feel confident that I could rapidly create an organization which would be able to handle the work in a satisfactory manner.

All that is necessary to give effect to your suggestion is for you to issue an executive order or letters directing me to undertake the work and directing the various Departments and Boards to furnish the requisite information fully and promptly. Directions along the lines of the enclosed draft suggestions would, I think, be sufficient.[1] These directions will enable me to have placed on your desk at stated intervals a condensed and digested summarization of the actual operations and results of the war activities in all departments, and it will give me great pleasure to undertake this work.

Yours very truly,   Bernard M Baruch

[1] "Dear Sir: I have requested Mr. Baruch, in connection with his work as Chairman of the War Industries Board, to arrange to have summarized and reported periodically all the information requisite for checking up and forming a judgment upon the actual operations and results of all the war activities of this Government. As a basis for such reports, I request that you will cause to be furnished to him periodically all the information requisite for this purpose concerning the war activities under your direction." T MS (WP, DLC).

My dear Mr. President: Washington May 28, 1918.

Replying to your letter of May 24th with reference to the estimates of the necessary expenditures of the War Industries Board for the use of the Committee on Appropriations: Such estimates in as much detail as possible have been furnished the Committee on Appropriations, and I understand from Mr. Sherley that they are in satisfactory form. The only further action which the Appropriations Committee desires that we take is to send them a formal request for an appropriation through the regular official channels. The request in the form which they asked for was outlined in my letter to you of May 24th.[1]

Mr. Sherley is also of the opinion that the War Industries Board should be made a direct administrative agency by executive action before money is appropriated. I outlined a suggestion as to this in my letter of May 24th.

Very sincerely yours,   Bernard M Baruch

TLS (WP, DLC).
  [1] B. M. Baruch to WW, May 24, 1918, TLS (WP, DLC).

From John Franklin Shafroth

My dear Mr. President: Washington, D. C. May 28, 1918.

I was very much distressed to read in the paper this morning that General Leonard Wood had been relieved of his command of the 89th Division of the National Army.

I have visited Camp Funston a number of times, that being the cantonment of the district in which Colorado is located and all of the young men in the National Army from our State have had their training there. I know that they are very much attached to General Wood. Of all things that will inspire soldiers to daring deeds the most important is the obeying of commands of officers whom they love and admire and I feel that it would be a great mistake as to them not to permit General Wood to command them in engagements in France.

I do not know what reasons Secretary Baker may have had for this order, but I do hope, if it is possible, that you will permit General Wood to retain command of his Division on the battle front in France.

With best wishes, I remain,

Yours truly,   John F. Shafroth

TLS (WP, DLC).

From Ben Johnson

My dear Mr. President: Washington, D. C. May 28, 1918.

Assuming and hoping that you will approve Senate Joint Resolution No. 152,[1] which finally passed the Senate yesterday, may I not suggest that you do so not later than the last day of this month?[2]

On the last day of the month a great number of leases expire; and on the next day, the first day of June, leases for the same premises will be let to the same or new tenants at greatly increased rates. In order that the tenants may have the benefit of the "present rates" provided for in the Resolution, it is necessary that you approve it before the new and further extortionate rates become the "present rates." Under the terms of the Resolution the rates which will prevail will be those in operation at the time of your approval.

Yours most respectfully,   Ben Johnson

TLS (WP, DLC).

[1] S.J. Res. 152, which was introduced by Senator Saulsbury on May 4, 1918, was designed to reduce rent profiteering in the District of Columbia during the war. It prevented landlords in the District of Columbia, during the present session of Congress, from evicting tenants in good standing and from then renting the premises at higher rates. Tenants who had a written or oral lease could be evicted only if a landlord required the rented premises for occupation by himself or his family while they were employed by the federal government.

The Senate debated and amended Saulsbury's resolution on May 6 and 7 and adopted it on May 7. It was referred to the House Committee on the District of Columbia on May 9, which reported it with further amendments on May 15. The House passed it with additional amendments on the same day. The House version was referred to the Senate on May 21, which disagreed with the suggested amendments and requested a conference. The conference report was introduced in the House on May 24 and was passed the next day. The Senate debated it on May 25 and 27 and adopted it by a vote of thirty-one to seventeen, with forty-eight senators abstaining. See *Cong. Record*, 65th Cong., 2d sess., pp. 6035, 6058-59, 6099-6107, 6155-59, 6299, 6553-64, 6823-29, 7030, 7063-67, 7080-83, and 7111-27.

[2] Wilson signed the resolution on May 31, and Representative Johnson was so informed by telephone. *Ibid.*, p. 7279; typed note on Johnson's letter to Wilson.

From James Cannon, Jr.

My dear Mr. President: Washington, D. C. May 28, 1918.

As a member of the Special Committee of the General Conference of the Methodist Episcopal Church, South, it was my pleasant duty to join in framing the telegram sent by the Committee to you on May 3rd, and the General Conference greatly appreciated your response,[1] emphasizing your gratitude for the sympathy, support and prayers of the men composing the body.

The General Conference later on, on the occasion of Secretary Daniels' visit, declared it to be the purpose of the people we represent that "nothing shall be left undone which will assist in securing the victory to us and our allies."

Later on, when Food Administrator Hoover, sent to the Conference an appeal for its co-operation, that co-operation was guaranteed with an enthusiastic rising vote.

Having thus declared its desire to support and to co-operate with the President and his Cabinet in every possible way, the Conference, by a unanimous rising vote, sent an appeal to the President, and to Congress, asking for War Time Prohibition Legislation, and the same protection for our soldiers and sailors abroad that is now given to them by law in the United States. Nearly every member of the General Conference has sons or grandsons in the army, and these fathers and grandfathers are intensely solicitous concerning the moral welfare of their boys.

The General Conference at its recent meeting organized a Commission on Temperance and Social Service, of which the undersigned was elected Chairman.

The General Conference instructed the undersigned, as Chairman of its Commission on Temperance and Social Service, to send a copy of its action on Prohibition legislation to the President, and the Secretary of War, to the Secretary of the Navy, and to both Houses of Congress, and the Commission on Temperance and Social Service has requested me to ask for an opportunity to make to you in person a statement of the deep convictions of the more than two and one-quarter million members of our Church on this subject.

I shall be glad to carry out the instructions of the General Conference Commission in this matter at any time you may designate after Monday, June 3rd.[2]

With great respect, I am,

Yours sincerely,   James Cannon Jr.

TLS (WP, DLC).
  [1] The committee's telegram and Wilson's reply are both missing in WP, DLC.
  [2] Wilson saw Cannon at the White House on June 4, 1918.

From Keith Neville[1]

Lincoln, Nebraska, May 28, 1918.

Nebraska allotment of White House wool sold to Judge Slama[2] Wahoo Saunders County, Nebraska, for five thousand dollars. Check being mailed to you by endorsement.[3]   Keith Neville.[4]

T telegram (WP, DLC).
  [1] Governor of Nebraska, a Democrat.
  [2] Charles H. Slama, a former county judge of Saunders County, at this time in the private practice of law in Wahoo, Neb.
  [3] Wilson and Mrs. Wilson had announced on May 17, 1918, that they wished to contribute to the Red Cross War Fund by having sold at auction throughout the United States approximately ninety pounds of wool recently clipped from a flock of sheep which

had been grazing on the White House lawn for the past three weeks. Each state, as well as Porto Rico, Hawaii, and the Philippines, would receive a share of two pounds of this "White House wool," and the governors would be asked to act as auctioneers. *New York Times*, May 18 and 20, 1918.

⁴ "This is all right, except don't you think you had better express my appreciation of the personal interest Governor Neville has taken in the matter? The President." WW to JPT, c. May 28, 1918, TL (WP, DLC).

From the Diary of Josephus Daniels

May Tuesday 28 1918

WW told of preacher who prays "O, Lord, you have doubtless seen from the morning papers[,"] &c. He said you have doubtless seen that Leonard Wood is here & I am to see him to-night. The papers will want to know why he is not sent to Europe. Then WW read paper he had prepared setting forth that Wood was an agitator and it was better that he agitate here than abroad—he could do less harm here for his agitation could be corrected in America. Most of cabinet opposed WW's saying anything. Baker said Pershing had not desired Wood & he had told Wood so & therefore he would not send him

Gregory had caught 5 Irishmen busy with German spies & suggested giving out facts. The British wished it as backing up their statement. WW said no. G.B. had been stupid in its dealing with Ireland & we should not be stupid likewise. Let the traitors be arrested & indicted, & the news go from the courts & not from the Administration

WW said Carnegie once said there was no more reason to study Greek than Choctaw. "Not to a man who couldn't understand the difference & see that there was a literature in Greek & not in Choctaw" WW thought it silly to forbid teaching German and tearing down German statues. Baker said statue of Frederick the Great ought not to have been taken down at War College

To Willard Saulsbury

My dear Senator: The White House 29 May, 1918

I have your letter of yesterday. You may be sure I am as much interested in maintaining the validity of the anti-profiteering rent bill as anyone can be, because I have felt deeply outraged by what has been going on in the District. It has been not only unjust, but distinctly against the interest of the country as interfering very seriously indeed with the efficiency of the government service. I

will see what the Attorney General thinks about the best method
of handling it.

          Cordially and sincerely yours,   Woodrow Wilson

TLS (W. Saulsbury Papers, DeU).

To Thomas Watt Gregory, with Enclosure

                    [The White House] 29 May, 1918
My dear Mr. Attorney General:

The enclosed letter speaks for itself. I am, as you know, intensely
interested in seeing that these rent profiteers are got at and defeated
of their piratical purposes, and I am sending Senator Saulsbury's
letter only that I may get from you the best suggestion as to how
we ought to act in order to maintain the restraints set up by the
new law.

          Cordially and faithfully yours,   Woodrow Wilson

E N C L O S U R E

From Willard Saulsbury

Dear Mr. President: [Washington] May 28th, 1918.

The so-called anti-profiteering rent bill will be before you for
consideration in the course of a day or two and assuming that you
will approve the resolution, I beg to suggest that you will instruct
the Department of Justice to uphold the law in the courts in whatever proceedings are brought to have it declared unconstitutional.

It is an open secret that the real estate agents are combining to
obtain a favorable decision in the courts and of course it is a hard
thing for the tenants to get together while if they knew that the
Department of Justice was going to support the law, it would I
think put an end to the tenants' panic which has been prevailing.

          Yours very truly,   Willard Saulsbury

TLS (JDR, RG 60, No. 191479-1-1, DNA).

To John Franklin Shafroth

My dear Senator: [The White House] 29 May, 1918

I appreciate the force of what you say to me in your letter of
yesterday, and you may be sure that the whole matter has given

me concern, for I wished to do the thing that is most serviceable to the Army and to the country.

There are many elements in this particular case which it is difficult to go into with any degree of particularity, but the resulting judgment in my mind is that General Wood is serving the country very much better in training men on this side than he could serve it in any other way at the present juncture. The training of men on this side of the water is more difficult, requires more imagination and a more detailed and accurate conception of what is needed on the other side than any other present task.

I shall be glad some time to have a talk with you about this whole matter.   Cordially and sincerely yours,   Woodrow Wilson

TLS (Letterpress Books, WP, DLC).

From Robert Lansing, with Enclosure

My dear Mr. President: Washington May 29, 1918

Allow me to call to your attention the attached copy of a telegram from the Minister at Stockholm, dated May 27, which summarizes the views of a well known Russian patriot and student of affairs, Mr. Bourtseff.[1] The views of Mr. Bourtseff may be taken as typical of a large element of socialist opinion which is now represented only in opposition. It is significant of quite a definite line of effort which is being made from Russia to influence opinion abroad.
                    Faithfully yours,   Robert Lansing

TLS (WP, DLC).
   [1] About whom, see RL to WW, Feb. 18, 1918 (first letter of that date), n. 1, Vol. 46.

E N C L O S U R E

                    Stockholm May 27, 1918

2168. Have had an interview with Bourtzeef, well known Russian Socialist who was persecuted by old regime, but who was not radical enough for Bolsheviks, and was imprisoned. He managed to escape and came to Sweden. He is convinced *this organization* (disorganization?) and anarchy in Russia so great that order within reasonable time can only be restored by outside armed force. Bourtzeef is extremely anti-German and sees in the present situation only downfall of Russia; and its complete political and economic subjugation to Germany. He states it seems to be consensus of opinion of Russian Socialists that they should do everything possible to secure Allied Intervention, and to this end are sending him through Europe and later to America.

Morris.

T telegram (WP, DLC).

From Robert Lansing, with Enclosure

My dear Mr. President: Washington May 29, 1918.

Senator Phelan called upon me this afternoon and left with me the enclosed memorandum prepared by Mr. T. P. O'Connor and Mr. Hazleton,[1] the representatives of the Irish Nationalist Party in this country. This, you perceive, gives a new point of view to the publication of information in regard to the Sinn Fein conspiracy in this country. In view of the source I think that we should give careful consideration to the suggestions made.

Senator Phelan was desirous that somebody from this Department should see and talk with the authors. I can see no particular harm in doing so, provided I can select a man sufficiently discreet. Will you be good enough to give me your opinion at your earliest convenience?   Faithfully yours,   Robert Lansing.

TLS (SDR, RG 59, 841D.00/9A, DNA).
[1] Richard Hazleton, Nationalist M.P. from North Galway.

E N C L O S U R E

Handed me by Senator Phelan
as prepared by T. P. O'Connor
and Hazleton—May 29/18/RL.

MEMORANDUM ON THE PRO-GERMAN CONSPIRACY CHARGE
AGAINST SINN FEIN IN IRELAND AND AMERICA.

1. The British Government has recently issued through the Press Bureau, an official statement setting forth part of the evidence on which it relies for its charges that the Sinn Fein leaders in Ireland have been guilty of treasonable conspiracy with Germany, as a result of which more than one hundred leading Sinn Feiners have been arrested and interned in England. At the same time the whole American press has announced that some of the evidence on which the British Government has acted was supplied by the American authorities. It is understood that this is correct, but that the State Department does not wish officially to confirm or deny the report.

2. Clear and convincing evidence against Sinn Feiners of a recent

pro-German conspiracy would react strongly against their party both in Ireland and the United States. While Sinn Fein has gathered very great strength in Ireland, the bulk of its following is not at all pro-German and would resent intrigues with Germany, especially since America entered the war. It would, therefore, be disastrous to the Sinn Fein movement if Sinn Fein leaders could be shown to be guilty of such action, on evidence which was above question in the eyes of fair-mended [minded] men.

3. On the other hand, failure to produce convincing evidence of plotting with Germany in any serious way, must bring Sinn Fein enormously increased strength both in Ireland and America. Indeed, it may well be that such failure would in Ireland be the determining factor in placing the Sinn Fein party in a position of supremacy in Irish politics.

4. Such evidence as has been produced in the statement of the British Press Bureau has utterly failed to convince Ireland of the reality of the charges made against Sinn Fein. The London Correspondent of the "New York World" in a despatch published in that paper on Tuesday, May 28th, says:

"Even the Unionists and the most violent of the anti-Sinn Fein Nationalists simply laugh at the Government's evidence. * * * Nothing but public proof need be expected to have the slightest effect upon Irish opinion * * * * I discussed with men in highly responsible positions the probable effect of such a document* * * * These men were Unionists and Government officials. They declared without exception that the effect must be injurious, that the Separatist movement would be enormously strengthened, and the last hope of putting Constitutionalism on its legs would disappear. The same opinions held in Dublin. 'We are all Sinn Feiners now' is the remark you hear everywhere."

5. If the American authorities can do anything to avert what must prove a serious disaster, this is surely the time. A despatch from Washington in the "New York Times" on Sunday the 26th of May, says:

"More evidence than that disclosed in the British Press Bureau's charges of the close connection between the Irish Sinn Fein and German influence is in the hands of the British and American Governments, according to an official statement made here today."

While this report speaks of "an official statement" it fails to state by whom the official statement was made. The situation is in urgent need of being cleared up. If valuable time is allowed to pass, the effect of damaging disclosures, if the materials for such are in the hands of the authorities, will be considerably lessened. If the American authorities have really important evidence in their possession its immediate production would do more than anything else to influence public opinion in Ireland, for the charge of a "frame-up" which is believed in Ireland against the British authorities would not be entertained against the American authorities. Either too little or too much has been said already on behalf of the American authorities—too little if important evidence of German-Irish plotting of a serious nature is in their possession, and too much if no such important evidence exists. As it now stands, the whole affair cannot fail to produce the most unfortunate results in Ireland, with consequent reaction on America itself. The arm of the Constitutional party in Ireland is being paralysed and that is not a situation which the American authorities can intend or desire. But it is not too much to say that for them to leave the matter in its present wholly unsatisfactory position has that effect. It is, therefore, respectfully urged that, even if it be impossible to publish the evidence gathered in America—which it is hoped is not the case—a general statement of the nature and importance of the evidence should be made with as little delay as possible, so that Irish opinion should be able to form some judgment of the issue at least so far as the American end of it is concerned. If the evidence thus disclosed is not conclusive the British, and not the American Government, must bear the onus of further proof.

T MS (SDR, RG 59, 841D.00/9A, DNA).

From Edward Prentiss Costigan[1]

Dear Mr. President: Washington May 29, 1918.

May I say to you in all frankness and earnestness that I am one of many who were distressed this morning to learn that the criminal charge in New York against Eastman, Reed and others is to be pressed to trial in June? There is nothing of fact or persuasion which I may add to what you already know and feel on the subject, but I ought perhaps to say that I find myself unable to understand the backward-looking attitude of certain prosecutors in an hour when forward-facing unity is increasingly desirable.

Contrasting past and present viewpoints, I remember less than two years ago one of the strongest appeals made on your behalf in the Middle West by Progressives, who then and continually since have supported your administration, was summed up in the sentence: "President Wilson believes peace honorable." Some men and women have bridged the long distance between then and now easily and without friction. Others according to their differences of en-

dowment and development have arrived, in doubting Thomas fashion, by halting steps and through criticism. Personally, I have no
question that Eastman, Reed and the rest are in accord with the
present overwhelming national mind and purpose, and, as one who
remembers seeing many a fine spirit tinged with cynicism by certain pre-war conditions, now generally condemned as un-ideal, I
hope something may be done by you to solve with wisdom the
problem presented by so understandable an evolutionary process.

I trouble you with reluctance, and trust you will not feel called
on to reply.

Believe me, as always, with deep respect,

Very sincerely,   E. P. Costigan

TLS (WP, DLC).
¹ Lawyer of Denver, founding member of the Progressive party in Colorado, and its
candidate for governor in 1912 and 1914. Costigan had long been active in such progressive causes as municipal, civil-service, and electoral reforms and had represented
the United Mine Workers during the congressional investigation of the Colorado coal
strike in 1914. Wilson had appointed him to the Tariff Commission in 1917.

From Anna Howard Shaw, with Enclosure

My dear Mr. President: Washington May 29/1918

May I submit to you the enclosed resolution which was passed
by the State representatives of the Woman's Committee of the Council
of National Defense, in convention assembled, at Washington, May
13-14-15? The resolution was also endorsed by the Woman's Committee in executive session, Thursday, May 23.

Believe me, my dear Mr. President,

Faithfully   Anna Howard Shaw

TLS (WP, DLC).

E N C L O S U R E

Washington
May 13-14-15/1918

WHEREAS, we believe that we can fulfil our obligations as women
citizens of the United States to do our utmost to win the war only
if we are given the opportunity to serve in such direct coöperation
with the Government as has made possible the magnificent war
work of British women; Therefore, Be It

RESOLVED that we respectfully urge upon the President of the
United States the immediate consideration of the following requests:

(1) That on all Government boards and commissions controlling

the work of women or affecting their interests, one (or more) properly qualified woman shall be associated with the central direction and administration in positions of authority and responsibility.

(2) That whenever great bodies of women are employed in war work, the conditions under which they work and live shall be under the immediate supervision and control of women officials with adequate authority.

(3) That in order to secure the highest efficiency at the present time we respectfully urge that women be appointed to the following positions:

a) Assistant Federal Food Administrator

b) Assistant Director of Housing, who shall deal with the housing of women workers.

T MS (WP, DLC).

From Henry Pomeroy Davison

My dear Mr. President: Washington, D. C. May 29th, 1918.

I venture to enclose herewith a copy of a statement I am giving to the press for publication Friday morning.[1] I am sure you will be gratified, as I have been, at the extraordinary response to our appeal for funds.

Will you allow me to say that I am more than ever conscious of the very great value of the way in which you, yourself, have supported the work of the Red Cross by word and act ever since the day of your appointment of the War Council? I have always said that I never thank anybody for what they do for the Red Cross (I only congratulate them), but I can thank you personally, Mr. President, for the way in which you have made it easier for me personally to perform the very great responsibility to which you called me, and this I do again from the bottom of my heart.

I think you will also be interested to see a copy of the cablegram I have sent to our commissions in France, England and Italy,[2] which will give you some idea of the spirit in which all of us are accepting the new responsibility created by the magnitude of the people's faith and expectation.

With high regard, I am, Mr. President,

Very respectfully yours,   H. P. Davison

TLS (WP, DLC).

[1] "Copy of Statement to Public by Mr. Davison," CC MS (WP, DLC). It announced the success of the recent second American Red Cross "War Fund" drive, which so far had brought in more than $166,000,000 in contributions.

[2] H. P. Davison to American Red Cross commissions in England, France, and Italy, May 28, 1918, TC telegram (WP, DLC).

Tasker Howard Bliss to Robert Lansing and
Newton Diehl Baker

Versailles. May 29th [1918].

Number 119 Secret Urgent.

For Secretary of State and Secretary of War.

Paragraph 1. Sixth session of Supreme War Council will be held at 3 pm Saturday June first.

Paragraph 2. As I will probably be asked the attitude of my government on subjects discussed at last session of Supreme War Council I request that I be informed if practicable before the hour set for next meeting what is the action of the President on resolutions reported in paragraphs 2, 4, 5, 7 and 8 of my cable number 103.[1]

Paragraph 3. I also request information whether United States accepts joint notes numbers 26, 27 and 28 of military representatives reported in my number 114.[2]

Paragraph 4. At their meeting yesterday the military representatives passed joint note number 29. After reviewing the evidence that the central Empires are actually suffering from a need of textile fabrics, thread and sewing silk and after noting the fact that only small quantities can be obtained otherwise than through neutral countries, especially Switzerland, this note concludes with the following statement: "Under these circumstances the military representatives are of opinion that the situation as disclosed above should be brought to the notice of the Supreme War Council in order that the governments may have the question studied by their ministers of *blockade*, or other appropriate agencies, and such action taken as may be opportune to restricting as speedily as possible, consistent with our policy, the supply of textile products to the central Empires from neutral sources" full text by mail.

Paragraph 5. For the Chief of Staff. British military representative requested from his war office certain information called for in your telegram No. 55.[3] Today he informs me that the army council in London cannot grant this request for the reason that "That at the specific request of the American Government an arrangement has been made by which all information required by the British and American war offices should be supplied solely through their respective military attaches. The army council regret that they do not feel themselves at liberty to depart from this agreement." My answer to your number 55 will contain best information about British I can obtain so that you may compare it with that which you obtain from military attache in London. French daily promise information desired but have not yet got it. Believe there is decided indisposition to make some of it known.

Paragraph 6. Not for publication. Information from Headquarters General Foch to noon today shows line substantially as follows: Betheny, Neuvillette, Branscourt, Serzy-et-Prin, south of Arcis-le-Ponsart, Longeville, Dole, Cuiry-Housse, Violaine, Vauxrot, east of Juvigny, Tours-des-Loups, Crecy-au-Mont. Possession of towns mentioned doubtful.   Bliss.

TC telegram (WDR, RG 407, World War I Cablegrams, DNA).
¹ T. H. Bliss to RL *et al.*, May 3, 1918, Vol. 47.
² Joint Note 26, dated May 19, 1918, concerned the advisability of reducing the number of horses on the western front, in order to lessen the need for oats. The text is "Supreme War Council, . . . JOINT NOTE No. 26," T MS (WDR, RG 120, Records of the American Section of the Supreme War Council, 1917-1919, No. 331-1, DNA). T. H. Bliss to P. C. March, No. 114, May 22, 1918 (WDR, RG 407, World War I Cablegrams, DNA), prints the text of Joint Note 27. It concerned the possibility of a German attack against Holland and suggested consultations with the Dutch government about measures of common defense. Bliss' No. 114 also summarized Joint Note 28, which recommended that the French Minister of Public Works serve as ex officio president of the Inter-Allied Transportation Council at all meetings which he might attend.
³ P. C. March to T. H. Bliss, No. 55, May 15, 1918, TC telegram (WDR, RG 407, World War I Cablegrams, DNA). This telegram requested detailed information about French, British, Belgian, Portuguese, American, Italian, and German fighting strength on the western front: artillery strength, machine guns, number of airplanes, etc.

Cary Travers Grayson to the Norman Foster Company

My dear Sirs: The White House 29 May, 1918

The President requests me, as his physician, to make a report to you, in connection with the accident policy he holds with your agency, of the burn caused his left hand on April nineteenth, last.

I will say that the burn was one of the third degree, requiring heavy bandages over all of the hand except the thumb for a period of three weeks; and that the hand could be put to no practical use for that time, namely, three weeks. Obviously, the burn did not completely disable the President in the performance of his duties at any time at all. He was partially disabled for the period named above.   Very truly yours,   Cary T. Grayson

TLS (received from Henry B. Cox).

A Translation of a Telegram from Jean Jules Jusserand to Stéphen Jean Marie Pichon

Washington, undated
received May 29, 1918.

Nos. 658-659. The English Ambassador has seen the President again about the Japan-Siberia question, has renewed his entreaties and based his arguments on the disturbing news now reaching us, but, from what he told me, all this was to no avail. Repeating the same objections, without countering our position with any definite plan of his own, Mr. Wilson has shown himself less disposed than ever to come over to our views. He has spoken of letting events take their course, manifesting even greater passivity than in his last conversation with me, in which, when asked what he foresaw in the future, he replied: the formation in Siberia of the kind of government which our agents could help to stand on its own feet.

It appears impossible, however, that he will not try something to justify the assurances of the fullest goodwill that he has recently given to Russia. And yet, if he has really settled on some plan, he has told my English colleague nothing to indicate its nature.

Perhaps he will embrace the ideas of Mr. Wright, Counselor of the American Embassy in Petrograd, recently returned from his post through Siberia and now in the Department of State. This diplomat recently revealed to me that nothing is closer to the hearts of the Siberians than the restoration of their railroad in good order. The mission of American engineers now halted at Harbin, which did a very useful job in Manchuria, could perhaps render them this service, under the cover of which foreign troops, presenting themselves more as police than as military, would (Mr. Wright thinks) be favorably received and could advance rapidly toward the Urals.

Lord Reading and I miss no opportunity to bring up again the urgent need for a decision, not only because of the German danger but also because of the shortness of the good weather in Siberia and Russia.

The differences in views of our governments about the Bolsheviks remain a very serious obstacle.

Mr. Masaryk, who has not yet seen the President, has published a new interview[1] in which he still insists on the necessity of working with the Bolsheviks, who, he claims, are "more and more anti-German." All speak against a military intervention and recommend industrial and economic aid.   Jusserand

T telegram (Campagne contre l'Allemagne, 1914-1918, 4 N 46, Conseil Supérieur de Guerre, Intervention en Sibérie, 1918-1919, FMD-Ar).
[1] In an interview published in the New York Times on May 27, 1918, Masaryk had

warned the Allies against an intervention in Russia, which, he claimed, would present insurmountable logistical problems. The Allies could best aid Russia by assisting the Russian government to restore the administrative and economic life of the country through the rebuilding of railroads, communications services, and mines and factories. The dispatch of American and Allied engineers, executives, and businessmen, Masaryk added, would also be of great value in offsetting the pernicious propaganda which the Germans were spreading throughout Russia. Masaryk claimed that the Bolsheviks were growing increasingly anti-German, and he strongly urged the Allies to cooperate with the Soviet government.

From Felexiana Shepherd Baker Woodrow

My dear Tommy: Columbia, S. C., May 30, 1918.

Forgive me for writing you a purely personal note when your heart and thoughts are so filled with matters of World-wide importance.

I thought you might be interested in knowing that Lottie's[1] boy Woodrow,[2] has just graduated with "highest honors" at Davidson College. He was also leader of the Orchestra, Manager of the Foot-Ball Team, and Champion Golf player.

In addition to this, he has passed the mental and physical examinations necessary, and has been appointed by Senator Tillman to West Point, where he is ordered to report June 14. In my Study window is a "Service Flag" with six Stars representing my six Grandsons who are trying to serve our Country.

So you see we are doing what we can to help you "Win the War."

Lottie's other boy, Washington,[3] is also graduating at "Porter Military Academy" in Charleston with "highest honors."

I am constantly thinking of you and praying that God will guide you, and protect you, and bless you, in your wonderful work for Him and for humanity.

With love to your dear Wife,

Yours most affectionately,   "Aunt Felie."

ALS (WP, DLC).
[1] Her daughter, Mary Charlotte Woodrow (Mrs. Melton) Clark.
[2] James Woodrow Clark.
[3] Washington Augustus Clark.

Sir William Wiseman to Sir Eric Drummond

[New York] 30th May, 1918.

No. 97. The President sent for me yesterday, and I had an hour's conversation with him. He asked me to tell him very frankly my views on the situation in Europe.

Starting with the question of JAPANESE intervention, he asked what was the genesis of the movement. I told him the idea was two-fold: First of all, to recreate a RUSSIAN front, and, secondly, to help the RUSSIAN people. I said that it was generally agreed among military experts that if an Eastern Front could be recreated it would have a decisive effect and might end the war in a few months in our favor. On the other hand, so long as the Germans could withdraw all their troops from Russia, there was a grave danger that we might be overwhelmed by superior numbers on the Western front. He said that he entirely agreed with everything I said, but no military man with whom he had talked had been able to convince him that there was any practical scheme which would recreate a Russian front. He remarked that he would go as far as intervening against the wishes of the Russian people—knowing that it was eventually for their good—providing he thought the scheme had any practical chance of success. The schemes put forward, however, were in his opinion impracticable, and would have the opposite effect to that desired. The Japanese themselves said they could not get any further than OMSK and were very doubtful if they could get as far as that. They were, he thought, anxious enough to have an invitation from us so that they might occupy the maritime provinces, but had no intention of engaging on a vast military enterprise sufficient to reach even the Ural Mountains.

If we could have put a large British-American force into Vladivostock, and advanced along the Siberian railroad, we might, he thought, have rallied the Russian people to assist in defence of their country. But if we relied mainly on Japanese military assistance we should rally the Russians against us, excepting for a small reactionary body who would join anybody to destroy the Bolsheviki. I remarked that in any case it was not possible to make the situation worse than it was now. He said that that was where he entirely disagreed. We could make it much worse by putting the Germans in a position where they could organize Russia in a national movement against Japan. If that was done he would not be surprised to see Russian soldiers fighting with the Germans on the Western Front. "Then," I said, "are we to do nothing at all." "No," he said, "we must watch the situation carefully and sympathetically, and be ready to move whenever the right time arrived."

His own idea was to send a Civil commission of British, French, and American[s], to Russia to help organize the railroads and food supplies, and, since currency is worthless, organize a system of barter. He would send such missions to Vladivostock and Murmansk. Of course, it would take a long time before any results could be expected from such a movement. If in the meantime we were invited to intervene by any responsible and representative body, we ought to do so. An oral or secret arrangement with TROTSKY would be no good since he would repudiate it. He realized that U. S. Government held the key to the situation in that Japanese Government would not intervene without their sanction; but it would be odious for him to use such power except the best interests of the common cause demanded it.

Regarding American infantry: He asked me to tell him what had happened. He thought the discussion somewhat academic as BAKER assured him that they were sending all the infantry and machine-gunners who were ready to go as quickly as possible. If PERSHING really stood in the way, he would be ordered to stand out of the way, but he thought that he was only asserting a principle which he was not putting into practice. For his part he stood on no ceremony regarding the use of American troops—they were to be used in any way that was necessary regardless if need be of national sentiment. It would, of course, distress him to have to override his Commander-in-Chief because he felt he ought to be loyal to him, and he did not like overriding a man so far from home and possibly only understanding part of his case. He could not see the advantage at present of a civilian representative. PERSHING had full authority, and the part America was playing in Europe was purely that of rendering military assistance. He hoped the question of the new agreement regarding American infantry would not be raised at the next Supreme War Council because (he repeated) they could not in any event send more than they were sending, and it was no good discussing questions of principle with PERSHING when in practice you could not get anything better than you were getting now. "In any event," he said, "why limit your arrangement to June, July, and August. It is possible you may need American infantry for several months after that. Why not leave the time indefinite until the emergency is passed?"

I took the opportunity of impressing upon the President once more the problem of the American higher command and staff. "It was quite impossible," I said, "that PERSHING could train his General Staff behind the line, and the greatest disaster might befall the American army if they went into battle with inexperienced leaders and staff." He agreed entirely, and hoped some means could be found which would remedy this without discouraging the keenness or hurt the pride of the American commanders.

AUSTRIA: He referred to the AUSTRIAN peace overtures, and said it was a thousand pities that CLEMENCEAU had acted as he did.[1] He had no great sympathy for the Emperor Karl, but thought he had been sincerely looking for a means of breaking away from Germany, and now CLEMENCEAU'S action had fixed them to Germany and rivetted them there permanently; and all this, he said, merely to score a personal triumph. Now we had no chance of making a separate peace with Austria, and must look to the other way—the way which he disliked most intensely—of setting the AUSTRIAN people against their own Government by plots and intrigues. We were not good at that work, and generally made a failure of it, but he saw no other way. He intended to support the Czechs, Poles, and Jugo-Slavs.

IRELAND: He hoped the Government would not force Conscription without Home Rule. I tried to explain that these were two entirely different problems. He said that he could well understand that himself—the mass of the people in America would not understand it. It would not have been wise for U. S. Government to make the Sein Fein revelations as we had asked them to. It would have been regarded here as too obviously helping the British Government in a political situation: the people would have resented it. He was afraid the way the revelations had appeared in the press here had not caused a particularly good impression. He deeply regretted the situation and had no sympathy whatever for Irishmen either here or at home who sought German aid.

I asked him his opinion as to the war generally. He said he hoped and believed the Allies would be able to hold back the German onslaught during the summer. That the Americans must speed-up in every way the creation of a great American army, so that in time we could beat the Germans and force them to accept a peace we thought right. He was, he said, telling everyone he came in contact with that we could hope for no satisfactory compromise with the present rulers of Germany.

Finally, I urged again that the American representation in Europe was unsatisfactory; that PERSHING had far more to do than should fall to the lot of a Commander-in-Chief; and urged him to send more fully empowered representatives to assist the military. He merely remarked that he realised the difficulties of the situation, and was even now considering what could be done to remedy it.

T telegram (W. Wiseman Papers, CtY).
    ¹ About this, the so-called Sixtus affair, see RL to WW, May 10, 1918 (first letter of that date), n. 1, Vol. 47.

From Robert Lansing, with Enclosure

My dear Mr. President: Washington May 31, 1918.

Lord Reading handed me on Wednesday the enclosed paraphrase of a telegram from Mr. Balfour, dated the 28th, relative to our sending troops to Murmansk.

As this is a military question, as well as a question of policy, I am sending it to you without comment because if physical impossibilities exist there seems to me little object in passing on the policy of such a step.   Faithfully yours,   Robert Lansing

TLS (SDR, RG 59, 861.00/1907½, DNA).

E N C L O S U R E

Handed to me by Lord Reading
May 29/18 RL.

PARAPHRASE OF A TELEGRAM FROM MR. BALFOUR
TO LORD READING.
May 28, 1918.

We understand from your reports that intervention at Archangel and Murmansk is regarded by the United States as a different question from that of intervention in the Far East.

I should be much obliged if you would urgently impress upon the United States Government and upon the President the following considered opinion of our Military and Naval authorities on this question.

On the Murmansk coast assistance from America is badly required and is, in fact, essential. Every day the position of Murmansk is more seriously endangered and, as the United States Government will of course be aware, it is of vital importance to us to retain Murmansk, if we desire to retain any possibility at all of entering Russia.

This danger has become so extreme that we are sending to Murmansk such small marine and military forces as we are able to spare during the present crisis in France. These forces will, however, clearly not be enough to resist the further efforts which the enemy are certain to put forward on this coast. The despatch of additional French or British reinforcements is impossible and it is therefore essential that America should help by sending a brigade, to which a few guns should be added. It is not necessary that the troops sent should be completely trained, as we anticipate that military operations in this region will only be of an irregular character.

It is possible that we may be asked why British troops are not sent. The reason is that Great Britain is now completely denuded of troops, and it is not feasible to take trained troops, even in small numbers, from France where they are being used more or less as cadres for the training of the American forces now reaching the West front. There is a further consideration which is worthy of careful consideration by the President. Great use has been made already of the divergence of view among the Allied countries with regard to the Russian situation, and for this reason it is of great importance that the United States should show their agreement with us on this matter by taking part in the steps adopted for preventing the closing of the only remaining door through which assistance can be given to Russia in her hour of need.

BRITISH EMBASSY
WASHINGTON.
May 29th, 1918.

T MS (SDR, RG 59, 861.00/1907½, DNA).

To Newton Diehl Baker

My dear Baker: The White House 31 May, 1918

The enclosed is a serious and delicate matter.[1] I should very much like to know from you how you think we can handle it.

Faithfully yours,   Woodrow Wilson

TLS (N. D. Baker Papers, DLC).
[1] Anna H. Shaw to WW, May 28, 1918, TLS (WP, DLC), enclosing Annie Eliza Pidgeon (Mrs. John W.) Searing to Anna H. Shaw, May 25, 1918, TCL (WP, DLC). Mrs. Searing, a writer, lecturer, and advocate of woman suffrage from Kingston, N. Y., wrote that her application as a director of one of the so-called hostess houses, which the Y.W.C.A. was establishing in cooperation with the Commission on Training Camp Activities at all army and navy camps, had been rejected on the ground that she was a Unitarian. At a recent interview at the national headquarters of the Y.W.C.A., she had been told categorically that only women who were members of an evangelical church would be accepted, and that Catholics, Jews, and Unitarians were specifically excluded. Mrs. Searing urged Dr. Shaw to bring the matter to Wilson's attention and to ask him to use his influence to nullify this policy of "terrible neglect and disregard" of a large number of American women who were willing to contribute their share to the war effort.
  In forwarding Mrs. Searing's letter, Dr. Shaw informed Wilson that, in her capacity as "chairman" of the Woman's Committee of the Council of National Defense, she had received many similar protests and appeals. She told Wilson that, in her opinion, the Y.W.C.A., which performed its work in the training camps under an agency of the federal government, would have to change its discriminatory policy, since it clearly violated the principle of religious liberty. She asked Wilson for advice as to the kind of answer which she should give to the many complaints and requested a message from Wilson which she could convey to inquiring women throughout the country.

To Edward Prentiss Costigan

My dear Mr. Costigan: [The White House] 31 May, 1918

You may be sure that I sympathize with the spirit of your letter of May twenty-ninth about Eastman, Reed and others, and I am going to look into the matter again.

In haste, which I am sure you will pardon,

Sincerely yours,   Woodrow Wilson

TLS (Letterpress Books, WP, DLC).

To Thomas Watt Gregory

My dear Gregory: [The White House] 31 May, 1918

This is only one of a number of earnest letters of the same sort and on the same subject which I have received, and I would be very much obliged to you if you would advise me whether you think we are in fact pursuing the best and wisest course in these prosecutions.

Cordially and faithfully yours, Woodrow Wilson

TLS (Letterpress Books, WP, DLC).

To Leo Stanton Rowe[1]

My dear Mr. Rowe: [The White House] 31 May, 1918

I always hesitate and am very much disinclined to differ from Mr. Hoover, but in this matter which you submit to me I do not find myself able to agree that it is wise to make the amended regulation which he suggests with regard to the brewers.[2] I realize that a hardship is suffered, but I do not think it would be wise to cure the hardship in that way. It would undoubtedly lead to the development of other and more serious aspects of the subject.

Cordially and sincerely yours, Woodrow Wilson

TLS (Letterpress Books, WP, DLC).
  [1] Acting Secretary of the Treasury.
  [2] L. S. Rowe to WW, May 28, 1918, TLS (WP, DLC). Rowe asked for Wilson's decision on an amendment proposed by Hoover to the existing regulations governing the use of grain in the manufacture of beer. The regulations, which had been issued on February 5, 1918, provided, among other things, that the amount of grain used by a brewery in 1918 was not to exceed 70 per cent of the amount used in 1917, and that the allotment for 1918 had to be used in the same breweries which had been operated during the previous year. Hoover's proposed amendment, which he had prepared in response to appeals from brewing companies in states which had recently passed prohibition laws, would have permitted brewers to transfer their grain rights from "dry" to "wet" states and to manufacture there that portion of beer which had previously been sold outside the state which had now voted "dry." In his detailed analysis of the proposal, Rowe pointed out that a liberalization of the grain regulations would weaken their intended effect on the conservation of food, and he argued strongly against the adoption of Hoover's amendment.

To Anna Howard Shaw

My dear Doctor Shaw: [The White House] 31 May, 1918

I realize the importance and the many bearings of the question raised by the letter of Mrs. Searing which you have been kind enough to send me, and I am going to look into the matter at once. Thank you for calling my attention to it.

Cordially and sincerely yours, Woodrow Wilson

TLS (Letterpress Books, WP, DLC).

From George Davis Herron

Dear Mr. President: Geneva Switzerland May 31, 1918.

It is in obedience to the urgence, not only of authoritative individuals, but of whole peoples whom these individuals truly represent, that I take the liberty of addressing you on the subject of the immediate establishment of the Society of Nations. Time after time, during the past quarter of a year, good and representative Europeans have urged me to cross the Atlantic and personally present to you their plea. I could wish that yourself, with your singular political sensibilities, could for a brief time be in the midst of these peoples. You would quickly understand, and no plea would be needed.

Not the lesser peoples alone are looking to you to speak soon the summoning word. For this word our greater Allies are even more anxiously waiting. I do not mean their governments; for there is a daily-widening mental cleavage between European governments and peoples. It is by faith in what America will do,—it is above all by faith in what you will do,—and not by faith in governors and diplomats that the nations are enduring the unimaginable strain and horror of this hour. When I tell you that it is solely the faith of the peoples in you, in the word they are waiting for you to speak, that for now these many weeks has saved the Continent of Europe from a condition akin to that of Russia, think not there is exaggeration or thought of personal compliment in what I say. I am telling you the truth as radically, as nakedly, as mortal words can be made to tell it. If anything is true, this is true—is sternly and divinely true: that this Continent would now be in a state of dissolution were it not for the hope of the peoples in you—in your championship of their liberties; in your shepherdship of the nationalities; in your commanding and creative call. The peoples are trusting you to speak the word that shall gather them all into one fold, that shall form them into a federate world.

But the times grow perilous and imperative. The German penetration, its elusive and occult evil power,—more to be dreaded by far than the triumph of German arms,—this increases apace, despite all you may hear to the contrary; and the peoples grow evermore clamorous for you to formulate the purpose and the faith whereby they may endure the months if not years of sacrifice and sorrow now so terribly before them.

Let me give you a single instance of the insistence upon this necessity. Among the best and most trusted of Frenchmen is Professor Edgard Milhaud, of both the University of Geneva and the University of Paris. He is the author of different vital books on political and social problems; but more especially is his book, "La

Société des Nations,"[1] a classic on the subject. He has been intrusted with important special missions by the French Government,
and fulfills certain intimate official duties. No man more thoroughly
understands the French people than Professor Milhaud, to whom
France is not only a country but a religion.

Professor Milhaud came, some weeks ago, urging upon me the
duty of seeking an audience with you to present the need,—the
saving necessity indeed,—of your immediate initiation of the Society of Nations. He declared that no matter what answer you may
have been led to expect, once the call were issued the whole French
people would instantly respond: no government would dare to resist
for a day. In order to make his plea more convincing, he recently
undertook a questioning tour among the French people, including
the French Government and the Army Headquarters. He spoke at
length with Monsieur Clémenceau, not about the Society of Nations, but with the result that he is convinced that it is not impossible that Clémenceau would now respond to your invitation. Among
the representatives of the French democracy, he heard not one
dissenting voice: there was unanimous and urgent assent to his
proposition. He consulted such men as Monsieur Brizon,[2] Minister
Albert Thomas (probably the ablest representative of the French
democracy)[3] and many others. While there are different opinions
as to method and detail, there is no difference as to the immediacy
of the great need.

As a result, Professor Milhaud has just returned to me with a
renewed entreaty that I appeal to you to speak now the initial word.
Two months from now, he avows, may be too late. The peoples are
everywhere asking, he says,—and so say all the good and wise men
who have come to me upon this errand,—that the peoples wish to
know if you literally mean to establish the Society of Nations. If
you do, send forth the summons now, they cry. With your spoken
word before them as their pledge, as their uttered faith, as their
"substance of the things hoped for," they are ready to endure the
immeasurable tortures and griefs that may await them, that most
probably do await them. They do not greatly trust either the wisdom
or the integrity of their governments and governors: *they do trust
you: they do trust America.* Already, you have prepared your own
way. Already, your messages, the hope of the principles they ex-
pound, have become the very texture of the political mentality of
European peoples. If you will make this a war not only against the

---

[1] Edgard Milhaud, *La Société des Nations* (Paris, 1917). A copy of this book is in the
Wilson Library, DLC.
[2] Pierre Brizon, French Socialist deputy.
[3] Leader of the Socialist party and former Minister of Munitions.

German dominion,—against the universal spiritual death that must issue from such dominion,—but a war for the establishment of the Society of Nations, a war for the creation of a new earth, then they are with you to the death. They will follow you as never mortal man was followed; nor will rulers or diplomats or financiers dare say them nay.

Not in the whole history of mankind, dear Mr. President, has the world turned to one man as it now turns to you. It is the supreme opportunity of mankind that stretches to you its appealing hands. So far as I can see,—so far as the infinitely wiser and better men than myself who have spoken to me can see,—no hand but yours can open the door of this unprecedented and predestinative opportunity.

Will you open it? If you will, I believe the whole race of man will pass through that door, no matter what the travail and the tragedy of the passing, and that therethrough the race will enter upon a world of such fellowship and felicity, such new and nobler progress, as now seems incredible and Utopian.

I first spoke of France; but you will find the same response in England. The new Labor Party, as it is now organized, includes the best intellectual life of England, and the whole of the real English democracy. Such men as Professors Gilbert Murray[4] and John G. Hobson[5] (the greatest living political economist) are among its members. England is absolutely in the hands of this party. The British ruling-class exists only by the Labor Party's sufferance. Completely organized and splendidly poised, it only bides its time, concentrating its first energies upon the war against the monstrous German. The moment the war is ended, this party will take possession of England; and the British Empire will then become a wondrous and free confederation of nations. If you call for the Society of Nations today, this party and its leaders,—the best leaders that England has had for generations,—will be altogether with you.

Italy, too, will respond. Day before yesterday, I put the question to Marquis Paulucci,[6] the Italian Minister here. "Would Italy give good answer," I asked, "and would Baron Sonnino now respond favorably, if President Wilson should call for the Society of Nations?" His reply was instantly and earnestly in the affirmative.

The Serbians, the Czechs, the Poles, the Lettonians, and all the weaker peoples Germany has practically annexed,—all the uprising nationalities of the doomed and dissolving Hapsburg Empire,—

[4] George Gilbert Aimé Murray, Regius Professor of Greek at Oxford University.
[5] That is, John Atkinson Hobson, prolific writer and lecturer on economics, imperialism, and the social sciences. He did not hold an academic position.
[6] Marquis Raniero Paulucci di Calboli, Minister of Italy to Switzerland.

would take your summons as their pledge of deliverance: they would hence proceed with such joyous assurance as would make their respective self-affirmations a power working vastly with the Allies for the overthrow of Germanism. The Czechs and Yougo-Slavs are already each a nearly-born nation, with their potential governments already formed and drilling. These wait only for your word. Once that is spoken, they will rise, and rise with noble effectiveness, against the seemingly triumphal German march.

Your summons would prove shattering to the German power itself. I have inquired of many Germans as to the effect of a call from you for the establishment of the Great Society. Such men as Professor Foerster and Jaffé[7] of Munich; such as Herr Dr. Muehlon, the former Director-General of the Krupp works, whose exposures of German diplomacy have recently filled the world with amazement;[8]

---

[7] Edgar Jaffé, Professor of Economics at the Commercial College of Munich.

[8] In August 1917, Muehlon had drawn up a memorandum about two conversations which he had had in July 1914 with Karl Theodor Helfferich, then the Director of the Deutsche Bank. According to Muehlon, Helfferich had told him that "the Austrians" had been in Berlin in early July 1914, and that William II had promised them Germany's full support in their policy toward Serbia. The Emperor had reportedly declared that, in case of a Russian mobilization, Germany, too, would mobilize and immediately declare war against Russia.

Muehlon had intended his memorandum, entitled "The Viennese Ultimatum to Serbia," solely for the use of members of the Reichstag, in order to help them evaluate recent Allied charges of a secret Austro-German conference in which the decision for war had been made. However, in late 1917, copies of the memorandum began to appear in pamphlet form all over Germany. On March 16, 1918, the German government finally reacted officially to the matter. In a debate in the Main Committee of the Reichstag, Vice-Chancellor von Payer denied the accuracy of Muehlon's disclosure and branded the author as a neurasthenic and as mentally unstable. Muehlon's memorandum was published in the *Berliner Tageblatt* on March 21, 1918. On the following day, a strongly worded denial appeared in the semiofficial Berlin *Norddeutsche Allgemeine Zeitung*.

Muehlon reacted to these denunciations by publishing a letter which he had written to Bethmann Hollweg in May 1917. Muehlon had told the Chancellor that he could no longer support the present German government, since its recent policy had clearly shown that it was not interested in a genuine peace. The letter was first published in a French translation in *L'Humanité* of Paris on March 31, 1918, and appeared in German in the Bern *Freie Zeitung* on May 4, 1918. In addition, Muehlon published two more articles in the Swiss press: "Toward the Truth," Zurich *Wissen und Leben*, May 1, 1918, and "Germany and Belgium," Bern *Freie Zeitung*, May 4, 1918. The first article was a strong rejoinder to the denials of the facts of his memorandum by the *Norddeutsche Allgemeine Zeitung*, the second a vigorous defense of Belgium against charges by the German government that Belgium had failed to remain neutral before the war.

Finally, Muehlon decided to publish the diary which he had kept during the first months of the war and which repeated in greater detail many of the points raised in his memorandum and his articles. Muehlon's diary was published in May 1918 as *Die Verheerung Europas: Aufzeichnungen aus den ersten Kriegsmonaten* (Zurich, 1918) and was translated as *Dr. Muehlon's Diary* (London, New York, Toronto, and Melbourne, 1918) and *The Vandal of Europe* (New York and London, 1918).

Muehlon's disclosures were widely circulated by the Allies and were reprinted, for example, in German and English as "Memoranda and Letters of Dr. Muehlon," trans. Munroe Smith, in *The Disclosures from Germany* (New York, 1918), pp. 183-223. For a detailed discussion of the "Muehlon affair," see Wolfgang Benz, "Der 'Fall Muehlon'; Bürgerliche Opposition im Obrigkeitsstaat während des Ersten Weltkriegs," *Vierteljahrshefte für Zeitgeschichte*, XVIII (Oct. 1970), 343-65. See also the *New York Times*, April 21 and 30, 1918. For more information about Muehlon and his earlier contacts with Herron, see H. R. Wilson to RL, Feb. 5, 1918, Vol. 46.

such as Herr Hausmann, the acting Vice-Chancellor, and Count Montgelas, who was formerly one of the ablest German commanders;—these are unanimous in their affirmation that your initiation of the Society of Nations would be the worst blow Germany could receive, and that the delayed formation of this Society has been the greatest mistake of the Allies since the beginning of the war, or especially since America's entrance thereupon.

Each of these authoritative men is of the opinion that even now such initiative on your part would do more to overthrow the power of the Prussian military class, of the dynasty also, than a formidable military defeat. It would bring to the German people a feeling of guilt and shame that nothing else could produce. They would at last know themselves as outcast and pariah among nations. They would also see that, by the establishment of the Society of Nations, their own just rights were secured, and that they had actually nothing to fight for except the perpetuity of their servitude and their masters. Your call would result in their first awakening from the Great Lie, the Great Delusion, the Great Hypnosis, under which they morally sleep while they yet physically put to shame the beasts of the jungle.

I have spoken of your immediate call for the Society of Nations as the only known anchor of common hope for the universal peoples. I have spoken of it as the shortest method of a moral conquest of Germany. I am also certain that it would prove to be a profound military tactic, a high and incomparable military strategy.

But there is now a more especial reason for the immediacy and urgency of this matter. It is the new peace offensive which Germany is preparing, and of which I am every day receiving information through German University friends. It is a peace offensive that will probably bring the nations to their most critical hour, and throw the whole responsibility for the yea or the nay as to the continuance of the war upon America—upon you, Mr. President.

This will not be an offensive which begins by sending chosen messengers to such as myself, or by secret messages to Englishmen like Lord Landsdowne: it will be a peace offensive employing the mass tactics of the German military: *it will be a vast and unexpected assault upon the whole moral front of the Allied peoples.*

Germany will suddenly propose, especially if she is as measurably successful as I fear she will be in France, such apparently frank and generous terms to the Allies as will awaken a militant response in all the latent pacifist element, as well as among the troubled and powerful financiers. She is seriously considering the question and the moment of offering Alsace-Lorraine to France, the African Colonies to England, independence and even restoration to Belgium, on condition that the territories east of the Rhine and the Adriatic shall not come into consideration at the Peace Congress. Let Germany have her way in the East; leave to her the future organization of Russian and Turkish territories; then shall France and England and Belgium be given complete satisfaction, and even some concessions made to Italy and Serbia.

"Why sacrifice yourselves for Russia?" Germany will ask. "Why bleed yourselves white, why each of you commit national suicide, for the Russia that failed you utterly, and for territories and peoples with whom you have no near or real concern? We will organize them, giving them civil and economic capacity, creating markets for you as well as for ourselves. Our proved efficiency will take them out of barbarism and chaos, and put them on the road to government and progress. You will thus be free to develop your own special cultures anew. We make no claims upon you. We give you all you ask for yourselves. Let us now make peace, and together put the world in order. You are exhausting yourselves; and you see that we are unconquerable, especially as the East, with all its resources, now lies open to us."

There is today, as Germany knows, among the war-wearied peoples, a sentiment that would cry for the acceptance of these seemingly generous terms. The Allied nations are now partly mooded to respond favorably to such a German appeal. For it would be an appeal, as I have already stated, not to individuals or to diplomats: it would be a public proclamation to the peoples.

What would result, supposing the Allied peoples even made such response as to paralyze partly the resisting power of their armies, and to gave [give] the Germans still further military advantage?

Germany would then have in hand the most compact and well-organized empire since the days of Rome at her greatest, and one more efficiently and tyrannically penetrated and ruled. Without interruption, the German Empire would stretch from the Rhine to the Pacific Ocean, so far as Northern Asia is concerned; and from Egypt to the gates of India, so far as the Near East is concerned, including inevitably all the present states of the Austro-Hungarian Monarchy, the control of the Mediterranean through Trieste and Saloniki, and the lordship of the Bosphorus and the shores of Asia Minor. She would establish a swift economic penetration and dominion, taking away from the subject peoples all weapons of defense, all power or chance of military organization, all economic freedom or initiative, forming them infallibly, without effectual resistance, according to the material and mental models of the essentially Satanic German "Kultur."

Furthermore, she is planning to make the peace proposals all the more appealing and effective by accompanying them with her own special plan for an organization of the Society of Nations. This is to be her great, her delectable surprise to the world. She thinks the surprise hidden in her diplomatic treasure-house for the moment, but it will be no surprise to some of us who know. She expects to be able to say to the nations: "Behold, that which President Wilson and the Allies promised and did not, we now propose to do without having promised." And there are millions, alas! who will yield to the strong lie, to the Gargantuan delusion.

What, or who, can now save the peoples from a surrender to this double assault of an anti-Christ Germanism? What, or who, can hold the peoples together through who knows what suffering, until America is ready with an effectual military leadership? What, or who, can stay the triumph of the German world-purpose when it masquerades in the terms of a broad and generous peace? What, or who, is sufficient to save mankind from the ages of iron darkness wherewith Germany is now more nearly overcoming the world than at any hour since she poured her well-nigh cosmical madness through Belgium's gates?

No one but yourself, Mr. President—nothing but your own immediate summons of the nations to the sacred convocation that shall prepare their federation in a league for the compulsion of the world's just and permanent peace. No other than yourself can now speak the word that shall preserve the world from a German darkness and despotism infernal—the word, too, creating while it saves, that renders conscious the common but yet unuttered soul of mankind, and precipitates it upon a new and comparatively divine plan of progress. No one but yourself is sufficient for proposing this world-revolution—this new creation of the world, in fact: a world wherein, when once it appears, men shall be no longer creatures but creators, cho[o]sing and directing the course of evolution, and writing hence the history of the future rather than of the past. No one but yourself can so speak to the present chaos as to compel the new creation's issue therefrom: no one but yourself is the recipient of the requisite universal confidence of mankind: no one but yourself is the possessor of an indisputable spiritual authority over the world.

You would wish to summon the best experts of America and the Allies to prepare the constitution of the Society. The details,—not so complicated and perplexing as they seem,—would have to be worked out. But you need not wait for these. Indeed, I make bold to say you dare not wait. You can boldly and broadly proclaim the Society's probable outlines. You can arch forth, for the high quick-

ening and resolute acceptance of the peoples, the commanding
perspective.

Do this now; and the whole world, so helplessly driven hither
and thither in one red wilderness of cynic confusion, will follow
you as never Moses was followed by his tribes. Not the total course
of human evolution, nor yet the stars in their courses, have committed unto man the shepherd's staff that now beseeches your
hands.

I wish, Mr. President, I could put the power and immediacy of
this appeal into words: I cannot. I wish there were words wherewith
the appeal could be adequately and livingly stated: there are none.
I wish you could know that it is no mere single individual who is
speaking to you: that it is rather the long hope, so ancient but
perennial, that striveth and groaneth in the whole history and heart-
ache of humanity. Yea, I dare to say to you that it is the appeal of
the immediate purpose of God in man to which you attend, as you
consider these words, beset and baffled as they are with the writer's
consciousness of their inadequacy and helplessness.

Let the League of the Nations be now, Mr. President. Unto you
it is divinely given, and unto you only, to speak the word that shall
bring the World-Society into being. Not I, but all the shattered and
sorrowing peoples entreat you to speak, and to speak while there
is yet time.

Praying you pardon the presumption of this appeal, even while
knowing as I do that it must be made, and remaining always your
obedient and devoted servant, I am,

                          Faithfully Yours,   George D. Herron

TLS (WP, DLC).

Thomas James Walsh to Joseph Patrick Tumulty

Dear Mr. Tumulty: [Washington] May 31, 1918.

When I talked with the President some time ago[1] about the woman's suffrage amendment on the eve of the contemplated vote, I
took the liberty to suggest to him that he send a letter to some
Senator expressing his hopes in the matter, as he did when the
resolution was about to come to a vote in the House. He was not
adverse to the idea, but indicated that he would be embarrassed
about finding something to say. I hesitate about offering any suggestion to the President along that line. No one ever accused him
of lack of fertility or want of facility in saying the appropriate thing
at the appropriate time. I am told, however, that a delegation rep-

resenting the women's trades unions is now seeking an interview with him on the subject. It occurred to me that such an occasion might be improved for the purpose we had in mind.

You might think the suggestion here made worthy of being brought to his notice.[2]   Very truly yours,   T. J. Walsh

TLS (WP, DLC).
   [1] At the White House on May 8, 1918.
   [2] "Dear Tumulty: I am hoping to take some such occasion very soon. The President." WW to JPT, c. May 31, 1918, TL (WP, DLC).

Newton Diehl Baker to Tasker Howard Bliss

Washington May 31st [1918]

Number 60 CONFIDENTIAL RUSH

Your cablegram 119, May 29th, received. Following is action on various questions submitted.

Paragraph Your number 103,[1] paragraph 2, deals with Milner-Pershing London agreement. President regards the Foch-Milner-Pershing agreement,[2] covering May and June, as in substitution for all previous arrangements, and we are attempting to live up to it. In view of the confusion arising from attempts to settle such questions here while they are being also considered in Europe, we feel that any modification of this program as set forth in your sub-paragraphs A, B, C and D, should be made only with concurrence of Foch, Milner and Pershing. If this or any other program is to be adopted for July and later months, it should be worked out by conference with British, French and American commanders all present. Pershing has been supplied full statement of available infantry and machine gun units and batteries who have had requisite minimum training. He is therefore prepared to confer on the subject. French and British Ambassadors here have sought to open discussion on this subject for July, but have been told that in my judgement General Foch should open the subject in Europe with Pershing and reach an arrangement there mutually satisfactory.

Paragraph Your number 103 paragraph 4. President concurs in the dissolution of Executive War Board and transfer of its functions to General Foch.

Paragraph Your number 103 paragraph 5. President believes extension of powers of Supreme Commander to Italian Front highly desirable, but defers to opinion of Italian Government upon a question so peculiarly affecting its own frontiers.

Paragraph Your number 103 paragraph 7, deals with Joint Note 25 covering transportation of Czech regiments from Russia. Pres-

ident concurs in recommendations of the note, but points out that
if Allied Military operations are in contemplation in Russia from
Murmansk and Archangel, these Czech contingents might be especially valuable in association with any such expeditions because
of their familiarity with Russian language and previous employment
on Russian Front.

Paragraph Your number 103 paragraph 8, deals with report of
Allied Naval Council, April 26th and 27, covering transfer of Italian
dreadnaughts. President concurs in recommendations.

Paragraph Your number 114,[3] Joint Note 26, covers recommendations reducing employment of horses for the conservation of for-
age. President concurs.

Paragraph Your number 114, Joint Note 27. President concurs
in analysis of situation. Believes that the continued neutrality of
Holland is of the highest importance and feels that no steps should
be taken which would give even a colorable pretext to the enemy
to claim that Holland had, by compromising her neutrality, justified
aggression against her.

Paragraph Your number 114, Joint Note 28. President concurs
in proposed mode of action of Inter-Allied Transportation Council.

Paragraph Your number 119, Joint Note 29. President concurs
in the importance of the study suggested.   Baker   McCain

TC telegram (WDR, RG 120, Records of the American Section of the Supreme War
Council, 1917-1919, No. 316, DNA).
  [1] That is, T. H. Bliss to RL et al., No. 103, May 3, 1918, Vol. 47.
  [2] See J. J. Pershing to P. C. March and NDB, May 15, 1918, printed as an Enclosure
with NDB to WW, May 16, 1918.
  [3] For all references to Bliss' 114, see T. H. Bliss to RL and NDB, No. 119, May 29,
1918.

To William Bauchop Wilson

My dear Mr. Secretary: [The White House] 1 June, 1918

In performing my obvious duty of presiding over the war activities
of the Government and trying to get them properly correlated, so
that they may cooperate and function in the most effective way, I
find myself hampered by the fact that I have nowhere a complete
picture (either in my mind or on paper) of the special war activities
which the several departments have undertaken or which have
been allotted to them from time to time through myself or through
other departments. I will be very much obliged, therefore, if you
would be kind enough to have prepared for me a succinct statement
of the special activities and functions which have fallen to your
department or any bureau or agency of it by reason of the war.

Just because my own knowledge in this matter is so incomplete, I cannot be more particular but must venture to leave the development of the idea to yourself.[1]

Cordially and sincerely yours,   Woodrow Wilson

TLS (Letterpress Books, WP, DLC).
[1] Wilson wrote the same letter, *mutatis mutandis*, as WW to WCR, June 1, 1918; WW to FKL, June 1, 1918; WW to DFH, June 1, 1918; and WW to WGM, June 3, 1918, all TLS (Letterpress Books, DLC).

Three Letters to Thomas Watt Gregory

[The White House]
My dear Mr. Attorney General: 1 June, 1918

The enclosed marked paragraph about W. R. Hearst[1] calls attention to a very extraordinary performance. In the Hearst papers, it would appear that my address concerning Memorial Day as a day of prayer was altered and, nevertheless, published with my signature. This constituted, I should suppose, something very like forgery, and I would very much like to know whether there is or is not some legal process which we could institute to bring this habitual offender to terms.

Cordially and faithfully yours,   Woodrow Wilson

[1] Wilson referred to a paragraph from W. W. Keen to WW, June 1, 1918, TLS (WP, DLC). William Williams Keen, a prominent surgeon of Philadelphia and an old acquaintance of Wilson's, complained at length about the alleged disloyalty of the Hearst press. As one example, he pointed out that the *New York American*, in printing Wilson's proclamation of May 11, 1918, had omitted that portion of the proclamation which called upon Americans to pray for victory in the war.

My dear Gregory: [The White House] 1 June, 1918

Here is a red-hot telegram about the District Attorneyship in Montana which I think you ought to see.[1] I wonder if Senator Walsh realizes the character of the heat that is accumulating out there?

Cordially and faithfully yours,   Woodrow Wilson

[1] This telegram about Burton K. Wheeler, federal district attorney in Montana, is missing.

My dear Gregory: [The White House] 1 June, 1918

Here is another letter about the Eastman-Reed prosecutions. Mr. Amos Pinchot is not always very wise, but he is always very sincere, I believe, and his letter, I must admit, has made some impression upon me.   Faithfully yours,   Woodrow Wilson

TLS (Letterpress Books, WP, DLC).

To Anna Howard Shaw

My dear Doctor Shaw: [The White House] 1 June, 1918
I have received your letter of May twenty-ninth, enclosing the important resolution of the Woman's Committee of the Council of National Defense with regard to the appointment of women upon all government boards and commissions controlling the work of women or affecting their interests, and to certain other positions in which women are directly dealt with or directly affected, and beg to assure you that I will give what is recommended the most serious consideration in consultation with my colleagues of the Cabinet.   Cordially and sincerely yours,   Woodrow Wilson

TLS (Letterpress Books, WP, DLC).

From Newton Diehl Baker

My dear Mr. President: Washington. June 1, 1918.
I return Dr. Shaw's letter with a suggested reply.[1] She sent me a similar letter and I have about made up my mind to send for the executives of the Young Women's Christian Association and tell them that they can have no privileges in any military camp unless they are willing to relax their rules so as to admit as fellow-workers Unitarians, Catholics, Jews, and persons of good character but without denominational affiliation.
The Young Women's Christian Association is erecting so-called hostess houses in the several camps. The houses are most attractive places for the families of soldiers to meet and visit with their soldier brothers and husbands. No other women's organization has undertaken this work. It is distinctly non-religious in character, and I have insisted from the first that the religious features of camp life should be left in the hands of the Army chaplains who are provided by law for that purpose, and that the social and recreational facilities supplied by the Young Men's Christian Association, the Knights of Columbus, and the Young Women's Christian Association should not be proselyting, sectarian, or religious in character, but social and recreative. I do not feel that we have a right to give to a frankly sectarian group an exclusive privilege of this kind, and if the Young Women's Christian Association can not broaden its basis I shall ask the Red Cross to undertake the work of supplying these hostess houses and withdraw the privilege from the Young Women's Christian Association. I do not commit you to this course, and if the suggested reply to Dr. Shaw about what I am about to do seems

too decided a course I would of course appreciate a word of caution
from you.   Respectfully yours,   Newton D. Baker

TLS (WP, DLC).
¹ "My dear Dr. Shaw: I have received your letter of May 28 and have read with regret
the enclosure. The social and humanitarian work about our Army camps and soldiers
is larger than any sectarian or denominational distinction, and I am glad to be able to
tell you that the Secretary of War has this matter in his mind with the view of bringing
about a broader and more generous attitude, if possible, on this subject." CCL, June 1,
1918 (N. D. Baker Papers, DLC). Wilson signed this letter, but decided not to send it.
The TLS of this letter is WW to Anna H. Shaw, June 1, 1918 (WP, DLC). See also WW
to NDB, June 3, 1918.

From Thomas Watt Gregory

Dear Mr. President: Washington, D. C. June 1, 1918.

I have received your letter of the 29th ultimo enclosing a letter
from Senator Saulsbury in relation to the Joint Resolution just
approved by you to prevent rent profiteering in the District of Columbia.

The Resolution does not provide for its enforcement by any proceeding instituted by the Government. The question of its constitutionality, therefore, would come before the courts in private litigation. The Government of course would have no standing as of
right in such a litigation. I have no doubt, however, that the court
would grant an application by the Department of Justice to appear
as *amicus curiae* in support of the constitutionality of the Resolution, and I think that such an application should be made as
soon as the issue is raised.

Respectfully,   T. W. Gregory

TLS (WP, DLC).

From William Bauchop Wilson

My dear Mr. President: Washington June 1, 1918.

I have read with a great deal of interest the paper attached to
Dr. Walcott's letter.¹ The Department of Labor has been pursuing
the policy recommended in Mr. Nunn's communication. I have
believed that the workers of the United States were inherently
patriotic, intelligent and efficient, and that more production could
be obtained for the great cause we are engaged in by presenting
and interpreting the facts to them than could be obtained by physical or mental repression.

Personally, I have gone into all kinds of meetings of union and
non-union workmen, commercial bodies, associations of manufac-

turers and professional men, and pointed out to them that if the purpose of the Government had been to promote the interests of capital, allowing it to profiteer to the fullest extent, we would have remained out of the war and permitted our business men to extort the highest prices for their goods which the needs of the European belligerants compelled them to pay; that our entrance into the war changed the situation so that it became necessary for us to inaugurate a policy of price fixing, thereby limiting the profits of employers, and that in doing so there had been no attempt made to fix a maximum wage for labor; that in addition it had resulted in our increasing income taxes and imposing an excess profits tax; that consequently this is not a capitalistic war.

That the action of the German Imperial Government in sinking our vessels at sea without warning and without giving the passengers and crew an opportunity of reaching points of safety, its destruction of our factories by the use of explosives, murdering our workmen while they were following their legitimate occupations, and then forbid[d]ing us to engage in ocean commerce with our neighbors with whom we were at peace, while audaciously granting us permission to send one vessel a week, demonstrates the purpose of the German Imperial Government to impose its will upon us, and that therefore this is a war for democracy, for freedom and for humanity; that it does not mend matters to assert that passengers should not have been permitted to travel upon these vessels, thereby endangering the peace of their country. There could be no passengers if there were no seamen to man the vessels. We either had to abandon our overseas trade altogether or protect these seamen in their right to earn their living in their usual way. That the seamen were just as much entitled to protection as any millionaire who happened to be a passenger and the Government decided to protect them.

That even in normal times employers and employees have a mutual interest in securing the largest possible production with a given amount of labor, having due regard for the health, safety and proper opportunities for rest and recreation of the workers, and that their interests only diverge when it comes to a division of that which is produced; that if nothing is produced there will be nothing to divide, and with a large amount produced there will be a large amount to divide; and that the wise course for them to pursue when it comes to the point where their interests diverge is to sit down around the council table and work the problem out on the most equitable basis that the circumstances surrounding the industry will permit; that notwithstanding the dark spots here and there in our industrial and social life, the American worker is the best paid in real wages and has the highest standard of living of any wage worker in the world; that this is due to the fact that the American working man produces more than any other, notwithstanding the boasts that have been made about German efficiency; and that efficiency in production becomes more essential in time of war; that we have taken millions of men from productive enterprise and in defense of our institutions have assigned them to destructive enterprise; that our standards of living are dependent upon the efficiency of the balance; that the more we now produce the longer we will be able to maintain our standards of living, which in any event must be materially changed before the conflict is over.

That the philosophy of the I.W.W. that reducing production through striking on the job, sabotage or any other process will eliminate the profits of employers, destroy the value of their property and enable the workers to take over the plants and operate them themselves collectively, is a fallacy clearly demonstrated by the historical facts that prior to the development of modern industry, at a time when nearly everything was produced by hand, the productivity per individual was very much less than anything that could result from the widest system of sabotage that the I.W.W. could possibly inaugurate, and even in those days there were profits for the employers, the effect being that the standard of living of the workers was much lower than anything in existence today, and if the I.W.W. succeeded in carrying its policy into effect the injury would fall upon the workers themselves in the form of lower living standards.

That the turnover of labor means a tremendous economic loss. Aside from the loss of time incident to finding one man to take the place that another has left, no man can reach his highest efficiency until he has become familiar with his shop, his machine, his associates, his foreman, the methods of routing and otherwise handling the work, and the hundred and one other things that go to make up his shop surroundings; that the turnover represents the individualistic strike. It is the non-union or union man dissatisfied with conditions unwilling or unable to interest his associates in a collective protest. It is nothing unusual in normal times to find establishments having two hundred or three hundred per cent turnover per annum. In these times in some congested localities where housing conditions are bad the turnover is frequently much greater. We discourage strikes because they interfere with production at this critical period. They attract attention and are items of news because they affect large bodies of men at the same time, but the economic loss resulting from the tremendous turnover of labor is greater by far than all of the strikes of union labor and spontaneous collective protests of non-union workers combined. The remedy is two-fold: (1) Make the conditions for the workmen such that they will have no just cause for complaint, and (2) in view of the unusual conditions caused by the rapid concentration of industry to produce material for the national defense a spirit of forbearance is necessary on the part of the workmen.

It has also been necessary to allay the uneasiness created in the minds of the workmen by various drives made for conscription of labor by taking the stand that there should be no conscription of labor for private employers even though the private employers may be engaged on public work; that if the demand for war material makes it advisable for us to conscript labor it should also include a conscription of the plants in which the labor is to be employed. I have been ably assisted by my official staff in presenting this and similar thought to the American wage workers and their employers.

In January, last, I came to the conclusion that it was necessary to organize a Speakers' Bureau to more rapidly reach the workers than we had been doing. The only fund we had available to meet the expense was the Immigration fund, but as many of the people we had to reach were aliens under the care and jurisdiction of the Department of Labor, I assumed the responsibility of using part of the fund for this purpose. Since then we have had fourteen or fifteen men taken from the ranks of labor presenting these thoughts to the union and non-union workers at noon and evening meetings in the industrial centers throughout the country. I am sending you two photographs indicative of the manner in which this work is being carried out.

In addition I am having posters prepared from time to time which are being widely distributed with the hope that they may assist in creating and maintaining the proper attitude of mind towards the whole industrial problem as it affects the winning of the war. I am sending you a few samples of these.

You will therefore see that I am in hearty accord with the suggestion contained in Mr. Nunn's letter.

Faithfully yours,   W B Wilson

TLS (WP, DLC).
  [1] Walcott's letter and its enclosure are missing in WP, DLC. However, WW to C. D. Walcott, May 29, 1918, TLS (received from Mary A. Strohecker), and a White House memorandum, May 29, 1918, T MS (WP, DLC), reveal that Walcott had written to Wilson on May 27 and had enclosed a "paper" by P. N. Nunn of Santa Barbara, California, about a "campaign of education" among American workers. Wilson had forwarded Walcott's letter and its enclosure to Secretary Wilson in WW to WBW, May 29, 1918, TLS (Letterpress Books, WP, DLC).

From the French, British, and Italian Prime Ministers

Versailles, June 2, 1918

Presented to the President by the French Ambassador June 6

We desire to express our warmest thanks to President Wilson for the remarkable promptness with which American aid, in excess of what at one time seemed practicable, has been rendered to the Allies during the past month to meet a great emergency. The crisis, however, still continues. General Foch has presented to us a statement of the utmost gravity, which points out that the numerical superiority of the enemy in France, where 162 Allied divisions are now opposed to 200 German divisions, is very heavy, and that, as there is no possibility of the British and French increasing the number of their divisions (on the contrary, they are put to extreme straits to keep them up), there is a great danger of the war being lost unless the numerical inferiority of the Allies can be remedied as rapidly as possible by the advent of American troops. He therefore urges with the utmost insistence that the maximum possible number of infantry and machine-gunners, in which respects the shortage of men on the side of the Allies is most marked, should continue to be shipped from America in the months of June and July to avert the immediate danger of an Allied defeat in the present campaign, owing to the Allied reserves being exhausted before those of the enemy. In addition to this, and looking to the future, he represents that it is impossible to foresee ultimate victory in the war unless America is able to provide such an army as will enable the Allies ultimately to establish numerical superiority. He places the total American force required for this at no less than 100 divisions, and urges the continuous raising of fresh American levies, which, in his opinion, should not be less than 300,000 a month, with a view to establishing a total American force of 100 divisions at as early a date as this can possibly be done.

We are satisfied that General Foch, who is conducting the present campaign with consummate ability, and on whose military judgment we continue to place the most absolute reliance, is not overestimating the needs of the case, and we feel confident that the Government of the United States will do everything that can be done, both to meet the needs of the immediate situation and to proceed with the continuous raising of fresh levies, calculated to provide, as soon as possible, the numerical superiority which the Commander-in-Chief of the Allied armies regards as essential to ultimate victory.

A separate telegram contains the arrangement which General Pershing and Lord Milner have agreed to recommend to the United

States Government with regard to the despatch of American troops
for the months of June and July.   G. Clemenceau
                                           D. Lloyd George
                                           V. E. Orlando

Telegram—Annex

An agreement concluded between General Foch, General
   Pershing, and Lord Milner with reference to the Trans-
   portation of American troops in the months of June and
   July

The following recommendations are made on the assumption that
at least 250,000 men can be transported in each of the months of
June and July by the employment of combined British and American tonnage.

We recommend:

(a) For the month of June—

1st. Absolute priority shall be given to the transportation of 170,000
combatant troops (viz.: six divisions without artillery, ammunition
trains or supply trains, amounting to 126,000 men and 44,000
replacement for combat troops).

2nd. 25,400 men for the service of the railways, of which 13,400
have been asked for by the French Minister of Transportation.

3rd. The balance to be troops of categories to be determined by
the Commander-in-Chief, American Expeditionary Forces.

(b) For the month of July—

1st. Absolute priority for the shipment of 140,000 combatant
troops of the nature defined above (4 divisions minus artillery, etc.,
amounting to 84,000 men, plus 56,000 replacements).

2nd. The balance of the 250,000 to consist of troops to be designated by the Commander-in-Chief, American Expeditionary Forces.

(c) It is agreed that if the available tonnage in either month allows
of the transportation of a larger number of men than 250,000, the
excess tonnage will be employed in the transportation of combat
troops as defined above.

(d) We recognise that the combatant troops to be despatched in
July may have to include troops which have had insufficient training, but we consider the present emergency is such as to justify a
temporary and exceptional departure by the United States from
sound principles of training, especially as a similar course is being
followed by France and Great Britain.

CC telegram (WP, DLC).

Lord Reading to Arthur James Balfour and
Walter Hume Long[1]

PERSONAL.   Washington. June 2, 1918.

Following for Mr. Balfour and Mr. Long.

Mr. Hughes of Australia[2] had interview with President at which I was present. Mr. Hughes impressed upon President that it was vital to the security of Australia that Germany should never be allowed to take any part of New Guinea or the Islands of the Pacific. Mr. Hughes made plain that Australia was not seeking all these Islands for herself that she had sufficient territory but that her life would be menaced if Germany with her predatory designs held any of these Islands and he emphasised the necessity of these belonging only to British Empire and friendly Powers. The President was sympathetic and said he would communicate with those to whom he had entrusted study of these and similar questions.

Mr. Hughes also spoke on same subject at dinner of Pilgrims to him. I have not yet seen or heard any comment upon his views. Americans are at moment too intent upon the winning of the War to think of peace terms.

T telegram (W. Wiseman Papers, CtY).
   [1] British Secretary of State for the Colonies.
   [2] That is, Prime Minister William Morris Hughes.

To Bernard Mannes Baruch

My dear Baruch: [The White House] 3 June, 1918

Thank you for your letter of June first.[1] I had already done substantially what you suggest. I have written to the departments of which we have not already a conspectus, and hope their first reports will be made pretty soon.

                    Cordially and faithfully yours,   Woodrow Wilson

TLS (Letterpress Books, WP, DLC).
   [1] B. M. Baruch to WW, June 1, 1918, TLS (WP, DLC).

To Alexander Mitchell Palmer

My dear Palmer: The White House 3 June, 1918

I don't wonder that you were prompted by what is going on in Germany to propose an even stiffer proclamation than the one you first brought to me,[1] but my own judgment is that it would not be wise to go further than that proclamation goes, at any rate at pres-

ent, and you will have noticed that even in the paragraph relating
to propagandists I thought it was wisest, for the present at any rate,
to strike out the word "native." These are matters upon which there
is a wide room for differences of opinion, but I think the more
slowly we go, the more wisely we shall handle the matter.

Cordially and sincerely yours,   Woodrow Wilson

TLS (A. Mitchell Palmer Papers, DLC).
  ¹ Palmer had conferred with Wilson at the White House on May 29, 1918, and had
handed him a draft of a proclamation which extended the meaning of the term "enemy"
to include certain other persons not covered by the previous definition and which authorized the Alien Property Custodian to take over their property. Whereas under the
existing regulations, only the property of aliens interned in the United States and that
of persons living within enemy territory could be seized, the new definition added five
additional categories of subjects of Germany or Austria-Hungary who were living anywhere outside the United States. It included the wives of officers or agents of Germany
or Austria-Hungary and women whose husbands were either living in enemy territory
or were doing business therein; enemy prisoners of war and other persons detained by
an ally of the United States; persons who were aiding the Central Powers by intriguing
or by the dissemination of propaganda; persons and companies included in the Enemy
Trading List; and persons who, at any time since August 4, 1914, had been living in
enemy territory. Wilson signed the proclamation on May 31, 1918. See 40 *Statutes at
Large* 1786. Palmer's draft is missing, but there is a printed copy of the proclamation, dated
May 31, 1918, in WP, DLC.
  On May 30, 1918, Palmer informed Wilson that the German government had recently begun
to seize the property of American citizens living in Germany, and he quoted at length from
a telegram from Stovall to the State Department of May 13, 1918, about the matter. A. M.
Palmer to WW, May 30, 1918, TLS (WP, DLC). On the next day, Palmer again wrote to
Wilson and enclosed copies of correspondence which he had received from the State Department to the effect that Germany was also taking over the property of British subjects who
were residing in neutral countries. Palmer suggested that Wilson respond firmly to these latest
German actions by issuing a proclamation which would be more far-reaching than he had
originally proposed. He enclosed a draft of a new proclamation which designated as enemies
all German and Austro-Hungarian subjects who were living outside the United States and all
natives or subjects of enemy countries, regardless of their residency, who were propagandists.
This draft proclamation, too, is missing in WP, DLC. However, Palmer summarized its main
provisions in A. M. Palmer to WW, June 1, 1918, TLS, enclosing Lord Reading to RL, May
14, 1918, and Lucy M. Muddock to the Director of Foreign Claims, March 21, 1918, both
TCL (WP, DLC).

To John Thomas Watkins¹

My dear Mr. Watkins: [The White House] 3 June, 1918

I know that you will understand me if I lay very frankly before
you the reasons why I think it would be unwise (both on your own
account and because of the general impression that would be made)
for me to write such a letter as you suggest in yours of the first of
June.² The record speaks for itself. I do not mean the Congressional
Record, but the record of votes and actions which you can have
verified either by the Clerk or the Speaker, and my personal feeling
is that it would weaken your position if you gave the impression of
personal dependence in any way upon me.

You will understand that I have had a number of such suggestions to consider, and one reason why I think that the decision I

have arrived at is wise is that these suggestions are very numerous and I am afraid there would presently grow up in the country a very unfavorable impression based upon an apparent effort on my part to certify members of Congress and to judge as between members of my own party who should be returned to the House.

You will understand, I hope, that I write this with the greatest cordiality and with a warm personal appreciation of the generous attitude you have always maintained towards the administration.

Cordially and sincerely yours,   Woodrow Wilson

TLS (Letterpress Books, WP, DLC).
  [1] Democratic congressman from Louisiana.
  [2] It is missing.

To Newton Diehl Baker

My dear Mr. Secretary: The White House 3 June, 1918

I have your letter of June first. I have no hesitation in saying that the conclusion you have come to with regard to the duty of the Young Women's Christian Association in dealing with the matters that they are dealing with on the other side of the water, to admit to their activities women who are Jews or Catholics or members of non-Christian bodies, or members of no religious denomination at all, is the right one, but I would suggest, in view of the splendid spirit the women of the Association have shown, that you put the matter to them as one duty and attach no threat of exclusion, merely pointing out to them that this is a policy upon which the Department of War as representing the Government would be obliged to insist.

But I must apologize for making the suggestion because I know how you will do the whole thing kindly. I am making the suggestion only because you were generous enough to ask me to say just what I thought of the course you were about to pursue.

Cordially and faithfully yours,   Woodrow Wilson

TLS (N. D. Baker Papers, DLC).

To Joseph Patrick Tumulty

Dear Tumulty: [The White House, c. June 3, 1918]

Please thank President Schurman for this suggestion[1] and tell him that I have again and again tried my hand at special messages and they simply won't "go" when I am cold and have no definite audience in my imagination. I am very much complimented that he should use extracts from my addresses.   The President.

TL (WP, DLC).
[1] J. G. Schurman to JPT, May 31, 1918, TLS (WP, DLC). Schurman told Tumulty that he had accepted an invitation from the Y.M.C.A.'s National War Work Council to address American soldiers in camps in Europe during the summer. In similar addresses in camps in the United States, Schurman had used quotations from Wilson's messages and had found them "exceedingly effective." He now asked Tumulty for "a special message of a sentence or two" from Wilson which he could use in his addresses in Europe.

To Henry Pomeroy Davison

My dear Mr. Davison: The White House 3 June, 1918

I am warmly obliged to you for your letter of May twenty-ninth. The results of the subscription are truly remarkable and make us additionally proud of the great country we are serving.

It gratifies me very much that you think that I have been useful in promoting the success of the organization, and I am particularly glad that you feel that I have been helpful to you. I congratulate you most sincerely upon the results.

Cordially and sincerely yours,   Woodrow Wilson

TLS (War Council File, DARC).

To Felexiana Shepherd Baker Woodrow

My dear Aunt Felie: The White House 3 June, 1918

There was certainly no need to ask me to excuse your letter of May thirtieth. It has brought me the greatest pleasure. It is fine to have the boys of the family making such a record and I share your pride in what they are doing. These are days of sacrifice, but every sacrifice seems to bring with it an exhilaration of a duty highly performed which is more than compensation.

I hope that you are well, and beg that you will give my love to all.   Affectionately yours,   Woodrow Wilson

TLS (received from James Woodrow).

From Edward Mandell House

Dear Governor,   Magnolia, Mass. June 3. 1918.

What Sir William and others have told me concerning the lack of coordination of our interests in France and their constantly increasing magnitude, leads me to suggest a plan looking towards a more orderly outcome.

It is clear that Pershing should confine his activities solely to the molding our Army into an efficient fighting machine and directing it against the enemy. If he does this well, he will have done more than any Allied commander has yet done.

There was no excuse for these recent German successes on the Western Front. We had as many men—better men—and better equipment. The failure has been with the higher command. The Germans have proven themselves greatly superior in generalship and in staff organization. The drive of March 21st caught the Allies napping, and the success of the present drive shows that our command learned but little from the first one. It does not much matter how many men we send over, if in the end they are not under leadership measurably equal to that of the Germans.

If Pershing had nothing else to think about I doubt whether he has the capacity to build up a staff adequate to the needs of the occasion. Certainly, he can never do it under present conditions. The French are the only ones of the Allies that have proven themselves at all equal to the task. The English have failed, and we will do no better unless we get at the problem now.

Our Civil War teaches a lesson which we should take to heart. The South by superior generalship repeatedly defeated the North, and no one knows better than you how much inferior both in numbers and equipment were the Armies of the South.

A beginning has been made to better conditions by the appointment of a Generalissimo, but I doubt whether Foch's authority goes far enough. There are indications that Haig and Pershing, to say nothing of Petain, assert themselves almost as positively as they did before. I doubt whether complete unity of command can be brought about until you, Clemenceau and Lloyd George insist that the commanders in the field subordinate themselves to Foch. This might lead, probably would, in the case of Haig, to a change in command.

What I have in mind to suggest to you is that Pershing be relieved from all responsibility except the training and fighting of our troops. All his requirements for equipping and maintaining these troops should be on other shoulders. He should be relieved of all questions of policy except where his opinion is asked. There should be no need for him to be in consultation with the Prime Ministers and Foreign Secretaries of England France and Italy. He should be in touch with Foch, and Foch should be in touch with these. Foch should build up the military end of the Supreme War Council and use it as an important part of the General Staff. It amounts to next to nothing now.

To give Pershing the free hand necessary I would suggest sending Stettinius over in his capacity as Assistant Secretary of War, and put him in charge of all army work behind the lines. I would suggest sending Vance McCormick over and making him Chairman of the American Board Overseas. His activities would be to bring about coordination between Crosby, Stettinius, Stevens, Skinner[1] and any others that are now there or may be sent. His headquarters should be in Paris, but he should go to London when necessary. He should keep in touch with you and keep you informed as to vital matters.

I may not have outlined the best plan of procedure, but it would do to start with, and until a better one could be brought about after trial and further experience.

Affectionately yours,   E. M. House

P.S. Until I read your address to Congress on the new revenue bill, I did not think it possible that so prosaic a subject had in it possibilities for such an appeal to the idealism and patriotism of a people.

TLS (WP, DLC).
  [1] That is, Robert Peet Skinner, the American Consul General in London. Raymond Bartlett Stevens, vice-chairman of the United States Shipping Board, was at this time also the American representative on the Allied Maritime Transport Council.

From Elizabeth Merrill Bass

My dear Mr. President: Washington, D. C. June 3rd, 1918.

Suffrage still continues to occupy the foreground, and it is taking from many of us who should be engaged in the work of getting ready to go into the Congressional campaigns with the woman voters of this country, hours of each day. Our time is taken up, not only in the endeavor to pick up the two or three necessary votes from among the group of southern senators, but also in making explanations and apologies in the way of letters and telegrams in reply to inquiries from all over the country.

I am venturing the hope that you have been able to communicate again with Senators Fletcher and Trammel, of Florida, Guyon[1] of Louisiana, who is reported to say that if it is put to him by you as a war measure he will vote for it, and Overman of North Carolina. In regard to the last named, the Federation of Women's Clubs met last week, which is not a suffrage organization and whose opinion, therefore, has more weight with him, and they sent him a message expressing the desire of the majority of the women of North Carolina for the ballot.

If nothing has resulted from your further communications with the above Senators, I believe, Mr. President, that the time has come for you to take the final step of making a public proclamation, either using the International communication sent for your attention, or by going directly to the Senate and placing before them the necessity of making this a war measure. You, more than anyone else in the world, are the voice of the world, and I believe you can make them see that they need the women of this country, not only in the work of the war, but in the work of rebuilding civilization, and that they must equip them for this high duty, not forgetting the claim of the constantly increasing army of the women in industry.

I believe the vote should be called for the middle of next week, say Wednesday June 12th, whether we had the pledges of the necessary two or three votes or not, providing of course you make your public statement, of whatever sort it may be. In the latter case we shall, of course, have to take the vote, not knowing what the effect will be, but whatever the result in the Senate, I can at least go about the business of the Congressional campaign with a clear defense of the Administration and its incomparable leader.

Respectfully yours,   Elizabeth Bass

TLS (WP, DLC).
[1] Walter Guion, appointed to succeed Robert F. Broussard, who had died on April 12, 1918.

From Henry Pomeroy Davison

My dear Mr. President: Washington, D. C. June 3, 1918.

Perhaps you know that Mr. Raymond Robins has left Russia and is now on his way home, but that our Red Cross Commission, in charge of Mr. Wardwell, still remains there.

The problem of relief in Russia by the Red Cross is one which is weighing heavily upon my mind. I would, therefore, appreciate it very much, if it is agreeable and convenient for you to see me for a few minutes, to favor me with your suggestions. I would also like to see you for a moment upon another Red Cross matter—a question of policy—but this is not urgent.[1]

As I think you know, I feel very reluctant to suggest taking a moment of your time, notwithstanding that you have made me feel very free to do so.

With esteem, believe me, my dear Mr. President

Sincerely yours,   H. P. Davison

TLS (WP, DLC).
[1] Wilson saw Davison at the White House at 5:30 p.m. on June 5, 1918.

From William Kent, with Enclosure

My dear Mr. President: Washington June 3, 1918

I inclose herewith a brief note from Max Eastman. I am greatly impressed with the statement by my old friend, Mr. Louis Post, Assistant Secretary of Labor, who is great and wise, who believes that it is extremely bad policy for the Government to be prosecuting what he deems is "folly." Every thoughtful Socialist is driven into our camp in the contest now on, and I do not believe that we can afford to throw away the opportunity of reclaiming for constructive work men like Max Eastman. When I think of Rose Pastor Stokes, I regret the absence of the ducking stool.[1] Ten years' imprisonment for foolish talk seems extreme.

Yours truly,   William Kent

P.S. I wish you could advise with Solicitor General John Davis. He has an open constructive mind and has talked with Eastman.

[1] Rose Harriet Pastor (Mrs. James Graham Phelps) Stokes, a social worker and lecturer of New York and a member of the Socialist party, had been arrested in Willow Springs, Missouri, on March 22, 1918, on charges of disloyalty. In several speeches and in a letter to the *Kansas City Star* of March 20, 1918, Mrs. Stokes, who had left the Socialist party in April 1917 but had rejoined it later, had stated her opposition to the American government and the war, which, she had asserted, was being fought solely for the benefit of American capitalists and profiteers. She was indicted in Kansas City on April 23, 1918, on three counts of violating the Espionage Act, was convicted on May 23, 1918, and was sentenced on June 1, 1918, to three concurrent terms of imprisonment for ten years. See the *New York Times*, March 18 and 24, April 24, May 22, 23, and 24, and June 2., 1918.

E N C L O S U R E

Max Eastman to William Kent

Dear Mr. Kent,   New York City May 31, 1918

Thank you for telling me that the President is concerned over our case, and in doubt about it.

If he is in doubt after hearing only the one side presented by those concerned in the prosecution, his doubts would resolve in my favor if I had an opportunity to present my side to him as it is.

I know he would not swerve for any personal or political reason from his one task and resolution to prosecute the war with relentless vigor toward the high aims he has set before the country. But I believe that if he could feel my attitude and my purposes as they are, he would not think an intervention in this situation altogether apart from those aims.

Is it beyond the possibilities that I should have ten minutes with him?   Yours sincerely,   Max Eastman

TLS (WP, DLC).

From Robert Lansing

My dear Mr. President: Washington June 3, 1918.

The matter of purchasing supplies in Russia which otherwise would be acquired either directly or indirectly by Germany and about which I wrote you on February 12, 1918,[1] appears to have been proceeding successfully. In response to my recommendation at that time[2] you placed at the disposal of our Military Mission in Russia $1,000,000 to be used in cooperation with British and French Military Attachés, who each received like sums from their Governments.

The Ambassador now telegraphs urgently for an increased allotment of funds for the same purpose. I am accordingly inquiring whether you will authorize me to telegraph Mr. Francis that he may draw upon the Department of State up to an additional $5,000,000 to enable the purchasing commission to continue its work under the supervision of the Ambassador.

As indicating what has already been determined by the French Government I think you will be interested in the enclosed copy of a letter from Mr. André Tardieu, the French High Commissioner, in which he reports that the French Ambassador at Vologda has received "carte blanche" from his Government to purchase Russian supplies needed in Germany and which he can control.[3]

Faithfully yours,   Robert Lansing

TLS (SDR, RG 59, 861.24/81a, DNA).
    [1] RL to WW, Feb. 12, 1918, CCL (SDR, RG 59, 861.24/39A, DNA).
    [2] If Wilson ever replied in writing to Lansing's suggestion, his letter is missing. See, however, the White House memorandum, Feb. 13, 1918, T MS (WP, DLC), which says that Lansing's letter was referred to the State Department with Wilson's approval.
    [3] A. Tardieu to FLP, May 13, 1918, TCL (SDR, RG 59, 861.24/81a, DNA).

A Memorandum by Robert Lansing

Monday, June 3, 1918.

After conference with the President on Saturday, June 1st, it was agreed that I should say to Lord Reading that this Government was entirely willing to send troops to Murmansk provided General Foch approved the diversion of troops and the necessary shipping for that purpose from those now going to France. Before doing this I saw Secretary Baker who entirely agreed with this action and today I saw Lord Reading and told him of our attitude. He made notes and said he would inform his Government.   Robert Lansing

T MS (SDR, RG 59, 861.00/1978½, DNA).

To Joseph Patrick Tumulty

Dear Tumulty: The White House [c. June 4, 1918].

It is hard for me to believe that the Governor of California will allow Mooney to hang.[1] Do you know anything further than the newspapers have stated? I hesitate to send another message to the Governor, because it might only serve to irritate him after all that I have said to him. The President.

TL (WP, DLC).
[1] Ida Reese *et al.* to WW, June 2, 1918, T telegram (WP, DLC). They urged Wilson to call on Governor Stephens to grant Mooney a new trial.

To William Dennison Stephens

[The White House] 4 June, 1918

I beg that you will believe that I am moved only by a sense of public duty and of consciousness of the many and complicated interests involved when I again most respectfully suggest a commutation of the death sentence imposed upon Mooney. I would not venture again to call your attention to this case did I not know the international significance which attaches to it.

Woodrow Wilson.

T telegram (Letterpress Books, WP, DLC).

To Leon Samuel Haas[1]

[The White House] 4 June, 1918

I hope that you will not think I am taking an unwarranted liberty in expressing my deep interest in the suffrage question now before your committee.[2] I cannot help regarding the settlement of this question as of world-wide significance and as affording a standard by which to judge our present interest in the complete establishment of democracy. I am moved to send you this expression of opinion by a very profound sense of the public interest.

Woodrow Wilson.

T telegram (Letterpress Books, WP, DLC).
[1] Chairman of the suffrage committee of the Louisiana Senate and banker and lawyer from Opelousas, La.
[2] Senator Ransdell had informed Wilson on June 3, 1918, that a bill for a woman-suffrage amendment to the Louisiana constitution had been introduced in the state legislature and that hearings on the measure would be held before the suffrage committee of the state Senate on June 4. He asked Wilson to send a brief message in support of the bill to Senator Haas. Such a message, Ransdell said, would also show Wilson's continuing interest in a national woman-suffrage amendment. The bill would be submitted to the Louisiana legislature, Ransdell concluded, and Wilson's message would probably help to secure a favorable vote on a national amendment from Senator Guion. J. E. Ransdell to WW, June 3, 1918, TLS (WP, DLC).

To Willard Saulsbury

My dear Senator: The White House 4 June, 1918

Upon receipt of your letter about the rent resolution, I got into communication with the Attorney General. I now have a letter from him from which I quote, as follows:

"The resolution does not provide for its enforcement by any proceeding instituted by the Government. The question of its constitutionality, therefore, would come before the courts in private litigation. The Government, of course, would have no standing as of right in such a litigation. I have no doubt, however, that the court would grant an application by the Department of Justice to appear as *amicus curiae* in support of the constitutionality of the resolution, and I think that such an application should be made as soon as the issue is raised."

This is evidently the only way we can get in, and I feel confident we can count upon the vigilance and interest of the Department of Justice in the matter.

Cordially and sincerely yours,   Woodrow Wilson

TLS (W. Saulsbury Papers, DeU).

From Robert Lansing

Dear Mr. President: [Washington] June 4, 1918.

It would seem to me advisable in view of the annexed memorandum, which was prepared from information derived from the War and Navy Departments,[1] that there should be concentrated at Galveston approximately six thousand marines so that we would be adequately prepared for any emergency which may arise in connection with the Mexican oil fields.

Faithfully yours,   Robert Lansing.

TLS (SDR, RG 59, 812.00/22199, DNA).
   [1] G. Auchincloss to RL, June 4, 1918, TLS (SDR, RG 59, 812.00/22199, DNA). This memorandum summarized the evidence of Germany's increasing involvement in Mexico and suggested that the United States take immediate steps to prepare for a possible abandonment of Mexico's neutrality. As proof of the alleged pro-German attitude of the Carranza government, Auchincloss cited Germany's financial assistance to Mexico, the shipment of raw materials, the dispatch of military advisers, and the installation of a new wireless station near Mexico City; the secret mission of Isidro Fabela, the former Mexican Foreign Minister, to Germany; the suppression of pro-Allied newspapers by the Mexican government and its support of newspapers opposed to the Allies and the United States; the establishment of a German espionage system in Mexico; and Mexico's break of diplomatic relations with Cuba. In light of these developments, Auchincloss said, the United States had to be prepared for an openly hostile action by the Mexican government. He therefore recommended the stationing of 6,000 marines at Galveston, who, if necessary, could be immediately dispatched to seize the Mexican oil fields at Tampico.

From William Phillips, with Enclosure

Dear Mr. President: Washington June 4, 1918.

I beg to send you enclosed a translation of a note dated May 28th which the Department has just received from the French Ambassador regarding the Russian situation. It is especially interesting to note that Count Mirbach has been authorized by the Emperor to announce that, if appealed to by any party of industry and order, he could have German troops at Moscow in forty-eight hours.

Faithfully yours, William Phillips

TLS (WP, DLC).

E N C L O S U R E

Jean Jules Jusserand to Robert Lansing

Mr. Secretary of State: Washington. May 28, 1918.

My Government has just cabled me information it has received from Vologda and Moscow which I deem it advisable to impart to Your Excellency at this time when the Allied Governments are equally interested in overlooking no information that is likely to throw light on the Russian situation.

Under date of the 19th of this month, the Ambassador of France telegraphed, in substance, that "the pro-German trend is making speedy headway" and that the Allied Representatives are unanimous in the opinion that:

1st—The trend is only growing because the hope of efficacious help from the Allies is dwindling.

2nd—On account of that lack of help, the Government which succeeds the Bolsheviki is bound to be like that of Ukraine, that is to say, to rest on Germany's support and adhere to her influence.

3rd—Without outside help, the Russian people cannot rally.

Mr. Noulens adds that he has reason to believe that his American colleague telegraphed Your Excellency in the same sense, sharing the opinion that unless action be taken, the situation will soon be wholly compromised. The Ambassador of France particularly points out to my Government the urgency of sending the two battalions that are wanted for Arkangel and of supporting Semenoff. Again the Consul General of France at Moscow[1] has it from a most reliable source that in the course of a private conversation with the political friends of Prince Troubetskoy and Mr. Krivosheine,[2] former Minister of Agriculture, Count von Mirbach declared that "although Germany had made it a principle not to meddle with Russian domestic affairs, all her sympathies went to the parties of industry and order. If those parties should succeed in setting up a Government, he was authorized by Emperor William to announce that if appealed to he could have German troops at Moscow in forty-eight hours."

Count von Mirbach supplements that important declaration calculated to bring the men of good will around to his country with the statement that "Germany would be disposed to revise the Brest Litovsk treaty as she never intended to make that instrument the true foundation of her future economic relations with Russia which she desires, in accordance with her interests and sympathies, to see restored to a normal and prosperous life." The German diplomat, thoroughly versed in that kind of propaganda, wound up in saying that the sentiments of his country toward Russia had not been altered by a war "for which as it well knows England alone is responsible."

Your Excellency will perhaps deem it appropriate to lay before the President of the United States those indications which, by reason of their source as well as of the grave perspective they disclose, demand in our opinion, the most earnest and prompt attention.

Be pleased to accept, etc.   Jusserand.

TCL (WP, DLC).
    [1] Joseph-Fernand Grenard.
    [2] Prince Grigorii Nikolaevich Trubetskoi, former head of the Near Eastern department of the Foreign Ministry, and Aleksandr Vasil'evich Krivoshein.

From Edward Mandell House

Dear Governor,   Magnolia, Mass. June 4. 1918.

Would it not be a move in the right direction if you formed a Committee on Russian Affairs to act in conjunction with you and the State Department?

The perso[n]nel of the State Department is hopelessly inadequate to handle any but routine matters. If such a committee was headed by John R. Mott it would command general confidence. One of its functions might be to prepare a list of men qualified to go to Russia as the occasion requires.

The subject is so vast, the ramifications so far-reaching, that only through some such organization can the problems arising be properly brought to your attention.

Affectionately yours,   E. M. House

TLS (WP, DLC).

To Joseph Patrick Tumulty

Dear Tumulty: The White House [c. June 5, 1918].

How long is Governor West[1] going to be in town?[2] I know what he wants to see me about. He wants to run for the Senate in Oregon and believes he can win if the Democrats who have been justly dissatisfied with the course Senator Chamberlain has pursued are prevented from being too hostile to him, West. Chamberlain first brought him into public life by appointment. He was subsequently Governor, as you know, and was Senator Chamberlain's campaign manager when Chamberlain was last elected to the Senate. He professes to disapprove of Senator Chamberlain's recent course, but I think disapproves very mildly. I cannot do anything in his behalf without condoning what I cannot condone on Senator Chamberlain's part. I tell you all of this to show you how delicate a matter it is for me to see him and how much I should like to avoid him if it can courteously be done.[3]   The President.

TL (WP, DLC).
    [1] Oswald West, Governor of Oregon, 1911-1915.
    [2] Wilson was replying to JPT to WW, June 5, 1918, TL (WP, DLC): "Governor West of Oregon asks for an appointment to see the President."
    [3] There is no record of a meeting between Wilson and West.

To Thomas Watt Gregory

My dear Gregory: [The White House] 5 June, 1918

The enclosed letter from Max Eastman to William Kent I thought you might like to see.
                    Cordially and faithfully yours,   Woodrow Wilson

TLS (Letterpress Books, WP, DLC).

To Frederic Clemson Howe

My dear Howe: [The White House] 5 June, 1918

Thank you for your little paper entitled, "Real Politik in Russia."[1] The thesis of it interests me very much and I am going to give it a very careful reading.
                    Cordially and sincerely yours,   Woodrow Wilson

TLS (Letterpress Books, WP, DLC).
    [1] It is missing. However, it was published as Frederic C. Howe, "Realpolitik in Russia," *The New Republic*, XV (June 15, 1918), 202-203. Howe argued that, for the Allied governments to begin to comprehend the perplexing situation in Russia, they had to understand the economic foundations of the country. Russia, Howe said, was basically divided into two economic groups: the landowning "Junker" aristocracy and the mass

of landless peasants. With the coming of the revolution and the expropriation of the large estates, the Russian landed nobility betrayed their country in order to save their property and turned for help to the Prussian Junkers, with whom they shared a common ideology. The bond between the Prussian and Russian Junkers, Howe stated, was so powerful and the economic union between them so inevitable that the Allies could never hope for support from the landed Junker and larger bourgeois classes in Russia. Hence, Howe concluded: "Our only hope in Russia lies with the revolutionary groups. Not necessarily with the Bolsheviki, but with whatever government the peasants and artisans may see fit to erect. And these are our natural allies. Whatever their form of government may be, it must be anti-German because the interest of the peasants and workers lies in preventing the Prussian government from reimposing the old feudal system in Russia, which is the one thing against which all revolutionary classes are united."

To Richard Hooker

Personal.

My dear Mr. Hooker: The White House 5 June, 1918

I hope you wll not be surprised to know that I subscribed almost in its entirety to the enclosed editorial from the Republican.[1]

I am keenly aware of and keenly sensitive to the implications which will be drawn out of the fact that I am not sending General Wood to the other side, and I want personal friends like yourself upon whose approval I depend for my encouragement to know why I am not sending him.

In the first place, I am not sending him because General Pershing has said that he does not want him and, in the second place, General Pershing's disinclination to have General Wood sent over is only too well founded. Wherever General Wood goes, there is controversy and conflict of judgment. On this side of the water we can take care of things of that sort, because the fighting is not being done here, but it would be fatal to let it go on at or anywhere near the front.

I have had a great deal of experience with General Wood. He is a man of unusual ability but apparently absolutely unable to submit his judgment to those who are superior to him in command. I am sorry that his great ability cannot be made use of in France, but, at the same time, I am glad to say that it is being made very much use of in the training of soldiers on this side of the water, a task for which he is eminently well fitted and which he is performing with diligence and success.

With sincere regard,

Faithfully yours,   Woodrow Wilson

TLS (received from Richard Hooker).
  [1] It is missing; however, it was "Gen Wood's Case," *Springfield* (Mass.) *Republican*, June 1, 1918. It commented on an editorial in the *Chicago Daily Tribune* which had severely criticized the Wilson administration for its alleged failure to utilize more efficiently the limited number of experienced American officers by refusing to send General Wood to France. The *Springfield Republican* stated that, if Wood was to be kept at

home, in spite of the fact that he could render exceptional service abroad, in order to "punish" him for past indiscretions, the President would, indeed, merit sharp criticism. Wood's military value should be estimated entirely apart from his political connections, his political escapades, and his opposition to Wilson. On the other hand, the editorial continued, Wood should not be given a command merely to satisfy his strong personal ambitions, and it was of no consequence that he wished to serve in France. His case was no different from those of other capable officers who had been kept at home without causing a debate in the newspapers and in Congress. The editorial pointed out that the real issue was how Wood could best be used to promote the winning of the war, and it concluded:

"The treatment of Gen Wood, then, is now a question mainly contingent on his capacity to fit into the military organization which has been created, that is to say, to do team work as a subordinate of Gen Pershing, if he is to be sent to France.

"In this particular, Gen Pershing's judgment should be controlling. It has been strongly intimated that the present difficulty is precisely at this point. It would be folly to order Gen Wood to France as commander of a division under Gen Pershing, if the appointment were obnoxious to Gen Pershing. Whether such an explanation covers the case no one seems to know authoritatively, however, and the administration must expect to be censured if it is impossible to satisfy Gen Wood's friends that he is not the victim of unfair discrimination."

From Newton Diehl Baker, with Enclosure

My dear Mr. President: Washington. June 5, 1918.

Mr. Juss[e]rand called on General March yesterday afternoon and told him he had an appointment to see you to-day at two o'clock, at which time he is going to present a request of Mr. Lloyd George, Mr. Clemenceau, and Mr. Orlando for the June shipment of troops to Europe. I do not know what this joint request from the three Prime Ministers contemplates, but in all likelihood it will urge for the month of June further preferential shipments of infantry and machine gun units. I understand the British and ourselves estimate the June transportation capacity at 300,000 men. Our program for shipment in June is based on that number and comprises 120,000 infantry and machine gun personnel as such, 20,000 infantry replacements, making in all 140,000 infantry and machine gun personnel; the remainder, as now planned, is 160,000, and comprises Engineers, Artillery, Medical units, Signal Corps (including Air Service), and Service of the Rear troops, the latter being of great, if not indispensable, importance, as we are already landing at the French ports from our cargo ships, month by month, larger stocks of subsistence and other stores than we are able to evacuate away from the port, creating a congested situation which of course can not be indefinitely continued.

I have received to-day, from General Pershing, a cablegram of which I enclose a copy. From it you will observe that General Pershing feels that to a larger and larger degree the burden of this fighting is going to fall upon the American Army. Already, from all accounts we have, the American divisional units are giving the best sort of account of themselves, while there seems to be marked loss of cohesion among the British and French troops. For this reason, General Pershing is clear that the greatest military strength we can add to the Allied defensive line lies in complete American divisions operating under their own commanders and having the esprit de corps which comes from serving in their own units. General March concurs very strongly in General Pershing's view, and feels that probably some part of the apparent disorganization of the French and British forces proceeds from the fact that American troops have been brigaded with them, thus depriving the French and British soldiers of the sense of responsibility and esprit de corps which comes to them when they are members of an established French or British division, by making them divide responsibility with their American associates. General March also feels that American soldiers brigaded with either the French or British, serving under officers whose language or ways they do not understand, and fighting under another flag than that of their own country, lose a great element of moral strength. So that on the whole case General Pershing and General March are very urgent that the rapid formation of complete American divisions is of the highest importance.

From the beginning of this pressure for the shipment of American infantry and machine gun personnel, I have felt that we ought not be put in the position of failing to do what was suggested to us as essential to hold the German line, chiefly because I did not want the possibility of failure being attributed to us even if the course recommended by our Allies would not have prevented the failure. Nevertheless, the present situation is one in which the best thing to be done has to be determined on the facts as they are, and these seem to point quite clearly to the soundness of General Pershing's judgment, particularly when one takes into account the fine and steady service of our organized divisions as contrasted with the wavering and unsteady service of the British and French divisions which are composite in character by reason of the brigading of American troops with them.

The program for June as made up, involving the transportation of 140,000 infantry and machine gun personnel, ought in my judgment to satisfy the French and British, since it is a number in excess of any expectation they have at any time entertained; and the transportation of the other personnel deemed necessary by General Pershing and General March can not be prejudicial and must be helpful to the Allied cause if it in fact expedites the formation of complete American divisions with the advantages above pointed out.

Should Mr. Jusserand suggest the depletion of French and British divisions as reason for supplementing them with American personnel, the obvious military answer is that it would be better for them to consolidate two depleted divisions into one homogeneous division, all French or all British as the case might be, and to have an independent American division, with the advantage in each case of national sympathy, officers, and traditions all of the same kind with the men comprising the division.

I wish, too, it could be possible for you to urge upon Mr. Jusserand the suggestion contained in General Pershing's cablegram to the effect that Great Britain and France in this crisis ought to use the maximum man-power available to them. I do not know how fully they are doing this, but in no case ought any uncertainty to be left in the minds of Mr. Lloyd George and Mr. Clemenceau that the United States desires its military effort to be supplementary to their maximum, rather than any replacement of any of their available strength.

I am sending these observations so that you may at least have them in mind in your conference with Mr. Jusserand.

Respectfully yours,   Newton D. Baker

TLS (WP, DLC).

E N C L O S U R E

Paris June 4, 1918, 8:22 A.M.

Number 1235. Personal and Confidential.

For the Chief of Staff and Secretary of War.

Paragraph 1. Consider military situation very grave. The French line gave way before what was thought to be a secondary attack and the 8 divisions that occupied that front have lost practically all their materiel and a large percentage of their personnel, although actual number of men and guns are yet unknown. The German advance seems to be stopped for the time being. The railroads in the areas they have taken are not available for their use principally because of the destruction of the tunnel at Vauxaillon. As already reported, the infantry of our third division is being used in Lorraine and the 5th along the Marne. Our 2d division entire is fighting northeast of Chateau-Thierry and has done exceedingly well. It is General Foch's plan to take the divisions from behind the British attacking line as needed and use them with French artillery in Lorraine to replace French divisions for the battle.

Paragraph 2. The attitude of the Supreme War Council which has been in session since Saturday is one of depression. The Prime Minister and General Foch appeal most urgently for trained or even untrained men, and notwithstanding my representations that the number of trained infantry in United States would be practically exhausted by the middle of July, they still insisted on a program of infantry personnel. The agreement entered into however was not entirely satisfactory as to July, but instead of sending raw infantry troops it is believed wiser to send more of the class we need for various services. I hope we shall be able to make heavy shipment of combat personnel in August and succeeding months.

Paragraph 3. The utmost endeavor should be made to keep up a constant flow of personnel to their full capacity of tonnage, and I very strongly urge that divisions be organized as rapidly as possible and be sent over entire after July, and also that auxiliary troops of all kind be shipped in due proportion. It should be fully realized at home that the time has come for us to take up the brunt of the war and that France and England are not going to be able to keep their armies at present strength very much longer.

Paragraph 4. I have pointed out to the Prime Minister(s) the necessity of both the French and British Governments utilizing every possible man at this time, including 1919 draft(s) who still lack a month or so of completing their training. Attention is called to general reference to this matter in the agreement which implies that both governments are doing this, but I am not sure however that this is the fact. It might be wise to request the respective ambassadors to urge their governments to put in every available man to meet this crisis and hold on until our forces can be felt.

Paragraph 5. In view of recent losses * * * the question of divisional artillery is also very serious. It is doubtful now whether the French will be able to supply us with the artillery we require. It is also reported that our program *at home it* (is?) very far behind. I most sincerely hope this is not so, as it is unlikely that France will be able to do more than meet her own requirements from now on. Will advise you more in detail later.

Paragraph 6. The urgent cables sent by the 3 Prime Ministers giving General Foch's views as to allied needs in troops and asking for an increased American program was read to me. I told them that the United States were fully alive to the necessity of doing everything possible and would do so. I can only add that our program should be laid out systematically and broadly and men called out as fast as they can be handled.   Pershing.

T telegram (WP, DLC).

From William Dennison Stephens

Sacramento, Calif., June 5, 1918.

Your message of yesterday received and in reply I beg to inform you that since my last wire to you[1] Mooney has moved the lower court to set aside the judgment. This motion was denied by the lower court. A bill of exception has been signed by the judge of that court who has stated that he will not sign the warrant of execution until the supreme court has decided whether or not it will issue a writ of probable cause. Consequently the case is not yet out of the hands of the courts. Please be assured that I am mindful of your deep concern in the matter.

William D. Stephens.

T telegram (WP, DLC).
[1] W. D. Stephens to WW, March 30-31, 1918, Vol. 47.

From the Diary of Josephus Daniels

June Wednesday 5 1918

Discussed coal & grain used in making beer & soft drinks. WW objected to Randall amendment because there was no temperance in it. Felt like making a trade—cut out beer &c if Congress would give war-time prohibition. Told Baruch, Hoover, Garfield & Mc-Cormick to study & make recommendations.

Irish attitude.

Two Letters to Robert Lansing

My dear Mr. Secretary,   The White House. 6 June, 1918.

I am quite willing to furnish the funds for this[1] provided we have reason to think that these supplies, if purchased by us, can be kept out of the hands of the Germans or the Irresponsible Bolsheviks in Siberia. I would not like to spend real money for them and then have both the goods and the money fall to the enemy. How can we safeguard them? Will it be possible in the circumstances to get the goods out of the country?   Faithfully Yours,   W.W.

WWTLI (SDR, RG 59, 861.24/82, DNA).
[1] See RL to WW, June 3, 1918.

My dear Mr. Secretary,   The White House. 6 June, 1918.

I shall be very glad to have you consult the Secretary of the Navy about this proposed movement of 6000 marines to Galveston. If that number of marines can be spared from immediate war service for this purpose, I will be glad to approve of the concentration and of preparation for their use if necessary, though I shall need to be convinced by very pressing and unusual circumstances before I can assent to disturbing the peace of Latin America.

Faithfully Yours,   W.W.

WWTLI (SDR, RG 59, 812.00/22199, DNA).

To William Bauchop Wilson, with Enclosure

My dear Mr. Secretary: The White House 6 June, 1918

Governor Harrington came to see me yesterday and requested a letter from me like the enclosed. I dare say you are much more familiar than I am with the working of the Maryland compulsory work law and I don't like to send this letter without seeking your approval of it. If you approve it, will you not be kind enough to have it posted at once without being returned to me? If, on the other hand, you think it ought to be altered or added to in any way, I would be very much obliged to you for suggestions.

Cordially and sincerely yours,   Woodrow Wilson

TLS (LDR, RG 174, DNA).

E N C L O S U R E

To Emerson Columbus Harrington

My dear Governor Harrington: [The White House] 6 June, 1918

Your letter of May twenty-first[1] calls my attention to the proposal for a nation-wide movement based upon the principles embodied in the Maryland compulsory work law. I can say without hesitation that I am heartily in accord with any movement intended to bring every citizen to a full realization of his responsibilities as a participant in this war.

Upon our entrance into the war I called upon our citizens to mobilize their energies for its prosecution in every way that was possible. The response has been exceedingly gratifying. The slogan "Work or Fight" has everywhere been taken up as a satisfactory expression of the spirit of the people. The instances of failure to appreciate its force and significance have been few. It is only natural, however, that those few cases should excite the feeling that the spirit of the community should in some way be enforced by law upon those who were not willing to cooperate of their own initiative.

This has made possible the effective operation of our selective service law and has found expression, also, in your compulsory work law.

The memorandum which you have prepared points out how wisely Maryland has acted in this matter. I particularly admire the care the Maryland Legislature has taken to be just in the provisions of the law which protect the honest working man in his rights and privileges. I hope that it will be possible to duplicate the action and experience of Maryland in other states.

Cordially and sincerely yours,   Woodrow Wilson[2]

TLS (Letterpress Books, WP, DLC).

[1] E. C. Harrington to WW, May 21, 1918, TLS (WP, DLC). Harrington said that the National Committee on Prisons and Prison Labor had asked for his support in a nationwide campaign for the enactment of compulsory work laws. He enclosed a letter from Ernest Stagg Whitin, the chairman of the executive council of the National Committee on Prisons and Prison Labor, which stated that the Maryland compulsory work law of June 1917 had set an example for other states in their search for a solution to the "slacker" problem. Whitin asked Harrington for a statement about Maryland's experience with the law which could serve as a guideline for states contemplating similar legislation. Whitin also suggested that Harrington write to Wilson to determine the President's views on the matter and to make sure that the proposed movement would not conflict with the recent "work-or-fight" regulations of the War Department. E. S. Whitin to E. C. Harrington, May 20, 1918, TCL (WP, DLC).

Harrington also enclosed the memorandum which he had prepared at Whitin's request. It reviewed the major provisions of the Maryland law, explained its operation, and summarized its results. E. C. Harrington, "Operation of the Maryland Compulsory Work Law," T MS (WP, DLC). For the main features of the Maryland law, see S. Gompers to WW, Aug. 10, 1917, n. 1, Vol. 43.

[2] As it turned out, this letter was not sent in its original form. See WBW to WW, June 8, 1918.

To William Phillips, with Enclosure

My dear Mr. Phillips: The White House 6 June, 1918

Thank you for sending me the notice from Cambridge University of the bestowal of the honorary degree of Doctor of Laws.[1] Will you not be kind enough to send the enclosed letter in the pouch and ask the Embassy in London if they will not be kind enough to see that it is delivered to Doctor Shipley?

Cordially and sincerely yours,   Woodrow Wilson

TLS (SDR, RG 59, 811.001W69/369, DNA).

[1] W. Phillips to WW, June 5, 1918, TLS (WP, DLC), enclosing I. B. Laughlin to RL, June 1, 1918, Nos. 10385 and 10386, T telegrams (WP, DLC). In his first telegram, Laughlin reported that, in Page's absence, he had received, on June 1, 1918, on behalf of Wilson the honorary degree conferred upon Wilson by the University of Cambridge and had signed the roll as Wilson's proxy. Laughlin's second telegram transmitted a message in Latin from Shipley which officially notified Wilson of the conferral of the degree. For earlier correspondence on this matter, see WW to RL, March 20, 1918, and ns. 1 and 3 thereto, and A. E. Shipley to WW, April 5, 1918, both in Vol. 47.

ENCLOSURE

To Arthur Everett Shipley

My dear Mr. Vice Chancellor: [The White House] 6 June, 1918

I do not know the right formal way in which to acknowledge the high honor which Cambridge University has so graciously conferred upon me *in absentia*, but I hope that you will overlook formality in the unusual circumstances and permit me to express to you and through you to the senate of the University my very deep appreciation of this generous action on your and their part. The terms of cordial friendship and the spirit of international unity in which the degree was conferred have given me great cheer and much additional courage in helping to perform the tasks which daily lie before all of us, and I shall feel that it is a great distinction to be so connected with an ancient University which I have all my life admired and which played so great a part in the foundation and development of the higher learning in America.

With warm personal regard,

Cordially and sincerely your,   Woodrow Wilson

TLS (Letterpress Books, WP, DLC).

To Anna Howard Shaw

My dear Doctor Shaw: [The White House] 6 June, 1918

After receiving your letter of May twenty-ninth, sending me the resolutions of the Woman's Committee of the Council of National Defense concerning placing women in positions of authority where the work of women was involved, I took the matter up not only with the Cabinet on Tuesday, but with the group of gentlemen whom I assemble about me every Wednesday for conference. I found that they gave the suggestion very sympathetic hearing, and I hope that you can rest assured that wherever it is possible to do so they will act upon it.

Cordially and sincerely yours,   Woodrow Wilson

TLS (Letterpress Books, WP, DLC).

From William Phillips

Dear Mr. President: Washington June 6, 1918.

I did not fail this morning to show Mr. Davison the enclosed letter[1] which you so kindly sent me. He asked me whether it would be a relief to you to know that Dr. Lowell was not going, to which I replied in the affirmative. An hour later he telephoned to me that the matter had been arranged and that Dr. Lowell would not go to Berne.[2] He added, also, that he would regard the matter in the strictest confidence and that Dr. Lowell would never know that you had expressed concern. I trust, therefore, that everything is settled to your satisfaction.

With assurances of respect, etc., I am, my dear Mr. President,

Faithfully yours,   William Phillips

TLS (WP, DLC).

[1] That is, C. J. Edwards to EMH, May 21, 1918, printed as an Enclosure with EMH to WW, May 25, 1918.

[2] The American Red Cross had intended to send Lowell to Bern as the head of its new Commission for Switzerland. The Red Cross had decided to increase its representation in Switzerland in order to care more adequately for the growing number of American and Allied prisoners of war in Germany.

From Thomas Watt Gregory

Dear Mr. President: Washington, D. C. June 6, 1918.

You have recently sent me original letter addressed to you by Mr. Upton St. Clair [Sinclair], dated May the 18th, last, accompanied by a copy of a letter addressed by Mr. St. Clair to United States District Attorney Caffey, at New York, dated May 3rd, last, and also a copy of Mr. Caffey's reply to Mr. St. Clair, dated May the 10th, last; also, original letter addressed to Mr. Kent by Max Eastman, bearing date May 31st, last; also, original letter addressed to you by Tariff Commissioner G. P Costigan, dated May the 29th, and original letter addressed to you by Mr. Amos Pinchot, dated May 24th.[1]

All of these relate to the further prosecution of the indictment against Max Eastman and others in the Southern District of New York. The matter having been disposed of at our personal interview this afternoon,[2] I send the enclosures for your files, retaining copies thereof.   Faithfully yours,   T. W. Gregory

TLS (WP, DLC).

[1] Sinclair to Caffey, May 3, 1918, and Caffey to Sinclair, May 10, 1918, are summarized in U. B. Sinclair to WW, May 18, 1918, ns. 1 and 2. Eastman to Kent, May 31, 1918, is printed as an Enclosure with W. Kent to WW, June 3, 1918. Costigan's and Pinchot's letters are printed at their own dates.

[2] Gregory had seen Wilson at the White House at 5 p.m. They had obviously decided that the Justice Department should proceed with its prosecution of Eastman, Reed, and other associates of *The Masses* and seek a retrial. The second *Masses* trial was held in the federal district court in New York from September 30 to October 5, 1918. Like the earlier trial, the second trial ended in a hung jury, with eight jurors in favor of conviction and four opposed. *New York Times*, Oct. 1, 2, 4, 5, and 6, 1918. See also Robert A. Rosenstone, *Romantic Revolutionary: A Biography of John Reed* (New York, 1975), pp. 330-33.

A Translation of a Telegram from Jean Jules Jusserand
to Stéphen Jean Marie Pichon

New York Washington undated
received June 6, 1918 4:15p.m.

Nos. 694-702. Following my telegram 689.

I have just delivered to Mr. Wilson, in the name of my colleagues
and myself, the message from the three prime ministers and the
note setting forth the accord of the generals.

The conversation was most satisfactory. The President told me
that he was perfectly aware of the situation, of the urgent need for
aid and of exactly what was needed, and that he would spare no
effort to satisfy fully the wishes of his cobelligerents, which were
supported by such a military authority as General Foch.

Just as my telegram of the day before yesterday predicted, he
told me as he did the first time: "It is only a question of tonnage;
if the ships are not lacking, all the troops requested will depart."

I insisted on the necessity for sending high proportions of infantry
and machine-gunners, which, from the nature of our losses, were
desperately needed. The President had no difficulty in falling into
accord with this.

I have been anxious to get from him a formal assurance.

As for the hundred divisions of American effectives (the response
to the English Ambassador's telegram came at the time allotted to
me for this subject), he replied that for the moment this figure did
not frighten him, but that if necessary it would be surpassed.

In this regard, however, he said, two points must be considered.
First, in view of the effort demanded of us by the three governments,
it will be necessary that each of them examine its military strength
and let us know that the number of combatants supplied by each
is really the maximum possible. Such a declaration could be useful
in certain circumstances to communicate to Congress and even, if
necessary, to the public in order to fend off possible criticisms.

Second, if we have but a relatively short time in which to prepare
the strongest army available for the front, do not be surprised if we
deem it indispensable for us to think this over from now until the
moment when it [this American force] must act as an army, and
if, even while we are sending on a priority basis the kinds of troops
which, above all others, are currently needed, we still apply ourselves to completing the divisions with the objective of a homogeneous and independent American army.

I replied that the earlier communications which the President
had received from us showed that formation of this army under the
best conditions was the Allies' wish as well as his own. Just now

it was necessary to deal without delay with the most urgent matter, to cut short an offensive which was now as close to Paris as Washington was to Baltimore, and for this purpose to continue the system of brigading troops which has given the best results.

The conversation ended with Mr. Wilson's assurances of the strongest good will.

As I was leaving, the Secretary of War and the Secretary of the Navy arrived at the White House. The latter told me that all suitable ships were chasing German submarines, which had just appeared in American waters. However, it has not yet been possible to destroy any enemy vessels.

I gave a report of my interview with the President to the English and Italian Ambassadors, who telegraphed it to their governments.

When the President spoke to me about the use of military resources by the three concerned governments, I told him of our situation, providing him with various facts and figures. He replied: "I have no doubt at all on this subject, but you will fully understand that it can be very useful to be able to cut short at the very beginning certain ill-intentioned criticisms in case these crop up."

After leaving Mr. Wilson, I went to the War Department and saw the Chief of the General Staff in order to satisfy myself that the good will shown me by the President would be demonstrated in actual measures of execution. On this score, I was able to convince myself that we need entertain no doubts. General March was very pleased with the support that I had received, and he told me that our requests were perfectly realizable and would be realized. It was above all vital that the Allies do their best regarding tonnage.

The 300,000 men which you expect for the month of June, the General told me, can leave immediately. They are trained, assigned, and ready to embark.

I spoke as I had spoken earlier to the President about the necessity of continuing the system of brigading troops, at least in June and July, and we shall see what comes after that.

Fearing possible delays resulting from training or instruction that were considered insufficient, I told the General that even though five months of training in the United States had been considered necessary at the beginning, now that the soldierly spirit was better aware of this crisis, and now that the ardor to learn had become truly impassioned, less time would suffice, especially for the infantry, and three or three-and-a-half months would be enough. By this means the troop movements could be continued at the high level we are counting on.

General March replied that he was of the same opinion and that he had even cabled General Pershing yesterday to this effect.

The organization on which the American authorities have settled involves maintaining on a permanent basis a total of a million men under the colors in training. Therefore, when a contingent is sent to France, an equal number is called up for training, thus reconstituting the million.

Some *mélanges* of untrained soldiers have in certain cases been joined at the last minute with trained ones, with great damage to the divisions thus manipulated.

General March assured me that nothing like this will be done again. They are forming special reserves of soldiers at various stages of training to serve as replacements in case they are needed at the time of departure.

I took advantage of my conversation today with the President to speak to him of the Russo-Siberian situation, reminding him of the grave indications of which we learn each day, and I said to him: In your last speech you assured Russia of your firm intention to assist her. May I ask if you have decided on a plan as to the form this assistance might take?

He replied: Despite certain appearances that are more or less serious, I continue to envisage an intervention that will be not only Japanese. The Japanese are too badly regarded in Russia for their auxiliaries not to be regarded as more dangerous than helpful. But I envisage now sending a shipment of American troops, a rather large shipment, several divisions. The realization of such a plan, however, like every similar plan (an allusion to the transport of the Czechs from Vladivostok) would have to receive General Foch's approval. These troops will be associated with the Japanese and with those troops which, according to their means, China, France, and England might furnish.

Mr. Wilson seemed to expect the latter two countries to provide only insignificant forces rather than real assistance.

When I asked if he had consulted Japan, he replied in the negative but said that if the aid was serious, as proposed, he thought that it would doubtless be gladly accepted.

At the bottom of his soul the President seems to me, even despite the projects similar to ours that he is now formulating, to believe that the solution of all problems, all at once, will be obtained on the western front; that it is necessary to concentrate his efforts there, to hasten his action and try to achieve definitive success before the Germans are able to take anything from Russia except the hatred that they have already sown there in abundance, as for instance in the Ukraine. With this success obtained, he told me, we could with one blow topple the peace settlements of Brest, the Ukraine, Finland, and Rumania.

I spoke to him of the rumor now circulating of his intention to send a political mission (socialist) and an economic one to Japan [Russia]. He replied that this rumor was false. Various personages have dreamt of making such a trip, but this would be on a private basis and not on a mission as such.   Jusserand.

T telegram (Campagne contre l'Allemagne, 1914-1918, 14 N 25, Archives du Maréchal Joffre, p. 73, FMD-Ar).

Remarks to Mexican Editors

[[June 7, 1918]]

Gentlemen, I have never received a group of men who were more welcome than you are, because it has been one of my distresses during the period of my presidency that the Mexican people did not more thoroughly understand the attitude of the United States toward Mexico.

I think I can assure you, and I hope you have had every evidence of the truth of my assurance, that that attitude is one of sincere friendship—not merely the sort of friendship which prompts one not to do his neighbor any harm, but the sort of friendship which earnestly desires to do his neighbor service.

My own policy and the policy of my own administration toward Mexico was at every point based upon this principle, that the internal settlement of the affairs of Mexico was none of our business; that we had no right to interfere with or to dictate to Mexico in any particular with regard to her own affairs.

Take one aspect of our relations which at one time may have been difficult for you to understand: when we sent our troops into Mexico, our sincere desire was nothing else than to assist you to get rid of the man who was making the settlement of your affairs for the time being impossible. We had no desire to use our troops for any other purpose, and I was in hopes that, by assisting in that way and thereupon immediately withdrawing the troops, I might give you substantial proof of the truth of the assurances that I had given your government through President Carranza.

And at the present time it distresses me to learn that certain influences, which I assume to be German in their origin, are trying not only to make a wrong impression, but to give an absolutely untrue account of the things that happen.

You know distressing things have been happening just off our coasts. You know of vessels that have been sunk. I yesterday received a quotation from a paper in Guadalajara which stated that thirteen of our battleships had been sunk off the capes of Chesapeake.

You see how dreadful it is to have the people so radically misinformed. It was added that our Navy Department was withholding the facts with regard to these sinkings. I have no doubt that the publisher of the paper printed this in perfect innocence and without intending to convey a wrong impression, but it is evident that allegations of that sort proceed from those who wish to make trouble between Mexico and the United States.

Now, gentlemen, for the time being, at any rate—and I hope that it will not be a short time—the influence of the United States is somewhat pervasive in the affairs of the world, and I believe it is pervasive because those nations of the world which are less powerful than some of the greatest nations are coming to believe that our sincere desire is to do disinterested service.

We are the champions of those nations which have not had the military standing which would enable them to compete with the strongest nations in the world. And I look forward with pride to the time, which I hope will come, when we can give substantial evidence, not only that we do not want anything out of this war, but that we would not accept anything out of this war, that it is absolutely a case of disinterested action.

And if you will watch the attitude of our people, you will see that nothing stirs them so deeply as the assurances that this war, so far as we are concerned, is for idealistic objects. One of the difficulties that I experienced during the first three years of the war—the years when the United States was not in the war—was in getting the foreign offices of the European nations to believe that the United States was seeking nothing for herself, that her neutrality was not selfish, and that if she came in she would not come in to get anything substantial out of the war, any material object, any territory, or trade, or anything else of that sort.

In some foreign offices, there were men who personally know me and they believed, I hope, that I was sincere in assuring them that our purposes were disinterested, but they thought that these assurances came from an academic gentleman removed from the ordinary resources of information and speaking the idealistic purposes of a cloister. They did not believe I was speaking the real heart of the American people, and I knew all along that I was. Now I believe everyone who comes in contact with the American people knows that I am speaking their purposes.

The other night, in New York, at the opening of the campaign for funds for our Red Cross, I made an address. I had not intended to refer to Russia, but was speaking without notes, and, in the course of what I said, my own thought was led to Russia, and I said that we meant to stand by Russia just as firmly as we would stand by France or England or any other of our allies.

The audience to which I was speaking was not an audience from which I would have expected an enthusiastic response to that. It was rather too well dressed. It was not an audience, in other words, made of a class of people who would have the most intimate feeling for the sufferings of the ordinary man in Russia, but that audience jumped to its feet in enthusiasm. Nothing else that I had said on that occasion aroused anything like the enthusiasm that single sentence aroused.

Now that is a sample, gentlemen. We cannot make anything out of Russia. We cannot make anything out of our standing by Russia at this time—the remotest of European nations, so far as we are concerned, the one with which we have had the least connections in trade and advantage—and yet the people of the United States rose to that suggestion as to no other that I made in that address.

That is the heart of America, as we are ready to show it by any act of friendship toward Mexico. Some of us, if I may speak so privately, look back with regret upon some of the more ancient relations that we have had with Mexico long before our generation; and America, if I may now so express it, would now feel ashamed to take advantage of her neighbor.

So I hope you can carry back to your homes something better than assurances and words. You have had contact with our people. You know of your own personal reception. You know how gladly we have opened to you the doors of every establishment that you wanted to see and have shown you just what we are doing, and I hope you have gained the right impression as to why we are doing it. We are doing it, gentlemen, so that the world may never hereafter have to fear the only thing that any nation has to dread—the unjust and selfish aggression of another nation.

Some time ago, as you probably all know, I proposed a sort of Pan-American agreement.[1] I had perceived that one difficulty in our past relations with Latin America was this: the famous Monroe Doctrine was adopted without your consent and without the consent of any Central American or South American states. If I may express it in the terms that we so often use in this country, we said, "We are going to be your big brother, whether you want us to be or not."

We did not ask whether it was agreeable to you that we should be your big brother. We said we are going to be. Now, that was all

---

[1] A reference, of course, to the ill-fated Pan-American Pact.

very well as far as protecting you from aggression from the other side of the water, but there was nothing in it that protected you from aggression from us, and I have repeatedly seen an uneasy feeling on the part of representatives of states of Central and South America that our self-appointed protection might be for our own benefit and our own interests and not for the interest of our neighbors. So I have said, "Very well, let us make an arrangement by which we will give bonds. Let us have a common guarantee that all of us will sign a declaration of political independence and territorial integrity. Let us agree that if any one of us, the United States included, violates the political independence or territorial integrity of any of the others, all others will jump on her."

I pointed out to some gentlemen who were less inclined to enter into this arrangement than others that that was in effect giving bonds on the part of the United States that we would enter into an arrangement by which you would be protected from us.

Now, that is the kind of agreement that will have to be the foundation of the future life of the nations of the world, gentlemen. The whole family of nations will have to guarantee to each nation that no nation shall violate its political independence or its territorial integrity. That is the basis, the only conceivable basis, for the future peace of the world, and I must admit that I was anxious to have the states of the two continents of America show the way to the rest of the world as to how to make a basis of peace.

Peace can only come by trust. As long as there is suspicion there is going to be misunderstanding, and as long as there is misunderstanding there is going to be trouble. If you can once get a situation of trust, then you have got a situation of permanent peace. Therefore, every one of us, it seems to me, owes it as a patriotic duty to his own country to plant the seeds of trust and confidence instead of seeds of suspicion.

That is the reason I began by saying to you that I had not had the pleasure of meeting a group of men who were more welcome than you are, because you are our near neighbors. Suspicion on your part or misunderstanding on your part distresses us more than we would be distressed by similar feelings on the part of those less near to us.

It is you who can see how Mexico's future must depend upon peace and honor, so that nobody shall exploit her. It must depend upon every nation that has any relation with her, and the citizens of any nation that has any relations with her, keeping within the bounds of honor and fair dealing and justice, because so soon as you can admit your own capital and the capital of the world to the free use of the resources of Mexico, it will be one of the most wonderfully rich and prosperous countries in the world. And, when you have foundations of established order, and the world has come to its senses again, we shall, I hope, continue in connections that will assure us all permanent cordiality and friendship.

Printed in the New York *World*, June 11, 1918, with minor corrections from the text printed in *Attitude of the United States toward Mexico . . .* (Washington, 1918).

David Franklin Houston to Albert Sidney Burleson, with Enclosure

Dear General: [Washington] June 7 [1918].

Here is the letter. I have read it to Lever. He thinks it "OK." He would like to receive it from the President this evening or early in the morning. It is understood that Lever is not to be known in this to the Senator.   D.F.H.

ALI (WP, DLC).

E N C L O S U R E

A Draft of a Letter to Asbury Francis Lever[1]

Dear Mr. Lever: [The White House, June 7, 1918]

I ⟨understand⟩ *know* that some time ago you submitted your name for nomination in the Democratic primary election in South Carolina as Senator from that State, and that the last day for the filing of papers is the 17th of this month. There now seems to be every reasonable assurance that no one will succeed in securing the nomination in South Carolina whose entire record does not make it plain that he will ⟨unqualifiedly loyally⟩ support the Nation and the Government *with unqualified loyalty* in the vigorous prosecution of this war to a successful conclusion. I am writing to ask if this is not also your own view and, if it is, whether you would not be willing to reconsider your decision and to remain in the House where you would continue to serve as Chairman of the very important Committee on Agriculture. It is clear to me that unless there are very compelling reasons to the contrary you should do this. The past five years have been exceptionally fruitful of legislation of vast importance not only to agriculture and rural life and to the fifty millions of people living in the rural districts but also to the whole Nation and the world as well. There are still, *as you know*, important and critical measures pressing for solution. The regular appropriation bill, not only providing for the highly important activities of the Department of Agriculture but also containing ⟨the⟩ *an* unfortunate proposal to change the price of wheat fixed ⟨by me in⟩ a proclamation issued some time ago, is still pending. It is important that this measure be disposed of wisely at the earliest possible moment. The emergency Food Production Bill, with two unnecessary and objectionable riders, *which* has passed the House, has not yet been taken up by the Senate, and will doubtless again require careful consideration by the House before it becomes a law. It is important ⟨also⟩ that this measure be passed before June 30; otherwise the Department may have to discontinue activities essential to the winning of the war or be greatly embarrassed in its efforts to stimulate production and render assistance to the farmers in the solution of emergency problems. The water power bill, which is under consideration by the special committee of which you are a member, is another urgent and important measure which should be acted upon as promptly as possible. It is obvious that many other matters of vast ⟨importance⟩ *consequence* to the Nation in the field of agriculture will continue to press for solution not only during the continuance of the war but also after the return of peace. Your long experience in the House as a member of the Committee on Agriculture and, for a number of years, as Chairman, *and* the important part that you have been able to play in securing wise action on vital measures already enacted into law, clearly point to the desirability of your continuing in the House for the time being, if possible. I hope, therefore, you will not feel that I am taking an unwarranted liberty in suggesting that, if feasible, you reconsider your decision and that you do not press your candidacy for Senator further.[2]

Assuring you of my appreciation of your cooperation in all matters of legislation, I am,   Very sincerely yours,[3]

T MS (WP, DLC).

[1] Words in angle brackets deleted by Wilson; words in italics added by him.

[2] Lever had entered the South Carolina Democratic preprimary campaign for the seat of the ailing Senator Tillman, who had repeatedly announced that he would not stand for reelection in 1918. Lever had received the support of the White House in his candidacy against former Governor Coleman L. Blease, an antiwar agitator and bitter opponent of Wilson, and Nathaniel Barksdale Dial, a conservative lawyer and banker. However, Tillman had changed his mind in March 1918 and decided that it was his patriotic duty to seek another term. Tillman's candidacy, together with Lever's refusal to withdraw from the contest voluntarily, put the White House in a quandary, since it threatened to divide the forces loyal to Wilson and raised the prospect of a victory by Blease. For a detailed discussion, see Francis B. Simkins, *Pitchfork Ben Tillman, South Carolinian* (Baton Rouge, La., 1944), pp. 535-46, and Livermore, *Politics Is Adjourned,* pp. 139-40, 160-61.

[3] In this revised form, this was sent as WW to A. F. Lever, June 7, 1918, TLS (Letterpress Books, WP, DLC).

To Newton Diehl Baker

My dear Baker,   The White House. 7 June, 1918

Here is a letter from House[1] which I would be very much obliged if you would read and return to me with such comment as you please to make.

While the letter is very frank (House knows that he can say what he pleases to me without parliamentary circumlocution) it is yet, as he himself says, not very specific in its outline of what ought to be done. You have been on the other side and can perhaps make a plan out of his suggestions better than I have been able to.

Faithfully Yours,   W.W.

WWTLI (N. D. Baker Papers, DLC).
[1] EMH to WW, June 3, 1918.

From Joseph Patrick Tumulty

Dear Governor: The White House 7 June 1918.

In the matter of the strike situation which you asked me to take up this morning with Secretary Wilson:[1]

After discussing the whole situation with him, he agreed with me that a statement from you *of a general character* which would carry no reference to the strikes now going on or about to be begun, would be very helpful and would prevent a great deal of future trouble.

I pass the following on to you as a suggestion for your statement:

We ought to establish the fact that strikes must not be begun or even considered until every instrumentality set up by the Government for their amicable settlement shall have been resorted to and the processes which it provides utterly exhausted. The first line of trenches is back home and while our boys "over there " are doing so much and sacrificing so much, it is disheartening to find that in the disputes between Capital and Labor, strikes have been proclaimed and labor disturbances have been permitted to continue without resorting to the agencies provided by the Government; that in this hour of crisis in the Nation's life, delay, interference or debating the rights of Capital and Labor result in crippling and paralyzing the industries that are so necessary to an expeditious prosecution of the War.

The lines of communication stretch far beyond the fields of Flanders where our boys are shedding their blood for the vindication of those conceptions of liberty which are so dear to all of us. Every class in America is generously giving its all to the needs of this war; the wealthy are paying their share in blood and treasure; the farmer by every means is increasing the productivity of the soil; the businessman is ungrudgingly giving his genius to the mobilization of our resources; the artisan, the small businessman and the ordinary man of the street are unselfishly devoting themselves to the cause of America.

We are all in the same boat. There are no classes in America. We are fighting as a united Nation for the life of the free peoples of the world. The men, whether they are representatives of Capital or Labor, who block the way of our men as they travel the glorious road of self-sacrifice, will be condemned in the court of public opinion not only as slackers but as guilty of the highest treason to their country. Let those who consider stopping the progress of industry pause and consider what the affect of any intermission in their labors will be. America is determined to see this war through to the end and those who hesitate or pause are striking a blow at the heart of America. We must fight and work and use every ounce of our energy in order to make the world free for the men, women and children who are generously sacrificing themselves in order to help in this consummation.

Sincerely yours,   J P Tumulty

TLS (WP, DLC).
¹ Although the number of strikes had decreased by 60 per cent in the first four months of 1918 as compared to the same period in 1917, controversies between capital and labor still resulted in frequent work stoppages which adversely affected the war effort. The potentially most serious among these conflicts in mid-1918 was a threatened nationwide strike by commercial telegraphers, about which see WBW to WW, June 10, 1918, and subsequent documents in this volume.

From Frank Lyon Polk

My dear Mr. President: Washington June 7, 1918.

Your comment on the Secretary's request to provide funds to enable the Ambassador to safeguard Russian supplies from German hands brings up the point which was especially emphasized in the Ambassador's instructions. No supplies are being purchased from the funds you have already set aside, except such as can really be controlled to the point of moving them in safety to Archangel or towards Vladivostok. It is the Ambassador's purpose to have members of the Purchasing Commission, aided by the additional American Consuls and Vice Consuls who have been appointed in European Russia and Siberia, and by the French and British, to follow all shipments and report at once if their safety is imperiled. The Ambassador's urgent demand for additional funds is prompted by the success of his initial efforts. He will report frequently to the Department, and whenever it seems that the plan is failing of success he will be instructed to cease expenditure.

The supplies in question consist of munitions, rubber, fats, hides, platinum and other products useful to Germany. It is believed that they can gradually be brought to this country. The Ambassador and the Military Attaché[1] seem confident that, in the meanwhile, the prospect of getting them beyond German control is favorable and worth the effort. It was on this account that the Secretary favored the idea of enabling the Ambassador to continue his present undertaking.   Faithfully yours,   Frank L. Polk

TLS (SDR, RG 59, 861.24/92a, DNA).
  [1] That is, Lt. Col. James A. Ruggles.

From Jouett Shouse

PERSONAL

My dear Mr. President: Washington, D. C. June 7, 1918.

When the Suffrage Amendment was pending before the House I took the liberty to address a letter to you concerning it, urging that insofar as you might feel you could with propriety do so you give it your support.[1] There can be no question that your announced attitude at that time was responsible for the passage of the amendment in the House.

I do not profess to be in any sense thoroughly in touch with the attitude or the sentiment of the United States Senate, but from what I can learn it seems that the amendment is apt to fail in the Senate. And if it should fail that failure will be due entirely to the lack of Democratic votes.

Those of us who come from Suffrage states are in position to realize much more definitely than those who live elsewhere the political effect of the failure to pass the amendment by a Congress in which our party has a majority in both branches.

I know that you have been altogether out-spoken in your attitude toward suffrage, and I read with interest and with gratification your recent public message to the Legislature of Louisiana on the subject.[2]

It seems now to be pretty well assured that the general work of this session of Congress will close during the month of June and that its labors beyond this month will be confined practically to the Revenue Bill. From a party standpoint it is of the greatest importance that the Suffrage Amendment shall be acted upon by the Senate and acted upon favorably. I know that you have given the situation deep thought and I hesitate to even seem to make a suggestion in view of the tremendous responsibilities and the vast burdens which are yours already. But not from any standpoint of self interest, not instigated by any selfish motives, simply because of my desire that the Democratic party, which has found such splendid justification in your wonderful leadership and in the accomplishments of the five and a half years of your administration, shall not intentionally put in its way obstacles for future success, I want to urge that to the uttermost point which you feel you can do so you shall exert your influence to see that the amendment goes through the Senate.

I believe a public statement from you given to the press, and particularly a statement made by you as the head of our party to some of those prominent in the leadership of our party in the Senate, will have such a sweeping effect as to assure successful action upon the amendment.

May I not be permitted, therefore, to offer the suggestion that you consider making such a statement and that you personally urge upon the Democratic leadership of the Senate the grave necessity, from a party standpoint, of giving Democratic support to the Suffrage Amendment?

While I am writing this letter personally I know that I voice very definitely and fully the sentiment of the entire Democratic delegation from my state in Congress.

With great respect, believe me

Sincerely yours,   Jouett Shouse

TLS (WP, DLC).
  [1] J. Shouse to WW, Jan. 8, 1918, TLS (WP, DLC).
  [2] That is, WW to L. S. Haas, June 4, 1918.

From Frank Lyon Polk, with Enclosure

My dear Mr. President,   Washington June 8, 1918.

Allow me to send you, enclosed herewith, a telegram from the American Ambassador at Petrograd, dated June fifth, giving the text of a communication from the Bolshevik Commissary for Foreign Affairs at Moscow announcing the appointment of a Bolshevik plenipotentiary representative in Washington. In a later telegram, dated the same day, the Ambassador recommends delaying any reply to this announcement and the Department concurs, if you approve.   Faithfully yours,   Frank L Polk

TLS (SDR, RG 59, 701.6111/221, DNA).

ENCLOSURE

Petrograd. June 5, 1918.

Following just received via Vologda, addressed American Ambassador: "Russian Government nominates as plenipotentiary representative in Washington Citizen Litvinov now same in Paris. Hopes friendship your Government, will not object, our purpose closer relations, intimate friendship between our peoples. Commissary Foreign Affairs, Chicherin." See my telegram of June 5, 6 p.m.[1]

T telegram (SDR, RG 59, 701.6111/221, DNA).
   [1] The relevant portion reads as follows: "I suggest delaying reply to request in my No. 1, June 5, 5 p.m., especially if inclined to make favorable reply which I do not anticipate." D. R. Francis to RL, June 5, 1918, 6 p.m., FR 1918, Russia, I, 552.

From Newton Diehl Baker

My dear Mr. President: Washington. June 8, 1918.

I return herewith the letter from Colonel House which you sent me yesterday. Substantially the same suggestions were made to General Pershing by General March before he left Europe and by me while I was in Europe. They resulted in a fairly complete separation of the Service of Supply from the purely military staff organization which General Pershing had built up in France.

At the outset, of course, General Pershing's problem was to prepare on the physical side for the receipt and maintenance of the army which was to come later. His headquarters at Chaumont became, therefore, principally offices of business administration. Later, as our troops began to go in increasing numbers, the purely military problem of training and combat grew more and more important, and General Pershing then concentrated the so-called Service of Supply at Tours, under General Kernan,[1] preserving at Chaumont only the military staff and such liaison officers as were necessary to keep him in touch with the Tours organization under General Kernan. This was a step in the right direction, but not so long a step as plainly will have to be taken and probably ought to be taken now. The problem is as Colonel House states it, and the solution is probably the one he suggests. There are three aspects of it: First, the purely military. This involves the command of the fighting army, the training of fresh contingents, and constant military study and cooperation with the High Commands of the other armies, and is all that a military commander can possibly be expected to accomplish. If General Pershing is able to do this, it will be all that he can do.

The Services of Supply for the American Army are, of course,

different from those of the French and British. Those armies have
their countries at hand and the vast civilian and military personnel
dealing with supply questions are under the immediate eye of Ministers of War, Munitions Ministers, Surveyors General of Purchases,
and other agencies which are three thousand miles away in our
forces. For this reason, very much more extensive warehouses and
supply systems generally are needed by the American Army in
proportion to its numbers than have been found necessary for either
the British or French. My judgment is that this entire burden should
be taken off General Pershing's shoulders, and the only hesitation
I have had about it has grown out of my inability to find a man of
sufficient breadth of view and swiftness of decision to put at the
head of the business. General Goethals is the one man in the Army,
so far as I know of its personnel, who could be surely entrusted
with the task. I do not believe it could be done by a civilian, for the
reason that it involves the actual command, at present, of 400,000
military people which in itself, of course, is a vast army and is
thoroughly military in its organization and activities, and because
of this fact I think Colonel House's suggestion that Mr. Stettinius
could head the matter up would hardly work.

The third aspect of the case, of course, deals with the so-called
diplomatic duties which General Pershing has from time to time
felt called upon to perform. His visits to London and P[a]ris have
of course necessarily been frequent, and his conferences with Prime
Ministers and other civilians even more frequent, but for all of this
he will have no time from now on and his mind ought not to be
burdened with any responsibility for such matters. The answer
which General Bliss suggested to this problem, when I discussed
it with him, was the appointment of a direct representative on the
Supreme War Council; I know there are considerations in your
mind which disincline you to that course. The only alternative
seems to be the more or less permanent presence in Paris of some
representative who will carry out for you all of the diplomatic negotiations of a purely war character, and thus relieve General Pershing and General Bliss from any responsibility for them whatever.
Mr. Page and Mr. Sharp are of course not available for this assignment, since each of them is an ambassador to a particular country,
while the representative suggested would have to move freely from
London to Paris and Rome and be able to attend conferences in
which four nations are represented. This I assume would be impossible for our ambassador to France, or England, or Italy, as each
of them has only one part of the territorial jurisdiction and it would
perhaps create difficulties if any one of them were selected to visit
the countries to which the others are officially accredited. Of course
the ideal solution of the problem would be to have Colonel House

in Paris. I fancy his health would make him reluctant to undertake so permanent a mission, and I know that his presence here is so helpful that permanent absence on his part would be a very serious loss. I do not think Mr. Stettinius would do for this phase of the work; he is essentially a banker and his knowledge is that of a banker dealing with industrial and commercial questions. Moreover, he does not speak French, which would be a serious handicap. I have thought over this problem for several months. Nobody occurs to me who would be as available as Vance McCormick, and if he could be spared from the War Trade Board, or replaced there, his permanent residence in Paris would be the most helpful relief I can figure out. Should he or anybody else be designated there as a permanent representative on the Supreme War Council, or as simply resident in Paris for the purpose of working out these war diplomacy questions, it would of course be necessary for him to be so accredited that General Pershing would look to him for any instructions he ought to have of a diplomatic character, and his relations ought to be direct with you and me so that many questions which have some sort of diplomatic color but are primarily military could be the subject of cable correspondence between him and me without unnecessarily taking up your time until they were matured and in some form for action or decision by you.

My reference above to General Goethals needs this much addition. Until now it has been impossible to spare him because there was a very large and indispensable task of organization to be done on this side, affecting storage and land and water transportation. This has now been so well done that in all likelihood it could be carried forward by someone else without serious loss of efficiency, and we are nearly, if not quite, to the place where it will be possible to send General Goethals to relieve General Kernan. When that is done, General Pershing will be able to rely on General Goethals for the whole supply question, and it will then be dissociated from his command just as the supply operations of the War Department in this country are dissociated from the command of the General operating in the field.

The suggestion of Colonel House's that we ought to do everything to magnify and strengthen the position of the Supreme Commander is, of course, sound. The British are reluctant in this matter, and therefore we should be the more zealous, as an example and an argument. General Pershing's duties under such a reorganization as Colonel House suggests would therefore be constant attention to his own troops, their preparation and their use, his own actual command of them in the field, and such conferences with General Foch or other Allied commanders as General Foch might from time to time direct, and I think in making any redistribution of these functions abroad we ought to emphasize to General Pershing our own conception of his task as being military and under General Foch to the fullest extent possible.

Respectfully yours,   Newton D. Baker

TLS (WP, DLC).
    [1] Maj. Gen. Francis Joseph Kernan, a former member of the General Staff and acting Assistant Chief of Staff, who had organized and now commanded the Service of Supply in France.

From Asbury Francis Lever

My dear Mr. President: Washington, D. C. June 8, 1918.

I am in receipt of your letter of the 7th in which you convey the impression that you desire me to continue as a Member of the House of Representatives.

I entered the Senatorial race in South Carolina only because of my belief that thereby I could best serve my State and Country.

You will pardon me for saying that this communication is a great and complete surprise to me, as I have been under the belief that I was performing the highest duty of a citizen in entering the race for the Senate, and also performing a sacrificial duty to the Administration. At no time did I believe that I was serving my own ambition solely. The one thought actuating me in retiring from the House of Representatives was that I believed that I was performing the highest duty to the people of my State, to the Nation, to the Administration, and yourself. I had every cause and reason to believe this. You have conveyed to me now the belief that there is still a higher and greater duty to perform to the Nation, and to yourself. You have impliedly commanded me to remain in the House of Representatives, and not to take the stump in South Carolina during the coming months. We are at war, you are the Commander in Chief of the Army and Navy, we have a Selective Service Act, and it is the duty of every man to be placed where he can best serve his Nation. If it is your belief, as I construe your letter to me, that my services can best be used in the House of Representatives, and you will say so to me in unmistakable terms so that "He who runs may read" no matter what my own judgment may be, or the desires of my friends, I wish to say to you that I am willing, and likewise my friends, most cheerfully to accede to your command.[1]

Respectfully yours,   A. F. Lever

TLS (WP, DLC).
    [1] As it turned out, Tillman, in whose favor Lever withdrew from the campaign, died on July 3, 1918. The Wilson administration thereupon threw its full support to Dial. About the outcome, see WW to T. H. Daniel, Aug. 14, 1918, n. 4.

From Willard Saulsbury

Dear Mr. President: [Washington] June 8th, 1918.

Thanks for your letter of June 4th regarding the rent profiteering resolution and the position of the Department of Justice regarding the matter.

I think the Attorney General's views are correct and the appearance by some capable representative of the Department amicus curiae will have the result I desired.

Yours very truly,   Willard Saulsbury

TLS (WP, DLC).

From William Cox Redfield

My dear Mr. President: Washington June 8th, 1918.

Information which we have been gathering concerning Russia from many sources points unanimously to the opportunity and to the obligation to make our influence felt through commercial lines in helpfulness to the Russian people. Our facts come, not only from our own permanent and traveling men in Russia and Siberia and through the Department of State, but from personal contact with Russians, with Americans long residents of Russia, and with Americans who have for many years carried on business in Russia. Many of these men have been long personally known to me. The general opinion deprecates military action but urges commercial action.

Confidentially but indirectly we learn that some plan has been suggested to you through the Department of State. Of its details we are not informed. I write simply to say that we are ready to act and we believe we understand what the situation requires. A considerable sum would be required but I can put no estimate upon it without knowing to what extent plans of the kind may have matured in your own mind and that of the Secretary of State. Of course our desire is to cooperate in the fullest way with the Department of State should our cooperation be desired.

I write, however, lest amid the urgent pressure brought from what seem to me authoritative sources for commercial action, I should be deemed negligent if I failed to put the matter definitely before you.   Yours very truly,   William C. Redfield

TLS (WP, DLC).

From William Bauchop Wilson

My dear Mr. President: Washington June 8, 1918.

I am in receipt of your proposed letter to Governor Harrington.

The habitual loafer is a greater menace to the honest workingman than to any other portion of the community. It is from this class that the professional strikebreaker is recruited. They are willing to exert themselves temporarily under the extraordinary inducement of large pay for strike-breaking purposes. Idleness interferes with production and the first person who suffers from insufficient production is the wage worker.

When, however, it is proposed to compel these people to work under penalty of law, the honest workman is interested in safeguarding such legislation so that the effect to compel the loafer to work may not be used as a club to beat down legitimate aspirations and activities. The Maryland law accomplishes that purpose more effectively than any that has come under my observation. It completely safeguards the rights of men who are temporarily unemployed by reason of differences with their employers, but it is doubtful whether the language would apply to the individual workman dissatisfied with his conditions. It also safeguards persons engaged or employed in seasonal occupations. It would seem, however, to leave the standards and conditions under which men are to be compelled to work entirely to the discretion of the authorities intrusted with the enforcement of the law. For that reason I am of the opinion that another sentence should be included in your letter to Governor Harrington immediately following the word "privileges" in the third last line, as follows:

"I assume that the safeguards of this legislation against the possibility of abuse include the maintenance of those standards and working conditions which the Council of National Defense and the National War Labor Board have set up as indispensable to the nation's full productive efficiency."[1]

This would make it clear that you had in mind the maintenance of these standards in such a manner as to protect the honest workman against unfair competition.

Faithfully yours,   W B Wilson

TLS (WP, DLC).
    [1] Wilson added this sentence to the draft printed as an Enclosure with WW to WBW, June 6, 1918, and sent it as WW to E. C. Harrington, June 6, 1918, TLS (Letterpress Books, WP, DLC).

Carrie Clinton Lane Chapman Catt to
Joseph Patrick Tumulty

My dear Mr. Tumulty: [Washington] June 8, 1918.

I have visited several states of late and upon my return to Washington for a few hours yesterday and talking the matter over carefully with Mrs. Park and Mrs. Gardener, we concluded that the only thing which will break the impasse in the Senate, is a public declaration by the President in favor of the Federal Amendment.

I found that the general opinion prevails that he does believe in suffrage for women but that he believes in it only state by state and that he is not sincere in his advocacy of the federal amendment. While this view does the President an injustice, it is a difficult matter to change that point of view since much propaganda is being spread broadcast to strengthen that view and no signed statement has ever appeared from the President with which to counteract it. The President did give permission to the Congressmen, who waited upon him in January, to use a statement which he authorized,[1] but as it was not a direct statement signed by him, it did not travel far.

It is with great distress that I make this appeal for I know how overtaxed the President is and were it an ordinary favor, I should certainly not press it. I feel myself such confidence that further delay in the Senate or the possible defeat of the federal amendment is going to lead to wide misunderstanding of our war aims throughout the world, that it seems to me vital to the fundamental psychology of the great world war that this amendment should be put through and now.

The eight years between 1904 and 1912, I was in Europe most of the time and my work brought me in contact with the leaders of the democratic movements in most of the European countries. I have had many letters from such sources asking whether the Senate has taken action and now [no] report made in the European press or whether it is delaying action and if so, why. An impulse to democracy on the other side has received a new intensity within the last year and I am proud to believe that the President's war message and his immortal slogan "we will make the world safe for democracy" had much to do with lifting the world conflict to a higher plane. If the world war is indeed to be "fought out in the souls of the people" as General Smutts puts it, the United States must not evade or avoid the clean issue of democracy and a frank out and out statement to this effect on the part of the President can do him and the Democratic Party no possible harm and it will give a stimulus to high thinking that is well worth while. The

following points seem to us important to be embodied in the statement:

    1. The aim of the Allies in the great world war is the establish-
ment of democratic institutions.

    2. It was the United States which stressed the point that we
were fighting for democracy.

    3. Great Britain and Canada have given the world pledge of their
sincerity that they are indeed fighting for democracy by cleaning
their own record and establishing democracy at home. Canada
has enfranchised her women and Great Britain has enfranchised
the men who had never had the vote before and also the women.

    4. The only Parliaments in the world which have turned down
bills for extending suffrage have been those of the Central Powers.   Carrie Chapman Catt

TCL (National American Woman Suffrage Association Papers, DLC).
   [1] It is printed at Jan. 9, 1918, Vol. 45.

To Asbury Francis Lever

[Dear Mr. Lever: The White House, June 9, 1918]

    I am in receipt of your letter of June 8th and in reply permit me
to say that I wrote you only after the most thoughtful consideration
of what I deemed to be my duty in the case. I do not wonder that
you thought yourself entitled by your long and distinguished service
in the House to consideration as a candidate for the Senate but, as
you yourself suggest in the last paragraph of your letter, we are at
war; the Selective Draft Act is applicable in principle to all of us.
It was this consideration that made me able as the present head of
the nation to ask you to remain in the House of Representatives.
It seems to me absolutely necessary that you should remain in
Washington through the present session because consideration of
legislation to which I alluded in my letter to you of the 7th instant
(matters which we believed would have been finished by this time).
You see how I view the clear basis of my judgment in this important
matter, which so nearly touches your own political career, about
which I would not in ordinary circumstances be at liberty to express
a judgment at all. I am convinced that the interests of the nation
make it in the highest degree desirable that you should remain as
long as possible in direction of the agricultural legislation of the
House.   [Cordially and sincerely yours,   Woodrow Wilson]

T transcript (WC, NjP) of WWsh MS (WP, DLC).

From Charles Richard Crane

Dear Mr President   Wood's Hole Mass. June 9 1918

Professor Masaryk plans to spend two weeks in Washington after June 16th and I hope that at sometime within that period you and he can have a good talk. I believe him to be—and I have known him well for nearly twenty years—one of the wisest and best of Christians. He has given up his whole life to helping solve the difficult problems of other people and I do not know of a more useful one. He has a wider touch with the people in this war than anyone else and his organizing of the Bohemian army in Russia last year—the only organized thing there—and, with anarchy all around him, providing it with food, ammunition and transportation, shows that he knew his way around even there. He is certainly the outstanding Slavic leader of the world and I should say one of the half dozen leading statesmen. As I still hope that Christians—New Testament Christians—will determine the conditions under which peace may come and be maintained for a long time, I believe no one else in Europe could make so valuable a contribution as he.

You made my daughter, Mrs. Leatherbee,[1] very happy the other [day] and I am happy also that she can have the memory of the little chat with you. Thank you!

Affectionate greetings to you, the pretty lady and your other aides,

Always   Charles R. Crane

ALS (WP, DLC).
[1] Frances Anita Crane (Mrs. Robert William) Leatherbee.

A Translation of a Letter from Jean Jules Jusserand to Stéphen Jean Marie Pichon

[Washington] June 9, 1918.

The Russo-Siberian Situation
Views of the President and of the Press.

No. 269. By a telegram of the fifth of this month, I reported to Your Excellency about the interview which I had with President Wilson on the subject of the Russo-Siberian situation. His statements to me about the intentions now maturing in his mind are important because at last they are coming perceptibly closer to our own plans. I am pleased therefore to think that they will have been received with satisfaction by the Department, which will no doubt inform me promptly of its views in this regard. It goes without saying that the sooner the better.

It will in fact be all the more important to take advantage of the views that the United States Government continues to receive from diverse sources, American as well as foreign, including information which is not in harmony with ours and often is not favorable to the realization of our plans: affirmations reiterated by Mr. Masaryk, Mr. Wright's plans, and the statistics furnished by Mr. Bakhmeteff, as noted in my telegram 710. It is certain that, if the Department of State takes seriously the unforeseen figures produced by the Russian Ambassador, who inclines, as we know, rather toward an economic and police action than to a military one, it will draw from them arguments against armed action, on a grand scale, which we hope for and to which the President no longer maintains the same absolute opposition as before.

Many newspapers proclaim the necessity of acting, and without delay, but hardly any define the kind of action which they wish. The English Ambassador has confirmed to me the news that the English agent Lockhart has now expressed himself in favor of intervention, but without being any more precise about the form it should take.

Mr. Masaryk's telegram *en clair* of the second, which I reported to Your Excellency in my No. 714, will contribute, however, one must conclude, to change his ideas about the Bolsheviks, whom he described in his most recent interview as more and more anti-German, whereas his lieutenants, who are more *au courant* with the course of events, report the redoubling of the ill will of the maximalists and state that "the German influence on the Russian government is incontestable."

Today's *New York Times* publishes a long article on the situation ascribed to Senator Poindexter,[1] who formulates some positive conclusions which conform to our own views: armed intervention, to be carried out by large contingents, principally Japanese, that will be explicitly anti-maximalist in character. He protests energetically against the Administration's tergiversations and against the opposition which it raised at the outset, contrary to the wishes of France and England, "to the generous offer by Japan." The rebuke is a stinging one, but its effect will be lessened by the fact that Senator Poindexter is a Republican and belongs to the opposition. The text of this article is attached.

The fact that dominates all the others, however, is the new disposition which the President has shared with me in confidence, and which, despite his reservations, marks a very noticeable shift to our advantage compared to his previous position.

TCL (Papiers Jusserand, Vol. 17, Lettres Politiques, 1918, pp. 166-68, FFM-Ar).

[1] "Senator Poindexter Urges Action in Russia. Wants Military Expedition Chiefly of Japanese Troops—U. S. Government, He Says, Has Misconceived the Bolsheviki. By Miles Poindexter." *New York Times*, June 9, 1918.

To Samuel Gompers

[The White House] June 10, 1918.

Please convey to the thirty-eighth annual convention of the American Federation of Labor my congratulations upon the patriotic support which the members of your organization have given to the war program of the nation in the past year, not only in the trenches and on the battlefield, where so many of our younger men are now in uniform, but equally in the factories and shipyards and workshops of the country, where the army is supported and supplied by the loyal industry of your skilled craftsmen. We are facing the hardships of the crucial months of the struggle. The nation can face them confidently, assured now that no intrigues of the enemy can ever divide our unity by means of those industrial quarrels and class dissensions which he has tried so diligently to foment. In these days of trial and self-sacrifice, the American workingman is bearing his share of the national burden nobly. In the new world of peace and freedom which America is fighting to establish, his place will be as honored and his service as gratefully esteemed.

Woodrow Wilson.

T telegram (Letterpress Books, WP, DLC).

To the American Alliance for Labor and Democracy[1]

[The White House] June 10, 1918.

The American Alliance for Labor and Democracy has my earnest hope for a successful convention that will give added strength to future activities. Called into being to combat ignorance and misunderstanding, skilfully played upon by disloyal influences, your organization has done a great and necessary work. It has aided materially in promoting the unity that proceeds from exact understanding, and is today a valid and important part of the great machinery that co-ordinates the energies of America in the prosecution of a just and righteous war.

The war can be lost in America as well as on the fields of France, and ill-considered or unjustified interruptions of the essential labour of the country may make it impossible to win it. No controversy between capital and labour should be suffered to interrupt it until every instrumentality set up by the government for its amicable settlement has been employed and its intermediation heeded to the utmost; and the government has set up instrumentalities wholly fair and adequate. And this duty to avoid such interruptions of industry wherever they can be avoided without the actual sacrifice of essential rights rests upon the employer as imperatively as upon the workman. No man can afford to do injustice at any time but at this time justice is of the essence of national defence and contests for any sort of advantage that at other times would be justified may now jeopard the very life of the nation.   Woodrow Wilson.

TLS (Letterpress Books, WP, DLC).
    [1] Creel wrote the first paragraph, Wilson the second. G. Creel to JPT, c. June 10, 1918, ALS (WP, DLC); WWhw comment on JPT to WW, June 10, 1918, TL (WP, DLC). There is a draft of this message in WP, DLC, of which the second paragraph is WWT.

Two Letters to Frank Lyon Polk

My dear Mr. Counselor,   The White House. 10 June, 1918.

    Thank you for this reassurance. I am quite willing, in view of it, to authorize a credit of the necessary amount, five million dollars ($5,000,000) for the purchase of these supplies.

                                    Faithfully Yours,   W.W.

WWTLI (SDR, RG 59, 861.24/93, DNA).

Confidential.

My dear Mr. Counselor: [The White House] 10 June, 1918

    I have your letter of June eighth enclosing the telegram from Ambassador Francis about the assignment by the Bolshevik Government of Citizen Litvinov as plenipotentiary representative of that Government in Washington. I write to say that I concur in the wisdom of following Ambassador Francis' advice and delaying a reply to the communication for the present.[1]

        Cordially and faithfully yours,   [Woodrow Wilson]

CCL (WP, DLC).
    [1] "Make no answer for the present or without consulting Department." RL to D. R. Francis, June 13, 1918, T telegram (SDR, RG 59, 701.6111/221, DNA).

To Frank Lyon Polk, with Enclosures

My dear Mr. Counselor,   The White House. 10 June, 1918.

    I think the instructions Francis asks for are safe, but I should prefer that they should be expressed in some form which would not seem to dictate just how the new government should be chosen, as, for example, "a government which it has reason to regard as representative of the people of Russia and chosen by their collective action."[1]   Faithfully Yours,   W.W.

WWTLI (SDR, RG 59, 861.00/2060, DNA).
[1] Wilson's revised language was incorporated in a telegram sent, presumably by Polk, over Lansing's signature. It reads as follows:

"In the event present Soviet Government abdicates or is deposed you may announce to the Russian people, whom the United States has never ceased to consider its associates against the Central Powers, that this Government will recognize a government of Russia which it has reason to regard as representative of the people of Russia and chosen by their collective action. The Department prefers that you should not make any announcements which would seem to dictate just how a new Government should be chosen. There is no change in this Government's policy towards Russia either in Europe or in the Far East." RL to D. R. Francis, June 12, 1918, T telegram (SDR, RG 59, 861.00/1945, DNA).

ENCLOSURE I

From Frank Lyon Polk

Dear Mr. President: Washington June 6, 1918.

I venture to bring to your special attention a telegram from Ambassador Francis, dated June 3rd, asking for instructions in view of the possibility of the collapse of the Bolshevik Government which he thinks likely to occur soon. He outlines the instructions which he would like to receive.

I should be very grateful if you would kindly indicate your views.
                    Faithfully yours,   Frank L. Polk

TLS (SDR, RG 59, 861.00/1945, DNA).

ENCLOSURE II

Vologda June 3, 1918

No. 239. Have been considering the situation which will confront us when Bolshevik Government collapses which may possibly be soon and broached the subject to my colleagues yesterday with suggestion that our respective Governments be prepared to instruct Allied Ambassadors here to support whatever Government should be formulated by Constituent Assembly fairly elected. Such instructions might be sent before down fall of Soviet Government but held until collapse occurs when they should be immediately promulgated before another Government formed as postponing action until thereafter would subject Allies to the same situation that has existed for seven months past. French Ambassador, Italian Ambassador agreed, former suggested that in the aforesaid instructions should be condition that all parties should be represented in new Government. I demurred advocating no conditions whatever as I thought such position more tenable and furthermore there are numerous parties in Russia, even five or more Socialistic party organizations, in addition to formidable international and Anarchistic parties.

Russian people require guidance, are helpless without it; we are decidedly most popular of Allies not only because Russians are satis[f]ied we have no territorial designs but because of President Wilson's eloquent, impressive utterances of sympathy and interest and probably because American Embassy was first to recognize the Republic and is only one that never left Russia or planned to do so.

Following instructions respectfully outlined: "In event present Soviet Government abdicates or is deposed, you are instructed to announce to the Russian people, whom this Government has never ceased to consider its ally against the Central Empires, that the Government of the United States will recognize that Government which will be adopted by the people through their representatives chosen at an election duly called and held under safeguards which will insure an honest expression of the popular will." Such an election could be held within thirty days, I believe, by a provisional government composed of unselfish patriotic Russians; experience of the last fifteen months has equipped Russia for prompt and emphatic expression of popular will and any Government so organized, and promised united support of Allies, would be immediately accepted and valiantly sustained by great majority of Russians.

Has the Department any other suggestions for deliverance from this impending dilemma? Please answer.   Francis

T telegram (SDR, RG 59, 861.00/2060, DNA).

To Leo Stanton Rowe

My dear Mr. Secretary: [The White House] 10 June, 1918

I am very much obliged to you for your letter of June eighth.[1] It pleases me very much to know that the Mexican editors were favorably affected by my little address.

I chided myself afterwards for not having pointed out to them the radical differences for Mexico in having Germany for her friend rather than the United States, in view of the uses which all the world now knows Germany makes of her "friendships."

          Cordially and faithfully yours,   Woodrow Wilson

TLS (Letterpress Books, WP, DLC).
    [1] It is missing in WP, DLC.

To Jouett Shouse

My dear Mr. Shouse: The White House 10 June, 1918

Your letter of June seventh was entirely welcome. I have been very much concerned about the whole matter of the suffrage amendment and just before receiving your letter had sent a message through Mrs. Catt to certain foreign representatives of the movement for woman suffrage[1] which I dare say will presently be published and which I hope will meet the purpose you have in mind.
        Cordially and sincerely yours,   Woodrow Wilson

TLS (J. Shouse Papers, KyU).
[1] See WW to Carrie C. L. C. Catt, June 13, 1918.

From Josephus Daniels

My dear Mr. President: Washington. 10 June, 1918.

I am in receipt of your favor[1] enclosing memorandum from the Secretary of State suggesting that there should be assembled at Galveston, Texas six thousand marines so that we might be prepared for any emergency that may arise with reference to the Mexican oil fields;[2] also your memorandum to the Secretary of State asking him to confer with me about the matter.[3]

I have taken the matter up with Admiral Benson and the Major General Commandant of the Marine Corps,[4] and while they feel it would not be easy to do so, these marines could be concentrated at Galveston. However, if it becomes necessary to do so, the necessity is imminent to provide ships to be ready to take them on short notice as we have no ships now that are not employed in other service.

The feeling of the Navy Department about this is that while there is, of course, always danger in and about the Tampico oil fields, and every few months it seems to become acute, it would be necessary not only to land but to go into Mexico to protect the oil wells, which would be, as I understand, an act of war against Mexico.

In the absence of Secretary Lansing, I talked with Acting Secretary Polk. He states that Mr. James A. Garfield and other gentlemen, interested in these oil fields, are in Mexico and will be in Washington in a few days and advised that we take no action until they return when we can get their advice.[5]   Upon receipt of your memorandum, I sent a message to the Naval Officer in command at Tampico,[6] and this morning received the following answer:

"Conditions in oil fields have been very quiet for last month. Have heard no complaints lately and both British and American Consuls report conditions very quiet. Will report further."

A copy of this cablegram has been sent to the State Department.
Faithfully yours,   Josephus Daniels

TLS (WP, DLC).
    [1] The Editors have not found Wilson's letter.
    [2] See RL to WW, June 4, 1918, and n. 1 thereto.
    [3] WW to RL, June 6, 1918.
    [4] Maj. Gen. George Barnett.
    [5] American oil companies had sent James Rudolph Garfield and Nelson Osgood Rhoades to Mexico in May 1918 to negotiate with the Mexican government about a change of its petroleum decree of February 19, 1918. Rhoades, Garfield's law partner, was a former engineering consultant to the Mexican government, an owner of large tracts of land in Mexico, and the president of several sugar companies in Mexico. For documents related to the negotiations of Garfield and Rhoades with Carranza and other Mexican officials, see FR 1918, pp. 720 ff., passim. For the major provisions of the petroleum decree of February 19, 1918, see H. P. Fletcher to RL, April 3, 1918, n. 5, printed as an Enclosure with RL to WW, April 15, 1918, Vol. 47. See also Robert F. Smith, The United States and Revolutionary Nationalism in Mexico, 1916-1932 (Chicago and London, 1972), pp. 117-26.
    [6] Capt. Louis Clark Richardson.

To Josephus Daniels

My dear Mr. Secretary: The White House 10 June, 1918

Thank you for your letter of today about sending marines to Galveston. I think your judgment in the matter is right, that we should at least wait until we have further advises about the conditions obtaining in the Tampico oil fields.

In haste
Cordially and faithfully yours,   Woodrow Wilson

TLS (J. Daniels Papers, DLC).

From Norman Foster

Dear Mr. President,   Trenton, N. J. June 10, 1918.

I am enclosing herewith the Company's sight draft for thirty-seven dollars and fifty cents, ($37.50), covering three weeks of partial disability at twelve dollars and fifty cents a week under your Accident Policy with this Company, in accordance with Dr. Grayson's report that you were partially disabled for that period.[1]

I am enclosing an original letter from the Chief Adjuster of the Company[2] to assure you that the claim will be given no publicity as I feel that is what you wish.

Assuring you of my respect and esteem, I remain
Very truly yours,   Norman Foster

TLS (WP, DLC).
    [1] C. T. Grayson to the Norman Foster Co., May 29, 1918.
    [2] It is missing.

From William Bauchop Wilson

My dear Mr. President: Washington June 10, 1918.

Relative to the status of the contemplated telegraphers' strike,[1] I am inclosing you a clipping from the Official Bulletin containing a statement authorized by the National War Labor Board.[2]

The essence of the decision of the Board is:

(1) The employees have a right to join a union if they so desire, and men discharged for joining the union shall be reinstated.

(2) The companies should not be required to deal with it or to recognize it.

(3) Committees of employees shall be recognized in presenting grievances.

(4) Where they fail to agree, the question in dispute shall be determined by the National War Labor Board.

(5) The Telegraphers Union shall not initiate strikes nor permit its members to initiate them, but shall submit their grievances to the National War Labor Board.

I am informed that the representatives of the union are willing to accept this. Mr. Newcomb Carlton for the Western Union Telegraph Company[3] declines to do so or to submit to the jurisdiction of the Board. The matter is therefore at an end so far as the Board is concerned.

I am advised confidentially that Mr. S. J. Konencamp,[4] President of the Commercial Telegraphers Union, has decided to issue a strike-order effective July 9th, unless in the meantime the telegraph companies accept the decision of the National War Labor Board. Heretofore the Commercial Telegraphers Union has not been strong numerically or otherwise. The present agitation may result in increasing its membership. It may or may not be able to cause any considerable walkout as a result of its strike-order. My judgment is that there would be no general walkout but in a number of important centers it would be sufficiently great to seriously interfere with telegraphic communication. In any event the decision of the National War Labor Board should be sustained if for no other reason but to maintain its prestige for the adjustment of future disputes, at least until the Board can be given power to enforce its decisions through clauses to that effect in Government contracts.

I therefore suggest that you communicate with Mr. Newcomb Carlton, President of the Western Union Telegraph Company, Mr. Clarence H. Mackay, President of the Postal Telegraph Company,[5] and Mr. S. J. Konencamp, President of the Commercial Telegraphers Union, insisting that they accept the jurisdiction of the National War Labor Board and abide by its decisions.

Faithfully yours,   W B Wilson

TLS (WP, DLC).

¹ The Commercial Telegraphers' Union had announced on April 21, 1918, that it would call out 30,000 telegraphers employed by the Western Union Telegraph Co. and the Postal Telegraph-Cable Co. unless the two companies ceased to discriminate against union members and agreed to reinstate about 100 employees who had been discharged because of their membership in the union. However, upon intervention by Secretary Wilson, who declared that the telegraph service was vital to the conduct of the war and that even a partial shutdown would have a serious effect on national defense, the union agreed to postpone the strike until the War Labor Board had had a chance to mediate the dispute. In spite of the board's request to the companies to refrain from discharging any more employees while the case was pending, the companies insisted that they would not change their policy and, by the end of May, had discharged some 800 telegraphers. The War Labor Board held its hearings in Chicago on June 1 and published its report on the following day. New York Times, April 22, 29, May 2, 11, June 2, and 3, 1918.
² Official Bulletin, II (June 4, 1918), 6-7.
³ He was president of the company.
⁴ The Editors have been unable to find Konenkamp's given names.
⁵ Clarence Hungerford Mackay, president of the Postal Telegraph-Cable Co. and other telegraph companies, and a pioneer in transoceanic cable communication.

To Clarence Hungerford Mackay

My dear Mr. Mackay: [The White House] 11 June, 1918

My attention has been called to the fact that the National War Labor Board, after a careful consideration of the questions at issue between the telegraph companies and their employees, have arrived at a decision the essential points of which are embraced in the following:

(1) The employees have a right to join a union if they so desire, and men discharged for joining the union should be reinstated.

(2) The company should not be required to deal with the union or to recognize it.

(3) Committees of employees should be recognized in presenting grievances.

(4) Where employees and employers fail to agree, the question in dispute should be determined by the National War Labor Board.

(5) The Telegraphers' Union should not initiate strikes or permit its members to initiate them, but should submit all grievances to the National War Labor Board.

I am informed that the representatives of the union are willing to accept this decision, but that the representatives of the telegraph companies have not accepted it.

May I not say that in my judgment it is imperatively necessary in the national interest that decisions of the National War Labor Board should be accepted by both parties to labor disputes? To fail to accept them is to jeopard the interests of the nation very seriously, because it constitutes a rejection of the instrumentality set up by the Government itself for the determination of labor disputes, set up with a sincere desire to arrive at justice in every case and with the express purpose of safeguarding the nation against labor difficulties during the continuation of the present war.

All these circumstances being taken into consideration, I do not hesitate to say that it is a patriotic duty to cooperate in this all-important matter with the Government by the use of the instrumentality which the Government has set up. I, therefore, write to ask that I may have your earnest cooperation in this matter, as in all others, and that you will set an example to the other employers of the country by a prompt and cordial acquiescence.

Very sincerely yours,   Woodrow Wilson[1]

TLS (Letterpress Books, WP, DLC).
[1] Wilson wrote the same letter, *mutatis mutandis*, as WW to N. Carlton and WW to S. J. Konenkamp, both June 11, 1918, TLS (Letterpress Books, WP, DLC). In his letter to Konenkamp, Wilson substituted the following final words: "and that you and those whom you represent will assist in setting an example to all those who have anything to do with the administration of the affairs of labor."

To Charles Richard Crane

My dear Friend: [The White House] 11 June, 1918

Of course, I will try to see Professor Masaryk.[1] I had been planning to have a joint conference with him and one or two others in order to work out a scheme for the relief of Russia, and I am very glad indeed to know when Professor Masaryk will be here.

Cordially and sincerely yours,   Woodrow Wilson

TLS (Letterpress Books, WP, DLC).
[1] Wilson saw Masaryk at the White House on June 19. For an account of the meeting, see WW to RL, June 19, 1918, n. 1.

From Edward Mandell House

Dear Governor,   Magnolia, Massachusetts. June 11, 1918.

The French Ambassador accredited to Japan[1] came to see me this morning.

He is going to ask Jusserand to present him to you in order that he may deliver a message from Clemenceau.[2] It is the old story of Japanese intervention. I suggested that he should not go into the subject in detail, assuring him that you knew it in its every phase. I advised him to merely give Clemenceau's message and ask if you approved the general plan of Inter-Allied Intervention provided a plan could be worked out that appealed to your judgment. He promised to do this.

The Swiss Minister and Madame Sulzer took lunch with us today. He is sailing for Switzerland tomorrow. I have a feeling that he is returning home at the instance of his Government, acting under a suggestion from the German Government. While I believe he is pro-Ally in his sympathy, at the same time, he has always seemed to me a good medium to convey to the Germans anything we desire them to know.   Affectionately yours,   E. M. House

TLS (WP, DLC).
    [1] Marcel-François Delanney (often spelled Delaney), who had been appointed to succeed Regnault on May 7, 1918.
    [2] Delanney saw Wilson at the White House on June 17. For an account of the meeting, see G. T. M. Bridges to Lord Reading, June 18, 1918, and J. J. Jusserand to the Foreign Ministry, June 18, 1918. For Clemenceau's message see the extract from the House Diary printed at June 11, 1918.

From Henry Morgenthau

My dear Mr. President: New York June 11, 1918.

I am sending you herewith the first three instalments of my book[1] and hope you can give them a superficial perusal. The chapter on the treatment of the Armenians, which will soon follow,[2] will disclose a state of affairs that ought to arouse the ire of the most callous of our citizens.

I am in hopes that when the book is completed you will permit me to dedicate it to you and that you will perhaps consent to write a short foreword for me.

My immediate object in writing you to-day is to obtain your opinion as to my consenting to have the book put into a moving picture. I am being pressed by my publishers and a number of moving picture firms who claim that the story would be a most effective anti-German propaganda. I myself think that nothing could so completely bring before the American people the true nature of the German aggression as a picture showing the Armenian massacres and the responsibility of Germany for them.

I would esteem it greatly if you would give me your personal advice about this matter. I deem it unnecessary to put any arguments before you.

With kindest personal regards,
                    Yours most sincerely,   H Morgenthau

TLS (WP, DLC).
    [1] Henry Morgenthau, *Ambassador Morgenthau's Story* (Garden City, N. Y., 1918), a copy of which is in the Wilson Library, WP, DLC. The book was serialized and published in nine installments in *World's Work* from May 1918 to January 1919. For the first three installments, see *World's Work*, XXXVI (May 1918), 42-73, (June 1918), 154-84, and (July 1918), 262-83.
    [2] *Ibid.*, XXXVII (Nov. 1918), 92-116.

From Newton Diehl Baker

My dear Mr. President:　　　　　　Washington. June 11, 1918.

The Council of National Defense at its meeting yesterday voted to recommend to you that you designate the Council as the agency to coordinate studies of reconstruction problems and to suggest methods of procedure in connection therewith.

The language of the resolution does not contemplate the taking of executive action, but merely the coordination of studies to be carried on concurrently. Unless you have some other agency in mind to centralize this inquiry, the Council will be very glad to accumulate such literature as there is and to cause the Director of the Council to report from time to time of the progress being made in the development of helpful suggestions for future action.

Respectfully yours,　Newton D. Baker

TLS (WP, DLC).

Arthur James Balfour to Lord Reading

[London] 11. June 1918.

No. 3599. Secret. Your tel. No. 2478.[1]

Following from Lord Milner. Begins.

We are anxious to obtain consent of U.S.G. to despatch following American force.

1. Three battalions with a quota of machine guns.
2. Three companies of engineers.
3. Two batteries of Field Guns preferably naval hand-drawn guns.
4. Necessary medical and administrative details suitable for above force.

In order to form part of Allied forces which are protecting Northern Russian port of Murmansk and Archangel under command of General Poole.[2] As regards 1. above if U.S.G. would find it as convenient to send an equivalent number of marines instead of infantry regiments this might be preferable in view of amphibious nature of the operations contemplated.

I gather that objections which President feels to Allied intervention at Vladivostock do not apply to Northern ports where there is no question of Japanese participating but that on the contrary he is favourable to keeping these ports under Allied control and recognizes importance of retaining this as our only means of access to European Russia.

Supreme War Council at its last meeting passed a resolution approving of these operations[3] and agreeing that for time being military and naval forces engaged should be under command of a British Officer and H.M.G. have assigned General Poole for this purpose because he is not only an able soldier but is very familiar with Russian conditions as he has spent the last two years in the country, gets on well with Russians and is on the spot.

Forces at present at his disposal are small consisting only of three men of war and their crews about 1200 British, a few hundred French and 1500 Serbians. They may be considerably increased by Czecho Slovaks if any proportion of these succeed in making their way to northern ports which is doubtful.

But it is important that absolutely reliable satisfactory nucleus should be strengthened. As you are aware we cannot at present spare British troops beyond the few already sent. General Poole thinks with assistance now asked for he could at least make sure of the ports themselves and of the railway lines ? connecting them at any rate for some distance. His relations with local authorities are at present friendly and in as much as inhabitants of these northern districts are almost entirely dependent on such supplies as we can give them for food and other necessaries there is reason to hope that they may even be prepared to give us active assistance and that small Allied force may in time become nucleus of larger one.

In order to make sure that proposed diversion of American troops might not clash with wider military interests I consulted General Foch on the subject during my recent visit to Paris on Friday, June 7th, and obtained his cordial assent to the proposal. He fully recognized importance of keeping Murmansk and Archangel in Allied hands from the point of view of general military situation and definitely expressed his opinion that if U.S.G. were willing to give help specified for that purpose force would be most advantageously employed.

Matter is very urgent. I understand there are no practical difficulties about conveying troops or supplying them but a great many arrangements will have to be made. I cannot however of course take any further steps in the matter until we have President's assent to employment of number of American troops specified in manner proposed.

T telegram (W. Wiseman Papers, CtY).
 [1] Lord Reading to A. J. Balfour, June 3, 1918, T telegram (W. Wiseman Papers, CtY). Reading told Balfour that Lansing had informed him that, provided General Foch agreed, the United States would be willing to send troops to Murmansk. However, Reading continued, the American government was still adamantly opposed to any kind of intervention in Siberia: "U.S.G. adhere to views already expressed and reported to you in regard to intervention in Siberia and which are applicable to your request to them to co-operate in protection of stores at Vladivostock. They are determined to avoid giving occasion for Russian suspicion or German propaganda of territorial designs on part of

U.S.A. They hold that any movement by U.S.G. in Vladivostock even if simply to protect stores would lead to mischievous results and might seriously embarrass their relations with the Russian people."

[2] Maj. Gen. Frederick Cuthbert Poole.

[3] This was Joint Note No. 31, dated June 3, 1918, "Allied Intervention at the White Sea Ports," T MS (WDR, RG 120, Records of the American Section of the Supreme War Council, 1917-1919, File No. 337-1, DNA), the text of which follows:

"At their Joint Meeting on the 23rd March, 1918, the Inter-Allied Naval Council and the Permanent Military Representatives considered the possibility of sending an Inter-Allied Military Expedition to Murmansk and Archangel with the object of protecting the stocks of military material warehoused in those ports.

"While recognising the impossibility for the moment of such an operation, the Representatives in their Joint Note No. 17 B expressed the hope that the naval effort at Murmansk should be continued in order to maintain Allied possession of that port as long as possible.

"The Permanent Military Representatives are of opinion that since the 23rd March the general situation in Russia and especially in the Northern Ports has completely altered.

"(1) The German threat to Murmansk and Archangel has become more definite and more imminent, Finland has completely fallen under German domination and is now openly hostile to the Entente and makes no concealment of its claims to Carolia, the Kola Peninsula and the Murmansk railway. The Germans are preparing for an advance on Petrograd.

"(2) We are urged to occupy these ports not only by the Allied Representatives in Russia but also by the majority of the Russian parties. Such occupation is an indispensable corollary of Allied intervention in Siberia.

"(3) The available Serbian and Czech units render the land defence of the maritime bases possible without the transport of any considerable expeditionary force.

"(4) The Serbian and Czech units gathered at these points cannot be conveyed immediately to France and, should the German Finnish Armies advance rapidly, they run the risk of capture unless organised and supported without delay. Further, the following considerations must be noted:

"(a) The lines of communication both by land and sea terminating at the ports of Murmansk and Archangel are the only routes the Allies have left by which to penetrate into the heart of Russia in order to watch its political evolution, to keep in touch with the various nationalities and to combat German influence.

"(b) These ports are the only free economic outlets towards Western Europe that are left to Russia and Siberia.

"(c) The occupation by Germany of Murmansk alone and its conversion into a first rate submarine base would make the sea route to Archangel impracticable for the Entente.

"(d) On the other hand, the occupation of Murmansk by the Entente would protect the flanks of the Allied Armies which may eventually operate in Siberia and facilitate and expedite liaison with them.

"(e) The agreement of the Czecho-Slovaks to the maintenance of a portion of their forces in those regions will be conditional on the moral and material support of a few Allied units on the spot to co-operate with them against the Germans.

"Hence the Military Representatives are of opinion:

"(1) That a military effort must be made by the Allies to keep possession first of the port of Murmansk, secondly (if possible simultaneously) of the port of Archangel.

"(2) That, to reduce to a minimum the force required, the National Czecho-Slovak Council should be asked to agree to maintain in those regions, for such time as may be necessary, some Czech units, with the understanding that only the minimum number will be required to stay, while the remainder as previously agreed will be shipped to France.

"(3) That provided the assistance above defined is obtained the Allies need only send to Murmansk and Archangel:

"(a) A few British, French, American or Italian battalions, 4 to 6 at the most:

"(b) Officers and specialists (Allied and Czechs from France) to complete the training and cadres of the Serbo-Czech troops and the general organisation of the corps of occupation:

"(c) Such material and supplies as could not be obtained locally.

"(4) That the organization of the Commands could be obtained in the following manner:

"There will be a single command with the duty of directing both the defence by sea and the defence by land of the Russian ports on the Arctic Ocean as well as of important points on the railway lines leading to those two ports: this command will be entrusted to a Commander-in-Chief chosen by the British Government, until such time as the Supreme War Council revises this decision."

From the Diary of Colonel House

June 11, 1918.

M. Marcel Delaney, the French Ambassador to Japan came this morning. Stephane Lausanne and Captain Martin[1] accompanied him. We had a conference of about an hour and a half. He impressed me as being an able Frenchman. He has a sonorous voice and I imagine is something of an orator. He was instructed to see me upon landing and before he saw anyone else, therefore he came to Magnolia having found that I had left New York. We discussed Japanese and Allied intervention in Russia, and Siberia in its every phase. He is to see the President almost at once and I advised him not to go into discussion with the President concerning the merits of intervention but merely to deliver Clemenceau's message, which is to the effect that he considers intervention imperative not only because he believes it will be effective, but because he believes it will stimulate the morale of the French people more than anything else, and that they need stimulating in this hour of trial.

He declared the situation to be critical. The Germans are within forty miles of Paris in two different directions along two valley routes. The nearer they get to Paris, the more air raids are possible and the harder it is to maintain the morale of the people.

After delivering Clemenceau's message, I advised him to ask the President whether he approved the principle of Interallied intervention, provided a plan could be found which seemed to him, the President, workable. I thought the President would answer in the affirmative, and I advised leaving the matter there as far as he was concerned. After his interview with the President, I suggested that he see Lord Reading, Viscount Ishii, Ambassador Jusserand and have a general conference. Ishii should be asked whether the Japanese were willing for interallied intervention or whether they held to exclusive intervention by the Japanese. I thought Ishii's answer would be favorable. In that event, I advised working out a plan to be submitted to London, Paris and Tokyo for approval. When that approval was had, the plan should be taken to the President for his decision.

The Ambassador accepted this advice and declared he felt fully repaid for coming to Magnolia. He was extravagant in his compliments and said the French people understood what a staunch friend I had been to France from the beginning. I assured him of my deep appreciation of his country's good will and of my admiration and affection for France.

I asked Lausanne to go to Washington with the Ambassador and to keep in touch with me through Gordon as to developments, so that I might advise further if necessary.

The Swiss Minister and his wife Madame Sulzer lunched with us. We had a long and intimate conference. I handed him a letter to the President of the Swiss Republic; a copy of which is attached to the record. I did not say in this letter all that I felt, and that is something I wish to mention here. I am seldom able to give all I have in mind, for the reason that I am so close to the President and am considered so nearly his mouthpiece that what I say is considered as his opinion.

The Minister asked my views upon the League of Nations, the reduction of armaments and peace questions in general. In answer to this I told him that all this country desired for itself, we were willing to concede to the Germans and Central Powers. The war must bring a peace based upon right, reason and justice. Unless it did, we would inevitably have another conflict. Treaties, leagues to enforce peace and what not, seemed to me not so important as the awakening of public sentiment in each country which would forbid its representatives acting in a way which would not be condoned in a private individual. Under the guise of patriotism, it has been thought permissable to lie, to steal and do things which if done by a private citizen would ostracize him from the society of his fellows.

I constantly hear prominent men in this country declare if treaties stand in the way of our success in this war, they would act as if they were not in existence. Unless this kind of view is changed, we can never hope for peace. A nation or state must be as honest as an individual of honor, and when that comes about we will have taken a long step toward a solution of our international difficulties.

I told the Minister that such a resolution should be placed before the Peace Conference, and I did not believe any nation would dare oppose it. If we could once get thus [this] resolution as a part of an international agreement it would not be difficult to educate the people to a sense of its importance and justice and they would not permit their representatives to violate it. They would not wish the name of their country smirched any more than an individual would desire the name of his family smirched.

This, to my mind, is the very foundation upon which the future amity of nations must be built. It is my purpose to ask the President to announce this doctrine to the world. I have talked with him about it, but I have not insisted upon his making a definite appeal concerning it.

¹ That is, Stéphane-Joseph-Vincent Lauzanne, about whom see EMH to WW, April 10, 1917, n. 3, Vol. 42; and Capt. Hugh S. Martin, former Assistant Military Attaché in Russia, who had just returned to the United States.

To Newton Diehl Baker

My dear Mr. Secretary: The White House 12 June, 1918

I have your letter of yesterday informing me that the Council of National Defense, at its meeting on June tenth, voted to recommend that I designate the Council as the agency to coordinate studies of reconstruction problems and suggest methods of procedure in connection therewith.

I am ashamed to say I am not clear as to just what you are referring to. Do you mean the specific questions like the re-allocation of labor and the assistance along those lines which it will be necessary for the Government to render after the war is over, or do you mean the whole field of economic readjustment? If you will clear my mind as to these questions, I need not say I shall be happy to consider the recommendation right away.

Cordially and faithfully yours,   Woodrow Wilson

TLS (N. D. Baker Papers, DLC).

To Thomas Watt Gregory, with Enclosure

My dear Gregory: [The White House] 12 June, 1918

I must say I have read the enclosed telegram with a good deal of concern. You probably know that the Non-partisan League referred to in this telegram has had persons connected with it whose loyalty to the highest interests of the country was at least questionable, but since the war began the League has rendered consistent assistance and very effective assistance where it could to the cause of the war. This telegram does not directly refer, as you will see, to anything done in connection with the League but only something done in connection with a branch of the State Grange which met at Walla Walla, Washington. There is a savage political fight on in the Northwest between the Republican organization and the Non-partisan League, which has recruited its membership for the most part, I am informed, from the rural districts.

Would it not be possible through the secret agents of your department to get a more complete picture of this incident at Walla

Walla and be ourselves in a position to judge more clearly about it?   Cordially and faithfully yours,   Woodrow Wilson

TLS (Letterpress Books, WP, DLC).

E N C L O S U R E

Seattle, Washn., June 10, 1918.

We, the Executive officers of the Washington State Grange, 9, Patrons of Husbandry, in session at Seattle, Washington, appeal to you for justice and for a Federal investigation to determine whether the officers and members of the State Grange are disloyal or whether it is the local authorities of Walla Walla, Washington, who so summarily broke up the annual meeting of the State Grange, who are disloyal. From the moment Patrons assembled in Walla Walla, every effort was made to show the loyalty of the Grange. The first act on assembling in convention was to pass strong resolutions pledging earnest, united support to you as our President and Commander-in-Chief, and these resolutions were wired you.[1] The Grange address at the public meeting in response to the address of welcome, was a ringing declaration of unswerving support of you in prosecuting the war, and, Mr. President, the only act or acts that could be honestly construed as disloyal at any of the Grange meetings was the refusal of the school board to allow the Grange to take up a collection for the Red Cross in the building. A collection was, however, taken up in the entrance way at the close of the meeting. We now believe the purpose of this refusal was to prevent the Grange from making any record of patriotism that would appeal to the people of Walla Walla, or that would interfere with the purpose of stamping the Grange disloyal. The treatment of the Washington State Grange at Walla Walla only differs from the treatment accorded other farmers meetings all over the northwestern states, in that it is the first, so far as we are aware, breaking up of the regular annual meeting of a large state organization by local authorities on the plea that the meeting was disloyal. But we firmly believe that the methods pursued by the local authorities of Walla Walla are indicative of the growing boldness of the reactionary controlled officials in large numbers of our northwestern cities and counties and several of our states taking advantage of war to destroy their political opponents under the pretense of disloyalty and pro-Germanism. This constant persecution of the organized farmers of the northwest, by state and local authorities and self-constituted patriotic societies and corrupt newspapers, on the pretense that the farmers are disloyal, has produced a situation terrible in its possible consequences. The charge that the farmers of the great northwest are so disloyal that their meetings must be broken up, must be encouraging to the enemy. The terrible consequences may be that the war will be prolonged, hundreds of thousands of our boys unnecessarily killed, and billions added to the war's cost. If we, or any of the members of our order, are disloyal in the face of such terrible possibilities, then we admit that no punishment would be too severe. On the other hand, if the officers and members of the Washington State Grange are loyal, as we claim honest investigation will show, then the local authorities of Walla Walla, who have placed the stigma of disloyalty upon us, are themselves disloyal and should be dealt with accordingly. They are giving aid and comfort to the enemy and for petty, ignoble purposes and will be responsible for all the terrible consequences that must inevitably follow if such high-handed practices are not suppressed. They, and not the farmers organizations, were the "shadow Huns"—the enemy within our gates. The crime with which the Washington State Grange is charged is, that it has given support and encouragement to the national non-partisan league by allotting [allowing] members on [of] the National Grange, who are also members of the non-partisan league, to address its meeting, and by re-electing state master, an avowed supporter of the League. For this offense the school board suddenly appeared on the evening of the third day of the session, and without previous warning gave the officers and members of the Grange a limit of thirty minutes in which the Grange meetings were being held. This notice was accompanied by a threat of ejectment by force if the buildings were not cleared by end of that time, and this threat was emphasized by the presence ·by [of] a body of about seventy five huskies held in readiness in the shadow of the building. On vacating the building the officers of the Grange got into touch with the mayor of the city[2] who disclaimed knowledge of the school board's action and assured us that the invitation of the city had not been revoked. We also were in conference with the official representative of the Council of National Defense, who promised the committee protection and aid in securing a meeting place, but although we waited patiently until noon of the following day, we got no further communication from him and were later advised that he had left the city. On formal appeal by a duly appointed committee of the State Grange, the mayor of the city refused to give the protection of the city government if attempts were made to hold meetings in any other hall in the city, and the sheriff of the county[3] advised this committee that he feared mob violence would result if the Grange attempted to hold meetings in either the city or county of Walla Walla. He further informed that a "home guard" armed with loaded Winchester rifles added greatly to the danger of the situation. We wired the Governor of the state[4] asking for protection in holding our meeting, but received no reply. As loyal citizens, pledged to give their earnest united support to you, as our President and Commander-in-Chief and mindful of your noble appeal to all loyal citizens to aid in maintaining the peace, we made no further attempt to hold meetings in Walla Walla or Walla Walla County, and advised our members to restrain their indignation and the outrage and return peaceably to their homes as early as possible. Then we, the officers and executive committee, with such members as we needed for consultation came to this city to consider the proper steps to be taken in this grave situation. Our members, men and women, after being ordered to vacate the High School building, retired singing the National anthem, and, Mr. President, among these six hundred farmers and their wives, grown sons and daughters, were, we believe, more people wearing service pins, more people who were active members of councils of defense workers in the Red Cross and other war activities than in any body of citizens of the same size. Many of the women were knitting for our boys at the front as they retired from the hall.[5] Also among these expelled members for disloyalty were wives of officers and men on the battle line in France. The Washington State Grange is one of the thirty three state organizations constituting the National Grange, with a total of a million members. It is in fraternal cooperation with other farm organizations throughout the nation aggregating another million members and with the labor organizations of our state. By its every act it has attempted to show its determination to stand solidly behind you, Mr. President, in prosecuting the war to speedy and successful issue, and we can only explain the action of the Walla Walla authorities on the ground that it is a part of the German propaganda, or a part of a widespread political movement to prevent, if possible, the capture or control of government, local, state or national, by any but the old by-partisan reactionary rings. That unworthily, and in this war time disloyal, political moves, are at the bottom of these persecutions of the farmers organizations, will be shown, we positively believe, if honestly investigated, and we most earnestly and respectfully submit than an investigation by you through your own chosen investigating body, will alone be adequate to meet the situation, and we appeal to you to order such investigation. We firmly believe that the successful prosecution of the war, at the minimum cost of men, money, and time, demands it.

Assuring you, Mr. President, that the farmers of the great State of Washington, both those who are members of the Grange and those who are not, are earnestly and unitedly behind you in the supreme task of winning the war, and firmly believing this to be true of the farmers of all states, and that when the world, both allies and enemy, know this, through you, it will have a powerful effect in helping to end the war by the encouragement it will give to our allies and the corresponding discouragement to our enemies, we place our case in your hands.

Respectfully submitted,   Executive Committee
Washington State Grange,
Wm. Bouck, Master; Fred W. Lewis, Sec'y; Herman
Nelsen, U. S. Case, J. T. Compton.

T telegram (WP, DLC).
   [1] It is missing in WP, DLC.
   [2] D. F. Powell.
   [3] Lee Barnes.
   [4] Ernest Lister, a Democrat.
   [5] For another account of this affair, see Harriet Ann Crawford, *The Washington State Grange, 1889-1924: A Romance of Democracy* (Portland, Ore., 1940).

To Champ Clark

My dear Mr. Speaker: [The White House] 12 June, 1918

I have your letter of June tenth[1] enclosing the telegram from Colonel Frank W. Buffum.[2] I appreciate the spirit of Colonel Buffum's suggestion and the public considerations which prompted it, but my own judgment is that it would not be wise for me to take the action he suggests. The people of the country will, I am sure, without any suggestion from me know what to do, but, besides that, I think any general suggestion of this sort would very likely be somewhat shocking to the religious sense of a very large proportion of our population.

With much regard,
Cordially and sincerely yours,   Woodrow Wilson

TLS (Letterpress Books, WP, DLC).
   [1] C. Clark to WW, June 10, 1918, TLS (WP, DLC).
   [2] It is missing. However, it suggested that "farmers forego Sunday holidays, and engage in usual agricultural pursuits, in order to help win the war." Hw note on the letter cited above. Frank Washburn Buffum, a businessman from Louisiana, Mo., had been Missouri highway commissioner from 1913 to 1917.

From Jean Jules Jusserand

Dear Mr. President,   Washington June 12. 1918

Our Prime Minister cabled me that the account I had sent him of our conversation the other day[1] was exactly what he expected from the head of the American state and gave him the greatest satisfaction.

Mr. Clemenceau states that there is no reason why you should abstain from any question concerning the using by us, as combattants, of the maximum of our available manhood. We have, he cables, nothing to conceal from President Wilson, and he will have in this respect full satisfaction.

The Prime Minister also fully agrees with you as to the importance and necessity of the American troops being employed at the proper time as armies, and every facility will be given in that view: the fine valor displayed by American troops forecasts, he says, splendid results.

Mr. Clemenceau begs that your kind attention be called to the importance of forming staff officers with the greatest care: according to his views, scientific method is, in the present warfare, of paramount importance; and such method cannot, of course, be improvised.

This morning's news is better, and I consider it a particularly good omen that it is so with respect to all allied troops, and especially the American and the French.

Believe me, dear Mr. President
Respectfully and sincerely yours   Jusserand

ALS (WP, DLC).
¹ J. J. Jusserand to S. J. M. Pichon, received June 6, 1918.

To Jean Jules Jusserand

My dear Mr. Ambassador: [The White House] 12 June, 1918

Thank you for your letter of this morning. I am very much gratified by the message which it contains from Mr. Clemenceau, and you may be sure that I shall in every possible way heed his suggestion as to the choice of staff officers, for I am sure that it is the advice which will be most acceptable to the Secretary of War.

Cordially and sincerely yours,   Woodrow Wilson

TLS (Letterpress Books, WP, DLC).

From Harry Augustus Garfield, with Enclosures

Dear Mr. President: Washington, D. C. June 12, 1918

I enclose, herewith, a memorandum concerning the matters discussed at the meeting this afternoon. Also I venture to add a memorandum upon another subject with apologies if it is an intrusion.

Cordially and faithfully yours,   H. A. Garfield

TLS (WP, DLC).

ENCLOSURE   I

MEMORANDUM FOR THE PRESIDENT

June 12, 1918

I have too little information of the details of the subject under discussion to justify me in offering criticism of those details, but I am deeply concerned as to the underlying principle which I believe ought to govern in setting up machinery which indirectly may affect by the decisions made, principles touching the aims of the war, as distinguished from items in the program for the conduct of the war.[1]

Of course, we must win the war, but neither our public, nor the people abroad, must be allowed for a single instant to forget the reason. I know how passionately you cling to this thought. My own preoccupations with the details of the Fuel Administration, lead me to understand how easy it is to fall under the spell of achievements connected with the program of administration, and while these things, including, of course, the great program of conduct of the war, can be accomplished only by bringing to bear all the powers we possess, their very accomplishment will be our condemnation, if, in the end, we have not safeguarded all that is summed up in your trenchant phrase "making the world safe for democracy."

The German Government with its peculiar thoroughness, is using every opportunity to make her people believe that we are intent upon crushing them, that their war is indeed a defensive war. To set up a tribunal in London which shall have power or may be construed to have power, to do with our financial strength and war supplies what it chooses, will play into the hands of the German Government in such manner as to still further strengthen its plea.

Moreover, to repeat the substance of my observations this afternoon, the control of the situation is, providentially I believe, in your hands, and were the power mine, I would insist that representatives of the Allies come here to Washington and here confer with your representative concerning the apportionment of the credits and supplies necessary to the prosecution of the war program.

I venture to suggest that the proposed administrations to be set up in London, be merely the eyes and ears of the conferees sitting here. It is difficult for me to believe that surer knowledge or calmer judgment will mark the counsels of conferees sitting in London than can be made to prevail in Washington. If the conferees are to be clothed with powers to determine policies, the foregoing applies with greater force.

There is this further and most important matter for consideration. If the conferees sit in Washington, they have at hand every source of information bearing upon production (information as essential to coordinated action as that concerning the allocation of supplies among the Allies), and in the event of disagreement, appeal may and should be made to you. In that event, the people of the world will have full confidence that the high aim which has led the United States into the war, will not be lost sight of.

Respectfully submitted,   H. A. Garfield.

[1] For a description of the plan then under discussion, see V. C. McCormick to WW, June 15, 1918, and its Enclosures.

E N C L O S U R E   I I

MEMORANDUM FOR THE PRESIDENT

June 12, 1918

Concerning the Russian situation, if anything in the nature of intervention ought to take place—about which I have not sufficient information to express an opinion—it is, of course, vital that the Russian people should be made to understand that what is proposed is done in accordance with the aim which you have set up as the governing motive of the United States in entering the war.

As I understand it, their people have taken the preliminary steps necessary to the holding of a Constitutional Convention. They, and no one else, have the right to determine what their Government shall be. If it is made plain to them *that the presence of a Commission or of an armed force in Russia is there for the purpose of enabling them to hold their Constitutional Convention and to determine for themselves their own form of Government*, it cannot be claimed that the United States and the Allies have intervened for selfish or ulterior purposes.

This suggestion has been made to me by Mr. Bentley W. Warren,[1] my Chief Counsel, and it seems to me is worthy of consideration, as furnishing an unimpeachable motive—provided, of course, it is adopted in good faith by all the nations participating—for complying with the request which the papers state has come to you from Russians interested in the establishment of a Constitutional Government.[2]   Respectfully submitted,   H. A. Garfield.

TS MSS (WP, DLC).
  [1] Bentley Wirt Warren, president and director of various railroad companies and investment firms and a former civil-service commissioner of Massachusetts, was the legal adviser to the Fuel Administrator.
  [2] The text of a resolution forwarded on June 10 by Bakhmet'ev to Lansing for Wilson, which is printed as an Enclosure with RL to JPT, June 19, 1918.

From Clarence Hungerford Mackay

New York, June 12, 1918.

In reply to your letter of yesterday, allow me to say that this company has done its very utmost since the beginning of the war to assume its full share of responsibility to the Government and to the public and that, in order to still further show its sincerity and earnest desire to be of service at this time of national trial, we cannot but respond to your request that we waive, during the war, our right to discharge employees who join a union, and you may rely upon our doing so.

Very respectfully,   Clarence H. Mackay.

T telegram (WP, DLC).

From David Franklin Houston

Dear Mr. President: Washington June 12, 1918.

In response to your letter of June 1, I am enclosing herewith a memorandum, in some detail, of the emergency activities of this Department.[1] Some of these activities are entirely new; others, such as are indicated especially under the heading "Special emergency food production and conservation activities," represent intensification of work which has been under way in the Department for a long time. Such work has been given emphasis and has been greatly extended because of its peculiar bearing on food supply and conservation.   Faithfully yours,   D. F. Houston

TLS (WP, DLC).
  [1] DFH, memorandum, c. June 12, 1918, T MS (WP, DLC).

A Memorandum[1]

[June 12, 1918]

After an analysis of the Russian situation, in which the President would find much of his own thought expressed, Mr. Browne suggests a programme, substantially as follows:

1. The Allies must decide whether the soviet government is really a power in Russia; then, if it is, they must begin immediate cooperation with that government. Mr. Browne goes to show that the soviet government is a power. "It has now been in undisputed power for five months without serious armed opposition, except in the Ukraine, where the reactionary rada, mortgaged to Germany, is bolstered up by German divisions. The soviet elements in the Ukraine are conducting an active guerrilla warfare against the German and rada troops. They retook Odessa. The authority of the soviet extends from Petrograd to Vladivostok and from Archangel to Baku. Only German or *Japanese* bayonets will prevent this soviet power from lasting many months longer."

"Recognition (of the soviet) is not absolutely essential. It desires the Allies' recognition more than anything else in the world, but next it desires the Allies' cooperation.

"The soviet asks the aid of American and French officers in organizing a new revolutionary army; also aid in removing large stores of military munitions beyond the Volga, where they would be out of reach of the Germans should the latter again advance."

2. We should foster and encourage the resentment which is already crystallizing in Russia against Germany, and also encourage the revolutionary spirit for war.

3. We should make no concerted invasion of Siberia and should not permit Japan to invade Siberia. Such an invasion would immediately result in the turning of Russian resentment away from Germany and against the Allies. "If we are able to assure the soviet government that such a move will not occur, we shall see a wonderful change in the Russian situation in the next six months."

4. Suggests sending of 40 to 200 American army officers for the purpose of helping to organize the new revolutionary army; also experts in oil and coal mining, to assist in the reorganization of the oil and coal fields.

5. Suggests industrial commission for the purpose of arranging tonnage and purchasing raw materials for shipment to America and England, to prevent the available natural resources of Russia from going to Germany through taking them ourselves; on a trade basis, of course.

Says some allied cooperation along these lines has already been started.

"Democratic Russia is getting angry with Germany for the first time since the world war began* * * * The Russian situation is better for the Allies today than at any other time since the revolution began* * * * Had we known Russian psychology or spent as much time studying Russia as Germany spent we should have understood* * * * Let us play our ally's government for better or for worse, lest Germany beat us to it!"

T MS (WP, DLC).
¹ The following summary of Louis Edgar Browne (staff correspondent in Russia for the Chicago *Daily News*), *New Russia in the Balance: How Germany's Designs May Be Defeated and Russian Democracy Preserved* (Chicago, 1918) was prepared by Tumulty, probably at Wilson's request. Browne's pamphlet, a copy of which is in WP, DLC, reprinted six of Browne's special dispatches from Moscow from April 11 to 15, 1918.

Shane Leslie to Joseph Patrick Tumulty

Dear Mr Tumulty,   Port Washington L. I. June 12, 1918

Sir Horace Plunkett I am afraid is seriously ill. However he writes to me on May 24,

"You and I have been sorely afflicted by the Government's mad folly in torpedoing the Convention¹ with Conscription.² I think however the chaos they have caused is bound to produce a reaction. The Convention really did good work in Ireland. Against stupidity the Gods strive in vain and we are both temporarily knocked out, but if we are right, our opportunity will come again and I do not regret any of the work either of us have done or regard it as wasted. The R. C. Church have been in an extremely difficult position. Personally I think the action they took saved us from a wild outbreak which would have deluged the country with blood.³ But in my judgment it was not right to question the sovereign power of the Imperial Parliament in military and naval matters, if the safety of these islands made it necessary."

As for us moderate Irishmen, we have no right now to allow even what is just to Ireland to embarrass America or to do otherwise than place ourselves unconditionally at the service of the President. Since Ireland is in his mind we have no right to ask for her to be on his lips. He has first right to the service of the Irish race all over the world.   your obedt servant   Shane Leslie

TLS (WP, DLC).
¹ The Irish Convention, about which see E. Drummond to W. Wiseman, April 2, 1918, n. 1, Vol. 47.
² On April 9, 1918, the day after Plunkett had submitted the final report of the Irish Convention, Lloyd George had introduced a manpower bill in Parliament which, among other things, empowered the government to extend military conscription to Ireland. The bill was adopted on April 16, 1918, and went into effect two days later. However,

throughout the debate on the measure, Lloyd George had insisted that the government would not enforce Irish conscription unless some form of home rule for Ireland could first be agreed upon. As a recent study suggests, Lloyd George realized that any attempt to impose conscription on Ireland would be met by massive resistance, and he never intended to enforce the measure. Since Lloyd George could be sure that any form of self-government which Parliament might propose would be rejected by at least one of the Irish parties, his insistence on home rule as a *quid pro quo* for conscription virtually assured the indefinite postponement of conscription in Ireland. See George Dangerfield, *The Damnable Question: A Study in Anglo-Irish Relations* (Boston and Toronto, 1976), pp. 264-84.

[3] The Irish Roman Catholic hierarchy had joined the Nationalists, the Sinn Feiners, and the trade unionists in their vehement opposition to Irish conscription. At a meeting at Maynooth on April 18, 1918, the bishops had ordered that a pledge be read at every mass in every parish on the following Sunday which denied the right of the government to enforce compulsory military service in Ireland and asked Irishmen to "resist conscription by the most effective means" at their disposal. At the same time, the bishops issued a manifesto to the effect that conscription forced upon Ireland was an "oppressive and inhuman law" which the Irish people had a right to resist "by every means consonant with the law of God." *Ibid.*, pp. 279-80. See also the *New York Times*, April 19, 1918.

To Raymond Poincaré

[The White House] 13 June, 1918

Mr. President: Your telegram of yesterday[1] was certainly conceived in the highest and most generous spirit of friendship and I am sure that I am expressing the feeling of the people of the United States as well as my own when I say that it is with increasing pride and gratification that they have seen their forces under General Pershing more and more actively cooperating with the forces of liberation on French soil. It is their fixed and unalterable purpose to send men and materials in steady and increasing volume until any temporary inequality of force is entirely overcome and the forces of freedom made overwhelming, for they are convinced that it is only by victory that peace can be achieved and the world's affairs settled upon a basis of enduring justice and right. It is a constant satisfaction to them to know that in this great enterprise they are in close and intimate cooperation with the people of France.

Woodrow Wilson.

T telegram (WP, DLC).
[1] R. Poincaré to WW, June 12, 1918, T telegram (WP, DLC), which noted the first anniversary of Pershing's arrival in France.

To Clarence Hungerford Mackay

My dear Mr. Mackay: [The White House] 13 June, 1918

May I not express my warm and sincere appreciation of your kind telegram of this morning, and may I not say I was sure of the response which my request would meet?

Sincerely yours,   Woodrow Wilson

TLS (Letterpress Books, WP, DLC).

To Joseph Patrick Tumulty, with Enclosure

Dear Tumulty: [The White House, c. June 13, 1918]

I have it in mind to do the very thing that is here suggested but not quite as the writer suggests it.   The President.

TL (WP, DLC).

E N C L O S U R E

Lester Aglar Walton[1] to Joseph Patrick Tumulty

My dear Mr. Tumulty: New York June 12, 1918.

Mr. Herbert Bayard Swope of the New York World, a personal friend of mine, has sent me word that he had taken up with you the matter I took up with him several days ago, to-wit-the advisability of President Wilson speaking out against the reign of mob law.

I am writing not as a colored man to a white man but as one good American to another good American with a view to securing your kindly interest in a matter which I regard of vital interest to the Nation. I believe that if Mr. Wilson can be brought to realize conditions as they really are he will speak out strongly against what has become a National evil. You are in a position to present the facts and arouse his deep concern, thereby playing a prominent part in winning over to the President twelve million loyal Americans.

As I told Mr. Swope, the colored people are depressed on account of the wholesale lynching of Negroes in this country without one word of protest from the chief executive of the Nation. Condemnation of mob law by Mr. Wilson would do more than any other agency to put a stop to this growing evil which puts this country in a none too enviable light before the world.

I should very much like to secure an interview from Mr. Wilson on the subject, or a letter for publication in the white and colored press. I can assure you that strong words from the President at this time would have a great psychological effect for good on colored Americans throughout the country.

Trusting you will give this matter the serious consideration it deserves, and with kind regards, I am,

Very truly yours,   Lester A Walton

TLS (WP, DLC).
[1] Managing editor of the *New York Age*, a weekly newspaper for blacks.

To William Cox Redfield

My dear Mr. Secretary: [The White House] 13 June, 1918

I want presently to have a conference with you, the Secretary of State and Doctor John R. Mott for the purpose of seeing if we can't between us organize an original kind of relief expedition for Russia. I know that you have been interested in the matter of organizing what I may call barter commerce with Russia, the only sort that is just now feasible, and I am writing this to suggest that by way of getting all the light possible on the subject of conditions in Russia before we meet, you seek out Mr. Henry W. Anderson,[1] the Red Cross Commissioner to Roumania who has just returned to Washington, and Mr. S. P. Elliott,[2] who can be reached in care of W. R. Grace & Company, Hanover Square, New York City, who has also just returned from Russia, and who I am told knows thoroughly the trading situation there.

Cordially and sincerely yours,   [Woodrow Wilson]

CCL (WP, DLC).
[1] Henry Watkins Anderson, a lawyer from Richmond, Va.; head of the American Red Cross Mission to Rumania from July 1917 to March 1918.
[2] Stewart P. Elliott, an executive of the W. R. Grace Steamship Co.

To Carrie Clinton Lane Chapman Catt[1]

My dear Mrs. Catt: The White House 7[13] June, 1918

May I not thank you for transmitting to me the very interesting memorial of the French Union for Woman Suffrage addressed to me under the date of February first, last. Since you have been kind enough to transmit this interesting and impressive message to me, will you not be good enough to convey to the subscribers this answer:

I have read your message with the deepest interest and I welcome the opportunity to say that I agree without reservation that the full and sincere democratic reconstruction of the world for which we are striving, and which we are determined to bring about at any cost, will not have been completely or adequately attained until women are admitted to the suffrage, and that only by that action can the nations of the world realize for the benefit of future generations the full ideal force of opinion or the full humane forces of action. The services of women during this supreme crisis of the world's history have been of the most signal usefulness and distinction. The war could not have been fought without them, or its sacrifices endured. It is high time that some part of our debt of gratitude to them should be acknowledged and paid, and the only acknowledgement they ask is their admission to the suffrage. Can we justly refuse it? As for America, it is my earnest hope that the Senate of the United States will give an unmistakable answer to this question by passing the suffrage amendment to our federal constitution before the end of this session.

Cordially and sincerely yours,   Woodrow Wilson

TLS (National American Woman Suffrage Association Papers, DLC).
¹ Wilson presented this letter to Mrs. Catt and a delegation from the National American Woman Suffrage Association at the White House at 4 p.m. on June 13. Other persons present included Dr. Shaw, Mrs. Gardener, Mrs. Park, Ruth White, the secretary of the association's congressional committee, and Rose Young, "chairman" of the association's press department, director of the Leslie Woman Suffrage Bureau, and editor of the *Woman Citizen.* Wilson wrote a shorter version of this letter on June 7, and Tumulty gave it to Mrs. Gardener soon afterward. Mrs. Gardener read it to Mrs. Catt over the telephone, and the latter asked Mrs. Gardener to request Wilson to add a sentence expressing the hope that the Senate would ratify the woman-suffrage amendment. JPT to WW, June 10, 1918, TL (WP, DLC). Wilson added the sentence, and Swem retyped the letter under the date of June 7. There is a WWsh draft of the letter in WP, DLC.

From Carrie Clinton Lane Chapman Catt

My dear Mr. President: Washington, D. C., June 13, 1918.

On behalf of the National American Woman Suffrage Association as well as on behalf of the suffrage associations of France, Great Britain, Belgium, Italy and Portugal, for whom we transmitted a memorial to you asking for a message to the world upon the subject of woman suffrage, I express most grateful appreciation for your letter of June 13th.

Particularly do I want to say that your strong stand for the early passage of the federal suffrage amendment is of both national and international import as a renewed guaranty to the world that America is indeed and in truth fighting for democracy.

But two parliaments since the beginning of the war have pronounced against woman suffrage. These two are those of Germany and Hungary, while the parliaments of several of our allies have either given or promised the ballot to women. Surely the United States Senate cannot longer stand with our enemy countries in this matter of fundamental democracy.

Your message will give courage and hope to the women of our allied countries who are bearing such tragic burdens in this titanic struggle for freedom, and it is a continual gratification to suffragists in this country to know that we have a loyal friend in the White House.   Sincerely yours,   Carrie Chapman Catt

TLS (WP, DLC).

From Robert Lansing

My dear Mr. President: Washington June 13, 1918.

The very active propaganda now being carried on in the press respecting the attitude of the Administration towards Russia combined with the fact that Great Britain, France, Italy and Japan, and indeed the Russian people, are eagerly awaiting the announcement by the United States of a constructive plan for meeting the present chaotic conditions in Russia leads me to make the following suggestions:

(1) The creation of the "Commission for the Relief of Russia." This Commission to be organized generally along the same lines as the "Commission for the Relief of Belgium," except that all of the funds required should be furnished for the time being at least out of your War Fund. This would obviate the necessity of going to Congress for the present for an appropriation.

(2) An announcement by you that in order to give some tangible evidence to the world that the United States proposes to stand by Russia and to assist the Russian people in the circumstances in which they find themselves you had concluded to create this Commission and to request Mr. Herbert Hoover to act as its head and that the Commission would act in close conjunction with the State Department and be guided in all questions of foreign policy by the State Department.

I feel sure that you will agree with me that unless the policy of such a Commission is controlled through this Department, so far as it relates to foreign affairs, hopeless confusion will result.

Your appointment of Mr. Hughes to assist the Department of Justice in its Aircraft investigation effectively cleared up what bade fair to develop into a most distressing situation. As I pointed out to you after Cabinet on Tuesday, I see signs in Congress and outside of a similar situation arising in connection with Russia unless you give concrete expression to the splendid encouragement you have already extended to the Russian people. I feel sure that Mr. Hoover's appointment to head such a Commission would be widely acclaimed as another evidence of the determination of the United States to assist the Russian people towards the establishment of an orderly Government independent of Germany.

The creation of this Commission would, for the time being, dispose of the proposal of armed intervention. The British, French, Italian and Japanese Governments could be told that armed intervention would have to depend on Mr. Hoover's recommendations after he had proceeded further with his work. Armed intervention to protect the humanitarian work done by the Commission would be much preferable to armed intervention before this work had been begun.

I know that you will hesitate to take Mr. Hoover from his present work. I have learned, however, that the organization of the Food Administration has proceeded to such an extent that, while much work remains to be done, nevertheless another man could easily step in and effectively continue the work. No doubt Mr. Hoover has told you, as he has me, that our food supply at the present time is most satisfactory and that the present problem is to dispose of properly the enormous supplies we have acquired through stimulation of production. I understand that Mr. Julius Barnes[1] is considered the ablest of Mr. Hoover's assistants and best equipped for his position.

I should very much appreciate an expression of your views with reference to these suggestions.

I am, my dear Mr. President,

Faithfully yours,   Robert Lansing.

TLS (WP, DLC).
  [1] That is, Julius Howland Barnes, former president of the Barnes-Ames Co., a wheat brokerage firm; president of the United States Food Administration Grain Corp. since August 1917.

From Edward Mandell House

Dear Governor,   Magnolia, Massachusetts. June 13, 1918.

In talking with Gordon yesterday he wondered what I thought of suggesting to you the substitution of Hoover for Mott. After thinking about it, it appealed to me and I asked Gordon to take it up with Lansing for his approval. Lansing was enthusiastic and instructed Gordon to draft the letter which you have received.

I hope you will think well of the plan. Hoover is no longer necessary where he is, and there are several who are able to carry on the work—notably his understudies, Julius Barnes or Alonzo Taylor.[1]

The Russians know Hoover and Hoover knows the East. If he heads "The Russian Relief Commission" it will typify in the Russian mind what was done in Belgium, and I doubt whether any Government in Russia, friendly or unfriendly, would dare oppose his coming in.

It seems to me fortunate that Mott declined to serve,[2] for Hoover has more ability as an organizer, his name will carry more weight in the direction desired, and his appointment will, for the moment, settle the Russian question as far as it can be settled by you at present.

Someone has been here almost every day since I arrived to talk about this vexatious problem, and to try and get me to transmit their views to you. I have not done so because no good way out was presented. This plan, however, seems workable, and I sincerely hope it will appeal to your judgment.

Affectionately yours,   E. M. House

TLS (WP, DLC).

¹ That is, Alonzo Englebert Taylor, M.D., Rush Professor of Physiological Chemistry at the University of Pennsylvania, at this time head of the department of research of the Food Administration and a member of the War Trade Board.

² There is no record in WP, DLC, that Wilson had formally requested Mott to serve on the commission and that Mott had declined. Wilson probably talked to Mott about the matter on the telephone, and Mott had probably indicated that he would prefer not to be appointed. However, on June 13, Mott asked Tumulty for an interview with Wilson. J. R. Mott to JPT, June 13, 1918, T telegram (WP, DLC). Wilson saw Mott at the White House at 4:30 p.m. on June 18 and discussed the question with him. Finally, Mott withdrew entirely in a telegram of June 27: "After prolonged consideration am not clear that at present time could render best service to nation and to yourself by undertaking that special mission. It is my hope and desire that I may be of service on the problem in other ways." J. R. Mott to WW, June 27, 1918, T telegram (WP, DLC).

From Newton Diehl Baker

My dear Mr. President: [Washington] June 13, 1918.

I send the following figures for your information as to troop shipments to June 1st:

Net, after deducting wounded and other men returned from France,	722,370
Sailings to and including June 12th,	101,013
Marines,	12,000
Grand Total,	835,383

You, no doubt, noted the fact that I spoke of 700,000 with the "Blue Devils"¹ at the foot of the monument the other day. I did this because Senator Lewis, and a number of others had talked about a million men, and there was coming to be an exaggerated notion on the subject in the country which I thought it necessary to sober by my statement. By the first of July I will make another statement which will undoubtedly add 100,000 to the figures here given.

Respectfully yours,   [Newton D. Baker]

CCL (N. D. Baker Papers, DLC).

¹ Baker addressed a group of 112 members of the *chasseurs alpins*, or "Blue Devils," at the Washington Monument in the late afternoon on June 10, 1918. Called the "Blue Devils" because of the color of their uniform, the *chasseurs alpins* were an elite unit of the French army which had distinguished itself in several battles during the war. The group had come to the United States on April 29 and had toured the country in support of the Third Liberty Loan and the Red Cross War Fund drives. Wilson had received them at the White House at 2:10 p.m. on May 13. Baker's address is printed in the *New York Times*, June 11, 1918.

From Herbert Clark Hoover

Dear Mr. President: Washington 13 June 1918

Certain discussions have arisen with regard to Allied relations to the Food Administration next year that I do not believe can be solved without a joint meeting of myself with the Food Administrators of France, England and Italy.

First, we must determine an arrangement of a cereal program next year, based upon the real needs of the Allies, and its adjustment to shipping conditions. Beyond this, as you are aware, we have a guaranteed price for wheat, and I am anxious that the three European Governments should prepare large storage for wheat reserves, in order that if shipping conditions improve in 1919 they could transport our surplus to Europe as a safety reserve for themselves, and thus will relieve us from the necessity of carrying this large amount of wheat at great investment.

A second problem arises in that the European demands for meat at the present time are larger on the beef side than our production will stand without conservation methods further than we can carry on a voluntary basis. On the other hand, we shall have apparently a large surplus of pork, and I have failed in my endeavors so far to persuade the European Food Administrators to substitute pork for beef in sufficient quantities to take care of our excess production and at the same time relieve us of strain on the beef side.

The broad issue in this matter is that in order to increase the animal food supplies from the United States our only hope was through an increased production of pork, which we were able to do over a period of less than twelve months, whereas to stimulate the beef production in the United States would have required at least three years and would have been of practically no importance during the war. From an economic point of view the same food values can be had from pork at an expenditure of much less than the amount of feeding-stuffs.

Our policy has been absolutely sound in this particular and was informally agreed by myself with European Administrators. But the Administrators have changed and the force of national habit and the desire in Europe to proceed on the lines of least resistance has so far not secured the cooperation from them in this particular that is necessary. I believe that a personal conference would effect this, as I am able to present to them strongly that they must support production in this country if they are to be safeguarded in the future. Any failure on our part to find a market for our large increasing pork production would discourage our producers to a point which might become a national calamity in production.

Thirdly, it is necessary that we should improve the organization of the "Executives," who now handle the detailed cereals, meat, fats, sugar, vegetable oils and fiber on the lines that we have discussed with you during the last few days. In many of these commodities we are importers as well as the Allies, and we must have better cooperation in securing supplies and the elimination of competition in common markets abroad.

Fourth, I believe it will have a considerable effect on the psychology of the American production and consumption if we can present to the American people a definite statement that our food supplies must be pooled with the Allies' and set out to them a definite program we must fulfill and to be able to state to them accurately what this program is. Furthermore, it will, I believe, be of utmost importance in maintaining morale in the civil population in Allied countries if I could state on your behalf that the American people will make any necessary sacrifice to maintain their food necessities. There is nothing they can ask next year that with common-sense management will be beyond our capacity on present promise of production and conservation.

I propose to be absent from a month to five weeks and to set up in my absence a committee of the principal divisional heads in the Food Administration. I will obviously assent to no plans without the reservation of your approval, and I would like to add an assurance to you that I shall confine myself absolutely to food problems. I will be glad to know if this program meets with your approval.

Yours faithfully,   Herbert Hoover

TLS (WP, DLC).

From Samuel Gompers

St. Paul, Minn., June 13, 1918.

Your message brought to the convention of the American Federation of Labor an inspiration impossible to express in words and by unanimous vote I was directed to make reply. It is my pleasurable duty to say that America's workers have come to regard you as the world spokesman for democracy and human justice and we confidently trust your leadership. We wish to express to you our determination to give wholehearted support to the government of our free country in this war to establish principles of freedom that will insure peace between nations. We are doing and will continue to do our part whether at the front or at home and will share the burdens and the sacrifice. We pledge loyal support and service until human freedom and equity shall be the common right of all peoples.

Samuel Gompers.

T telegram (WP, DLC).

From the Diary of Colonel House

June 13, 1918.

Wiseman is here and we have been in conference nearly all day and largely upon the Russian situation.

Gordon telephoned last night suggesting that Hoover head a "Russian Relief Commission" as part of an intervention plan. The idea appealed to me strongly at once. This morning he called again and we decided that he should go to Hoover and ask whether he would be willing to serve in that capacity. I asked Gordon to say that I thought he had been so entirely associated with food problems, that for his own sake, it would be a good thing to show the world that he was capable of just as good work in other directions.

Hoover told Gordon he was willing to serve wherever the President and I thought he could do so best. He was enthusiastic over the suggestion and thought it the best solution of the Russian problem. We then mentioned the plan to Lansing who greeted it with enthusiasm and asked Gordon to draft a letter to the President which he, Lansing, would sign. Gordon drew up the letter, read it to me, I made a suggestion or two which he incorporated, and Lansing signed it. The letter was then sent to the President. It was really an admirable letter and I do not wonder Lansing accepted it without change.

The next move was to let the President know that I approved. We did this by Gordon writing a note to Mrs. Wilson calling attention to the letter and to my approval of it. In addition, I wrote the President today expressing my views on the subject. This letter is attached.

Sir William is enthusiastically in favor of the plan and we agreed that he should intercept Reading at Princeton, where he goes tomorrow for a degree, tell him the story, and get him to cooperate with us in putting it through. I cautioned Sir William that no one should be told of the plan except Reading, for it is necessary that it should come in the nature of a surprise. Wiseman intended remaining overnight, but because of the importance of the matter, he left at once for Boston and New York.

To Herbert Clark Hoover

My dear Mr. Hoover: The White House 14 June, 1918

I think that the reasons you give for your plan to go abroad and consult with the Food Administrators of France, England and Italy are entirely conclusive, and I believe that your visit to the other side will probably result in a better situation all around with regard to food supplies. My best wishes will certainly follow you.

Thank you for the arrangements you are making for taking care of the Administration during your absence.

Cordially and sincerely yours,   Woodrow Wilson

TLS (Hoover Archives, CSt-H).

To Henry Morgenthau

My dear Friend: The White House 14 June, 1918

Thank you for sending me the first installments of your book. Mrs. Wilson and I have been following them in the World's Work with the greatest interest and I am warmly obliged to you for the little inscription on the fly-leaf of the copy you send me.[1]

I appreciate your consulting me about the question whether the book shall be translated into motion pictures, and I must frankly say that I hope that you will not consent to this. I have been very much distressed that Mr. Gerard should have put his narrative into that form,[2] and personally I believe that we have gone quite far enough in that direction. It is not merely a matter of taste,—I would not like in matters of this sort to trust my taste,—but it is also partly a matter of principle. Movies I have seen recently have portrayed so many horrors that I think their effect is far from stimulating and that it does not, as a matter of fact, suggest the right attitude of mind or the right national action. There is nothing practical that we can do for the time being in the matter of the Armenian massacres, for example, and the attitude of the country toward Turkey is already fixed. It does not need enhancement.

With renewed appreciation,

Cordially and sincerely yours,   Woodrow Wilson

TLS (photostat in WP, DLC).
  [1] The copy is missing in WP, DLC, and in the Wilson Library, DLC.
  [2] Gerard's *My Four Years in Germany* (New York, 1917), had been made into a motion picture by Henry M. Warner and released early in 1918.

To Joseph Patrick Tumulty

Dear Tumulty: The White House [c. June 14, 1918].

Please answer this letter for me and tell Mrs. Levine how much I appreciate the suggestion but that I feel that I must ask that it be not acted on, as it would embarrass me.[1]

The President.

TL (WP, DLC).
    [1] Evelyn L. Levine to JPT, June 12, 1918, TLS (WP, DLC). Miss Levine, assistant to
the "Headworker" of the Arnold Toynbee House in New York, asked if Wilson would
object to the distribution of a button bearing his picture, under the caption, "WILSON,
THE MAN OF THE HOUR."

From Robert Lansing, with Enclosure

My dear Mr. President: Washington June 14, 1918.

Representative Gallagher[1] called on me this morning and submitted the draft of a proposed resolution relative to Poland, which
is practically an adoption of the declaration of the Premiers attending the Supreme War Council at Versailles.

He asked me for my views as to the propriety of introducing such
a resolution and I told him that I would take it under consideration.

Would you be good enough to give me your judgment in the
matter, and any suggestions as to change in phraseology which
would meet your wishes?

Faithfully yours,   Robert Lansing.

TLS (SDR, RG 59, 763.72119/1803½A, DNA).
    [1] Thomas Gallagher of Chicago, Democratic congressman.

E N C L O S U R E

Whereas, the President of the United States in his address to the
Congress of the United States on January 8, 1918 said: "An independent Polish State should be erected which should include the
territories inhabited by the indisputably Polish populations, which
should be assured a free and secure access to the sea";

And, Whereas, on the fifth of June, 1918, at the session of the
supreme war council at Versailles the British, French, and Italian
representatives agreed that: "The creation of an independent Polish
state, with free access to the sea, constitutes one of the conditions
of a solid and just peace and of the rule of right in Europe."

Be it therefore Resolved by the House of Representatives, that
the House of Representatives consider the creation of a free and
independent Polish state, with access to the sea, to be one of the
objects for which the United States is fighting in the present war,
and as one of the necessary provisions in any treaty of peace which
may be concluded.

T MS (WP, DLC).

From Herbert Clark Hoover

Dear Mr. President: Washington June 14, 1918.

With regard to the monthly report on the activities of the Food Administration, I have asked for a report from each division head and from each State Food Administrator and will furnish these reports as an appendix to a short summarized report from myself.

I have instructed that the reports shall be prepared as quickly as possible covering the month of May, but the initial report will require a little more time for preparation than the subsequent one.

In order to have the matter constantly in hand, I have appointed Mr. Robert A. Taft,[1] son of ex-President Taft, who is a volunteer in our Legal Division, to take charge of this reporting work. I trust that this will meet with your approval.

Yours faithfully,   Herbert Hoover

TLS (WP, DLC).
[1] Robert Alphonso Taft, a lawyer of Cincinnati.

From Samuel Gompers

St. Paul, Minnesota, June 14, 1918.

In pursuance of the unanimous decision of the convention of the American Federation of Labor I take pleasure in transmitting to you the following resolution: "That the American Federation of Labor in convention assembled respectfully represent to the President of the United States that the Western Union Telegraph Company and the Postal Telegraph Cable Company should immediately be taken under government control for the period of the war and as long thereafter as may be deemed advisable."

Samuel Gompers.

T telegram (WP, DLC).

David Wark Griffith to Edith Bolling Galt Wilson

(PERSONAL)   Los Angeles, Calif., June 14, 1918.

Spent a sleepless night and a troubled day after receipt of your unexpected wire, trying to think why the play had made such an effect on you.[1] Also to get the public to come in numbers to our plays, we must give them what they want and are not always able to play our story as we would like it. However, I believe I understand what the trouble is and how you are absolutely right. In this effort, which has cost a year and a half in time and a small fortune in sacrifice in a very sincere effort in a cause through which I believe I could do more good than in any work.

When we deal with the general public as a whole, we deal with a very very stolid hard animal to move or impress. We must hit hard to touch them. In trying to bring home the truth of what they have suffered over there in an intimate human way, so that our people so far away from the struggle could understand and want to strain every nerve to help them, I fell into the error which you so generously reminded me of, and overshot the mark.[2]

I am already at work restudying and re-editing. While practically the entire press in all the plays we have shown and the thousands that have by word or mouth spoken of its great value, I myself, have not been satisfied. The greatest help in all work is sincere constructive criticism. The little play has, I believe, done quite good work which I am, of course, naturally anxious for you to know, particularly in touching the stolid public. In one city in California we had nine hundred recruits who attributed their enlistments to seeing what was being done by the Germans in France in this play, and to right this great wrong being committed by German autocracy. From Thrift Stamp salesmen, Four-Minute-Men, California to New York, who said it was best help that they ever had to sell bonds and Thrift stamps. From the papers in many cities that have been kind enough to speak of its patriotic value, while practically the entire press in all the places we have shown, and the thousands that have by word or mouth spoken of its value I, myself, have not been satisfied. The greatest help in all work is sincere constructive criticism, as you know, and I think your's has shown me the light, and I shall struggle hard to deserve it.

I think that by eliminating the two powerful acting scenes, particularly where the Germans are concerned, and leaving more to the imagination, we will have a play that will not only hit the masses but not offend the refined and sensitive spirits, such as yourself; otherwise, I shall, indeed, be a very disappointed, broken individual, for my hopes and work and prayers have been so bound up in this that, unless it is pleasing in your household, I feel that everything has been in vain.

You will pardon this long message, I know, when you realize how important the matter is to me. I thoroughly believe your kind advice will be the means of making a most effective weapon to help in the great cause of humanity. I have instructed my New York representatives to go to Washington. Here they will await your convenience, in the hope that you will give them a little time on this matter. They have instructions to carry out your suggestions, after which, I will incorporate them finally in our picture.

Most respectfully,   D. W. Griffith.

T telegram (WP, DLC).

¹ Mrs. Wilson's telegram is missing. It referred to *Hearts of the World*, which Griffith had produced in cooperation with the War Office Committee of the Ministry of Information of Great Britain. The film, the story of a French village occupied by Germans, included scenes of actual fighting made by Griffith at the front. It featured Lillian Gish and Dorothy Gish. *New York Times*, April 5, 1918. Wilson, Mrs. Wilson, Margaret Wilson, Helen Bones, and the McAdoos had seen the movie at Poli's Theater on June 10.

² Arthur S. Friend, treasurer of Famous Players-Lasky Corporation, had written to Tumulty as follows:

"Those who have seen the picture state that it is, without professing so to be, the greatest piece of propaganda work done since the war began. It is hard indeed for any man to see it without wanting very much to go over and do his damndest against the Huns, and it is hard for any woman to see it without feeling that she wants her men, and all of them, to go to the Front at once." A. S. Friend to JPT, June 1, 1918, TLS (WP, DLC).

Sir William Wiseman to Sir Eric Drummond

[New York] June 14th. 1918.

Most Secret. Intervention in Russia.

As reported in my cable No. 627¹ of May 30th. I discussed with the President the question of intervention in Russia and found that, while he realised the importance and urgency of action, he did not approve the plans we proposed. Since then House has been endeavouring to evolve a policy which would be acceptable to the President and has e[x]changed views with members of the Administration and others.

I have not troubled you with the various suggestions which have been put forward, but now a concrete proposal is being prepared and is likely to be accepted. Please treat this information as very secret for the present.

The President is still firmly opposed to intervention by the Japanese alone. He is also opposed to Allied-cum-Japanese intervention on the ground that this amounts to practically the same thing because the Japanese would supply the greater part of any military force. He is, in fact, totally opposed to armed intervention without invitation either from the de facto Russian Government or some body really representing Russian opinion. His objection is simply that such action on the part of the Allies would play into the German hands, and, quite apart from the moral issue involved, would do our cause more harm than good from a military point of view. He despairs of receiving any invitation from the Bolshevic Government. As reported in my cable No. 627 of May 30th. his mind has been working on the lines of a Civil commission, and this is what is now proposed:

It was at first suggested that the Commission should be under John R. Mott of Y.M.C.A. fame. While Mott has many admirable qualities he was clearly not the man for the task. The proposal now under consideration is that Hoover should proceed at once to Vladivostock at the head of an important Allied Relief Commission. In the first instance, the object of this commission will be to bring all the relief the Allies can spare in the way of food and other supplies, and, more particularly, to help the Russian people to organize their resources to better advantage. Mr. Hoover would take with him a large staff, and he has, as you know, a world-wide reputation for organization of food supply. A military force would accompany Hoover sufficient to protect his mission, and further troops would be held in readiness and sent later if Hoover so advised. When all is ready the Bolshevic Government will be asked to invite this Relief Commission, and I think they will find it very difficult to refuse if the suggestion if [is] properly worded. In any event the commission would go. The Japanese Government would be requested to assist as well as the other allies. Having thus started the movement, the President would, I think, be very largely guided by Hoover's advice, and if he told the U.S.G. armed intervention (even mainly Japanese) would be acceptable to the Russian people, the President would probably support the proposal.

The objection which will no doubt occur at once to your mind is the delay between the sending of the Civil Commission and serious armed intervention. My reply is that at any rate we should be on the right road, and I do not believe it is possible to persuade the President to agree to armed intervention without some such preliminary movement. The advantages of the proposal seem to lie in the personality of Hoover, who knows Siberia, having spent some time there as a mining engineer. He is by no means a sentimentalist, but an ambitious and energetic man, and his recent achievements have gained him the confidence of the President and the country. He is, moreover, friendly disposed towards the British. We would, I think, be able to persuade U.S.G. to pursue their military preparations, and, if possible, to send with Hoover the nucleus of an armed force, such as a staff, to prepare the way for further troops.

This scheme has not yet received the approval of the President, but is now being considered. The information, therefore, is very secret.

T telegram (W. Wiseman Papers, CtY).
[1] Another series number for Wiseman's No. 97, printed at May 30, 1918.

From the Diary of Colonel House

June 14, 1918.

Among the callers today were Herbert Swope of the New York World and Dr. Henri Bergson, who has just arrived from France.[1] Someone said recently "Magnolia is the first port of call for foreigners coming over, and the last port before returning home."

Bergson was sent over by his Government about Siberian intervention. He started to argue the question, but I explained that I had had the matter before me, in one way or another, almost every day since last November, and that I knew every argument for and against so perfectly that I had no difficulty in repeating them in my sleep. The main trouble was that no concrete plan of value had been formulated. He admitted this and said a mission should go in to help Russia. He was glad to know that I had reached this same conclusion, and that I had presented such a plan to the President.

Bergson asked if he might convey this information to his Government by a carefully worded cable. He wrote a cable which I did not approve. I then dictated one which was acceptable to him.[2] Acting under instructions from his Government, he desires to meet the President. I advised him what to say to the President about the matter and what to leave unsaid. I asked him to assume that the President knew everything that a man in his position should know. I advised that he state that Russia could not compose herslef [herself] without aid from either the Central Powers or the Entente, and if the Entente did not attempt it, Russia would turn to Germany. I asked him to suggest as a beginning, a relief commission, and then to talk of other subjects—subjects which he and the President, of all men, have so much in common.

Bergson said he had noticed upon his last visit that Ambassador Jusserand resented Frenchmen coming to this country, or interfering in any way with diplomatic matters. He was wondering whether he had best try to reach the President without Jusserand or through him. I advised the latter. He asked how long I thought he should remain in Washington, and how long in this country. His stay in Washington, I thought, should be governed solely by his relations with Jusserand and conditions as he found them there. His stay in the United States I hoped would be for a lengthy period.

He remained for an hour and a quarter, and apologized by saying he understood my time was as wholly occupied here as in New York. I asked him to come again and talk about international affairs in general. I advised him to keep in touch with Gordon while he was in Washington, so I might have an inti[mate] view of what was going on in his immediate circle.

¹ About Bergson's mission to the United States, see H. Bergson to S. J. M. Pichon, June 26, 1918, n. 1.

² H. Bergson to S. J. M. Pichon, June 15, 1918, T telegram (Papiers Jusserand, FFM-Ar): "He [House] told me that he would not be unfavorable to the idea of a Japanese and Allied intervention in Siberia if an acceptable plan was proposed to him. I at once submitted to him a plan for forcible and rapid action which we would conduct at least to the Urals and probably beyond. We have discussed it in detail, and we are agreed among ourselves on certain of the principal points." (Our translation.)

A Platform for the Indiana Democratic Party[1]

[c. June 15, 1918]

I. The immediate purpose of the Democratic party, the purpose which takes precedence of every other, is to win the war. The fate of true democracy everywhere depends upon its being won. Its object is to rid the world once for all of the threat of violence and injustice which must hang over it so long as there is ⟨any⟩ *anywhere an* autocratic government which can disturb its peace or dominate its fortunes. The outrages against right which Germany has committed have directly touched our own citizens and our own liberties; and they have done much more than that. They have threatened right and liberty everywhere, and Germany must be brought to terms by such a victory as will leave no doubt in the minds of her rulers and her people as to what forces control mankind.

II. Because we mean to win the war, it is our purpose to support and sustain to the utmost the administration of Woodrow Wilson. His administration can better be supported by those who believe in it and trust it than by those who are constantly eager to ⟨discover⟩ *make a selfish use of what they conceive to be* its mistakes. It is therefore, our purpose to supply the administration in our nominees with men who are its real and unquestionable friends.

III. We are confirmed and strengthened in our purpose to support the administration because our judgments have been won to its support, not merely because we are at war and must stand behind the only common instrumentality through which we can win it, but also because the administration has deserved our confidence by its record. ⟨⟨See record of achievements attached. As much of this can be used as desired.⟩⟩

IV. Our purposes look also beyond the period of the war. We recognize that the war must of necessity be followed by a period of reconstruction, to whose problems it will be necessary that the best, most sympathetic and most liberal minds of the country ⟨must⟩ *should* be devoted. Those problems will some of them be new; and many of them, ⟨be⟩ *though* old problems, ⟨with⟩ *will wear* a new aspect and significance. They must be approached without regard to old party catchwords, formulas or prepossessions, in full recognition of the fact that they are new and must be dealt with in a new way.

V. As full a development as possible of vocational training must be undertaken, particular attention being given to the rehabilitation of those who have been in one way or ⟨other⟩ *another* disabled by the war. Opportunities for their ⟨economic⟩ *industrial* employment must be sought and found and they must be equipped to take advantage of those opportunities.

VI. And not in their case alone must the *sympathetic* aid of the Federal Government be given to the allocation of labor, the development of its skill and the establishment of proper labor conditions, but such services must be rendered all laborers and a systematic effort must be made to raise the whole level of labor conditions and facilitate the ⟨whole process of the placing of labor⟩ *access of labor to employment* and the ⟨enhancement⟩ *improvement* of its preparation and training.

VII. We must seek to avoid in the future the conflicts between capital and labor which have been all too frequent in the past, and must seek to do so by measures of coordination such as we have hitherto not attempted. The statesmanship of the country must be devoted to this fundamental and all-important task whose successful working out is a condition precedent to harmonious democracy. Provision must be made for the settlement of all questions upon the single basis of fairness and justice.

VIII. The whole industry of the country must be dealt with in the most liberal and enlightened manner. Raw materials and all universal essentials, like coal and electric power, must be made accessible to all upon equal and equitable terms. The natural resources of the country must be systematically developed where they have been neglected or their development delayed. Arid *and waste* lands must be reclaimed *and agriculture in general further sustained and encouraged.* New industries *must be* fostered and the barriers removed which have stood in the way of old ones, and the thought of the nation devoted to every impartial process by which the industrial prosperity of the country may be secured, by methods which will absolutely exclude monopoly.

IX. Railway transportation must be controlled in such a way as to assure complete coordination, adequate development and the equal service of the railways in every field of economic activity. The water transportation of the country must be developed in such a way as adequately to supplement and, wherever ⟨necessary⟩ *advantageous*, parallel the transportation systems of the railways.

X. A budget system for the Federal Government has become an imperative necessity, and the legislative and executive branches of the Government should work together for its establishment.

XI. There must be a single test and standard for every public policy. Every measure must be put to this test: Is it just? Is it for the benefit of the average man without influence or privilege? Does it in real fact embody the highest conception of social justice and of right dealing without regard to person or class or special interest?

As an evidence of the achievements of the ⟨Wilson⟩ *Democratic* administration, the following brief ⟨review of the conduct of the war⟩ *record* is submitted:[2]

T MS (A. S. Burleson Papers, DLC).
    [1] A handwritten note on this document by Burleson reads: "Draft of platform prepared by me and reformed by Presdt. It was in substance used in many of the States."
    It seems highly likely that Burleson either misremembered or was boasting when he wrote this note. The document was obviously typed by Swem on the plain paper which he always used. More important, the vocabulary and phrasing of the document are clearly Wilsonian. Finally, it hardly seems likely that Wilson would have entrusted the task of writing a model Democratic platform for the campaign of 1918 to the most conservative member of his cabinet, indeed to anyone except himself.
    We conclude that Wilson dictated this platform to Swem, that Swem typed up this draft, and that Wilson then emended it and sent it to Burleson for duplication and distribution.
    Words in angle brackets were deleted by Wilson; words in italics were added by him.
    This platform was repeated verbatim in the platform which the Indiana Democratic state convention in Indianapolis adopted on June 18, 1918. The full text of the "Indiana platform" is printed in the *Indianapolis News*, June 19, 1918.
    [2] This sentence was emended by Burleson and was not typed by Swem.

Remarks to a Delegation from the United States Employment Service

[June 15, 1918]

Mr. Secretary and gentlemen: The word of encouragement I can give with all my heart. I wish I could give more by way of counsel that would be of service to you, but after the consultations and interchanges of views which you have had, you know more about the problem than I do.

I can only say that the thing you are doing is one of the most necessary and serviceable things to be done. Because while it is easy, relatively, to organize an armed force, it is infinitely difficult to mobilize the working force, the industrial force of the nation, and America has never tried before to do so. Therefore, the task that you are attacking is novel as well as difficult, and I am delighted that there should be so great a force of thought and energy and enthusiasm back of this necessary and useful thing.

I am therefore very glad to utter not only a word of encouragement but a word of very sincere thanks to you that you have been good enough to associate yourselves with us in this thing which would be so necessary to do, and if at any time I can be of service to you, I will be at your service to render any counsel or assistance that you may desire.

I don't know that I have very much to offer of my own. I have been where every day in recent months that I not only had to use all the brains I had but all I could borrow, and you are here in order that I may borrow yours. But if there is anything of my brain that is serviceable to you, you are more than welcome to it. You have all that is in my heart.

JRT transcript (WC, NjP) of CLSsh MS in the C. L. Swem Coll., NjP.

From Newton Diehl Baker

My dear Mr. President: Washington June 15, 1918.

The Council of National Defense, understanding that its functions are advisory and not executive, has been distributing as rapidly as possible among the executive departments of the government, such executive or semi-executive functions as it has undertaken through force of circumstances.

This action has raised in the minds of members of the Woman's Committee of the Council the question as to whether their work should not be either discontinued or distributed among several executive agencies of the government. The Council has given serious consideration to this matter and is unanimous in the opinion that the Woman's Committee, as at present constituted, is indispensable to the successful organization of the woman power of the country.

The Council, under the law, has the duty of "the creation of relations which will render possible in time of need the immediate concentration and utilization of the resources of the nation." In accordance with this provision the Woman's Committee have caused to be established committees of women in each State with subordinate committees in each county and community. The function of these women's committees in the States is to organize the women within the State for war work and to carry into execution such activities as the federal government may wish.

The fact that the Treasury Department, Food Administration, and to a lesser extent some other departments, have created their own national organizations of women to assist in Liberty Loan, Food Conservation, and other special work, has caused the feeling on the part of the Woman's Committee of the Council and many of their State committees that their nation-wide organization is perhaps unnecessary and tends to confusion. The Council believes it is unfortunate that it has been impossible to develop closer working relations between the organizations of women developed by executive departments and the country-wide organization of the Woman's Committee of the Council, but it feels strongly that much would be lost if the Woman's Committee of the Council and the organization it has created throughout the country were dissolved. It seems to the Council most important that the women of the country generally have a definite channel both for the expression of their wishes and desires in war time, and for instruction and direction as to the work they can do for the war, and the Council considers that the Woman's Committee of the Council both is, and will continue to be the only satisfactory agency that can be created for this purpose.

The Council of National Defense is desirous of having your views on the matter in order that the work may proceed along lines which will have your entire approval.

Respectfully,   Newton D. Baker Secretary of War and
Chairman, Council of National Defense.

TLS (WP, DLC).

From Thomas Watt Gregory

Dear Mr. President: Washington, D. C. June 15, 1918.

I acknowledge receipt of yours of the 12th, accompanied by wire to you, dated Seattle, Washington, June 10th, and sent by the Executive Committee of the Washington State Grange. I assume that this is a part of the general political fight to which you refer in your letter. I return the wire, keeping a copy for my files.

We have heretofore insisted that crime was personal and that we would neither denounce nor endorse the Non-Partisan League or any branches thereof, but would hold its membership to the same responsibilities to which other citizens are held. Unless the suppression of this meeting grew out of some disloyalty it would probably be impossible for the Federal Government to deal with the situation.

I am instructing the head of my Bureau of Investigation[1] to have the meeting at Walla Walla, Washington, carefully investigated and report just what occurred and the attending circumstances. I will report to you as soon as this is received.

Faithfully yours,   T. W. Gregory

TLS (WP, DLC).
[1] That is, A. Bruce Bielaski.

From Robert Russa Moton

Dear Mr. President: Tuskegee Institute, Ala. June 15, 1918

You already have more difficulties than any one person ought to be asked to face; and may I say you are facing them with wisdom and courage, and succeeding in such a way as to deepen the respect of every true American citizen for his country and its Chief Executive.

What I want to say frankly is, that there is more genuine restlessness, and perhaps dissatisfaction, on the part of the colored people than I have ever before known. I have just recently returned from trips in Alabama, Georgia, North and South Carolina. It seems to me something ought to be done pretty definitely to change the attitude of these millions of black people; and this attitude, which is anything but satisfactory, not to use a stronger word, is due very largely to recent lynchings and burnings of colored people. The recent lynching in Georgia of six colored people in connection with a murder, and among them a woman who it is reported was a prospective mother, has intensified tremendously this attitude of colored people.

A great many of the leading colored people throughout the country have been most wise and patriotic in their attitude and efforts to allay this feeling. Mr. Emmett J. Scott, Secretary of this institution, now Special Assistant to the Secretary of War as you may remember, has been most wise and vigilant in his efforts to bring about a changed attitude on the part of the Negro.

I have the feeling that every ounce of effort of these twelve million Negroes, physically and morally, ought to be thrown in, and it seems to me the whole question is worth your serious personal consideration. These Negroes should not be permitted to become indifferent or antagonistic, not to say quietly hostile, in this emergency.

The one concrete suggestion that I wish respectfully to make is that, I think a strong word, definitely from you on this pynching [lynching] proposition will have more effect just now than any other one thing, and I think you could say that word in such a way as not to offend the South or the North or the Negro.

I am enclosing herewith a recent editorial from the Atlanta Constitution, in which the feeling is freely expressed that the Federal Government will have to come in and take charge if things continue to go as they are.[1] Similar expressions have been made by perhaps a half dozen leading Southern papers recently.

I know you will forgive me for writing frankly, or for adding another ounce to your already too heavy burden.

You can count upon my loyalty to you absolutely, and I shall be

glad of course to be of any possible service along any line whatsoever.

Thanking you for all past courtesies which you have shown, and
with best wishes for your continued good health, I am,

Yours very respectfully,   R. R. Moton

TLS (WP, DLC).
  ¹ "Dealing with Lynch Law," *Atlanta Constitution*, June 13, 1918, clipping, WP,
DLC.

From Vance Criswell McCormick, with Enclosure

Dear Mr. President: Washington June 15th, 1918.

In accordance with your wishes as expressed at our meeting on
Wednesday, Mr. Hoover, Mr. Baruch and I have revised the memorandum on the co-ordination of the activities of the governments
of the United States, Great Britain, France and Italy, and hope it
meets with your approval.

If it is in the form you desire we would appreciate your confirming
it, so we can proceed in perfecting our organizations under this
plan.

I am sending this to you in this manner because both Mr. Hoover
and I expect to be away the first part of next week, and will not be
present at our Wednesday meeting.

Sincerely yours,   Vance C. McCormick

TLS (WP, DLC).

E N C L O S U R E   I

COORDINATION OF THE ACTIVITIES OF THE GOVERNMENT OF THE UNITED

STATES, GREAT BRITAIN, FRANCE AND ITALY.

****

1.   The activities exclusive of military and naval in which joint

action should be secured fall into the following groups:

    (a) Finance
    (b) Shipping
    (c) Export and Import relations
    (d) Foodstuffs
    (e) Raw Materials or manufactured or partly manufactured
       products exclusive of foodstuffs.

2.   Each of these groups is at present organized in the four

governments, where ministers are charged with the formulation of

national programs. Responsibility for the formulation and execution

of a common program for the four countries will naturally be vested in

these same ministers. By "Ministers" is meant the departmental head

responsible directly to the President or the Premiers of the respective

governments, whether called ministers, secretaries, departmental heads,

chairmen of boards or whatever the title may be.

3.   Where the subject matter to be dealt with by the ministers is

intricate, voluminous or requires continuous attention, the ministers

will appoint committees or "executives" to make studies upon which the

ministers will formulate a common program, and which committees or

"executives" may be charged with the carrying out of programs which

have been adopted. These "executives" should be composed of a re-

presentative of each of the four governments, named by and responsible

to the appropriate minister of that government.

-2

It being the premier

4.   ~~The~~ object of this ~~recommendation being primarily~~ to insure
in   *method of Conference*
which have to do with
better cooperation ~~of~~ activities ~~in respect to~~ the provision of
the
supplies, programs ~~will~~ primarily be formed by or under the direction

of the ministers representing ~~groups (d) and (e), namely~~, foodstuffs,
and
raw materials, manufactured or partly manufactured products. The
in these matters will be limited
formulation of ~~such~~ common programs ~~may be limited~~ to cases,

    (a) Where two or more governments are interested in supplies *wh. mu*
         ~~to~~ be transported over seas ~~in~~ supplement ~~to~~ deficiencies
         in local production; or,
         the several   *supply sh. be agreed*
    (d) Where ~~there should be an agreed~~ source of ~~supplies and~~
upon and the   ~~an agreed~~ distribution or utilization ~~of supplies~~; or,
                              without agreement
    (c) Where there might ~~otherwise~~ be competition between
         governments in procuring supplies or a wasteful
         duplication of productive effort.

5.   When provisional programs respecting the commodities mentioned

in paragraph four above and subject to the limitations therein specified

have been determined upon by the ministers in charge of such commodities

such programs will be;

    (a) Coordinated with finance through the Inter-Allied
         Commission.

    (b) Coordinated with shipping through the Inter-Allied
         Maritime Council.

    (c) Coordinated with export and import relations through
         an Inter-Allied body made up of the heads of representatives
         of the United States War Trade Board and similar depart-
         ments of the other three governments.

6.   If it is impossible to secure acceptance of a program by the

various ministers, the difference of opinion must ~~necessarily~~ be
of the U.S.
submitted to the President and the three allied Premiers for final

-3

determination. *Thus (♀ ζ*

7. ILLUSTRATION: Cereal needs for the three importing countries
France, England and Italy, will be considered, first, by the Cereal
"Executive" and a recommendations submitted for approval to the four
food ministers. A provisional program will then be adopted by these
ministers which will be submitted to the corresponding ministers
dealing with finance, shipping and export and import relations. After
approval by these ministers, the finally determined program will be
turned over to the cereal executive for execution, in such manner and
through such agencies as ministers may determine.

8.   In the event that the Ministers in charge of any of the five
groups of activities here dealt with, feel that the formulation of
programs is delayed or rendered difficult by a geographical separation
of such ministers which cannot be obviated consistently with the other
duties of such ministers, then any such minister may appoint a personal
representative to sit at a foreign capital. This representative may
exercise such control as the minister may determine over the minister's
appointees on "executives" sitting at such capital.

ENCLOSURE II[1]

The Government of the United States recognizes that in addition to military and naval action a careful coordination is necessary between the governments now associated in the war against Germany in
Finance
Shipping
Export and Import relations
Foodstuffs
Raw Materials and manufactured or partly manufactured products exclusive of foodstuffs.

The activities which should be grouped under each of these heads are at present organized in the several governments, where in each field Ministers are charged with the formulation of national programmes. Responsibility for the formulation and execution of a common programme for the associated governments will naturally be vested in these Ministers. By "Ministers" is meant the departmental heads responsible directly to the President or the Ministries of the respective governments, whether called Ministers, Secretaries, departmental heads, chairmen of boards, or by whatever title.

The Government of the United States agrees that where the subject matter to be dealt with is intricate, voluminous, or in need of continuous attention, the several Ministers should appoint representatives to sit upon joint committees or "executives" charged with making studies upon which the Ministers are to formulate a common programme, and that these committees or "executives" should be charged with the carrying out of such programmes as have been adopted by the Ministers upon their recommendation.

It being the primary object of this method of conference to insure better cooperation in activities which have to do with the provision of supplies, programmes should primarily be formed by or under the direction of the Ministers representing foodstuffs, raw materials, and manufactured or partly manufactured products. The Government of the United States understands that the formulation of common programmes in these matters will be limited to cases

(a) Where two or more governments are interested in supplies which must be transported overseas to supplement deficiencies in local production; or,

(b) Where the several sources of supply should be agreed upon, and the allotment and method of their distribution or utilization; or,

(c) Where there might without agreement be competition between governments in procuring supplies or a wasteful duplication of productive effort.

When provisional programmes respecting the commodities mentioned above have been agreed upon within the limits specified by the Ministers in charge of such commodities, such programmes will be

(a) Coordinated with finance through the Inter-Allied Commission.

(b) Coordinated with shipping through the Inter-Allied Maritime Council.

(c) Coordinated with export and import relations through an Inter-Allied board made up of the heads or representatives of the United States War Trade Board and similar departments of the other governments.

If it is impossible to secure a unanimous acceptance of a programme by the various Ministers, differences of opinion will be submitted to the President of the United States and the Premiers of the Allied Governments represented for final determination.

In the event that the Ministers in charge of any of the groups of activities here dealt with feel that the formulation of programmes is delayed or rendered difficult by the geographical separation of the Ministers from one another, and that the difficulties cannot be obviated by personal conference consistently with their other duties, any such Minister may appoint a personal representative to sit at a foreign capital. This representative may exercise such control as the Minister by whom he is appointed may determine over the Minister's appointees or "executives" sitting at such capital.

T MSS (WP, DLC).
¹ The following document is a copy of the draft with Wilson's revisions.

From S. J. Konenkamp

St. Paul, Minnesota, June 15, 1918.

I have the honor to acknowledge receipt of your letter today and it has increased my determination to do all that I can to avoid a strike among the Commercial Telegraphers. In agreeing to accept the decision of the National War Labor Board the commercial telegraphers union of America has been actuated by an earnest desire to cooperate with you. I can readily pledge you that if the telegraph companies will in turn accept the decision of the National War Labor Board and be governed by its rules and awards industrial peace in the telegraph service will be certain at least until victory for our great cause has been achieved.   S. J. Konenkamp.

T telegram (WP, DLC).

Newton Diehl Baker to Tasker Howard Bliss

[Washington] June 15, 1918

Number 61 Confidential Rush.

Paragraph 1. Subparagraph A. The President has received from Lord Milner an urgent request[1] that an American force be dispatched to the ports of Murmansk and Archangel, consisting of 3 battalions of infantry and Machine guns, 2 batteries of Field Artillery, 3 companies of Engineers, and the necessary administrative and medical services, aggregating more than 4,000 men, to be placed under the command of the British General Poole who is already at Murmansk with 1200 British troops, 1500 Servians, a few hundred French, and is supported by the presence of 3 British ships of war in the port. This force, it is suggested, may be supplemented by Czecho-Slav troops now in Russia, and it is expected that this force will be able to protect the ports of Murmansk and Archangel. Lord Milner's dispatch says that he discussed this matter with General Foch and found that he realized its importance from the standpoint of the General Military situation and believed the proposed use of American troops most advantageous. The President does not know how fully the matter was presented to General Foch and desires you to see him, lay before him the fact that while it is entirely possible for the United States to supply the troops in question, it will necessarily be at the expense of American troops on the Western front, since there are no American troops who are not available for use on the Western front, and the United States is now using all available shipping for the transportation of troops to France. Does General Foch believe that it would be wise to divert the troops in question and the shipping in question to Murmansk, rather than to send these troops to France? It is possible that Lord Milner's dispatch means the diversion of these troops from those transported to England by the British, but in any case it would mean the withdrawal of the number sent from those available for use in France.

Subparagraph B. Lord Milner's dispatch states that the Permanent Military Representatives of the Supreme War Council passed a resolution approving of this expedition and recommending that the force be placed under command of a British General for the present.[2] I can see no reason why a British General Officer should command an expedition in which a large majority of the soldiers are Americans, and it is my personal belief that politically it would be much wiser to have an American officer in command because the known separation of America from all European interests would at once impress the Russians favorably while with an European commander the question might be raised as to the particular national interest of the government which he represented. Will you let me know confidentially whether the recommendation of the Permanent Military Representatives in this behalf was of such a character that we ought to yield to it in spite of my strong feeling of opposition on both grounds. Baker.   McCain.

TC telegram (WDR, RG 407, World War I Cablegrams, DNA).
  ¹ That is, A. J. Balfour to Lord Reading, June 11, 1918.
  ² That is, Joint Note 31, the text of which is printed in n. 1 to the document just cited.

Sir William Wiseman to Sir Eric Drummond

[New York] June 15, 1918.

No. 100. For some time HOUSE has been endeavoring to frame a suitable scheme for American representation in Europe. As reported in my cable No. 97 of May 30 PRESIDENT was opposed to the idea of permanent political American representative, and there have been moreover various departmental difficulties.

A scheme has now been prepared, and accepted in principle but not in detail by the President. It is as follows:

VANCE MCCORMICK is to be appointed Chairman of the Board of American Commissioners in Europe, with headquarters at Paris and offices in London. The other members of the Board will probably be CROSBY, Financial Commissioner; STETTINIUS, Assistant Secretary for War and in charge of munitions and supplies; and STEVENS may also join the Board as Shipping Commissioner.

If this plan is carried out MCCORMICK will have wide powers over all American war missions, except, of course, that he would not interfere with PERSHING as Commander-in-Chief of the Expeditionary Force. MCCORMICK would be the man with whom Allied statesmen could discuss any war problems, and, even if he could not give a decision himself, his recommendations to the President would have the greatest weight.

The above is very secret as it is now being considered by the President and his Cabinet.

T telegram (W. Wiseman Papers, CtY).

William Graves Sharp to Robert Lansing

Paris, June 16, 1918.

4221. Strictly confidential. In connection with my weekly report which will follow later I have thought the Department might be interested in getting the views of Marshal Joffre upon the military situation at the present moment. This statement was delivered yesterday by the Marshal to Mr. Dawson of this Embassy,[1] for my information. In former telegram I have taken occasion to attest to the very high value which I place upon the judgment and opinion of Marshal Joffre whether upon military or political subjects. His statement embraces the following in its entirety:

"For the present, at all events, Paris may be considered as safe. The Chateau-Thierry, Villers-Cotterets, Compiegne front is stable. There may be slight local engagements but the Germans plan no further attack there just now. They realize that they cannot take Paris in this manner and they are not going to run the risks of a big failure at this juncture when they must succeed if they are ever to succeed. They have done a great deal of thinking in the last month largely owing to the American troops. They fully realize now what America's intervention means for they have felt the American soldier at work. They would have taken Paris if they could but their real objective was and is to destroy the French and British Armies before America can put a big army in the field. Now they recognize the necessity for haste especially since one month from now we may expect to see an entire American army corps fighting with its individuality as an army corps and this will continue.

According to such information as we can get, the Germans now *dispose of* between thirty and forty entirely fresh divisions in the north. I believe they are going to try their supreme effort of the 1918 campaign against the English, planning to turn again towards Paris after smashing the British army. Such preparation might require some weeks but these new divisions may already be in position for all we know, and in that case the attack might be imminent. I myself incline to think it will come within the next two weeks and probably within a few days. They have everything to gain by promptness, especially in view of the rapidity with which American troops are arriving. The attack may come anywhere between Amiens and Arras but I foresee it will be to the south and west of Albert where there are only British troops. The reports we receive of the spirit and the condition of the British troops are not at all encouraging. Should the Germans succeed in their attack it would mean a separation of the French and British armies with very serious consequences. Then, of course, the way would be opened for a further drive towards the Channel after which another attempt towards Paris might be undertaken." Sharp.

T telegram (SDR, RG 59, 763.72/10397, DNA).
[1] Francis Warrington Dawson, at this time an unofficial attaché in the American embassy in Paris.

Lord Reading to Arthur James Balfour

[New York] June 16, 1918.

No. CXP 652. *Following from* LORD READING *for* MR. BALFOUR: URGENT & SECRET.

A. On Friday, 21st June, I shall be conferring with HOUSE near Boston, and should wish to be fully acquainted with your latest views in reference to intervention in Siberia and Japanese forces.

B. The difficulty in persuading the President to armed intervention by Japanese forces plus Allied and American contingents arises from military and political considerations: (1) No military plan has ever been submitted to him which in his military advisers' opinions need or would cause withdrawal of German forces from West; (2) The sum of his information leads to conclusion that Russians would not look favourably upon entry of Japanese troops and in such event Russians would be likely to become more friendly to Germany with all the possible consequences and dangers to Allied interests.

C. I am not unmindful of all you have cabled in answer to above but the present opportunity in view of most recent developments both here and in Russia should be used to present your latest ideas upon this subject.

D. Cable in answer to be sent through Wiseman. R.

T telegram (W. Wiseman Papers, CtY).

An Appeal

The White House, *June 17, 1918.*

For more than a year it has been our pride that not our armies and navies only, but our whole people is engaged in a righteous war. We have said repeatedly that industry plays as essential and honorable a role in this great struggle as do our military armaments. We all recognize the truth of this, but we must also see its necessary implications—namely, that industry, doing a vital task for the Nation, must receive the support and assistance of the Nation. We must recognize that it is a natural demand—almost a right of anyone serving his country, whether employer or employee, to know that his service is being used in the most effective manner possible. In the case of labor this wholesome desire has been not a little thwarted owing to the changed conditions which war has created in the labor market.

There has been much confusion as to essential products. There has been ignorance of conditions—men have gone hundreds of miles in search of a job and wages which they might have found at their doors. Employers holding Government contracts of the highest importance have competed for workers with holders of similar contracts, and even with the Government itself, and have conducted expensive campaigns for recruiting labor in sections where the supply of labor was already exhausted. California draws its unskilled labor from as far east as Buffalo, and New York from as far west as the Mississippi. Thus labor has been induced to move fruitlessly from one place to another, congesting the railways and losing both time and money.

Such a condition is unfair alike to employer and employee, but most of all to the Nation itself, whose existence is threatened by any decrease in its productive power. It is obvious that this situation can be clarified and equalized by a central agency—the United States Employment Service of the Department of Labor, with the counsel of the War Labor Policies Board—as the voice of all the industrial agencies of the Government. Such a central agency must have sole direction of all recruiting of civilian workers in war work; and, in taking over this great responsibility, must at the same time have power to assure to essential industry an adequate supply of labor, even to the extent of withdrawing workers from nonessential production. It must also protect labor from insincere and thoughtless appeals made to it under the plea of patriotism, and assure it that when it is asked to volunteer in some priority industry the need is real.

Therefore, I, Woodrow Wilson, President of the United States of America, solemnly urge all employers engaged in war work to refrain after August 1, 1918, from recruiting unskilled labor in any manner except through this central agency. I urge labor to respond as loyally as heretofore to any calls issued by this agency for voluntary enlistment in essential industry. And I ask them both alike to remember that no sacrifice will have been in vain, if we are able to prove beyond all question that the highest and best form of efficiency is the spontaneous cooperation of a free people.

Woodrow Wilson.

Printed in the *Official Bulletin*, II (June 18, 1918), 3.

To Joseph Patrick Tumulty

Dear Tumulty: The White House [c. June 17, 1918].

It is practically impossible to do this without going into some matters which I am sure Mr. Sherley would agree should remain confidential for the present.[1] The President.

TL (WP, DLC).
[1] JPT to WW, June 15, 1918, TL (WP, DLC). Tumulty reported that J. Swagar Sherley, chairman of the House Appropriations Committee, had telephoned to request a more detailed breakdown of the allocations made from Wilson's discretionary war fund. The statement previously given to Sherley listed allotments, for example, of over $1,000,000 to the Treasury Department, a similar sum to the Navy Department, and so on, but did not specify any particular branches of these departments or the amounts given to each.

To Robert Lansing

My dear Mr. Secretary, The White House. 17 June, 1918.

Mr. Page need not concern himself about Horodyski.[1] We are not likely to trust him in any way.

Faithfully Yours, W.W.

WWTLI (SDR, RG 59, 763.72119/1762½, DNA).
[1] The letter to which this was a reply is missing in all collections.

To Robert Lansing, with Enclosure

My dear Mr. Secretary, The White House. 17 June, 1918.

There seems to me to emerge from this suggestion the shadow of a plan that might be worked, with Japanese and other assistance. These people are the cousins of the Russians.

Faithfully Yours, W.W.

WWTLI (SDR, RG 59, 861.00/2145½, DNA).

E N C L O S U R E

Peking, June 13, 1918.

It is the general opinion of Allied representatives here in which I concur that it would be a serious mistake to remove the Czech-Slovak troops from Siberia.[1] With only slight countenance and support they could control all of Siberia against the Germans. They are sympathetic to the Russian population, eager to be accessories to the allied cause, the most serious means to extension of German influence in Russia, their removal would greatly benefit Germany and further discourage Russia. If they were not in Siberia it would be worth while to bring them there from a distance.

Representatives of the Moscow Central Supply Committee here at present describe the nature of their organization elective in its communal district and central bodies devoted to task of filling crying needs Russian population, saving lives, resisting extension of German influence, preventing supplies to regions under German control. They seem an organization which allies could support with good results. They are working here for relaxation of Manchurian export embargo. Do you desire that I support release of merchandise addressed to that committee.   Reinsch.

T telegram (SDR, RG 59, 861.00/2014, DNA).
    ¹ About the situation at this time of the Czech troops in Siberia, commonly called the "Czech Legion," see Victor M. Fic, *The Bolsheviks and the Czechoslovak Legion: Origin of Their Armed Conflict, March-May 1918* (New Delhi, 1978). For a brief narrative, see Kennan, *The Decision to Intervene*, pp. 136-65. For a narrative by a contemporary participant, see the Enclosure printed with T. G. Masaryk to WW, Aug. 6, 1918. And for a study which lays out in full for the first time the role which the Czech Legion played in the Russian Civil War, see the forthcoming book by Betty Miller Unterberger. We are grateful to Professor Unterberger for supplying us with a draft of this book.

From Newton Diehl Baker

My dear Mr. President: Washington. June 17, 1918.

I ought to have been more explicit in my note to you of June 11th; but I was absent from the meeting of the Council of National Defense at the time its resolution was passed, and so could not advise as to the discussion leading up to it.

The studies of reconstruction problems which the Council feels itself an appropriate agency to coordinate, deal with the specific questions of re-allocation of labor to which you refer; but cover a somewhat wider field. For instance, we are already suggesting through the State Councils of Defense the wisdom of maturing as many municipal and State improvement projects as possible, but deferring their execution so that when the war is over these deferred public improvements will afford a considerable demand for labor. As the Secretary of Labor is a member of the Council, and also the Secretary of Commerce, we have the two Departments represented which, through existing bureaus, are able to keep track of the changes in labor and industry which the war is causing.

The suggestion of the Council, however, is that it coordinate studies and suggest procedures, and not that it actively undertake any present executive action. The Director of the Council has collected from England, France and Canada the printed studies which are being made in those countries, and our object is more to discuss the activities of others for the present than to undertake the instigation of any affirmative things here.

Respectfully yours,   Newton D. Baker

TLS (WP, DLC).

From Newcomb Carlton

Dear Mr. President,   New York June 17th, 1918.

Permit me to thank you for your letter of June 11th, which I acknowledged by wire on Friday.

The foundation upon which rests the procedure of the National War Labor Board is contained in the following clause of the official paper issued with your proclamation of the eighth of April:

"When the board, after due effort of its own, through sections, local committees, or otherwise, finds it impossible to settle a controversy, the board shall then sit as a board of arbitration, decide the controversy, and make an award if it can reach a *unanimous* conclusion. If it cannot do this, then it shall select an umpire, as provided, who shall sit with the board, review the issues and render his award."[1]

In view of this required procedure, I think we are entitled to state the facts, which are that the Walsh-Taft plan which has been referred to as the decision of the board was rejected by the board under the above procedure by five votes. Following this failure of unanimous action, there was no appointment of an umpire and therefore, under the prescribed procedure of the board itself, no decision.

Let me assure you, Mr. President, that our desire to support the National War Labor Board in their conciliatory and mediatory functions is expressed in our willingness to submit to their arbitration any dispute which might arise between the management and the employes over a question of pay or working conditions. We believe, however, that we are entitled during the war to maintain the dictum which the Secretary of Labor has so well expressed in these words:

"Where either an employer or an employe has been unable under normal conditions to change the standards to their own liking

[1] Carlton's citation is inaccurate. This quotation is not from Wilson's proclamation of April 8, 1918 (printed at that date in Vol. 47) or from the report of the War Labor Conference Board of March 29, 1918 (printed as Enclosure II with WBW to WW, April 4, 1918, Vol. 47), which was the "official paper" issued with Wilson's proclamation. It comes, rather, from the plan of procedure adopted by the National War Labor Board on May 13, 1918, which is printed in the *Official Bulletin*, II (May 14, 1918), 1-2.

they should not take advantage of the present abnormal conditions to establish new standards."[2]

We have for years maintained the position that our essential employes, those working the wires, should not affiliate with organizations employing the strike either for their own benefit or sympathetically for the benefit of others. This policy has long been known to our employes and we have considered abstention from such affiliation a condition of their service, and to-day there are no members of such organization in our employ.

We desire to be perfectly frank with you, Sir, as we have been with the Board. We are not favorable to sharing the responsibility of conducting a great public service with the peculiar features of the telegraph, which the exigencies of the war have increased many fold, with members of an outside organization whose interests are personal rather than public.

The telegraph business that comes to us is about 80 per cent of the total and this volume involves about 1,500,000,000 handlings per year. Obviously, properly to handle so vast a volume promptly and accurately requires complementary effort and a cordial cooperation between all employes.

The quality of telegraph service depends absolutely upon the spirit of individual employes. For the telegraph service, unlike the railroad, there is no time table by which the individual patron may measure whether or not his message is being handled expeditiously. Neither the public nor the management is able to determine whether small delays or slight inaccuracies are warranted or not. It is essential, therefore, that every employe of this company sustain an attitude not only of loyalty toward the management itself, but of friendliness and desire to cooperate with all their fellow employes. Thus it becomes peculiarly true in the telegraph business that a small minority of operators not cordially cooperating may seriously interfere with the speed and accuracy of messages.

Under the plan of Mr. Walsh, concurred in by Mr. Taft, an outside union which has for many years been frankly hostile to the company would, under the pretext of a war emergency, waive its right to

---

[2] Carlton took this quotation out of context. In a conference with labor leaders on April 23, 1917, Secretary Wilson had commented as follows: "The Council of National Defense takes this position, that the standards that have been established by law, by mutual agreement, or by custom should not be changed at this time; that where either the employer or the employee has been unable under normal conditions to change the standards to their own liking, they should not take advantage of the present abnormal conditions to establish new standards." *Monthly Review of the U. S. Bureau of Labor Statistics*, IV (June 1917), 808-809. Secretary Wilson then said that working people had a special concern about the "standard" involved in the question of union recognition and that, in his opinion, employers had no right to interfere with workingmen who were trying to organize their fellow workers. For an extensive quotation of Wilson's opinion on this latter point, see W. Catchings to WW, Aug. 17, 1917, n. 1, Vol. 43.

strike during the war, but carry on a propaganda for the purpose of enlisting sufficient of the Company's employes for no possible result that it could attain during the war, but only that it might furnish the nucleus for the disorganization of our service through demoralized discipline and the use of the strike immediately after the exigencies of the war had ceased and released it from its promises. As indicative of the character and temper of this Union, permit me to quote the following words from an official circular issued by it calling a meeting in Chicago for June 9th: "Come armed if you deem it necessary."

I need not remind you, Sir, that the primary obligations of a telegraph service are to provide continuity and competence and that we desire to protect these essentials not only during this emergency but at all times. To this end there are, it seems to us, two plans of procedure. One, compulsory arbitration which, as we recall, you urged upon Congress at the time the great railway strike was imminent. The other is found in the suggestion of our employes that they form their own union or organization upon the theory that the normal relationship between employer and employe is that of peace and mutual cooperation in the adjustment of their relations and not that of strife, and that a spirit of hostility and efforts of warfare are not necessary for industrial progress or the adjustment of mutual relations.

In order that our operating employes might give free expression to their wishes respecting this outside union or an organization of their own, we suggested to the National War Labor Board the submission of the questions to the employes through a referendum to be taken under the direction of the National Board and we agreed to abide by the event of the ballot, but for reasons unknown to us this proposal was not adopted.

Now that our employes have determined upon their own association, I am sure they would be glad to have the advice and counsel of the National War Labor Board in the formation of their organization to the end that it may be representative of the employes' interests as well as free from any influence that might limit its effectiveness in dealing with the rights and privileges of the employes. Nothing that can be accomplished by the Walsh-Taft plan is not accomplished by the employes' association, but there is this important distinction—that unionism established under conditions of coercion and hostility is not the same thing as the right to bargain collectively, a right which is given the employes by their association.

We ask you to believe that our view is based upon a most careful re-examination of our experience in the operation of telegraph service. There is no dispute between the company and its employes over pay or hours of labor. There is no likelihood of a strike of our employes, a body of men and women of high patriotism who have borne great burdens uncomplainingly as a part of their contribution to the Nation's cause.

The Board of Directors and the executives concerned in the management of the property, with primary responsibility to the public and Government, would deeply deplore being forced to lay aside the safeguards that experience has shown to be requisite and which are believed essential to the preservation of effective telegraph service.

I am, my dear Mr. President,
                              Yours faithfully,   Newcomb Carlton.

Postscript: I am sending herewith a copy of a pamphlet which was in press when your letter reached me containing a full record of the Company's position and collateral facts and papers.[3]

TLS (WP, DLC).
  [3] It is missing.

From Helen Hamilton Gardener

My dear Mr. President: Washington, D. C. 17, June, 1918.

As president of the National and of the International Associations for Woman Suffrage, Mrs. Catt left with you on June 13th her official letter of thanks for your comprehensive response to her request that you give out one of your inimitable statements to the world, as it's leader in the onward march toward a real democracy.

I trust that you will not think it amiss for me to add a word of my own in this connection, since I have been the envoy to ask you for so many helpful acts for women during the past two years.

In your response to the appeal of the women of France and of our other allies, you have now securely linked together in the public mind the cause of *human* liberty and justice, and removed the idea that a democracy can be a government of male domination. You have planted the idea that humanity is a unit, and that justice has no sex. You have furnished the political imagination so lacking where vision is needed to plan and to build for the future.

It is unthinkable that the United States Senate can now vote to range itself on the side of Germany and Hungary, who, alone of all the warring countries, have denied to women the ballot since this "war for democracy and self-determination" began.

With your attitude now made clear to the dullest (or most reluctant) senator and *to his constituents*, that the fundamental principle for which the war is being fought is at stake in his vote—

namely, self-government and not sex government, I do not believe that the voters of the various states will sustain their senators in lining up with Germany on this issue against our allies; against the women of the world and against the President of the United States to whom the world is looking for leadership in the matter of self-determination of the nations.

To my mind, therefore, Mr. President, this last stand you have taken in the fight to establish a real democracy at home, as well as in the world at large, is to be in history about the most far-reaching state document that even you have put forth. I hope that it may take its place *as* a state document in the next issue of your messages in book form.

Whatever the United States Senate now elects to do "at this session" it, alone, is on trial before the world as to its power to grasp the principles of democracy and as to the integrity of purpose for which we are fighting.

Finally, Mr. President, I have a deep feeling of personal gratitude and pride in what you have done, since it has been to me that was intrusted the work of dealing with the Executive branch of the government in bringing about this happy result.

I have always believed (and said so to our officers) that it was only a question of the right time to do it when you would make the country understand clearly that a fight for democracy did not, and could not, exclude women.

We do not ask, and do not want it given as a "reward" for war work and war sacrifice. Those are our loyal duty and pleasure to give even under the humiliation of disfranchisement, but how much more whole-heartedly, cheerfully, joyfully we can and will make those duties our *first* thought and pleasure when we can feel that we are a part of the government which we gladly sacrifice so much to protect and to make safe! I doubt if even you can grasp how deep that feeling is in the women who think.

From the bottom of my heart I thank you for your powerful help at this critical moment.

I have the honour to remain,

Yours sincerely,   Helen H. Gardener.

TLS (WP, DLC).

From George Creel

My dear Mr. President: Washington, D.C. June 17, 1918.

As you may know, the colored population of the country, from a variety of causes, has been torn by rumor and ugly whisperings

ever since we entered the war. Their leaders have been working
with the Administration splendidly in combatting this dangerous
unrest, and in order to get a working agreement and organization
that will take care of this situation, and others that may arise, we
have asked the negro editors of the country to come here for a three
days' conference.

The Secretary of War and the Secretary of the Navy will address
them, and I am very eager to bring them to you for one of your
informal talks. There are about forty-five of them, all loyal and
enthusiastic, and seeing you and hearing you is just the inspiration
that they need.

May I suggest Thursday afternoon?

Sincerely,   George Creel

TLS (WP, DLC).

From Antoinette Funk[1]

My dear Mr. President: Washington 17th June, 1918.

I am writing in response to your request[2] that I put before you
the attitude of the farmers of the Northwest toward the government,
according to my understanding.

It seems beyond question that the farmer group has been the
slowest to grasp the meaning of the war and its direct bearing upon
the life of the nation, and also that they have failed to respond to
the spiritual side of the war, if I may use the word spiritual.

This is true of the entire group, but it is a little less pronounced
in the Middle West and the South West, and most notable in the
great wheat-growing districts, Wisconsin, Minnesota, the Dakotas,
Montana, Idaho, Oregon and Washington.

I think the underlying reason for this condition is a lack of national consciousness—the inevitable result of isolation, where their
world is bounded by their line fences, and the members of their
households are their only associates. Not knowing the world, they
are suspicious of everybody in the world, and while the farmers as
a class have many pronounced virtues—integrity, industry, and so
forth—my observation of them leads me to the belief that suspicion
is very often their dominant characteristic.

Generally speaking, farmers have never organized for purely constructive purposes. Their only mass activity for years was the annual

[1] A suffrage leader, formerly a practicing lawyer in Chicago. At this time she was a
member of the Woman's Committee of the Council of National Defense and vice-
chairperson and executive officer of the National Woman's Liberty Loan Committee of
the Treasury Department.
[2] Made orally at the White House on June 10.

state fair. But it is noteworthy that the members of this particular group did organize for defense, or for what they deemed to be defense. This, in my judgment, is the crux of the situation. This is what happened in the Northwest.

Owing to their distances from market, railroads, freight rates and elevators became vital factors in their existence. And railroads, freight rates and elevators being susceptible of control by law, but in fact being in control of law-making bodies, came in a vague sort of way to represent to them the powers of government, and when they had been exploited by the railroads and the elevators, always cooperating under one guise or another, there grew up a feeling that the government was at the very best remote or indifferent to their welfare.

It was at this juncture that La Follette entered the ring as the farmer's champion, and because he battled with the railroads and exposed their back-door, and indeed, very often their front-door connection with the elevators and the resultant combination against the grain growers, he became in a measure their leader. He was, I believe, their very earliest leader, and this accounts in part for their luke-warmness at this time.

If the farmer group had been concentrated, I believe they would have become socialists, but as socialism seldom develops in scattered communities, this did not come about and they developed into protestants instead. Thus a fertile field was created for the seeds of discontent.

About the same period, the question of power rights came to the front. A great number of power sites have been developed at government reclamation dams and the farmers naturally feel that these in part should be controlled and operated by the government and that they should not be permitted to be leased to private concerns or operated for private advantage. In addition to this, every power site is a natural monopoly. It is one of those things which seem to be dedicated by nature to the public at large and ought in the minds of the farmers particularly and more and more in the minds of the community to be operated and controlled by the government or the states, in other words by public ownership and control.

This is a live, burning issue in all the Western communities and hundreds of thousands of these people have reached the conclusion that if they do not own the power and operate the power plants the power trust will own them. You will recall that this is one of the four fundamental planks of the Non-partisan League and the Grange platforms.

The Northwestern farmer has not grown rich as has the farmer of the Middle West, and this may add to his general discontent. In any event, when the war broke out, the various societies—all with ostensible legitimate purposes—became agencies for German propaganda and breeding places for disloyalty.

Due allowance must be made for the make-up of these people nationally. There is a large sprinkling of Germans, together with a great many Scandinavians, and in certain localities, particularly in Minnesota, there is a strong anti-Canadian feeling growing out of the Soo Railroad and from other causes. Unless one has come in contact with the people of this section of the country, it is hard to believe how remote they are from sources of information. I have traveled the length and breadth of those states west of Minnesota and have scarcely been able to buy a magazine of even average importance. The metropolitan papers do not reach them. The local papers are entirely inadequate. Columns will be given to a murder in a near-by community, and four inches of space to the most important happenings of the war.

Naturally they believed every wild rumor and report, and anything like criticism of a governmental activity, such as the Hog Island matter[3] or the Aircraft investigation, and so forth, takes on an exaggerated importance. Their trend of feeling has been that the capitalistic class is the controlling class, and this feeling has been aggravated by the unfortunate condition which I am informed and which I believe prevails with reference to war activities in the several localities.

The Councils of Defense have been most unfortunate in their appointments. Very few farmers belonging to the great farmers' organizations have been recognized and this, I understand, is true in the appointment of Red Cross representatives, Food Administrators, Liberty Loan Committees, and so forth. There is a feeling that there has been a definite plan to penalize them by excluding them. To my mind, this is extremely unfortunate. These very activities should have been used as agencies to build up their loyalty and promote their education.

In spite of these things, I am convinced that the situation has materially improved in the past few months. May I repeat what I said to you over a week ago, that the trip of Mr. Vrooman through the Northwest was big in results, and may I say again that the Department of Agriculture is the strongest link binding them to the government. Mr. Vrooman has a peculiarly human quality, and he made that Department seem alive and real to them. I have this information largely from farm women, and I find this a most trustworthy source. I am certain, too, that the administration of the

[3] About this matter, see EMH to WW, Feb. 16, 1918, n. 1, Vol. 46.

railroads by the government will be of enormous advantage, and that the attitude of our people toward the outrageous conduct of Mr. La Follette is commencing to have an effect upon them.

My feeling, dear Mr. President, is that this important group of people are now at the parting of the ways. In a crisis such as this they are like children. They want the feel of personal leadership—they must have it. They want a human hand to guide them through the darkness. The Little Father idea is inherent in all of us. The farmer is simple. Once he forms an alliance he does not break it easily. Once he accepts a leader, he does not desert him. It is my hope that in some way these may come to really know their leader. If it were possible—this is perhaps too much to hope or expect—I wish that you might go among them, travel across their great fields of waving grain, see them in their homes, talk to them at one of their state fairs or elsewhere. The way is prepared, and among us all they need you most.

If such a plan would be an impossible demand upon your precious time, then I wish that some of them might come to Washington; not officers of the Grange nor teachers in their agricultural institutions, but the real farmers who have struggled along to pay for their land and lost their crop and gone through all of the phases of farmer life.

You know it is the belief of many people that the Non-partisan League will be the Labor Party of the future. I doubt it. The farmer has an inherent antipathy for the industrial classes. But whatever this or any other organization may develop into, they now need your inspiration and your guidance; they need a foreword on the day of reconstruction. You and no one else can make them understand the dire need of their country for their support at this time. There is no one except yourself who can save them entirely from the evil effects of the La Follettes and the I.W.W.'s and the German propagandists.

My letter has extended to an unconscionable length. I seem not to be able to accomplish a desirable brevity.

With my deepest devotion, dear Mr. President,

Yours most sincerely,   Antoinette Funk.

TLS (WP, DLC).

To Joseph Patrick Tumulty

Dear Tumulty: The White House [c. June 18, 1918].

I wish you would be kind enough to explain to these ladies that the substance of these resolutions[1] was conveyed to me some time ago by the Woman's Committee of the Council of National Defense[2] and was discussed on my initiative at the Cabinet. The members of the Cabinet and I both fully appreciate the importance of the suggestions, and you can assure the ladies that we shall do everything possible in the circumstances to act upon them. This would seem to render an interview supererogatory!

The President.

TL (WP, DLC).
[1] Association of Collegiate Alumnae, n.d., T MS (WP, DLC). This document embodied a series of resolutions adopted by the council of the association on April 12 and 13, 1918. These resolutions requested the President and Congress to make use of trained and qualified professional women in positions of real executive authority in all governmental agencies involved in the war effort whose activities directly affected women. The resolutions also urged that women physicians and nurses be employed in the armed forces, not only in the United States, but also at the front. Tumulty had also enclosed Gertrude S. Martin to JPT, June 12, 1918, ALS (WP, DLC). Mrs. Martin listed a large number of other women's organizations which had endorsed the resolutions and noted that, if the requested interview with Wilson was granted, the resolutions would be presented to him by Martha Carey Thomas, chairperson of the War Service Committee of the Association of Collegiate Alumnae, which had drafted the resolutions.
[2] See the Enclosure printed with Anna H. Shaw to WW, May 29, 1918.

To George Creel

My dear Creel: The White House 18 June, 1918

I have your letter of yesterday suggesting that I see the negro editors who are to assemble here for conference.

My own judgment is that it probably would do no good for me to receive them. I have received several delegations of negroes and I am under the impression that they have gone away dissatisfied. I have never had an opportunity actually to do what I promised them I would seek an opportunity to do. I think probably it would be best just to carry out the programme without me for the present, until I am able to act in a way that would satisfy them.

Cordially and faithfully yours,   Woodrow Wilson

TLS (G. Creel Papers, DLC).

To Robert Russa Moton

My dear Major Moton: [The White House] 18 June, 1918

Thank you for your letter of June fifteenth. I have been seeking an opportunity to do what you suggest and if I do not find it soon, I will do it without an opportunity.

In haste Sincerely yours,   Woodrow Wilson

TLS (Letterpress Books, WP, DLC).

To Helen Hamilton Gardener

My dear Mrs. Gardener: [The White House] 18 June, 1918

Your letter of yesterday has given me a great deal of pleasure. I want to thank you for it most sincerely. I hope that the anticipations you have of a favorable result will be abundantly realized, though I don't think it safe by any means to take it for granted that they will be. Cordially and sincerely yours, Woodrow Wilson

TLS (Letterpress Books, WP, DLC).

From Joseph Patrick Tumulty

Dear Governor: The White House 18 June 1918.

In the matter of the Fall elections which we discussed over the telephone on Saturday, I beg to lay before you the following:

The impression has been industriously circulated by our Republican friends that in Iowa, Minnesota and Michigan, the President had endorsed the non-partisan idea by openly advocating the re-election of Senators Nelson and Kenyon, and the election of Henry Ford.[1] You will recall that at the time I told you that Senator Nelson's friends were using your name in connection with his re-nomination but you thought it wise not to repudiate the idea at that time.

The visit of Henry Ford to the White House and your urging him to accept the Democratic nomination has given momentum to this movement with the result that it is liable to spread so as to be a cause of great embarrassment to us as the days of the campaign approach. There is a certain value in having the movement spread and the idea gain root in the minds of the people that you wish the campaign to be carried on without regard to partisanship. The dangers of repudiating this movement are so obvious that we must consider some counter move in order to clear the mists away and make the issue plain to the people. I think the attitude of the leaders of the Republican party as reflected in speeches of Mr. Hays, the National Chairman, and Senator Penrose on Saturday last give you the opportunity *to strike and define the issue at the psychological moment.* I think our policy at the present time should be one of silence and even indifference to what the leaders on the other side are saying and doing. This will embolden them to make rash statements and charges, and by the time you are ready to strike, the whole country will realize how necessary it is for you to ask for the re-election of a Democratic Congress.

In the speech on Friday night, last, in Philadelphia by Mr. Hays, was contained the following:

"We will bring the Government back to the limitations and principles of the Constitution in time of peace and establish policies which will again bind up the wounds of war, renew our prosperity, administer the affairs of government, with the greatest economy, enlarge our strength at home and abroad, prevent the further spread of the socialistic tendency of the times toward Federal ownership of all the creation and distribution of wealth as a panacea for all the real and fancied ills of society and put the nation's feet once more firmly on the path of progress, etc."

Senator Penrose went further than Mr. Hays and after charging the Democratic party with inefficiency, said,

"I want to say to the Republican party: Keep it vigorous and virile all through the United States, successful whenever it can be successful and if under guidance of the chairman of the National Committee, we can secure a Republican majority in the House of Representatives at Washington, I believe that we have reached a point in the development of the situation when it will be best to replace the Democratic party for military improvement and economical efficiency. We are all pulling together in order to stop the war as soon as we possibly can stop it, and then, Mr. Chairman, over and above all the people, by an overwhelming vote, we will vote the Republican party in control of the American people; as the country has never prospered economically unless it has been under Republican control. Let us keep up an efficient Republican organization in Pennsylvania and all through the United States, and make a successful Republican contest at every opportunity in every congressional district and at the next presidential election, and endeavor to assure the election of Republican candidates."

He further says that the protective tariff will be of more importance than ever before in the history of our country. "We will have to make proper economic preparations for these conditions of low-priced products which will threaten to invade our market, and the Republican party should keep up its organization and keep up the courage and the spirit of its personnel and be ready to make a contest at the earliest opportunity to secure control of the Government," he says.

I think these speeches will give you an opportunity some time in September flatly to state just what your attitude is toward the coming campaign, and to show the real purpose that lies behind the Republican campaign, and thus set forth before the whole country what the Republicans hope to gain by bringing about the election of a Republican Congress.

I would suggest that some man of distinction in the country write you a letter calling your attention to these speeches, paying particular attention to the parts I have mentioned and asking your opinion with reference to the plan of the Republican party to get back into power. In other words, we ought to accept these speeches charging incompetency and inefficiency as a challenge, and call the attention of the country to the fact that the leadership of the Republican party is still reactionary and stand-pat; that their spokesmen including Penrose and others openly state what the objects of the Party are; that they sneer at everything progressive and characterize the fine things as socialistic tendencies. I think a letter along the lines of the Indiana platform which I suggested a few weeks ago (copy of which I attach herewith)[2] would carry to the country just the impression we ought to make. This letter should be issued, in my opinion, some time in September and should be followed in October by your participation in various parts of the country in the Liberty Loan campaign when speeches of a non-partisan character could be made.   Sincerely yours,   J. P. Tumulty

TLS (WP, DLC).
    [1] About Wilson's alleged endorsement of Senator Knute Nelson for reelection, see WW to V. C. McCormick, March 18, 1918, Vol. 47. There is no record of Wilson's having recommended the reelection of Senator William S. Kenyon.
    Josephus Daniels had initiated the effort to persuade Henry Ford to run for the Senate in Michigan. The strategy was to enter Ford in both the Democratic and Republican primaries, then permissible under Michigan law, in the hope that he would win both nominations and thus run unopposed in the general election in November. However, during a lengthy interview in Washington, Daniels could not persuade Ford to run. Daniels brought Ford to the White House at 5:15 p.m. on June 13. Wilson said that it was Ford's patriotic duty to make the Senate race. Ford agreed to do so and that same evening issued a public statement saying that, "at President Wilson's request," he had decided to accept the nomination for senator if it was offered to him. *New York Times*, June 14, 1918; Ray Stannard Baker, *Woodrow Wilson: Life and Letters* (8 vols., Garden City, N. Y., 1927-39), VIII, 209; Josephus Daniels, *The Wilson Era: Years of War and After, 1917-1923* (Chapel Hill, N. C., 1946), pp. 293-98.
    [2] The enclosure is missing, but see the platform for the Indiana Democratic party printed at June 15, 1918.

From Samuel Gompers

St Paul, Minn.,   June 18, 1918.

The convention of the American Federation of Labor unanimously instructed me to convey to you the protest of the delegates constituting the convention against the action of Newcomb Carlton of the Western Union Telegraph Company in issuing a call for a convention of employees of the Western Union for the purpose of

perfecting an industrial constitution in order to control all employees, the expenses of the convention to be paid by the company.
The action of the Company is intended as a continuance of its policy
of denying its employees their right to belong to a bona fide legitimate trade union and refusal to reinstate employees discharged
because of membership in a trade union affiliated to the American
Federation of Labor. The policy of the Western Union Telegraph
Company is out of harmony with the labor policy of the Administration and the War Labor Board and renders it very difficult, if not
impossible, to prevent interruption of work essential to the successful conduct of the war.   Samuel Gompers.

T telegram (WP, DLC).

From Henry Morgenthau

My dear Mr. President: New York June 18, 1918.

Many thanks for the frank opinion contained in your letter of
June 14th.

I at once informed the publishers that I have decided not to have
the narrative put into a motion picture.

With kindest regards,

Very sincerely yours,   H Morgenthau

TLS (WP, DLC).

From John Humphrey Small

Dear Mr. President: Washington, D. C. June 18, 1918.

May I trespass upon your time sufficiently to express briefly my
opinion upon the proposed additional legislation affecting intoxicating liquors and the attitude of the Anti-Saloon League. We have
forbidden the use of grain and other food material in the distillation
of liquor during the period of the war and you have been vested
with discretion regarding beer and wine. You have reduced the
alcoholic contents of beer. The tax on all kinds of intoxicating
liquors has been increased. All this was done in the name of food
conservation and in the interest of the war, and while every good
citizen is willing to concede that Congress did not exceed its war
powers in such legislation, we have in my opinion reached the limit
and should proceed no further.

I may submit several reasons. As the quantity of distilled spirits
on hand decreases and the price increases the tendency on the part

of those who will gratify their appetite will be to resort to light beer and wines. This in itself will be a decided improvement. I am almost inclined to the opinion that restricting the use to beer and wine will in itself work better results in the cause of temperance and sobriety than would absolute prohibition.

Again, regardless of what long-haired theorists may contend, there is quite a large proportion of laborers in the congested industrial districts who have formed a life-long habit of drinking beer and any sudden deprivation of this beverage would certainly contend to create intense dissatisfaction and resentment and add to the present labor difficulties.

May I say further that every intelligent citizen recognizes that the Federal Government has no power to regulate or prohibit the manufacture, sale and use of intoxicating beverages and that it belongs to the States. We have gone far enough in this direction as a war exigency.

Any normal man dislikes to impugn the motives of another but I am persuaded that the active leaders of this propaganda, the head and front of which is the Anti-Saloon League, care nothing for the fundamentals of the Government and in large degree are using the war as a mere pretext to enable them to accomplish what they could not lawfully do in a time of peace. Apparently they have to a large extent hypnotized Congress. I happen to know that quite a number of intelligent Members of the House have, against their better judgment, followed the Anti-Saloon League in some of their votes. I think I stand for good morals and will say without egotism that I am willing to compare my own activities for things worth while in my own community and State with some of these uncompromising zealots, but I have not followed them in every movement but have voted my own convictions. I always voted for local option in my home town, and for State-wide prohibition, but I have on each occasion in the House voted against the proposed Constitutional Amendment for so-called nation-wide prohibition.

Some one whose voice will command attention should speak words of sanity and soberness and I know of no one whose voice would carry further and command greater respect and attention than that of our President.

Do not take the time to answer this. I have simply gotten tired of witnessing Pharisees stand on street corners and proclaim themselves as the elect who were ordained to reform a sinful world.

Very respectfully,   Jno. H. Small

TLS (WP, DLC).

From Lydia Wickliffe Holmes[1]

Baton Rouge, La., June 18, 1918.

We believe that your telegram to Senator Haas giving the Louisianians your ideals of democracy have put suffrage over in this State. It is the first Southern State to refer the question of full suffrage to its people and we believe that we will adopt the amendment November sixth. This could not have been done we believe except through Senator Ransdell whom the women of Louisiana will never forget and our State Senator Leon S. Haas. We thank you.

                                        Lydia Wickliffe Holmes.

T telegram (WP, DLC).
  [1] State "chairman" of the Woman Suffrage party of Louisiana.

From Leon Samuel Haas

My dear Mr. President: Baton Rouge, La., June 18, 1918.

The Senate this afternoon finally passed the Woman Suffrage Constitutional amendment. Will now be submitted to people of this State for ratification in November. I express to you my deep appreciation of your telegram of June fourth which materially aided the movement in this State.   Leon S. Haas.

T telegram (WP, DLC).

George Tom Molesworth Bridges to Lord Reading

Dear Lord Reading,   Washington, D. C. 18th June 1918.

I got your note and will observe due caution and certainly will not commit myself to anything. So far I have confined myself to working behind the scenes.

General Berthelot[1] and M. Delaney had their interviews with the President[2] M. Jusserand acting as interpreter. I dined with the Jusserands last night and I heard a good deal of what occurred and M. Jusserand told me the rest this morning. The only features of the conversations worth repeating to you are

(I) When General Berthelot put forward his proposition for intervention in Siberia[3] the President was interested and made the remark that we had now nominated a military chief and that he, the President, would not set the bad example of not following his advice or even abiding by his decisions. This confirms the view that I have frequently expressed to the War Office, and what I believe, you yourself have repeated to the Prime Minister, that any expression of opinion on this subject from General Foch will have effect.

(II) When M. Delaney proposed to the President that he should declare whether he would accept the principle of intervention or not, and that if he accepted it the Ambassadors might at once meet in Conference and submit a proposal of joint action to him, the President demurred. He said that although he trusted the Japanese he received such conflicting statements as to the possible effect of intervention on the Russian people that he could not as yet make up his mind but that he was going to see other people on this question.

M. Jusserand told me that other people were Professor Mazeryk and also some American (*Robins probably*)[4] arriving from Russia.

General Berthelot has left for France.

I had also yesterday a long interview with General March on this subject. He is still very sticky about using the Japanese. One of his arguments is that of command. He affirms that no American troops would ever serve under Japanese command. I think he exaggerates this difficulty. He is at the present moment an ultra "Western Fronter" but merely, I fancy, because his nose happens to be pointing that way. He did however, discuss details of such an expedition as General Berthelot proposed with me which is a step forward.

I also laid before him certain proposals of the War Office as to details of the Murmansk expedition. He informed me that the subject had been referred to Versailles for revision and that as soon as the answer was received and the President had given a definite decision he would call me in for a Conference. I am given to understand that the number of troops asked for by Lord Milner is considered in excess of requirements. Mr Charles Crane came to see me this morning. He told me that the President had now definitely taken up the question of carrying the war into the East via Siberia, and that his mind was now occupied with it to the exclusion of other things and that we could expect progress and definite decision before very long also that the President was now seeing people who he thought could give him good information on the subject. Mr Crane is going to Archangel as perhaps I told you and asked me to try and fix up his journey for him.

Mazeryk has arrived and I saw him this afternoon because I was very anxious that he should not confuse the issue with his Czech views, especially as I believe he will carry great weight with the President having been recommended to him by Mr Crane as the best information he is likely to get on the Russian problem.

On the whole his views appear to me to be quite sane. There is this difference between him and the French. He wants to use the whole Japanese Army for war against Russia with Allied contingents to co-operate. He will have nothing to do with the policy of the nucleus army which is to gather Russians like a snowball. In conversation however he was prepared to accept my view that we should get to work and occupy Siberia up to the Urals as a first phase on the Napoleonic doctrine of "J'engage et puis je vois." He expects to have several conversations with the President and volunteered to keep me informed of his progress.

Colonel Edwards[5] was sent for by Mr. Baker—they have mutual Cleveland friends—and had a long conversation on conditions in Russia and Mr Baker appeared much interested and said he was going to send for him again. He has also been unofficially asked by the State Department for a general statement of the conditions in the country. He has given them this and sent a copy to the Embassy. It does not contain any controversial matter.

I am keeping the War Office fully informed of any progress. I may be an optimist but I cannot help feeling that we are getting nearer business and I shall be glad when you get back. I may meet you in New York as I have to be there on Saturday. Shall go up tomorrow Thursday night & be at the Plaza Friday.

I should add that Mazeryk is emphatically of my view as to the improbability of forcing any decision on the Western Front that will affect the situation in the East and he hopes to make this clear to the President.

I fear this missed the messenger as we were kept much later at Camp Meade than we intended, but I send it by special.

Yours sincerely   Tom Bridges

I only heard after you left that your boy[6] had got the Military Cross. It is splendid news and means a lot these days. My best congratulations to yourself & Lady Reading.[7]   T.B.

TLS (Reading Papers, FO 800/223, PRO).
[1] Gen. Henri Mathias Berthelot, most recently chief of the French military mission in Rumania.
[2] On June 17 at 2 p.m.
[3] "The ideas of General Berthelot relative to an action in Siberia can be thus summarized:

"Action of a defensive character but pushed to the Vologda (Nijni)-Samara line. It is a question of secure protection of the food supplies of Siberia (the only center of provisioning from now until the autumn of 1919; in the Ukraine the harvest will be nothing in the next autumn on account of the failure of the planting) and of the minerals of the Urals. Employ a modest number of effectives who would constitute the center to rally to and would represent one will: in Russia now anyone who commands is obeyed. The expeditionary corps could include 30,000 Americans, double that number of Japanese, and, in order to emphasize its inter-Allied character, a French and an English detachment.

"But what should this limited number of effectives do in case the Germans push as far as to the line thus indicated? The General did not believe that they would risk this, just as he does not believe in the reconstitution of the eastern front in the course of the present war. But putting the food supplies and minerals beyond reach [of the Germans] is in his eyes of first importance. Jusserand." J. J. Jusserand to the Foreign Ministry,

No. 762, n.d., received June 19, 1918, T telegram (Campagne contre l'Allemagne, 1914-1918, 16 N 3211/2-98, FMD-Ar). (Our translation.)

⁴ Reading's insertion.

⁵ Lt. Col. George Maitland Edwards of the Royal Engineers, formerly a member of the British military mission in Russia, at this time on special mission to the United States.

⁶ Gerald Rufus Isaacs, Viscount Erleigh.

⁷ Alice Edith Cohen Isaacs, Lady Reading.

A Translation of a Telegram from Jean Jules Jusserand to the Foreign Ministry

Washington, no date
received June 18, 1918.

No. 755. I have just presented M. Delaney to the President and he asks me to transmit the following telegram:

"In accordance with the instructions of the President of the Council, I requested an audience with President Wilson who accorded me one today. After conveying to him, as former Prefect of the Seine, the sentiments which the Parisian population profess regarding the United States and the person of the President, I pointed out to him the desire manifested by public opinion that nothing be left undone which could contribute to winning the war.

"It is this sentiment which the government, after having called me to the post at Tokyo, asked me to impress upon the highest American authorities when I came into contact with them.

"I indicated that, following the expressions of M. Clemenceau, intervention in Siberia was considered as a response to a military necessity, as being of an urgent character on which the Allies were in accord, and the success of which required only an adhesion in principle by the President.

"Mr. Wilson replied to me that this adhesion in principle was not clear-cut in character on account of the contradictory advice which came to him from different sides. But that if, to respond to the desires of M. Clemenceau, he was not yet convinced, he was trying to be. He declared that, contrary to what had been declared, he had confidence in Japan and that his hesitation revealed, not a sentiment of reserve vis-à-vis this country, but sympathetic preoccupations regarding the Russian people.

"He concluded by saying that he would see Masaryk next week and divers nonofficial persons coming from Russia, and that the information and impressions which they would convey to him would help him to form an opinion."

M. Jusserand asked the President if Mr. Robins would be among that number. No, said the President, and he expressed himself with severity on the poor judgment ["le peu de bon sens"] of this American.   Jusserand.

T telegram (Série E, Japon, Intervention en Sibérie, E 6212/18-20, FMD-Ar).

From the Diary of Josephus Daniels

1918 Tuesday 18 June

In Naval Allied Council the Italian Ad[miral] was not willing to act in concert. Sims wanted pressure. WW said tell L to talk to Italian Ambassador and tell him how embarrassing it was.

Clemenceau said might have to move valuable papers from Paris. WW not pleased.

WW said Empy's[1] play "Pack Up Your Troubles["][2] & talk would have America go into war with as much brutality as Germany.

Burleson: "If you induced Ford to enter race for Senate in Mich. it was a slick trick."

Roosevelt to go to England. WW said "He ought not to decline to run for Gov. of N. Y. if it is tendered to him.["] I talked to FDR who was pleased at the Presidents view.

[1] Arthur Guy Empey, author and soldier of fortune who had served in both the British and American armies in France, best known at this time for his book describing life in the British army, *Over the Top* (New York and London, 1917). He was making his first appearance as an actor in *Pack Up Your Troubles*.

[2] A "war comedy" written by George Cochrane Hazelton, which opened at the National Theatre on June 17. The *Washington Post*, June 18, 1918, described the play as follows: " 'Pack Up Your Troubles' takes up in an easy, sketchy way the life of the American soldier boy from the moment of his arrival in a cantonment to his baptism of blood in the trenches. The comedy note, however, is kept supreme. Hazing, rough camp jokes, good singing of familiar songs and a reasonable amount of disconnected, sporadic love making is utilized to fill in the conventional period allotted for an evening's entertainment. The story is a very frank bid for the laughs of the light-hearted and the cheers of auditors who, naturally, are easily moved to enthusiasm these days by judicious references to the Huns and what our husky young fighters propose to inflict upon them. A dash of extra zeal was provided last evening by the presence of President Wilson and various members of the Washington government."

To Joseph Patrick Tumulty

Dear Tumulty: The White House [c. June 19, 1918].

I would be very much obliged if you would get into communication with Griffith in some way and tell him that we shall be very glad to make any suggestions that we can make to his representatives in this part of the country with regard to this film.[1]

The President.

TL (WP, DLC).
[1] Wilson saw Griffith's representatives, Albert L. Grey and a Mr. Kane of New York,

at the White House on June 21. In response to Wilson's "few hints" (WW to JPT, June 20, 1918, TL [WP, DLC]), Grey made "quite a few changes." A. L. Grey to WW, June 26, 1918, TLS (WP, DLC). In this letter, Grey also wrote: "I am leaving tomorrow, however, for the Coast to convey personally to Mr. Griffith your suggestions and see just what can be done along the lines suggested by you."

Three Letters to Newton Diehl Baker

My dear Mr. Secretary: [Washington] 19 June, 1918

The enclosed paper is not signed.[1] It was handed to me by a friend the other day[2] with the information that it was a sort of composite of the views of a group of men, some of them thoroughly informed, or supposing themselves to be thoroughly informed, about the actual state of affairs in the various parts of Siberia. Do you think that General March would have time to look the paper through and express for me briefly a judgment as to the military value of the plan of campaign suggested?

Cordially and faithfully yours,   Woodrow Wilson

[1] See n. 1 to the Enclosure printed with P. C. March to NDB, June 24, 1918.
[2] Probably Charles R. Crane.

My dear Mr. Secretary: [The White House] 19 June, 1918

Thank you for your letter of the seventeenth about the relation of the Council of National Defense to the study of reconstruction problems.

I think it will be entirely appropriate and desirable that the Council should coordinate the studies that have been made and suggest procedures. After that preliminary work has been done, it will be possible for us in counsel with one another to form a clearer and more trustworthy judgment as to how the plans shall be executed and under what guidance and supervision.

Cordially and sincerely yours,   Woodrow Wilson

My dear Mr. Chairman: [The White House] 19 June, 1918

Replying to your letter of June fifteenth, I entirely concur in the judgment of the Council of National Defense that not only is the usefulness of the Woman's Committee of the Council not at an end, but that it is indispensable that the Committee continue to exercise the functions originally assigned to it. I believe that it would be possible, and it is certainly desirable, for the Council to bring about such a conference between the women's organizations of the Treasury Department, the Food Administration, and such other departments as have organized auxiliary committees of women as would coordinate what I entirely agree with you in thinking it is not desirable to have separated, and if I can assist in any way in effecting such a coordination, you may count upon my assistance.

I think we should not only continue the Woman's Committee but that we should in every way seek to assist the Committee in performing its functions, in enriching them, and in adding to them along appropriate lines.

Cordially and sincerely yours,   Woodrow Wilson

TLS (Letterpress Books, WP, DLC).

To Robert Lansing, with Enclosures

My dear Mr. Secretary,   The White House. 19 June, 1918.

This despatch has interested me very much. These associations may be of very great service as instruments for what we are now planning to do in Siberia.

By the way, I saw Professor Masaryk today[1] and he seemed to think well of the plan.   Faithfully Yours,   W.W.

WWTLI (SDR, RG 59, 861.00/2148½, DNA).
[1] Wilson saw Masaryk at 5 p.m. The only contemporary record of the conversation was a brief note made by Masaryk. Victor S. Mamatey, *The United States and East Central Europe, 1914-1918: A Study in Wilsonian Diplomacy and Propaganda* (Princeton, N. J., 1957), pp. 285-86, summarizes this document as follows: "According to his contemporary note, he [Masaryk] began the conversation, which was to last exactly forty-five minutes, by thanking the President for the 'honor and opportunity' of recommending to his attention the Czech and Slovak peoples. Wilson replied that he had a 'sincere interest' in them and was glad for the opportunity to talk with him about a 'serious problem': about Russia, and how to 'help' her. He explained at length the Allied plans to use the Japanese for intervention and inquired what effect that move would have on Russia and whether Czechoslovak soldiers could be used. Masaryk then launched into an unenthusiastic discussion of intervention, considering it only from a technical point of view. Allied plans, he said, were not clear. He had heard only of a 'nucleus' of a small intervention force of between 50,000 to 100,000 men. He had really never received any other information. As for Japanese intervention, he would be for it, but there, too, were difficulties, mainly, 'how to pay the Japanese.' The President interjected that the Allies would 'finance' the Japanese expedition, but Masaryk thought that this would not be enough, and that the Japanese would want territory. He also wondered whether they were militarily prepared. The President said that, according to his information, they had 250,000 men and the same number of reserves, but he doubted whether they could scrape together a million men—the figure Masaryk thought necessary if intervention was to succeed. The President wound up the conversation by saying that he felt bound by the Allies and would abide by the decision of Marshal Foch in the matter."

Thomas Garrigue Masaryk, *The Making of a State: Memories and Observations, 1914-1918* (London, 1927), pp. 273-79, conflates several conversations between Wilson and Masaryk during the late spring and summer of 1918 and thus is not a reliable source for the Wilson-Masaryk conversation on June 19.

Speaking at Mount Vernon, July 4, 1918. Mrs. Wilson at Wilson's left.

David Rowland Francis

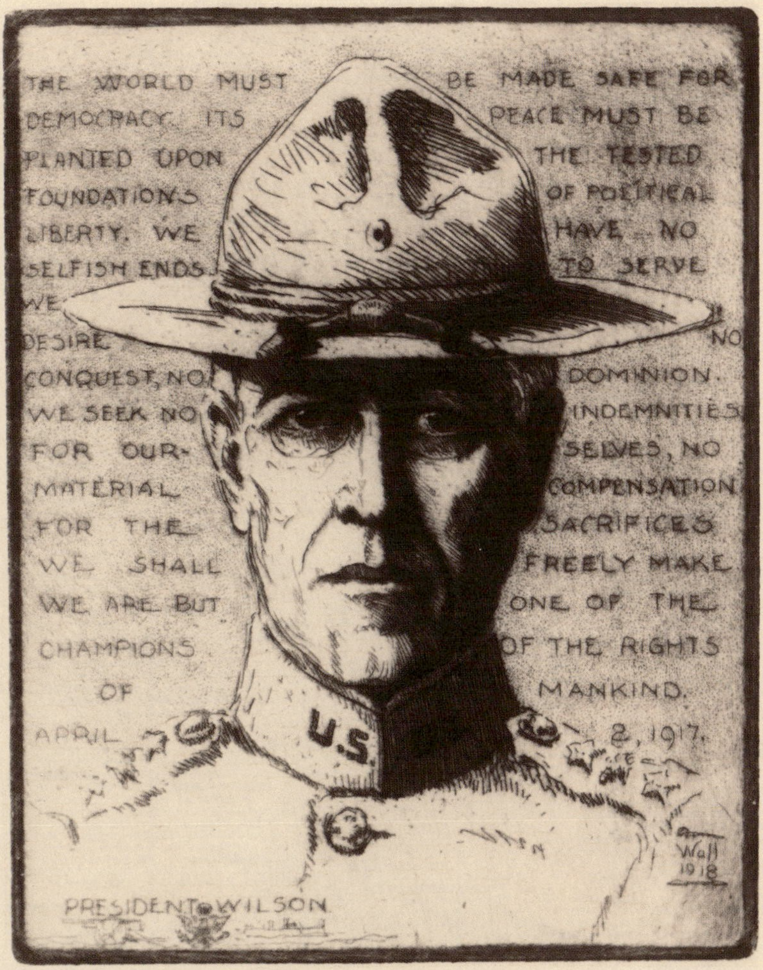

Etching by Bernhardt Wall

DeWitt Clinton Poole, Jr.

John Kenneth Caldwell

Austin Melvin Knight

Thomas Garrigue Masaryk

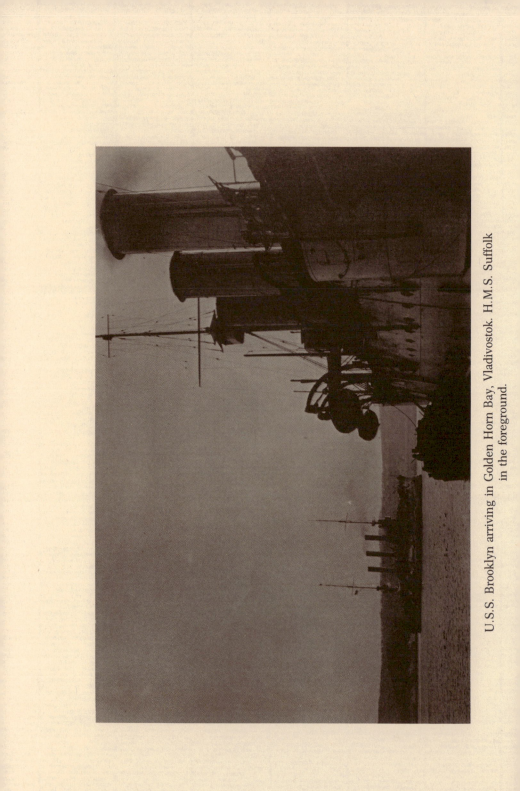

U.S.S. Brooklyn arriving in Golden Horn Bay, Vladivostok. H.M.S. Suffolk
in the foreground.

E N C L O S U R E   I

From Robert Lansing

Dear Mr. President: [Washington] June 19, 1918.

It has occurred to me that you will wish to take especial note of this very interesting telegram from our Consul at Moscow, dated June 12th, and accordingly I desire to bring it to your attention. It is the reply to an effort which I recently made to find out the attitude of the Russian Cooperative Societies on the present situation.

Faithfully yours,   Robert Lansing

CCL (SDR, RG 59, 861.00/2053, DNA).

E N C L O S U R E   I I

Moscow June 12, 1918

628. Confidential. Alexander Birkenheim, member of the Board of the All Russian Union of Cooperative Societies, which includes Moscow National and Siberian Union at Novo Nikolaievsk and is in close relation with Siberian Union of butter makers, has authorized consulate general to transmit to the Department statement given below as an exact and confidential expression of his personal views on points stated in Departments unnumbered June 5, 12 midnight.[1] B. is considered the most solid leader among the cooperatives of Siberia and Russia on the purely business side. Commended for his participation in the Moscow Conference,[2] he has carefully refrained from all political activity and he desired it to be understood that he gives the statement below as a business man and humanitarian worker, not as a politician. Every one whom Consulate General has consulted agrees that B is the most dependable spokesman for the rank and file of the Cooperatives, especially those of Siberia.

The statement is as follows "The Cooperative Societies are non political organizations. Our rule that the leaders should not be politicians has been broken only when the Cooperatives, under my leadership, took part in the Moscow conference of last August, we thought it was our duty to help save the country at a crisis. Our efforts were in vain. The country has perished.

Now an economic calamity surpassing the imagination impends, and it is the duty of the cooperative societies to endeavor to save the people from starvation. For this, outside help is necessary.

The weariness of the great masses of the people in European Russia has become such, as a result of disorganization and Bolshevik terror that they desire only the reestablishment of normal economical order; and although as a rule antagonistic to Germany, was now prepared to accept the reestablishment of order through the interference of either the Allies or even the Central Powers. As for the cooperatives, we have worked under the Bolshevik regime and now, if necessary, we can work under German (?), as our main duty is to relieve the masses of their suffering.

However, the political sympathies of the cooperative are with the Allies. In Siberia, where the cooperative societies represent the people here in the fullest measure, there is a special feeling of friendliness fixed and upholding in America. On the other hand there is distrust of Japan.

We have no means ourselves of stopping the German advance or of preventing the spread of all German influence.

Direct military aid from the Allies is the only means of making resistance against Germany.

We are practical men and understand that for intervention there must be compensation of some sort. Many of us fear that if Japan is allowed to enter Siberia by herself without the control of other nations she may demand compensation such as none of us is prepared to grant.

It is my personal view that the Allies should take the leaders of the cooperatives, as well as other pro-Ally leaders, into their confidence stating definitely their objects and intentions, what compensation is expected, especially by Japan, the manner of intervention and the approximate date at which it will come. Speed is especially important as the suffering of the people has reached such a pitch that it cannot be endured much longer.

I believe that in view of the confidence of the Siberian people in America, American assurances respecting the preservation of what we consider our vital interests would be acceptable, and that intervention begun after such assurances have been given would be welcome by the Siberian cooperatives, and the Allies could count upon our support and the support of the Siberian people in carrying out a combined resistance to German aggression."

Poole.

T telegram (SDR, RG 59, 861.00/2053, DNA).
  [1] F. L. Polk to D. C. Poole, Jr., June 5, 1918, T telegram (SDR, RG 59, 861.00/1967a, DNA). Polk asked Poole to ascertain the views of the Union of Siberian Cooperative Societies and of the Moscow Cooperative Societies "in regard to maintaining resistance against Germany and how they believe it should be accomplished."
  [2] About this conference, see WW to the President of the National Council Assembly, Aug. 24, 1917, n. 1, Vol. 44.

To Antoinette Funk

My dear Mrs. Funk: [The White House] 19 June, 1918

I have read with close attention and a great deal of interest your letter of June seventeenth about the state of affairs and of opinion among the farmers in the West, and it has given me a great deal of food for thought.

I have myself had the hope that I might come into personal contact with bodies of Western farmers. I should like nothing better. It remains to be seen whether I can work it out, since I am already doing about all that it is possible for me to do intelligently.

In haste
Cordially and sincerely yours,   Woodrow Wilson

TLS (Letterpress Books, WP, DLC).

From Edward William Bok

Confidential

Merion Station Pennsylvania
June nineteenth nineteen hundred
My dear Mr. President: and eighteen

I want very much to do what I know you don't like to have done. But in this instance there is, it seems to me, a distinct call, a need, and a reason. Besides, I agree with Mr. David Lawrence when he recently wrote this about you:

"True enough, the public impression of Mr. Wilson is quite different from the actual personality of the man. The President himself has remarked that of all the sketches and articles that have been written about him since he entered public life he has been able to recognize himself in only a few of them. He is portrayed either as a cold, methodical mental machine, devoid of sentiment and emotion, or described as a dilettante and dreamer, full of abstract visions, discouragingly impractical in concrete performance.

"For these conflicting versions Mr. Wilson himself is partly to blame. He shuns personal publicity; it is genuinely odious to him. Since he has been President he has seen fewer correspondents and writers by far than any of his predecessors."

As you know so much better than I do, the casualty lists are growing, and everywhere throughout our country the fateful "We regret to inform you" notices are causing sadness. But worse than that, they are creating doubts. The cry is going up that "christianity has failed," else this war and its fearful results would not be. The letters to us are already beginning to come in from apparently earnest women and strong men: believers in christianity, but all, nevertheless, asking "Why?"

You will agree with me that the morale of the nation must be kept up: its faith must not totter. All that we do for our soldiers will be as naught if we lose our faith. But even where faith is not lost or wavering, courage is necessary, whether in afflicted homes or in circles close to them and affected by the army losses.

It is into this situation that I want to project what I believe would be the most needful and successful article that I could print: an article to be called "A Sunday With the President," the opening part of which would be, briefly, to show how a typical Sunday is spent by you and your family—not differently from the average home-circle, I know, but it is always interesting to the people to know that their President does what they do. Then, let the article gradually melt into the vital and important part: a talk with you along spiritual lines, a talk that would give heart to the depressed: courage to the faltering, and light to those in the darkness of sadness.

I know you will immediately say that you are not a spiritual leader, but, my dear Mr. President, you *are* the leader, today, of the American people in every aspect of their lives. Your voice is *the* voice to which they listen, and your voice used at this juncture along spiritual lines would have a heartening effect that you perhaps little dream of. It is a wonderful opportunity really that your position gives you, and I have the power in my hands to spread that opportunity for you into over five million lives, allowing me three readers to each copy of my magazine.[1] These people are worldwide. Tens of thousands of copies of our magazine are now going abroad: to subscribers in our allied countries, to our women in service and, curiously enough, by the thousands to our boys "over there."

Thousands of our American people are going to face the next winter with fear-thoughts based on last year's experiences. I want very much to put faith-thoughts in their place, and I can do it through no other way so effectively as through you.

A half-hour's talk on some early Sunday would be all that this real service would cost you in time. My idea would be to send either David Lawrence to you with a series of questions, or Bruce Barton,[2] himself the son of a Presbyterian clergyman, or I will act as "interviewer" myself, as you prefer.

But may I ask that you will not turn aside from this request without stopping for a few moments in your busy life to try, in thought, to visualize what this article may mean to thousands: what the opportunity means to you, and what a privilege you can confer on me to publish such an article?

I won't take up any more of your time, except to say that I daily grow in my loyalty to you and my faith in your purposes.

Believe me, Mr. President,

Yours sincerely,   Edward Bok

TLS (WP, DLC).
  [1] That is, *Ladies' Home Journal.*
  [2] Journalist of New York, most recently editor of *Every Week.*

From Elizabeth Merrill Bass

My dear Mr. President: Washington, D. C. June 19, 1918.

The Senate Committee on Woman Suffrage met this afternoon and voted to have Senator Hollis, who is the Acting Chairman, rise in the Senate tomorrow and ask for a vote on Suffrage on next Thursday. He did this at the request of the National Woman Suffrage Association of which Mrs. Catt is the President. They have been pressing for a vote for some time, and since the receipt by them of your answer to the communication from the Women of the Allied Countries, they have wished to have an almost immediate vote so that the effect of your widely published letter might be taken advantage of. The Senate Woman Suffrage Committee, having a Democratic majority, would not consent to a vote unless I, too, were willing. I have joined in the request principally for the reason that Mrs. Catt gives, but also because the militant suffragists are taking up a great deal of my time and stirring women all over the country to write and wire me that they are holding the Democratic party and you responsible for the delayed suffrage vote. I am also influenced by the fact that even the friendly Association of which Mrs. Catt is President, constantly urges me to secure the two or three necessary Democratic votes, and they, too, gently intimate that if we do not take the vote soon, the Republicans are going into the congressional campaigns and use the Democratic delay as an issue.

If I have to go into the congressional campaigns in the western states, with the Republican candidates using our delay as an issue, I believe that we might as well have the vote and let it be seen just [as] the group that defeats the Amendment, if it loses, both Democrats and Republicans. Then we shall, in every possible public way (press and platform) clear the Administration of blame and put it entirely upon the individuals of both parties. I am confident, however, that the Amendment will pass, though we are two short the pledged number still.

I am sending you this explanation because it is quite possible that some of the Democratic members of the Woman Suffrage Committee are feeling that it is unwise to have the vote called until we absolutely have the pledged number. Senatorial courtesy goes rather far sometimes, and even those senators who are perfectly willing to vote for the Amendment have a friendly sympathy toward those who oppose it but who do not wish to have it figure at all in their states against them. Candidates who are coming up for re-election dislike to record themselves against it, preferring to leave it still in the air until their nominations are assured.

Faithfully yours,   Elizabeth Bass

TLS (WP, DLC).

Robert Lansing to Joseph Patrick Tumulty, with Enclosure

My dear Mr. Tumulty: Washington June 19, 1918.

I beg to enclose herewith, for the attention of the President, a copy of a note from the Ambassador of Russia dated June 10, 1918, in which he transmits a copy of an extract of the resolution recently adopted by the Central Committee of the Constitutional Democratic (Cadet) Party concerning Allied intervention in Russia.

I am, my dear Mr. Tumulty,

Very sincerely yours,   Robert Lansing

TLS (WP, DLC).

E N C L O S U R E

EXTRACT OF THE RESOLUTION ADOPTED BY THE CENTRAL
COMMITTEE OF THE CADET PARTY CONCERNING ALLIED
INTERVENTION IN RUSSIA.

"We never recognized the conditions of the Brest-Litovsk peace and consider that the disastrous situation in which they have placed Russia can only be ameliorated with the aid of the Allies.

The movement of the Germans on Russian soil, their perpetual seizure of new regions still continues and there seems to be no limit to such occupation. Under such conditions we cannot restrain from appealing to our Allies to whom we have frequently given proof of the loyalty of our feelings.

We proclaim our conviction that the appearance of a new powerful factor on the scene of struggle undoubtedly will have a decisive bearing on the issues of the war and on the conditions of peace.

We can assure in the most conclusive manner that the information picturing that the Russian democracy does not approve of Allied aid is false. If such information has reached the President of the United States it must originate from Bolshevik sources. The Bolsheviki in no way are representative of the Russian democracy. Their regime, a fictitious rule of democracy, is really oligarchy, demogogy and despotism, which at the present moment relies only on physical force and daily becomes more and more odious to the popular masses.

Nevertheless, we consider it our duty to emphasize that the attitude of the Russian public opinion towards the Allied action is conditioned by the forms of its realization. Its success depends on the whole-hearted support of national feeling in Russia. It is furthermore imperative for the Russian public opinion to receive assurances that the compensations due to Japan and to the other powers who will take part in the expedition be co-ordinated with the inviolability of rights and interests of Russia and that the actions of all the Allies on Russian territory be performed under international control."

T MS (WP, DLC).

To Elizabeth Merrill Bass

My dear Mrs. Bass: [The White House] 20 June, 1918

Allow me to acknowledge the receipt of your letter of June nineteenth and to say that I think you exercised good judgment in joining Mrs. Catt and her associates in asking for an early vote on the suffrage amendment.

Cordially and sincerely yours,   Woodrow Wilson

TLS (Letterpress Books, WP, DLC).

To Lord Reading, with Enclosure

My dear Mr. Ambassador: [The White House] 20 June, 1918

When Prince Arthur of Connaught was here, he was kind enough to hand me a letter from King George.[1] Enclosed you will find a reply to the King's letter which I would be very much obliged if you would be good enough to forward at your convenience to His Majesty. His letter I greatly appreciated. As I was parting with

Prince Arthur, I asked him through what medium I should convey an answer and he suggested that I request this kindness of you.

Sincerely yours,   Woodrow Wilson

TLS (Letterpress Books, WP, DLC).
  [1] George V to WW, May 10, 1918, Vol. 47.

E N C L O S U R E

To George V

Sir,   The White House 16 June, 1918

Your Majesty's letter, which Prince Arthur of Connaught was kind enough to hand me on his brief visit to Washington, gave me a great deal of pleasure. You may be sure that the generous message of friendship which it conveyed met with a very warm response in my own sentiments towards yourself and the great people for whom you speak. It has been delightful and inspiriting to feel the temper of our people here as it has responded to the great task to which, with your own people, we have now set our hands. You have evidently yourself felt it in the American soldiers with whom you have talked. It is not a mere spirit of adventure. It is a high spirit of duty. It is a genuine eagerness to fight,—to *fight*—for the deepest convictions of our lives. And I am sure that I am speaking for my fellow countrymen when I say that it is a great satisfaction to know that we are standing shoulder to shoulder with the people of the indomitable British lands who hold like convictions with our own of right and justice and liberty

I am glad that you have known Colonel House in his true quality and have had the opportunity to learn from him at first hand just what our purpose and our spirit are. May I not express the hope that, as these trying months of comradeship in the tremendous struggle of the war go by, the two nations and the men who guide them may be drawn closer and closer together in sentiment, understanding, and coöperation? The victory is certain, if we but keep the vision true!

It was a real pleasure to meet your cousin, Prince Arthur of Connaught and to know him for the sincere and straightforward gentleman he is.

Please accept my assurances of cordial friendship. I hope that some day we may meet face to face and that I may have the same opportunity that Colonel House has had to make you feel with what reality of unaffected sentiment I subscribe myself

Your sincere friend,   Woodrow Wilson[1]

ALS (George V, Q. 1550/XIV, Royal Archives, Windsor).
  ¹ There is a WWsh draft of this letter in WP, DLC.

From Newton Diehl Baker, with Enclosure

Dear Mr. President: Washington. June 20, 1918.

The enclosed cablegram from General Bliss is in response to my inquiries of him after my consultation with you over the memorandum handed by Lord Reading to the Secretary of State, and by him to me, covering Lord Milner's proposed American assistance at Murmansk.¹

As I understand it, you have from the first insisted that we would not participate in any such enterprise unless it met with General Foch's approval. In that view, I would be very happy to show the enclosed cablegram to Lord Reading. This, of course, has to do only with the first part of Bliss's cablegram; the second part dealing with the command can be more appropriately taken up when the fact of the expedition and its constitution have been definitely determined, and I would not raise that question with Lord Reading at this time. I am making this suggestion only to save you the necessity of taking it up with Lord Reading, if you prefer to have me do so.

Respectfully yours,   Newton D. Baker

TLS (N. D. Baker Papers, DLC).
  ¹ That is, A. J. Balfour to Lord Reading, June 11, 1918.

E N C L O S U R E

Versailles June 18 [1918]

Urgent—Number 135—Confidential

For Secretary of War.

Paragraph 1. In further reference to your 61 June 15, I presented subject matter of your paragraph 1, subparagraph A, to General Foch at his headquarters last night. He sent for General Weyg [and]¹ and all papers on the subject. Finally he wrote and gave me a statement of which the following is a translation:

"Paragraph 1. The value of the occupation of the port of Murmansk by the Allies is indisputable.

"Paragraph 2. The Supreme War Council at Versailles has decided that the occupation of the port should be realized.

"Subparagraph A. By the Czechs;

"Subparagraph B. By the British, French, Americans and Italians.

"Paragraph 3. There is nothing further to be done but to undertake the realization of this program which contemplates the use of one or two American battalions and the same for the French. The dispatch of one or two American battalions in June or July would not sensibly retard the arrival of American troops in France."

Paragraph 2. With reference to his written statement and in reply to specific questions General Foch stated in substance as follows:

Subparagraph A. He mentioned only the port of Murmansk because that is the place of first importance but the occupation of Archangel is also contemplated.

Subparagraph B. Joint note 31[2] of Military Representatives approved by Supreme War Council is based on the assumption that a force of some 20,000 Czech troops would arrive at Archangel and Murmansk which would be sufficient for ordinary purposes provided it was stiffened by not more than a total of six allied battalions.

Subparagraph C. General Foch says that Lord Milner's despatch to the President is apparently based on the assumption that the Czechs will not arrive at Archangel and Murmansk and that therefore Milner must have in view a much larger allied expedition of unknown ultimate strength than has ever been contemplated or studied; that if such be the case he objects to one of the parties in the Supreme War Council making a new allied plan without the knowledge or approval of the others; that this new plan would commit the French to he does not know what.

Subparagraph D. General Foch says that he has not discussed this plan with Lord Milner; that he stands by the plan of joint note 31; and that if American forces of more than one or at most two battalions of American infantry are demanded he will object.

Subparagraph E. He thinks that Lord Milner should be definitely asked whether his present demands for American assistance is based on the assumption of the nonarrival of the Czech troops and that if such be the case he should be told that it constitutes a new allied problem that should be carefully examined by the Supreme War Council.

Paragraph 3. The outline of Joint Note 31 is in paragraph six of my number 125.[3] Full text sent by mail.

Paragraph 4. In my opinion Lord Milner's despatch to the President may be based not only on the assumption that the Czechs will not arrive but also that no other troops but Americans will be available for the expedition. If this be so, the question of the ultimate force we may have to despatch to Murmansk must be carefully studied as well as the tonnage that will be involved because we may be committing ourselves to a more serious enterprise than appears at first sight. The American section has always assumed

that under the plans of Joint Note 31 the one or possibly two American battalions would be Marines going in Navy tonnage. This
would avoid diversion of any troops from France.

Paragraph 5. Reference subparagraph B of your 61, the question
of command as recommended by the Military Representatives must
be considered in the light of their joint note 31 and not of Lord
Milner's entirely new proposition which was never before us. The
question of command has proved a delicate one. The force to be
assembled at Archangel and Murmansk was assumed by the military representatives to be composed, first, of more than 20,000
Czecho-Slavs with whom are a considerable number of French
officers and, second, a small force of English and French now there
and, third, an additional expeditionary force of not more than six
battalions in all of British, French, Americans and Italians. The
French demanded command on land, leaving command on sea to
the British. The British said that safety demanded a single command; that they had an experienced general already there to exercise this command; that everything at those ports depended upon
British assistance in tonnage, et cetera; that they therefore demanded the single command. The matter remained unsettled when
the Supreme War Council met June 1. The latter thought the question urgent and suspended its last meeting to enable the Military
Representatives to further consider it. Lord Milner appeared before
us to represent the views of the British War Cabinet. He flatly
demanded single command for the British. My view was that if the
expedition was ever to be undertaken the question must be settled
at once. As the total force of Americans in the expedition would be
only about one thousand or at most about two thousand in a force
of three naught thousand (30,000) troops, I do not see my (our)
way to demanding command for an American. I therefore proposed
that at the outset there be a single command appointed by the
British Government and that the Supreme War Council should
decide later in its discretion any changes that should be made in
this arrangement. The French accepted this arrangement and it
was adopted and approved by the Supreme War Council. You will
see that Lord Milner's present proposition has nothing to do with
the foregoing and raises anew the question of command. If the
proposed expedition is to be entirely or largely an American one
our prestige and influence with the Russian people will require an
American Commander even though this should involve a separation
of the land and sea commands. I do not regard this latter as of
much importance which is further shown by the fact that the British
are themselves now proposing, on account of differences between
their Army and Navy, to divide the single command between a

British admiral and a British general. Replying specifically to question in last sentence of your subparagraph B my opinion is that Lord Milner's present proposition involves an entirely new plan which was not under consideration by the Military Representatives when they recommended in their Joint Note 31 a single command to be appointed by the British Government and that our recommendation is null with respect to his proposition.

Paragraph 6. Finally I recommend that action along the line indicated in interview with General Foch.   Bliss.

TC telegram (N. D. Baker Papers, DLC).
    [1] Gen. Maxime Weygand, previously the French military representative on the Supreme War Council, was at this time Foch's chief of staff.
    [2] Printed in n. 3 to A. J. Balfour to Lord Reading, June 11, 1918.
    [3] T. H. Bliss to H. P. McCain, June 3, 1918, TC telegram (WDR, RG 407, World War I Cablegrams, DNA).

From Joseph Patrick Tumulty

Dear Governor: The White House. 20 June 1918.

I have it from a very good source that Senator Shields of Tennessee would vote for suffrage if you would send for him and ask him to do so; and that Senator Wolcott of Delaware will favor it if requested by you. These two votes will put suffrage over. Isn't it worth while trying it? The vote is to be taken on the 22d of June.
                        Sincerely yours,   J P Tumulty

TLS (WP, DLC).

To Joseph Patrick Tumulty

Dear Tumulty: [The White House, c. June 20, 1918]

I have already tried out Senator Wolcott of Delaware and have met with no success.[1] I am writing to Senator Shields today. Having written to a number of other Senators rather than sent for them, I don't like to act differently now for fear some of the others might since their replies to me have changed their minds.
                        The President.

TL (WP, DLC).
    [1] See WW to J. O. Wolcott, May 9, 1918, Vol. 47.

To John Knight Shields

My dear Senator: [The White House] 20 June, 1918

I feel so deeply the possibilities latent in the vote which is presently to be taken by the Senate on the suffrage amendment that I am going to take a liberty which in ordinary circumstances I should not feel justified in taking and ask you very frankly if it will not be possible for you to vote for the amendment.

I feel that much of the morale of this country and of the world, and not a little of the faith which the rest of the world will repose in our sincere adherence to democratic principles, will depend upon the action which the Senate takes in this now critically important matter. If it were merely a domestic question, or if the times were normal, I would not feel that I could make a direct request of this sort, but the times are so far from normal, the fortunes of nations are so linked together, the reactions upon the thought of the world are so sharp and involve such momentous issues, that I know that you will indulge my unusual course of action and permit me to beg very earnestly that you will lend your aid in clearing away the difficulties which will undoubtedly beset us if the amendment is not adopted.

With much respect,

Sincerely yours,   Woodrow Wilson

TLS (Letterpress Books, WP, DLC).

Two Letters from Robert Lansing

My dear Mr. President: Washington June 20, 1918.

The subject of making a loan or loans to China again presents itself. Conditions are different at present from what they were when this subject was up a while ago, and entirely different from what they were when the American group withdrew from the Consortium. The last time it was under discussion the Secretary of the Treasury expressed the feeling that our commitments to European countries and our needs in America were such as to make a loan to China then impracticable.

I have recently been advised by the Secretary of the Treasury that the affairs of the Treasury will probably permit some such loans to be made, provided the diplomatic situation warrants so doing, and I feel that it does. The question immediately arises as to the nature of the loans, the purposes for which they are to be used and the character of the loan, that is, as to whether it shall be a Government loan or one by private bankers. After consultation between the officials of this Department and of the Treasury, it is felt that loans for war purposes by private bankers would be best under the circumstances. With that object in view, it is being proposed to call together the representatives of a few of the banks which have been interested in making loans in the Far East, and that they, or any of them, and such others as they may desire, form an American group. Those who would fall in this category are the officers of the Guaranty Trust Company, J. P. Morgan and Company, Kuhn, Loeb and Company, of New York, the Continental and Commercial Trust and Savings Bank of Chicago, and Lee, Higginson and Company of Boston.

There are three matters in prospect which offer opportunities for such a group to operate in, in which it will be very advisable to have American financiers interested. They are as follows:

1st. The Continental and Commercial Trust and Savings Bank of Chicago made a loan to China some time ago, taking as security the income from the wine and tobacco tax. As part of the contract they obtained a preference on any additional loans looking to the same security up to twenty-five million dollars. Japanese interests are at present negotiating with China to make a loan on the same security, having in contemplation a liquidation of the existing five million dollar loan above referred to, and including in the contract provision for the organization and control of the whole tobacco and wine industry of China—its manufacture, production and sale. Consummation of this loan under those conditions would mean the establishment in China in favor of Japanese interests of a monopoly of the tobacco business, and would automatically exclude the very large American interests now existing there in the form of the British-American Tobacco Company, which, though organized under the laws of Hongkong, is officered controlled and almost entirely capitalized by Americans. The Chicago Bank has less than sixty days in which to exercise its option to make additional loans but the exercise of it would prevent the execution of the proposed loan by Japan and would automatically protect the British-American Tobacco Company's interests. The Chicago Bank has graciously offered its option to the Department to be used in any way we choose, to be exercised either by the Bank or by the Government, or by any group of bankers we may designate, or to let it expire.

2nd. The railroad service projected from Canton to Hankow was under British control. The line is not completed. It will take about thirty million dollars to finish it. The British financiers have not been able to proceed with it and have called in the American International Corporation and their subsidiary, the Siems-Carey Company, and have asked them to proceed with the construction. The

Siems-Carey Company is unable to finance it, but is able, in case they can make financial arrangements, to agree with the British interests that American engineers shall be used and American control exercised over the road during the period of the contract existing between the British interests and the Chinese Government which extends over a number of years. The financing of the road at this time would enable American interests to control a very important railroad. It is understood between the Siems-Carey Company and the British and French interests concerned that their governments would, because of such aid, be likely to withdraw their claims to the spheres of influence of the regions affected.

3rd. The loan for currency reform purposes, which will amount to a sum variously estimated between one hundred million and two hundred million, must under the contract, be made with the old Consortiun [Consortium] from which the American group withdrew, and with which neither the British nor the French groups are now able to proceed. That leaves Japanese capital in control. They have several times requested American participation and have expressed a real desire to have us join them. This is not imminent but will become active within the next three or four months. China has renewed the option several times but has declined to extend it again so that unless we are able to participate Japan can and probably will proceed alone with this large and important loan.

China has expected some financial assistance from the United States. Japan has made her many loans recently. We have made none. It was at our invitation she entered the war, and it is to us that she is looking for some financial help to guard against possibilities now that the scenes of war are nearing her borders. The indications are that her disappointment at not receiving what she has felt she had reason to expect has made her somewhat resentful against this country. If we are able to give permission to American banks to make the loans in connection with the tobacco tax and with the railroad, and to co-operate with Japan on the question of currency reform, it will be pleasing no doubt both to China and Japan.

The proposal is made to form an American group, composed of interests which have made loans in the Orient and to allow them to carry out the details. It would be necessary to assure them of the support of the Government for these three projects, and for such other legitimate and non-political enterprises upon which they may enter.

In view of the present circumstances and of the situation in China, and of the conversations which have been had with the Treasury Department and their informal and verbal assurances that

the plan above suggested would be feasible, I have the honor to
request whether it receives your approval that we organize an American group for the purpose indicated and have your permission to
proceed therewith subject to consultation and agreement with the
Treasury.   Faithfully yours,   Robert Lansing

TLS (SDR, RG 59, 893.51/2513a, DNA).

Dear Mr. President: Washington June 20, 1918.
    The Russian Ambassador has asked me whether I would receive
Mr. Konovaloff[1] who just arrived in this country, and whether, in
my opinion, you also would be willing to receive him. You will
recollect that Mr. Konovaloff was the Vice Premier with Kerensky
and that in view of Kerensky's resignation he is technically the
head of the so-called provisional government.
    I told Mr. Bakhmeteff I would be glad to talk to Mr. Konovaloff
at my house but that his reception by you would create considerable
discussion and perhaps be misunderstood in Russia. Mr. Bakhmeteff now asks whether you would be willing to say that in view
of your many engagements you find it difficult to arrange to receive
Konovaloff but that you have authorized Colonel House and myself
to talk to him and to receive his views.
    As the Ambassador is pressing for a reply, I should be grateful
if you could indicate your wishes tomorrow morning is [if] possible.
                      Faithfully yours,   Robert Lansing.

TLS (SDR, RG 59, 861.00/2162A, DNA).
    [1] That is, Aleksandr Ivanovich Konovalov.

From Francis Patrick Walsh

Kansas City, Mo., June 20, 1918.
    In view of statements in the press as well as circulars which are
being sent broadcast by the Western Union Telegraph Company,
I beg to submit the following facts for your information:
    The principles rejected by the Western Union Telegraph Com-
pany were unanimously adopted by the War Labor conference board,
approved by the Secretary of Labor and specifically made a part of
your proclamation creating the National War Labor Board and declaring the principles which would rule its action.
    Unanimity of action on the part of the War Labor Board under
its principles and practices is only required where the board is
acting as arbitrator in specific cases of grievances submitted to the

arbitration of the board in conformity with the principles declared in your proclamation. In all other cases, including that of the Western Union Telegraph Company, a majority decision of the board governs. Otherwise it could not function. There has been no vote cast upon this board in which Mr. Taft and myself have been in disagreement.

Under the principles rejected by the Western Union more than one hundred thousand workers already upon strike have been taken from the streets and returned to their employment. Upon next Saturday at Schenectady, N. Y., Mr. Taft and myself, under an application of the same principles, are to pass upon the case of twenty thousand workers of the General Electric Company, a most essential war industry. Upon Monday, the twenty fourth instant, we are to take up the cases of more than fifty thousand street railway employees, who have submitted to the jurisdiction of the board under the same principles. In practically all of these cases the application of these principles is opposed to what might be termed the financial or selfish interest of the workers.

Another misstatement which should be corrected is the one carried by the press associations and contained in the circulars of the Western Union to the effect that its employees have made no complaint to the National War Labor Board respecting hours of labor, rates of pay or general working conditions. The records of the War Labor Board will show that the telegraph operators filed a formal written complaint with the board alleging that the telegraph operators were habitually compelled to work to the point of utter exhaustion and the wages paid to the vast majority were far below the standard necessary for bare subsistence.

Under the submission of the Postal Telegraph Company I have no doubt that all differences between that company and its employees will be justly composed without any cessation of work.

Frank P. Walsh.

T telegram (WP, DLC).

From Charles Edward Russell[1]

My dear Mr. President,   London. June 20th, 1918.

A Committee of Russian residents of London has asked me, because of my interest in Russia, to forward to you the enclosed Memorial.[2] I am asked to say that the signers include members of many political parties. Among them are writers, correspondents, a former Director of the Economic Department of the Ministry of Foreign Affairs under the Provisional Government, the Russian

Consul General in London, a former Commissioner of the Kerensky Government, a President of the Siberian Co-operative Union and a Rear Admiral. I understand that Mr. J. Gavrousky,[3] whom I have known for some time, and who came to me very highly recommended from trustworthy sources, endorses the signatures.

With earnest wishes for your good health,

I am, my dear Mr. President,

Yours very truly,   Charles Edward Russell

TLS (WP, DLC).

[1] At this time, the London representative of the Committee on Public Information.

[2] "To the President of the United States of America," June 1918, TS MS in Russian with English translation (WP, DLC). The numerous signers of this memorial urged that the Allies and the United States immediately undertake military intervention in and economic assistance to Russia, in order to prevent her from falling under complete German domination.

[3] Jacob O. Gavronsky, a Russian living in England, probably a scientist, author of *The Truth about New Russia* (London, 1917). He was one of the signers of the memorial cited in n. 2 above.

From Adolph Joseph Sabath[1]

Dear Mr. President: Washington, D. C. June 20, 1918.

Believing to be thoroughly acquainted with the labor conditions and the mode of living of the vast number of foreign born and those born of foreign parentage, of whom it can be safely said ninety per cent are of the working class, employed in our mines, in our mills and in our factories, doing the hardest manual labor and making it possible to increase the production of the essentials needed for our Army, Navy and shipbuilding, I feel it my duty to express my views on the present unjustifiable demand for prohibition.

The most rabid restrictionists and prohibitionists must admit that these people, especially the Poles, Galicians, Bohemians, Italians, Slovaks, Croatians, Lithuanians and Hungarians who are employed in the hardest work are showing the proper patriotic spirit. They are loyal and in every way desirous of being of the greatest service to our Nation at this time when the country is so much in need of their cooperation. Living in Chicago, a city thickly populated by the people constituting these nationalities, and, as a member of the Foreign Affairs and Immigration and Naturalization Committees, I have had special opportunity to familiarize myself with their loyalty, with their customs and mode of living not only in that city, but in the entire United States. I am convinced, should they be deprived of their beer at their dinner and supper, which their systems and hard work demands and which to them represents nourishment and stimulation, it would create such dissatisfaction as to endanger the present contented conditions prevailing in the industrial sections of our country. Their whole cooperation has been obtained because of your sympathetic, sincere and high minded efforts, the irresistible influence of the great Samuel Gompers and other patriotic leaders in the labor world; also by those of us who have striven with all our energy to impress upon all the foreign born people the duty they owe to our Republic, thus encouraging them to still greater efforts, activity and increased production.

In most instances, the noon meal of these men employed in the mines, mills, plants and factories usually consists of dry sandwiches made of bread and meat, sausage or cheese and a glass of beer. Deprived of that beer something would have to be furnished to take its place, containing an equivalent ratio of nourishment and stimulation.

Notwithstanding the contention of un-informed advocates of prohibition who seem to think more of their pet theory than they do of the welfare of the Nation, I am satisfied that a much greater amount of grain would be consumed in the production of unsatisfactory and less invigorating substitutes than is now used in the production of beer itself.

It is a noteworthy fact that our Allies though dependent on us for grain, after four years of careful observation and most thorough investigation on the part of several commissions, and even though compelled to issue cards for bread and flour, have found it unwise to abolish malted liquors as a beverage and the main reason assigned was that they feared it would disturb labor conditions in Great Britain.

Within the last six months those who are making conditions of labor their study have been unable to explain the unusual percentage of turn-overs. Were they to tabulate the sections of the country for the purpose of analysis it would most likely surprise them to find the greatest turn-over in labor to have occur[r]ed, in spite of increased pay offered as an inducement to remain, in those labor districts where prohibition has been forced upon the citizens therein.

It is not my province at this time to deal in figures and elaborate statistics which are unquestionably at your demand should you desire them. Suffice it to say for the above reasons I believe it unwise at this time to disturb the living conditions, lest it prove detrimental to the best interests of our country and to the successful prosecution of the war which is, and ought to be, the main aim in the minds of all patriotic and well meaning citizens, as against the hysterical notions of professional prohibitionists who are the only ones asking at this time for this unwise legislation.

With kindest regards and assurance of esteem, I remain,

Very respectfull[y] yours,   A. J. Sabath

TLS (WP, DLC).
[1] Democratic congressman from a Chicago district.

Two Telegrams from Arthur James Balfour to Lord Reading

[London] June 20th, 1918.

No. 82, to be read in conjunction with No. 83, which follows:

Your telegram No. 652 of the 16th[1]: I have little to add to the exhaustive presentation of the case for intervention contained in my many previous communications. But I would call attention to the draft memorandum prepared by the French Ambassador and Mr. LOCKHART: see latter's telegram No. 287 of June 18th[2]: and to a memorandum prepared at the War Office, which put in high relief the military view of the situation. I fear that this last is not exactly what the President asks for; but it may be nevertheless helpful.

Memorandum:

1. Unless Allied intervention is undertaken in SIBERIA forthwith we have no chance of being ultimately victorious, and shall incur serious risks of defeat in the meantime.

2. By first of June 1919 the exhaustion of British and French reserves of man-power will have necessitated very serious reduction in the number of divisions that they can maintain in the field. The growth of the American army, even under the most favourable circumstances, will not suffice to equip, train, and place in the line enough divisions to restore original balance in our favour. Thus the Germans, reckoning on a similar scale of battle casualties for them as for the Allies, will in the first half of 1919 still have formidable army on the Western Front even without withdrawing any further divisions from the East.

3. But if Central Powers are not threatened by any military force in the East they will by that time be in a position to withdraw from there many more divisions, still further increasing their superiority. In view of unfavourable strategic situation of the Allied armies in France it is possible that the Germans might with this superiority obtain a decision in their favor in the West.

4. On the other hand, if intervention is started now it is estimated that by the spring of 1919 sufficient Allied force could be deployed west of the URALS to rally to the Allied cause all those Russian elements which are in favour of law and order, good government and economical development, and which would render possible the reconstitution of democratic Russia as military power.

5. The greater part of this force must for the time being be Japanese, as it would be strategically unsound to divert forces that can be used in the Western theatre, except such small detailments of the other allied powers as are necessary to give the operation an international character.

In this manner too German troops would be held by allied force which would not otherwise be employed. Ultimately there may be a surplus of American troops over and above what can be maintained in France, and this should be used in support or in substitution of Japanese.

6. Immediate effect of this force would be, first, to prevent withdrawal of any further German troops from the East; second, to oblige them to withdraw divisions from the Western Front and thus give the allies a real chance of obtaining a military success in the West even in 1919.

7. Finally, it is not considered that any military success which it is within the power of the allies to obtain on the Western front can be decisive enough to force the Central Powers to tear up the Brest-Litovsk treaty, or to prevent Russia and most of Asia from becoming a German colony.

The immense spaces at the enemy's disposal for manoeuvre in the West and his superior communications would enable him to fight for an unlimited time without a decision being obtained. Even if driven completely out of France, Belgium, and Italy, the Central Powers would be still unbeaten. Unless therefore Russia can re-constitute herself as a military power in the East against the time when the allied armies are withdrawn nothing can prevent the complete absorption of her resources by the Central Powers, which would imply world domination by Germany, and only means by which resurrection of Russia can be brought about is by immediate allied military intervention in that theatre.

8. *To sum up*:

No military decision in the Allies' favour can ever be expected as the result of operations on the Western front alone; nor will such a measure of equality as may be looked for in that theatre in any way secure objects for which the allies are fighting, unless combined with the maximum military effort that can be made in the East.

9. Matter is urgent not merely politically, but also because it is necessary to take advantage of the summer, which is rapidly passing away, and because the agricultural districts should be secured before the harvest is gathered in.

[1] See Lord Reading to A. J. Balfour, June 16, 1918.
[2] It is quoted in the next document.

[London] June 20th 1918.

VERY URGENT. *No. 83.* Following for Lord Reading from Mr. Balfour, to be read in conjunction with my telegram No. 82:

Following from LOCKHART, *No. 287, June 18th:*

I forward herewith a draft of a memorandum which I have prepared in conjunction with the French Ambassador, and which has been sent to U. S. Ambassador. French Ambassador hopes U. S. Ambassador will himself adopt this draft as text for resolution which he will put at VOLOGDA Conference, which everyone is most anxious to have as soon as GENERAL POOLE arrives.

Begins:

"1. Intervention must be inter-allied.

"2. It must take place immediately because Bolshevics, having lost power very sensibly during the last month, there is good reason to fear that the Germans will forestall us by creating a counter-revolution with pro-German tendencies which will render our intervention more difficult for us and less favourable in the eyes of Russians.

"3. It must take place immediately to prevent the Germans from arming war-prisoners and organizing serious resistance to our intervention in Siberia.

"4. It must take place immediately so as to profit by favourable situation created by CZECHO-SLOVAKS, who are masters at the moment of the most important points on trans-Siberian line, but who evidently cannot hold on indefinitely.

"5. It must take place immediately because those Russian elements who remain loyal to the allies are beginning to lose patience and every day's delay drives them on to German side.

"6. It must take place with the greatest possible eclat, because Russian people will only support it in the event of an initial success.

"7. For this reason it should take place simultaneously at MURMANSK, ARCHANGEL, and in the FAR EAST; being of chief importance, since force in possession of SIBERIA will be economically master of CENTRAL RUSSIA.

"8. Intervention should be preceded by a declaration to Russian people guaranteeing integrity of Russian territory and promising not to interfere in Russian internal affairs.

"9. Consent of Bolshevics will not be given. This is no longer of vital importance. Bolshevics are clearly convinced of imminence of inter-allied intervention. We would gain nothing by abstaining and we have every reason to act immediately.

"10. Minimum intervention must be URAL district, if enterprise once undertaken is to have a decisive effect on Germans and is to define mutual obligations of the allies.

"11. It is probable that on news of our intervention Germans will immediately occupy PETROGRAD and MOSCOW. This should not disturb us, since in doing so they will increase their effectives and increase their difficulty of provisioning.

"12. Inter-allied intervention is designed to cement such Russian elements as remain favourable to the allies, to revive energies of our friends, and perhaps revive national spirit in Russia, which, should it be created, would have a decisive effect on the issue of the war."

CC telegrams (W. Wiseman Papers, CtY).

From the Diary of Colonel House

June 20, 1918.

Wiseman also came to lunch and out-stayed Stettinius so we might have one of our intimate talks. He says the British Ambassador's sensibilities are hurt because the President refused to see him the other day upon request of the State Department. Sir William characterized the refusal as bad manners and tending to upset the good relations between the two countries. He thought Reading should warn Lloyd George and Balfour of how impossible it is to see the President as often as they desire, but he also thought when an ambassador made a request of that kind at the instance of the head of his government, the President should see him. If an ambassador made too many requests, it would be within the province of the President to have the State Department inform his government that their ambassador was asking for too many interviews. This would enable his government to caution him to see the Secretary of State instead of the President, excepting matters of vital importance.

Reading claims, as an excuse for wanting to see the President so often, that he has found from experience it is utterly useless to see Lansing. He says they smoke a cigarette together, have a pleasant talk and that is the end of it. Nothing is ever done, and it is waste of time to undertake any sort of negotiation through the Secretary. I told Sir William that this was largely the President's fault, because he refused to see Lansing and other members of his Cabinet, just as he refused to see the Ambassador. I tried to excuse the President by telling how terribly engrossed he was, and of the demands upon him, and of his temperamental objection to seeing anyone when he could avoid it.

Sir William thought the President could never be on as confidential terms with Reading as he was, for instance, with himself, for the reason that he had observed that Reading always approached the matter with the air and caution of a lawyer. The President insensibly assumed a similar attitude, and close, confidential relations between the two could hardly be brought about.

Two Letters to Robert Lansing

My dear Mr. Secretary: The White House 21 June, 1918

Will you not be kind enough to say to Mr. Bakhmeteff that in view of my many engagements I find it impossible to arrange to have an interview with Mr. Konovaloff, and that I am glad to think that it would be of not particular service to me, inasmuch as I know that you and Colonel House will have an opportunity to talk with him informally?

Cordially and sincerely yours,   Woodrow Wilson

TLS (SDR, RG 59, 861.00/2162½, DNA).

Confidential.

My dear Mr. Secretary: The White House 21 June, 1918

I approve of the course proposed in this letter. I take it for granted that everything necessary would be done to protect the Chinese Government against such unconscionable arrangements as were contemplated by the former Consortium, because I am afraid it is not less but rather more likely that the Chinese Government would permit unfair advantage to be taken of it at the present time of stress than formerly.

Cordially and sincerely yours,   Woodrow Wilson

TLS (SDR, RG 59, 893.51/2513, DNA).

To Edward William Bok

My dear Mr. Bok: The White House 21 June, 1918

I am very sorry but my judgment is against this suggestion of your kind letter of June nineteenth. In the first place, if I do this in one instance, I must do it in a number of others, and, in the second place, my judgment is different from yours as to the timeliness and serviceability of what you suggest.

You are quite right in thinking that we spend Sundays here as other normal American families spend it, but while it is true that the shock and distress of the war are beginning to be felt in a good many homes, nothing like the full effect of it is yet perceptible, and I think we ought to reserve our processes of reassurance until the moment arrives, if it should arrive, when it is obviously necessary to use them.

For my own part, my impression is that the women of the country are standing up under the strain in the most wonderful and beautiful way. Of course, their hearts cry out and sometimes the cry is audible, but that does not mean that those hearts are rebelling or that there is any unwillingness of sacrifice, and I think we do not know enough yet of the psychology of the whole thing to deal with it.   Cordially and sincerely yours,   Woodrow Wilson

TLS (WP, DLC).

From Newton Diehl Baker, with Enclosure

My dear Mr. President: Washington. June 21, 1918.

I enclose a letter of very recent date from General Bliss. I send it because of its intrinsic interest and also because of the fact that it seems to show that Lord Milner took up the proposition, which Lord Reading submitted, with General Foch and Mr. Clemenceau before sending it through Lord Reading here, which puts a better face on the whole matter, but still leaves in my judgment the wisest course to be the one you outlined for me to communicate to Lord Reading.   Respectfully yours,   Newton D. Baker

P.S. I send a copy so that you can tear it up when read and I shorten it by leaving out unimportant parts.

TLS (WP, DLC).

E N C L O S U R E

Extracts from letter of General Bliss—June 8, 1918.

I told you in my No. 7 (June 1)[1] of my interview with M. Soukine[2] on Friday afternoon, May 31, and of the outline of the plan which he told me had been drawn up in M. Clemenceau's office, and his statement that he had personally seen it. This plan was for a Japanese intervention in Siberia under conditions that they thought might be accepted by the President. I knew that all military men and high political men had long ago given up the idea of Japanese intervention with a small force such as M. Soukine spoke of. I asked him what he thought would be the attitude of the Russians if, instead of a small Allied force, including some Japanese, a very great Japanese Army should come in. He said that he believed the Russians would bitterly oppose it, and that he himself, if he were at home, would fight it. He informed me to his certain knowledge

---

[1] It is missing in all collections.

[2] Jean (John, Ivan) Sookine, who had been Secretary attached to the Russian embassy in Washington at the time of the November Revolution.

the plan prepared in M. Clemenceau's office would be brought up for action before the Supreme War Council at its Session the following day. When I saw Mr. Lloyd-George the next morning I asked him if he knew anything about it, and he replied that he had not heard of it. He said that in his opinion the Japanese would have to come in with every man that they could put in the field, even up to the extent of 2,500,000 men, because they must be strong enough to overcome any possible resistance and reach the Germans in the West as rapidly as possible; and after they reached the Germans they must be amply strong enough to fight them.

If such a plan as M. Soukine spoke of was actually prepared, it did not come before the Supreme War Council. On Sunday, the Prime Ministers agreed that the question (in some form which they did not state) should be taken up by the Foreign Ministers of Great Britain, France and Italy, at the Ministry of Foreign Affairs, on Monday morning. At the meeting of the Supreme War Council that afternoon, M. Pichon made a report the substance of which you will find in the Procès-Verbaux that I send you herewith.[3] The Foreign Ministers agreed that their Governments should approach the Japanese Government on the question of military intervention, putting up to it three questions, satisfactory answers to the first two of which would result in taking the subject up with the Government of the United States. So far as I can see now, the Supreme War Council will not again ask the views of the Military Representa-

[3] "M. Clemenceau said the next item for consideration was 'The Situation in Russia and Action to be taken.' Under this heading the main subject was the question of Japanese intervention. M. Clemenceau asked M. Pichon to explain what agreements had been reached among the Foreign Ministers who had met in Paris that morning.
"M. Pichon said that an agreement had been reached on two points:
"1. That Allied intervention in Russia to protect the Murman Coast and Archangel was necessary.
"2. That all the Allies, with the exception of America, thought Japanese intervention in Siberia desirable.
"On the second point they had found that as yet no precise official proposals had been made to Japan. The Foreign Ministers of Great Britain, Italy, and France had therefore considered that their Governments should approach the Japanese Government and enquire from it whether intervention was acceptable under the following conditions:
"a. That Japan should undertake to respect the territorial integrity of Russia.
"b. That with due regard for the acknowledged principle of the self-determination of peoples, Japan should undertake to take the side of no party in the internal politics of Russia.
"c. That the Japanese force should go as far west as possible for the purpose of encountering the Germans.
"The three Foreign Ministers had all agreed that these conditions were indispensable, and before sending their proposals to Tokio wished to submit them to the Supreme War Council.
"M. Pichon added that when the Japanese reply had been received it would then be possible to explain to the President of the United States exactly what Japan's intentions were, and it might then be easier to overcome his evident reluctance to acquiesce in Japanese intervention." SUPREME WAR COUNCIL. Procès-verbal of the Third Meeting of the Sixth Session of the Supreme War Council, held at the Trianon Palace, Versailles, on Monday, 3rd June, 1918, at 3 p.m., printed document (WDR, RG 120, Records of the American Section of the Supreme War Council, 1917-1919, DNA).

tives,—this is as it should be. I have repeatedly said here that the Military Representatives had expressed all of the opinions from the military point of view, that they could express; and that it is doing no good to "fire" Joint Note after Joint Note to the President, simply reiterating in different words what they said before. If there is anything that can be said that will cause the Government of the United States to cordially accept the proposition of intervention it must come from the Governments here, themselves. It is, of course, possible that Japan may reply to the overtures of the three Governments with a proposition that would require new study from the military point of view. In that case, it would again come before the Military Representatives; but as the case now stands I do not see that they have anything further to say.

The question which consumed more time of the Supreme War Council than any other was the question of naval action by the Italians in the Mediterranean. As you know, the Italian Navy has kept itself for the most part shut up in ports where the enemy cannot attack it and where it cannot attack the enemy. This has proved a safe but inefficient procedure. The Inter-Allied Naval Council has for a long time been trying to get the Italian Navy to take more active participation in operations in the Mediterranean. A resolution of the Inter-Allied Naval Council came before the War Council at its meeting on June 1st, with the general purpose of agreeing on a combined Allied Naval Commander in the Mediterranean. It was for the purpose of this discussion that there were present Admiral de Bon, Commanding the French Navy, the First Lord of the Admiralty, the First Sea Lord and Chief of the Naval Staff, and four Italian Naval Officers, including Admiral di Revel, the Italian Naval Commander-in-Chief.[4] They discussed the matter for the rest of the day. The Italians hung out for a continuance of their present policy; the English and the French were unanimous against it. The meeting broke up late, without any decision having been arrived at, and the three Heads of Government present took the matter up among themselves with a view to settling it themselves in view of the fact that there were irreconcilable differences of opinion among the technical naval men. There is nothing official of record to show what conclusion they arrived at but it is commonly understood that they tentatively agreed upon the appointment of Admiral Jellicoe of the British Navy as Allied Commander-in-Chief in the Mediterranean. This, of course, would have settled what was to be done with the Italian Navy, whether the Italian Commander-in-Chief liked it or not. I assume that his own naval officers then proceeded

[4] That is, Vice Admiral Ferdinand Jean Jacques de Bon, Sir Eric Campbell Geddes, Vice Admiral Sir Rosslyn Erskine Wemyss, and Admiral Paolo Thaon di Revel.

to "lay down" on Mr. Orlando, because the next day he challenged the decision (whatever it was) reached by the Heads of the Governments late the previous evening and asked to have the matter rediscussed between the three Prime Ministers and their Naval advisers. All the rest of us then withdrew from the Council Room and the discussion lasted for pretty much all the rest of the day with no decision being reached—and that was the status of the question on final adjournment of the Supreme War Council. Presumably, therefore, the Italian Navy will continue to remain "bottled up."

The first paragraph of your cable No. 60 to me,[5] signed by yourself and McCain, was regarded by everyone here as very important and most eminently satisfactory. This session of the Supreme War Council was called, primarily by the French in order to discuss the features in the Milner-Pershing-Foch agreement at Abbeville in regard to the coming and allocation of American troops after the month of May, which were unsatisfactory to the French. It would almost certainly have resulted in interminable discussion with no more satisfactory results than had previously been attained.

As soon as I received your cable I took it to General Pershing who was at his house in town, and told him that it seemed to me that for the first time it put the matter on a perfectly satisfactory basis; that it was evident that you and the President had decided to accept whatever arrangement he made with the military authorities (including Lord Milner) here; and that I proposed to ask the Prime Ministers to withdraw the subject from discussion at the Supreme War Council and leave the matter entirely in the hands of the people indicated in the first paragraph of your cable. He agreed with me and said that there was no doubt at all that he and General Foch and the others could reach a satisfactory result. I showed the cable to the Prime Ministers and they saw at once that it was no longer a question for their consideration. Pershing, Milner, and Foch got together and reached the agreement which has already been cabled to you[6] and a copy of which is one of the Procès-Verbaux that I send herewith.

In addition to the Italian Naval question, there is another illustration which I may give you of the difficulty which the Allies find in coming to cordial agreement about important military and naval matters.

It appears that General Foch, in connection with the present critical situation, issued an order directing the transfer of certain

[5] NDB to T. H. Bliss, May 31, 1918.
[6] See the French, British, and Italian Prime Ministers to WW, June 2, 1918.

British Divisions in which American infantry units are now incorporated, from the British Front to a point toward the extreme right of the French line, toward the Swiss frontier. This was to enable the relief of certain French Divisions which would then be put on the line opposing the present German drive. Marshal Haig, taking advantage of the provision in the Agreement of Beauvais,[7] protested to his Government that such a move endangered the British Army, and, meanwhile, he declined to obey it. This resulted in an important secret conference held here yesterday between Lord Milner, Marshal Haig, and General Foch. Whether any agreement was reached or not, I do not know, but the British Representative has promised to keep me informed.

If General Foch's proposition be as it is said here to be, it is difficult to understand it. It is generally believed that the Germans are preparing a final effort which will take the form of a drive from the North to the South, somewhere on the line Montdidier-Noyon, combined with a powerful thrust from the East to the West. General Foch, himself, told me, the day before yesterday, that he expected this movement to begin at any moment. If such a combined movement should succeed, it would give the Germans possession of all-important railroad lines and it might very possibly open a direct route to Paris. If it succeeded, it could only do so by rushing all of the French Divisions that are included in the angle of the present line at Noyon and back of the more or less straight line running from about Montdidier to Viller-Cotterets. If this should take place everything would depend on the troops further to the North,—the few French Divisions still north of the Somme and the entire British Army.

(Later) The British Military Representative has just been in my office to give me the result of yesterday's secret conference to which I referred above. It appears it has been agreed, much against the wish of the British, that the American infantry now in five British Divisions, should come South, to go in as regiments in French Divisions, somewhere toward the extreme right of their line, toward the Swiss Frontier. This may result in the relief of a few French Divisions there for use on the present battle-front. It further appears that there was a misunderstanding as to an order supposed to have been given by General Foch directing the transfer to the South of certain British Divisions. General Foch directed that a study be made of the possibility of doing this in the event that the Germans should move all of the Reserves with the army of Prince Rupprecht,[8]

---

[7] For the text of the Beauvais agreement, see T. H. Bliss to P. C. March, April 3, 1918, Vol. 47.

[8] Rupprecht Maria Luitpold Ferdinand von Wittelsbach, Crown Prince of Bavaria.

who commands all of the German forces north of the Somme. The British agreed that if these German reserves were moved to the South they will have to send forces of their own below the Somme.

The British Military Representative also told me that Lord Milner expressed great anxiety on the part of his Government to have a regiment of American troops sent to Murmansk, as contemplated in one of the Joint Notes passed by the Supreme War Council at its last session. He says that there are no British troops that can be sent there. Lord Milner sent word that he had hoped to have a conference with me but that he had had to leave for London immediately after the conference of yesterday. I fancy that this is what he wanted to talk about. The British also think that if we could make a strong effort at Red Cross assistance in Siberia, it would have a most excellent effect on Russian sentiment.

It is possible that before this reaches you the Military Representatives may have adopted a Joint Note on the subject of the procedure that ought to be followed by the several Governments in respect to action on their Joint Notes. In order that you may know just what is in question I will state the following: * * *

I inclose a study made by the American Section here on the subject of the present offensive of the Germans.[9] The day before yesterday I took it to General Foch's Headquarters and discussed it with him and General Weygand and find that it is in substantial accord with their own views. I feel quite sure that before this reaches you one of the most critical events of the war will have been decided.

(Later) Under instructions of its Government here, the British Section is quietly preparing for a move. They are gradually sending their personnel further West. I do not want to make any movement in this direction before it should prove to be necessary but, of course, have made all my plans on the supposition that it may become necessary. I have arranged with General Pershing's Chief Quartermaster for motor transportation for my personnel and such records as should not be destroyed except in the last emergency. Of course, there is always, in doing this sort of work, a rapid accumulation of material which it is not absolutely necessary to preserve and which would do a great deal of harm if it got into the wrong hands. This I am quietly destroying, as the British have been doing. I have agreed with the British Representative that in case a move should be necessary his section and mine will stick together. If we

---

[9] "Comments on Present Offensive," June 26, 1918, CC MS (WDR, RG 120, Records of the American Section of the Supreme War Council, 1917-1919, File No. 346, DNA). It predicted coordinated German attacks in the immediate future on the approximate line, Montdidier-Noyon, and on the western face of the Soissons salient, and it recommended rapid concentration of Allied reserves in the general area of Clermont.

move at all, it would almost certainly be to the westward, probably to some place in the vicinity of Tours. It would be necessary that we be in cable communication with our Governments. I, personally, do not believe that it will be necessary to move but it would be foolish not to contemplate the possibility. The Germans are already in a position from which, if they could get up their long-range naval guns they could bomb Paris. If they can make a little further advance, we all expect that this is what will happen, accompanied by most intense bombing by avions. That is what has been steadily going on along the rear of the Allied front against which the German thrusts have been made. The newspapers and reports lay great stress on the claim that the Allies have two aeroplanes to the Germans one. This may be true, but it does not mean that they have the mastery of the air. The Germans, apparently, use one aeroplane as efficiently as the Allies do two or three.

Since the Supreme War Council Session at Abbeville at the beginning of May, that city has been effectively smashed by German bombing expeditions. At Abancourt, the English had what was perhaps the largest ammunition dump in France. On the night of the 19-20 of April the Germans bombed this and practically destroyed it with all the ammunition. They have bombed Marshal Haig's Headquarters, General Foch's Headquaters, and Beauvais and every important town in the rear of the Allies has been badly shattered. One of my officers returned last night from a trip as far as St. Omer. He tells me that the Germans in that vicinity are constantly bombing every place where they suspect aerodromes to be located or ammunition dumps, or troops to be concentrated.

Two nights ago Boulogne was heavily bombed. Of course, the German hope would be that by terrorizing Paris they may cause the overthrow of the present Government. Signs are not wanting of French political pressure that may be brought to bear on the military conduct of the campaign. Yesterday M. Clemenceau had to yield to this to the extent of organizing a Committee, largely political in character, charged with the defense of Paris. I know that General Foch's view is that if it should be necessary to temporarily lose Paris he would let it go and not be diverted from the real purpose of his campaign, and thereby play into the hands of the Germans, by attempting to hold it. And in any event, the loss of Paris, temporarily or not, would have a tremendously depressing effect upon the French. It is for that reason I do not like to see the initiation of a movement which looks to a re-concentration of a large part of the American forces down towards the Swiss frontier. I should very much prefer to see them on the left flank of the French line and where they could, if necessary, operate with the British. However, a few days will probably show what there is in this. (Signed) Tasker H. Bliss.

T MS (WP, DLC).

From Edward Mandell House

Dear Governor: Magnolia, Mass. June 21, 1918.

Lord Reading, who has been in Cambridge getting a degree, has spent the better part of the day with me. While here he received a cable from Balfour about Russian intervention. I suggested that he send you a copy for your information before he sees you, which he hopes to do on Monday.[1]

It is a panicy document in the main, and neither Reading nor I agree to the statement that a decision is not possible on the Western Front without an Eastern Front as well. The memorandum attached and which was drawn up by their representative in Russia together with the French Ambassador there, is worthy of notice.[2]

I believe something must be done immediately about Russia, otherwise it will become the prey of Germany. It has become now a question of days rather than months. I have this to suggest and recommend:

Make an address to Congress setting forth the food situation in this country; telling of the speeding up of our food products in one year time to a point where after August it will not be necessary for the Allies to continue on rations except as to beef and sugar. This statement in itself will enormously stimulate the morale in France, England and Italy and correspondingly depress that of the Central Powers.

Hoover has planned to make this statement himself in London around the middle of July, and may not like your anticipation. Nevertheless, you are the one to make it and now is the time.

Then set forth your plan for sending a "Russian Relief Commission," headed by Hoover, with the purpose of helping Russia speed up her food production by the same methods we have used. While this is being done, the Commission to be instructed to coordinate all such relief organizations as the Red Cross, Y.M.C.A. etc. etc. and supply the Russian people with agricultural implements necessary to make their potential arable lands as productive as ours and with a like beneficent result.

To do this it would be necessary for the Relief Commission and their assistants to have a safe and orderly field to work in, and you have therefore asked the cooperation and assistance of England,

France, Italy and Japan which they have generously promised, and they have also given the United States the assurance that they will not either now or in the future, interfere with Russia's political affairs, or encroach in any way upon her territorial integrity.

This program will place the Russian and Eastern situation in your hands, and will satisfy the Allies and perhaps reconcile the greater part of Russia towards this kind of intervention.

Lord Reading is enthusiastic over this plan, and I asked him to discuss it with you when you receive him.

The main difficulty that I see is getting Japan's consent to your taking such a dominant position, but Reading thinks she can be persuaded to yield.   Affectionately yours,   E. M. House

TLS (WP, DLC).
 [1] A. J. Balfour to Lord Reading, two telegrams, June 20, 1918. These telegrams are not in WP, DLC.
 [2] That is, the memorandum embodied in the second of the two telegrams cited in n. 1.

From the Diary of Colonel House

June 21, 1918.

Lord Reading and Sir William Wiseman spent the better part of the day with me. Besides them, I invited to lunch Mrs. T. Jefferson Coolidge, Jr. and Mrs. Francis L. Higginson Jr.[1] to take Loulie's place since she had gone to town. After lunch I had to listen again to Reading's story of his ill treatment by the President in regard to the engagement he wished to make before he left Washington[.] I minimized it by calling his attention to some of the things that had happened which seemed inexplicable, but which turned out to be easily explained. For instance, when Lady Reading first came to Washington she wrote Mrs. Wilson asking when she might call. By some inadvertence, this note was put in the British pouch, sent to London and returned and was received by Mrs. Wilson some six weeks after it was written. If I had not happened to be in Washington at the time, and upon intimate terms with both parties, it would have resulted in strained relations.

I also called his attention to the time when the President wrote Lansing a note for his own (Lansing's) information, which Lansing sent to the French Ambassador without revising. The President had not intended him to do more than convey, in a diplomatic way, to the French Ambassador the substance of what he had said. Reading evidently felt better when I finished. Nevertheless, I know, and, down in his heart, he knows that the President treated him rudely. . . .

The most important matter he wished to discuss was Russian intervention. I outlined my ideas, and told him what I had suggested regarding Hoover. I amplified this and asked him to make notes so he might tell the President when he sees him Monday just what my views are, and of his concurrence in them.[2] Reading wrote the notes and read them to me, but he did it so badly and set them forth so much less clearly than what I had in mind, that I concluded to write the President a letter myself which I have done and which is a part of the record.

[1] That is, Clara Amory Coolidge and Hetty Appleton Sargent Higginson.
[2] "COPY OF NOTES MADE BY LORD READING, Notes of conversation with Col. House on Friday 21 June/18 to be submitted to P. for speech," T MS (Reading Papers, Add. MSS Eur. F 118/ 117, IOR).

To Joseph Patrick Tumulty, with Enclosure

Dear Tumulty   The White House. 22 June, '18.

Please let Mr. Brookings know that I have approved this and then give it out in the usual way.   W.W.

ALI (WP, DLC).

E N C L O S U R E

From Robert Somers Brookings

My dear Mr President: Washington June 22, 1918.

At a meeting of the Price Fixing Committee with the steel interests yesterday, after a careful consideration of costs sheets furnished by the Federal Trade Commission, it was finally agreed that there should be no change in the price of finished steel products, but that the price of Lake Superior ore should be advanced 45¢ per ton, and that the basing point for certain steel products should be made Pittsburgh, Penna., all of which is more clearly set forth in the enclosed statement[1] which I present for your consideration and approval.

The railroads connecting the Lake Superior ore mines with the lake were private property owned largely by the United States Steel Company. The rate heretofore prevailing on ore from the mine to the lake has been about 63¢ per ton, at which rate it was said to have been the most profitable transportation in the country. On the taking over of the railroads, however, by the Railroad Administration, this rate was arbitrarily fixed at a flat advance of 33¢ or 35¢ per ton, over 50%, taking effect June 25th. At this advanced rate, nearly 50% of the mines were being operated without profit, so that the advance agreed upon yesterday was to cover this advanced freight rate and some additional advance in labor. We had some difficulty in persuading the pig iron manufacturers to pay this advanced rate without advancing the price of pig iron and some finished steel products, but, as usual, after an all day discussion, everybody agreed to make some concession and the price of finished steel products remained unchanged.

As price fixing regulates profits, and as excess profits taxes is at present one of our acute problems, I am necessarily in close touch with Mr Kitchen and the Ways & Means Committee, furnishing him with such information as I am able to gather regarding the prospective profits for this year and such suggestions as I hope may prove helpful.

Will you kindly either return the enclosed statement to me with your approval, or send it direct to our publicity agent, Mr Newdick,[2] as you may prefer.   Sincerely yours,   Robt. S. Brookings

TLS (WP, DLC).
    [1] It is printed in the *Official Bulletin*, II (June 24, 1918), 1.
    [2] Edwin W. Newdick, formerly a reporter for the *Christian Science Monitor* and the C.P.I.

From William Bauchop Wilson

My dear Mr. President: Washington June 22, 1918.

In connection with the correspondence from Mr. Newcomb Carlton and others relative to the action of the National War Labor Board in the telegraphers' dispute, Mr. Carlton in his letter to you quotes the foundation upon which rests the procedure of the National War Labor Board, as follows:

"When the Board, after due effort of its own, through sections, local committees, or otherwise, finds it impossible to settle a controversy, the Board shall then sit as a Board of Arbitration, decide the controversy, and make an award if it can reach a unanimous conclusion. If it cannot do this, then it shall select an umpire, as provided, who shall sit with the Board, review the issues and render his award."

If Mr. Carlton is willing to accept the jurisdiction and procedure expressed in the paragraph he quotes, there need be no further discussion of the matter. The National War Labor Board would then be in a position to proceed to adjust the questions in dispute in accordance with its prescribed method, and the fear of a strike would be over. Mr. Carlton on behalf of the Western Union Telegraph Company expresses his willingness to recognize the jurisdiction of the Board upon the question of wages and working conditions, but refuses to recognize its jurisdiction in the matter to the right of its employees to join a union, although the denial of this right may lead to stoppage of work which would interfere with the operation of the wires.

By a majority vote the National War Labor Board decided contrary to the company's contention. If its only reason for objection was that the vote was not unanimous and that, therefore, it was entitled to have the questions in dispute submitted to an umpire, it would be our duty to insist that the demand be complied with. But that is not the only reason for objection, nor is it the principal one. The real reason is the contention of the company that the Board has no jurisdiction over the question of permitting employees to join a union. Unless the company acknowledges this jurisdiction and agrees to abide by the result, it will be useless to insist either upon a unanimous vote by the Board or a submission to the decision of an umpire. It is immaterial whether or not the motion passed by a majority of its members constitutes a decision of the Board, as long as the jurisdiction of the Board itself is denied. Mr. Walsh as one of the makers of the report moved that it be adopted. Mr. Osborne offered an amendment that "with a statement to the public that this report has been adopted, it be shown who voted for and against it." The amendment was carried unanimously. The original motion was then carried by a vote of the workers and the two chairmen, all of the employers voting against it.

The report contains this language:

"The construction of our principles as set forth in Mr. Taft's telegram to Mr. Carlton leads to the conclusion that the Western Union Telegraph Company should accept this compromise as therein stated. It declines, however, to do so, *or to submit to the jurisdiction of this Board*." The last sentence constitutes the meat of the situation.

If instead of attempting to draw a distinction between different kinds of disputes, admitting the jurisdiction of the Board in some and denying it in others, he will agree to its jurisdiction in all matters of labor dispute and will abide by its awards when made, the National War Labor Board can go on to the uninterrupted consideration of the questions in accordance with the method of procedure adopted for its guidance.

I am therefore of the opinion that you should insist upon the Western Union Telegraph Company accepting the jurisdiction of the National War Labor Board and abiding by its decisions when made.   Faithfully yours,   W B Wilson

TLS (WP, DLC).

From Kenneth Douglas McKellar

My dear Mr. President: [Washington] June 22nd, 1918.

Further in reference to the call of Mr. Keating and myself about the Civil Service Retirement Bill, I enclose, first, a copy of the Bill, second, a succinct statement of its various sections, and third, a statement made by Doctor Beach, which refers particularly to the very pertinent question of expense during the war raised by you.[1]

I dislike very much to burden you with this matter at a time when I know you are already overburdened, but this Bill has been agreed upon[2] and I think is a very moderate retirement measure, and of course those affected by it are very anxious to have it enacted into law.

We have had very extended hearings running over nearly a year's time and this is the result of our efforts. I think our Committee, with perhaps one exception, is favorably inclined towards the Bill.

Should you desire any further information it will give me the greatest pleasure to furnish it at once if I can.

With great respect, I am

Sincerely your friend,   Kenneth McKellar

TLS (WP, DLC).

[1] 65th Cong., 2d sess., S. 4637 . . . A Bill for the retirement of employees in the classified civil service, printed bill; Provisions of Retirement Bill, printed summary of the bill; and John Staats Beach to K. D. McKellar, June 22, 1918, TLS, all in WP, DLC. The bill, introduced by McKellar on June 3, provided for a pension plan for classified federal employees under which a person could receive a maximum annuity of $600 after thirty years of service. The plan was to be financed largely through deductions of 2½ per cent from the salaries of eligible employees. Beach, a clerk in the Pension Office of the Department of the Interior and president of the Washington branch of the National Federation of Federal Employees, listed arguments in favor of the bill. One of these was that the lack of a pension plan forced many superannuated employees to remain in governmental service because they could not afford to retire, thus impairing the efficiency of the civil service during the war emergency.

[2] Apparently, McKellar meant that the Committee on Civil Service and Retrenchment, to which the bill was referred, had agreed on it. It was not reported back to the Senate until autumn.

Lord Reading to David Lloyd George and Lord Milner

Washington. 22nd, 1918

No. 2833. Very Urgent and Secret.

Following for Prime Minister and Lord Milner.

Lord Milner's telegram No. 3599 and my reply No. 2652.[1]

The U.S. Administration has made enquiries of General Bliss as Lord Milner's request in his above mentioned cable did not appear to be specifically authorised by the Supreme War Council at Versailles. Further the U. S. Administration had not received report of the reconsideration of joint note No. 31 of Military representatives at Versailles communicated to me in telegram No. 3510.

I have seen Secretary Baker today who after informing me of the substance of General Bliss's answers to questions submitted to him gave me a copy of the cable from General Bliss which is as follows: (begins)

"June 18 Confidential For Secretary of War.

Paragraph 1. In further reference to your 61 June 15,[2] I presented subject matter of your paragraph 1, subparagraph A, to General Foch at his head quarters last night. He sent for General Weyg[and] and all papers on the subject. Finally he wrote and gave me a statement of which the following is a translation:

'Paragraph 1. The value of the occupation of the port of Murmansk by the Allies is indisputable.

Paragraph 2. The Supreme War Council at Versailles has decided that the occupation of the port should be realised.

Subparagraph A. By the Czechs;

Subparagraph B. By the British, French, Americans and Italians.

Paragraph 3. There is nothing further to be done but to undertake the realisation of this program which contemplates the use of one or two American battalions and the same for the French. The dispatch of one or two American battalions in June or July would not sensibly retard the arrival of American troops in France.'

Paragraph 2. With reference to his written statement and in reply to specific questions General Foch stated in substance as follows:

Subparagraph A. He mentioned only the port of Murmansk because that is the place of first importance but the occupation of Archangel is also contemplated.

Subparagraph B. Joint Note 31 of Military representatives approved by Supreme War Council is based on the assumption that a force of some 20,000 Czech troops would arrive at Archangel and Murmansk which would be sufficient for ordinary purposes provided it was stiffened by not more than a total of six allied battalions.

Subparagraph C. General Foch says that Lord Milner's despatch to the President is apparently based on the assumption that the Czechs will not arrive at Archangel and Murmansk and that therefore Lord Milner must have in view a much larger allied expedition of unknown ultimate strength than has ever been contemplated or studied; that if such be the case he objects to one of the parties in the Supreme War Council making a new allied plan without the knowledge or approval of the others; that this new plan would commit the French to he does not know what.

Subparagraph D. General Foch says that he has not discussed this plan with Lord Milner; that he stands by the plan of Joint Note 31; and that if American forces of more than one or at most two battalions of American infantry are demanded he will object.

Subparagraph E. He thinks that Lord Milner should be definitely asked whether his present demands for American assistance is based on the assumption of the non-arrival of the Czech troops and that if such be the case he should be told that it constitutes a new allied problem that should be carefully examined by the Supreme War Council.

Paragraph 3. (not material).

Paragraph 4. In my opinion Lord Milner's despatch to the President may be based not only on the assumption that the Czechs will not arrive but also that no other troops but Americans will be available for the expedition. If this be so, the question of the ultimate force we may have to despatch to Murmansk must be carefully studied as well as the tonnage that will be involved because we may be committing ourselves to a more serious enterprise than appears at first sight. The American section has always assumed that under the plans of Joint Note 31 the one or possibly two American battalions would be Marines going in Navy tonnage. This would avoid diversion of any troops from France.

Paragraph 5. Finally I recommend that action along the line indicated in interview with General Foch.

(signed) Bliss."

Please treat text of above cable as confidential for your information only. I send it in full so that you may know what has been reported here.

The President's answer to Lord Milner's request is that the problem now presented of occupying Murmansk by American and Allied troops without the assistance of Czecho-Slovak troops is new and that it must be considered by the Council at Versailles. The President holds the view that requests for military assistance should be based upon recommendation of the Versailles Council and General Foch.

Whenever there is such a recommendation I think he will give effect to it immediately.

The result of General Bliss's cablegram is to produce the impression that something different from the plan originally agreed upon is now proposed which will mean increased demands upon U. S. military effort and which has not been considered by all the parties interested. The proposal means the sending of about 5,000 men from U. S. which is more apparently than originally intended according to U. S. reports from Versailles.

T telegram (Reading Papers, FO 800/223, PRO).
¹ That is, A. J. Balfour to Lord Reading, June 11, 1918, and Lord Reading to A. J. Balfour, June 16, 1918.
² See NDB to T. H. Bliss, June 15, 1918.

From Robert Lansing, with Enclosure

My dear Mr. President: Washington June 23, 1918.

I received yesterday from the British Embassy the enclosed paraphrase of a telegram from Lockhart at Moscow.

The situation of the Czecho-Slovak forces in western Siberia seems to me to create a new condition which should receive careful consideration. Prof. Masaryk assured me that these rebels against Austria-Hungary, collected from the Russian prison camps and from deserters, would not fight against the Russians but only sought to pass via Vladivostok to the western front.

Now it appears that their efforts to reach Vladivostok being opposed by the Bolsheviks they are fighting the Red Guards along the Siberian line with more or less success. As these troops are most loyal to our cause and have been most unjustly treated by the various Soviets ought we not to consider whether something cannot be done to support them?

There are, it seems, between 10,000 and 15,000 at Vladivostok and some 40,000 to 60,000 in western Siberia. In the latter territory Omsk and Tomsk are reported to be in their hands. Is it not possible that in this body of capable and loyal troops may be found a neucleus [nucleus] for military occupation of the Siberian railway?

I would like to confer with you on the subject after cabinet-meeting Tuesday if you find it convenient.

Faithfully yours,   Robert Lansing

TLS (SDR, RG 59, 861.00/2164½, DNA).

ENCLOSURE

Sent to my house
June 22/18 RL

PARAPHRASE OF A TELEGRAM FROM MR. LOCK-
HART, MOSCOW, TO THE FOREIGN OFFICE.

From numerous sources which I regard as reliable reports of a very disquieting nature have reached me with regard to the plans of the Germans for executing in Moscow a coup d'état similar to that in the Ukraine.

It is of course very difficult to estimate reports of this sort because the Germans make one statement to the reactionaries and another to the Bolshevists. But it is evident that the reactionaries have received vague promises from the Germans, and it would also seem from the very strong language used by Mirbach in his last note[1] that Germany desires to bring over the middle class element to her own side.

It is also clear that the Germans are conducting a strong prop-
aganda campaign among the various organizations of officers at
Moscow and are dispersing large sums of money for this purpose.
It is further the case that the number of people supporting the
Allies is daily decreasing owing to our refusal to spend money for
the purposes of a counter revolution or to take any decisive action.

I also hear from various directions that the Germans are endeavouring by means of bribery to bring over the Lettish regiments on
which the Bolshevists mainly depend, and these attempts are said
to have been to some degree successful.

It seems to me particularly clear, firstly, that there is a rapid
decrease of the Bolshevist power and, secondly, that there is now
immiment danger of a counter revolution on pro-German lines.

In this situation we shall clearly be compelled to intervene sooner
or later either willingly or unwillingly. It will surely be realized that
we shall be placed at a serious disadvantage if our intervention is
carried out after a counter revolution of a pro-German character,
and that we have much better excuse or reason for intervention at
the present moment, while Russia is in a condition of anarchy and
while the greater part of the Russian people is demanding intervention of whatever kind it may be.

I know of no further argument which I can use, but I must again
point out that if we leave the Czechs to their fate and if we fail to
intervene now we shall suffer a blow to our prestige in Russia from
which it will take years for us to recover.

BRITISH EMBASSY
WASHINGTON.
June 20th, 1918.

T MS (SDR, RG 59, 861.00/2164½, DNA).

¹ This may refer to Mirbach's note of June 6, which was printed in the official Soviet
gazette of June 8, 1918. This note referred to "continued unfounded complaints" by
Russian authorities about illegal German activities in Russia. Mirbach countered by
accusing the Russians of issuing false reports which were "pure inventions having
propaganda purpose." German troops, he added, had the right to be protected against
such reproaches, and he found the behavior of the Russian government "all the more
striking" since nothing was known of "similar conduct toward the Allied powers or with
regard to the violation of international law through the presence of Allied troops on
Arctic coast." Mirbach's note was quoted and summarized in D. C. Poole, Jr., to RL,
June 8, 1918, printed in FR 1918, Russia, I, 555-56.

Mirbach was assassinated in Moscow on July 6. One week previously, he had written in a
private letter to Kühlmann as follows: "After two months' careful observation, I can now no
longer give Bolshevism a favourable diagnosis. We are unquestionably standing by the bedside
of a dangerously ill man, who might show apparent improvement from time to time, but who
is lost in the long run." To fill an expected vacuum, Mirbach wrote, Germany should look to
a "nucleus . . . composed of moderates from the right wing, Octobrists and Kadets (these
reaching as far to the left as possible), especially as such a combination would ensure that
we had a large percentage of the influential men of the industrial and banking worlds serving
our essential economic interests." Mirbach did not count on much help from the Monarchists
but thought that there were some possibilities among the Siberians. W. v. Mirbach to R. v.
Kühlmann, June 25, 1918, Z. A. B. Zeman, ed., Germany and the Revolution in Russia,
1915-1918: Documents from the Archives of the German Foreign Ministry (London,
1958), pp. 137-39.

From Edward Mandell House

Dear Governor: Magnolia, Mass. June 23, 1918.

In the event you think well to address Congress on the Russian situation I would suggest that you also state the number of men we have in France.

I notice that the Germans are saying it will be 1920 before we can have as many as a million men there. We already have them and the German people should know it. I was under the impression, and Reading confirmed it, that we have sent men across the Atlantic more rapidly than the English have ever sent them across the Channel, and the shipping facilities of the Allies are increasing so rapidly that we can soon do even better.

England, France and Italy need now constant stimulation and no one can do it as well as you. If their morale can be kept up until Autumn, in my opinion, our fight against Germany will be largely won. I believe Austria is already at the breaking point, and I also believe the German people will take the supreme power from the military extremists this Autumn if they do not have a decisive victory on the Western front.

I hope you will have this message given as wide and accurate publicity as your former ones, so that not only the Allies will be stimulated but the nearby neutrals be influenced and in turn influence the Central Powers.

Affectionately yours,   E. M. House

TLS (WP, DLC).

From Helen Hamilton Gardener

My dear Mr. President: Washington, D. C. 23, June, 1918

On Thursday, June 27th will come the final test of whether women are to begin all over again the long, sickening contest for their right to be counted as units and not ciphers in the problems of democracy.

Tomorrow—Monday—a number of senators led by Senator Shafroth are coming to you for a final word of direction and inspiration on this subject.

They may touch largely on the political or party side of the matter, but may I not ask you to give out to and through them, in your own unapproachable method and form some points along the enclosed lines?

A "war measure" blast from you is, I believe, our one best hope. My good friend and yours, Senator John Sharp Williams, told me

the other day that he "would back the President in all war measures," but felt that he must vote against us at this time to protect
Mississippi because of the colored race.

Perhaps he might be induced to accept this as a war measure
(by you) *or* refrain from voting with the explanation that because
he fears it would be bad for his state, he can't vote for the measure,
but that because of its war and world democratic significance to
the nations in this struggle, he will not vote against it.

It seems to me he might do that if you can make him see that
it has such significance in world politics now.

He loves and admires you very much, and he is too fine and
honorable a man to be easily let go wrong on this great and fundamental principle at this critical time in world determination.

I hope that you can save him from himself.

I hope, too, that I shall not have to trouble you again on this
topic, because we hope to "go over the top" on Thursday—but the
poll is dangerously weak yet, and this is "a cry from Macedonia."!

I have the honor to remain,

Yours sincerely,   Helen H. Gardener

TLS (WP, DLC).

Tasker Howard Bliss to Peyton Conway March

Versailles, June 23d [1918].

URGENT Number 137 Confidential.

FOR THE CHIEF OF STAFF:

Paragraph 1. In further reference your 61 from Secretary of War
subject Murmansk and Archangel and my number 135 same subject the following is submitted:

Paragraph 2. Joint Note 31 expresses opinion of military representatives that if assistance can be obtained from Czech units now
in Russia military efforts to be made by allies for retention of Murmansk and Archangel can be limited to four or six allied battalions.
A study prepared by French section Supreme War Council in connection with Joint Note 31 expressed view that Czech forces to be
retained at Arctic port for this purpose should comprise 15 infantry
battalions. These battalions together with six battalions to be furnished by allied and contingents now at Murmansk would afford
combatant force of approximately 25,000 men. It is probable that
additional troops for non-combatant services would swell total to
about 35,000 men.

Paragraph 3. The following are estimates of tonnage required for
maintenance of this force under alternative assumption indicated.

Subparagraph A. Assuming that supplies to be despatched will average 30 pounds per man per day, of which ten will originate in England and 20 in the United States; and that replacements, estimated at 2,500 monthly will be obtained from Czech or other allied sympathizers in Vladivostok; maintenance of force will involve constant employment of about 77,000 dead weight tons of shipping.

Subparagraph B. If ports be isolated by enemy's force so that all replacements must come from United States, amount of tonnage for maintenance will be increased to total of about 109,000 dead weight tons.

Subparagraph C. If no assistance be obtained from Czechs or Russians and the entire force be provided by the United States, the dispatch of that force would involve the employment for about two months approximated 175,000 gross tons of shipping. Tonnage required for maintenance would be the same as in subparagraph B.

Paragraph 4. It is now reported that German forces in Finland equivalent to two divisions and that three Finnish divisions of 27,000 each are being organized under German supervision. In that event enemy will have a force of about 100,000 men to oppose to allied intervention at Arctic ports and allied force will have to be increased to from two to three times that stated in paragraph 2, requiring a correspondingly increased amount of ocean tonnage for maintenance. Capacity of Murmansk railroad 200 wagons per day is probably sufficient for supply of enemy's force of about 150,000 men while capacity of Archangel railroad is four times that of Murmansk railroad.

Paragraph 5. Projected allied occupation Murmansk and Archangel is intended to serve double purpose of preventing use of those ports, more particularly Murmansk, as enemy's submarine base and of retaining only routes still open to allies for access to central Russia. It is assumed that retention of these ports would afford latter bases *in the interest of* military operations on eastern front. Present project for allied intervention is based on the assumption that bulk of troops will be drawn from elements in Russia still friendly to allied cause. If that assumption be not realized it would appear unwise to attempt occupation of these ports on a scale that would offer reasonable hope of their retention in the face of determined enemy opposition. This belief based upon following:

Subparagraph A. Enemy can employ troops unfit for use in both decisive theatres of war to contain approximately equal number allied troops suitable for and needed on Western Front.

Subparagraph B. Because of marked difference in communications conduct of such campaign would involve a considerable greater expenditure of military effort on the part of allies than upon the part of enemy and would involve draft upon common military resources of allies for troops and tonnage that should not be diverted from decisive theatre of war.

Subparagraph C. In view of German domination of Finland allied advance from these ports to districts of any allied political importance would be wholly impracticable unless supported in major part by Russian element.

Paragraph 6. In my opinion port of Murmansk and Archangel can not be retained by allies without an unwise expenditure of military effort unless major part of forces required for the purpose be drawn from Czech units now in Russia or from Russian sources; and further, that until definite assurance is had that such assistance will be obtained the allied forces maintained at those ports should be sufficient only for defense against small enemy operations or in the event of major enemy operations to insure removal or destruction of stores and destruction in as far as practicable of port facilities that would be of service to enemy in establishment of submarine bases.

Paragraph 7. All of foregoing emphasizes statement in my 135 June 18th that before entering on a new and vague plan calling for large increase in original proposed American forces, that plans must be carefully studied and a common agreement of the allies reached. A suggestion to this effect by Washington government will probably be sufficient.   Bliss

TC telegram (WDR, RG 407, World War I Cablegrams, DNA).

To Newton Diehl Baker

My dear Baker: [The White House] 24 June, 1918

This man behaved after his abominable crime in so sodden a way that I cannot help drawing the conclusion that he was not fully aware of the heinousness of what he had done, in short, that he was in some real sense abnormal, and that impression has led me to doubt the justice of subjecting him to capital punishment. Would you be kind enough to look the case over and tell me whether you share that impression and whether you do or not think, as I am inclined to think, that a life sentence could be substituted?[1]

Cordially and faithfully yours,   Woodrow Wilson

TLS (Letterpress Books, WP, DLC).
[1] Baker never replied in writing to this letter.

To Helen Hamilton Gardener

My dear Mrs. Gardener: [The White House] 24 June, 1918

I have your letter of yesterday but I am very much afraid that a statement such as you suggest would not be wise. I mean that it would not accomplish the object in view. I think that I have said so much that there are indications that some of the Senators might become irritated if I said more, and I have done a good many things privately which are not known, adding thereby to the impression on the part of some of the Senators at any rate that I am bringing unusual and, perhaps in their minds unwarranted pressure to bear.

In haste

Cordially and sincerely yours,   Woodrow Wilson

TLS (Letterpress Books, WP, DLC).

To Ollie Murray James

My dear Senator: [The White House] 24 June, 1918

Do you think you could stretch a point and give up your pair against the suffrage amendment to meet a situation which is more than national? The action of the Senate in the matter of suffrage is, I can assure you from abundant evidence in my hands, of international importance, and critical international importance. It would be a matter of very serious embarrassment to the party not only, but to the country and to our influence in the final democratic settlement of the present struggle if the vote should go against the amendment.

If you could see your way clear to cancel the pair, I believe the amendment would pass, and I am wondering if you would yield to my judgment in this matter and make that indirect contribution.

I was rejoiced to hear from Grayson that you were very much better. It warms my heart to think of seeing you "on deck" again.[1]

Cordially and faithfully yours,   Woodrow Wilson

TLS (Letterpress Books, WP, DLC).
[1] James was in the Johns Hopkins University Hospital.

To Samuel Gompers

My dear Mr. Gompers: The White House 24 June, 1918

I received through your letter of the twenty-first[1] the very impressive resolutions of the American Federation of Labor with regard to the case of Thomas J. Mooney. I need not tell you how deep and sincere my personal interest in that case is.

The resolutions refer to the "exercise of such power" as may be vested in me. Unhappily, in cases of this sort there is absolutely no power vested in me.

I believe that the Governor of California is himself very much impressed with the significance of this case and that he is awaiting the decision of the courts before making up his final decision in the matter. I hope with all my heart that it will be a decision for clemency.

Cordially and sincerely yours,   Woodrow Wilson

TLS (photostat in RSB Coll., DLC).
[1] S. Gompers to WW, June 21, 1918, TLS (WP, DLC).

To Thomas Watt Gregory

[The White House]

My dear Mr. Attorney General: 24 June, 1918

I have had a good many people speak to me recently about the fact of the (very just) conviction of Rose Pastor Stokes and at the same time the apparent injustice of convicting her when the editor[1] of the Kansas City Star seems to be, to say the least, a direct participant in her offense. Don't you think that there is some way in which we could bring this editor to book?

Cordially and faithfully yours,   Woodrow Wilson

TLS (Letterpress Books, WP, DLC).
[1] Ralph Emerson Stout.

From Bernard Mannes Baruch

My dear Mr. President: Washington June 24, 1918.

This is to remind you of the Power Bill, concerning which Mr. Sherley spoke to you, and you told him you would communicate with me. May I suggest that if anything is to be done it should be done now, as the next Congress would be too late. If you remember, I took this matter up through Mr. Martin and Mr. Kitchin sometime ago. In my opinion, if the suggestion of Mr. Sherley for a conference is carried out I believe we can pass the bill, which I think is urgent and necessary to carry out our war program.

Very truly yours,   Bernard M Baruch

TLS (WP, DLC).

From Robert Lansing, with Enclosure

My dear Mr. President: Washington June 24, 1918.

I hope you can find time to read this memorandum by Mr. Konovaloff before I see you tomorrow in regard to the Siberian situation. It is, to my mind, well worth careful consideration.

                    Faithfully yours,   Robert Lansing.

TLS (SDR, RG 59, 861.00/2214½A, DNA).

                    E N C L O S U R E

                              Handed me by Konovaloff,
                              Vice Premier of Kerensky Govt.
                                        June 24/18 RL

The present situation in Russia represents but a certain phase in the general progress of the revolution. Under normal conditions, if unobstructed, this process after certain fluctuations would finally settle Russia in certain forms of social existence which would exemplify the liberty loving aspirations of the people and would correspond to the real constituency of Russia's economic powers. However, at present Russia is performing her transformation under the tightening grip of German domination. On the other hand having entered the revolution at a moment when after three years of war the country was on the verge of economical exhaustion, Russia through further disorganization is approaching a degree of disintegration where disappears the very possibility of constructive social activity. The consequence of these factors is, that under present circumstances, if abandoned to herself, Russia will unavoidably return to reaction which under actual conditions means German Caesarism.

The extermination of intellectual elements, the destruction of industries, followed by an exodus from the cities, is bringing Russia back to a state of an elementary agricultural Peasant country, to be ruled by an autocrat restituted by German complacency, pledged to his benefactor and bound by different agreements of an economical, political and military character. A German industrial aristocracy and the eastern vassal supplying its virtual master with all the necessary food, raw products and contributing an unlimited peasant military force.

It is unnecessary to obviate the threat of such an issue. These prospectives are not only incompatible with the final goal of the democratic Alliance, but do as well represent an immediate military danger of the gravest import. General political strategy, therefore, imperatively demands that such aspirations be most energetically frustrated unless the Allied cause be fatally molested. This cannot be achieved unless through a national consolidation of the Russian democracy. The consolidation of Russia on the lines of a politically united and economically independent national democracy not only would represent the most effective menace to German penetration, but in the very process of its realization will carry the necessity of counteracting German effort while defending its own independence and integrity. While at this moment one is unable to foresee the concrete forms and the scope of future anti-German resistance, one should, however, conceive that effective military action, if any, is possible solely as a result of a similar process of national reconstitution.

Under present circumstances, such an achievement is conceivable only in result of an active Allied policy in Russia, as a consequence of active assistance to Russia of an economic and military character.

Russia has issued manifold appeals for such assistance. Political parties, cooperative workers and different organizations in Russia and abroad, have voiced the call for Allied action. If the desire of the people in Russia could not receive a more tangible expression it is only because the present conditions within the country do not allow for any assertion of free will and concentrated action. There is no doubt that action on the part of the Allies will be welcomed by the great majority of the Russian population. It is necessary only that the aims and procedures should assume proper forms and purposes.

The aims of Allied assistance should be expressed as an endeavor: (A) To protect the Russian people from German aggression and seizure and, (B) To enable them to obtain an unhampered and unembarrassed opportunity for the independent determination of their own political development and national policy and for the constituting of institutions of their own choosing—aims which have been so fully expressed by the President of the United States in clause VI of his address to Congress on January 8, 1918. A proper Inter-Allied statement should remove any possible doubts as to violation of Russian territorial integrity.

Allied action in Russia should be unpartisan in essential. The aims of the expedition should broadly unite all who earnestly strive for a consolidation of a democratic State and are sincerely anti-German in their aspirations and activities.

Allied action should be performed by an Inter-Allied Commission with a Civil Commissioner at its head, which should start its activities in the eastern end of Siberia and should be supported by an Inter-Allied military contingent, sufficient to impose authority and counterfeat any possible attack by German elements, outlaws or deliberate anarachists. In so far as politics, Allied action should enable the people to create on broad democratic principles stable and efficient organs of local government, municipal and rural. The Allies should not interfere with the institution of such governments. The military force should frustrate only any violence or interference contrary to the free expressions of the people's will. It should further render assistance to the newly constituted authorities in suppressing crime and lawlessness.

The local governmental units will naturally present the basis of the reconstitution of Russia, provincial and later national government being formed in the natural process of constructive synthesis. Local Legislatures and executives will present the lawful constituencies with which the Inter-Allied Commission will enter into regularized relations and in particular shall cooperate economical reconstruction. A necessary period of relief should be followed by systematic activity in order to restitute normal production, distribution and exchange. It should be noted on this occasion that economical assistance can be effectively performed only if a certain stability of social conditions is previously obtained. Economic assistance otherwise will not only be resultless but can eventually evoke disappointment through inadequacy of possible achievement.

The Inter-Allied Commission backed with its armed force will serve a[s] a nucleus, a rallying point for all elements of Russia, who after suffering and experience, are eager to enter the constructive period of national consolidation, but under present conditions of violence are unable to initiate this process on their own behalf.

At the outset of the activities of the expedition the number of troops required will be relatively small, conditions may substantially change in measure as the movement will proceed westward and will approach and eventually emerge into European Russia.

The progress of national consolidation will naturally be met with anxiety by Germany and active endeavors on the part of the Teutons to oppose its success is to be anticipated. While an accumulation of Russian military force is naturally to be expected with the progress of the movement, it is nevertheless obvious that to frustrate successfully possible German opposition, it may require a more extensive usage of Allied military power. It is clear that at this stage of events with the eventual development of military operations, it is only Japanese forces which will be able to meet adequately the situation.

With reference to similar plan of Allied active assistance, certain objections are frequently raised: It is contended that a landing of an expeditionary force on Russian territory will be used by German and extremist propaganda in Russia as a proof of imperialistic attempts of the Allies and will enable Germany's agents to turn the Russian population heart and soul over to Germany. The reply is that the experience and sufferings of the last months have clearly shown to the Russian people the actual aims of German aspirations and have given them a clearer understanding of social and political realities. Ample evidence is given that such a process of national education has been performed to a great extent. One cannot further conceive why any Russian with unbiased opinion would prefer German slavery to the brotherly hand of Allied assistance bringing liberty and economic welfare. It is brought forward that the Bolsheviks being threatened in their power will turn to the Germans and join their efforts with those of the Teuton powers. As far as elements will prefer affiliation with German autocracy to the possibilities of honest democratic constructive work this will only elucidate the situation and dispose of pro-German activities concealed under democratic veil. The Bolsheviks in such occasion would not have a following.

It is further contended that an active Allied assistance to Russia followed by a consolidation of a national democracy will call immediate active counteraction on the part of Germany which, infracting the Brest-Litovsk treaty, will militarily invade Russia. The Brest-Litovsk Peace has never been recognized and least of all this "scrap of paper" would never prevent Germany from military or other movements in Russia which she may feel desirable to bring to effect. Moreso, it will not be the pact of Brest-Litovsk which will determine the future destinies of Russia, but the ultimate results of the world's war. It is the extent of Allied victory which will determine the future existences of nations and which is to reestablish the rights and repair the wrongs inflicted by Germany. Russia's hope, therefore, lies with the issues of the world's war and Russia's vital interests imperatively demand concentrated efforts to the winning of the war. From this point of view that or other dislocation of German troops within Russia is a secondary point, the main object from the strategical point of view being to detract as much forces as possible from the Western front and create in the East the necessity for Germany of a military campaign with all the burdens of organization, transportation and administration. The more troops and the sooner will be withdrawn from the Western front the better. To this should be added that a campaign in Russia would greatly facilitate the Allied governments in combatting the deteriorating influence of a peace offensive which one can expect will be brought forward by Germany with proposals of a liberal peace on the West at the expense of Russia.

T MS (SDR, RG 59, 861.00/2214½A, DNA).

From Josephus Daniels, with Enclosure

Dear Mr. President: Washington. June 24, 1918.

On Friday Mr. W. T. Ellis, of Penna,[1] a capable and conscientious gentlemen I have known many years, was in the Department. He had recently returned from Russia and I asked him what he thought of the Russian situation and what our attitude ought to be. His knowledge seemed to be such that I asked him to make a memorandum. He did so and am enclosing it, feeling sure you would like to read it.

If you have not seen to-day's New York Herald, may I suggest that Herman Bernstein's letter[2] would interest you?

Sincerely,   Josephus Daniels

ALS (WP, DLC).
[1] William Thomas Ellis, journalist and war correspondent, who had spent some six months in Russia in 1917 and had been there at the time of the November Revolution.
[2] Herman Bernstein, "The Greatest Crime of History; Iron Hun Rule Has Made Russia a Hell Beyond Self-Redemption," New York Herald, June 24, 1918. As the headline implies, Bernstein followed the interpretation, familiar by that time, that the Bolsheviks in general, and Lenin and Trotsky in particular, had betrayed Russia and allowed her to become a German puppet state by ratifying the Treaty of Brest-Litovsk. He held the Bolsheviks and their German overlords solely responsible for the political, economic, and social chaos then afflicting Russia.

E N C L O S U R E

William Thomas Ellis to Josephus Daniels

My dear Mr. Secretary: Washington, D. C., June 21, 1918.

Pursuant to your request, I am glad to submit to you a memorandum on what I think our course should be in Russia. As you suggest, my background is that of personal travel over more than 15,000 miles of Russia within the past year. I have intimate personal experience of the new mood in that sadly perturbed land, so I shall follow your suggestion that I write in terms of what America ought to do in the present situation.

First and obviously, we ought to recognize clearly, as we are doing, that Russia may become Germany's greatest asset. There is a real possibility that she may raise a Russian army to do her will in the West; for the Russian peasant is as clay in the hard hands of the German drill-master. How completely she can dominate is shown by her experience in Riga. Of course, there is also the ominous likelihood of all the vast material resources of Russia being utilized by the Germans.

Above all, we must recognize the existence of one dominant state of mind in Russia. That is, the peasantry and the working men are obsessed by the spirit of the revolution. Ninety per cent. of the people of Russia care more for the revolution than they do for Russia. The passion for freedom—a fire which was lighted by America's torch—burns brightly in the breast of the people, even during these dark and bewildered days. I have seen soldiers who were deserting from the front fight heroically when they thought the revolution was in danger. The master word of the bolsheviks is "counter revolution." Whenever they can persuade the people that the revolution is menaced, and that there is danger of a return to anything like the old order, then they may be sure of the support of the masses. It is a tragic imitation of liberty that these people of the darkened mind now enjoy, but they would not relinquish even this for anything which smacks of the old regime.

So whatever is done in or for Russia must reckon with the dominance of the revolutionary sentiment, strongly tinged with bolshevikism. There is no shadow of a government in Russia except that of the soviets. No party or group or class would presume to say that it is the real Russia government or nation as opposed to the bolsheviks. Were the foreign powers to ally themselves with the theoretically right but thoroughly discredited Cadet Party, or with the representatives of business and autocracy, they would at once alienate the bulk of the Russian population. Whatever dealings we may have with Russia must be, for the present, with the soviets. (Needless to say, I am not a supporter of the bolshevik regime, and thoroughly disapprove of their methods and of most of their principles. I consider bolshevikism a real and great menace to the world.)

The principal asset of the Allies in Russia to-day is the good will of the Russians toward America. Only those who have passed through the mobs and riots and disorganization of Russia, by means of the magic word "Americansky," can understand how general and how deep is the friendship of all classes of Russians for the people of the United States. They know us better than we suppose, and they trust us entirely. We are their brother democracy. To take any action that would forfeit this friendship would not only be recreancy to a trust, but it would also be to shut ourselves off entirely from the possibility of fulfilling our unique mission to this sorely distressed nation—for, after the tribulations of many years, there will again be a great Russia.

What is the bearing of all this upon the proposed military intervention in Russia? We owe it to the Russians and to ourselves to interpose all possible barriers against German advance, especially in Siberia. At the best, there are serious physical obstacles to be overcome by such an expedition. If we can secure an invitation from the Siberian Soviet to enter Russia to help save the country from the Germans, we should do so up to the utmost limit of our power. Three months ago, I am persuaded, it would have been easily possible to get such an invitation. These soviets are rather easily handled. Let us remember how immature and how used to subordination are the men who are now ruling in Russia. They are really but children of a larger growth, unreasoningly dominated by a few distorted ideals. Even yet it should be possible to secure such an invitation from the Siberian Soviet. It is unlikely that anything could be done with the Central Council of Soviets which assumes to govern the nation.

This invitation can be secured only by America. Men of a sensitive social spirit, keen to understand the Russian people, men like Raymond Robins and A. C. Hart[1] (in charge of the Prison Work of the Y.M.C.A.) could be entrusted with this delicate task of sitting down with the Siberian soviet and winning its confidence to the extent of securing an invitation for an allied relief force.

Such special emissaries as I have suggested should be accompanied by wise propagandists and by relief workers and economic and administrative helpers. In a friendly way, America should go in with evidences of her desire to help Russia, and then secure from Russia the request for the larger means of staying the advance of the Germans. No matter what military steps are taken, they should be accompanied by a great ministry of helpfulness to the Russian people.

The underlying religious spirit of the Russian people may also be utilized to save the nation from the twin perils of Prussianism and Bolshevikism.

To enter Russia in military force, without the invita[tion] or consent of the Russian soviets, would be *invasion*, and practically on all fours with Germany's invasion of Belgium. It would give the bolsheviks the best of excuses for reasserting their leadership, and it would surely drive the people into the hands of Germany. Under such conditions, an allied force would have to fight Russians before it could fight Germans,—and that is unthinkable to anybody who takes the American viewpoint.

May I add that the clamor which is being raised by exiled Russians who, for whatsoever reason, failed to stay in their own land to protect and serve her, is given undue weight in the press of

America? There is much to be said about the character and state of mind of these exiles, but it is enough to remark that apparently their zeal for the reclamation of Russia is not entirely distinct from their desire for a return of their former estates and privileges.

I think I have written enough, Mr. Secretary, in this hastily dictated memorandum, to fulfill your request. I am so sensible of the gravity of the Russian situation that there is no work of my own that I would not set aside in order to come to Washington at any time to give to the Government any shred of information or judgment that I may possess. I feel deeply that we must serve and save Russia; but with equal confidence I feel that we dare not *invade* Russia with a military force and against her will.

It is implied in what I have said in the foregoing that should the way be opened for a military expedition to co-operate with the Russian people against the Germans, it should be not exclusively a Japanese enterprise, but that there should be at least a represen-tation of America and our other allies upon it.

With sincere esteem, I remain as ever,

Faithfully yours,   Wm. T. Ellis

TLS (WP, DLC).
  [1] Archibald Clinton Harte, International General Secretary for War Prisoners' Aid of the Y.M.C.A.

From Morris Sheppard

My dear Mr. President: [Washington] June 24, 1918.

I send you herewith copy of the bill S. 4036 to insure the secrecy of military dispatches, information, and correspondence.[1]

I introduced the bill and was chairman of the sub-committee of the Committee on Military Affairs which considered the bill. Rep-resentatives of the War and Navy Departments appeared before the sub-committee and favored the enactment of the bill, saying that it might be necessary at any time that such authority should be invoked, and that therefore it ought to exist. I refer to the authority given you by the bill for military reasons, to take over marine cables, telephone or telegraph systems, etc.

I shall present the bill to the full committee soon, and would be glad to have a letter from you advocating it, if you think the measure is warranted by the situation.

With highest regards,   I am Morris Sheppard

TLS (WP, DLC).
  [1] The enclosure was returned. Since no action was taken on the bill after its intro-duction on March 8, there is no text of it in *Congressional Record* or among the pub-lications of the Sixty-fifth Congress. However, Sheppard describes the measure.

From Samuel Reading Bertron

My dear Mr. President: New York June 24, 1918.

The time for decisive action in Russia I think has arrived. The demand for it is of the same character and is as wide-spread as it was for war in April, 1917. The feeling is shown through the newspapers all over the Country, by public speech and private conversation. It is the one topic. Your Red Cross speech crystallized thought in this direction.

Our Allies, who admit that their action heretofore in many important matters has been too late, seem to be agreed on the necessity of immediate and urgent action.

Our friend M. Bergson is here, representing France in this connection and indicates complete agreement between our Allies along the lines of the plan I discussed with you when I last had the honor of meeting you.[1] He is here for the purpose of laying this matter before you. We cannot afford to be too late in making this all important decision.

There confronts Russia either Bolshevism or Germanization. The masses want neither but unless we offer a means of national expression, the better people I am advised will turn to Germany as against the former, while the lower classes will become subservient to German domination, even to the extent of being forced into the German army. This is the belief of many of the best posted on Russia. Many Russians of the better class think our delay in action is due to sympathy with the Bolsheviki.

The time would seem opportune by developments in Russia as well. There will undoubtedly be opposition from Lenine's followers who are pro-German but all indications are that they are few in numbers and that the Soviets are gradually being joined by some of the better element. This would be greatly facilitated by an announcement of Allied action.

A Clarion Call from you will have a great effect in Russia and it will be exceedingly encouraging to the morale of our Allies and equally discouraging to our enemies. The prospect of opposition in Russia would also facilitate favorable developments in Austria. It will increase guer[r]illa warfare in Russia and necessitate a movement of German troops to the East rather than the West.

Through the Russian-American Chamber of Commerce I have ascertained that there are about $10,000,000 worth of supplies in this Country for Russian account, other than Government supplies and that there are about $4,000,000 worth of material in Russia ready for exchange. We could begin with material aid which will cement our relationships with the co-operative organizations throughout Russia, which touch at least 60,000,000 people, all of whom are anxious to do business with us. Our failure to do this will necessitate their trading with Germany.

A small business Commission, gathering all facts and figures with recommendations for you might save you an infinite amount of trouble, to which might be added representatives of the Red Cross, the Y.M.C.A. and the Food Administration.

Mr. Konovalov, former Vice President of the Duma, and Vice Premier under Kerensky, is here with the Russian Ambassador and could give you very valuable information if you could see him.

Please, Mr. President, forgive me for writing you again on this all important matter, but I am convinced that the time has come when we must move in order to save the great Russian Democracy, not only for itself but for the good of the World, and take such action as will lead to the re-establishment of the Eastern Front. This is the only path to permanent Peace and the privilege of making this, is by common wish of the world, properly delegated to you.

There are other phases of the International situation which are exceedingly important, but which I do not like to trust to paper, even though I shall send this letter to you by hand.

Please believe me,   Faithfully yours,   S R Bertron

TLS (WP, DLC).
  [1] The most recent meeting between Wilson and Bertron listed in the Executive Appointment Diary and the Head Usher's Diary had taken place on March 20.

From Jean Jules Jusserand

Dear Mr. President,   Washington June 24, 1918

I am asked by Premier Clemenceau[1] to submit to you the following statement from Gnl. Foch:

"I learn from a source leaving no room for doubt, that the Germans have recalled from Russia during the last weeks, a certain number of divisions. This seems to be a decisive military argument in favor of an intervention by the Allies, since those divisions are destined for the Western front."

I take the liberty of recommending to your kind consideration the views thus expressed by the commander in chief, and I beg you to believe me, dear Mr. President

Very sincerely and respectfully yours   Jusserand

ALS (WP, DLC).
  [1] In G. Clemenceau to J. J. Jusserand, No. 1317, June 23, 1918, T telegram (Série E, Japon, Intervention en Sibérie, E 6212/18-20, FMD-Ar).

A Translation of a Telegram from Georges Clemenceau to Jean Jules Jusserand

Paris, June 24, 1918

No. 1322. Please transmit the following telegram to President Wilson on behalf of the President of the Council.

To the decisive opinion which has been submitted to you by General Foch, I take the liberty of adding a necessary remark: it is only until the end of October that the temperature will permit the organization of an expedition in Siberia. If we do not wish to permit the slaughter of the Czechs, then we have no more than three months.   G. Clemenceau.

T telegram (Série E, Japon, Intervention en Sibérie, E 6212/18-20, FMD-Ar).

From Robert Russa Moton

Tuskegee Institute, Ala.

Dear Mr. President: June 24, 1918

May I thank you for your very kind letter of the 18th; and permit me to make just this one more suggestion regarding the matter on which I wrote you on June 15th. I might say I made this suggestion to Secretary Baker.

The suggestion was that you might think it wise to call together the Governors of the states in which mobbings and lynchings have occurred. That will take in three or four Northern states as well as certain Southern states. Or, you might think it wise to have Governors from more states, and put the situation to them in your own way, especially as a war measure. Whatever action taken thereafter, local authorities would feel at least their chief executives would have been advised with by yourself. Then, too, I am sure these Governors would appreciate the compliment of being invited by you for such a conference.

Please forgive me for again taking your time. If I seem overanxious, it is solely for the good of my country by serving as best I may its Chief Executive.

I beg to remain,   Yours very respectfully,   R. R. Moton

TLS (WP, DLC).

Robert Lansing to Elbridge Gerry Greene[1]

[Washington] June 24, 1918.

Your June 5, 6 p.m., June 11, 2 p.m., 16, 6 p.m., 21, 5 p.m., 23, 8 p.m.[2]

You are instructed immediately to inform the Government of Panama that the Government of the United States has given very careful consideration to the postponement of the elections which was done by issuance of decree of June 21 by acting President; that result of this consideration has led to the following conclusion: In the opinion of the Government of the United States, the issuance of the above mentioned decree postponing the said elections is of doubtful effect and probably a direct violation of the provisions of the constitution of Panama, and therefore cannot be looked upon with favor by the Government of the United States. In the event that the Government of Panama does not withdraw the above mentioned decree, the Government of the United States will be on account of these unconstitutional or questionable practices constrained to give very careful consideration to the advisability of according recognition to any President of Panama assuming office as a result of elections, postponed under decree of June 21. You will furthermore inform the Government of Panama that the Government of the United States is not impressed with the reasons given for the issuance of this decree, as it is ready at any time to fulfill its obligation as the guarantor of the independence of Panama and also to carry out the provisions of Article 7 of the Convention of 1903.[3] The Government of the United States feels constrained to advise the Government of Panama to withdraw this decree.

CONFIDENTIALLY: You are instructed to show this telegram to the American Military Authorities and the Governor of the Canal Zone[4] and discuss with them the advisability of making this telegram public. The Department desires you to use your discretion as to publicity.

In view of the fact that your June 21, 5 p.m. states that decree of President Urriola gives reasons for its promulgation quote to avoid possible riots end quote, and in view of notorious unsatisfactory police conditions existing in Colon and Panama the Department is seriously considering whether it may not be necessary immediately to invoke Article 7 of the Convention and take over policing of cities as provided in such Article.[5]

CC telegram (WP, DLC).
[1] Chargé d'Affaires of the American legation in Panama.
[2] E. G. Greene to RL, June 5, 11, 16, 21, and 23, 1918, T telegrams (SDR, RG 59, 819.002/37, 819.00/652, 819.00/653, 819.00/657, 819.00/661, DNA). Greene reported on events following the death of Ramón M. Valdés, the President of Panama, on June

3. The point of the telegrams of June 5, 11, and 16 was that the Acting President, Ciro Luis Urriola, a partisan of former President Belisario Porras, intended to postpone the municipal elections and the elections to the National Assembly, scheduled for June 30 and July 7 respectively, in order to forestall a victory of the anti-Porrista faction. The new National Assembly would choose a new President later in the year. On June 21, Greene reported that Urriola had indeed issued a decree postponing the elections indefinitely. Alleging that this action represented a coup d'état and the establishment of a virtual dictatorship by the Porras group, Greene repeatedly urged the State Department to instruct him to make the statement which Lansing in fact did embody in the above telegram.

3 Under Article VII of the Hay-Bunau-Varilla Treaty of November 18, 1903, the United States had the right to intervene to maintain public order in the cities of Panama and Colón, if the Republic of Panama should, in the opinion of the United States Government, be unable to do so. For the text of this article and a discussion of its implementation on various occasions, including the present one, see Raymond Leslie Buell, "Panama and the United States," *Foreign Policy Reports*, VII (Jan. 20, 1932), 410-16 *passim*.

4 Col. Chester Harding, U.S.A., was Governor of the Panama Canal Zone.

5 The War Department on June 28 did in fact order Brig. Gen. Richard M. Blatchford, commander of the Department of Panama, to take over the policing of Colón and Panama City. The offending decree was quickly repealed, and the elections took place as scheduled on June 30 and July 7, with United States army officers acting as observers at the polls. *Ibid.*, p. 416, and *New York Times*, June 29, 30, and July 2 and 8, 1918. Porras won the election and was installed as President in October 1918.

Peyton Conway March to Tasker Howard Bliss

Washington, June 24, 1918.

Number 64, Confidential

Reference your 137, the British Ambassador has been informed that the president will not consider any project for the use of American troops emanating from a single nation, but that such recommendations must come from the Military Representatives at Versailles representing all the nations. It is understood that Lord Reading is cabling that decision to Lord Milner. March.   McCain.

TC telegram (WDR, RG 407, World War I Cablegrams, DNA).

Peyton Conway March to Newton Diehl Baker, with Enclosure

Washington. June 24, 1918.

MEMORANDUM for the Secretary of War:

In accordance with the President's letter of June 19, 1918,[1] I am enclosing herewith a memorandum upon the plan of campaign suggested in Siberia, with return of all papers in the case.

P. C. March

TS MS (WP, DLC).
1 See WW to NDB, June 19, 1918 (first letter of that date).

E N C L O S U R E

Washington. June 24, 1918.

MEMORANDUM.

The unsigned memorandum dated June 17, 1918,[1] which accompanied the letter of the President, has been carefully examined by me. Considered purely as a military proposition, it is neither practical nor practicable. The occupation of the Trans-Baikalian portion of Siberia by the force suggested would have no effect upon the actual conduct of the war. It would not divert a single German division from the western front to the old eastern front or to the present general line now occupied by the most advanced German forces in Russia.

To make a substantial diversion of German forces would require the occupation of the Trans-Siberian Railroad to Russia proper, and the maintenance of a force in Russian territory entirely beyond the possibility of the present resources of the United States to maintain; we have neither men nor shipping to divert from the western front. The portions of Russia which are of the greatest value to Germany lie in the Ukraine, and that is the portion toward which they are devoting most of their energies. The mineral wealth, the oil and the grain which Germany needs in her conduct of the war are found in the Ukraine.

The project of intervention in Russia which presents the greatest possibilities from the military standpoint is the expedition to Murmansk and Archangel recommended by the Inter-Allied War Council; and that too presents the greatest difficulty in arriving at any solution which will not be merely sentimental.

All responsible military opinion believes that the War will be won or lost on the western front, including Italy; and that any substantial diversion of troops from that one object is a serious military mistake. We are now utilizing all our available shipping to transport and supply our troops for the western front, and in addition, all we can borrow or obtain from the Allies and Neutrals. It is calculated that even the expedition to Murmansk would necessarily absorb over 100,000 gross tons of American shipping, provided we contemplated going in there with the force recently suggested by Lord Milner.

All such schemes are absolutely futile. I have not yet found a single military man who, when advocating expeditions to various other portions of the world, was asked the question "Would you divert troops from the western front to form such an expedition?" did not invariably reply that he would not divert a man from the

western front:—the most recent case of that kind being that of
General Berthelot, of the French Army.

The solution of the Russian question which involves giving Japan
a portion of Siberia as the price of intervention is wholly inadmissible from any American standpoint. No other nation but Japan is
in a position to intervene in Siberia. I served in Manchuria as
attaché with the Japanese army during the Russo-Japanese war,
and at that time formed a definite opinion as to the Russian character and attitude, which has been confirmed and strengthened by
the developments of the present war. Large numbers of prisoners
and Russian dead were seen by the attachés. Notebooks, letters,
scraps of paper containing messages home, which had not been
sent, were translated for me by European attachés who had served
at St. Petersburg; and great numbers of such writings were not
only against the war in which they were engaged, but clearly against
all war. I do not believe that any man, or men, or combination of
men representing the Allied Nations will ever be able to re-constitute Russia into a military machine. I am perfectly convinced, however, that if there is one influence in the world which would draw
Russia together and throw her into the arms of Germany, it would
be the advent of Japan in Russia. There is no doubt whatever in
my mind that as between Germany and Japan *as their master* they
would infinitely prefer Germany. The situation in Russia, while
superficially hopeless and impossible of solution, will in reality be
solved by our concentrating the entire energies of the nation on
putting such a number of men on the western front as will permit
us to drive through to Berlin, where the terms of peace which we
would dictate should include a just and satisfactory solution of the
internal troubles of Russia. Certainly none of the schemes looking
to the restoration of the Romanoffs, or a government of that country
without the consent of the governed, which I have heard advanced
by people in Europe, should be permitted for a moment.

Considering specifically the size of the expedition which is proposed in the unsigned memorandum: the forces enumerated would
be wholly inadequate for the expedition in question. General Semenoff's force has already been reported as having been defeated
by the Bolsheviks. The only part of the force that would be of any
value would be the Japanese troops said now to be in Korea and
the small Japanese force in Manchuria. "The 10,000 or 15,000
American, British, French and Italian troops" who, it is assumed,
would live off the country and get all their arms and ammunition
from Japan, would, in the ultimate analysis, be expected to be
largely furnished by America, as is now expected in the case of the
proposed Murmansk expedition. In this connection, it is to be noted

that while the supply of grain and cattle in Siberia was properly used in the Russo-Japanese war for the feeding of their own people, it is now proposed, without regard to the inhabitants of Siberia, to subsist this army of invasion on the food supplies which naturally would go to feeding the inhabitants themselves. This, to my mind, is practically out of the question, and no expedition could be launched in that territory without a regularly organized source of supply,— as is necessary for the subsistence of any well organized army anywhere. All this involves a diversion of much tonnage to the Far East, and there is no such tonnage to divert as far as the United States is concerned.

The whole matter comes down to a decision as to whether the Japanese should be given a free hand in Siberia. The Supreme War Council, when that proposition was presented to it, would not take action on it in the face of the attitude of the Government of the United States toward that problem. I am strongly of the opinion that the position of the Government in this matter is wholly correct.

P. C. March.

TS MS (WP, DLC).
¹ "Memorandum," June 17, 1918, T MS (WP, DLC). The first half of this memorandum considered the effect of Allied intervention, especially in Siberia, on the Russian people. The author concluded that the more conservative elements would rally around an Allied army and that it did not matter how the pro-Bolshevik groups felt about an intervention. The second half of the document discussed the military aspects of intervention in very general terms. The author was quite sanguine in his belief that most of Asiatic Russia could be seized and controlled by a force of 10,000 to 15,000 American and Allied troops, supplemented by the Czechs and by anti-Bolshevik Russian forces already operating in Siberia. The memorandum bore the address "Washington, D. C."

To Jean Jules Jusserand

Confidential.

My dear Mr. Ambassador: [The White House] 25 June, 1918

Thank you for your letter of yesterday quoting a statement from General Foch about intervention in Russia. I was very anxious to get a direct expression from General Foch about this perplexing matter. I am sorry that he does not explicitly say whether he thinks we would be justified in sending troops from this country to Russia if there were involved in doing so a subtraction of that number of men from those whom we could send to France. If he has expressed any opinion along these lines, I would be very much obliged to you if you would let me know of it.

Cordially and sincerely yours,   [Woodrow Wilson]

CCL (WP, DLC).
¹ Jusserand transmitted this message to Clemenceau and added: "Please put me in a position to answer this question, which is very important and which reveals a marked

disposition to act in the sense of our wishes." J. J. Jusserand to G. Clemenceau, Nos. 799-800, received June 26, 1918, T telegram (Série E, Japon, Intervention en Sibérie, E 6212/18-20, FMD-Ar).

In a telegram to Pichon, Jusserand added that Wilson's letter showed a desire, "very favorable to the rest of our views," to be given something more concrete than general recommendations of intervention and a regret that General Foch's declarations had not been accompanied by specific indications concerning the use of American troops in Siberia. "The President is more and more inclined to act," Jusserand concluded, "and we should take advantage of his state of mind." J. J. Jusserand to S. J. M. Pichon, [No. 796] June 26, 1918, T telegram, *ibid.* (Our translations.)

To Samuel Reading Bertron

My dear Mr. Bertron: [The White House] 25 June, 1918

Thank you for your letter of yesterday. You may be sure I have the Russian situation very much in mind and am constantly seeking a feasible line of action.

Cordially and sincerely yours,   Woodrow Wilson

TLS (Letterpress Books, WP, DLC).

From Thomas Watt Gregory

My dear Mr. President: Washington, D. C. [c. June 25, 1918]

I have your letter of June 24, 1918, calling attention to the apparent injustice of the conviction of Rose Pastor Stokes in the absence of any prosecution of the editor of the Kansas City Star, the paper which printed and published the letter upon which the charge against Mrs. Stokes was based. You ask whether there is some way in which this editor could be brought to book.

Upon the facts of the situation I believe you will agree with me that no action should be taken against the editor for the publication of Mrs. Stokes' letter. The facts may be summarized as follows:

On March 16th, Mrs. Stokes delivered an address before the Woman's Dining Club of Kansas City. This address produced considerable public discussion in and out of the newspapers. In the issue of March 18th, in addition to the discussion of the address, the Kansas City Star contained an alleged interview with Mrs. Stokes, headed "Mrs. Stokes for the Government and Anti-War at the Same Time," in which she is quoted as having expressed sentiments decidedly favorable to the prosecution of the war.

Mrs. Stokes felt that this interview did not correctly state her views, and she thereupon wrote the letter which formed the basis of the charge against her. This letter read as follows:

"To The Star: I see that it is, after all, necessary to send a statement for publication over my own signature, and I trust that you will give it space in your columns.

A headline in this evening's issue of The Star reads: 'Mrs. Stokes for Government and Against War at the Same Time.' I am not for the government. In the interview that follows I am quoted as having said 'I believe the government of the United States should have the unqualified support of every citizen in its war aims.'

I made no such statement, and I believe no such thing. No government which is for the profiteers can also be for the people, and I am for the people, while the government is for the profiteers.

I expect my working class point of view to receive no sympathy from your paper, but I do expect that the traditional courtesy of publication by the newspapers of a signed statement of correction, which even our most Bourbon papers grant, will be extended to this statement by yours.

Yours truly,   Rose Pastor Stokes.

March 18, 1918.["]

You will see from the text of the letter, that she insisted upon its publication as an act of courtesy to her, to correct the misstatements about her sentiments which had been printed in the next previous issue of the same paper. I am attaching hereto the article in which the letter was published; you will note,[1] that the editor took the pains, in this very article, to repeat the alleged pro-war utterances of Mrs. Stokes.

In the trial of the Stokes case, the attorneys of the defendant attempted to make capital out of the failure of the Government to prosecute the editor of the Star. The court, in its charge to the jury, referred to this in the following language:

"The point has been made here that the editor of the Star, Mr. Stout, was guilty of improper conduct in publishing this letter which was sent to him, after, in his opinion, knowing and feeling that it was an improper and disloyal letter. Gentlemen of the jury, this letter was sent to the editor of the Star with a very urgent request that it be published; with an appeal practically to the chivalry and courtesy of the editor to right what was conceived to be a wrong, by publishing a letter of correction over one's own signature. That was strong reason for its publication. No matter what the editor of the Star thought of it, and he said he knew nothing with respect to the legal effect of it, he did this: He immediately sent that letter to the law officers of the Government for their examination and investigation and to determine what, if anything, ought to be done with it; and the publication was made, as he says, upon this urgent appeal and upon this, practically an insinuation, that he would probably refuse to publish it, and that if he did refuse to publish it, it would not be a proper courtesy."

In view of Mrs. Stokes' insistence upon the publication of her letter as a matter of courtesy and fairness toward her; in view of the fact that, in the same article, the editor repeated her alleged pro-war sentiments; and in view of the foregoing remarks of the court, it would obviously be difficult to attribute to the editor a disloyal intent or purpose in publishing the letter. Consequently, action against him is, I feel, inadvisable.

My Department has repeatedly received complaints against the Kansas City Star with suggestion of prosecution. These have had their source partly in the fact that the managing editor of the paper, one August F. Seested,[2] is a German who secured his citizenship papers as late as July 2, 1917, almost four months after the declaration of war, and partly in the paper's persistent criticism of your administration. My Department has carefully examined all issues that have been sent in, but has not found anything on which to base a hope for successful prosecution.

Faithfully yours,   T. W. Gregory

TLS (WP, DLC).
  [1] A clipping from the Kansas City *Star*, March 20, 1918.
  [2] August Frederick Seested, who was actually of Danish birth.

From Edward Mandell House, with Enclosure

Dear Governor: Magnolia, Mass. June 25, 1918.

I am enclosing you a copy of a letter which I have written Lord Robert Cecil in response to one from him in which he asks for my personal views.

The sentiment is growing rapidly everywhere in favor of some organized opposition to war and I think it essential that you should guide the movement. It will not wait for the peace conference and, while I can understand that you would not want to commit yourself to any plan until the war is ended, yet, there are other ways by which you can direct it.

The trouble that I see ahead is that the English, French or the groups here may hit upon some scheme that will appeal to people generally and around it public opinion will chrystalize to such an extent that it will be difficult to change the form at the peace conference. It is one of the things with which your name should be linked during the ages. The whole world look upon you as the champion of the idea, but there is a feeling not only in this country but in England and France as well that you are reluctant to take the initiative.

If you do not approve the letter which I have written Lord Robert, I can stop it.[1]

Everywhere the most popular slogan is, "This is a war to make future wars impossible," and I believe that sentiment animates not only the people but the soldiers as well.

Affectionately yours,   E. M. House

TLS (WP, DLC).
¹ The letter was sent: EMH to R. Cecil, June 24, 1918, TLS (FO 371/4365, pp. 133-34, PRO).

E N C L O S U R E

Edward Mandell House to Lord Robert Cecil¹

Magnolia, Massachusetts.
Dear Lord Robert: June 25, 1918.

There seem to be as many opinions concerning a league of nations as there are groups working at a solution.

To me there is something pathetic in the faith which the people of nearly every country have in the ability of their statesmen to work out this problem in a way that will insure an enduring peace.

I believe we should use as our guide the experience which mankind has gathered in solving the questions of law and order between individuals. The more advanced states of the world have worked out a fairly satisfactory civilization. But, internationally, thanks to Germany, we are thrown back to the Stone Age.

One of the most essential features of any league seems to me to be the installation of a moral standard such as that maintained among individuals of honor. Even before Germany smashed the international fabric, reprehensible action was condoned under the broad cover of patriotism; actions which in individuals would have been universally condemned and the perpetrators ostracised from society.

I believe that the most vital element in bringing about a world-wide reign of peace is to have the same stigma rest upon the acts of nations as upon the acts of individuals. When the people of a country are held up to the scorn and condemnation of the world because of the dishonorable acts of their representatives, they will not longer tolerate such acts.

To bring this about will not I think be so difficult as it would seem, and when this condition is realized, a nation may be counted upon to guard its treaty obligations with the same fidelity as an individual guards his honor.

I do not believe at the start it would be possible to form any court or to have an international force at the disposal of the court to enforce its decisions. It seems to me that in forming the league we could not go further than to agree that:

(1) Any war, no matter how remote or how insignificant the country involved, is the concern of all nations.

(2) Some country like Switzerland or Holland should be selected for a centralized peace ground. The ministers sent there should be ipso facto peace delegates.

When there is a rumor or murmur of war these delegates should by previous agreement automatically meet and

(a) Insist that the proposed belligerents agree to settle their differences by arbitration according to the agreement, which as members of a League of Nations, they have signed.

(b) The arbitrators to be selected as follows: one by each belligerent and these two to select a third. In the event the two could come to no agreement as to the third, then the selection of the third arbitrator should be made by the League.

(c) Either nation to the arbitration may, if dissatisfied with the findings, have the right to appeal to the League.

(d) The finding shall be set aside only by a three fourths vote.

(e) If the belligerent against whom the finding is made insists upon going to war, then it shall become obligatory upon every nation in the League to immediately break off all diplomatic, financial and economic relations of every character and, when and where possible, also exert physical force against the offender.

(3) One of the fundamental principles of the League shall be a declaration that each signatory nation shall bind itself forever to maintain the same standard as that maintained among people of honor so that any nation that failed to live up to the letter and spirit of this agreement shall be held up to public condemnation.

(4) The members of the League shall guarantee each other's territorial integrity. Any violation of this guarantee shall be visited by the same penalties as sent forth in Paragraph (2), section (e).

These are my personal views at the moment and do not represent either the President or the groups over here that are working at the problem.

I would appreciate your letting me know what you think of the plan I have proposed.

I am, my dear Lord Robert,

                                    Your very sincere,   [E. M. House]

TCL (WP, DLC).
    [1] House was prompted to write this letter by reading the interim report of the Phillimore Committee, about which see Lord Reading to WW, July 3, 1918 (second letter of that date), n. 1, which Wiseman had given House on June 20, 1918.

From John Knight Shields

My dear Mr. President: Washington June 25, 1918.

Your valued letter, concerning the joint Resolution proposing an amendment to the federal constitution favoring equal suffrage now pending in the United States Senate, has challenged my most thoughtful consideration, as do all your views upon public matters.

The Resolution involves fundamental questions affecting the sovereignty and powers of the federal and state governments, most important and vital to the people of the state which I have the honor in part to represent in the United States Senate, and those of states with which they are closely allied, in all social, economical and governmental interests, upon which I have most profound convictions, unfavorable to it, known, and I believe approved, by the great majority of the people of Tennessee,—arrived at after full consideration of conditions existing when I voted against a similar one some years ago and those now confronting our country.

The reasons for my conclusions are those controlling the majority of my colleagues from the Southern states, well known to you and which would not be interesting to here restate.

If I could bring myself to believe the adoption of the Resolution would contribute to the successful prosecution of the war we are waging with Germany, I would unhesitatingly vote for it, because my whole heart and soul is involved in bringing it to a victorious issue and I am willing to sacrifice every thing save the honor and freedom of our country, in aiding you to accomplish that end, but I have been unable to do so.

We can not reasonably expect the proposed amendment to be ratified within less than two years and the discussion of it would, unquestionably, divert the minds and energies of the people from the one great absorbing subject before us—the winning of the war—by involving those of many states in a most bitter controversy contrary to our earnest desire for that unity of thought and action of the American people now so imperatively required.

These are my sincere convictions; but, out of my very high respect for your views, I will continue to give your suggestions grave consideration.

With the highest respect, I am,
                    Sincerely yours,   Jno K. Shields

TLS (WP, DLC).

From George Creel

My dear Mr. President: Washington, D. C. June 25, 1918.
I would suggest four o'clock in the afternoon as the best time for your speech at Mt. Vernon.[1] This does not interfere with your day or with your dinner arrangements. Will you please let me know whether the time suits you, and if not, indicate your desire?
I am arranging the Washington end of the day so that you will only be required to witness the finish of the Pageant at the Capitol between eight-thirty and nine o'clock, and without speaking.
In our statement to the papers, I will give the names of the twenty-three foreign groups who are making the pilgrimage, and simply state that you have accepted their invitation.
Respectfully,   George Creel

TLS (WP, DLC).
[1] On July 4.

A Memorandum by Charles Lee Swem

The White House [June 25, 1918].
If the Jones amendment gets attached by the Committee to the Bill, the President hopes the Senator[1] will vote for it.[2]
C.L.S.

T MS (WP, DLC).
[1] Senator Tillman.
[2] Wilson was replying to JPT to WW, June 25, 1918, TLI (WP, DLC). Tumulty reported that Tillman had asked him several times what Wilson "wished him to do about the Jones amendment." Senator Wesley L. Jones, on June 10, had introduced an amendment to H.R. 11945, an agricultural appropriation bill, which, for the duration of the war, prohibited absolutely the manufacture, transportation, or sale of alcoholic beverages in the United States. The amendment had been referred to the Committee on Agriculture and Forestry. *Cong. Record*, 65th Cong., 2d sess., p. 7557.

John Kenneth Caldwell to Robert Lansing

Vladivostok June 25, 1918.
9. Allied Consuls here just met with the two principal members Czech national council, who state that even if willing, Soviets are powerless to prevent armed prisoners from interfering with movement Czech troops east, that Trotsky has ordered all Czech troops disarmed arrested and imprisoned and that the 15,000 Czech troops now here must return west to assist their fellows. To do this they require arms and munitions, and these they request from Allies, together with a supporting armed Allied force.
Allied consuls all agreed to recommend to their respective gov-

ernments that favorable action be taken immediately on requests of Czechs, both as to supplying arms and supplies, and also the sending of an Allied force into Siberia for the double purpose of assisting a splendid body of Allied troops in their just fight against armed war prisoners, and of checking German activity in Siberia.

The strength of Soviets is decreasing, that of armed war prisoners is increasing constantly. Only a few days ago, the most important official of Soviet in Easter[n] Siberia stated in the presence of Consul McGowan,[1] in answer to question put by private American, that Soviets will never ask foreign intervention. I believe intervention is necessary, and there is evidently no use in waiting for it to be requested by Soviets. If intervention is to be undertaken, favorable situation created by holding of large section of railway by Czechs should be taken advantage of.

Czechs (*) that action must be begun here within three weeks. They estimate that they require 13,000 rifles, three mounted batteries, 100 machine guns and 1,000,000 cartridges, and should be supported by from 50 to 100,000 Allied troops, to establish permanent front against Germany.   Caldwell.

(*) omission.

T telegram (WP, DLC).
[1] David Bell Macgowan, at this time an assistant to Caldwell at the consulate in Vladivostok.

Lord Reading to Arthur James Balfour

Washington. June 25th, 1918

No. 2863 Following from Lord Reading to Mr. Balfour.
Very Secret.
My telegram of June 16th through Wiseman to you.
Intervention in Russia.
During last fortnight administration circles and the press have been discussing intervention or allied assistance in Russia. The public has become very interested and on the whole favours policy of intervention in a general and somewhat vague way. Various persons from Russia are now at Washington trying to influence the policy of the Administration. The proposal that holds the field and is the only one which is receiving the serious consideration of the President is that a Relief Commission should proceed to Siberia supported by a protective armed guard and headed by a Special Commissioner who would carry the complete confidence of the President. That the President has such a concrete proposal before him is known to very few even of the Administration. All the reports

and rumours that you may hear and which are very prevalent of other modes of intervention are quite beside the mark.

I visited Colonel House last Friday June 21st in accordance with intention notified to you. Wiseman accompanied me at my request. The situation was discussed at length and the result is to show that Colonel House has certainly changed his views and is distinctly favourable to some definite step being taken immediately by the United States and the Allies in support of Russia. I came to the conclusion and he agreed with it that I should see the President and put to him the substance of the long conversation between House and me.

Accordingly I saw the President yesterday evening June 24th and had a long discussion upon intervention in Russia. I informed him that I had had no communication from you upon the subject of the Relief Commission proposal and that I was merely speaking personal views and repeating Colonel House's opinions at his request to the President. I approached him because I am convinced that the best means of obtaining the President's assent to an armed intervention through Siberia is to use the Relief Commission as the advance guard. As I have reported to you in the past he has persistently referred to such a Commission as the best policy to be pursued. I think his views have changed to this extent that he now recognises that such a Commission would be useless unless of vast dimensions and importance and protected by a military force. It is the accompaniment by a military force which to my mind is of such importance in this new proposal. It is obvious that once that military force has entered Siberia it must be supplemented as and when necessities arise as they assuredly will.

From the interview with the President it is clear that the policy above indicated will commend itself to him if he can be satisfied that it is feasible, although he has not yet expressed any conclusion. For the moment the problem is being studied by the War Department and elsewhere to report upon the number of persons who will be required for the Commission and particularly the number and composition of the military force together with the requirements as to supplies and shipping. The President wants a definite worked out plan before him and until he has it and is satisfied that it is practicable he will not announce his decision at least publicly.

The suggestion arrived at by Colonel House and myself in order to meet difficulty of the introduction of Japanese forces only which was communicated by me to the President was that he should consult the Allied Powers of course particularly including Japan and propose that the armed guard should in the main consist of American troops supplemented by Japanese and a smaller number of the other Allies. Thus the dominating force would be composed of those viewed most favourably by the Russians whereas if it consisted entirely or in the main of Japanese it would be viewed most unfavourably. This argument could be advanced to the Japanese who have hitherto said here that their entry would produce hostility in Russia. I told the President that I was convinced that the Japanese will go very far to secure his co-operation. It should be explained that as and when the Japanese troops were introduced as they must be in ever increasing numbers to supplement the small force of the armed guard Japan would be entitled to the general command. The President thought this might be a means of getting over the difficulty with Japan although as he stated the Japanese always insisted that the intervention must be under their command from the first.

My view is that if only a small force perhaps not more than fifteen to twenty thousand men of which the larger number should be Americans were once introduced into Siberia there would be little difficulty hereafter in getting the President's agreement to a more advanced policy of military intervention.

The President feared that the sending of American troops in any numbers must be in subtraction of the assistance to be given on the Western front. As stated in other telegrams if the Supreme War Council and General Foch were to express a view in favour of the utilization of some American troops in Siberia it would of course have a very important effect upon the President.

I presented a paraphrase of the Lockhart telegram of June 18th[1] but not of the War Office memorandum[2] which you sent me although I used arguments therein contained more particularly those showing the necessity for the creation of an Eastern front to obtain a decisive victory over Germany.

No decision was reached at the interview but I regard it as of considerable importance because it showed (A) that it is only by means of the Relief Commission that the President can be got to agree to intervention (B) that the President is in favour of an armed guard for the Commission, and (C) that he is still not convinced of the purely military policy of intervention by a large army of Japanese supplemented by contingents of Allied forces.

It is possible that the President may make a public announcement of U. S. policy regarding Russia on the occasion of the 4th July celebrations.

T telegram (FO 115/2447, pp. 146-51, PRO).
[1] See A. J. Balfour to Lord Reading, June 20, 1918 (second telegram of that date).
[2] See A. J. Balfour to Lord Reading, June 20, 1918 (first telegram of that date).

From the Diary of Josephus Daniels

June Tuesday 25 1918

Went before Agricultural Committee in favor of war-time prohibition bill. Burleson & shipping board had opposed bill.

Cabinet. Houston told how farmers said they could not plant full
wheat crop unless guaranteed $2.50 Have not only done that but
raised biggest rye, barley &c & they now wished to be assured high
prices for these

Can President regulate street car fares? Baker thought not & that
Congress could not either. Street car co's cannot, so they say, pay
higher wages unless they raise fares. Secy Wilson will get Mr. Taft
& Mr. Walsh of Labor Board to file memorandum

A News Report

[*June 26, 1918*]

WILSON PLANS TO AID RUSSIA WITHOUT ARMY
MISSION TO ENTER SIBERIA
To be Purely Economic, Possibly With Escort of Troops
HELPFULNESS ITS SOLE AIM

Washington. June 26.—President Wilson has determined upon
the basic principles of a plan for extending aid to Russia and is
now engaged in formulating the details. Last night at a Cabinet
council, called hastily for the purpose, he outlined his proposals
and invited suggestions as to the best means of carrying the policy
into execution.

The President's plan does not contemplate military intervention
to restore Russian nationality and save the Russian people from the
German yoke. It aims at the commercial, industrial, and agricultural
upbuilding of the great territory, formerly ruled by the Czar, through
a policy of mutual helpfulness arranged between the United States
and whatever Russian authority is established through the efforts
of this Government along the lines of the proposals which will be
advanced in the President's name. At the same time it has features
somewhat similar to those in what has been regarded by many
friends of Russia as the most feasible scheme for saving Russia
from complete political and economic disintegration.

Although no authoritative disclosure has been made concerning
the President's views on the subject, it is the understanding that
his plan contemplates sending to Russia a commission of distinguished civilians with offers of assistance and with powers to discuss and arrange with Russian representatives a plan of co-oper-

ation designed to set that perturbed country on its feet. Troops might be sent to give protection to the commissioners and to police territory where native local Governments might be established to carry out the policy inaugurated by the United States, but it is contemplated that there shall be no military intervention in any sense of the term. The whole project, according to information obtained today, is of an economic and non-military character, and there is good reason to believe that the Administration will not tolerate any suggestion that the upbuilding of Russian nationality shall be accompanied by force of arms.

In certain of its features the plan coincides in a qualified way with the plan for intervention proposed by Senator King of Utah in a resolution recently offered in the Senate,[1] and in an article in THE NEW YORK TIMES by Senator Poindexter of Washington.[2] The Senators' plan, however, provided that the commission should be accompanied by an allied army, in which all the nations party to the plan would be represented, this army to give protection to the commission and the local native governments established, and to be used, wherever necessary, to stay the German invasion.

It has not yet come to light whether the President's policies contemplates joint action with America's allies in seeking to assist Russia. So much of the plan discussed at the White House Cabinet conference is still a secret. It is believed, however, that Great Britain, France, Italy, Japan, and China will be invited to join with the United States in the measures contemplated for the upbuilding of Russia. They must be consulted, at any rate, and their views doubtless will have weight with the President.

The proposed Administration policy follows the line of prior suggestions in that the commission would enter Russian territory through Siberia.

Without doubt the President's plan will bring strong dissent from those who have been insisting that, while the Russian people must have plenty of time and opportunity to organize local governments in Siberia under the encouragement of the allied commission, this cannot be accomplished without the backing of a strong military force, composed of soldiers of all the principal allied nations, which would afford protection from German and radical native elements.

Under the plan which is being formulated, this Government would seek to help Russia through furnishing the means of restoring agriculture and commerce. The commission would propose, it is understood, that the United States furnish Russia agricultural machinery and implements and undertake to purchase some of the products of Russian agriculture or take these and other Russian products in exchange for American products necessary to Russia.

Commerce between Russia and the United States would be encouraged, also, and there would be a general effort on the part of this Government to make Russia strong and self-supporting in an economic way. The whole plan is based on the principle of mutual helpfulness.

It is gathered that the entire plan of co-operation between Russia and the United States, and perhaps the Allies generally, will not be formulated until the proposed civilian commission has had the opportunity of discussing a definite policy with representatives of Russia, who will be met by the commission when it enters Russian territory through Siberia.

It should be understood that in the absence of any authoritative statement the President's views are not fully known and there are phases of the plan that are to be disclosed when the President believes that the proper time has arrived. For the present the most that can be said is that the President's policy, while contemplating sending a civilian commission to Siberia with sufficient armed forces to give police protection in the territory in which the commission will operate, does not embrace the idea of military intervention, and this cannot be too strongly emphasized.

The Cabinet council to discuss the Russian situation was called, apparently, in some haste. There had been a regular session of the Cabinet on Monday afternoon at which nothing was said, it is understood, as to the President's views as to the upbuilding of Russia. Soon after this meeting adjourned five members of the Cabinet were notified by telephone that the President desired to see them at the White House at 8:30 o'clock last night. These five were the Secretary of State, the Secretary of War, the Secretary of Agriculture, the Secretary of Commerce, and the Secretary of Labor. Each has jurisdiction over a branch of the Government that must be intimately associated with the plan that the President outlined.

Printed in the *New York Times*, June 27, 1918.

[1] Senator William Henry King, Democrat of Utah, had introduced S. Res. 262 on June 10. The significant portion of the resolution reads as follows:

"*Resolved*, That it is the sense of the Senate of the United States that a commission be sent to Russia to cooperate with the American ambassador and other representatives of our Government to overcome and neutralize German propaganda in Russia and to aid in Russia's economic, industrial, and political freedom; and be it further

"*Resolved*, That it is the sense of the Senate of the United States that a military expedition be organized and sent by the United States of America in conjunction with its allies, including Japan and China, to cooperate with the armies of the Russian people to repel the advance of German arms and to expel from Russia German military power and establish therein the authority of the people and Government of Russia."

The resolution was referred to the Committee on Foreign Relations, which took no action upon it. *Cong. Record*, 65th Cong., 2d sess., p. 7557.

[2] See J. J. Jusserand to S. J. M. Pichon, June 9, 1918, n. 1.

To Robert Lansing, with Enclosures

My dear Mr. Secretary,   The White House. 26 June, 1918.

I agree with you that we can no longer respect or regard the integrity of the artificial Austrian Empire. I doubt if even Hungary is any more an integral part of it than Bohemia. I base this judgment in part upon a very interesting and illuminating conversation I had a month or two ago with a group of Magyar Americans, who spoke very plainly to that point.[1]

I approve of the interpretative note to the Serbian minister which you here suggest, with the query, Would it not suffice to say German and Austrian and leave out Magyar in the closing sentence?

Faithfully Yours   W.W.

WWTLI (R. Lansing Papers, NjP).
[1] Wilson had met at 4:30 p.m. on February 5 with a committee of the New Freedom Society, an organization of American citizens of Hungarian descent, who were introduced to him by Senator J. Hamilton Lewis. Neither the Executive Appointment Diary nor the Head Usher's Diary lists any more recent meeting with any group of Hungarian origin.

E N C L O S U R E   I

Handed to the President
pm June 25/18 RL.

MEMORANDUM ON THE POLICY OF THE UNITED STATES IN RELATION
TO THE NATIONALITIES INCLUDED WITHIN THE
AUSTRO-HUNGARIAN EMPIRE.

June 24, 1918.

In the first place we should be perfectly frank with ourselves and admit that as long as there was a chance of entering into a separate peace with Austria-Hungary it was wise and expedient to attempt to do so, even though it was contrary to the just claims of the nationalities within that Empire which sought independence, because the primary object of this Government was and is to win the war against Prussianized Germany and nothing could so soon or so effectively accomplish it as breaking the alliance between the Austro-Hungarian Monarchy and the German Empire.

When the informal negotiations were brought to an end by the unwise publication of the Prince Sixtus letter[1] and the resulting declaration of the Emperor Karl of his loyalty to the German alliance, a declaration based undoubtedly upon fear rather than desire, a new situation was presented.

Manifestly it would be useless to pursue further a policy which would be ineffective and in no way beneficial in winning the war.

As that was the only argument in favor of encouraging the Austro-Hungarian Monarchy in the belief that the United States and the Allies would support its continued existence within its present frontiers, and as the principle of "self-determination" was hostile to the idea of holding in subjection to the imperial rule of Austria Hungary the Poles, Czecks, Ruthenians, Rumanians, Italians and Jugo-Slavs composing so large a part of the population of the Empire, it would seem wise to abandon a policy which will contribute nothing to success in the war and which is unjust to the nationalities subject to the dual crown insofar as it affects their nationalistic aspirations.

We have already gone part of the way, first in declaring in favor of an independent Poland, and, second, of expressing "sympathy with the nationalistic aspirations" of the Czecho-Slovaks and the Jugo-Slavs. It would seem to me not only politic at this time of political and social unrest in Austria-Hungary and of the failure of the offensive against Italy, but just to the nationalities concerned to declare without reservation for an independent Poland, an independent Bohemia, and [an] independent Southern Slav State, a return of the Rumanians and Italians to their natural allegiance.

That would mean in effect the dismemberment of the present Austro-Hungarian Empire into its original elements, leaving these independent nationalities to form such separate states or federal states as they might themselves decide to form, especially if the severance of Austria and Hungary resulted.

The Austro-Hungarian Monarchy was organized on the principle of conquest and not on the principle of "self-determination." It was held together after its formation chiefly by fear of the power and greed of the Russian Empire. When the Czar was overthrown, the dread of absorption by the Muscovite power disappeared and the desire for national independence became dominant.

The consequence of such a dismemberment or partition of Austria-Hungary would be that in addition to the independent states already referred to the Empire would probably be divided into the Arch-duchy of Austria and the Kingdom of Hungary. In the former would be included the German-speaking people of the Empire and in the latter those speaking the Magyar langauage.

I believe that the announcement of this policy, which is founded on the just principle that nationalities possess the inherent right of self-government, would exert a decided, if not a decisive, influence in eliminating Austria-Hungary as a factor in the war. If the political and military results would be such as we may reasonably expect they would mean the defeat of Prussianized Germany, the destruction of Mittel-Europa, the emancipation of Russia from German domination, and the restoration of peace on a just and therefore on a firm basis.

If this is the wise policy to adopt, it should be done *now* when the political, military and social conditions of Austria-Hungary are in the greatest confusion and when the spirit of revolution is rife. It should be done unconditionally and without ambiguity. The entire surrender of the Dual Monarchy to the German Empire should remove all sympathy and compassion for the Hapsburg rulers. They are no longer entitled to merciful or considerate treatment since they have become vassals of the Hohenzollerns.

The time has arrived in my opinion for the determination of a very definite policy and that determination should be clear and unequivocal.

T MS (R. Lansing Papers, NjP).
[1] About which, see RL to WW, May 10, 1918 (first letter of that date), n. 1, Vol. 47.

E N C L O S U R E   I I

Robert Lansing to Ljubo Mihajlović

[Washington] June 24, 1918.

No. 72

Sir:

I have the honor to acknowledge the receipt of your Note of June 14th,[1] enclosing a copy of a letter sent by you to the Ambassadors of France, Great Britain, and Italy, concerning the allied declaration at the Versailles conference on the fate of the oppressed nationalities of Austria-Hungary.[2]

In this connection, in order that there may be no misunderstanding concerning the meaning of the statement issued by the Department of May 29th to the effect that the nationalistic aspirations for freedom of the Czecho-Slovaks and Jugo-Slavs have the earnest sympathy of the United States Government,[3] I beg to state that the position of the United States Government is that all branches of the Slav race should be completely freed from German and Austrian rule.[4]

Accept, Sir, the renewed assurances of my highest consideration.

CCL (SDR, RG 59, 763.72119/1747, DNA).
[1] L. Mihajlović to RL, June 14, 1918, *FR-WWS 1918*, 1, I, 812. Mihajlović was the Serbian Minister to the United States.
[2] L. Mihajlović to Lord Reading *et al.*, June 14, 1918, *ibid.*, pp. 812-13. Mihajlović called the Ambassadors' attention to a statement made by the Allied Prime Ministers at

a meeting of the Supreme War Council on June 3 which, he said, had "puzzled the Czecho-Slovaks and the Yugo-Slavs and also furnished to our enemy—Austria-Hungary—the opportunity to turn it to advantage." He urged that in the future the Allies take greater care to coordinate their policies with the interested representatives of the minority nationalities.

The puzzling aspect of the statement issued by the Supreme War Council grew out of the apparent distinction which it drew between the nationalistic claims of the Czechoslovaks and Yugoslavs, on the one hand, and those of the Poles, on the other hand. The relevant portion reads as follows:

"The Allied Governments have noted with pleasure the declaration made by the Secretary of State of the United States Government and desire to associate themselves in an expression of earnest sympathy for the nationalistic aspirations towards freedom of the Czecho-Slovak and Jugo-Slav peoples.

"The creation of a united and independent Polish state with free access to the sea constitutes one of the conditions of a solid and just peace, and of the rule of right in Europe." A. H. Frazier to RL, June 4, 1918, *ibid.*, pp. 809-10.

[3] The statement is embodied in RL to T. N. Page, May 29, 1918, *ibid.*, pp. 808-809. It reads as follows: "The Secretary of State desires to announce that the proceedings of the Congress of Oppressed Races of Austria-Hungary, which was held in Rome in April, have been followed with great interest by the Government of the United States, and that the nationalistic aspirations of the Czecho-Slovaks and Jugo-Slavs for freedom have the earnest sympathy of this Government."

[4] "Magyar" omitted in this final version of the letter.

To Thomas Watt Gregory, with Enclosure

My dear Gregory: The White House 26 June, 1918

There are statements of so serious a character in the enclosed letter from Mr. Gompers that I am taking the liberty of sending it to you and asking if you will not have the Mr. Rubin[1] to whom Mr. Gompers refers interviewed in order that we may see the substance that lies back of his judgments.

Cordially and faithfully yours,   Woodrow Wilson

TLS (JDR, RG 60, Numerical File, No. 193271, DNA).
[1] William Benjamin Rubin, lawyer of Milwaukee, who specialized in work with organized labor.

E N C L O S U R E

From Samuel Gompers

Sir: St. Paul, Minn., June 17, 1918.

Enclosed, I beg to submit for your consideration two resolutions adopted by the Convention of the American Federation of Labor whose sessions have just come to a close at St. Paul, Minnesota.[1] The subject covered by these resolutions has been a matter of serious anxiety for several years, particularly so since our entrance into the war. During the hearing of the Industrial Relations Commission I felt it incumbent upon me to expose much of the chicanery of the private detective agencies and which has been made part of the printed hearings of the Commission.[2] Since then we have become fully convinced that many of the operators of the private detective agencies are not only pro-German but particularly anti-American, and that their efforts are directed to create dissension and division in the labor movement so that the unity, loyalty and wholehearted support of our movement in our Government's mission in the war shall be less effective or nullified.

Evidence has been submitted that the operators of the detective agencies have been instrumental in engendering strikes, cessations of labor. We have been advised that the "operators" activity has been suborned by the propaganda of our country's enemies.

Recently, that is, about a week before the opening of our St. Paul Convention, I had the honor of a conference with the Honorable Secretaries of War, Navy and Labor, Messrs. Baker, Daniels and Wilson. At the conference Mr. William B. Rubin, an eminent attorney, one who has given splendid service to the cause of justice and who has served labor faithfully and well, participated.

Mr. Rubin has given the subject much study and consideration, and the means and methods suggested by him to cope with the situation appear logical, convincing and practical as a solution of this most important problem. Mr. Rubin has the confidence of all who know him. He has broad ability and zeal and is faithful in his work. Without his uncompensated assistance it would have been impossible to have made the investigations by reason of their costliness.

Permit me therefore to suggest that the subject of the resolutions receive your early attention and to suggest further that Mr. Rubin will I know be very glad to serve his country without remuneration by assisting in the investigation.

Yours very respectfully,   Saml. Gompers.

TLS (JDR, RG 60, Numerical File, No. 193271, DNA).

[1] Resolutions No. 39 and 111, clipping from printed source (JDR, RG 60, Numerical File, No. 193271, DNA). The preambles of both resolutions asserted that the private detective agencies employed in labor disputes were made up chiefly of "despicable" men who spent most of their time spying on workingmen and attempting to destroy labor unions. The first resolution called for a federal governmental investigation of such agencies, and both resolutions urged enactment of legislation by Congress to abolish them.

[2] United States Commission on Industrial Relations, *Industrial Relations: Final Report and Testimony* (11 vols., Washington, 1916), VIII, 7642-44, 7655.

To George Creel

My dear Creel: The White House 26 June, 1918

Four o'clock in the afternoon will be the best hour for the Mount Vernon affair, and I write to say that Mrs. Wilson and I will hope to have the members of the Diplomatic Corps and the representatives of the foreign language groups, if they are not too numerous, as our guests on the Mayflower.

I dare say we shall leave the dock at the Navy Yard about two o'clock, and we shall expect to serve light refreshments on the way back.   Faithfully yours,   Woodrow Wilson

TLS (G. Creel Papers, DLC).

To John Knight Shields

My dear Senator: [The White House] 26 June, 1918

Thank you very sincerely for your frank letter of yesterday about the suffrage amendment. I realize the weight of the arguments that have controlled your attitude in this matter, and I would not have written as I did if I had not thought that the passage of the amendment at this time was an essential psychological element in the conduct of the war for democracy. I am led by a single sentence in your letter, therefore, to write to say that I do earnestly believe that our action upon this amendment will have an important and immediate influence upon the whole atmosphere and morale of the nations engaged in the war, and every day I am coming to see how supremely important that side of the whole thing is. We can win if we have the will to win.

Cordially and sincerely yours,   [Woodrow Wilson]

CCL (WP, DLC).

To Morris Sheppard

My dear Senator: [The White House] 26 June, 1918

You may be sure I have no objections to the enclosed bill, Senate 4036, but I wish that the authority might be less restricted. There are reasons why we should control the telegraph systems of the country which are not immediately connected with the conduct of the war, and I feel that there would be the same advantage in possessing a general authority to take over the telegraph lines as there proved to be in the authority to take over the railroads.

Cordially and sincerely yours,   Woodrow Wilson

TLS (Letterpress Books, WP, DLC).

To Frank Lyon Polk

My dear Polk: [The White House] 26 June, 1918

I have been very late in hearing the distressing news of the death of your father.[1] My heart goes out to you in the warmest and deepest sympathy. I know something of what your father was and can realize what he must have meant to you, and it distresses me to think that you should have been so bereaved. I hope that you will realize how the affection of your friends goes out to you with particular warmth at this time.

Cordially and sincerely yours,   Woodrow Wilson

TLS (Letterpress Books, WP, DLC).
[1] William Mecklenburg Polk, M.D., a distinguished physician and Dean of the Cornell University Medical School, had died in a sanitarium in Atlantic City on June 23.

A Translation of a Telegram from Henri Bergson to Stéphen Jean Marie Pichon

Washington, undated [June 26, 1918];
received [June] 28 at 3 a.m.

Nos. 809-12. URGENT. For the Minister of Foreign Affairs. Personal—from M. Bergson.[1]

The attitude of Colonel House, who had discussed with me the details of a plan for intervention in Siberia and Russia, led me to believe that President Wilson was closer to our point of view than he really is. In a long conversation which I have just had with the President, I have pressed our case most forcefully. I have asked him for an energetic intervention, pointing out to him that this was vitally important and that, long before achieving its full effect, it would alter the situation on our front. I spoke of the grave responsibility that he would assume by doing nothing. He replied right away that, some time ago, when General Foch was sounded out as to the possibility of diverting some troops from our front, the latter had hesitated to give an affirmative reply, that, besides, we did not know if there was enough tonnage available to transport an Allied and American contingent to Vladivostok. I observed to him that, according to reports I had received, certain freighters now in the Pacific could be converted into troopships, as these would suffice for the task. He declared to me then that he had had the matter studied, but that in any case a military intervention in Siberia would require steel and coal, and that the production of coal and steel in the United States was already insufficient for American war industries.

I replied that, even before the heavy pressure struck our front,

French and British public opinion had not resigned itself to regard such difficulties as insurmountable, that we had to take into account this state of opinion, that we recalled how the Japanese had conducted their war, and that one did not understand why the Allies (and the Americans) were hesitating to use such efficacious assistance.

The President immediately pointed out to me that people greatly exaggerated the military power of Japan, that the troop strength in the Russo-Japanese war had been relatively inconsiderable, that in fact the Japanese have about 200,000 men under arms and that they would have, at most (500,000) including their reserves; that, moreover, if they engaged most of their military power, they would expect to command the expedition. I replied that we would settle for adding to a Japanese military command an interallied (or, at the very least, an American) civil commission, which would have supreme direction. But the Japanese, Mr. Wilson responded, will also claim compensations, and I warn you that we will not accord them any territorial compensation: it is contrary to our principles to dispose of other people's property. I replied that the Japanese would probably content themselves with certain commercial advantages in China, and the President acknowledged that such advantages might be conceded, provided that China consented to them. In any case, Mr. Wilson declared, cautioning me to the greatest discretion, he is at this very moment having studies made of a plan for intervention in Siberia, but an intervention that is limited in principle to distribution of manufactured articles. A certain military force would accompany those who were sent to supervise the distribution. I thought I understood that, in the mind of the President, this military force would be susceptible of growth and could become a threat for Germany in Russia, but I am not sure of this.

The argument drawn from recent developments on our front is evidently the most telling; I constantly returned to it, and the President never responded. But he cannot decide to do right away that which is necessary to inflict a significant blow on Germany in Russia.

In summary, here is my impression: From a mélange of information, whose source he did not reveal to me, President Wilson has been led to the conviction that Russia, detesting Germany, runs no risk in submitting definitively to German ascendancy, and will reject everything German after the war. During the war itself, he feels the necessity to do something, but he does not wish to proceed except with an extreme prudence that is certainly excessive, a little through fear of chilling Russian sentiment, but more, I think, so as to have recourse to Japanese assistance only in the smallest measure possible.

I shall remain some days in Washington to work on certain of President Wilson's personal friends. Then I shall return to Boston to see Colonel House, who has advised me to keep in touch with him, and, following that, I will return to Washington. I believe that a detailed study of the conditions in which an intervention would be possible will lead the President to a solution close to ours, and then this solution will impose itself. But we must work so that this does not come too late.   Jusserand.

T telegram (Campagne contre l'Allemagne, 1914-1918, 4 N 46, Conseil Supérieur de Guerre, Intervention en Sibérie, 1918-1919, FMD-Ar).
    [1] Bergson had returned to the United States on a special mission. Its purpose, as Pichon described it, was "to employ his persuasive eloquence and his great authority with President Wilson and some of the latter's friends, in the question of Japanese intervention." This mission was to remain strictly confidential, and Bergson had specified that he wished to have no official status so as to obviate any problems arising as to Jusserand's authority or his, Bergson's, own relations with American officials. S. J. M. Pichon to J. J. Jusserand, June 4, 1918, T telegram (Papiers Jusserand, Vol. 30, p. 2, FFM-Ar). Before leaving Paris, Bergson had conferred with Berthelot and Clemenceau. Henri Bergson, "Mes Missions (1917-1918)," Hommes et Mondes, III (July 1947), 372.
    Evidently in order to prepare for his interviews with Wilson on June 26 and July 25, Bergson wrote in English, in draft form, on the stationery of a Washington hotel, a paper which began as follows: "I am much surprised to see how you complicate here a question which *we* think very simple. . . . For us, the question is simple enough: we must win the war, and the war cannot be won, or we shall spend years before we win it, if something—and we know exactly what we mean—if some particular thing is not done in Russia."
    Noting that the German offensive had not succeeded, Bergson then wrote that the Germans would now revert to trench warfare on the western front and raise armies in Russia to replace gradually the German troops in the West, who could then leave the trenches to resume the offensive there. "That is what they are bound to do," he went on, "and what they will do. If they do not do it, they are lost, because you Americans are going to send us more and more of your men." The Germans had "nothing left to do but to utilize Russian troops." Bergson contrasted the German single-minded "will to conquer" with the western more balanced "wish to conquer."
    Bergson then wrote that the French, after much study, had found a simple solution, namely, that it would be very easy to control the Trans-Siberian railway. Indeed, a few thousand Czechs and Slovaks had just proved that this could be done. The French, he pointed out, were not interested in Russian internal problems and did not care whether the Bolsheviks were expelled or not so long as the Germans did not gain the advantage. In due course, Bergson continued, the Russians would see that aid from the Allies was disinterested: "They might not believe words, but they will believe deeds." Occupation of the railway would take time, he added, and the question of Japanese participation had not yet been settled. Bergson wrote that he and his colleagues did not consider any of the difficulties insurmountable. They did not believe that *much* Japanese assistance would be needed, and they expected enough Russian support to overcome any German resistance. The Allies should be in Russia to prevent the Germanizing of that country, because the Russians could not get out of their difficulties alone. Bergson did not think that Japanese assistance would be dangerous or that supplying Japan would drain American resources during the current crisis. He also noted that some persons said that "it would be a pity to win the war with the help of Japan, an autocratic country," but he considered that the existing situation gave a unique opportunity to draw Japan toward democratic principles. In fact, Bergson noted, some Japanese had said that their country was at a crossroads, hesitating between Germany and the Allies. Bergson was "perfectly sure" that, if this opportunity was missed, there would be "another immense war," with "Japan uniting with China and probably with Germany and probably with Russia (Russia autocratic again) against us." The current danger for democracy, Bergson warned, was "nothing compared to the danger for democracy when the three autocracies unite together."
    Bergson dismissed the idea that Japan would ask for territorial compensation in Siberia and thought that Japan would expect only commercial advantages in China. As he saw it, if the Allies did not accept Japanese assistance, they might some day have to come to terms with Germany at the expense of Russia. An offer by Germany to give the French

people everything they wanted in the West, in return for a free hand in the East, would be very tempting, Bergson conceded, but the Allied peoples would persevere so long as they knew that everything possible had been done to shorten the war and that Germany would be crushed within a reasonable time.

The remainder of Bergson's manuscript appears to have been written after his interview of July 25 with Wilson. H. Bergson, Hw MS, undated [June-July 1918] (Papiers d'Agents, Henri Bergson, 2ème Mission aux U.S.A., FFM-Ar).

From Joseph Patrick Tumulty

Dear Governor: The White House. 27 June 1918.

There has been a great deal of speculation regarding the meeting of the Cabinet with you on Tuesday night. Do you wish anything said about it, even in an unofficial way?   The Secretary

TL (WP, DLC).

To Joseph Patrick Tumulty

Dear Tumulty: [The White House, June 27, 1918]

The members of the Cabinet present on Tuesday night, as you no doubt know, were the Secretary of State, the Secretary of War, the Secretary of Agriculture, the Secretary of Commerce, and the Secretary of Labor. As a matter of fact, we were matching ideas about Russia, but I would be very much obliged if the questions asked about the meeting should be left unanswered for the present.
                                        The President.

TL (WP, DLC).

To Kenneth Douglas McKellar

My dear Senator McKellar: [The White House] 27 June, 1918

I have your letter of June twenty-second in further reference to the Civil Service Retirement Bill, but I have not yet heard anything from Mr. Keating with regard to the attitude of the House leaders towards action on the bill at this session. I hope I shall hear from him soon.   Sincerely yours,   Woodrow Wilson

TLS (Letterpress Books, WP, DLC).

From Joseph Patrick Tumulty

Dear Governor: The White House 27 June 1918.

I hope you will have a chance to read the attached letter from Mr. Gompers with reference to the Borland amendment.[1] I am afraid of the effect on the labor of the country of the attitude taken by Congress in this matter. The effect of your action in approving it is bound to be nation-wide and it will result in a reaction that may be very hurtful.

No matter what may be said about the Government employees, there is nobody who has dealt with them who is not willing to say that they will work overtime when the occasion requires. The effect of this legislation would be to force them into labor organizations that will harrass and interfere with the Government at every turn.

Your approval of this measure would seem to sanction every effort on the part of employers to increase the hours of labor. You will recall some months ago that you sent a letter to Governor Brumbaugh[2] (copy attached) at the time when the Pennsylvania Legislature was considering the increase of hours of labor, advising him that this was a bad time to consider legislation of this character. I think a veto by you of this particular provision would do more to hearten labor throughout the country, and would give you first call upon their services, than anything you could do. Nobody will argue that the efficiency of the departments will be increased one iota by this provision.   Sincerely yours,   J P Tumulty

TLS (WP, DLC).
    [1] S. Gompers to WW, June 27, 1918, TLS (WP, DLC). Gompers called Wilson's attention to the fact that Congress had just passed H.R. 10358, the legislative, executive, and judicial appropriation bill. Gompers objected to an amendment to the bill by Representative Borland which had the effect of increasing the average working day for federal employees from seven to eight hours, without providing additional compensation or making any provision for time and a half for overtime beyond eight hours or on weekends. Gompers argued that this amendment violated statements made by the Council of National Defense and by Wilson himself to the effect that the existing standards of labor should not be altered during the war emergency. Gompers asked if it might not be possible for Wilson to persuade Congress either to delete the Borland amendment or to pass a supplementary measure which would "recognize the eight hour workday as a basic day" for governmental workers and "provide time and a half for service after eight hours work." Gompers requested Wilson, in the event that Congress did neither, to veto the entire appropriation bill.
    The Borland amendment, introduced on March 14, reads as follows: "No increase herein shall apply to salaries or personal services in any department, bureau, office, or independent establishment of the United States which does not, subject to the provisions and exemptions of section 7 of the legislative, executive, and judicial appropriation act approved March 15, 1898, require eight hours of labor each day." *Cong. Record*, 65th Cong., 2d sess., p. 3518.
    [2] WW to M. G. Brumbaugh, June 4, 1917, Vol. 42.

From Ferdinand Foch[1]

Washington, le June 27th. 1918

TELEGRAM OF GENERAL FOCH
TO THE PRESIDENT.

In my opinion the sending by you of American troops to Russia is justified, for no appreciable diminution of the number of troops to be sent to France will result therefrom. I conceive the expedition to Siberia as having to be mainly formed with Japanese elements. The Allies' contingents would be reduced to modest numbers: some 12.000 men or thereabouts. America could supply at once two regiments, and the Allies the rest. Under those conditions the American troops sent to France would only be reduced in an insignificant way.

More than ever, in the interest of military success in Europe, I consider the expedition to Siberia as a very important factor for victory, provided action be immediate, on account of the season being already advanced, I take the liberty of insisting on this last point.   Foch.

TC telegram (N. D. Baker Papers, DLC).
    [1] The following document was typed on the stationery of the French embassy.

A Translation of a Telegram from Jean Jules Jusserand to Stéphen Jean Marie Pichon

Washington, undated [June 27, 1918]
received June 29, 1918, at 10:40 a.m.

Nos. 822-25. Extremely urgent. I have just given the President the telegram from General Foch that was included in your No. 1356.[1] He expressed his satisfaction at receiving this information, which was exactly what he wanted, and he said that he would give the problem, thus clarified, his most serious attention.

Since the conversation on this subject was prolonged, I took the opportunity once again to place before him our principal arguments, signaling to him that, even though, as he said, a certain time inevitably must pass before the expeditionary corps could encounter the Germans, the mere news of its dispatch, quite apart from other consequences, would cause them worry, and this would mean strength for us and weakness for them.

I made much of the good fortune that the Czech contribution and the remarkable success of their troops were for us: from the political point of view it would have been a great error not to profit by it, and, from the moral point of view, to abandon them to their fate would have been an act entailing the most humiliating culpability.

I strongly urged the necessity of acting quickly because of the season: the possibility of making arrangements for assistance; and the probability of attaining great results with meager means, provided that these were used without delay. I told him of the judgment of many noted Americans, who had just returned from Russia, which they knew well (one group garbled), and a recent assurance that a Japanese action would be gladly accepted.

He asked me what contingent we could provide, but, not having had a reply to my telegram 796, I was not in a position to respond.

To counteract the bad effect that the report which will be made to him about the Japanese Ambassador's démarche[2] might have, I made the first move, and, as he had mentioned how little inclination the Japanese show to act in this matter, I told him that to us it had appeared necessary to clarify it; we had noted that they were ready to accept the three points of the Council of Versailles and that their only qualms came from the lack of any assent to their action from the President of the United States. We ask (one group garbled) then, with a stronger insistence.

The President (one group garbled—repetition of telegram requested) repeated, in the course of the conversation, several of the objections that always permeate his study of this subject and which he expressed most recently to Mr. Bergson. Taking coal as an example, he said, the estimate of our needs for the coming year is 640 million, which is more than we have ever extracted: and, without speaking of adding anything there, we do not know how we can attain this figure, given the shortages of labor and even more of transport. I replied that the much-reduced plan to which all parties have agreed would require only the most modest efforts and that the English had the tonnage necessary for their own contingent, which was certainly important for us. In summary, the possibility but still the certainty of a favorable solution and for* * * *

Jusserand.

T telegram (Campagne contre l'Allemagne, 1914-1918, 4 N 46, Conseil Supérieur de Guerre, Intervention en Sibérie, 1918-1919, FMD-Ar).
  [1] S. J. M. Pichon to J. J. Jusserand, No. 1356, June 27, 1918, T telegram (Série E, Japon, Intervention en Sibérie, E 6212/18-20, FMD-Ar).
  [2] That is, the presentation by Viscount Chinda to Balfour on June 24 of the Japanese government's reply to the proposals of Great Britain, France, and Italy concerning Japanese intervention in Siberia (about which see the Enclosure printed with RL to WW, June 27, 1918, and the notes thereto). An expanded version of the Japanese reply is printed as Enclosure III with Lord Reading to WW, July 3, 1918.

From Robert Lansing

My dear Mr. President: Washington June 27, 1918.

I am very glad that you have determined this Government's policy in regard to the Austro-Hungarian Empire so that the oppressed nationalities within its boundaries will be assured of our entire support of their just rights as independent peoples.

An opportunity should be taken or made, it seems to me, to

announce this policy to the world, and the sooner this can be done the more effective it will be because of present conditions. Would not such an opportunity be the occasion of your addressed [address] to oppressed races on the 4th of July?

Provided you decide to announce this policy on some public occasion would it not be wise to avoid offense or a charge of lack of frankness to inform the Allied Governments in advance of our attitude? If you intend to make the announcement and if you think it advisable to communicate the policy beforehand to the other Governments, would you be good enough to indicate the form of communication by telegraph or what I may say to the diplomatic representatives here in regard to the matter?

Faithfully yours,   Robert Lansing.

TLS (WP, DLC).

From Robert Lansing, with Enclosure

My dear Mr. President: Washington June 27, 1918.

I enclose for your information a paraphrase of a telegram received by Viscount Ishii, which he was good enough to read to me yesterday. Will you please return it after reading?

Faithfully yours,   Robert Lansing.

TLS (SDR, RG 59, 861.00/2215½, DNA).

E N C L O S U R E

Sent me June 26/18 RL

CONFIDENTIAL

Paraphrased copy of cablegram received by
Viscount Ishii from his Government.

As the result of the Versailles Conference, His Britannic Majesty's Principal Secretary of State for Foreign Affairs, in the name of the Governments of Great Britain, France and Italy, had recently proposed to the Imperial Government to consent to undertake certain common action in Siberia, subject to the concurrence of the American Government.[1] The Imperial Government still hold the same view as expressed to the American Government on the 19th March last[2] and attach great importance to the positive support of the latter in considering any action of intervention in Siberia. Accordingly, a reply has been sent in the sense that the Japanese Government, while deeply appreciating the proposal, could not feel at liberty to express their decision before a complete and satisfactory understanding on the question was reached between the three Powers and the United States.

T MS (SDR, RG 59, 861.00/2215½, DNA).

¹ At the third meeting of the sixth session of the Supreme War Council on June 3, 1918, Lloyd George, Clemenceau, and Orlando had decided to ask the Japanese government to accept three conditions for an intervention in Siberia. First, Japan would agree to respect the territorial integrity of Russia; second, Japan would take no side in Russia's internal politics; and third, the Japanese forces would advance as far west as possible for the purpose of encountering the Germans and establishing a new eastern front. Once Japan had agreed to these conditions, the four powers would approach Wilson *en bloc* in the hope that he would then be more willing to commit the United States to a joint intervention.

Balfour handed the formal request of the Allies to the Japanese Ambassador in London, Viscount Chinda, on June 7, 1918. Bliss informed Washington about the latest developments in T. H. Bliss to H. P. McCain, June 3, 1918, No. 125, T telegram (WDR, RG 407, World War I Cablegrams, DNA), and in T. H. Bliss to NDB, June 8, 1918, printed as an Enclosure with NDB to WW, June 21, 1918. For a brief discussion, see also Morley, *The Japanese Thrust into Siberia*, pp. 225-26.

² See R. S. Morris to RL, March 19, 1918, Vol. 47.

From Grenville Stanley Macfarland

Personal

My dear President Wilson: Boston June 27, 1918.

I have labored industriously over a memorandum for you on the Russian situation, concerning which I have given a great deal of study and thought since the Revolution. But the more I revise the memorandum, the more I have reduced it, until now it seems best, in view of the pressure upon you, to reduce it to a few headnotes.

First: The result of my study and reflection, and of such investigation as our publicity organization has enabled me to make, is the conclusion that the Soviet government (as distinguished from the Bolsheviki majority which now cont[r]ols it), ought to be recognized either officially or by such favorable public attitudes on the part of our responsible public men as will convince the Soviets that our attitude is friendly.

Second: That the contiguity of the German Frontier to Russia, her present military penetration, her recognized efficiency and her manifest interest, will enable and incite the Germans eventually to effect a kultural penetration of Russia when the inevitable reaction against the present radical control sets in, unless we take adequate propagandist measures against it.

I eliminate military intervention from the Pacific as too absurd for consideration. I eliminate also *any* military intervention, unless it is with the co-operation of the majority of the Russian people as expressed through their established government. I eliminate any military intervention whatever, until the opposing forces on the Western and Italian fronts reach such a state of equilibrium as will enable us to pin every Austrian and German soldier on the Western front, thus preventing them from repeating their operations against Russia of last year. It will take some time before we are sure of our power to do this, and this time will be about the period required to organize an effective propaganda which could immediately precede the plan for a military intervention from some European point of entry like Archangel.

I assume also that any propaganda, in order to compete successfully with the propaganda to which the Germans would resort to oppose it, must be in the nature of a surprise, and must be so complete and overwhelming that it would do its work before the Germans could organize a counter attack.

I have been able to think of no method which could meet these requirements so well as a moving picture campaign greater in its magnitude than was ever seen in this world before. This leads me to the object for which I submit this plan.

From the investigation I have been able to make, it appears practicable to organize a moving picture offensive on such a scale as to move the Russian people to action, if they can be moved at all by any appeal of propaganda, almost in a single night. This would, of course, require nearly as much effort and preparation as a military offensive. The campaign would have to open simultaneously throughout Russia. That would require a great deal of waste work through elimination and selection of scenarios, but it would have this advantage: It would appeal to the Russian illiterates as no other form of propaganda could, and if it failed, it would do no harm, except through the loss of effort.

                    Yours sincerely,   G. S. Macfarland

TLS (WP, DLC).

From Charles Richard Crane

Dear Mr President   [New York] June 27 1918

I have just had two very helpful and informing talks about Russia, Siberia and eastern Asiatic affairs with Professor Ross of Wisconsin[1] and Professor Abbott of Washington University.[2] Professor Ross was six months in Russia, travelling more or less under my direction and authorized to make an intensive study of existing social and political forces.

Like everyone else who devotes any time to the Russian people he comes home full of enthusiasm and affection for them and anxious to help in any way. He had long and intimate talks with the actual political leaders and I believe understands present day affairs there better than any other American. I find that his views very much accord with the views of Professor Masaryk.

Professor Abbott has spent much time in the East and was the author of an excellent book before he went out there for me.[3] He especially knows his Japan well, speaks Japanese and understands her methods of advancing. He has some most illuminating ideas about her present day activities and the social struggle going on within her. Perhaps they could make some notes for you or you could fit them in in some way.

Yours always sincerely   Charles R. Crane

ALS (WP, DLC).
[1] That is, Edward Alsworth Ross.
[2] James Francis Abbott, formerly Professor of Zoology at Washington University, at this time serving with the Military Intelligence Division of the General Staff of the United States Army in Washington.
[3] James Francis Abbott, *Japanese Expansion and American Policies* (New York, 1916).

From John Joseph Pershing

My dear Mr. President: [Chaumont] France, June 27, 1918.

Permit me to thank you most cordially for the very kind message brought me personally by your nephew, Major Wilson.[1]

It is more than gratifying to know that you impose in me the confidence which your words convey. While I have felt sure of it from the beginning, this direct message has given me new encouragement.

I have not for a moment failed to realize the tremendous task that has been allotted to me, and in my humble way try to realize to the utmost my obligations to you and to the American people.

The splendid army that you have sent so rapidly is an inspiration to our allies. With sufficient training and under young and vigorous leaders, the fighting qualities of our men will be unequalled in Europe. I sincerely trust that the War Department may exert every effort to send a sufficient force to end the war next year and profit by the splendid spirit of aggressiveness that prevails throughout the country and throughout the army.

I can see no other end than a victorious one, and strongly endorse your view that we must fight on until we bring Germany completely to her knees.

I am happy to say that our relations with the other allies are most cordial. With the principle of unity of command established, the cooperation among the armies is quite satisfactory.

With my prayers for your personal welfare and the continued success of your administration, also with a new pledge of the patriotic support of the army in France, I again thank you for your kind message and extend to you expressions of my sincere loyalty and devotion.

Believe me, with high esteem and admiration,

Yours faithfully,   John J. Pershing.

TLS (WP, DLC).
¹ Undoubtedly an oral message. Maj. Alfred McCalmont Wilson, U.S.A., at this time an assistant quartermaster with the A.E.F. He was the son of John Adams Wilson, first cousin of Woodrow Wilson.

From Scott Ferris

My dear Mr. President: Washington, D. C. June 27, 1918.

I have been very anxious to see you about the Waterpower Bill. I had planned to come down and see you today in company with Judge Sims. I had an acute attack of tonsilitis last night and my throat is swollen shut until I don't feel able to get down today. Judge Sims will present the situation to you. The situation in a word is this:

For the past ten years the waterpower people have contended for four distinct things:

1. To have a grant of the waterpower sites of the country in perpetuity, as distinct from a term of years.

2. To have waterpower sites granted to them without paying any royalty.

3. To have waterpower sites granted to them without any reservation to the Government of power to regulate them.

4. In the event they could not secure a grant in perpetuity and were compelled to accept a grant for a term of years; they have always insisted upon having a recapture clause, framed in such a way that it would be impossible to get Congress to appropriate a sufficient sum of money to ever retake them.

As to the first three contentions we have succeeded in heading them off. As to the last one they have succeeded in getting precisely what they want through this so-called "net investment scheme." This so-called "net investment scheme" in a word, requires the Government at the expiration of the term as a condition precedent to any retaking to pay the waterpower interests not what the property is actually worth, but to pay them back the original investment, plus all improvements, extensions, etc.

It will be observed at a glance that this requires the Government not to pay what the property is worth at the time of retaking, but to pay them back what they have paid for it, after they had used it fifty years and made profits and dividends from it.

This renders the Government an insurer of all their investment; this affords them a subsidy which no other legislation has ever dreamed of; this cannot be in the public interest. This is allowing them to get by indirection what no one would think of giving them by any direct method.

Four times the House of Representatives, during your administration, has passed on this matter, and each time until now it has been decided rightly and by an overwhelming majority. I cannot see why we should now make this surrender.

It seems to me during war times we ought to be more vigilant than ever in preserving natural resources and particularly the correct principles with reference to them.

I have prepared a minority report and am sending it down to you attached herewith.[1] I don't want to file it until I have had a chance to go over the matter with you.

Of course you will observe that this so-called "net investment" scheme was not a part of the Bill you delivered to us at the White House conference when the four Committees were present.[2] This was an afterthought, and I cannot believe is in the public interest.

I will ask Judge Sims to hand you this letter and a copy of my minority report. If you will be good enough to let Judge Sims know what your wishes are I shall try to carry them out.

With great respect, I am   Sincerely yours,   Scott Ferris

TLS (WP, DLC).
    [1] "Minority Report on Senate Bill No. 1419," CC MS (WP, DLC). In this report, Ferris discussed at length the objections to the bill which he outlines in the above letter. The report is printed in 65th Cong., 2d sess., *House Report No. 715*, pp. 40-46.
    [2] On January 4, 1918. See WW to FKL, Jan. 3, 1918, n. 1, Vol. 45.

Lord Reading to Arthur James Balfour

Washington. June 27th, 1918

No. 2888 Very Secret. From interview with Secretary Lansing today I think opinion here is crystallizing in favour of an Economic Commission to Russia. There is an idea of using the Czecho-Slovaks at Vladivostock of whom he said there were 15,000 there for the purpose of protection of the Commission, but that these and remaining Czecho-Slovaks were insufficiently armed. The U. S.

Administration had ascertained that there were altogether in the U. S. approaching 600,000 Russian rifles and some 2 to 3 million cartridges. He said that in England there were over 800,000 Russian rifles according to his information and many millions of cartridges. The U.S. Administration would be able to secure the rifles in their country and he asked if it would be possible to reserve the Russian rifles and ammunition in England which had not yet been converted for British use.

You must not assume that this is a definite policy decided by the President. Secretary Lansing's mind was turning to the equipment and arming of the Czecho-Slovaks both at Vladivostock and elsewhere and of such Russians as might join these forces, but it does not at all follow that the President intends to adopt it.

Later in the day I saw the French Ambassador who had had news of the desire to re-arm the Czecho-Slovak troops at Vladivostock. His information was that Russian rifles were there in the town under English control and in sufficient numbers. The British Consul had been notified of the wish to use these rifles and had undertaken to inform H.M.G.

M. Jusserand further informed me that he had had cable that General Foch said that the Germans had quite recently withdrawn several divisions from Russia and that it had become necessary to create a diversion. M. Jusserand has given this information to the President. This is timely as impression prevails here that General Foch is not favourable to intervention.

T telegram (Reading Papers, FO 800/223, PRO).

From the Diary of Colonel House

June 27, 1918.

The Russian Ambassador and Kornaloff[1] came from Washington to see me. The latter was a Minister in the Cabinets of both Miliukoff and Kerensky. They came at the President's direction. The President evidently thought I had more time to waste than he had, for, after all, it was a waste of time. They both wanted military intervention and in a way that would immediately antagonize the Soviets and Bolsheviki. Their theory is that if this is not done, the Allies will not be able to rally around them the public opinion in Russia antagonistic to the Bolsheviki. I was non-committal on this point, but satisfied them as to my attitude on sending in a relief commission with sufficient force to maintain order.

[1] That is, Aleksandr Ivanovich Konovalov.

A Message to Teachers[1]

[June 28, 1918]

Having myself been a teacher for twenty-five years, I am glad to avail myself of this occasion to greet my fellow-teachers, to congratulate you on your opportunities for public service, and to address a few words to you with regard to the peculiarly solemn public obligation which now rests upon you.

May I not earnestly suggest to you the necessity that you should by study and reflection acquire a deep spiritual understanding of the fundamental principles of our Government, whereof our Constitution is only a single though the chief expression, in order that you may be the better able to communicate the spirit of our institutions to your pupils? The country must rely chiefly upon you to interpret America to the children of new generations, to make them understand that it was by the law of its own nature that this nation was led into the world war, in order that for all time to come the principles which brought about its own birth should be made secure; that it was no new or strange doctrine which drew our country into association with European nations in this supreme enterprise, but rather fulfillment and extension of the principles for which Washington fought, a necessary application, indeed, of those principles to new conditions and to an age wherein it is no longer possible for one nation to live apart and to itself.

Under your instruction the children should come to see that it was the high logic of events and the providence of God that the United States and Germany, the one the most consistent practitioner of the new creed of mankind and the other the most consistent practitioner of the old, should thus meet in battle to determine whether the new democracy or the old autocracy shall govern the world, and under your instruction the children should be made to understand the stern duty and the supreme privilege which belong to the United States of being chief interpreter to the world of those democratic principles which we believe to constitute the only force which can rid the world of injustice and bring peace and happiness to mankind. The objects for which this war is being waged with indescribable pain and sacrifice cannot be kept secure in the future unless the children of this new generation, for whose sake the war is in fact prosecuted, themselves understand democracy, not as a mere word but as a living and vital thing. It is for them that the sacrifice is made, and by them that the fruits of the sacrifice must be gathered and safeguarded.

You who are in daily contact with young minds have a unique opportunity to instruct them in the true meaning of such words as

LIBERTY and DEMOCRACY, to interpret phrases too often used lightly or thoughtlessly, and convert them into realities which shall quicken the understandings of your pupils and thereby make them the more valiant and determined defenders of the faith.

Instruction in patriotism has always been a duty in American schools. It is now more than ever a duty to teach a burning, uncompromising patriotism which will admit of no divided allegiance but demands all that the heart and energy of the citizen can give, and at the same time a patriotism so pure and enlightened, so free from sham and subterfuge, that it leaves room for intelligent sympathy with other peoples living under other flags. A due regard for the rights of other nations is as necessary to enlightened patriotism as an insistence upon the rights of our own nation. The meaning of this war and of America's part in it is not fully comprehended unless we understand the claims of humanity as well as of our own country upon us. It is our present glory that we are battling for oppressed humanity everywhere as well as for our own rights, and that America seeks no selfish ends.   Woodrow Wilson.

TS MS (Letterpress Books, WP, DLC).
    [1] Stockton Axson was about to begin a coast-to-coast lecture tour, appearing chiefly before groups of teachers. At the suggestion of Howard Washington Odum, at this time Professor of Educational Sociology at the University of Georgia, Axson had drafted a message for Wilson which he proposed to incorporate in his lecture. Wilson approved the idea and sent Axson the revised text printed above. S. Axson to JPT, June 25, 1918, TLS, enclosing draft, T MS, both in WP, DLC; WW to S. Axson, June 28, 1918, TLS (Letterpress Books, WP, DLC). Wilson's text closely followed Axson's draft.

Three Letters to Robert Lansing

My dear Mr. Secretary,   The White House. 28 June, 1918.

The French Ambassador told me this afternoon that some proposal for a joint declaration about this matter[1] was on its way over the cables to him, our assent, or dissent, being desired by to-morrow, in order that the declaration, if agreed to, should be uttered on Sunday; but the message was then incomplete and he gave me no intimation of its character.

I had assumed that we would make no formal public declaration, but that we would make public our communication to the Serbian ministry *after* acquainting the governments with which we are associated with its contents. I do not now know of any nearby public occasion on which I could embody it *naturally* in what I might have to say.[2]   Faithfully Yours,   W.W.

WWTLI (WP, DLC).
    [1] Recognition of the right of the South Slavs to self-determination.
    [2] See RL to WW, June 29, 1918 (first letter of that date).

My dear Mr. Secretary   The White House. 28 June, 1918.

I have read this communication[1] with genuine pleasure.
                              Faithfully Yours,   W.W.

WWTLI (SDR, RG 59, 861.00/2216½, DNA).
 [1] The Enclosure printed with RL to WW, June 27, 1918 (second letter of that date).

My dear Mr. Secretary,   The White House. 28 June, 1918.

I hope that you will warn the legation at Berne to be very careful indeed not to burn their fingers by touching in any way this questionable business.[1]   Faithfully Yours,   W.W.

WWTLI (R. Lansing Papers, NjP).
 [1] Wilson was responding to P. A. Stovall to RL, June 24 and 26, 1918, T telegrams (SDR, RG 59, 763.72/10512 and 763.72/10518, DNA). In both telegrams, Stovall reported that, in the wake of the fall of the Bulgarian government of Premier Vasil Radoslavov, Bulgarians in Switzerland were beginning to put out feelers looking toward a separate peace with the other Balkan powers and/or the Allies. Stovall believed it very likely that someone would approach him to this end, and he asked for instructions as to how he should deal with Bulgarian territorial aspirations in the Balkans, with possible requests for American financial aid to Bulgaria, and with a possible request that he serve as an unofficial intermediary between the Bulgarians and representatives of other Balkan states.

To Charles Richard Crane

My dear Friend: [The White House] 28 June, 1918

Thank you for telling me about Professor Ross (who, by the way, I know very well myself) and Professor Abbott. Would it be possible for you to suggest to them that a brief thesis from each of them on the aspects of the Russian situation which are most hopeful to them would be very warmly welcomed by me?

With the warmest regards from us all,
                         Faithfully yours,   Woodrow Wilson

TLS (Letterpress Books, WP, DLC).

From Thetus Wilrette Sims

Dear Mr. President: Washington, D. C. June 28, 1918.

I beg to call your attention to the enclosed House Joint Resolution introduced by Mr. Aswell,[1] which resolution speaks for itself.

Will you kindly give me your opinion as to the desirability and advisability of the immediate passage of this resolution. If you will kindly give me in detail your reasons for supporting the resolution or for opposing it, if you are opposed to its passage, I shall be glad to have you do so.   Very truly yours,   T. W. Sims

TLS (WP, DLC).
¹ James Benjamin Aswell, Democratic congressman from Louisiana, had introduced a resolution (H.J. Res. 309) on June 27, 1918, to "insure the continuous operation of electrical communicating systems, to guard the secrecy of war dispatches, and to prevent communications between public enemies." It authorized the President, if he deemed it necessary, to "take possession and control of any telegraph, telephone, marine cable, or radio systems" and to operate them under the same provisions which were governing federal control of the railroads. The resolution was referred to the House Committee on Interstate and Foreign Commerce on the same day, and it was later referred instead to the Committee on Military Affairs. It is missing in WP, DLC; however, it is printed in *Cong. Record*, 65th Cong., 2d sess., p. 8719.

To Thetus Wilrette Sims

My dear Mr. Sims: [The White House] 28 June 1918

Thank you for consulting me about the enclosed. I endorse entirely the enclosed letter from the Postmaster General,¹ which I herewith return, and think that the reasons are stated by him truly and comprehensively.

Cordially and sincerely yours,   Woodrow Wilson

TLS (Letterpress Books, WP, DLC).
¹ Sims had also sent a copy of Aswell's resolution to Burleson, Baker, and Daniels on June 28, 1918, and had asked for their comments. Burleson replied on the same day and stated, among other things, the following:

"At this moment the paralysis of a large part of the system of electrical communication is threatened with possible consequences prejudicial to our military preparations and other public activities that might prove serious or disastrous. We are reminded that there is not a nation engaged in the war that intrusts its military or other communications to unofficial agencies.

"I deem it, therefore, my duty not merely to approve but to urge the passage of the resolution, in order that the President may act, if necessary, to safeguard the interests of the country during the prosecution of the war." Burleson's letter, together with the replies of Baker and Daniels, is printed in *Cong. Record*, 65th Cong., 2d sess., p. 8719.

From Robert Lansing, with Enclosure

My dear Mr. President: Washington June 28, 1918

Allow me to bring to your attention a telegram from Admiral Knight to the Navy Department, dated June 26th, which gives a more complete statement regarding the aims and plans of the Czecho-Slovak troops than that contained in the telegram from the American Consul at Vladivostok which you have already seen.¹

Admiral Knight's report seems to present with some definiteness the question of Czecho-Slovak operations against German and Austrian prisoners of war in Siberia and the attitude of this Government and the Allies. I have not been inclined to attach weight to Major Drysdale's² conclusions in the past, but in this matter which the Admiral reports, his views are endorsed by Mr. Langdon Warner³ who is conservative and sound and whom I regard as a reliable observer.   Faithfully yours,   Robert Lansing.

TLS (WP, DLC).

¹ That is, J. K. Caldwell to RL, June 25, 1918.

² Walter Scott Drysdale, U.S.A., Military Attaché at Peking since February 23, 1918.

³ Warner, an archaeologist and museum director from Philadelphia, had been appointed Vice Consul at Harbin on March 28, 1918.

ENCLOSURE

PARAPHRASE

From: Flag BROOKLYN
To: Secnav.

Members of Czecho-Slavak National Council have today visited me and desire to communicate to me and through me to the U. S. Government the present situation of Czecho-Slavak Military forces in Siberia and attitude of those forces and of the National Council towards the Soviet Government of Russia and the Austrian-German prisoners of war. Intelligence from the westward and central Siberia is not complete but it is understood that Czechs have control Siberian Railroad from Penza to Nijniendiensk¹ with force of approximately 40,000. Their relatively small emigration at Nijniendinsk is opposed by perhaps 20,000 Austrian German prisoners armed by Soviet government and commanded by German officers. The railroad Eastward is held by mixed force, prisoners and Red Guard but with prisoners heavily predominating. There are several thousand at Chita and the same at Habarosk² and Nikolsk. The indications now are that prisoners instead of acting with and under Soviets are out of hand and compelling obedience.

The Soviets have been overthrown in region controlled by Czechs and largely as result of their presence but without their active assistance, and replaced by a new Government wholly Russian but anti-Bolshevic and made up largely of delegates elected some months ago to Constitutional Convention to local Dumas and Zem[s]tvos. This Government appears to be supported by large majority of people including entire peasant population. All observers coming over Amur line recently say that popular sentiment whenever it finds free expression is strongly anti-Bolshevik and that Soviet power from Nijnieudinsk eastward would fall at once if it were not supported by prisoners of war. As stated by the Czech National Council all the foregoing is fully confirmed by Major Drysdale, American Attaché at Peking, and Langdon Warner who arrived last night from Marinsk. Drysdale who has heretofore minimized danger from war prisoners, admits they have now gone beyond control Soviets. Czech forces Vladivostok have received orders from Commander at Novonikolaevsk to proceed Westward to open and hold railroad and join forces from the Westward to attack on Austro-German forces Irkuts. The object of the National Council in visiting me was not only to lay out situation before me for transmission to my government but put out the following questions:

1. In view of many difficulties involved for the Czech forces in making their way to Irkuts, holding the road open behind them and finally cooperating efficiently with their Western detachments, they ask to be informed whether help can be expected from the other Allied Powers whose ally they consider themselves to be and in whose interest as well as in their own they consider that they are acting against the many thousand of armed Austro-German prisoners in Siberia.

2. If they succeed with or without help in obtaining control of the Siberian Railroad from Vladivostok to the Volga they ask to be informed whether the Allies desire that they continue to hold the road with the exception that the allies will join them in the establishment of a new eastern front.

3. If they remain in Russia to fight on a new Eastern front they ask to be informed minimum this force will be accepted by the allies as the equivalent of fighting on the Western front and as entitled them to same consideration when terms of peace are finally agreed upon as if they had proceeded to the Western front in accordance with their original agreement with the French Government. The foregoing questions were submitted by the members of the council in the finest spirit of loyalty and with no intimation of intent to abate in any degree their determination to fight on one front or the other, whatever the reply to their question might be. They appeared doubtful as to possibility of working their way back to Irkutz against the combined opposition of Bolskeviki and prisoners without allied help but am convinced they will attempt it if necessary and I should feel confident of their success if it were not for the ease with which bridges and tunnels can be destroyed.

I stated that I was not in a position to reply to any of their questions but that I should take pleasure to comply with the request to forward them to my Government. It is my understanding that the same question will be submitted to the other allied governments through Naval or Consular channels. I request, if it is not considered advisable to reply to those questions, that I be so informed. Acknowledge. Flag Brooklyn.

T telegram (WP, DLC).
1 Actually, Nizhneudinsk.
2 That is, Khabarovsk.

From Robert Lansing, with Enclosure

My dear Mr. President: Washington June 28, 1918.

I send you a letter which I have received from Mr. F. N. Doubleday[1] in which he encloses the memorandum of a conversation with Baron Goto last March.

Will you be good enough to return the letter and its enclosure to me after reading?   Faithfully yours,   Robert Lansing.

TLS (SDR, RG 59, 894.00/142½, DNA).
[1] Frank Nelson Doubleday, president of Doubleday, Page & Co., publishers.

E N C L O S U R E

Memo. of Conference with Baron Goto,
Minister of Home Affairs, at Tokyo,
March 22, 1918.

1. Japan would be in great danger if she had Germany as a near neighbor, and at whatever cost she must do what she can to keep Russia between as an independent state. Because Russia has no unity, Japan must help to create unity, as German civilization means a terrible menace.

2. Seven tenths of the Japanese people are agitating in favor of an invasion of Siberia for purpose of conquest. The Jingoes are most active, but they cannot control. Baron Goto repeatedly said that he agreed with Mr. Wilson, but the man in the street did not understand and failed to appreciate that Japan was bound to lose by an aggressive policy.

3. There is one influence which is saving and will save the situation; viz., the late Emperor[1] wrote some 30,000 poems; the Genros[2] and the whole people venerate these messages and the ethical teachings which they carry. The verses, as President Wilson knows, severely condemn war, and call upon the people to avoid war at all cost, the Emperor having seen its horrors in the two conflicts with China and Russia. He makes the appeal, which is virtually a command from a higher power, and this will prevent any violent outbreak of war sentiment. Prince Yamagata[3] knows and counts upon this. Baron Goto asked that this statement should be given to President Wilson, not as a personal message, but as an official one:

That the old Emperor's wishes, as expressed by his poems, will enable the present Government to control the people.

That they (the Japanese) have little or no skill in shaping public opinion, which they greatly need. That with the single exception of General Grant many years ago, no foreign influence has helped public opinion towards Japan; but the present Government is eager for help in this particular, and he welcomes the plan of supplying more and better news from America.

Regarding China—Baron Goto accepted as true the statement that Japan would have to do something big and generous to obtain China's goodwill, and this they are prepared to do. The Japanese, who were her nearest neighbors, had seen all countries but the United States take an aggressive attitude toward China for many years, and to China's great loss. It was very hard to convince the Japanese people that Japan should stay her hand, but he (Goto) knew that the United States had been in the right, and was doing his utmost to make his countrymen realize it.

One difficulty came about through the fact that China was Japan's earliest teacher; now Japan had grown in power and she was acting as teacher, which perhaps created friction; also she was becoming more of a competitor in trade, which produced irritation.

In conclusion, Baron Goto thanked me for having expressed myself so frankly; he was glad to know facts even if they were not pleasant. He thought the United States would greatly help Japan by her policy of frank diplomacy. No matter how discouraging it seemed at first, this policy was bound to win in the end, and he asked that I communicate his sentiments to the President.

I had previously explained that I was in Japan only as a Red Cross man, and I may say that I visited him at his invitation, and my frank statements and suggestions were made only as the result of his distinct request.   F. N. Doubleday.

CC MS (SDR, RG 59, 894.00/142½, DNA).
    [1] That is, Mutsuhito, the Meiji Emperor, who reigned from 1867 to 1912.
    [2] Usually called the Genro, or Elder Statesmen, a small, extralegal group of retired governmental officials, most of whom had played vital roles in the transformation and modernization of the Japanese government in the Meiji era, who now served as informal but very powerful advisers to the Emperor. They customarily dictated the choice of a Prime Minister and advised on other important matters of foreign and domestic policy. The group, which never numbered more than about eight, consisted of four men in 1918, three of whom were past eighty years of age and the fourth seventy years old. See the index references in Robert A. Scalapino, *Democracy and the Party Movement in Prewar Japan: The Failure of the First Attempt* (Berkeley and Los Angeles, 1953).
    [3] Prince Aritomo Yamagata, age eighty, principal creator of the modern Japanese army, Premier of Japan, 1889-1891 and 1898-1900, at this time the dominating figure of the Genro.

From James Hardy Dillard

My dear Mr President: New York June 28. 1918

You may recall meeting for a few moments the University Commission on Southern Race Questions.[1] This Commission is about to publish its minutes,[2] including three open letters to College men

of the South, which have been published in most of the Southern
College papers. In view of present agitation I thought that perhaps
you would like to see the letter on Lynching.[3]

With highest admiration and respect,

Very truly,   James H. Dillard

ALS (WP, DLC).
[1] About both the meeting and the commission, see n. 1 to remarks on the race question,
printed at Dec. 15, 1914, Vol. 31.
[2] *Minutes of the University Commission on Southern Race Questions* (n.p., n.d.).
[3] W. S. Sutton *et al.*, January 5, 1916, printed galley proof sheet (WP, DLC). This letter
called upon college men in the South to speak out against lynching. It said that lynching
was "a contagious social disease" which attacked the very fabric of civilization, and it
cited statistics on lynching in the United States for 1914 and 1915 to show that the
grounds given by perpetrators of the crime had spread far beyond the original ones of
punishment for rape and/or murder. This open letter is printed in *ibid.*, pp. 45-46.

From Lord Reading

My dear Mr. President   Washington June 28th/1918

This afternoon I received a very urgent request from the Prime
Minister and the British War Cabinet to deliver a message to you
to the following effect:

The British Delegates have been instructed by the British War
Cabinet to lay before the next ensuing meeting of the Supreme
War Council (July 2nd) proposals for the assistance of the Russian
people in their present unhappy situation.

The British War Cabinet therefore earnestly hope that the President will not decide upon the policy to be pursued by the United
States of America with regard to Russia until they have had the
opportunity of communicating to him the resolution of the Supreme
War Council upon the proposals.

I have been anxious not to trouble you unnecessarily with a visit
and therefore have adopted this means of conveying the message
to you.

I am my dear Mr. President

Yours with the highest respect   Reading.

ALS (WP, DLC).

Charles Lee Swem to the White House Staff

[The White House, c. June 28, 1918]

Please call Miss Lathrop on the telephone and tell her that the
President is in this embarrassing situation:[1] When Congress refuses
an appropriation, he is not at liberty to use public moneys for a

purpose for which they refused to expend them. Tell her that he hopes that if it is feasible, she will keep her little force together until the Secretary of Labor returns, at any rate, and we can confer as to the practicable course of action. The President is deeply grieved to learn that the appropriation has been refused.   C.L.S.

T MS (WP, DLC).
    [1] Swem was responding to the White House Staff to WW, June 28, 1918, two TL (WP, DLC). These memoranda relayed a request from Julia Lathrop that she be permitted to see Wilson before noon on June 29. She explained that, because of the failure of Congress to provide an appropriation for the Children's Bureau, she would have to discharge her staff on June 29 unless something could be done. She hoped that Wilson might be able to supply money from his discretionary funds.
    Although there is no further correspondence in the Wilson Papers on this subject, Wilson did succeed in obtaining an appropriation by Congress of $268,160 for the Children's Bureau for the fiscal year 1918-1919. Wilson added $229,000 from his war emergency fund. Of this latter sum, $150,000 was spent in the continuation of the "Children's-Year Campaign," begun on April 6, 1918. This was an effort to stimulate public and private efforts to promote the welfare of children. "Seventh Annual Report of the Chief, Children's Bureau," *Reports of the Department of Labor, 1919* (Washington, 1920), pp. 723-27.

Two Letters from Robert Lansing

My dear Mr. President: Washington June 29, 1918.

    Day before yesterday I telegraphed to all our embassies and legations an extract from our note to the Serbian Minister in regard to the Slav peoples,[1] and yesterday, before I received your letter telling me of the French Ambassador's statement as to some proposal for a joint declaration, I had already issued to the press a statement embodying our declaration to the Serbs.[2]

    I am not at all sure but that this has been fortunate though inadvertent because by acting independently we avoid the declaration being subjected to objection and suggested amendment induced by the jealousies and differences of European politics which would result in prolonged discussions. The Allies are constantly seeking to have us act jointly with them in political matters, and this is another effort in that direction. I believe that to keep our hands free and to act independently is our best policy, since we can in that way avoid taking sides in the conflict of interests.

    Will you be good enough to tell me if I have rightly interpreted your wishes in this regard?

                    Faithfully yours,   Robert Lansing

    [1] RL to W. H. Page, June 28, 1918, T telegram (SDR, RG 59, 763.72/10568a, DNA), printed in *FR-WWS 1918*, 1, I, 816.
    [2] "U. S. Position Is That Slav Race Should Be Entirely Free From Teutonic Rule," *Official Bulletin*, II (June 28, 1918), 1.

My dear Mr. President: Washington June 29, 1918.

Since telephoning you yesterday afternoon further activity of the Department of Commerce in connection with a Commission to Russia has been brought to my attention. In one case an officer of the Department of State was told by an individual whose name the officer did not feel at liberty to disclose that he (the informant) had been asked to confer with Mr. Willard about going to Siberia with him on the Commission. In the other case, an official of one of the Government Boards (who requested me not to mention his name) said that one of the officers of the Department of Commerce spoke of the commission being organized by his Department and expressed the hope that the Department of State would not meddle with it as it was a Department of Commerce matter. In addition to this I find in the Washington POST today an article stating that a commercial commission is being organized.[1] This article causes me considerable embarrassment since I have declined absolutely to discuss the question with the correspondents.

In view of the situation which is thus being created I feel that it is my duty to call the matter to your attention. Please do not think that I am criticizing Secretary Redfield for I am convinced that he is not to blame for the unfortunate impression which these reports cause or for the publicity which is being given to the proposed commission. I believe that the fault lies with his subordinates who appear desirous of obtaining control of the commission or at least of gaining a measure of notoriety. I am sure that Secretary Redfield would not be influenced by such improper motives and would seek rather to cooperate rather than to monopolize the work of the commission.

You can understand that in the circumstances I have been disturbed by these reports because of the difficulties which may arise if they indicate correctly the spirit of the officers of the Department of Commerce. I naturally am fearful of a lack of harmony and cooperation which seem to me essential for success.

Whatever may be the most effective agency for penetration in Siberia, whether industrial, commercial, social or political, I believe that we must be guided by the political effect and for that reason I suggested a subsidiary council in this country to analyze and study the work of the commission and to compare it and in a measure regulate it by the reports received from other sections of Russia. I do not feel, therefore, that the Department of Commerce, which only represents one branch of the work, should be permitted to dominate the activities of the commission.

I would not trouble you with this matter except that I am so anxious for the success of the commission that I am afraid it will be endangered if subordinate officers of the Department of Commerce seek to take over its entire direction, as appears to be the case, and which you told me yesterday was not your plan.

In any event I think publicity at the present time is unfortunate and may defeat the purpose of the commission.

Faithfully yours,　Robert Lansing.

TLS (WP, DLC).

[1] "Help to Russia Waits," *Washington Post*, June 28, 1918.

From James Duval Phelan

My dear Mr President　　　　　　　　Washington June 29 18

I called at the White House to ask, if agreeable to you, to have a brief talk on this subject: British American relations can only be improved by a frank statement of Ireland's right to autonomous government (without necessarily defining the kind) and the prompt granting of it.

Your July 4th speech might be a favorable time, should you see fit to make a statement. I am told Lloyd George wants your support to win over Tory opposition & to clear the way in England.

If you grant an interview a committee of about four will be in the party—Judge Dowling[,] Bishop Harding[1] and two others to be selected. I am asked to make this request by representative men interested in the cause.

I am, Respectfully yours,　James D. Phelan

ALS (WP, DLC).

[1] That is, Victor James Dowling, justice of the Supreme Court of New York and president of the Friendly Sons of St. Patrick, and the Rt. Rev. Alfred Harding, Protestant Espiscopal Bishop of Washington. Harding had been born in Lisburn, Ireland.

From Herbert Clark Hoover

Dear Mr. President:　　　　　　　　Washington *29 June 1918*

As I shall be leaving for Europe in the course of a few days, I am anxious to secure your approval to the plans I have in view:

First: I propose, in conference with the Food Administrators of England, France and Italy, to study the world harvest supplies, the Allied and United States requirements of the principal food commodities for the next twelve months and the distribution necessary at each point.

In order that these studies may be carried out expeditiously, I propose to make use of the staffs which the Food Administration has already in Europe and I propose to be accompanied by three or four assistants representing the technical side of different food commodity groups. Through these conferences I propose that we shall draw up as nearly as may be the general programme for the ensuing twelve months' requirements, sources and supplies in each commodity group.

After these preliminary programmes are drawn up, I would propose that they should be submitted to the International Maritime Council for consideration on the shipping side and, upon the settling of these issues, to the Inter-Allied Finance Council for their consideration.

Second: You will recollect that during the past year we have built up certain bodies for co-ordinated action, that is, an "Executive" for cereals, another for meats and fats, and a third for sugar. I propose to add to this a fourth, covering jute and hemp. We have also consolidated the direction of overseas buying into these bodies to eliminate competition. There is some complaint as to these "Executives" and we need more effectual relations to them as, in every commodity, our interest in distribution extends outside the United States. I propose therefore to endeavour to arrange that either these "Executives" themselves, or their policies, should be controlled by a committee representative of each of the four Governments; they, of course, operating within the programmes agreed.

For this purpose I propose to add somewhat to the staff the Food Administration already has in Europe so as to carry out this work efficiently. The necessity for these "executives" increases daily by virtue of our common interest in supplies from all quarters of the world. One point in having these "executives" is to have proper advice here as to the fluctuating requirements and supplies of the different Allied nations in order that we may properly formulate our production and conservation policies at this end.

It may prove necessary in order to obtain co-ordination between these different food "executives" that I should constitute some one of the gentlemen that I leave in Europe as the responsible head of our American food group, who can represent me personally in relations with the different Allied Food Ministers and who can represent in common the relation from our point of view with the American War Trade, Finance and Maritime representatives in Europe.

In all these programmes and arrangements I shall, of course, immediately submit any programmes for your approval, and if we consider it desirable to vary from the above form of organization, I shall, of course, secure approval first; and, as is customary, I shall assume it is my duty to approach the various European Food Ministers through and in co-operation with our Embassies abroad.

Third: I feel the food problem is for fundamental reasons a problem of marked distinction from all of the other Inter-Allied supply problems. This revolves around the points of psychology and morale which arise in this class of supplies as they so much affect the minds of the civil population both abroad and in the United States to a degree not touched by the more abstruse and less personal problems of war trade, finance and munitions.

During the whole of the past year we have built up a devotion of the American people to the issue that we must make any sacrifice of food short of damage to public health that the necessity of the Allies calls for. In other words, we have had morally and effectually a pooling of foodstuffs with the Allied peoples. The confidence this has inspired in Allied populations, of which I could furnish you many particulars, has been very great. I would therefore like to maintain this attitude in negotiation as being a direction from you that "the American people are gladly willing to make any sacrifice in consumption and production of foodstuffs short of damage to our own efficiency in the war that will maintain the health, comfort and courage of the people of the Allied countries. That we are, in fact, eating at a common table with them." I have in view endeavouring this year, if our supplies warrant, the establishment of a universal bread of about 20% other cereals than wheat over the United States and the Allied countries and to take off the quantity restrictions in Europe. This will be a much better bread than now prevails. It would give us a much better moral background here to effect economies and would have a great moral effect in Europe. It would also have a depressing effect in Germany where much comfort has been taken out of our bread difficulties.

In all this matter it seems to me fundamental that no financial restrictions should be placed upon the supplies of money for the purchase by the Allies of staple food commodities of United States production. Unless this can be assured, we cannot hope for continuity of policy in either production or consumption. On the other hand, problems will arise which are purely Treasury problems, as to the finance of supplies that may be purchased by the Allies from overseas sources outside the United States where they may want financial assistance.

I would indeed be glad to know if the above meets with your approval.   Yours faithfully,   Herbert Hoover

OKeh   W.W.

TLS (Hoover Archives, CSt-H).

Lord Reading to Arthur James Balfour

Washington. June 29, 1918.

No. 2933. Your telegram No. 3983.[1]

The anxiety that the President might make a declaration of policy with regard to Russia very shortly is allayed for the moment. Most reliable information is that nothing has yet been settled although the tendency is still that indicated by me to you; first the sending of an Economic Commission of a very comprehensive character with the intention that it shall penetrate at least as far as the Ural mountains as quickly as possible and secondly that there shall be some protective force to guard the Commission and its supplies. The second point is more in doubt than the first. The presence of the Czecho-Slovaks in Vladivostock may be looked to by the Americans as the guard thus avoiding the immediate necessity of the despatch of troops.

Your message will be conveyed to the President today and I shall communicate later with you.

T telegram (W. Wiseman Papers, CtY).
  [1] A. J. Balfour to Lord Reading, June 28, 1918, T telegram (W. Wiseman Papers, CtY). About this telegram, see Lord Reading to A. J. Balfour, July 3, 1918 (second telegram of that date).

From Jean Jules Jusserand

Dear Mr. President,   Washington June 30, 1918

I was greatly struck by what you told me friday of the views of that remarkable woman, Marie Botchkarevas,[1] which views did not tally with what I had heard of her.

It seems that her sayings have more than once suffered from her translators who have not always been quite accurate (*traduttore, traditore*). I have it from, I think, one of the best possible sources, that she is ardently in favor of a military action on the part of the allies, Japanese included, all she would recommend concerning these is that, in the first contingent sent to Siberia, they be not in a majority; their number could be increased afterward to any extent.

As nothing that concerns so important a problem should be neglected, I feel confident that you will kindly excuse me for sending you this note

Believe me, dear Mr. President,

Very respectfully and sincerely yours   Jusserand

ALS (WP, DLC).
  [1] Maria Leont'evna Frolkova Bochkareva, a Russian woman of peasant origin, who had become world famous as the organizer and commander of an all-woman army unit,

the Women's Battalion of Death, which was formed in May 1917 and served at the front from July to November. The battalion was disbanded shortly after the November Revolution. After harrowing experiences at the hands of the Bolsheviks, Mme. Bochkareva was allowed to sail from Vladivostok for the United States on May 1, 1918. She reached Washington about May 29, on which date she had interviews with Robert Lansing and Newton D. Baker. *New York Times*, May 30, 1918. She saw Wilson at the White House on July 10.

Sir William Wiseman to Sir Eric Drummond

[Washington] June 30, 1918.

No. 106. I have been at the Embassy all this week, and return tomorrow.

(A). The absorbing topic in Washington is intervention in SI-BERIA, and it is full of enthusiasts who are seeking interviews with the President.

(B). I see no reason to change the views expressed in my No. 98 of June 14th,[1] except that there appears less chance of HOOVER heading the commission.

(C). The most interesting change is the awakening of American public opinion to the worthlessness of the BOLSHEVIC Government, and the importance of the Allies doing something in RUSSIA. Public opinion, however, has not yet adopted any definite policy, though it is far more favorable to JAPANESE intervention than three months ago. The President's attitude has not altered, but in this, as in other questions, he is liable to modify his views if he feels the majority of American public opinion is against him. I know he feels the responsibility of the situation, and is anxious but unconvinced. He hesitates—wondering where intervention would lead the United States. It would be, he thinks, a political adventure, the far-reaching effects of which it is impossible to foresee.

(D). There is a general impression here that GENERAL FOCH is not an advocate of intervention on a large scale. If FOCH declared himself very strongly on the subject, and stated that he thought intervention necessary from the military point of view, and desirable even if it meant so many less American troops for France, it would have more influence on the President than anything else.

(E). READING realises that undue pressure on the President, and particularly too many interviews with him, may have the opposite effect to that desired, but he is taking every opportunity of pressing firmly, but tactfully, the policy of His Majesty's Government.

T telegram (W. Wiseman Papers, CtY).
[1] W. Wiseman to E. Drummond, June 14, 1918.

A Veto Message

The White House,

TO THE HOUSE OF REPRESENTATIVES: *1 July, 1918.*

Though I realize very keenly the inconvenience to the Government of returning without my signature H.R. 10358, making appropriations for the legislative, executive, and judicial expenses of the Government for the fiscal year ending June 30, 1919, and for other purposes, I feel constrained to do so because of the provision contained in the last paragraph of the bill which increases the hours of work for the employees of the Government within the District of Columbia from seven to eight hours per day.

At the outset of the war I felt it my duty to urge all employers in the United States to make a special effort to see to it that the conditions of labor were in no respect altered unfavorably to the laborer. It has been evident from the first how directly the strain of this war is to bear upon those who do the labor which underlies the whole process of mobilizing the nation, and it seemed to me at the outset, as it seems to me now, that it is of the highest importance that the advantages which had been accorded labor before the war began should not be subtracted from or abated.

Having taken this position in an earnest appeal to other employers, I do not feel justified in assenting to a measure in which the United States as an employer changes the conditions of the labor of its own employees unfavorably to them, and I feel the freer to take this position because I have not learned from any quarter that the employees of the Government in the District have been slack in their labor or have demurred from doing any of the necessary additional tasks which the time and the exigency require. On the contrary, I have learned that they have cheerfully done additional labor and have not needed the compulsion of law.

Woodrow Wilson.

Printed in *Message from the President of the United States, Vetoing H.R. 10358 . . .* (Washington, 1918), p. 3.

To James Duval Phelan

My dear Senator: [The White House] 1 July, 1918

I received your note of June twenty-ninth and was sorry that I missed your personal call.

I realize, of course, the critical importance of the whole Irish question, but I do not think that it would be wise for me in any public utterance to attempt to outline a policy for the British Government with regard to Ireland. It is a matter, of course, of the utmost delicacy, and I must frankly say that I would not know how to handle it without risking very uncomfortable confusions of counsel.   Cordially and sincerely yours,   Woodrow Wilson

TLS (Letterpress Books, WP, DLC).

To William Fellowes Morgan

My dear Mr. Morgan: [The White House] 1 July, 1918

The plan laid before me in your letter of June twenty-eighth is certainly a most interesting and important one.[1] Frankly, I must say to you that I am sorry that any large plans of this sort should be undertaken without first consulting the administration. All of our relations with Russia, and indeed some very critical aspects of the general European situation, are dependent upon our following exactly the right course in our dealings with Russia and everything that affects her, and it seems to me absolutely necessary so long as the war lasts that no plans should be privately developed with which the Government has not been previously acquainted and which it has not previously sanctioned. I do not mean that there is any legal obligation of this kind, but merely that there is an obvious practical obligation.

The plan you outline is most intelligently conceived, of course, and the objects sought are excellent, but I cannot form a judgment about it until I have more particular information about the Russian gentlemen named. I should like to know, for example, what their international connections were before the present chaos came upon Russia. The memorandum[2] you were kind enough to send me does not show whether they had German business connections or not, and I am unable to judge also as to their political sympathies, whether they wish to see a return to the old regime in Russia or not. I think you will agree with me that these particulars are of very considerable importance.

We all want to help Russia, but my own experience has been that each plan in succession has been thrown out of gear by a sudden change of circumstances in Russia, and it is of the utmost importance that there should be intimate cooperation in everything of this kind.   Sincerely yours,   Woodrow Wilson

TLS (Letterpress Books, WP, DLC).
[1] W. F. Morgan to WW, June 28, 1918, TLS, enclosing Vance Thompson to Merchants' Association of New York, June 3, 1918, TCL, both in WP, DLC. Thompson, American author of many works of fiction and nonfiction, who had spent many years in France and had most recently been serving as a director of French soldiers' homes, had proposed to the Merchants' Association a plan to reestablish in Russia "orderly government upon

strictly constitutional bases." He was acting on behalf of the Russian Union, which was "composed of the great Russian liberals of all parties" and which had within it "the germ of the future Russian government." The democratic future of Russia depended almost entirely, Thompson added, upon "the sympathy, support and immediate collaboration of the United States of America." Under the proposed plan, eight Russian industrial leaders, then in exile in France, would be brought to the United States to work in American business and industrial concerns in order that they might subsequently return to Russia as "missionaries of American trade and commerce—of American ideals and friendship." Morgan announced in his covering letter that the Merchants' Association had appropriated "ample funds" to carry out this project.

² T MS (WP, DLC). This undated and unsigned memorandum, which is filed with the above letter, gave further details of the project and included vitae of the eight Russians to be brought to the United States, as well as a lengthy list of names and addresses of other Russian exiles in France who were members of Union des Patriotes Russes, an organization in Paris which was also backing the project.

To Jean Jules Jusserand

My dear Mr. Ambassador: [The White House] 1 July, 1918

I am afraid that I did not leave the right impression upon you as to what I had heard quoted as the opinion of Madame Botchkarova with regard to military action in Siberia. I had heard that she said just what you quote with regard to joint military action there, but that she had said it would be a fatal mistake to send the Japanese in alone, so that, after all, the two versions do not differ.

Cordially and sincerely yours,   Woodrow Wilson

TLS (Letterpress Books, WP, DLC).

To Robert Lansing, with Enclosure

My dear Mr. Secretary,   The White House. 1 July, 1918.

Will you not be kind enough to have the enclosed message coded as soon as possible and sent to our Minister at Berne?

Faithfully Yours,   W.W.

WWTLI (SDR, RG 59, 763.72119/1770½, DNA).

E N C L O S U R E

The President requests that you immediately convey the following message to Professor George D. Herron at Geneva QUOTE I have just received your letter of the thirty-first of May and am deeply moved by it. Please let the Minister transmit to me by cable your answer to this question: Do you think that the immediate formation of a Society of Nations would have the effects you predict if its only members at the outset were the nations now associated in war against Germany? The neutral nations of Europe would in all likelihood not dare to enter such a Society now in such company for fear of becoming involved in the present conflict since some of them lie almost at the mercy of Germany.[1]

WWT MS (SDR, RG 59, 763.72119/1770½, DNA).
    [1] There is a WWsh draft of this document in WP, DLC. The message was conveyed in RL to Amlegation, Bern, July 1, 1918, T telegram (SDR, RG 59, 763.72119/1770a, DNA).

To Bernard Mannes Baruch

My dear Baruch: [The White House] 1 July, 1918

I see rather serious objections to adding to the membership of the Price Fixing Committee.[1] If we are to have a representative there of the farmers, why not representatives of many other classes of producers, and if the Shipping Board is to be represented, why not all the other purchasing agencies of the Government? I think we ought to go very slowly in this matter.

Cordially and faithfully yours,   Woodrow Wilson

TLS (Letterpress Books, WP, DLC).
    [1] Wilson was replying to B. M. Baruch to WW, June 27, 1918, TLS (WP, DLC).

To Edward Keating

My dear Mr. Keating: [The White House] 1 July 1918

Thank you for your letter of June twenty-ninth.[1] I would be obliged if you would remind me of the matter when the legislation is reached.

In unavoidable haste,
                        Sincerely yours,   Woodrow Wilson

TLS (Letterpress Books, WP, DLC).
    [1] E. Keating to WW, June 29, 1918, TLS (WP, DLC). Keating reported that he had spoken with Claude Kitchin in regard to the civil-service retirement bill (about which see K. D. McKellar to WW, June 22, 1918, n. 1). Kitchin did not want the bill brought up before the proposed summer recess of Congress but had no objection to its consideration in the autumn. Keating was sure that the bill could be passed at that time, provided it had Wilson's endorsement.

To Grenville Stanley Macfarland

My dear Mr. Macfarland: [The White House] 1 July, 1918

Let me personally acknowledge the receipt of your memorandum of June twenty-seventh about Russia, and thank you for it sincerely.
                        Very truly yours,   Woodrow Wilson

TLS (Letterpress Books, WP, DLC).

To Homer Peter Snyder[1]

My dear Mr. Snyder,   The White House 1 July, 1918.

I am pleased to know that the Washington quota of the White House wool sold for the benefit of the Red Cross has passed into your hands. I hope that it will in some form serve as a fitting memento of the splendid success of the recent effort to assist an organization of which we are all proud.

Very truly yours,   Woodrow Wilson

ALS (WP, DLC).
[1] Republican congressman from New York.

To Maria Leont'evna Frolkova Bochkareva

My dear Madame Botchkarova: [The White House] 1 July, 1918

The Secretary of State handed me the other day the little image of Saint Anne which you were generous enough to leave with him for me. He tells me that you wore it throughout your experience in the army and that it has been especially valued by you, and I am therefore very much touched and gratified that you should wish me to have it. I shall treasure it as among my most interesting possessions and also as an evidence of your very gracious friendship.

With the best wishes,

Sincerely yours,   Woodrow Wilson

TLS (Letterpress Books, WP, DLC).

Two Letters from Newton Diehl Baker

My dear Mr. President: Washington. July 1, 1918.

I have been much disturbed and my anxiety is growing at the situation in this country among the negroes. The reports of the Military Intelligence Branch of the Army seem to indicate more unrest among them than has existed before for years. Mr. George Foster Peabody has written me, expressing considerable apprehension, his fears being based upon reports of one sort and another which come to him naturally because of his philanthropic relation to questions of negro education.

Last week, a conference called at my suggestion brought together here at Washington some thirty or forty negroes who edit the most influential papers devoted to the interests of their race and two or three men like Dr. Moton of Tuskegee. I had the conference called in order that I might in a very authoritative way deny and disprove some rumors afloat in the country to the effect that negro soldiers were being badly treated in France and were being exposed in places of special danger in order to save the lives of white soldiers. I was able, I think, both from my own observations in France and from very specific cablegrams which I secured from General Pershing, to convince them of the baseless character of these rumors. They all admitted, however, that such stories were being circulated among their people and were to some extent being believed. I think the meeting resulted in a very helpful understanding and that the influence of the negro press is going to be sounder; but at the meeting Dr. Moton spoke with great frankness, admitted that there was unrest among the negroes of the country and that it was chiefly due to the apparently increasing frequency of lynchings of brutal and barbarous character. Every negro at the conference confirmed Moton's observations on this point.

Would it not be wise for you to write to the governor of some State in which a lynching has quite recently taken place a strong letter urging full use of the power of the State to search out and prosecute the offenders, and pointing out the unpatriotic character of these acts of brutality and injustice. Such a letter, if given to the press, would, I am sure, have a wholesome effect. It seems to me that in a spirit of cooperation you might even offer the assistance of the Department of Justice with its agencies of investigation to cooperate with the State authorities, both in the detection and prosecution of offenders. Apparently the negroes of the country feel that Federal agencies alone will be able to deal with such a situation, and, while of course no Federal legislation is likely on the subject, the voluntary and sympathetic cooperation of the Department of Justice would operate as a deterrent and would certainly allay some feeling among the leaders of the negro people.

Respectfully yours,   Newton D. Baker

My dear Mr. President: Washington. July 1, 1918.

More than one million American soldiers have sailed from the ports in this country to participate in the war in France. In reporting this fact to you, I feel that you will be interested in a few data showing the progress of our overseas military effort.

The first ship carrying military personnel sailed May 8, 1917, having on board Base Hospital No. 4 and members of the Reserve Nurses Corps.

General Pershing and his staff sailed on May 20, 1917. The embarkations in the months from May, 1917, to and including June, 1918, are as follows:

1917,	May	1,718
	June	12,261
	July	12,988
	August	18,323
	September	32,523
	October	38,259
	November	23,016
	December	48,840
1918,	January	46,776
	February	48,027
	March	83,811
	April	117,212
	May	244,345
	June	276,372
	Marines	14,644
	aggregating	1,019,115

The total number of troops returned from abroad, lost at sea, and casualties, is 8,165, and of these, by reason of the superbly efficient protection which the Navy has given our transport system, only 282 have been lost at sea.

The supplies and equipment in France for all troops sent is, by our latest report, adequate, and the output of our war industries in this country is showing marked improvement in practically all lines of necessary equipment and supply.

Respectfully yours,   Newton D. Baker

TLS (WP, DLC).

From Charles Turner Williams

Sir: Baltimore JULY First 1918

As Secretary and Treasurer of the American Red Cross Mission to Roumania, which trip gave me an opportunity to observe conditions in Russia, and having recently returned from that distracted country, I am taking the liberty of submitting to you my impressions of conditions prevailing there when I left.

My stay in Russia covered the period from the latter part of August, 1917, to December 7th, 1917, exclusive of a short stay in Roumania.

While in Russia I made it a point to meet and converse with people of high and low rank, the idea being to get the point of view of all elements, so far as possible, residing in that country.

My travel in Russia included a trip across the Trans-Siberian from Vladivostock to Moscow, thence to Petrograd, thence north to Archangel, and after considerable stay in the latter port, a trip south through to Roumania on a freight train with American Red Cross Supplies. I returned to this country, through Russia, early in December, when the Bolsheviki was in the height of its power.

The following is a summary of conclusions overwhelmingly forced upon me, and which as a loyal American citizen I take the liberty of submitting to you:

I. The Russians feel more friendly toward America than any country.

II. Germany is the least popular.

While many of the more ignorant are tired of war, and do not understand the issues, the masses of partly educated people with whom I came in contact on my long journey from Archangel to Roumania, express chagrin and mortification at Russia's failure to stand with the allies.

III. Next to Germany, Japan is by far the most unpopular nation with every class. The Russians do not trust the Japanese. The officers and the better class of Russians seem to feel that Japan has some ulterior purpose to serve in Russia. The Russians consider the Japanese their racial inferiors, and resent the defeat administered to the Russians by the Japanese in the Russian-Japanese war, which they explain by saying that this war was never a popular war in Russia.

IV. Next to Japan, the Russians dislike England. The English in Petrograd were all very much alarmed when I was there. I will not enter into an explanation why this feeling exists, except to say that any intelligent, observing man who had the opportunities that I had could not fail to be impressed with this fact.

And what is true in Petrograd is true in Archangel. The Russians in Archangel, of both high and low degree, resent the activity of the English at that port. The English are not diplomatic. And not only in Archangel, but in parts of Russia far removed therefrom, one would hear unfavorable comment about the English.

Since my return from Russia, January first, I have been watching with intense interest the course of the administration with respect to possible intervention in Russia by Japan. It seems to me that an all wise Providence is guiding our beloved President in these trying days.

But it is my opinion that if Japan alone were to send an armed force into Russia it would be a serious mistake from the standpoint of the allies. Such a move would be resented by Russia, and this resentment, aided by the usual German propaganda, would alienate the masses of Russia from the cause of the allies (and the masses are not yet past redemption).

On the other hand, I believe that armed intervention in Russia of American, English and French—and some Japanese, if necessary (but not more than necessary)—would result in bringing to the cause of the allies thousands of Russian soldiers, officer[s] and leaders who are only waiting for some such display of force to take sides against the present impossible Bolsheviki.

Respectfully submitted,   C. T. Williams

TLS (WP, DLC).

From Harper & Brothers

Dear Sir: New York, N. Y. July 1, 1918

We are having sent to you, by express today, an unusual set of books, which it has given us a great deal of pleasure to make. It has been a labor of love to put a fine book in a fine binding—ten books in fact—and they go to you with our compliments.

This set of the new Documentary Edition of "A History of the American People" is bound in three-quarter polished Turkey morocco, with the simple Jensen style of lettering.

Our attempt has been to match the inside of the books with an outside harmonious in dignity and strength, and that human warmth of style which the reader finds so abundantly as he turns the pages.

We beg to remain,

Most cordially yours,   Harper & Brothers

TLS (WP, DLC).

Basil Miles to Robert Lansing, with Enclosure

My dear Mr. Secretary: [Washington] July 1, 1918

I have just handed General March a copy of the telegram from Vladivostok giving details about the equipment and condition of the Czecho-Slovaks there.

General March tells me the President has discussed this question with Mr. Baker and that General March has given him a memorandum covering it. The General has informed Mr. Baker that he can procure 13,000 Russian rifles and one million rounds of ammunition and that he will take up with Admiral Benson the question of having these supplies carried to Vladivostok in naval vessels; that if the President decides to help the Czecho-Slovaks he may possibly find some machine guns for them. I gathered that the General believes military intervention hazardous, extremely difficult, and unsound policy.   Basil Miles

TLS (WP, DLC).

E N C L O S U R E

Paraphrase

From Commander in Chief Asiatic Squadron at Vladivostok.
TO Secretary of Navy. June 29, 1918

The following information is furnished at request of Consul and replying to telegram from State Department.

Czecho-Slovak forces Vladivostok 14,000 men, 5,000 officers, 2,500 with rifles, 26 machine guns, 586,000 cartridges, 1800 hand grenades. No other arms or ammunition; no other stores of arms and ammunition available. Large number of rifles in possession of Bolsheviki Government at Vladivostok without cartridges. Czechs not considering these available as absolutely unwilling to give ground for charges hostile Bolsheviki, insist wholly oppose Austro-Germans.

Morale troops magnificent; relations officers men most cordial. Organization two and a half regiments 11,500. Three batallions of infantry, one company telegraph experts, one company engineers, no equipment except above.

Officers: Major General Bloick,[1] Russian chosen for command by Czech Colonel. Each regiment commanded by Captain with necessary subordinates. Ability officers excellent.

Following material needed following expedite Irkutsk but suggest 50% increase for reserve: 13,000 rifles, one million cartridges; 18 light mounting guns, eighteen thousand rounds of ammunition; 60 trench mortars with 6,000 bombs; 100 machine guns with three million rounds of ammunition; 60 thousand hand grenades; engineer gear, and in addition, equipment including pontoons and material for temporary bridges with material for repairing railroad bridges and tunnels. All kinds of medical supplies and Red Cross. Water proof coats.

It is proposed to avoid as far as possible inopportune political questions. Will avoid associations Semenoff. Anxious to move as soon as possible. If assured Allied help will wait. If refused will proceed with 2,500 men for whom arms available. Specially request assistance railroad engineer for repair work, not fighting. Armed

Allied force would be welcomed. Request this be forwarded to State Department. Acknowledge.

NB: This is of course from Admiral Knight.

T MS (WP, DLC).
¹ Either Knight was in error or the name of the general was badly garbled in transmission. The Russian general in charge of the Czech forces in Vladivostok was Mikhail Konstantinovich Dieterichs. It was he who led the Czechs in seizing control of the city from the Bolsheviks on June 29.

Newton Diehl Baker to Tasker Howard Bliss

Washington July 1st [1918]

Number 66

Paragraph With reference to your 138,¹ General Foch and General Pershing have joined in a recommendation that the United States greatly enlarge its military program and send to France during 1918-1919 much larger forces than the present program contemplates. Possibilities of compliance are being studied here. Many questions of material and industrial output are involved, and no immediate determination can be made. It is of great importance that no expectations be held out of ability to comply with this enlarged program until studies are completed. Meantime, it is highly desirable that the July rate of shipping of troops from America be maintained through August. If Military Representatives will so recommend, the British will no doubt continue their shipping, upon which we must depend in the matter.

Paragraph The Macedonian Question. Our Government has no interest in this subject. Our troops, of course, could not participate and no action should be taken predicated upon action to be taken by the United States, nor should the Military Representatives undertake to advise the United States about its relations in this matter; but any proposed action to be carried on by the European Allies will not embarrass this Government. Baker   McCain

TC telegram (WDR, RG 120, Records of the American Section of the Supreme War Council, 1917-1919, No. 316, DNA).
¹ T. H. Bliss to NDB and P. C. March, No. 138, June 29, 1918, TC telegram (WDR, RG 407, World War I Cablegrams, DNA):
"A session of Supreme War Council has been called for July 2. Subjects to be discussed are, First, Intervention in Russia and Siberia, Second, The arrival of American troops for August and thereafter and, Third, The general situation in Macedonia and the Balkans.
"Reference your number 64 [P. C. March to T. H. Bliss, No. 64, June 24, 1918] the British Government has not requested any further study of the military expedition that should go to Murmansk and Archangel if any goes. My present opinion is that the sending of a considerable force will be abandoned unless at the same time there is intervention through Siberia."

To Newton Diehl Baker

My dear Mr. Secretary: [The White House] 2 July, 1918

Your letter of July first contains a very significant piece of news and an equally significant report of the forwarding of troops during the past year to the other side of the water. It is a record which I think must cause universal satisfaction, because the heart of the country is unquestionably in this war and the people of the United States rejoice to see their force put faster and faster into the great struggle which is destined to redeem the world.

Cordially and sincerely yours,   Woodrow Wilson[1]

TLS (Letterpress Books, WP, DLC).

[1] This Baker-Wilson exchange was published in the *Official Bulletin*, II (July 3, 1918), 1-2.

To Oscar Terry Crosby

My dear Mr. Crosby: [The White House] 2 July, 1918

I have your letter of yesterday[1] about Mr. Greenough,[2] and am sorry to say I doubt the wisdom of taking Mr. Greenough with you to the other side. Mr. Whitney C. Warren,[3] his father-in-law, is one of the most active, troublesome, and officious critics, I can perhaps justifiably say opponents, of this Government in Italy. His activities have been of a very mischievous kind and, while I dare say Mr. Greenough may have an entirely different attitude, I do not think that it would be wise to go into the family.

Cordially and sincerely yours,   Woodrow Wilson

TLS (Letterpress Books, WP, DLC).

[1] O. T. Crosby to WW, July 1, 1918, TLS (WP, DLC).

[2] William Greenough, a lawyer of New York.

[3] Whitney Warren (he apparently had no middle name), distinguished architect and member of the firm of Warren and Wetmore, who designed, among other buildings, Grand Central Station and the Vanderbilt, Ritz Carlton, Biltmore, and Belmont hotels. Warren had gone to Paris in 1914 and remained there (not Italy) throughout most of the war. An ardent critic of Wilson's foreign policy during the period of American neutrality, he had managed to convince many leading Frenchmen in interviews and lectures that he was one of the most authoritative representatives of American public opinion. See Robert Dell, "Amateur Diplomacy Abroad," *The New Republic*, VIII (Aug. 12, 1916), 35-37.

To Harper & Brothers

My dear Sirs: [The White House] 2 July, 1918

I have just received the very beautifully bound set of the documentary edition of my History of the American People which you were thoughtful and generous enough to have prepared for me, and wish to thank you most warmly. I shall value it very highly as an evidence of your generous thought of me.

　　　　　Cordially and sincerely yours,　Woodrow Wilson

TLS (Letterpress Books, WP, DLC).

Two Letters from Newton Diehl Baker

Dear Mr President　　　　　　　　　Washington. July 2, 1918

You asked me the total German strength on the Western front. It is believed to be 3,382,000 men.

The British have somewhere between 1,000,000 and 1,500,000. The French between 2,000,000 and 2,500,000.

These numbers are difficult to get, and are regarded as very highly secret. The[y], of course, change more or less from day to day.

I regret that I forgot to say today that a Fourth of July engagement in Chicago will cause me to leave before the meeting tomorrow afternoon　　　　　　　Respectfully,　Newton D. Baker

ALS (WP, DLC).

Dear Mr. President:　　　　　　　Washington. July 2, 1918.

There are two regiments in the Philippine Islands—the 27th and 31st Infantry—which can be recruited to war strength by sending recruits from the United States, and for the transportation of which—both the recruits from this country and the regiments from the Philippine Islands, sufficient space is available to the War Department. Arms, ammunition and supplies will have to be sent from the United States. The question of tonnage is being inquired into, with a strong likelihood that such tonnage in adequate quantities can be secured, but with the possibility of making arrangements for the storage and dispatch of additional supplies via the Chinese Southern branch of the railroad after the main expedition shall have arrived with its initial supplies. These two regiments will comprise about 7,000 men. The War Department has more than 13,000 rifles and more than 1,000,000 rounds of Russian ammunition which could be dispatched for the Czech troops at Vladivostok. England has large stocks of this ammunition and would doubtless be willing to supplement the supply. It is not unlikely that these rifles and the first 1,000,000 rounds of ammunition for the Czechs could be sent on a naval vessel.

The question of docks and storage facilities at Vladivostock is now being investigated. This report is preliminary, but it would seem that the military part of the expedition can be fitted out and be able to leave the United States in about one month from the time you give the order. Should greater speed be desired, the Philippine regiments could be moved out from present peace-strength and the recruits follow for organization at Vladivostok.

I will retain the regiments as they now are in the Philippine Islands and not start assembling recruits and supplies in this country until I hear further from you.[1]

Cordially yours,   Newton D. Baker

TLS (WP, DLC).
[1] This letter was based on a detailed memorandum: P. C. March, "Memorandum for the Secretary of War," July 2, 1918, printed in Peyton C. March, *The Nation at War* (New York, 1932), pp. 120-23.

From Herbert Clark Hoover

Dear Mr. President: Washington 2 *July, 1918*.

In accordance with your instruction that we should prepare for you a recommendation in connection with the systematic curtailment of non-war industries, we have asked a special committee, comprising:

Messrs. Clarence M. Woolley of the War Trade Board
        Edward Chambers of the Railway Administration
        Edwin F. Gay of the Shipping Board
        P. B. Noyes, of the Fuel Administration
        Theodore F. Whitmarsh of the Food Administration
        Edwin B. Parker of the War Industries Board.[1]

to make a detailed study as to the general policy to be pursued in connection with such industries. The conclusions of this committee, to which we unanimously agree, except in those relating to the brewing industry, upon which subject we are seeking further information, pending possible action by Congress, are:

That the approach to curtailment of non-war industries should be made by way of systematic and scientific reduction in their activities rather than by total and initial annihilation. They do not find that there are any industries which should be instantly cut off but there are many which should be reduced in activities at the earliest possible moment. These gentlemen are all members of the Priorities Board of the War Industries Board. This problem, in certain phases, lies outside the present conception of priorities in the use of material.

As to further action in the matter, we recommend that the above committee be constituted a special committee of the Priorities Board to study each industry from the aspect of what can be curtailed and what is a desirable curtailment, and to make such recommendations to the Priorities Board from time to time, and that the Priorities Board should advise the various departments of the action of the Board and the departments which will effectuate the conclusions of the Board.

The committee has furnished us with a recommendation that the brewing industry should be curtailed to 50% of the normal barrelage. A copy of this report we enclose herewith.[2] We have asked the committee to further consider whether, in addition to the curtailment at once of 50%, the industry should not be notified that no further foodstuffs are to be purchased and that, with the exhaustion of their present materials in process, they are to cease operation.

We are also asking the committee to make a further report, if possible, on the reduction that we recommend in connection with other non-war industries.

Yours faithfully,   Herbert Hoover

Okeh W.W.

TLS (Hoover Archives, CSt-H).
    [1] Clarence Mott Woolley, president of the American Radiator Co. and the representative of the Secretary of Commerce on the War Trade Board; Edward Chambers, a railroad executive and director of the Division of Traffic of the Railroad Administration; Edwin Francis Gay, Dean of the Graduate School of Business Administration of Harvard University and director of the Division of Planning and Statistics of the Shipping Board; Pierrepont Burt Noyes, president of Oneida Community, Ltd., and director of the Bureau of Conservation of the Fuel Administration; Theodore Francis Whitmarsh, a grocery wholesale merchant from New York and vice-president and treasurer of Francis H. Leggett and Co., at this time head of the Distribution Division of the Food Administration; and Edwin Brewington Parker, a corporation lawyer of Houston, Tex., priorities commissioner of the War Industries Board.
    [2] It is missing in WP, DLC, and in the Hoover Archives, CSt-H.

From Charles Richard Crane

Dear Mr President   Washington, D. C. July 2 1918

Ross and Abbott will prepare the notes for you. Lansing's note last week about the Slavic people was fine and has met with a cordial response.

Sometime you might call the attention to the Slavic people of the damage Germany has done to them and their wonderful mission in the world by keeping them divided—Russian against Pole, Serb against Bulgar and Bohemian kept away from all the rest—and urge them from now on to adjust their differences and bring out the best there is [in] the whole race.

To do this of course it will be the duty of the rest of us after this war to see that the various Slavic states are so well established that it will be possible for this to come about.

With cordial greetings for the "Fourth"

Yours always sincerely   Charles R. Crane

ALS (WP, DLC).

From Herbert Bayard Swope

[Washington]

Dear Mr. President: Tuesday night [July 2, 1918]

I have just read your Mount Vernon speech,[1] and its impulsion is such that I feel I must tell you of the deep reaction it produced in me. It has the touch of sublimity. I do not think you have been ever better in utterance. You are speaking a creed of world liberty in tones of serenity and confidence, born of a spirit that never falters and never loses sight of the goal. That you are able to say so much in so few words is not the least attribute of the speech, and the restatement of aims at the moment America becomes seriously effective in her war efforts, through a million men in France, takes on a timeliness that is very valuable. The address will take its place alongside the Gettysburg oration.   In sincerity   Swope

ALS (WP, DLC).
[1] An advance copy of the address printed at July 4, 1918.

From Arthur Capper

Dear Mr. President: Topeka July 2, 1918.

Kansas will support you to a man in any course you may take to grapple with the profiteers who prey on their country and their countrymen in this time of need. They are doing more to hamper us than all the devices of the enemy by making the necessities of life and industry cost more than the people can earn. To be shamelessly and continually exploited for the necessaries of living by a great commercial plunderbund, which they and their sons are defending in a war that taxes their every resource, is an outrage on the patriotism of the people, too intolerable to be borne. Such insatiable greed will stop at nothing short of stern and drastic compulsion.

Our continued fitness in the Middle West, depends on a speedy solution of the profiteering problem and the equitable financing of the war, or upon a thoroly effective solution of the problem of price regulation which shall include all necessary commodities. A practical solution of either will amount to a remedy for both and will strengthen and enhearten the people amazingly for all the trials and demands of the war.

The shocking report of the Federal Trade Commission[1] further emphasizes the force and truth of your statement of May 17 to Congress that information with regard to conscienceless *profiteering* is available and indisputable,[2] and justifies my appeal to you of 6 months ago for relief on behalf of the people of Kansas.[3] This state has suffered grievously and is suffering more and more seriously, from widespread and excessive profiteering by nearly all the big industrial gougers. Eventually this will defeat all our efforts, unless thorogoing and drastic regulation of the big industries can soon be effected. More than all other problems of the war, the one of reaching the brigands of profit who are demanding excessive toll from their country and their countrymen, at this critical time, is giving the people of Kansas deep concern and anxiety.

Kansas wishes to do more, not less. It cannot stand by and see the morale of the people slowly but surely undermined by a greed that knows no country, recognizes no duty and has no flag except the skull and crossbones.

Very respectfully,   Arthur Capper

TLS (WP, DLC).

[1] In response to Wilson's statement in his address to Congress of May 27, 1918, about wartime profiteering and his request for higher taxes on war profits, Senator Borah had introduced a resolution (S. Res. 255) on May 31, 1918. It directed the Federal Trade Commission to furnish the Senate with any evidence for the existence of profiteering, in order to enable Congress to remedy the situation through new revenue legislation or through more effective criminal statutes. The resolution was adopted on June 10, 1918. *Cong. Record,* 65th Cong., 2d sess., pp. 7232, 7558.

The Federal Trade Commission submitted its report to the Senate (S. Doc. No. 248) on June 29, 1918. The report discussed the financial operations of several industries vital to the war effort and found that, in general, profits were far higher than would be warranted in any circumstances. Many industries were making "unusual profits"; some, such as meat packing and flour milling, were making "outrageous" profits. In a number of instances, profits had been increased to unfair and extortionate levels through such practices as the juggling of accounts, the padding of salaries, bribery, manipulation of the market, and other devious methods. The report concluded: "The commission has reason to know that profiteering exists. Much of it is due to advantages taken of the necessities of the times, as evidenced in the war pressure for heavy production. Some of it is attributable to inordinate greed and bare-faced fraud." *Ibid.*, pp. 8458-62. See also the *Official Bulletin,* II (June 29, 1918), 1, 11-16, and the *New York Times,* June 30, 1918.

[2] That is, Wilson's address to a joint session of Congress of May 27, not 17, 1918.

[3] A. Capper to WW, Jan. 18, 1918, TLS (WP, DLC).

From Robert Somers Brookings

My dear Mr President: Washington July 2, 1918.

At a meeting of the Price Fixing Committee with the copper producers held this day, an advance of 2½¢ per lb from 23½¢ to

26¢ was agreed upon subject to your approval. This advance was made after a most thorough investigation by the Federal Trade Commission of the effect upon the cost of producing copper by reason of recent advances in cost of transportation, labor, smelting and refining, etc.

While this advance is much less than the industry feels it is entitled to, we have, as the result of several meetings, finally convinced them that it is the highest price to which the Government feels itself justified in giving consent.

I herewith enclose the usual press announcement,[1] a copy of which I have handed to Mr Newdick, our publicity agent, with instructions to release as before on receipt of a telephone communication from Mr Tumulty. As there is always some indiscreet person attending these meetings who gives to the press advance information, and as an increase of this amount in copper will probably lead to speculation in copper stocks, it seemed necessary, in order to protect the public, that the information be given out this evening subject to your approval.

Respectfully yours,   Robt. S. Brookings

TLS (WP, DLC).
[1] It is missing in WP, DLC. However, it is printed in the *Official Bulletin*, II (July 5, 1918), 4.

From the Diary of Josephus Daniels

1918 Tuesday 2 July

Went with Baker & Burleson before House Committee in advocacy of bill to take over telegraph and telephone companies for the war. I advocated it for a permanent government policy.

Cabinet. I asked WW to see that S—[1] did not build two big plants—it would lead to scandal & we will have enough to build the ships we will need.

Discussed whether the President should tell Congress that he would veto certain bills if they embodied objectionable features. Burleson said no. Baker said if he wrote open message it would be O.K. Lansing thought a veto was more impressive

Pres. objects to fixing higher price for wheat when the biggest crop in history is being harvested Burleson fears Germany will recruit its man power from Russia and thinks President should act now.

[1] That is, Charles M. Schwab, who had been appointed Director General of the Emergency Fleet Corporation on April 16, 1918.

To Robert Somers Brookings

My dear Mr. Brookings: [The White House] 3 July, 1918

I have your letter of yesterday containing a statement concerning the change in the price of copper. Unfortunately, your letter was not laid before me yesterday but I have approved the statement this morning and it will be given to the Press.

Sincerely yours, Woodrow Wilson

TLS (Letterpress Books, WP, DLC).

To Robert Lansing, with Enclosure

My dear Mr. Secretary: The White House 3 July, 1918

Thank you for having let me see the enclosed. The suggestions are certainly much more sensible than I thought the author[1] of them capable of. I differ from them only in practical details.

Cordially and faithfully yours, Woodrow Wilson

TLS (SDR, RG 59, 763.72/10614½, DNA).

[1] Raymond Robins. The Editors are unable to add anything by way of detail to Kennan's narrative of Raymond Robins' last days in Moscow, his meeting with Lenin, his return to the United States, and his meeting with Lansing at the State Department on June 26, 1918. Kennan, *The Decision to Intervene*, pp. 215-31. However, the Editors venture the following observations:

a. There is no solid evidence that Robins presented or read Lenin's offer of economic cooperation with the United States to Lansing (about which see Kennan, pp. 217-19) when Robins conferred with Lansing on June 26. To our knowledge, the manuscript embodying Lenin's proposal is not and never has been in the files of the Department of State. If Lansing knew anything about the document, he never mentioned it to Wilson.

b. It is not accurate to say (Kennan, pp. 230-31) that Wilson never did Robins the courtesy of "receiving him and permitting him to present his views in person." There is no evidence that Robins or any friend of Robins asked Wilson to grant him an interview at this time.

c. We cannot be sure that Wilson saw or read Robin's printed memorandum summarized in n. 1 to the following Enclosure. The memorandum, when found among the group of Lansing's confidential papers which were published as *The Lansing Papers* in 1939 and 1940, was separated from Wilson to Lansing of July 3, 1918, in which Wilson returned Robins to Lansing of July 1, 1918. As the file number on the memorandum indicates, the memorandum was at some time filed with Robins' letter and given the same file number as Robins' letter, but with the prefix, "F.W.," that is, "File With."

E N C L O S U R E

Raymond Robins to Robert Lansing

Sir: Washington, D. C., July 1, 1918.

Pursuant to your request I have the honor to present to you herewith a brief printed statement of my recommendations concerning the Russian situation.[1]

It seems to me that in all the confusion of statement and conclusion surrounding the Russian situation the following propositions are reasonably clear:

First, that Germany hesitates to employ in Russia armed forces in sufficient number to subjugate the land but desires—as clearly indicated by a consistent course of conduct in Ukrainia, Finland and the Baltic Provinces—to establish so-called governments of law and order which are too weak to support themselves in the great class struggle but which may be maintained and controlled by German force.

Second, that through such governments Germany hopes to control and utilize Russian resources and, if possible, Russian manpower against the Western Allies in this war, and to conclude the war with Russia completely under the economic dominion of Germany.

Third, that forcible Allied intervention opposed by the Soviets would be essentially analogous to what Germany is doing in the Ukraine, in Finland and in the Baltic Provinces.

Fourth, that such intervention unless welcomed by the great mass of the Russian people would be destructive in principle of the entire basis of President Wilson's democratic war policy.

Fifth, that forcible Allied intervention, if uninvited by the Soviet power, will certainly be opposed and will result in civil war.

Sixth, that forcible Allied intervention can not be justified upon grounds of military necessity, and will not prevent but will hasten and make easy the consummation of Germany's war aims in European Russia.

Seventh, that American economic co-operation with Russia will open the way for effective Allied intervention with force and the creation of an actual fighting front opposed to Germany in Russia.

The recommendations enclosed herewith are stated with as much brevity as possible.   Respectfully,   Raymond Robins

TLS (SDR, RG 59, 763.72/10610½, DNA).
[1] R. Robins, *American Economic Cooperation with Russia*, July 1, 1918, printed memorandum (SDR, RG 59, 763.72/10610½, DNA). Robins argued that, given America's democratic war aims, an Allied intervention by force in Russia was inconceivable unless it was desired by the Russian people. However, the recent invitation from the Soviet government for the cooperation of the United States in the economic reconstruction of Russia presented an opportunity for an initial step toward economic and military cooperation in the creation of a new eastern front. According to Robins, the Soviet leaders realized that their social and economic revolution would fail and that Russia would fall under the complete dominance of autocratic Germany unless they could obtain immediate assistance in the reconstruction of the country's economic life as a necessary prerequisite for the creation of an effective military force to oppose German power. If, with the help of the United States, such economic reorganization as was needed to support a revolutionary army could be accomplished, the Soviet government would undoubtedly form such an army and would gladly accept the military assistance of the Allies.

Robins then suggested the general purposes of an American economic commission to Russia: to reconstruct the country's commercial system in order to assure the consumption of Russia's resources in Russia and to prevent their use by Germany; to reestablish trade with Russia, which would furnish the Allies with necessary products from Russia via Archangel; to convince the Russian people that the interests of Russia and the Allies in overthrowing German autocracy were identical and that American assistance was given solely for the purpose of enabling Russia to contribute to the destruction of the German menace; to assist in the organization of a revolutionary army and to create the necessary economic organization for its support; to convince the Soviet government that the Allies had no imperialistic purposes in Russia and to obtain the Soviet government's consent to the dispatch of Allied troops to reestablish the Russian front; and to keep the American and Allied governments informed about the actual facts of the Russian social, economic, and political revolution.

Russia, Robins continued, was suffering not so much from lack of resources as from a breakdown of the ordinary processes of distribution. However, a competent American economic commission, in cooperation with the Soviet government, could solve this problem. Robins emphasized the need for the commission to cooperate with the Soviet leaders, regardless of ideological differences. In any event, the Soviet leaders were beginning to realize that the economic realities made it necessary for them to modify their rigid adherence to the formulas of radical socialism.

Robins then went on to list the specific tasks of the commission and stated that it would be necessary to create an elaborate organization with representatives in all important centers of Russia. Since the work of the commission would be extensive, the burden of its supervision should not be placed upon any of the existing governmental agencies. Thus, Robins suggested that a new department be created under the Overman Act, whose head would be responsible only to the President. The commission, in turn, would be responsible only to this independent department and, through it, to the President.

To George Gladden[1]

My dear Mr. Gladden: [The White House] 3 July, 1918

May I not express to you and through you to the other members of Doctor Gladden's family the very profound regret with which I have heard of his death?[2] I had come to share the affectionate regard for him which was common to all who knew him. His death has impoverished us.

Cordially and sincerely yours,   Woodrow Wilson

TLS (Letterpress Books, WP, DLC).
[1] Son of Washington Gladden; a newspaper and magazine editor and contributor to several encyclopedias and yearbooks; at this time, associate editor of *Mother Nature's News*.
[2] Washington Gladden had died on July 2, 1918.

To Jean Jules Jusserand

My dear Mr. Ambassador: [The White House] 3 July, 1918

I was very much pleased and complimented that you should have thought of sending me your little volume, "The French and American Independence,"[1] and I was deeply gratified by the generous inscription on the fly leaf.[2] Will you not accept my most heartfelt thanks?   Cordially and sincerely yours,   Woodrow Wilson

TLS (Letterpress Books, WP, DLC).
¹ Jean Adrien Antoine Jules Jusserand, *The French and American Independence* (New York, 1918).
² "To President Wilson, champion of Independence for all nationalities & nations, from an admirer of his noble efforts in the greatest of causes Jusserand Independence Day—1918[.]" From the copy of the book in the Wilson Library, DLC.

To Charles Edward Russell

My dear Mr. Russell: The White House 3 July, 1918

Thank you for the memorial signed by a committee of Russian residents of London. I have read it with great interest and am trying hard to think out a practicable method of assisting Russia.

Cordially and faithfully yours,   Woodrow Wilson

TLS (C. E. Russell Papers, DLC).

To Herbert Bayard Swope

My dear Swope: [The White House] 3 July, 1918

Thank you with all my heart for your little note about the Mount Vernon speech. It has touched and pleased me very deeply.

Cordially and sincerely yours,   Woodrow Wilson

TLS (Letterpress Books, WP, DLC).

To Sallie Starke Tillman

My dear Mrs. Tillman: [The White House] 3 July, 1918

I am deeply and sincerely grieved by the death of your husband.[1] I had learned to have a warm affectionate regard for him, and I hope that you will let me express to you my profound sympathy in your irreparable loss. I am sure the heart of everyone who knew the Senator will go out to you with the warmest feeling and with the sincere hope that this loss may be softened for you in some degree by the unusual general esteem in which the Senator was held.   Cordially and sincerely yours,   Woodrow Wilson

TLS (Letterpress Books, WP, DLC).
¹ Benjamin Ryan Tillman had died in the early hours of July 3, 1918.

To Charles Turner Williams

My dear Mr. Williams: [The White House] 3 July, 1918

I am very much obliged to you for your letter of July first which I have read with interest and profit.

Sincerely yours,   Woodrow Wilson

TLS (Letterpress Books, WP, DLC).

From Lord Reading, with Enclosures

My dear Mr. President,   Washington July 3rd/18

I send you herewith the four cablegrams to which I referred in my interview with you today. These are the full text of the Supreme War Council Resolution, the reply of the Japanese Government to the British French and Italian Governments and two reports from H.M.S. Suffolk.

The complete text of the Resolution only reached me this evening. It is of such importance that I would ask you to grant me a further interview when you have considered it.

I am, my dear Mr President

Yours with the highest respect   Reading.

ALS (WP, DLC).

E N C L O S U R E   I

Washington. July 3rd, 1918.

PARAPHRASE OF A TELEGRAM FROM MR. BALFOUR TO LORD READING.
July 2, 1918.

The Admiralty have received the following message from H.M.S. "Suffolk,"[1] dated June 26th:

Begins:

A conference was held yesterday between members of the Czech National Council and the Allied Consuls and, in accordance with a request made by the former, the Consuls communicated to their Governments by telegraph the request of the Czechs that help should be furnished by the Allies. In addition to the armaments needed for their own troops, as already telegraphed to you, they estimate that an Allied force of a strength of 100,000 men will be required in order to deal with the armed enemy prisoners. The railway line is occupied by the Bolshevists. The General in command of the Czech troops[2] asked me to-day to defer the despatch of transports from Hong Kong until such time as the decision of the Allied Governments in regard to sending assistance had been made known. The necessary instructions have been sent to Hong Kong accordingly. The gravity of the situation is confirmed by all reports from Central Siberia, as the war prisoners under German command and acting in concert with the Bolshevists have now obtained control. Ends.

[1] Then at Vladivostok.
[2] That is, Gen. Dieterichs.

E N C L O S U R E   I I

Washington. July 3rd. 1918.

PARAPHRASE OF A TELEGRAM FROM MR. BALFOUR TO LORD READING.
July 2, 1918.

The following telegraphic report has been received from H.M.S. "Suffolk." Begins:

On June 29th at 10 a.m. the Czechs presented their ultimatum and, having received no definite reply at 10.30, they proceeded to take possession of the buildings of the Soviet and to provide for a general disarmament, three of the chief members of the Soviet being placed under arrest. In the Naval barracks 600 sailors surrendered, and permission was asked through the British Consul for four destroyers to go to sea, but this was refused by the British and Japanese naval authorities.

The Bolshevists made no resistance with the exception of that offered by a party of Red Guards who were in occupation of houses near the railway station. Just before sunset, however, they were surrounded and overcome after a brisk fight; the Bolshevist losses are not yet ascertained: ten Czechs were killed.

The central parts of the town were patrolled by Japanese and British landing parties numbering 700, who isolated the districts in which the foreign Consulates are located and also provided guards to protect munitions belonging to the Allies outside the districts in the occupation of the Czechs.

Later in the day landing parties were sent by American and Russian ships. The population is giving support and sympathy to a coalition Siberian Government which has now declared itself.

The Czechs are now occupying the city, which is at present quiet. Ends.

E N C L O S U R E   I I I

Washington. June 29, 1918.

COPY OF A NOTE HANDED BY THE JAPANESE AMABASSADOR
IN LONDON TO THE BRITISH SECRETARY OF STATE
FOR FOREIGN AFFAIRS.

Text received by telegraph June 28th.

The Japanese Government have been always anxious to co-ordinate their policy as far as possible with the policy of the Governments with which they are associated in the War, respecting the measures to be taken to meet the exigencies of the situation in Siberia. At the same time, they have on more than one occasion made it clear that they place particular importance on the moral and material support of the United States to any undertaking of a military nature in which they may embark in Siberia. They understand that their attitude of thus counting on the support of the United States was fully appreciated and kept in view by the Governments of Great Britain, France and Italy in formulating the proposals embodied in the memorandum which His Britannic Majesty's Principal Secretary of State for Foreign Affairs was so good as to hand to the Japanese Ambassador in London on June 7th last. Having regard, however, to the conviction of the Japanese Government, declared in their communication to the United States Government under date March 19th last, they do not feel themselves at liberty to express their decision on the question of Allied intervention now suggested before a complete understanding is reached between the three Powers and the United States. The correspondence which passed between the Japanese and United States Governments on the subject was at that time communicated to the three Governments, and the Japanese Government trust that their intention in this respect will not be misunderstood or misconstrued.

They have also carefully examined the three conditions which it is proposed should be fulfilled in the event of common action being taken in Siberia, and they believe it due to frankness to offer the following observations for the confidential information of the British Government, in anticipation of the eventuality contemplated by the three Governments. The principles enunciated in the first and second points of those conditions are in entire accord with the repeated declaration of the Japanese Government, and are quite acceptable to them. With regard to the third condition, requiring the Allied expedition to advance as far West as possible, the Japanese Government, in full sympathy with the object which it is sought thereby to attain, has submitted the question to their most serious consideration. They regret that they should find it impossible for them to engage to extend Westward their military activities beyond the limits of Eastern Siberia, in view of the grave difficulties with which such operations will be practically confronted.

The Japanese Government further desire to point out that they attach great importance to unity of command, in case common action is taken in Siberia. Considering the geographical position of Japan, as well as the strength of the military forces which she will be called on to employ for the proposed undertaking, the Japanese Government feel themselves justified in expressing the hope that the supreme command of the whole international contingents in Siberia be placed in the hands of Japan.

E N C L O S U R E   I V

TELEGRAM FROM MR. BALFOUR, PARIS, TO LORD READING.[1]
July 2, 1918.

The Supreme War Council this afternoon discussed the question of Allied armed assistance to Russia and the following represents the considered views of the French, Italian and British Governments.

The Military views set forth are those of General Foch and the Military Advisers to the three Governments, who fully concurred in the memorandum and resolution.

After consultation with your French and Italian colleagues, the views of the Supreme Council should at once be placed before the President.

Begins:

The Supreme War Council consider that since its last meeting a complete change has come over the situation in Russia and Siberian Russia, which makes Allied intervention in these countries an urgent and imperative necessity.

In the first place, the recent action of Czecho-Slovak troops has transformed the Siberian situation. There is now a force of 50,000 troops of Slav nationality, totally disinterested in the internal politics of Russia, yet determined to fight Germany for the liberation of their own country, in control of the railway in Western Siberia. This success of the Czecho-Slovak troops proves that the bulk of the Siberian population are no longer sympathetic to the Bolshevists, and must be friendly disposed to the Allied cause. It also removes the apprehension that Allied intervention will meet with such serious opposition from the local population East of the Urals as would

---

[1] The original of this telegram is A. J. Balfour to Lord Reading, July 3, 1918, T telegram (W. Wiseman Papers, CtY).

make penetration through Western Siberia to the Urals very difficult. Provided that intervention takes place in time, there will be a Slav army in Western Siberia on [to] which the Russian patriots can rally, which eliminates the risk of Russian public opinion being thrown into the arms of Germany, as might have been the case if intervention were effected by forces almost entirely Japanese. This Czecho-Slovak force, however, is in grave danger of being cut off by the organization of German-Austro-Hungarian prisoners-of-war at Irkutsk, and an appeal for immediate military assistance has been made by the Czech National Council to the Allied Consuls at Vladivostock. The Allies are under the responsibility of taking immediate action if these gallant Allies are not to be overwhelmed. To fail in bringing support to these faithful troops, now desperately fighting for the Allied cause, would not only for ever discredit the Allies, but might have a disastrous effect on the Slav population both of Russia itself and of Austria-Hungary and the Balkans, as proving that the Allies are unable or unwilling to exert themselves effectively to save the Slav world from falling wholly under German domination. On the other hand, to push a force through to Irkutsk to overwhelm the German prisoners organization and join hands with the Czecho-Slovaks would probably be a simple and rapid matter if it were taken in hand immediately. Intervention in Siberia, therefore, is an urgent necessity both to save the Czecho-Slovaks and to take advantage of an opportunity of gaining control of Siberia for the Allies which may never return.

In the second place, a great change has come over the internal situation in Russia itself. There is no doubt that the Bolshevists power is waning. It is daily becoming clearer to all classes in Russia, including ex-soldiers, peasants and workmen, that the Bolshevists cannot fulfil their promises of a social millenium and that anarchy, disorder and starvation lie ahead under the Bolshevist regime. The accounts from all our representatives agree upon this. It is further clear that the Bolshevists have not real power with which to support their rule. They have entirely failed to raise an effective army. They remain in office simply because Russia is too divided to create any alternative organization with which to supplant them.

There is much evidence, however, that the best Liberal and Democratic elements in Russia are beginning to lift their heads and to get into touch with one another. They are animated partly by disgust with autocratic methods of the Bolshevists, partly by determination not to submit to the humiliation and partition of the Brest-Litovsk Treaties, and partly by a growing fear of German domination.

Practically all elements of the Russian population, indeed, except the dwindling minority of Bolshevists, now recognize that intervention of some kind is necessary and inevitable, because it is the only alternative to continuous anarchy and disorder, ending in universal starvation.

The only difference of opinion is as to whether intervention should be Allied or German. The reactionaries and pro-German agents amongst the Bolshevists naturally prefer German intervention. The Liberal and Democratic elements urgently ask for Allied intervention and make it clear that, while they desire economic assistance, the essential need is military support. Unless they can secure effective Allied support in the field and a base upon which to rally, the Reactionary forces, backed by German bayonets, will inevitably crush the movement for national freedom and regeneration.

Allied intervention, therefore, is urgently necessary in order to save Russia from the establishment of autocracy by German bayonets. If, however, the Allies are to bring effective assistance to Liberal Russia, not only must they occupy Murmansk and Archangel in order to retain the bridge heads into Russia from the North from which forces can eventually advance rapidly to the centre of Russia, but they must also control Siberia to the Urals without delay. If the Germans gain control of Western Siberia as well as of Archangel and Murmansk, they close the last means of contact between Russia and the outside world, and they obtain possession of supplies of food without which Russia will be starved. The Germans have already made the Black Sea a German lake, they are advancing as fast as they can on the Caspian, which will give them control of the Volga and its water communications with Western Siberia, and they are preparing to occupy the Murman coast before the winter. If they once succeed in these objects German domination of Russia will be complete. They will then not only control Russian resources but, under penalty of starvation, they may be able to compel the Russian people to serve as labour and possibly even as recruits for their armies in the field. All hopes of the regeneration of Russia on truly democratic lines depend upon seizure by the Allies of the granary of Western Siberia without delay.

In the third place Allied intervention is essential in order to win the war. There is no doubt that if the Germans fail to gain a decision in the West in the next few weeks they will turn East and endeavour with all their power to paralyse any possibility of the national regeneration of Russia during the war. They know as well as we know that there is but the smallest chance of an Allied victory on Western front in 1919 unless Germany is compelled to transfer a considerable amount of her strength back again from the West to the East. It will therefore be a primary object of her policy to prevent the re-creation of an Eastern Allied front during the forthcoming autumn and winter and she will endeavour to do this either by establishing in Russia a Government favourable to herself, or destroying all possibility of organised resistance to her domination. If the Allies are to win the war in 1919 it should be a primary object of their policy to foster and assist the national movement in Russia in order to reform an Eastern front or at least to sustain a vigorous spirit of independence in the occupied territories behind the German line as will compel Germany to maintain large bodies of troops in the East. Allied intervention at the earliest moment is therefore a necessity if any headway is to be made in organising that Eastern front, which is essential if the Allies are to win the war in 1919, before Germany has concentrated her whole strength once more on enceintement and domination of Russia.

At the present moment intervention as a practical policy is easier than it has ever been. The Japanese have now agreed to send an expedition into Siberia provided they are assured of the approval and active support of the United States Government; and, though they have not engaged themselves to go beyond Irkutsk, there is no ground for thinking that this necessarily represents the limit of their effort. They have also accepted the two conditions which the Supreme War Council has considered as necessary conditions of Allied intervention, viz: Disinterestedness in Russian internal politics and guarantee to evacuate Russian territory after the war.

The Czecho-Slovak forces are already in occupation of Western Siberia. In addition, American and Allied detachments would create a force really Allied in character, and acceptable both to Russian and Allied public opinion, especially if the Russian forces, under Russian leaders, were associated with it as soon as it was established in Russian territory. If action were taken immediately, it ought to be possible for the Allies to gain control of the railways through the whole of Siberia as far as the Urals, in a very few weeks. Only the assent and the co-operation of the U.S.G. is now required in order to set in motion a policy which promises success and which if successfully accomplished is bound to have decisive effect on the future of the war.

On the other hand S.W.C. (Supreme War Council) feel bound to point out that in their judgment failure to intervene immediately must inevitably cause effects which can only be described as disastrous to the allied cause. In the first place it would mean abandoning the people to triumph of militarism of Germany and the destruction of all hope of resuscitation of Russia as a liberal ally of the Western democracies during the war. In the second place it would mean the permanent impairment of the blockade, for if Germany were to establish effective control over Central Russian Siberia her chief anxiety as to supply both of raw materials and food would be removed. In the third place it would mean the indefinite prolongation of the war and the surrender of any real prospect of victory for the Allies in 1919. Fourthly it would mean the abandonment of yet another little nation the Czecho Slovaks to the mercies of Berlin with inevitably disastrous consequences on the sentiment of Slav peoples of Russia, the Balkans and throughout the world.

If policy of intervention however is to be really successful an adequate military force must be employed. Allied Representatives in Russia are agreed that while economic assistance is important military intervention is absolutely essential. The Czech Slovak leaders have informed the Allied Consuls at Vladivostock that in their judgment 100,000 men are necessary to save the situation. It is evident therefore that while rest of Allies should send what troops they can the bulk of the force must be provided by the Japanese.

For these reasons the Supreme War Council, having carefully considered the military situation and the prospects of the Allies in all the theatres of war, have come to the conclusion:

1. That immediate armed assistance to Russia is imperatively necessary for following reasons.

(a) To assist Russian nation to throw off their German oppressors and to prevent unlimited military and economic exploitation of Russia by Germany in her own interests.

(b) For decisive military reasons given by General Foch in his telegram to President Wilson i.e. that the Germans have already called back from Russia a number of divisions and sent them to the Western front.[2] Allied intervention will be the first step in stimulating national uprising in Russia against German domination, which will have an immediate effect in renewing German anxiety in regard to the East and compelling her to refrain from removing further troops Westward and perhaps to send troops back to the East.

C. To shorten war by constitution of Russian front.

D. To prevent isolation of Russia from Western Europe.

They are advised that, if action is not taken in Siberia, existing Allied forces in Northern Russia may have to be withdrawn and Russia will be completely cut off from the Allies.

E. To deny to Germany supplies of Western Siberia and important military stores at Vladivostock and to render them available for Russian population.

F. To bring assistance to Czecho-Slovak forces which have made great sacrifices to the cause for which we are fighting.

[2] See J. J. Jusserand to WW, June 24, 1918.

2. That intervention should be allied in character should be accompanied by pledges to Russian people as agreed at last Versailles Conference, and should include the following:

A. An Allied force to operate in Siberia. Circumstances render imperative that force shall be adequate in number and in character, and Allied in composition, and that above all things it should operate immediately. Delay would be fatal. It is recognized that owing to geographical and shipping conditions Japanese troops will comprise larger portion of force, but its Allied character must be maintained and it must include American and Allied units. Force should be under a single Command appointed by Power that provides the largest number of troops.

B. Such additions of Allied forces in Murmansk and Archangel as Military Advisers of Allies may recommend.

C. Relief expeditions under American direction and control to supply wants and alleviate suffering of Russian peoples.

Primary object of Allied action being to co-operate with the Russian nation in recreating the Eastern front, as a first step towards freeing Russia, the closest co-ordination must exist between the above forces and Russian population.

3. Therefore in view of:

A. The unanimous opinion of General Foch and Allied Military Advisers of Supreme War Council that immediate despatch of an adequate Allied force to Siberia is essential for victory of the Allied armies.

B. The fact that no adequate expedition can be sent without Japanese co-operation, and that Japan will not undertake effective action without encouragement and support of the United States Government:

and

C. The short time available before the winter for initiating active operations in Siberia and rapid German penetration into Russia.

Supreme War Council appeal to President Wilson to approve the policy here recommended and thus to enable it to be carried into effect before it is too late.

T MSS (WP, DLC).

From Lord Reading

My dear Mr. President:　　　　　Washington July 3, 1918.

I have the honour to forward to you, herewith, a copy of an interim report drawn up by a committee appointed by His Majesty's Government to consider the question of a League of Nations.[1]

You will notice that this Committee was presided over by Sir Walter Phillimore, who commands the highest reputation both as an English lawyer and an international jurist, while the other members of the committee are especially well qualified to deal with the subject.

The interim report has been submitted to the War Cabinet, and, although it has not been formally approved by them and must not, therefore, be considered as setting forth the policy of His Majesty's Government, it has nevertheless received the warm support of various members of that Government.

I have been requested by Mr. Balfour to communicate a copy of the report to you for your confidential information, giving at the same time the above brief explanation of the position in regard to its adoption. Mr. Balfour also asks me to inform you that His Majesty's Government would be glad to learn any views which you may be kind enough to express with regard to this report.

I have the honour to be

    My dear Mr. President,

        Yours with the highest respect,   Reading

TLS (WP, DLC).

¹ The Committee on the League of Nations, *Interim Report*, March 20, 1918, printed copy (W. Wiseman Papers, CtY). Balfour had appointed the committee on January 3, 1918, to inquire into various schemes, including a league of nations, for the peaceful settlement of international disputes. The chairman of the committee was Sir Walter George Frank Phillimore, a distinguished judge, ecclesiastical lawyer, and international jurist. The other members of the committee were the historians, Albert Frederick Pollard, Sir Julian Stafford Corbett, and John Holland Rose; the Foreign Office's representatives were Sir Eyre Crowe, Sir William George Tyrrell and Cecil James Barrington Hurst; Alfred Ravenscroft Kennedy, a legal assistant in the Foreign Office, was secretary.

The interim report, which the committee submitted to Balfour on March 20, 1918, consisted of a draft convention for a league of nations and a lengthy introduction which explained its principal features. The committee refused to offer an opinion as to whether the establishment of a league or the mere modification of the existing diplomatic structure could best maintain peace. It stated that it had found none of the existing schemes entirely practical or likely to meet with acceptance. Even so, the committee submitted a draft convention as a basis for discussion, on the assumption that a league of nations might be regarded as the best solution.

The committee's proposed league of nations was basically an alliance, whose principal objectives were the preservation of peace between its members and the provision of means for settling disputes among them. Under the first section of the draft convention, entitled "Avoidance of War," each of the allied states would agree collectively and separately not to go to war with another allied state without previously submitting the matter in dispute to arbitration or to a conference of the allied states, and until an award or a report had been handed down by the conference. Each member would further agree not to go to war with another of the allied states which had complied with the award or recommendation of the conference. If a member of the alliance broke any of these commitments, it would "become *ipso facto* at war with all the other Allied States," which would agree to support each other in taking all military, naval, financial, and economic measures necessary to restrain the breach of covenant. Any allied state not able to contribute effectively to a military or naval force should at least join in the financial and economic sanctions.

The second section of the draft convention described the procedure for what it called the "Pacific Settlement of International Disputes." The committee recommended that any legal dispute involving, for example, a question of international law, the interpretation of a treaty, or the breach of an international obligation, should be submitted to arbitration. If, for any reason, arbitration proved impossible or impractical, the disputants could take the matter before a conference of the allied states. This conference would have a permanent seat in a certain country. The head of state or government of that country would convene the conference, and his representative would preside over its deliberations. The allied states would be represented at the conference by their diplomatic representatives accredited to the country or by such other representatives as they might designate. The conference would ascertain the facts of the dispute and make a recommendation. This recommendation, however, would not have the force of a decision. The committee could not agree whether unanimity or a simple majority vote should be required for a recommendation, and it included two alternatives. In either case, the recommendation would be addressed to the parties in dispute, who were free to accept or reject it. The last article in the section on the peaceful settlement of international disputes provided that any allied state involved in a dispute could apply to the conference for relief from the commitment to await the report of the conference before going to war, on the ground that a continuing injury existed or that the injury would be irreparable unless prompt restitution was made. The conference, without deciding on the merits of the dispute, could either approve this request or suggest terms for a temporary arrangement as a condition for not exempting the applicant from the moratorium. In the event of relief from the moratorium, any of the allied states might come to the assistance of the relieved state.

The third section of the convention discussed the relations between the allied states and states not party to the convention. It stipulated that, in case of a dispute between a member of the alliance and a nonmember, the latter would be invited to submit the matter to arbitration or the conference. If the invitation was accepted, the nonmember would be treated as a member, and the normal procedure would be followed. Should the nonmember decline, the conference could inquire into the conflict *ex parte* and make a recommendation in the same way as if both parties were present. In the event that the allied state was attacked by the nonmember state, any of the members might come to the assistance of the allied state. A dispute between states not party to the convention could be brought before the conference by any of the allied states, and the conference could use its good offices to prevent war.

The final section of the draft provided that membership in the league would require the abrogation of all treaty obligations inconsistent with the terms of the convention and required the allied states to take immediate steps to procure their release from such obligations.

From Peyton Conway March, with Enclosure

Washington, D. C.
9:50 P.M. July 3/18

My dear Mr President.

I am enclosing herewith, an important cablegram from General Bliss, just decoded. This in the absence of the Secretary of War.

Sincerely,   P. C. March.

ALS (WP, DLC).

ENCLOSURE

Versailles, July 2d [1918].

Number 140 URGENT Very Confidential. For the Secretary of State and Secretary of War and Chief of Staff.

Paragraph 1. First meeting of seventh session Supreme War Council held at Versailles at Four PM. Before the meeting the three Prime Ministers held a secret session in which they agreed upon an important document apparently prepared by the British War Cabinet on the subject of intervention in Russia. This document covers seven legal cap pages. It was presented at the open session of the Supreme War Council and was there discussed only by the Prime Ministers and the ministers of foreign affairs of the three governments. After discussion it was decided that it should be transmitted to Washington by Mr. Balfour in English, in order to save time and that the other two governments should notify their ambassadors at Washington that it had been so transmitted. In the draft of the long preamble to the resolutions of the three Prime Ministers there were two references to Mr. Kerensky as a source of information. On the suggestion of Baron Sonnino the Italian minister of foreign affairs reference to Mr. Kerensky was omitted. The preamble to the proposed resolution of the Supreme War Council states, among other things, that "The Czeco Slovak leader has informed the allied consuls at Vladivostok that in their judgment one hundred thousand men are necessary to save the situation. It is evident, therefore, that while the rest of the allies should send what troops they can, the bulk of the force must be provided by the Japanese." One clause of the proposed resolution reads, in part, as follows "An allied force to operate in Siberia. Circumstances render imperative that the force shall be considerable in number, military and allied in composition, and that above things, it shall operate immediately." After discussion, on suggestion of Italian minister of foreign affairs, the above word "considerable" was changed to "adequate" for the reasons as stated that the word "considerable" might produce a bad effect in Washington. The original preamble to the resolution stated, among other things, "The Japanese have now agreed to send an expedition into Siberia as far as Irkutsk provided they are assured of the approval and active support of the United States Government." After discussion by the Prime Ministers this was changed to read "The Japanese have now agreed to send an expedition into Siberia provided they are assured of the approval and active support of the United States Government, and though they have not engaged themselves to go beyond Irkutsk, there is no ground for thinking that this necessarily represents the limits of their efforts." One paragraph of the proposed resolution reads as follows: "To shorten the war. They are advised that, [unless] the Russian front is reconstituted, there is no reasonable probability of such a superiority over the enemy being concentrated by the allies as will insure victory on the Western Front in 1919." General Foch states that he has already committed to the view in the telegram to Washington signed by himself and General Pershing that the 100 American Divisions program will give us the necessary superiority.[1] On his recommendation the above words were changed to read "shorten the war by the reconstitution of the Russian Front." The resolution adopted by the three Prime Ministers the unanimous opinion of General Foch and the allied military advisement of the Supreme War Council is that "immediate despatch of an adequate allied force to Siberia is essential for the victory of the allied armies: etc." You will note that no opinion has been expressed by the American military representative favoring military intervention in the form now proposed and without a careful prepared military plan.

Paragraph 2. At the moment of meeting of Supreme War Council today I was furnished with the following copy of a telegram received by the French minister of foreign affairs from their Ambassador in Tokyo "Mr. Jusserand, Ambassador of the French Republic at Tokyo,[2] received on June 24, 1918, a reply from the Imperial Japanese Government to the proposition which had been made on the 7th of June, 1918, by Mr. Balfour, in the name of the British, Italian and French Governments, on the subject of intervention at Washington. From this communication it appears that Japan does not think that it ought to join the three Governments in exerting influence upon Mr. Wilson. Baron Goto prefers from Washington a free acceptance and does not wish to exert any pressure on the United States. As for the rest, Japan has decided to act if the American Government promises it its unconditional material and moral support. It adheres to the principles set forth in the memorandum, but does not engage itself to push military action beyond Eastern Siberia. According to Baron Goto, Irkutsk would be the extreme limit, but he added that it is possible that they might go still further; everything depends upon the turn of events." It was this telegram that caused the three Prime Ministers to eliminate the words "as far as Irkutsk" and add the words given in my paragraph above. The military representatives were not called upon to present a plan. The only plan thus far prepared is a British plan which calls for a minimum of 600,000 combatant troops to go as far as Cheliabinsk and from there to push forward to control the railroads running through Ekaterinbourg to Vologda. The British have constantly maintained that this is necessary in order to prevent supplies from western Siberia going into European Russia. No plan has been submitted showing what the force of 100,000 Japanese going as far as Irkutsk would accomplish in effecting the desired object. When I mentioned these things in conversation after today's meeting I was told by a member of the conference that "The principal thing is to get the allies committed to this intervention and the rest will follow" In the telegram that the three Prime Ministers agreed that Mr. Balfour should transmit through the British Ambassador at Washington, the Government of the United States must understand that no definite military plan has been agreed upon.

Paragraph 3. When the subject of one hundred American divisions program came up for discussion, I presented a paraphrase of the first paragraph of War Department cable number 66 dated July 1st.[3] The Supreme War Council then adopted its resolution number two of this session as follows: "First, that General Tasker H Bliss is requested to ascertain in what measure the American Government can furnish the tonnage necessary to transport to France the troops called for in the approved program (100 divisions by August 1, 1919) both for men and supplies. Second, That after this estimate has been obtained, the British Government will examine to what extent it can make up any deficiency."   Bliss

CC telegram (WP, DLC).
[1] J. J. Pershing to P. C. March and NDB, June 25, 1918, printed in *United States Army in the World War, 1917-1919* (17 vols., Washington, 1948), II, 482-83.
[2] An obviously confused statement. As has been mentioned, Marcel François Delanney was the new French Ambassador to Japan and was at this time still on his way to Tokyo via the United States. The Japanese government undoubtedly gave its note to the French embassy in Tokyo, which probably forwarded it to Delanney in Washington. Jusserand then must have transmitted the note over his own name to Paris.
[3] That is, NDB to T. H. Bliss, July 1, 1918.

From Robert Latham Owen

My dear Mr. President: [Washington] July 3, 1918.

I inclose copy of a resolution[1] which I think is of the highest importance, if it should meet with your approval.

In effect it proposes an organization of the belligerent nations opposing the Teutonic autocracy, declaring against the entry into the belligerent countries of any of the products of Germany until the menace of militarism is removed. It proposes a world-wide boycott against German commerce until the German people agree to remove the menace of German militarism. The effect of this as a treaty would be to strike Germany's finance and commerce in a vital spot and would give those interests a powerful motive to use their influences against the maintenance of German militarism. We command the seas and will be able to continue to command the seas more and more completely. We therefore have a deadly weapon with which to influence the financial and commercial interests, not to mention the covetous elements, of Germany.

Will you not in the name of liberty swing this mighty club and let it fall on the head of the Kaiser?

                    Yours faithfully,   Robt. L. Owen

TLS (WP, DLC).
[1] *Joint Resolution Requesting the President to Invite the Entente Allies to Declare the Rules of International Law and Require the German Government to Accept such Rules under Penalty of Progressive International Boycott, and so forth.* S.J. Res. 153, 65th Cong., 2d sess., copy in WP, DLC.

From William Byron Colver and Others

Sir: Washington 3 July 1918

On 7 February 1917, you directed the Federal Trade Commission to "investigate and report facts relating to the production, owner-ship, manufacture, storage, and distribution of foodstuffs and the products or by-products arising from or in connection with their preparation and manufacture; to ascertain the facts bearing on alleged violation of the anti-trust acts and particularly upon the question whether there are manipulations, controls, trusts, com-binations, conspiracies, or restraints of trade out of harmony with the law or the public interest," to the end that "proper remedies, legislative or administrative may be applied."[1]

On July 1, 1917 funds for carrying out this direction became available and the Commission undertook the task.

The work fell naturally into various divisions and reports have already been made to you with reference to the milling and jobbing of wheat flour and the preparation and distribution of certain canned food products. Other divisions will be the subject of reports to you as rapidly as the results of our studies can be reduced to proper form. At this time we are reporting to you on the meat-packing industry.

Answering directly your question as to whether or not there exist "monopolies, controls, trusts, combinations, conspiracies, or re-straints of trade out of harmony with the law and the public interest" we have found conclusive evidence that warrants an unqualified affirmative.

This evidence in summary form accompanies this letter[2] and will be set forth in more detailed form in seven (7) reports in support of our findings and recommendations which will be placed in your hand at the earliest possible moment.

While we have found and will disclose to you an intricate fabric of "monopolies, controls, combinations, conspiracies and restraints" which would seem to indicate a similarly complex and minute sys-tem of legislative or administrative remedies, we believe that an adequate remedy may be more simply arrived at.

We believe that if the fundamental and underlying evils are rooted out that the whole structure of conspiracy, control, monopoly and restraint must fall.

If we are correct in this judgment, the task of applying legislative and administrative remedy is greatly simplified.

[1] WW to W. J. Harris, Feb. 7, 1917, Vol. 41.
[2] *Food Investigation: Summary of the Report of the Federal Trade Commission on the Meat-Packing Industry July 3, 1918* (Washington, 1918). The fate of this report will be revealed in documents which follow.

It appears that five great packing concerns of the country, Swift, Armour, Morris, Cudahy and Wilson have attained such a dominant position that they control at will the market in which they buy their supplies, the market in which they sell their products, and hold the fortunes of their competitors in their hands.

Not only is the business of gathering, preparing and selling meat products in their control, but an almost countless number of by-product industries are similarly dominated, and not content with reaching out for mastery as to commodities which substitute for meat and its by-products, they have invaded allied industries and even unrelated ones.

The combination has not stopped at the most minute integration but has gone on into a stage of conglomeration so that unrelated heterogeneous enterprises are brought under control.

As we have followed these five great corporations through their amazing and devious ramifications; followed them through important branches of industry, of commerce and of finance, we have been able to trace back to its source the great power which has made possible their growth. We have found that it is not so much the means of production and preparation, nor the sheer momentum of great wealth but the advantage which is obtained through a monopolistic control of the market places and means of transportation and distribution.

If these five great concerns owned no packing plants and owned no cattle and still retained control of the instruments of transportation and of storage, their position would not be less strong than it is.

The producer of livestock is at the mercy of these five companies because they control the market and the marketing facilities and to some extent the rolling stock which transports the product to the market.

The competitors of these five concerns are at their mercy because of the control of the market places, storage facilities, and the refrigerator cars for distribution.

The consumer of meat products is at the mercy of these five because both producer and competitor are helpless to bring them relief.

The stock-car is a part of the equipment of the common carrier whose services are necessary to the producer of meat animals so that he may reach the market. The railroads furnish suitable cars for the transportation of other kinds of freight and as to the use of such cars, the miner of coal or the manufacturer of furniture are on an equality, but in the matter of the transportation of livestock to a small degree there comes in a private ownership and a control

and a manipulation of the means of transportation—the stock-car—
so it is that we recommend:

1. That the Government acquire through the Railroad Administration, all rolling stock used for the Transportation of meat
   animals and that such ownership be declared a Government
   monopoly.

In the transportation of all other kinds of freight, the transportation companies provide proper and suitable freight depots. The
proper and suitable freight depot for livestock is a stock-yard with
its equipment of exchange buildings, terminal railways, and means
of distributing full, unbiased and helpful market information. We
therefore recommend:

2. That the Government acquire through the Railroad Administration the principal and necessary stockyards of the country,
   to be treated as freight depots and to be operated under such
   conditions as will insure open, competitive markets, with uniform scale of charges for all services performed, and the acquisition or establishment of such additional yards from time
   to time as the future development of livestock production in
   the United States may require.

A requisite for the proper transportation of fresh meat and dairy
products is that type of rolling stock known as refrigerator cars.
The railroads supply proper, special types of cars for other classes
of freight but the refrigerator cars and the icing facilities which are
absolutely necessary for the transportation and distribution of fresh
meats are in private ownership. This ownership furnishes these
five great packing companies one of their most powerful means for
controls, manipulations and restraints. Lacking access on equal
terms to these facilities competitors of the five great packers are at
their mercy, and competition being stifled, the consumer similarly
is helpless. We therefore recommend:

3. That the Government acquire through the Railroad Administration, all privately owned refrigerator cars and all necessary
   equipment for their proper operation and that such ownership
   be declared a Government monopoly.

Proper freight houses are provided by transportation companies
for the various sorts of freight except meat and dairy products. The
indicated freight depot for such commodities is a cold-storage house.
Such a depot used as a distributing station, if free of access to all,
would constitute an agency for fair and free competition. Such a
depot in private hands, as now, constitutes an invincible weapon
for monopoly and control and manipulation. We therefore recommend:

4. That the Federal Government acquire such of the branch houses,

cold-storage plants and warehouses as are necessary to provide facilities for the competitive marketing and storage of food products in the principal centers of distribution and consumption. The same to be operated by the Government as public markets and storage places under such conditions as will afford an outlet for all manufacturers and handlers of food products on equal terms. Supplementing the marketing and storage facilities thus acquired, the Federal Government establish through the Railroad Administration, at the terminals of all principal points of distribution and consumption, central wholesale markets and storage plants, with facilities open to all upon payment of just and fair charges.

The Commission believes that these four suggestions strike so deeply at the root of the tree of monopoly that they constitute an adequate and simple solution of a problem, the gravity of which will be unfolded to you in the pages which follow.

Out of the mass of information in our hands, one fact stands out with all possible emphasis. The small dominant group of American meat-packers are now international in their activities, while remaining American in identity. Blame which now attaches to them for their practices abroad as well as at home, inevitably will attach to our country, if the practices continue. The purely domestic problems in their increasing magnitude, their monopolization of markets and their manipulations and controls, grave as those problems are, are not more serious than those presented by the added aspect of international activity. This urgently argues for a solution which will increase and not diminish the high regard in which this people is held in international comity.

Some show of competition is staged by the five great packing companies. It is superficial. There is the natural rivalry of officials and departments and this is made much of as indicating the existence of real competition. It is not real. How sham it is will be fully set out in the accompanying summary and the complete reports.

Some independent packers exist by sufferance of the five and a few hardy ones have survived in real competition. Around such few of these as remain the lines are drawing in.

Having answered affirmatively the question to which you directed our attention and having summarized what we believe to be the simplest form of an adequate remedy, and before proceeding to a more detailed discussion of the subject, we wish to make acknowledgement to the tireless industry, the fidelity to the public interest, and the patience and forbearance of the men who in the public interest, have composed the Commission's staff in this inquiry.

These men have met and overcome every obstacle that ingenuity and money could devise to impede them. Space forbidding individual mention, we make this general acknowledgement and this seems the proper time to call to your attention again and especially, the work of Mr. Francis J. Heney whose conduct of the case, because of its success, has met with condemnation, misrepresentation and criticism. We contrast Mr. Heney's legal ethics with the legal ethics of the men by whom he was opposed.

The Commission through Mr. Heney, had to meet deliberate falsification of returns properly required under legal authority; we had to meet schools for witnesses where employees were coached in anticipation of their being called to testify in an investigation ordered by you and by the Congress of the United States; we had to meet a situation created by the destruction of letters and documents vital to this investigation; we had to meet a conspiracy in the preparation of answers to the lawful inquiries of the Commission.

We will not trespass upon your time to go into details as to the legal and business ethics employed, but on the foregoing statement, which we are prepared to substantiate in every detail, we contrast the ethics of the Commission's legal and investigating staff with the legal staffs of the five great companies. And in leaving this part of the subject, we say as we have said repeatedly to you during the time of the investigation, that Mr. Heney's conduct of the case as well as that of the other agents and attorneys of the Commission, were under the direct supervision of the Commission, the acts were performed with the knowledge and under the direction of the Commission, and the Commission assumes all responsibility for them.

Respectfully,   William B Colver. Chairman
                  John Franklin Fort
                  Victor Murdock.

TLS (WP, DLC).

Two Telegrams from Lord Reading to Arthur James Balfour

Washington. 3rd July 1918

No. 3024 Upon receipt of your telegram from Paris of July 3rd[1] I saw my French and Italian colleagues. It was agreed between us that I should take advantage of an appointment previously made for me to see the President this afternoon to communicate the decision of the Supreme War Council.

At my interview today with the President I presented the note from the Japanese Government cabled June 28th No. 3988.[2] The President commented on the passage stating that the Japanese Government found it impossible for them to extend their military activities beyond the limits of Eastern Siberia which was what he had always understood was the limit of any Japanese plan. I observed that this statement would not prevent their going further should the circumstances be sufficiently favourable. There was not much discussion with regard to the note first because the President was already aware of the substance of the communication if not of the text[3] and secondly because I intimated to him that I had other important communications to make.

I then informed him of the messages from H.M.S. Suffolk communicated in your No. 4088 and 4097. The substance of this information had already reached the President from Admiral Knight the U. S. naval commander at Vladivostock.[4]

I then referred to the resolution of the Supreme War Council representing the considered views of the French Italian and H. M. Governments. Unfortunately the cable reached me in various sections owing doubtless to the congested traffic and I had not received the full text at the time of my interview with the President. I did however lay great stress on the position of the Czecho-Slovaks and the grave injury that would result to our cause if we were unable to afford fully adequate protection to them against German or Austro Hungarian prisoners of war and on the necessity for immediate action taking advantage of present favourable conditions as indicated in the resolution. The President held firmly to his opinion that it was not possible to intervene with the object of creating an Eastern front. He rested this conviction upon the limitation contained in the Japanese note and referred once more to the impossibility of supplying troops other than Japanese except in very small numbers. He further said that notwithstanding the many persons whom he had seen recently he had heard no opinion which had caused him to come to a different conclusion. I gathered also that the military advisers of the President are of the same opinion. I called his attention to the importance of the resolution of which the text was only partly before him and me and especially to the fact that General Foch and the military advisers of the three Governments so strongly urged armed intervention. I promised to forward to the President the full text of the resolution as soon as it was received and he assured me that he would give it that very full and careful consideration that such a document emanating from such a source deserved.

The President said that although we could not create an Eastern front at the moment we should consider intermediate courses and he informed me that he had been still considering and examining the plans for an Economic Commission on a great scale and that he recognised that it would be necessary to protect this Commission. His idea was that the Commission should be of the first importance, that the policy of economic assistance to Russia should be kept to the front and that the military force should play a secondary part. I argued that above all we must not permit a failure or defeat of any protective or military force and that whether it was sent to protect the Czecho-Slovaks or to protect the Economic Commission it must necessarily be reasonably adequate for the purpose intended.

The President then referred to a report of the War Department to the effect that the maximum number of 7,000 American troops could be despatched to Vladivostock[5] and if 100,000 men were to be sent 80 or 90 per cent. must be Japanese and this would mean that the Japanese must have the supreme command. The President informed me that he was having plans worked out which when completed he would discuss with the Japanese in order to obtain their assent.

I then said to the President that I presumed that he would also consult the three allied Governments before publicly announcing a policy or even arriving at a conclusion. He said that he certainly would not act without having communicated with our three Governments. The President was ten minutes overdue at a Cabinet meeting and had to leave. I asked how long it would be before he communicated with us as immediate action was urged by the Supreme War Council. He answered that he must again consider the matter by the light of the text of the resolution and in any event complete plans which must take some few days.

My general impression is

(a) That there is no prospect at present of the President agreeing to the full policy of armed intervention with the object of creating an Eastern front.

(b) That the President's mind is still firmly fixed on a great Economic or civil Commission.

(c) That he realises the necessity for armed protection of the Commission so that as it advances it may be protected from attack in the rear or from being cut off, and

(d) That it is incumbent upon U. S. and Allies to assist and protect the Czecho-Slovaks and that immediate action must be taken.

It must be remembered that the President had not the full text of the resolution before him and in any event had had no time to consider the reasons recited in the resolution and that indeed I myself had only seen a comparatively small part of the resolution.

JULY 4, 1918

The importance of the interview is that it shows that the President's mind is crystallizing (if he has not already decided) in the direction of the Economic Commission and the armed protective force. The addition of the Czecho-Slovak incidents in Vladivostock and elsewhere and the resolution of the Supreme War Council endorsed by General Foch will I think cause him to decide in favour of a military force accompanying the Commission and of a more important character than he had originally intended.

I have given copies of the above to my French and Italian colleagues.

CC telegram (W. Wiseman Papers, CtY).
¹ That is, the document printed as Enclosure IV with Lord Reading to WW, July 3, 1918. It had been transmitted to Reading in two parts as A. J. Balfour to Lord Reading, July 3, 1918, T telegrams (W. Wiseman Papers, CtY).
² That is, the document printed as Enclosure III with Lord Reading to WW, July 3, 1918.
³ Actually, Wilson had received a communication from Frazier conveying the first part of the Supreme War Council's resolution shortly before he received Reading at 2 p.m. on July 3. W. G. Sharp to RL, July 2, 1918, No. 100, received July 3, 1918, 10:20 a.m., T telegram (WP, DLC).
⁴ See the Enclosure printed with RL to WW, June 28, 1918 (first letter of that date).
⁵ See NDB to WW, July 2, 1918 (second letter of that date).

Washington. July 3rd. 1918.

No. 3009. Very urgent.

Your telegram No. 3983.

In answer to my request based on your telegram the President has assured me that he does not intend to make a declaration of policy with regard to Russia in his speech tomorrow.

T telegram (FO 115/2447, p. 294, PRO).

An Address at Mount Vernon

[July 4, 1918]

GENTLEMEN OF THE DIPLOMATIC CORPS AND MY FELLOW CITIZENS: I am happy to draw apart with you to this quiet place of old counsel in order to speak a little of the meaning of this day of our nation's independence. The place seems very still and remote. It is as serene and untouched by the hurry of the world as it was in those great days long ago when General Washington was here and held leisurely conference with the men who were to be associated with him in the creation of a nation. From these gentle slopes they looked out upon the world and saw it whole, saw it with the light of the future upon it, saw it with modern eyes that turned away from a past which men of liberated spirits could no longer endure.

It is for that reason that we cannot feel even here in the immediate presence of this sacred tomb that this is a place of death. It was a place of achievement. A great promise that was meant for all mankind was here given plan and reality. The associations by which we are here surrounded are the inspiriting associations of that noble death which is only a glorious consummation. From this green hillside we also ought to be able to see with comprehending eyes the world that lies about us and should conceive anew the purposes that must set men free.

It is significant,—significant of their own character and purpose and of the influences they were setting afoot,—that Washington and his associates, like the barons at Runnymede, spoke and acted, not for a class, but for a people. It has been left for us to see to it that it shall be understood that they spoke and acted, not for a single people only, but for all mankind. They were thinking, not of themselves and of the material interests which centered in the little groups of landholders and merchants and men of affairs with whom they were accustomed to act, in Virginia and the colonies to the north and south of her, but of a people which wished to be done with classes and special interests and the authority of men whom they had not themselves chosen to rule over them. They entertained no private purpose, desired no peculiar privilege. They were consciously planning that men of every class should be free and America a place to which men out of every nation might resort who wished to share with them the rights and privileges of free men. And we take our cue from them,—do we not? We intend what they intended. We here in America believe our participation in this present war to be only the fruitage of what they planted. Our case differs from theirs only in this, that it is our inestimable privilege to concert with men out of every nation what shall make not only the liberties of America secure but the liberties of every other people as well. We are happy in the thought that we are permitted to do what they would have done had they been in our place. There must now be settled once for all what was settled for America in the great age upon whose inspiration we draw to-day. This is surely a fitting place from which calmly to look out upon our task, that we may fortify our spirits for its accomplishment. And this is the appropriate place from which to avow, alike to the friends who look on and to the friends with whom we have the happiness to be associated in action, the faith and purpose with which we act.

This, then, is our conception of the great struggle in which we are engaged. The plot is written plain upon every scene and every act of the supreme tragedy. On the one hand stand the peoples of the world,—not only the peoples actually engaged, but many others also who suffer under mastery but cannot act; peoples of many races and in every part of the world,—the people of stricken Russia still, among the rest, though they are for the moment unorganized and helpless. Opposed to them, masters of many armies, stand an isolated, friendless group of governments who speak no common purpose but only selfish ambitions of their own by which none can profit but themselves, and whose peoples are fuel in their hands; governments which fear their people and yet are for the time their sovereign lords, making every choice for them and disposing of their lives and fortunes as they will, as well as of the lives and fortunes of every people who fall under their power,—governments clothed with the strange trappings and the primitive authority of an age that is altogether alien and hostile to our own. The Past and the Present are in deadly grapple and the peoples of the world are being done to death between them.

There can be but one issue. The settlement must be final. There can be no compromise. No halfway decision would be tolerable. No halfway decision is conceivable. These are the ends for which the associated peoples of the world are fighting and which must be conceded them before there can be peace:

I. The destruction of every arbitrary power anywhere that can separately, secretly, and of its single choice disturb the peace of the world; or, if it cannot be presently destroyed, at the least its reduction to virtual impotence.

II. The settlement of every question, whether of territory, of sovereignty, of economic arrangement, or of political relationship, upon the basis of the free acceptance of that settlement by the people immediately concerned, and not upon the basis of the material interest or advantage of any other nation or people which may desire a different settlement for the sake of its own exterior influence or mastery.

III. The consent of all nations to be governed in their conduct towards each other by the same principles of honour and of respect for the common law of civilized society that govern the individual citizens of all modern states in their relations with one another; to the end that all promises and covenants may be sacredly observed, no private plots or conspiracies hatched, no selfish injuries wrought with impunity, and a mutual trust established upon the handsome foundation of a mutual respect for right.

IV. The establishment of an organization of peace which shall make it certain that the combined power of free nations will check every invasion of right and serve to make peace and justice the more secure by affording a definite tribunal of opinion to which all must submit and by which every international readjustment that cannot be amicably agreed upon by the peoples directly concerned shall be sanctioned.

These great objects can be put into a single sentence. What we seek is the reign of law, based upon the consent of the governed and sustained by the organized opinion of mankind.

These great ends cannot be achieved by debating and seeking to reconcile and accommodate what statesmen may wish, with their projects for balances of power and of national opportunity. They can be realized only by the determination of what the thinking peoples of the world desire, with their longing hope for justice and for social freedom and opportunity.

I can fancy that the air of this place carries the accents of such principles with a peculiar kindness. Here were started forces which the great nation against which they were primarily directed at first regarded as a revolt against its rightful authority but which it has long since seen to have been a step in the liberation of its own people as well as of the people of the United States; and I stand here now to speak,—speak proudly and with confident hope,—of the spread of this revolt, this liberation, to the great stage of the world itself! The blinded rulers of Prussia have roused forces they knew little of,—forces which, once roused, can never be crushed to earth again; for they have at their heart an inspiration and a purpose which are deathless and of the very stuff of triumph![1]

Printed reading copy (WP, DLC).
 [1] There is a WWT outline and a WWT draft (which Wilson sent to the Public Printer) of this address in WP, DLC.

To Robert Lansing, with Enclosures

My dear Mr. Secretary,   The White House. 4 July, 1918.

I approve the draft Mr. Long has made for the signature of the bankers[1] and also (with the one or two verbal changes I have taken the liberty of making) the draft of a reply made by yourself.[2] If we are to support these bankers, they must let us know of every step and arrangement, and especially what banks they have included,— for we cannot allow the shut outs they have repeatedly attempted.

                              Faithfully Yours,   W.W.

WWTLI (SDR, RG 59, 893.51/2514, DNA).
 [1] Printed as Enclosure III.
 [2] The draft which Wilson emended is missing. The letter as sent is printed as Enclosure IV.

E N C L O S U R E   I

PERSONAL AND CONFIDENTIAL.

My dear Mr. President: Washington July 3, 1918.

I enclose herewith a letter from Mr. Long telling of the progress of the negotiations with the Bankers relative to Chinese loans, which amount, in round numbers, to something like $200,000,000.

Attached to the letter is a draft of a proposed letter to me by the Committee which was named in New York last Friday.[1]

Following it is a substitute draft prepared by Mr. Long.

And, finally, there is the proposed reply to the Bankers' letter which I drafted to meet as far as possible the Bankers' wishes and at the same time lay down a proper declaration of policy as modified by the present war conditions.

Mr. Long had already started on a few weeks' vacation when I asked him to attend the Bankers conference in New York on Friday. From there he came here with the document which they had drafted, and will remain until a decision can be reached. I am sure you will pardon me, therefore, for asking you to give this matter your immediate attention, as I feel that Mr. Long should take a rest at the earliest possible time.   Faithfully yours,   Robert Lansing.

TLS (SDR, RG 59, 893.51/2514A, DNA).
  [1] It is missing.

E N C L O S U R E   I I

Breckinridge Long to Robert Lansing

Dear Mr. Secretary: [Washington] July 2, 1918.

Attached is the proposal of the bankers you met in Washington recently. They formed a Committee consisting of Messrs. Morgan, Vanderlip and Abbott,[1] held a number of meetings in New York, evolved the attached written informal memorandum and met finally yesterday afternoon at Mr. Morgan's office. They had asked me to be there and I had requested Mr. Williams[2] to be present. Mr. Strauss[3] represented the Treasury in the absence of and at the request of Mr. Leffingwell.[4]

The proposal will be formally presented if they are assured a favorable response will be made. It is now presented for consideration and for alteration as a basis upon which to build something concrete and definite.

It contains several apparently unnecessary clauses. To eliminate these I have drawn a substitute for it which it is proposed be submitted to them as the one they shall write to us and in response to which they shall receive an answer a draft of which is also attached for your consideration.

I feel that the time is opportune to bring this to a conclusion and think that if I talked with Mr. Morgan on the matters which will be embodied in his proposal and your reply we could soon come to a definite conclusion.   Breckinridge Long

TLS (SDR, RG 59, 893.51/2515, DNA).
[1] John Jay Abbott, vice-president of the Continental & Commercial Trust & Savings Bank of Chicago.
[2] That is, Edward Thomas Williams, chief of the Division of Far Eastern Affairs of the State Department.
[3] Albert Strauss, a banker from New York and member of J. & W. Seligman & Co. At this time he was the representative of the Secretary of the Treasury on the War Trade Board and a special adviser to the Treasury Department on matters relating to gold and currency.
[4] Russell Cornell Leffingwell, Assistant Secretary of the Treasury.

E N C L O S U R E   I I I

A Draft of a Letter by Breckinridge Long[1]

Sir:

We have been giving very earnest considerations to the suggestion you made in Washington respecting a loan to China, and wish in the first place to assure you of our disposition to be of service in the matter, and to help in finding some way in which the wishes of the Administration can be carried out.

In the course of our discussion the following points have seemed to us to be fundamental:

First: An arrangement of this sort which contemplates transactions spread over a considerable period of time, in our opinion should be made on the broadest basis in order to give the best protection to our investors, and with the right foundation established confidence would follow and anxiety and jealousy disappear. At the conference held in Washington recently there was mentioned as a course perhaps advisable that Americans and Japanese co-operate in a loan to China. We are disposed to believe that it would be better if such international co-operation were to be made broader. We suggest therefore, that this can best be accomplished if a four-power group be constituted consisting of financial members to be recognized by the respective Governments of Great Britain, France, Japan and the United States; our Government to recognize as their member of such group the American banks or firms which may become associated for this purpose, and which we should hope to have representative of the whole country. Although under the present circumstances it would be expected that Japan and the United States should carry England and France, such carrying should not diminish the vitality of the memberships in the four-power group.

One of the conditions of membership in such a four-power group should be that there should be a relinquishment by the members of the group either to China or to the group of any option to make loans which they now hold, and all loans to China by any [of] them should be considered as four-power group business. Through co-operation of England, France, Japan and the United States much can be accomplished for the maintenance of Chinese sovereignty and the preservation of the "open door"; and, furthermore, such cooperation might greatly facilitate the full development of the large revenue sources from only a very few of which China at present realizes a satisfactory income.

It would seem to be necessary if now and after the war we are successfully to carry out the responsibilities imposed upon us by our new international position, that our Government should be prepared in principle to recognize the change in our international relations, both diplomatic and commercial, brought about by the war.

Second: We have considerable doubt whether under the present circumstances the people of the United States could be induced to buy the debt of any foreign country on any terms. We feel quite certain that no loan could be sold unless the Government would be willing at the time of issue to make it clear to the public that the loan is made at the suggestion of the Government; with such an announcement we think it possible that a reasonable amount of Chinese loan could be placed in this country.

If these two fundamental conditions are agreed to by our Government we hold ourselves at your disposal to go further into the details of any proposed loan, and will co-operate with you most earnestly and sympathetically.   Yours very truly,

TLS (SDR, RG 59, 893.51/2176, DNA).
 ¹ To this draft was added, "New York City, July 8th 1918" and the signatures of representatives of J. P. Morgan and Co., Kuhn, Loeb and Co., National City Bank of New York, First National Bank of New York, Chase National Bank, Continental & Commercial Trust & Savings Bank of Chicago, Lee, Higginson and Co. of Boston, and Guaranty Trust Co. of New York.

Robert Lansing to J. P. Morgan and Company and Others

Confidential.

Gentlemen: [Washington] July 9, 1918.

Your letter of July 8, 1918, has had my very careful consideration. It contains several elements of an important nature which I will take up in order.

This war has brought the countries of Great Britain, France, Japan, the United States and some others into a state of harmony and helpfulness, and has supplanted an intense spirit of competition by a spirit of mutuality and co-operation in matters relating to their interests abroad. Doubtless this situation is in a measure due to the absence of capital seeking foreign investment at the present time because of the demands upon it for war purposes.

If international co-operation is necessary, as seems to be the case, for the successful flotation of the proposed loan, I realize that the support of Great Britain and France would be desirable even if it should be necessary for the United States and Japan to carry for the time being their respective portions of the loan. All four powers are of course deeply interested in any measures taken to strengthen China and fit her for a more active part in the war against the central European powers. Japan is already considering rendering financial assistance, while two of the loans that have been mentioned as desirable are loans by which the interests of British and French citizens would be directly affected and it would, of course, be unwise to undertake their negotiation without consulting parties so immediately concerned.

In these circumstances the formation of a four-power group, to consist of financial interests of the United States, Great Britain, France and Japan to deal with the Government of China for purposes of making loans to that Government seems advisable and it is my hope that in this way the whole subject of finance in China can ultimately be treated in a broad way. If the terms and conditions of each loan are submitted to and approved by this Government, and the other co-operating Governments and by the Government of China, this Government would not only interpose no objection, but, on the contrary, would consider such an arrangement an assurance that the welfare of China and the proper interests of the other Governments were of such a mutual character as to permit of close and friendly intercourse for their common good. I think that I should say frankly that this Government would be opposed to any terms or conditions of a loan which sought to impair the political control of China or lessened the sovereign rights of that Republic.

In response to your inquiry, as to whether the Government would be willing at the time of its issue to state that the loan was being made at the suggestion of the Government, I will say that the Government has suggested that this loan be made and would have no hesitancy in formally stating that fact at the time of issue.

The question of relinquishment by the members of the American Group of any options to make loans now existing in favor of any of them seems to be a reasonable condition of membership in that group. Such relinquishment by a member of a foreign group is a matter over which this Government would have no control. However, I may say that if the members of the American Group come to the conclusion that they desire it, this Government will use its good offices, in so far as it can properly do so, to bring about such relinquishment.

The war has created a community of interest between certain governments and their citizens and those of other governments and has broken down barriers that once have existed and made easier the intercourse between them. With the consequent expansion of our interests abroad there must be considered also the element of risk which sometimes enters into the making of loans to foreign governments and which is always inseparable from investments in foreign countries where reliance must be placed on the borrower's good faith and ability to carry out the terms of the contract. This Government realizes fully that condition and in order to encourage and facilitate that free intercourse between American citizens and foreign states which is mutually advantageous is willing to aid in every proper way and to make prompt and vigorous representations and to take every possible step to insure the execution of equitable contracts made in good faith by its citizens in foreign lands.

Your suggestion that the members of the proposed American group may be representative of the whole country is one which is entirely satisfactory since it removes a possible ground of objection. Various sections of the country are interested in enterprises of this character and undoubtedly would be glad to join any constructive movement such as is proposed. As so much depends upon the proper organization of the American financial group I assume that in the event of its formation you will submit the names of the proposed members to the Government before a final organization is made.

The spirit of co-operation you manifest is very gratifying and you are assured of the interest of the Government and of all proper aid which it can render in bringing this matter to a satisfactory conclusion.

I am, Gentlemen,

Your obedient servant,   Robert Lansing

CCL (SDR, RG 59, 893.51/2176, DNA).

Sir William Wiseman to Arthur Cecil Murray[1]

My dear Arthur,   [New York] July 4, 1918.

I am writing this in rather a hurry tonight to catch tomorrow morning's mail. It is just to thank you ever so much for your nice letter of 3rd June, and to acknowledge the reports you sent at the same time.

I had intended writing you some observations on these which had occurred to me while I read them, but I shall not have time to do so this evening, and for the last two weeks I have been either at the Embassy or with House in Magnolia. We have been, as you know, engaged almost exclusively on the question of intervention in Russia. I have not cabled you much about it because I have been with Reading, and have helped him draw up all his F.O. cables, so that I had practically nothing to add to them.

Nor will I attempt to write to you at any length now because by the time this letter reaches you the situation will certainly have changed. I may say, however, that the President remains quite unconvinced by all the political arguments in favor of Allied intervention, nor was he more impressed by the military arguments in favor of re-creating an Eastern front. From the political point of view, he has always thought—and still thinks—it would be a great blunder for the Allies to intervene without an unmistakeable invitation from the Soviet Government. Anyone who has studied his Mexican policy will understand the remarkable parallel which the Russian situation presents, and realise that this is to him more than a passing political question, but a matter of principle. I am not saying that he is right, but I think we should realise that we are up against a new conception of foreign policy which no amount of argument will reconcile with, for instance, traditional British policy. With regard to the military point of view, he is relying a good deal on the advice of his own military advisers who are against the scheme on the ground that it will not lead to any effective pressure on the East and would divert our energies from the West. In this, of course, they are not considering the question of man-power so much as supplies and equipment.

The Czech-Slovak position has, in my opinion, materially altered the situation, and will be, I think, the determining factor. The President recognises that both the Allies and the United States are responsible for the Czechs, and if possible must render them assistance. You may be sure that Reading is acting with great tact and firmness, and we are being helped by the much fuller information which we now receive from the F.O. by cable.

With regard to Reading, I want to tell you in great confidence what he has in mind regarding his future plans. I will not repeat what I said in my letter of June 15th, which still holds good. Of course, I would not like him to know that I had written to you about his personal affairs, and it may be a presumption. My object is that you may be acquainted with the situation and have an opportunity of discussing it with Eric,[2] and thinking it over, so that you have some suggestions to make when he arrives. Briefly the position is as follows: Reading feels that he came out here not as ordinary Ambassador, or High Commissioner, but because he thought, owing to his close connection with the Cabinet at home and his friendships on this side with members of the Administration, that he would be able to gain the President's confidence to such an extent that he would be able to discuss with him and consult with him on important questions affecting the war. He has now come to the conclusion that it is quite impossible to break down the barrier between the President and the foreign representatives and that he is unable to do more than any ordinary Ambassador could accomplish. In this I think he is quite wrong, and I have told him so. In the first place, the President does trust him and values his opinion very highly, but it simply is not the President's nature to be communicative or to discuss affairs of state with anyone. In this respect Reading achieves far more than anyone else I can think of whom the Government could send out. Furthermore Reading does not realise that the many problems (almost daily problems) which arise regarding finance, shipping, food, supplies, etc., which he negotiates and settles with comparative ease, would present real difficulties to anyone else, and furthermore would probably lead to friction. He has a particular gift for putting his case in a way that will appeal to the American officials and a very nice sense of how far he can go without causing trouble. He is worried, too, about the question of the Chief Justiceship. He feels more and more that if he stays out here any longer he must resign his position, and, of course, that would be a terrible wrench for him, and in my humble opinion a sacrifice he ought not to be called upon to make. His present plan is to go home and put this position to the Prime Minister, and agree to come back again for a short time, say a month or six weeks, in order to clear up here and hand over to somebody else; but I am afraid that his mind is very much against coming back here permanently. I have discussed the whole situation frankly with House, and more cautiously with the State Department. The opinion is unanimous that it would be a disaster to the Allied Cause if Reading did not remain here until the war is over. I must say, however, that I think it is a pity for him to stay here too long without going home. He soon begins to feel out of touch (much more out of touch than he really is) and becomes restless and very anxious to have a full discussion of problems with the Cabinet at home. I have suggested to him that the ideal arrangement would be something on the lines of Tardieu's new appointment; that is to say, a member of the Cabinet, without portfolio, specially charged with all American affairs, and that he should divide his time between London and Washington. I feel certain the best results could be achieved in this way. I think it would be advisable to have a good permanent head of the Missions, but as far as the Embassy is concerned I would leave that in charge of Barclay while Reading is away. Frankly, I dread the idea of a new Ambassador who would not know the position here and the very peculiar way in which business is done.

I have written freely exactly what I think, and would be glad if you would show this to Eric and tell him it represents also the view of Col. House.

Reading wants me to remain here while he is in London, and, although I shall be very disappointed not to go with him and see you all, I can understand that it may be of use for him to be in close touch by cable with House and others through me.

Ascherson[3] writes to me that so far as he is concerned the arrangements we made in London are working admirably. Many thanks for looking after all this.

With very best wishes,

Yours ever, [William Wiseman]

CCL (W. Wiseman Papers, CtY).
    [1] Lt. Col. Arthur Cecil Murray, M.P., former Parliamentary Private Secretary to Sir Edward Grey (1910-1914) and assistant Military Attaché in Washington from July 1917 to March 1918, was at this time attached to the American section of the Department of Political Intelligence of the Foreign Office. Murray had resigned his post in Washington and had returned to London upon Wiseman's request for the specific purpose of serving as House and Wiseman's contact with the Foreign Office. See Arthur C. Murray, *At Close Quarters: A Sidelight on Anglo-American Diplomatic Relations* (London, 1946), pp. 4-14.
    [2] That is, Sir Eric Drummond.
    [3] Charles S. Ascherson, probably Drummond's private secretary.

To Thomas Staples Martin

My dear Senator: [The White House] 5 July, 1918

I have just learned that the House is expected to act tonight on the resolution with regard to authorizing the taking over of the telegraph lines. Would it be imposing too much upon your kindness to ask if you would not endeavor to ascertain the possibility of an early action before adjournment by the Senate on the same matter? I am sure you will indulge me in this anxiety because of the practical importance of the subject.

Cordially and sincerely yours,   Woodrow Wilson

TLS (Letterpress Books, WP, DLC).

From Joseph Patrick Tumulty, with Enclosure

Dear Governor: The White House. 5 July 1918.

Nothing that you have been called upon to do since the War began is fraught with so much danger as is this suggestion. I do not want to burden you with a memorandum in the matter. Indeed it has so many angles that I could not make myself clear. I would be glad to talk with you any time about it.

Sincerely yours,   J P Tumulty

TLS (WP, DLC).

E N C L O S U R E

To Joseph Patrick Tumulty

Dear Tumulty: The White House [c. July 5, 1918].

Will you be kind enough to look over these[1] and summarize them for me briefly? I happen to be in a special rush. Apparently the Board's own counsel holds that I have not the legal power to change the rates. In that case the matter is simplified.

The President.

Dear Governor: 5 July 1918.

The members of the Labor Board "acting under the principles outlined by you" in establishing the War Labor Board, in view of the increased cost of living, recommend

(1) a general increase of railway rates;

(2) they are of the opinion that you have no power under the Act

of Congress to increase these rates but suggest that you ask Congress to legislate in the matter;

(3) they urge the appointment of an administrator to act for you in respect of each electric railway invoking relief.

They conclude their memorandum to you by saying:

"We expect to be able to hand down our award in a number of these street railway cases on or before the first of August. Indeed, to prevent a serious defection and withdrawal of the workers, not by concerted action, but individually, it is necessary for us to make a decision by that time. We venture to suggest, therefore, that to avoid widespread national embarrassment, assurance of relief to the companies, by securing them an income commensurate with their increased cost of operation, be given on or before the date of our award. We are authorized to say that the members of the National War Labor Board unanimously concur in our recommendation."   Sincerely yours,   J. P. Tumulty

TL and TLS (WP, DLC).
¹ W. H. Taft and F. P. Walsh to WW, July 1, 1918, TLS (WP, DLC), and R. A. Taft, "Memorandum on Power of President to Raise Street Railway Rates," TS MS (WP, DLC). W. H. Taft and Walsh informed Wilson that the National War Labor Board would soon try to settle more than twenty controversies between large street railway companies and their employees, in which the workers were asking for considerable wage increases. Since, in view of the high cost of living, the present pay of street railway employees was too low, Taft and Walsh expected that the board would have to grant the workers substantial pay raises in order to avoid possible widespread strikes. However, given the precarious financial situation of street railway companies across the country, additional operating expenses would probably force most of them into bankruptcy unless they were permitted to increase their fares. Considering the supreme importance of the street railways for war production and the need for their continued operation, Taft and Walsh urged upon Wilson, "with all the emphasis possible," the necessity of increasing the rates of fare on many of the electric street railways of the country. They then discussed the question of whether, under existing legislation, the federal government had the power to set the rates of street railways without actually taking them over and concluded: "If the requisite power be found to exist, we urge the appointment of an administrator to act for you in respect of each electric railway invoking relief and that, after a hearing of the parties and local public in interest, proper relief be granted. If you, as you may be advised, conclude that existing law does not give the needed power, we recommend that Congress be asked promptly to vest it in you." The other members of the War Labor Board concurred in this recommendation.

The accompanying memorandum by Robert Alphonso Taft examined the legal aspects of the question in detail. Taft argued that none of the present laws authorized the President to regulate the rates of electric railways, and he concluded: "The only power apparently conferred by these laws is to physically take over or assume control of the street railway properties. If this is done the title to the properties will vest in the United States during the War, and the United States can make such changes for the use of its property as it sees fit."

From Josephus Daniels, with Enclosure

Dear Mr. President: Washington. July 5th, 1918.

Will you indicate what reply should be made to the enclosed cable from Admiral Knight? The telegrams to which he has received no replies were somewhat along the same line. No definite answer was made because I wished to know your views before giving instructions. I think he ought to have an answer today.

Sincerely,   Josephus Daniels

ALS (WP, DLC).

E N C L O S U R E

From: C in C Asiatic
To: Secy of the Navy

At meeting representatives all Naval forces CZECHS General explained military situation and plans. Considered necessary move westerly immediately seize tunnels and bridges before these destroyed by war prisoners of whom expects encounter fifteen thousand twenty thousand. Has seized enough rifles to arm his full force but little ammunition. Consider unsafe to leave Vladivostok, Siberia unguarded as many Germans known to be in hiding with arms, and 7000 war prisoners between Vladivostok Siberia and Habarosk. I agree this view. Is willing leave one thousand CZECHS and requests Naval force guarantee second thousand ready in event necessary. Allied representatives agreed to refer question their Governments. As Bolshevic power entirely overthrown and as threatened danger is from war prisoners and spies, I consider it essential to act as may be necessary for securing of city and protection CZECHS rear and base. Request instructions.

As communications very bad and as I assume that Government wishes me to take all precautions against Germans, shall utilize full landing force if necessity arises before Department's reply received. Have no reply my 23320, 22023, 20025, 19028, 21029, 23022.

(No time group)
C in C Asiatic.

CC telegram (WP, DLC).

From George Creel, with Enclosure

My dear Mr. President,   Washington, D. C. July 5, 1918

I enclose you a report from Emmett Scott, one of the great negroe leaders, now serving as special assistant to Secretary Baker, and the man that I am using in my approach to the negroe problem.

May I ask that you read the resolution and, if possible, address a letter to Mr. Scott that we can use widely.

The conference, after the first day of ugly feeling, was all that we could have wished in the way of support and understanding.

Respectfully,   George Creel

ENCLOSURE

From Emmett Jay Scott

Dear Mr. President: Washington. June 26, 1918.

Mr. George Creel, Chairman of the Committee on Public Information, authorized me last week to call to Washington a group of the more important Negro editors and other leaders of thought and opinion among the Negro citizens of Our Country.

Practically everyone invited attended this three-day Conference which was held on June 19, 20, 21, 1918, in Room 112 of the Interior Department Building, 18th and F Streets.

At this Conference there were present men who heretofore have entertained divergent views on many matters of racial interest and national policy, and full opportunity was given for the expression of their thoughts and opinions on a number of important matters of present interest to our Race, after first discussing the greater question of how colored Americans could best cooperate and help to win the present war.

It is highly significant and encouraging to note that, at the close of the three-day Conference, a resolution, reading as follows, was *unanimously* adopted, viz:

"We, the thirty-one representatives of the Negro press which has a circulation of more than a million copies, principally among the colored people of America, and representatives of other activities, wish to affirm FIRST OF ALL, our unalterable belief that the defeat of the German government and what it today represents is of paramount importance to the welfare of the world in general and to our people in particular.

"We deem it hardly necessary, in view of the untarnished record of Negro Americans, to reaffirm our loyalty to Our Country and our readiness to make every sacrifice to win this war.

"We wish, however, as students and guides of public opinion among our people, to use every endeavor to keep these 12,000,000 people at the highest pitch, not simply of passive loyalty, but of active, enthusiastic and self-sacrificing participation in the war.

"We are not unmindful of the recognition of our American citizenship in the draft, of the appointment of colored officers, of the designation of colored advisors to the Government departments, and to other indications of a broadened public opinion, nevertheless we believe today that justifiable grievances of the colored people are producing not disloyalty, but an amount of unrest and bitterness which even the best efforts of their leaders may not be able always to guide unless they can have the active and sympathetic cooperation of the National and State governments. German propaganda among us is powerless, but the apparent indifference of our own Government may be dangerous.

"The American Negro does not expect to have the whole Negro problem settled immediately; he is not seeking to hold-up a striving country and a distracted world by pushing irrelevant personal grievances as a price of loyalty; he is not disposed to catalogue, in this tremendous crisis, all his complaints and disabilities; he is more than willing to do his full share in helping to win the war for democracy and he expects his full share of the fruits thereof,—but he is today compelled to ask for that minimum of consideration which will enable him to be an efficient fighter for VICTORY."

I have been directed, as Chairman of said Conference, to transmit these resolutions to you as expressing the sentiments which were adopted unanimously at said meeting, and, if agreeable, I shall be pleased to receive such acknowledgment and reply as you may deem suitable.

Mr. Creel will doubtless state to you that the Conference was characterized by a splendid spirit of patriotism and eager willingness to serve our Government during this period of national emergency and need.

A word from you at this time, Mr. President, addressed to colored Americans generally through this group of leaders will accomplish great good. Pains are being taken to see that a satisfactory report of the proceedings of this Conference of sane, patriotic leaders is given full publicity.

Dr. Robert R. Moton, Principal of Tuskegee Institute, was present continuously at this Conference, and his sound judgment helped to draft the resolutions which were adopted unanimously.

Very respectfully yours,   Emmett J Scott

TLS (WP, DLC).

From Robert Latham Owen

My dear Mr. President: [Washington] July 5, 1918.

I wish to add my voice to that of many others who believe we should encourage the oppressed peoples of Austria, such as the Jugo-Slavs, the Czechos, the Bohemians and the Poles by promising them our support in their aspirations for self-government. We can in this way encourage them to greater hostility to the Hapsburg Monarchy. Anything which will help to disorganize Austria and which is consistent with our faith in the principle that government should rest upon the sound foundation of the consent of the governed is justified as a policy in this world-crisis.

I hope you will see your way clear to emphatically declare for this principle.   Yours faithfully,   Robt. L. Owen

Your great address July 4th gave me great happiness. You voiced the heart of America.   R.L.O.

TLS (WP, DLC).

From Caesar Augustus Rodney Janvier[1]

My dear Wilson: Landour, India. July 5th, '18

Last evening we missionaries had a patriotic prayer-meeting, and I, as acting pastor of our Kellogg Mem. Presb'n. Church (I serve in that capacity during six weeks of nearly every Summer vacation), was asked to send you our formal greetings and to express to you our loyal devotion. There were British and Canadians and Americans present, & a representative of each spoke, with an extra American thrown in: and I really believe the Canadian and the Britisher were as enthusiastic as the Americans. All felt the tremendous significance of our share in the war, one (the Englishman) putting it that it was essentially a war between Americanism & Prussianism; all recognized, with thanksgiving to God, your position of leadership; and all hailed with joy the boundless possibilities for humanity and for the Kingdom of God in the alliance of the Anglo-Saxon peoples. It was both a solemn and an optimistic gathering. You will have word of ten thousand such, but perhaps none so far away and surely none more loyal and enthusiastic.

I have spared you for a long time! It has not been because you have not been constantly in my thought and often in my prayers. Two & a half years ago I gave a lecture in All'd[2] (at which the Lt. Governor[3] presided!) trying to define and defend the American (and the Wilsonian) position. I was asked to—and did—repeat it in Lucknow. Then came a time when we Americans were a bit unpopular. When questioned, I used to say that I didn't quite understand, but that I did know the man at the helm, and so was sure that things would come out all right. And of course they did! How we rejoiced—not without a profound sense of what it must cost—when you got us all into the game! I cannot doubt that God guided you, and brought us in when our help would count for the most possible. The final issue—at whatever cost—I do not for a moment question. We are bound to win: the consequences of anything else are simply unthinkable.

I wish I could be doing something to help. I *have* been serving as Presb'n Chaplain in Allahabad so that someone else could be at the front, and I came near getting to "Mespot" this summer for Y.M.C.A. work for a couple of months; but my college duties tie me fast—and I am only thankful that just now Gov't. has appointed me one of the members of the provincial publicity committee. But I would like to be at least a chaplain at the front!

Ernest,[4] whom we rather hoped to welcome out here this year, has somewhat reluctantly decided to stay one more year and complete his work in Sanskrit and Arabic at the U. of Pa. We out here are both well, and both overwhelmingly busy.

But I have no right to ramble on: you are not likely to have time to read even this much, unless you happen to be indulging in a few days vacation somewhere! Well, God bless you, old fellow, and give you his fellowship in your own heart, as well as his guidance in your place of overwhelming public responsibility.

As ever, your devoted friend,   C. A. R. Janvier

We have had 520 students this past year—bigger, isn't it, than Jimmie's[5] "me college"?

ALS (WP, DLC).
[1] Princeton 1880, former pastor of the Hollond Memorial Presbyterian Church in Philadelphia and an old friend of Wilson's; principal of the Ewing Christian College, Allahabad, India, since September 1913.
[2] That is, Allahabad.
[3] Sir James Scorgie Meston, Lieutenant Governor of the United Provinces of Agra and Oudh.
[4] His son, Ernest Paxton Janvier.
[5] That is, James McCosh.

From Thetus Wilrette Sims

PERSONAL

My dear Mr. President: Washington, D. C. July 6, 1918.

I am proud of the fact that we secured the passage of the wire control resolution without any adverse amendments.[1] There has been almost open charges that the introduction and support of this resolution was brought about by Mr. Burleson and the two secretaries[2] with my connivance, intended to be a first step in government ownership. It has been insinuated that you are not ardently supporting the legislation. There will probably be an effort to recess today until August 10, upon the idea that you will not oppose deferred final action upon this resolution. The House has done its part. Only four adverse votes were given on final passage of the resolution.

I do hope that you will immediately inform the leaders of the Senate and the House, if such are the facts, that you wish this resolution passed before a recess is taken. I believe anything less upon your part will result in a recess without action upon the resolution.

I can see no reason why it should take any considerable time to consider the resolution in the Senate as every principle involved and every question of law that can arise upon the consideration of this resolution was thoroughly discussed during the consideration of the Railroad Control bill. If two great corporations can prevent consideration of this resolution at this time it seems to me that it is a time for resignations rather than recesses.

Sincerely yours,   T. W. Sims

TLS (WP, DLC).
[1] After Sims, on July 2, 1918, had successfully blocked a move to transfer H.J. Res. 309 to the Committee on Military Affairs, the Committee on Interstate and Foreign Commerce reported the resolution with amendments (House Report 741) on July 4, 1918. The House debated and further amended it on July 5, 1918, and adopted it on the same day by a vote of 222 to four. *Cong. Record*, 65th Cong., 2d sess., pp. 8639, 8648-51, 8669, 8715-35.
[2] Baker and Daniels.

To Thetus Wilrette Sims

My dear Mr. Sims: [The White House] 6 July, 1918

I am deeply gratified that the House acted so promptly and so emphatically in the matter of the control of the wires, and I want to thank you and all who were associated with you in getting the measure adopted.

I feel the critical importance of the whole thing very keenly and am hoping that members of the House may be influential with members of the Senate in pressing for action by that body before the recess.

Cordially and sincerely yours,   Woodrow Wilson

CCL (WP, DLC).

To Thomas Staples Martin

My dear Senator: [The White House] 6 July, 1918

I understand that some people who for one reason or another do not want action on the matter which the House acted on last night, the control of the wire service, are spreading the report that I do not wish immediate action. Will you not be kind enough to assist me in correcting that impression? I not only wish it, but think it of vital consequence to the country and believe that delay in action might have very serious results.

I feel the responsibility in this matter so keenly that I know you will forgive me for making this additional request of you that you will see to it that there is no misunderstanding among Senators as to my hope.

Cordially and faithfully yours, [Woodrow Wilson]

CCL (WP, DLC)

To Atlee Pomerene

My dear Senator: The White House 6 July, 1918

It is of vital consequence to the country that the Senate should concur with the House in the action taken last evening with regard to the wire service, and I write to beg very earnestly that you will be generous enough to give me your active support in the effort to obtain immediate action.

I think I need not assure you that I would not speak in these terms if I did not believe that very serious consequences might ensue upon delay in this matter. Interruptions of the telegraphic service are sure to occur in the early future, and those interruptions might at a critical time be of the most serious consequence. I have found one of the great telegraphic companies quite unwilling to do what every other great service of the country has done in responding to the suggestions of the Government, and it has become absolutely necessary that the Government should have control while the war lasts.

You have always been so generously ready to respond to my appeals for assistance that I turn to you in confidence.[1]

Cordially and sincerely yours, Woodrow Wilson

TLS (received from Elmer Kaysen).
[1] H.J. Res. 309 was introduced in the Senate on July 6 and was referred to the Committee on Interstate Commerce. *Cong. Record*, 65th Cong., 2d sess., pp. 8739, 8741-47.

From Atlee Pomerene

My dear Mr. President: Washington, D. C. July 6th 1918.

Your letter of even date received, relative to the Telegraph legislation.

Senator E. D. Smith, the Chairman of the Committee on Interstate Commerce, is now in South Carolina. Within the last day or two this subject has been informally discussed by the members of the Committee, as well as by other Senators. I feel confident, as it is your desire that this legislation should be taken up, your wishes will be respected by the Committee. However, many of the Senators have already made their arrangements to go home in view of the statement that was circulated sometime ago to the effect that you had expressed the view that there was no reason why Congress could not take a recess.

Members of the Committee with whom I have talked believe that an opportunity should be given to interested parties to be heard, and I share this view. I can hardly think that either the employers or employees would be so disloyal as to attempt to tie-up lines of communication during this war.

I understand Senator Martin hopes to have an interview with you within the hour,[1] and I shall confer with him immediately upon his return to the Senate.

Shall be glad to call to see you at anytime if you should like to confer with me further.   Very sincerely,   Atlee Pomerene

TLS (WP, DLC).
[1] Wilson conferred with Senators Martin and Simmons and Representative Kitchin for one hour at the White House at 3:30 p.m. on July 6. During the interview, Wilson made it clear that he considered passage of the telegraph and telephone legislation vitally important and that he was eager for the Senate to adopt H.J. Res. 309 as soon as possible. The senators told Wilson that, since the Senate Committee on Interstate Commerce planned to conduct hearings on the measure, it would take at least three to four weeks before the resolution could be presented to the Senate. They asked Wilson, therefore, whether, in these circumstances, he would give his express consent to the contemplated recess of Congress. Wilson replied that he could not endorse a recess; that was for the Senate to decide. However, if it would facilitate and expedite the committee's action and the consideration of the resolution by the Senate, there could be no objection to a recess. Martin assured Wilson that he would not put the question of a recess before the Senate unless he could also secure a pledge from the committee that it would stay in session during the recess and begin immediate hearings on the resolution. See Kitchin's speech in the House, July 6, 1918, *Cong. Record*, 65th Cong., 2d sess., p. 8836.
After his interview with Wilson, Martin conferred with several members of the committee and decided that a recess of thirty days would get the resolution before the Senate earlier than if Congress remained in session. Thus, he introduced a resolution (S. Con. Res. 20) in the evening of July 6 to the effect that Congress would adjourn until August 12. The resolution was adopted by a vote of twenty-seven to twenty-six. *Ibid.*, pp. 8774-77. However, on the same night, Kitchin withdrew his motion that the House concur in the Senate's decision to recess and thus prevented the adjournment of Congress. *Ibid.*, pp. 8835-36.

From Newton Diehl Baker, with Enclosure

Dear Mr. President: Washington. July 6, 1918.

I enclose a dispatch from General Bliss which you will find important to read before your conference with Lord Reading on Monday.   Respectfully yours,   Newton D. Baker

TLS (WP, DLC).

E N C L O S U R E

Versailles July 5th [1918].

Number 143 Confidential.

For Secretary of State, Secretary of War and Chief of Staff.

Paragraph 1. The following is in reference to *your* numbers 61 and 64.[1] Sir Eric Geddes First Lord of Admiralty made report in person to Supreme War Council afternoon July 2d reference visit to Murmansk from which he has just returned. Sent there by British Government to confer with General Poole about plans for occupation Northern Ports. Latter now has force of three British warships and their crews, 1200 British troops, 200 French artillerymen without guns and 1500 Servians. With this force he says he can hold Murmansk Peninsula during this winter. He wants six *additional* battalions two batteries artillery and three companies of Engineers and necessary administrative personnel. He asked British for this force to carry out general plans in joint note 31.[2] As British could contribute nothing to their men now there; as French could send only three colonial companies and a machine gun company and Italians only one or possibly two battalions, Lord Milner said that British War Cabinet considered it necessary to ask Washington for the troops indicated in your number 61. They believed their request to carry out Pooles plans was in substantial accord with joint note number 31. Poole insists that immediate action is of vital consequence. Ice at Archangel *is* one *month* late. As soon as ice clears it is proposed to take possession of Archangel with larger part of additional force now asked for. With this force as a nucleus he believes he can rally one hundred *thousand* Russian troops between Archangel and Vologda inclusive. The Supreme War Council considers this attempt to be of vital importance and adopted the following resolution: "The Supreme War Council, having heard a statement on the naval and military situation in Northern Russia by Sir Eric Geddes, who had just returned from a visit to Murmansk, decided that the British, French and Italian Governments should expedite the despatch of the forces agreed on to carry out Joint

Note number 31 of the Military Representatives and that the American Government should be asked to send a force of three American Battalions and other units already asked for by the British Government in their telegram dated June 11th, 1918.[3] The Supreme War Council invited the British Government to take the initiative in regard to the transportation of the allied forces." The French reported their battalions now below a *channel* port ready for embarkation. Supreme War Council asked Italians to contribute two battalions and request has gone to Italy to that effect. British can contribute nothing except additional warships which they propose to send. This leaves forces to be contributed by *United States* as already requested. Supreme War Council asked me to communicate this to Washington government emphasizing *necessity of* immediate action in view of approach of winter at northern ports. British Colonel Steele[4] who accompanied Sir Eric Geddes emphasized desirability of sending men accustomed to colder climate in United States; also that 30 per cent of additional strength of each organization be sent because of difficulties of replacement. Subsequently I had conference with Lord Milner and General Pershing. General Pershing authorized me to say that he approves sending the *infantry* and engineers from troops now in France. Lord Milner intimated that possibly only the personnel of two batteries would be required. I am waiting exact information from him on this point. I recommend concurrence as to our participation in general plans and suggest prompt decision. Our troops could probably reach Murmansk from France within three weeks from date of decision. With respect to command, War Council believes that it should remain with General Poole until circumstances indicate a change. As there will be one commander on land and sea proposed arrangements seem best for the present. If subsequently inter allied expedition should proceed inland with considerable American forces question of its commander could be taken up. Please notify me of decision as soon as possible.

Paragraph 2. Resolution of Supreme War Council transmitted in my number one *four* one was prepared by Prime Ministers in closed session and adopted by them without discussion. *After further* conference with General Foch it was changed in two important points in paragraph 2 of my number 141[5] as follows. Change sentence beginning with the words "Their duty is" to read as follows: "Their task is, so far as the Anglo-French-American front is concerned in consultation with General Foch, and so far as other theaters are concerned in consultation with the allied Chiefs of Staff and Commanders in chief, et cetera." Omit sentence beginning "This duty can not be." Change last paragraph of resolution to read as follows

"The Military representatives present the results of their study of the situation in the form of advice to the Supreme War Council. Such advice may be furnished on *particular* questions referred to them by the Supreme War Council, or by the Governments, or on any matters considered desirable by the Military Representatives themselves, or on any question which General-in-Chief Foch may refer to them. The decisions belong to the *Supreme War Council*. More particularly it is the task of the Military Representatives in the present state of affairs to study the allied plan of campaign for the approaching Autumn and Winter, and for the Summer of 1919, but without intruding on the personal studies of General Foch in regard to which he is accountable only to the heads of Governments. They consult with the other competent authorities in regard to the other theaters of war and are to present their conclusions to the Supreme War Council at an early date."   Bliss.

T telegram (WP, DLC).
    [1] NDB to T. H. Bliss, June 15, 1918, and P. C. March to T. H. Bliss, June 24, 1918.
    [2] See A. J. Balfour to Lord Reading, June 11, 1918, n. 3.
    [3] That is, the telegram cited in n. 2.
    [4] Probably Lt. Col. Richard Alexander Steel, a General Staff Officer in the Division of Military Operations of the Imperial General Staff.
    [5] T. H. Bliss to H. P. McCain, July 4, 1918, T telegram (WDR, RG 407, World War I Cablegrams, DNA), which had already been partly corrected when it was received by the War Department. The resolution which Bliss transmitted defined the role of the permanent military representatives on the Supreme War Council and was designed to distinguish their tasks from the duties and functions of General Foch. It stated that the military representatives were the "competent advisers of the Supreme War Council on general military policy." In consultation with General Foch and the Allied chiefs of staff and commanders in chief, they would study the military situation in its broadest strategic aspect. They would take into account such factors as political developments, the naval and shipping situation, and the utilization of new instruments of warfare and new tactical methods, and would consider them over the whole field of actual or potential warfare. As originally adopted, the resolution had circumscribed the tasks of the military representatives less narrowly than the revised version, and, in particular, had been less specific about the independent authority of General Foch.

From George Davis Herron

Pontarlier (Berne) July 6th, 1918.

3889. Confidential. Department's 2214, July 1, 5 p.m.[1] Professor Herron reply as follows: "Dear Mr. President: My unhesitating and urgent answer to your crucial question is altogether affirmative.

In the course of a year if the war continues there will be no neutral nations. Both economic pressure and German intrigue will make neutrality impossible. Regardless of whether or not you now call for the Society of Nations the nations still outside of the conflict will be compelled to enter therein choosing one camp or the other of the belligerents. The initiation of the great society by you, even if the neutrals delay to enter it, will place before them an almost unescapable motive for fighting side by side with America.

I cannot say as to the present mind of all the neutrals. I do not know, for instance, the mental stand of Sweden or of Spain. But I do know that with the sacred sign of the Society of Nations before them no *equivocal* power could compell the Swiss people and their formidable army to fight upon the side of Germany. The same would be true of Norway; and I am of the opinion that your call would have a like effect upon Holland. In every case the neutrals would be left without moral excuse for deciding against us.

Also in each of these neutral countries your proclamation would do more than all else to render powerless the malignant and penetrative German propaganda. And each of them I believe, even if none of them at first dare accept the great invitation, would hail it with rejoicing. It is all to their interest to have the league formed: their self-preservation, the development of their respective national beings absolutely depends on the Society's formation. And even though they hesitated for a while to enter the new international (regime?) they would no less regard themselves as morally members thereof from the first.

Thus calling the society into being you will complete America's ongoing spiritual conquest of Europe by lifting the cause of America above reproach. And in lifting the cause of America above reproach you will lift the whole cause of the Allies above reproach also. The peoples will then indeed believe the war against the Central Powers to be a war for the realization of a honorable and liberating ideal.

Permit me to say that if you will propose reciprocal trade relations between the members of the society you will by this one proposition destroy the despot of modern war. You will also undermine the fear of the German peoples—the fear so persistently cultivated by their masters—that if they sue for a peace that shall be acceptable to our allies these allies will then take advantage of the surrender to encircle them with an impassable economic wall making them virtually prisoners for a long period of years in an economic penitentiary. You would practically paralyze, by thus giving a moral basis to the congress of nations, the power of the German masters over the German people. Our moral conquest: even Germany would thus begin rendering the military conquest less costly and more redemptive saving a million or more young American lives by shortening the war. Indeed I have reasons for knowing it, as you will see by despatch sent yesterday from Legation,[2] that American moral conquest of Germany is already beginning and only needs this great work of yours to proceed apace.

May I make bold to urge you not to be influenced by the recent speeches in the British House of Lords. These men do not know the mind of Europe nor even the mind of the English people. It is true as the British Lords contend that the constitutional government and juridical details of the society will have to be worked out with care but even so the society itself can be initiated and its broad principles stated without delay. If we long wait to summon the society into being, if we continue to make caution our master, (*) *will take months* there may be no organized nations left in Europe to associate with each other.

Of course the governmental wise and prudent will be against immediate action but it is these wise and prudent who have brought the world to its present abysmal plight. Before the judgment bar of the present unimaginable cripples wisdom and prudence of this world are an inexpugnable and devastating foolishness.

I beg you not to hesitate, not to doubt. The destinies of mankind for long centuries to come depend upon your instand [instant] decision. Tomorrow may be too late. You can project before the nations the sign that will lift them out of an impasse present difficulty, already abysmal, and that is fast becoming literally infernal. You can expand our American Declaration of Independence into a declaration of the rights of all peoples—into a declaration of the freedom and unity of humanity. You can speak the word that will pitch the whole crazy history, the whole sojourn of man, upon a new and comparitively divine plane of progress. You can wipe away the tears and the shames, the treasons and defeats of two thousand years of universal disappointment.

In fact, Mr. President, by your immediate initiation of the Society of Nations you will perform the most redemptive and creative act that has been performed mankind since the paling lips of Him who initiated our era pronounced His divine work finished.

Your devoted and obedient servant,   George D. Herron."

                                                    Stovall

T telegram (WP, DLC).
   [1] That is, the Enclosure printed with WW to RL, July 1, 1918.
   [2] Printed as an Enclosure with WW to RL, July 8, 1918 (third letter of that date).

Two Letters from Edward Mandell House

Dear Governor: Magnolia, Massachusetts. July 6, 1918.
    Viscount Ishii motored out from Boston this afternoon to see me.
    We had a very friendly and frank talk. Among other things I told him was that many thought Japan stood at the parting of the ways, and had not determined whether she would follow the German or American civilization. I pointed out the advantage to his country of following the international ideals set forth by you. If Japan would do this, I thought she would find America ready to help her extend her sphere of influence.

He was very receptive, and said that the foundation of your policy was justice to all nations, and that he hoped Japan was to be included. He stated that within recent years there had been a growing tendancy upon the part of Russia to exclude the Japanese from Siberia, although they continued to let Koreans and other Asiatics go in. He thought that the position of Japan would become intolerable if her citizens were to be deprived of such an outlet.

I expressed my sympathy with this view and believed he would find the United States cooperating with the Japanese to bring about a more liberal policy. If this could be done, he was sure that Japan would be willing to follow our lead in any policy that might be determined upon regarding Siberia.

It has been my opinion for a long time that unless Japan was treated with more consideration regarding the right of her citizens to expand in nearby Asiatic, undeveloped countries, she would have to be reckoned with—and rightly so.

Affectionately yours,   E. M. House

I want to congratulate you and felicitate with you over your Mount Vernon speech. It is in your happiest vein, and will have a heartening effect throughout the Allied and Neutral world. I wish I might have been privileged to hear it.

Dear Governor: Magnolia, Mass. July 6, 1918.

Every now and then a piece like this[1] appears in the press.

I would like you to know that Gordon went before an Army Medical Board for examination for the line, and without their knowing who he was, and he was rejected on account of his eyes.

This is all of record, but I take it that both he and I will have to submit to the unfair charge of favoritism.

Affectionately yours,   E. M. House

TLS (WP, DLC).

[1] "House's Son-In-Law Is Exempted from Draft. Auchincloss not Included at Request of Lansing," clipping (WP, DLC) from the New York *Evening Sun*, July 3, 1918.

A Memorandum by Robert Lansing

MEMORANDUM OF A CONFERENCE
AT THE WHITE HOUSE IN REFERENCE
TO THE SIBERIAN SITUATION.
July 6, 1918.

PRESENT: The President, the Secretary of State, the Secretary of War, The Secretary of the Navy, General March and Admiral Benson.

After debating the whole subject of the present conditions in Siberia as affected by the taking of Vladivostok by the Czecho-Slovaks, the landing of American, British, French and Japanese forces from the naval vessels in that port, and the occupation of the railroad through Western Siberia by other Czecho-Slovaks with the reported taking of Irkutsk by these troops; and after reading and discussing the communication of the Supreme War Council favoring an attempt to restore an eastern front against the Central Powers; and also a memorandum by the Secretary of State

The following propositions and program were decided upon:

First: That the establishment of an eastern front through a military expedition, even if it was wise to employ a large Japanese force, is physically impossible though the front was established east of the Ural Mountains;

Second: That under present conditions any advance westward of Irkutsk does not seem possible and needs no further consideration;

Third: That the present situation of the Czecho-Slovaks requires this Government and other Governments to make an effort to aid those at Vladivostok in forming a junction with their compatriots in Western Siberia; and that this Government on sentimental grounds and because of the effect upon the friendly Slavs everywhere would be subject to criticism if it did not make this effort and would doubtless be held responsible if they were defeated by lack of such effort;

Fourth: That in view of the inability of the United States to furnish any considerable force within a short time to assist the Czecho-Slovaks the following plan of operations should be adopted, provided the Japanese Government agrees to cooperate:

(a) The furnishing of small arms, machine guns, and ammunition to the Czecho-Slovaks at Vladivostok by the Japanese Government. This Government to share the expense and to supplement the supplies as rapidly as possible;

(b) The assembling of a military force at Vladivostok composed of approximately 7000 Americans and 7000 Japanese to guard the line of communication of the Czecho-Slovaks proceeding toward Irkutsk; the Japanese to send troops at once;

(c) The landing of available forces from the American and Allied naval vessels to hold possession of Vladivostok and cooperate with the Czecho-Slovaks;

(d) The public announcement by this and Japanese Governments that the purpose of landing troops is to aid Czecho-Slovaks against German and Austrian prisoners, that there is no purpose to interfere with internal affairs of Russia, and that they guarantee not to impair the political or territorial sovereignty of Russia; and

(e) To await further developments before taking further steps.

T MS (SDR, RG 59, 861.00/2240½, DNA).

Josephus Daniels to Austin Melvin Knight

[Washington] July 6, 1918.

23002 This government desires Vladivostok kept available as a base for the safety of CZECHS comma and as a means of egress for them should the necessity arise period. In order to accomplish this and to indicate our sympathy and support you are authorized to utilize the force at your disposal and to request similar action by allied naval forces in holding the city period. Avoid any action tending to offend Russian sentiment or to become involved in any political question period. Keep in close touch with leader of CZECH-SLOVAKS and inform Department daily of progress of events comma development of any new situations and sentiments of various parties. 16006 Secnav.

TC Telegram (NDR, RG 45, Naval Records Coll. of the Office of Naval Records and Library, Telegrams—Outgoing, Feb. 6, 1917-May 31, 1919, DNA).

Lord Reading to Arthur James Balfour

Washington. July 6, 1918.

No. 3058.

1. Secretary Baker has informed me that he is examining with his military and other advisers the questions of supply and equipment for the force of 100 Divisions which the U.S. are asked to place in field in France by July of next year. He tells me that an exhaustive investigation is being made to ascertain the possibilities of production in the U. S. of the necessary equipment. When this is completed there will be deficiencies particularly I gather in artillery. The War Department will then seek information as to possibilities of production in England and France of the deficiencies. Secretary Baker said the assurance of the supplies and equipment was essential in order to determine whether programme could be carried

out. There is no difficulty in calling up the requisite number of
men but there is anxiety as to the other matters abovementioned.
2. Secretary Baker wishes to receive from me a definite assurance
that H.M.G. will continue the use of British ships hitherto employed
in carriage of troops for assistance in the transport of 6 Divisions
in the month of August as in previous months. He told me he had
assurances for July of sufficient assistance of British shipping with
the American shipping to carry six Divisions but he must know
whether similar assistance could be given for August, that is whether
our ships would be available for U. S. in military transport service
for August. Also if it be possible now to give it he would like similar
assurance for September so that the programme could be arranged
well ahead.

T telegram (FO 115/2461, pp. 357-58, PRO).

From the Diary of Josephus Daniels

1918 Saturday 6 July

Conf. at W H on Russia
WW—Lansing, Baker, Daniels, Benson, Marsh.
Chezk-Slovaks have taken Vladovostock & wish to reach the
Western front. Pres. feels we must assist them, but does not believe
in big Japanese army going in. Decided to send equal force J & US
& to ask J to furnish guns & ammunition for Chezk-Slovak forces
so they can march to join their brethren 1,000 miles in the interior.
Knight ordered to land marines to help C-S hold Vladivostock. Baker
fears Japs. W.W. thinks Germans can get little help from Russia
in 18 months. Wishes to send a mission into Russia to help with
provisions & clothes & give practical evidence of our sympathy

From Newton Diehl Baker, with Enclosure

Dear Mr. President: Washington. July 7, 1918
    From this message it seems that the British have agreed to send
the necessary rifles and ammunition to the Czechs in Siberia. I will
tell Mr Lansing in the morning so that he need not request this of
Mr Ishii unless he has already done so
                              Respectfully,   Newton D. Baker

ALS (WP, DLC).

ENCLOSURE

Versailles. July 6th [1918].

Number 144. Very Confidential.

For Secretary of State, Secretary of War and Chief of Staff.

Paragraph 1. In addition to resolutions concerning Allied intervention in Siberia and Russia and the 100 American division program, both reported in my number 140,[1] and concerning the functions of the Military Representatives at Versailles, reported in my copy of resolution 141 and in paragraph 2 of my number 143, and concerning the expedition to Northern Russian ports reported in paragraph 1 of my number 143; the Supreme War Council at its 7th session considered the following subjects and reached the conclusions indicated below.

Subparagraph A. On July 3rd on request of Czecho-Slovak force(s) for 14,000 rifles and ammunition the Supreme War Council approved the proposal of the British Government to send at once to Vladivostok from stock held by them in the United States the rifles and ammunition required.

Subparagraph B. On July 4th in regard to situation in the Balkans the Supreme War Council decided that the Military Representatives should report as to the desirability of undertaking an offensive; and that diplomatic representatives of France, Great Britain and Italy should be attached to the Military Representative(s) for this inquiry; that pending the result of the inquiry no general offensive will take place; and finally that the appointment of the Commander in Chief of the Allied army of the East shall in the future be subject to approval of the three Governments concerned.

Subparagraph C. The Supreme War Council considered Joint Note 32[2] of the Military Representatives which had been passed on July 2nd on the subject of the voluntary enlistment of Austrian prisoners of Servian race for replacements in the Servian army and took note of the undertakings Messrs. Orlando and Sonnino to facilitate to the utmost of their ability the maximum recruitment of volunteers for the Servian Army among prisoners of Servian race at present in Italy. They also noted the statements made by Messrs. Orlando and Sonnino concerning the earliest possible incorporation of Yugo-Slav priority now in Italy in national units to fight with Italy against the common enemy.

Subparagraph D. With reference to paragraph 3 of my 140 as soon as you inform me of total tonnage required for the one hundred division program of June 23 and the amount that can be furnished by the United States I shall ask the Military Representatives to adopt a resolution asking the British to make up the deficiency.

Reference last sentence of first part of paragraph of your 66,[3] Mr. Clemenceau informed Supreme War Council at meeting of July 3rd that Mr. Lloyd George had assented to continue for the month of August same British tonnage as has been supplied in July.

Bliss.

TC telegram (WP, DLC).
  [1] Printed as an Enclosure with P. C. March to WW, July 3, 1918.
  [2] "The Utilization of Yugo-Slav Prisoners of Serbian Race in the Serbian Army," July 3, 1918 (T MS, WDR, RG 120, Records of the American Section of the Supreme War Council, 1917-1919, File No. 336-1, DNA).
  [3] That is, NDB to T. H. Bliss, July 1, 1918.

From William Bauchop Wilson

My dear Mr. President: Washington July 7, 1918.

I am sending you herewith copy of telegram sent to Mr. Konenkamp by Mr. Gompers and one sent by myself.[1]

Since sending the telegrams and before their arrival at Chicago, we talked over the long distance telephone with Mr. Konenkamp and have been given his assurance that he will immediately telegraph to all of their organizations throughout the country postponing strike action until he can have further conferences with us.

I am giving the telegrams to the Press with the statement that we have assurance from Mr. Konenkamp that the strike will be postponed for the present.   Faithfully yours,   W B Wilson

TLS (WP, DLC).
  [1] WBW to S. J. Konenkamp, July 7, 1918, and S. Gompers to S. J. Konenkamp, July 7, 1918, TC telegrams, WP, DLC. W. B. Wilson emphasized the vital importance of the prompt transmission of communications during the war and asked that the telegraphers' strike be postponed until he and Konenkamp had had an opportunity to confer about the situation. He reminded Konenkamp of President Wilson's repeated statements that, during the war, strikes were unjustified if any other means of settling grievances were available or in sight. Since Congress had now taken up the matter, Secretary Wilson concluded, a just solution would undoubtedly be found soon.
  Gompers told Konenkamp that he agreed entirely with Secretary Wilson's views. He stated that, while there was a good chance for an early and honorable settlement of the controversy, a strike would generally be considered unjustifiable. Of course, Gompers continued, he was in full accord with the telegraphers' demands. However, he urged Konenkamp, in order to avoid even the slightest interference with the war effort, to postpone the strike and to permit all parties to bring about a fair and just settlement of the dispute.

From Lincoln Ross Colcord

Dear Mr. President: Washington, D. C. July 7, 1918.

The knowledge, recently confirmed by competent advices, that the statements contained in my letter to you of December third, 1917,[1] suggesting a special mission to Russia and outlining my convictions regarding the situation there, were fully justified by the facts on the ground, emboldens me to write you once more, at a time when every man should tender his support to the truth he sees.

The world is on the brink of committing one of its terrible historic crimes. It is determined to do this; the overwhelming majority has gone astray. I have no hesitation in affirming my opinion that the Versailles Council is wrong, that all of the Governments of Europe are wrong, and that most of the peoples' groups, too, are wrong, as well as the Russian intelligencia. They are wrong because of selfish interests, jealousies, and abnormal state of mind, and because the facts have been perverted and the truth withheld.

You only possess the true facts, and see clearly; I would not be writing if I lacked the conviction that you are preparing to do an extraordinary thing. The task before you is hard and thankless, but the future will repay you with that honor reserved only for those who dare to stand alone. I believe that America's heroic opportunity has come. For there can be no compromise on this issue without ultimate defeat. I believe sincerely that anything short of full and outright action in co-operation with the Soviets will drench Russia in blood from end to end, and throw her body and soul into the arms of Germany.

If the Allies intervene in Russia in support of any counter-revolution whatsoever, there will be a wrong peace compacted with the Imperial German Government this fall, and Russia will be the spoils of the world. If America cannot stop them now, she cannot stop them then.

The tragic fact which, from a future social plane, history will record if this summer goes wrong, is that Russia all the while in her present phase has actually been striving towards the same new world for which the peoples everywhere are fighting. She has been doing it with shocking directness, according to her own lights, and in keeping with her own social fundamentals. She has been seeking to attain industrial democracy. The western world has consistently refused to recognize the almost total difference in social fundamentals between itself and Russia; but thereby hangs the whole stroy [story]. No other nation presents a proletariat in such a vast majority, an agrarian problem so acute and universally distributed, and a training in local self-government so ancient and indestructible.

How was it possible for Russia, under these conditions, to follow a common course with the west in the search for industrial democracy? How was it possible, with such an insignificant minority of the bourgeois[i]e, for the revolution to have resulted in anything

short of temporary injustice, especially when the bourgeoise refused to co-operate in the greater plan? It was our task and our
privilege to catch the vision, to discern in the loosing of pent-up
forces the working out of profound laws, to recognize in chaos and
destruction the promise of order, justice, and sublime attainments,
and with faith to discover in the countenence of the illiterate peasant the lineaments of truth and leadership. We saw only the tangled
protruding roots; but life was there, the roots were true roots, and
they would rise into a great tree.

The Bolsheviki have been fatally unwise, pathetically cruel, but
they have had scant help from us who are wise and kind. They
have had no hope of support on which to build a compromise with
their own stark program. The world has been ungenerous to men
who, charged with a mission that would not be denied, and bent
by the terrible responsibility of convictions and events, have with
evident sincerity tried to see the greater good. And in spite of hand-
icaps the Bolsheviki have learned many lessons. In my letter to you
of December 8, 1917, I ventured the prophecy: "Lenine and Trotsky, under the pressure of responsibility, will suffer a change of
heart. This will come about most powerfully with respect to domestic affairs* * * *" This prophecy has now been justified by events.
Lenine is preaching to the Soviets a measure of capitalism; and is
going so far, in fact, that he is being openly accused of leaning
towards the bourgeoise.

I still believe that the Russian situation could be turned into a
triumph of democracy. I still believe that, if outright support of the
Soviets were to be established and maintained by America, the right
men could go to Russia and persuade Lenine to stand behind the
Russian debt. I still believe that an active Red army could be put
into the field against Germany, though the re-establishment of the
eastern front would be a physical impossibility. I still believe that
the Bolshevik program towards confiscation could be modified, and
that the bourgeoise could be brought into co-operation with the
Soviets. I still believe, in short, that certain keynotes could be struck
in the name of the Soviets on the strength of which it would be
possible to create a change of sentiment in America and the Allied
countries towards Russian affairs, providing the original disposition
to do this were frank and cognitive, and providing definite action
in support of the course were taken at every opening; and that
Russia under her present Government could be brought into a
workable state of co-operation with the western democracies.

There is good ground for the claim that such a policy would be
more likely to succeed to-day than it would have been three months
ago. Had it been instituted at the beginning, six months ago, I think

there could have been no difficulty; but three months ago nothing had been proved. Now the west, in its very madness and inconsistency towards Russia, shows that it is ready for the true lines to be struck out. And Lenine, on the other hand, sees that if America turns against him, he and the Soviets, in the face of Russia's economic distress, are in all probability doomed to tempor[ar]y defeat.

But it is inevitable that the defeat would be only temporary. By setting up our own standards there we cannot change Russia's social fundamentals. They are written in the book of the race. Russia would boil with revolution until she had won her own government back again.

By one brave address, Mr. President, you could pull up the public opinion of the world in its headlong rush to disaster, and shame it into silence. By guaranteeing the Russian debt in the name of the American people you could effect a diplomatic coup of the first proportions, bringing both sides under the profound obligation of your idealism. With the right men to explain the act to Russia, the Soviets would quickly assume the burden and clear the air.

Such a policy would, of course, entail political action of a definite and unmistakable sort. But I think the Soviets would not respond in this sense to a purely economic mission, because they would be aware that under existing circumstances a mission to Russia inherently could not be purely economic in its functioning, but that the political function unavoidably exercised by any such mission in its choice of ground would logically take precedence over the other. I think the Soviets would be apt to hold a mission ostensibly specified as purely economic to be an evasion of the issue.

I am, my dear Mr. President,

Faithfully and respectfully yours,   Lincoln Colcord

TLS (WP, DLC).
[1] Printed at that date in Vol. 45.

To Edward Mandell House, with Enclosure

My dear House,   The White House. 8 July, 1918.

Will you not rewrite to [the] enclosed constitution of a League of Nations[1] as you think it ought to be re-written,—along the lines of your recent letter to Lord Robert Cecil?[2] That will be the best means of expressing a definite judgment and furnish me the full basis for the comment and opinion with regard to it for which the British Government is asking.

I wish you would read the enclosed very remarkable letter from Herron[3] and tell me what you think of it. It is a moving document, but I am not sure that it moves my judgment as much as it moves my feelings. Let me have it back, please, when you have read it.

I have not written recently because I have been sweating blood over the question what it is right and feasible (*possible*) to do in Russia. It goes to pieces like quicksilver under my touch, but I hope i See and can report some progress presently, along the double line of economic assistance and aid to the Czecho-Slovaks.

I hail your letters with deep satisfaction and unspoken thanks go out to you for each one of them, whether I write or not, and the most affectionate appreciation of all that you do for me.

I am very tired, for there never were so many problems per diem, it seems to me, as there are now. But I am well. *We* are well. And all unite in the most affectionate messages.

Your affectionate friend,   W.W.

WWTLI (E. M. House Papers, CtY).
   ¹ That is, the interim report of the Phillimore Committee, about which see Lord Reading to WW, July 3, 1918 (second letter of that date), n. 1.
   ² That is, EMH to R. Cecil, June 25, 1918, printed as an Enclosure with EMH to WW, June 25, 1918.
   ³ That is, G. D. Herron to WW, May 31, 1918.

To Lord Reading

My dear Mr. Ambassador: The White House 8 July, 1918

I have received with your kind note of July third the interim report drawn up by a committee appointed by His Majesty's Government to consider the question of a League of Nations. I have given it a hurried examination but will take the liberty of going over it more carefully and of communicating through you at a later date, if I may, my deliberate comments upon it.

Pray express to your Government when you have the opportunity my appreciation of their courtesy in letting me see this report.

I am, my dear Lord Reading,
          Cordially and sincerely yours,   Woodrow Wilson

TLS (FO 115/2427, p. 163, PRO).

To Wenceslao Braz Pereira Gomes

[The White House, c. July 8, 1918]

Allow me to express my very warm and cordial thanks for your generous message of the fourth of July.¹ It is a subject of peculiar gratification to the people of the United States that the people of Brazil should have come to their sides in this great and final struggle for the rights of free peoples. They are happy that such additional bonds of friendship and common purpose should unite them with neighbours whom they so highly respect and so sincerely admire and I am sure that I am speaking for them in assuring Your Excellency of their deep satisfaction at being accounted the close friends and associates of the Brazilian Republic.

WWhw MS (WP, DLC).
[1] W. Braz to WW, July 4, 1918, T telegram (WP, DLC).

To Venustiano Carranza

The White House, July 8, 1918

In response to your generous telegram of greeting and good will[1] may I not express to you the sincere friendship of the people and government of the United States, their earnest desire that the bonds of association and mutual helpfulness between the two countries may be drawn closer and closer, and their confident hope that as the friendship of the two countries ripens their common championship of political freedom may become more and more effective.

WWhw MS (WP, DLC).
[1] V. Carranza to WW, July 4, 1918, T telegram (WP, DLC).

Two Letters to Robert Lansing

My dear Mr. Secretary,   The White House. 8 July, 1918.

My clear judgment about this is, that it is not wise to take such action piecemeal about the items of a final settlement.[1] Our attitude is clearly spoken by our actions. The world has no doubt where we stand, and we have already recognized the representatives of a Polish State. If we are to be definite in the case of this particular national aspiration, why not in the case of others, and where shall we stop, definition being at each step increasingly difficult.[2]

Faithfully Yours,   W.W.

WWTLI (SDR, RG 59, 763.72119/1804½, DNA).
[1] See the Enclosure printed with RL to WW, June 14, 1918.
[2] The State Department informed Representative Gallagher of Wilson's views on July 11.

My dear Mr. Secretary,   The White House. 8 July, 1918.

Thank you for the enclosed,[1] which I return for your files.

Faithfully Yours,   W.W.

WWTLI (SDR, RG 59, 894.00/144½, DNA).
    [1] That is, the Enclosure printed with RL to WW, June 28, 1918 (second letter of that date).

To Robert Lansing, with Enclosure

My dear Mr. Secretary,   The White House. 8 July, 1918.

I am a bit in the dark about this, for I do not remember the conversation with Herron to which reference is made,[1] but the general import of the despatch is plain enough. It seems to me a pity that Herron should even be tempted to lead these conversations further without having his attention called to the fact that no nation east of Germany is so much as mentioned in these "terms." I would not even discuss a settlement which did not put all the Russian, Turkish, and eastern cards on the table. This is the game: to give up in the West in order to get a vast, incalculable gain in the East.

Faithfully Yours,   W.W.

WWTLI (R. Lansing Papers, NjP).
    [1] The relevant dispatch, summarized in n. 1 to the Enclosure printed below, was received in the State Department as early as July 2, 1918, but was not read in the Division of Near Eastern Affairs until July 8. Wilson probably never saw it.

E N C L O S U R E

Pontarlier (Berne). July 5, 1918.

3884. My despatch 3544, June 22nd.[1] De Fiori called again on Herron at Geneva and informed him that after his conversation with Herron he had returned to Munich instead of to Berlin, as he had previously intended, and presented to Professor Foerster, the Bavarian Minister of War and the Bavarian Minister President,[2] the memorandum of his conversations with Herron (practically identical to that submitted my despatch). De Fiori states that both these Bavarian officials later conferred with him stating they were much impressed with memorandum, believing that it represented genuine American opinion. They stated: "If war continues we will be defeated in the end. We must bring influence on Prussia towards conciliatory peace."

De Fiori learned that copies of memorandum were furnished Ludendorf and Hertling, who in turn distributed additional copies to about all members of Reichstag. He states that he was summoned Berlin by telegraph but did not go.

According to De Fiori the memorandum was also laid before the King,[3] Crown Prince of Bavaria,[4] and Bavarian Cabinet, which debated whether discussion of peace was possible and subsequently indicated to De Fiori a tentative peace program which later submitted to Herron who had it taken down verbally. Program follows: "The restoration of Belgium; contracts concerning the liberty of German navigation on Schelde and Rhine; elevation of Alsace-Lorraine to a free confederate state with complete home rule; equal free trade with France and Germany; contracts for the customary free exchange of coal, potash, and iron between Germany and France (personally I put here complete freedom of the press, of language and school, and in all national and political things). I attract your attention to the fact that the representation *that is*, and by parliamentary representation of the new German confederate state, would not stand on any other basis than it does now, because they have now already the direct right of vote for the Landtag in Alsace-Lorraine.

Self-administration for all the Austrian peoples, including the Germans, according to the principles agreed upon with Professor Lammasch; self-administration for the Italian provinces, with Trieste as capital and free port; repeal of all existing *different*[ial] contracts in favor of Trieste, which are greatly to Italy's damage; reorganization of the traffic of Trieste with the Lombardy and Venice, like before 1859, wherewith Trieste would remain, and would have to remain, a completely Italian city. Under the term self-administration of Trieste, I understand also the political and police administration, so that the state and not the monarchy would have the right to *hinder* in any way the political intercourse with Italy. The political relations of the *territory of* administration of Trieste with Italy would therefore be taken same as those of the canton of Ticino with Italy. Self-administration for all non-Magyar peoples of Hungary.

Complete restoration of Servia, with free access to the Adriatic, perhaps Durazzo becoming a Servian port, and the Servian port of Albania given to Servia.

Restoration of Poland in full freedom and independence. I do not mean that Galicia should go to Poland, nor that Prussia should give Posen. (I avoid these questions on purpose, because they would create confusion. I personally and confidentially would say that it would be a great injustice to leave Posen with Prussia, if Posnanian Poland would not get complete self-administration like

Alsace-Lorraine). Poland should receive freedom of the flag on Weichsel and (?),[5] and a free access to the East sea, through Lithuania. Reopening of the peace of Bucharest and the peace of Brest-Litovsk.

All the Balkan questions should be referred to the peace conference for their final settlement. America should mediate between England and Germany in all questions of the colonies; also in all German English questions of the Balkans, till a satisfactory arrangement was arrived at. (Return to the policy of contracts, which already before the war was on its best way).

Disarmament; the society of nations."

De Fiori then stated to Herron: "Can you say to me that you believe President Wilson would be favorable to at least debating peace on these terms? We ask you, Doctor Herron, to give your opinion. If you think the President would be willing to discuss peace on this tentative program Bavaria would try to round up other German states to bring pressure to bear on Prussia to end that Imperial Government should make formal peace offers in this sense. This program is not the last word. These terms may be called middle terms. We feel it is America which must umpire between England and Germany."

Herron stated: "I cannot express an opinion; I must reflect. When I have arrived at answer I will send for you in Zurich."

Herron stated to me that he shrank from assuming responsibility of giving his own views even though requested in view of magnitude of question. He stated to De Fiori however: "If I could believe for one moment that as a result of such peace a new Germany would emerge, if I believed we could trust Germany loose in the world without cutting her fangs, if I felt we could trust her word, I would give my life to open the door to peace. There are many reasons to make me wish to be convinced but I cannot achieve such conviction."

Herron believes that it is possible to reconcile Muehlon's statements representing it in my *cipher telegram 3774, June twenty-sixth* concerning De Fiori[6] with latter's statements of activity in Munich since De Fiori's immediate chief was Bavarian Minister of War. Herron feels also that De Fiori was speaking honestly and that Muehlon was somewhat mistaken in his characterization. It should be borne in mind however that few people can speak as authoritatively on such subject as Muehlon.

My feeling in the matter is that Ludendorf is searching the way *sympathetic* to America to put through his compromise program in case of failure on western front. It is also highly probable that Ludendorf thus makes use of liberal elements so that on receipt of anticipated refusal from America it will be clearly demonstrated to liberals that serious endeavor for peace was made and failed. These terms are more precise but not far different from Kuehlmann's statements in his first speech which raised a tempest in military party.[7] Can it be assumed that the Bavarian Government could put through a program on which the Prussian Government itself failed?[8]

Stovall.

T telegram (R. Lansing Papers, NjP).

[1] Actually, P. A. Stovall to RL, No. 3519, June 17, 1918, TLS (SDR, RG 59, 763.72119/1774, DNA). This letter enclosed a TCL of F. W. Foerster to G. D. Herron, dated Munich, May 8, 1918, introducing Dr. Robert de Fiori, a Bavarian who had for thirty-five years been the Rome correspondent of the Vienna *Neue Freie Presse*. De Fiori, Foerster said, was a member of the Social Democratic party and would give Herron "valuable information about the present state of public opinion in Germany and how to influence the better circles of that public opinion."

Stovall also enclosed a forty-seven-page memorandum by Herron which recorded his conversations with De Fiori at four meetings at Herron's home in Geneva from June 7 through June 9 or 10, 1918. A stenographer was present and, according to Herron, made a stenographic record of the conversations.

De Fiori said that he had a message which he wanted Herron to convey *verbatim* to President Wilson; also that the substance of his and Herron's conversations would be conveyed directly to Count von Hertling. De Fiori outlined a possible basis for peace discussions between Germany and the United States. The suggested terms are well summarized in this telegram, that is, Stovall's No. 3884 of July 5, 1918.

If one may believe Herron's report, Herron did most of the talking during the interviews. Speaking only for himself, Herron said that Germany had become an outlaw and a pariah among the nations; that Americans would fight one hundred years if need be to extirpate German militarism and imperialism; and that Americans would accept, as a basis for peace, nothing less than the unconditional acceptance by Germany of President Wilson's peace program.

[2] Philipp von Hellingrath and Otto von Dandl, respectively.

[3] Ludwig III.

[4] Prince Rupprecht Maria Luitpold Ferdinand.

[5] That is, the Vistula and Memel rivers.

[6] P. A. Stovall to RL, June 26, 1918, T telegram (SDR, RG 59, 763.72/10525, DNA). It stated that Herron had been informed by Muehlon that De Fiori was "one of Ludendorff's most intelligent agents." According to Muehlon, De Fiori was the first of a series of agents whom Ludendorff would send to prepare the way for a conciliatory peace in case the present offensive in France should fail. Ludendorff, Muehlon stated, was taking precautions, since he recognized the tendency in Germany toward peace and realized that this tendency would be beyond control if the offensive should prove unsuccessful. Muehlon urged Herron to avoid the impression that the United States would agree to something less than a peace of absolute redress. If the United States stood firm, Muehlon concluded, the crash in Germany would come soon. For brief discussions of the Herron-De Fiori talks, see Klaus Schwabe, *Deutsche Revolution und Wilson-Frieden* (Düsseldorf, 1971), pp. 80-81, and Mitchell Pirie Briggs, *George D. Herron and the European Settlement* (Stanford, Calif., 1932), pp. 50-53.

[7] Kühlmann had addressed the Reichstag on the second reading of the budget on June 24, 1918, and, as was customary on this occasion, had given an overview of the general political and military situations. An Anglophile with close personal connections to Sir William Tyrrell and other officials in the British Foreign Office, Kühlmann had recently arranged secret meetings between German and British representatives in Holland to explore the possibilities for a negotiated peace. His speech was thus intended to encourage these talks and to serve as a reply to certain conciliatory statements made by General Smuts. Kühlmann stated that Germany was not necessarily committed to a peace of conquest and was not seeking world domination, but merely a free, strong, and independent existence within the boundaries drawn by history. Germany's aims were the complete freedom and integrity of its territorial possessions, with colonies corresponding to Germany's wealth and importance, the freedom of the seas, and the freedom of trade. Kühlmann continued that Russia, not Britain, was primarily responsible for starting the war. He hoped that the Entente realized that victory on the battlefield had become an illusion and that it would soon approach Germany with peace offers which would "correspond with the situation and Germany's vital needs." Germany's position

on peace, Kühlmann concluded, was the same as that expressed by former Prime Minister Asquith—that a deaf ear would not be turned to any position clearly stated.

Kühlmann's speech caused a furor among the military leadership and the annexationist parties. Led by the Conservative leader, Count von Westarp, they accused Kühlmann of defeatism and demanded his immediate resignation. Although Kühlmann qualified many of his statements in a second speech on June 25, he was ordered to Spa for a conference with the Emperor and was dismissed on July 9, 1918. See the *New York Times*, June 26-29, and July 1 and 10, 1918. For Kühlmann's speeches and the reactions to them in the Reichstag, see *Schulthess' Europäischer Geschichtskalender*, LIX (1918), Part 1, pp. 202-21. See also Richard von Kühlmann, *Erinnerungen* (Heidelberg, 1948), pp. 569-81, and Gerhard Ritter, *Staatskunst und Kriegshandwerk* (4 vols., Munich, 1954-68), IV, 365-87.

[8] Lansing replied as follows: "2265. Your 3884, July 5, 9 p.m. It seems obvious that the German peace plan is to sacrifice in the west in order to obtain a vast incalculable gain in the east. Herron's attention might be called to the fact that the Eastern Question is not dealt with in the Bavarian tentative peace program and told that a discussion of a settlement which did not put all the Russian, Turkish, and Eastern cards on the table was not even remotely possible." RL to P. A. Stovall, July 10, 1918, *FR-WWS 1918*, 1, I, 282.

To Arthur Capper

My dear Governor Capper: [The White House] 8 July, 1918

I quite understand the earnest feeling with which your letter of July second was written and have read the letter with real appreciation.

Just what the remedy is to be I admit it is difficult to see, but that we are all willing and anxious to work out a remedy constitutes an atmosphere, at any rate, in which we may hope for a solution.

Sincerely yours,   Woodrow Wilson

TLS (Letterpress Books, WP, DLC).

To David John Lewis

My dear Mr. Lewis: The White House 8 July, 1918

I appreciate your letter of June sixth,[1] but, alas, I am afraid that prompt action by the Senate on the wire legislation is past hoping for.[2] I am going to have a conference with the Acting Chairman of the Senate Committee on Interstate Commerce this morning;[3] and you will notice what took place in the House on Saturday when the motion to concur in the Senate's resolution for a recess was withdrawn.

In haste

Cordially and sincerely yours,   Woodrow Wilson

TLS (D. J. Lewis Papers, NcD).
[1] D. J. Lewis to WW, July, not June, 6, 1918, TLS (WP, DLC). Lewis asked Wilson to urge the Senate to act with the same promptness as the House had done on the resolution authorizing the takeover of the telegraph and telephone lines.
[2] As it turned out, Wilson's prediction proved to be wrong. The Senate Committee on

Interstate Commerce had voted in the late afternoon on July 6 to hold full hearings on H.J. Res. 309. Since, at this point, it still seemed virtually certain that Congress would immediately adjourn for four weeks, most members of the committee left Washington soon afterwards. However, when it turned out that Congress would not recess, Senator Smith conferred briefly at 2 p.m. on July 8 with the six committee members who had remained in Washington. They decided, by a vote of four to three, to abandon the original plan for hearings and to report H.J. Res. 309 immediately without recommendation. When Smith reported the resolution an hour later, the Senate, after a heated debate, refused to receive it on the ground that it had not been concurred in by the number of committee members required to make a report. Thus, the committee met again on July 9 and heard a brief statement by Newcomb Carlton. It then decided not to hear any more witnesses and voted to report the resolution to the Senate again with a recommendation that it be adopted. As a result, Senator Smith reported H.J. Res. 309 favorably on July 10, 1918. *Cong. Record*, 65th Cong., 2d sess., pp. 8841, 8842-43, 8860-67, 8934.
    [3] Wilson saw Senator Pomerene at the White House at 11 a.m.

To Bernhardt Wall[1]

My dear Mr. Wall: The White House 8 July, 1918

I warmly and sincerely appreciate the sentiment which led you to make the etching of which you were kind enough to send me a copy,[2] but I feel bound, in replying to your letter of June seventeenth which was laid before me only the other day,[3] to say that there is a sense in which putting me in uniform violates a very fundamental principle of our institutions, namely, that the military power is subordinate to the civil. The framers of the Constitution, of course, realized that the President would seldom be a soldier and their idea in making him the Commander-in-chief of the Army and Navy of the United States was that the armed forces of the country must be the instruments of the authority by which policy was determined. It is for that reason that we can so truly say that our organization is in no sense and can in no sense be militaristic.

I do not think this is a mere formal scruple on my part. I believe it goes to the root of things, and I am sure I may thus candidly express it to you without creating the impression that I do not fully appreciate the motive and the idea of your etching, by which I am very much complimented.

                    Sincerely yours,   Woodrow Wilson

TLS (received from Mark Heefner).
    [1] Well-known etcher of New York.
    [2] It is reproduced in the Illustration Section.
    [3] B. Wall to WW, June 17, 1918, ALS (WP, DLC).

Two Letters to John Sharp Williams

My dear Senator: [The White House] 8 July, 1918

My heart goes out to you in profound sympathy. I have just read in the papers of the death of your daughter,[1] and know how your heart must be darkened by such a bereavement. I have been able to realize, if you will let me say so, in my intercourse with you how hard and sincerely you can love and therefore I can form some conception of what this loss must be costing you. I hope that you will not think that I am intruding in expressing my warmest and most heartfelt sympathy.

Cordially and sincerely yours,   Woodrow Wilson

¹ Julia Fulton Sharp Williams (Mrs. Thomas Reeves) Boykin, who had died on July 5, 1918.

My dear Senator Williams: The White House 8 July, 1918.

I have conferred with the Secretary of War on the subject of the soldier vote in France,¹ and he has pointed out to me difficulties which seem inherent in the problem but which do not lie on the surface so that they can be appreciated generally without a statement of them.² The laws of many of the States make no provision for taking the vote of absent soldiers, so that any facilities extended by the Army could be taken advantage of only by those States which have in some way made provision for such an emergency. In some States the soldier vote is authorized to be taken by mail, but the guarantee of the secret ballot stands in the way, because uncensored correspondence can not be permitted for military reasons. In some States commissioners are authorized to be appointed to visit the soldiers and take their votes, and the Secretary of War tells me that the military authorities will cooperate with such commissioners as far as possible, but he points out the danger of allowing any sort of responsibility for the purity of the ballot, or of the thoroughness of the opportunity to vote, being allowed to rest on the military authorities, as disappointed expectations on the part of candidates would undoubtedly lead to accusations of unfairness among military men in whom the public confidence ought not to be shaken by such charges.

I enclose an order of the War Department³ and that Department would be very glad indeed if you could suggest to me for the Secretary of War, or directly to him, any improvement of opportunity for further cooperation which seems possible to you in the circumstances.   Cordially and faithfully yours,   Woodrow Wilson

TLS (J. S. Williams Papers, DLC).
¹ J. S. Williams to WW, June 24, 1918, TLS (WP, DLC). Williams called Wilson's attention to the necessity for some arrangement by which soldiers in the A.E.F. could vote in the forthcoming elections. He said that most of the men in the army were loyal supporters of the administration, while the "slackers and skulkers" who had stayed at home were likely to vote for Republican candidates. Thus, Williams concluded: "In every State in the Union, unless some active, administration initiative is taken in order

to give men a chance to vote while firing their rifles, you and your crowd and I and my crowd may be left out, and when we are, it means America is left out."

² NDB to WW, July 5, 1918, TLS (WP, DLC). Wilson's letter summarizes Baker's arguments well.

³ P. C. March, "General Order No. 63," June 28, 1918, CC MS (WP, DLC). It stated that the War Department was willing to make arrangements for members of the A.E.F. to vote in both primary and general elections. It called on the states to amend their election laws as soon as possible in such a way as to validate the votes of soldiers which had been cast under the limitations prescribed by the War Department. These limitations provided, among other things, that it would not be possible to take votes of soldiers on active duty in military operations unless these votes could be transmitted through the mails as ordinary correspondence; that the War Department would not forward blank ballots or other election literature to the men in the field; that the censorship provision on all letters from France would not be waived; that military officers would be permitted, but not required, to administer oaths and issue certificates in order to validate votes whenever necessary under state law; and that the dispatch of election commissioners to take soldiers' votes would in most cases be impractical.

From Robert Lansing, with Enclosure

My dear Mr. President: Washington July 8, 1918.

I telephoned you this morning the result of my conference with the Japanese Ambassador regarding the Siberian situation. I now enclose to you a copy of a memorandum of the Conference.

Faithfully yours,   Robert Lansing

TLS (WP, DLC).

E N C L O S U R E

MEMORANDUM OF CONFERENCE
WITH JAPANESE AMBASSADOR
CONCERNING A SIBERIAN
PROGRAM.
10 a.m. July 8, 1918.

The Ambassador came to the Department at my request and I laid before him orally the propositions and program determined upon by the President after the Conference at the White House.

He told me that he was favorable personally to the views expressed and the plan proposed and that he would immediately communicate with his Government and ask their agreement to the plan.

He said that I would be pleased to know that on his return to Washington last night he found a telegram from Tokio directing him to advise me that the leader of the Czecho-Slovaks at Vladivostok had asked his Government to furnish that force with arms and ammunition and that his Government were ready to do this at once if it met the approval of this Government. I said that this news was most gratifying as that was the first step in our program, and that I hoped that he would urge the shipment with all possible speed. He replied that he would.

We discussed more in detail the possible effect of landing troops by this country and Japan with an identical announcement at Washington and Tokio as to the purpose of the expedition and the preservation of the integrity of the political and territorial sovereignty of Russia. We also considered the possibility of a friendly attitude by the Russians toward the Czecho-Slovaks thus aided and also the possible consequence of their forming a nucleus about which the Russians might rally even to the extent of becoming again a military factor in the war.

We both agreed, however, that, while we had these possibilities in mind, no plans should be predicated upon them; and that the objective for the present should be limited to furnishing facilities for the Czecho-Slovaks at Vladivostok to form a juncture with those near Irkutsk by obtaining control of the Amur branch of the Trans-Siberian Railroad.

In discussing the foregoing Ishii said: "The possibilities of extending the program will depend very much upon the way the Siberian people view the present plan (if it is adopted) and how other Russians will look upon it. This we cannot tell until our forces are actually landed at Vladivostok. That will test the question. If they are very friendly, we can revise our program."

The Ambassador spoke as if he was sure the suggestion of a small force of 14,000 men equally divided between the United States and Japan would be acceptable to his Government.

I impressed upon him that time was an essential factor in carrying out the program and I urged him to emphasize to his Government the great importance of a speedy decision and prompt action.

This he said he would do.

CC MS (WP, DLC).

From Robert Lansing

My dear Mr. President: [Washington] July 8, 1918.

In connection with the Siberian Affair I would like to call your attention to two matters which I think should be considered at once.

First: As Chinese troops are holding the Manchurian Railway east, and I believe west, of Harbin, ought they or ought they not be considered in connection with the guarding of the Siberian Railroad in aid of the Czecho-Slovaks?

Second: Ought we or ought we not to advise the Allied Governments, including the Chinese, of our program before we hear from Tokio? There is the possibility that the Japanese may consult them before we mention the matter. If they do, we may be embarrassed in our relations with those Governments who will consider us not frank. I am very sure that a secretive attitude will deeply offend Reading and Jusserand, and, to a lesser degree, Cellere and Koo. My own disposition is to be candid with them, now that the Japanese Government has had time to consider our proposed program.

Faithfully yours,   Robert Lansing

CCL (SDR, RG 59, 861.00/2292½A, DNA).

From Edward Mandell House, with Enclosure

Dear Governor: Magnolia, Massachusetts. July 8, 1918.

I am enclosing you a copy of a letter from Lawrence Lowell which explains itself.

I should be sorry to see this matter placed in the hands of such a committee as the Executive Committee of the League to Enforce Peace suggests, for it would add to the difficulties rather than solve them.

The letter I wrote to Lord Robert Cecil, a copy of which I sent you,[1] was merely my tentative views. I am giving the subject considerable thought and when I see you—which I hope may be soon—I would like to go into it in detail.

Do you think it would satisfy Taft, Lowell, Root and others if you told them that you expected the Peace Inquiry to cover this ground?

Affectionately yours,   E. M. House

TLS (WP, DLC).
[1] That is, the Enclosure printed with EMH to WW, June 25, 1918.

E N C L O S U R E

Abbott Lawrence Lowell to Edward Mandell House

Dear Mr. House: Cambridge. July 5, 1918.

Not on my initiative, I assure you—though I do not see how I could very well oppose it—at the meeting of the Executive Committee of the League to Enforce Peace the following vote was passed:

"Resolved, that the Chairman of the Executive Committee be asked to lay before the Government at Washington the advisability of the appointment of a committee in connection with similar committees of our Allies to consider the establishment of a League of Nations now."

Now I do not want to lay this suggestion before President Wilson, because I know that he has already disapproved of it; at least, expressed disapproval of some such plan; and therefore I thought I had better consult you about what had better be done. Although I should not myself have thought it wise to propose such a vote in the League to Enforce Peace, I do think it would be eminently wise for President Wilson to appoint some committee, because, as I said to you the other day, if he does not keep the lead in his own hands, it will pass into the hands of others.

Very truly yours,   A. Lawrence Lowell.

TCL (WP, DLC).

From Herbert Clark Hoover

Dear Mr. President: Washington 8 *July, 1918*

I am enclosing you rather a lengthy letter[1] in reply to the Trade Commission's report on the Food Administration maximum profits allowed the packers.[2] I have the feeling that if the Trade Commission report is made public then this reply, in justice, should be given co-incident publicity. I do not, however, believe that any useful purpose is served by public ventilation of inter-departmental disagreements as to governmental policy.

The matters at issue are matters of considerable importance and principle. If Congress passes sufficiently strong excess profits legislation, it will automatically correct the situation and meet the views of both the Trade Commission and ourselves. If Congress does not do so, I am afraid you will need to make some decision in matters of principle.

My proposal is, therefore, that the whole matter shall be laid aside until the action of Congress is determinable. If, however, you think it desirable to have the matter inquired into at once, I would like to suggest that the Trade Commission report, together with the letter which I enclose should be submitted to some independent person, say Mr. Baruch, or ex-Governor Stuart of Virginia,[3] both of whom could advise upon the matters of principle involved, without necessarily entering into details of fact.

Yours faithfully,   Herbert Hoover

TLS (WP, DLC).
[1] HCH to WW, July 8, 1918, TLS (WP, DLC). After a detailed criticism of the F.T.C.'s report (about which see n. 2 *seq.*) and a comprehensive analysis of the earnings of the meat-packing industry, Hoover admitted that the meat packers might, indeed, reap excessive profits under the Food Administration's present regulations. However, Hoover sharply disagreed with the commission over the methods best suited to regulate the industry and over the actual percentage of the packers' profits. According to Hoover's

calculations, these profits were far less inordinate than the F.T.C. had claimed. Moreover, to narrow the industry's profit margins and to prohibit earnings on "borrowed capital" would run counter to sound business practice. Many of the companies had borrowed funds to increase their stocks in storage in order to be prepared for any emergency during the war. Their compensation, therefore, had to bear some relation to their borrowed capital. The prime difficulty in all regulation of profits in advance, Hoover continued, was that it had to stimulate production, encourage support of the war effort, and provide sufficiently wide margins to cover all possible risks. If too strictly drawn, an advance profit regulation would curb incentive, destroy production, and limit efficiency. The sound method, Hoover argued, was "to give a fairly loose profit regulation, sufficiently strict to prevent speculation, stabilize price levels and then, by taxation, to appropriate to the Government any extraordinary profit that may have arisen." Thus, Hoover recommended that the present regulations of the Food Administration should remain unchanged but should be supplemented by strong excess-profits legislation.

[2] W. B. Colver *et al.* to WW, June 28, 1918, a revised version of which is printed as an Enclosure with J. F. Fort to WW, July 30, 1918. The original version has not been found.

[3] Henry Carter Stuart, at this time a member of the Price Fixing Committee of the W.I.B.

From Robert Somers Brookings

My dear Mr President: Washington July 8, 1918.

Pardon me for calling your attention to the urgency of the cotton goods situation. Practically all important transactions are being held up pending your approval. I appreciate how impossible it must have been for you to have given matters of this kind attention last week, and would not trouble you with this communication were it not very important that your approval should be given to the press today.   Respectfully yours,   Robt. S. Brookings

TLS (WP, DLC).

From Franklin Delano Roosevelt

My dear Mr. President   [New York] July 8 [1918]

I entirely forgot on Sunday evening to speak to you of a personal matter which might come up during my absence[1]—the question of my nomination for the Governorship of New York. I have tried in every way to stop it, but some of your friends & mine have talked of the possibility of forcing this while I am away, and of asking you to encourage me to accept it.

I sincerely hope the matter will not come up—I have made my position entirely clear that my duty lies in my present work—not only my duty to you and to the country, but my duty to myself. If I were at any time to leave the Assistant Secretaryship it could only be for active service.

Furthermore, may I say that I am very certain that it would be a grave mistake for either you or any member of the Administration to ask that I give up war work for what is frankly very much of a local political job in these times. I cannot accept such a nomination at this time either with honesty or honor to myself. I think I have put off all danger of it, but in case you are appealed to I want you to know what I feel—and I know too that you will understand and that you will not listen to the appeal.

Faithfully yours   Franklin D Roosevelt

ALS (WP, DLC).
    [1] Roosevelt was about to leave for Europe to inspect American naval bases in Great Britain and France.

From Robert Bridges

White Sulphur Springs West Virginia

Dear Mr. President: July 8, 1918

I've had five delightful days here—and am starting back to New York tonight. The evening with you[1] gave me a fine beginning for my little vacation. It did my heart good to see you so well—and to know that the terrible questions put up to you are in your able hands. That speech on July 4th you can rest your case upon for all time. It had perfection of form and real beauty, as well as a big plan and a chart to steer by.

Every day I have ridden for about three hours, on horseback, over high mountain trails. This would be the place for *you* to rest. You could lose the secret-service men completely, and do up any man on a motor-cycle. The sun is warm, but the air has just the right quality. I feel as though I had had a month's vacation.

It has been a pleasure to see Mrs. Grayson here—also that baby[2] which is worthy of all praise.

Thanking Mrs Wilson and you for your kindness to me, I am

Faithfully Yours   Robert Bridges

ALS (WP, DLC).
    [1] On July 3, 1918.
    [2] James Gordon Grayson, born on January 7, 1918.

Charles Lee Swem to Joseph Patrick Tumulty

The White House [July 8, 1918].

Please acknowledge this;[1] say that the President appreciates it and will take the liberty of withholding it from publication for the present for reasons which he will be glad to explain to them when he has the opportunity.   C.L.S.

T MS (WP, DLC).
  [1] That is, the F.T.C.'s report on the meat-packing industry: W. B. Colver *et al.* to WW, July 3, 1918.

Lord Reading to Arthur James Balfour

Washington. July 8th, 1918

No. 3083 I saw the President to-day. He had been informed by cable from the U. S. Representative at the Supreme War Council of the decision of the Council with regard to Murmansk and also of the memorandum of Sir Eric Geddes communicated to me in telegrams of July 3rd from Paris.[1] He informed me that he had held a conference last Saturday afternoon which was attended by the Secretaries of State War and Navy and the Chief of the Military and Chief of the Navy Staff. The Military and Naval Advisers produced reports which had been referred back for further elucidation of certain points and would be re-submitted to the President.

It was evident that the President's mind was disturbed as to the possibility of providing necessary supplies and equipment for the proposed Siberian expedition. An investigation has already been commenced for the purpose of determining programme as to the 100 divisions to be placed in the field in France by July next year as explained in my telegram No. 3058.[2] In addition to the requirements for France there would be requirements for these proposed expeditions which would in the main fall upon the United States and the question was whether it would be possible to produce sufficient for these additional purposes. He explained that vast as it was the productive capacity of the U. S. was limited and was being already very heavily taxed by the requirements for so large a force as 100 divisions and he assumed that it was not in contemplation to reduce this programme in order to carry out either the Siberian or Murmansk proposals. To my reply that Murmansk was quite a small matter he answered that it was small at present but in view of Sir Eric Geddes' memorandum it was a very risky proceeding and that although it may be advisable to take the risk we must be prepared to support the troops we send there and no one could say what this might mean both in men and supplies. He agreed that there might be possibilities of increasing production but these were all being taken into account in ascertaining the productive capacity for the next twelve months. The President said that there was no doubt that Japan would have to depend upon the U. S. for assistance in supply both of material and finance which would add considerably to present and prospective burdens. He was concerned lest these requirements could only be satisfied by subtracting from the assistance to be given in the West. He had been considering these matters with his advisers in the morning and it was plain that his mind was filled with the possible difficulties of providing the necessary supplies and equipment or the materials therefor.

I asked whether he was prepared to give an answer to the Allied Governments to the questions submitted to him. He replied that he desired to defer his answers for a short period first because he had not yet received the complete reports of his expert advisers and secondly because he must await the result of discussion proceeding between Mr. Lansing and the Japanese Ambassador. The President stated that he did not wish to give an answer piecemeal and was not in a position to give the complete answer at this moment for the reasons above stated. He added that until he knew the result of the discussions with the Japanese Ambassador he would not be in a position to give his reply. He would communicate with me as soon as he was ready to answer. I again referred to the urgent necessity for immediate action as explained in the resolutions of the Supreme War Council. He assured me that he was fully alive to the urgency of the matter and that he would reply in a very short time.

The President also informed me that there were some cabled observations of General Bliss upon the Murmansk expedition which he had not yet seen.

I hesitate to express a forecast of his decision but I am little disposed to alter the general impression stated in my report of last interview in my telegram No. 3024.[3]

Copies of above text have been given to French and Italian Ambassadors.

T telegram (FO 115/2448, pp. 135-38, PRO).
[1] About this matter, see T. H. Bliss to RL et al., July 5, 1918, printed as an Enclosure with NDB to WW, July 6, 1918.
[2] That is, Lord Reading to A. J. Balfour, July 6, 1918.
[3] Lord Reading to A. J. Balfour, July 3, 1918 (first telegram of that date).

Lord Robert Cecil to Edward Mandell House

[London] July 8th, 1918.

No. 680. Following for COLONEL HOUSE *from* LORD ROBERT CECIL:
You were good enough to tell me when you were over here last year that I might communicate with you, if there were anything which I thought you ought to know. May I venture therefore to say this?

I am convinced that there is growing up in this country a very strong feeling that Allied intervention in SIBERIA is being unduly delayed. So far public expression of opinion on the subject has been strongly discouraged by the Government. Till lately the newspapers have been warned not to discuss it, and even now they have been asked to treat it with great caution. Attempts to raise matter in Parliament have been prevented. But I am afraid that sooner or later feeling will become too strong to be repressed and a dangerous explosion may follow which might produce very un-welcome results, possibly even giving rise to international criticism and recrimination. From one point of view these are matters with which you may rightly say you have no concern. But knowing how very much you have at heart the maintenance and increase of cordial friendship between our two countries, I thought you would forgive me if I let you know how the situation strikes one, part of whose business it is to watch public opinion and who has given very close personal attention to this particular question for the last six months.

T telegram (W. Wiseman Papers, CtY).

To William Howard Taft and Francis Patrick Walsh

My dear Friends: [The White House] 9 July, 1918

I have received and thought very earnestly about your communication of July first with regard to the electric urban and suburban railway systems in connection with federal relief,[1] and find myself obliged to say in reply that I do not believe that the policy suggested is the wise one. In practically every state there is a board constituted under the laws of the state which is authorized to pass upon the question of rates, which seems to lie at the heart of the difficulties which you and the gentlemen associated with you on the Board have been so intelligently attacking, and I believe that it is the duty of those boards to address themselves to this subject in active cooperation with such federal instrumentalities as your own Board, in order that all local circumstances and conditions may be considered along with the federal interests.

In the case of New Jersey, for example, there is a Public Utilities Board, with full power, which has looked into the question of rates for the electric urban and suburban railway systems of the state as no federal authority would have the time or the opportunity to do, and I believe that it is their imperative duty to arrive at a decision at as early a date as possible and give it publicity and effect.

The danger in the present circumstances is that we will hasten to erect federal machinery which cannot promptly enough deal with complicated questions of this sort and which will unnecessarily supplant thoroughly organized and entirely competent bodies already in existence in their several states, and I hope that the Board will exercise its full influence in bringing about a coordination with such local instrumentalities.

Cordially and sincerely yours,   Woodrow Wilson

TLS (Letterpress Books, WP, DLC).
    [1] It is summarized in n. 1 to the Enclosure printed with JPT to WW, July 5, 1918.

To Lincoln Ross Colcord

My dear Mr. Colcord: [The White House] 9 July, 1918

I thank you for your letter of July seventh. Your thoughtful suggestions about Russia are always welcome and you may be sure I am trying to think out the right action. I hope and believe, too, that I am close upon the heels of it.

In haste   Sincerely yours,   Woodrow Wilson

TLS (Letterpress Books, WP, DLC).

To Olive Child Mitchel[1]

[The White House] 9 July, 1918

May I not express to you my very deep and sincere sympathy?[2] The tragical death of your husband has been a shock to the whole country and I am sure that I am speaking the feeling of multitudes in thus expressing my personal feeling.   Woodrow Wilson.

T telegram (WP, DLC).
    [1] Mrs. John Purroy Mitchel.
    [2] Her husband had been killed in a flying accident on July 6, 1918.

From Newton Diehl Baker

[Washington, c. July 9, 1918]

VERY CONFIDENTIAL

For the President's information[1]   Baker

ALS (WP, DLC).
    [1] J. J. Pershing to H. P. McCain, July 8, 1918, No. 1428, T telegram (WP, DLC). Pershing discussed in detail the present combat strength of the British, French, and German forces on the western front and the number of men available for future reinforcements. He concluded: "Resumé of this information shows: Combatant strength on French front: Great Britain 1,044,000; France 1,333,000, Italy 14,000; total 2,402,000. Germany 3,557,000. Additional prospective reenforcements that will form on the French

front in 1918: Great Britain 677,000; France 616,000; total 1,293,000; Germany 340,000."
However, Pershing wrote, his own calculations seemed to show that both Britain and
France had more men available for combat service than they were willing to admit.
These figures and statements, Pershing continued, had to be considered as extremely
confidential and should under no circumstances be published, since there was at present
an "acrimonious dispute" between the French and British governments as to whether
Britain was throwing its full weight against the Germans. The French claimed that the
British were holding an organized force of about one million men as a home army in
England and Ireland.

To Viscount Kikujiro Ishii

My dear Mr. Ambassador: [The White House] 9 July, 1918

May I not give myself the pleasure of saying how much I have
been interested in reading your addresses at Fairhaven, Massachusetts, and how gratified I am that the people of that region
should have had an opportunity of showing you their genuine cordial feeling for yourself and for the great country you represent?
The story of Manjiro Nakahama has particularly interested me.
Such links between Japan and America are delightful to remember.[1]

Cordially and sincerely yours,   Woodrow Wilson

TLS (Letterpress Books, WP, DLC).
    [1] Wilson's letter was prompted by a letter from Charles Sumner Hamlin (C. S. Hamlin
to WW, July 8, 1918, TLS [WP, DLC]), in which Hamlin had told Wilson about the
occasion of Ishii's visit to Fairhaven and New Bedford on July 4 and had enclosed
clippings about the event from the New Bedford *Morning Mercury*, July 4, 1918, and
the *New Bedford Evening Standard*, July 5, 1918. Ishii had presented to the people of
Fairhaven a thirteenth-century Samurai sword on behalf of Dr. Toichiro Nakahama, a
prominent Japanese physician, in gratitude for the kindness shown by the town of
Fairhaven to his father, Manjiro Nakahama. The latter had been stranded as a young
boy on a small island in the China Sea in 1841 and had been rescued by William H.
Whitfield, a whaling captain from Fairhaven. Captain Whitfield had taken Manjiro back
to Fairhaven, where he became the first Japanese boy to be educated in the United
States. After a number of years in Fairhaven and participation in several whaling expeditions, Manjiro returned to Japan in 1851. Due to his knowledge of western science
and culture, he soon rose to national prominence. He was called to Yedo (Tokyo) by
the Shōgun, became a teacher of navigation and English, and, in 1853, served as an
interpreter in the historic negotiations with Commodore Perry. He later continued to
teach shipbuilding, navigation, and whaling, led several Japanese whaling expeditions,
and was the first Japanese to navigate a ship across the Pacific. He was named vice-
principal of the school which was to become Tokyo Imperial University, and, in 1870,
was chosen to accompany a military delegation to Europe to observe the Franco-Prussian
War. See Emily V. Warinner, *Voyager to Destiny: The Amazing Adventures of Manjiro
the Man Who Changed Worlds Twice* ... (Indianapolis and New York, 1956), and
Hisakazu Kaneko, *Manjiro, the Man Who Discovered America* (Boston, 1956).

From Viscount Kikujiro Ishii

Mr. President: Washington July 9, 1918

It is difficult for me to express how highly I am honored and how
deeply I am touched by the cordial letter with which you favored
me under today's date.

The cordial feeling abundantly shown by the good people of Massachusetts to my country as well as to myself on the occasion of my recent visit to Fairhaven is the source of my sincere gratitude. You can well imagine therefore with what a pride I learn from your letter that this local affair and the episode of Manjiro Nakahama could have secured high appreciation on your part.

Thanking you sincerely for your so cordial message, I beg to remain, Mr. President,

Yours respectfully and gratefully,   K. Ishii

TLS (WP, DLC).

From Charles Richard Crane, with Enclosure

Dear Mr President   Woods Hole Massachusetts July 9 1918

I enclose you the notes you asked for by Professor Ross. Within the last two weeks another fine, patriotic and well-informed Russian has arrived in America—the former Minister of Commerce and Industry, Konavaloff. Bakhmetieff was his aid. Someone in your group would do well to have a full conference with Konavaloff as he is in every way to be trusted.

We are all glad and relieved to learn that McAdoo has returned in good condition.   Always sincerely   Charles R. Crane

ALS (WP, DLC).

E N C L O S U R E

NOTES ON METHODS OF HELPING RUSSIA
Prepared for President Wilson

by Edward A. Ross, Professor of Sociology, University of Wisconsin

The writer was in Russia July 5, 1917 to January 1, 1918 and his conclusions are fully set forth in his book RUSSIA IN UPHEAVAL published recently by the Century Company.[1]

The Meaning of the Bolshevik Revolution

The Revolution of last November, far from finding its cause in Lenine and Trotzky resulted from the craving of the Russian masses for the comfortably-off, thought of the March Revolution as a bestower of liberties—liberty of thought, of speech, of press, of agitation and organization. But the impoverished masses thought of it as a bringer of economic relief—more land to the peasants, more wages

[1] Edward A. Ross, *Russia in Upheaval* (New York, 1918).

to the workers. When the Lvov and Kerensky governments showed no disposition to correct the concentration of productive wealth, and therefore of income, in the hands of a small class, the masses—who had no vision of the meaning of the War but knew their immediate necessities—were ready to support the Bolshevik program. They had been encouraged in their hope by the hundred thousand political exiles who reentered Russia from Siberia and abroad between March and August 1917, scattered to their former homes and at once began to agitate for an expropriation of the monopolizers of the means of production. Once one visualizes this army of repatriated radicals, one assigns no great rôle to German propaganda in bringing on the *debâcle*.

Attitude of the Bolsheviks toward Foreign Governments

As orthodox Marxians the Bolsheviki characterize a society in economic terms. If it is not socialistic, it must be "capitalistic." That it is "democratic" does not interest them. To them democracy without socialism is an empty political form. Hence, for a long while, they saw little to chose between the Germans and the Allies. In every capitalistic government they saw a natural enemy and the conduct of the British and the French Governments went far to confirm them in that belief. The course of the American Government has not fitted into the Marxian formulae and they are at a loss to characterize it. Meanwhile the German Government is enlightening them as to the spirit of "autocracy." Normally the spontaneous reaction of the Russian people against the deplorable political and economic state to which they have been reduced by the Brest-Litovsk peace will presently bring them to the fighting point and then will be the time to cooperate with them. On the other hand, an attempt to overthrow the *de facto* government by force will undo the salutary education of the folk leaders in the meaning of "democracy." "See," they will say, "all these capitalistic governments are tarred with the same stick. Let us then come to terms with Germany because she is nearest and can offer the most kinds of help."

The Sovyet Republic and the Bolshevist Government

A clear distinction should be drawn between the *Sovyet* system and the Bolshevist government. The latter is no more to be identified with the former than the Lloyd George Government is to be identified with the Parliamentary system. The ascendency of the left (Bolshevist) wing of the Social Democratic party may soon pass, but it is extremely unlikely that the Sovyet system will in the near future be voluntarily abandoned by the Russian people. A system so broad-based is like a dinner plate—hard to tip over.

The chief faults of the system as a scheme of government are:

1. The exclusion of representatives of brain workers and property holders.

2. Weakness of the Central government resulting in an unreasonable freedom of action by the local Sovyets.

It is possible to modify the system so as to cure these faults without abandoning the principle of popular sovereignty and of representation of economic groups rather than of areas. Undisturbed the Russians would gradually learn through experience the necessity of improving their system; but an attempt to overthrow it by violence from outside would be resisted to death.

The Agitation for Armed Intervention

The extensive, well-organized, and well-financed propaganda among us for armed Allied intervention probably emanates from the British and French holders of Russians bonds bent on overthrowing at any cost the present government of Russia because of its repudiation of Russia's public debt. One cannot blame these bondholders who stand to lose nearly five billions of dollars, but their impatience to protect their loans ought not to seduce the Allies into a disastrous policy. It would be cheaper for the allied governments to recoup their citizens who hold Russian bonds than to cast the present government of Russia into the arms of Germany.

Perhaps a twelfth of the Russian people hate the Sovyet system because under it they are politically null and have lost their property. Unable to overthrow the system themselves they would be only too happy to have the Allies pull their chestnuts out of the fire. No doubt they abhor the Brest-Litovsk peace but they will lend their aid to an allied invasion only on condition that the hundred thousand noble landowners get back their estates and the capitalists regain control of their factories.

In time Russia will have to recognize the services of the entrepreneur and create conditions under which he will function. For the sake of agricultural enterprise she will have to go over to private property in land and give a skillful farmer the chance to build up a good-sized farm. But the eventual appearance of a new and chastened race of capitalists and landholders is no reason for spilling blood to reinstate the Russian proprietors. No doubt they will become a nuisance like the French noble emigres for the twenty years after the French Revolution, but they have no function and should be left to their fate i.e. having to go to work.

The Russian peasants whose per capita consumption of bread stuffs is but three-fifths of that of West European peasants, and whose average family holding is less than half of what it was fifty years ago will fight like wildcats to keep the one hundred-and-forty millions of arable acres in the estates they have recently divided among their village communities. The wresting of the land out of their hands by means of foreign bayonets would be a bloody business, and would make a mockery of our cry "A world safe for Democracy."

The launching of an Allied expedition from Vladivostock would be taken by the Russian masses as a capitalistic counter-revolution and would justify the Bolsheviki in at once inviting German aid. For four thousand miles our troops would find the railroad destroyed in front of them, and the Germans would occupy the passes of the Urals while our military efforts lost themselves in the vast void of northern Asia.

Of course if the Siberians should form a stable anti-Bolsheviki government and invite Ally cooperation the outlook would be very different. The Siberians are more intelligent and aggressive than the Russians and what they champion is likely in the end to prevail in Russia.

Friendly Aid

Every movement engineered by the dispossessed classes in Russia will masquarade as "national," but if the Allies join it, they will find themselves involved in the horrors of a social war. Until there is a genuine national movement against those responsible for the Brest-[Litovsk] treaty our activities in Russia should be confined to the following:

1. Propaganda.
2. Red Cross Service both military and civilian.
3. Development of the work of the Y.M.C.A. and the Y.W.C.A.
4. Gratuitous services of our railroad and technical experts to aid the Sovyets in coping with their difficulties respecting transportation and industry.
5. The establishment of an Ally-Russian joint commission to bring about the barter of Russian surplus raw materials for our goods needed by the Russian people.

In case our services are so urgently needed that we are in a position to exact a *quid pro quo* for them our political demand should not go beyond insisting upon the convening of an All-Russian constitutional assembly elected by universal, secret and equal suffrage.

T MS (WP, DLC).

From Robert Lansing

My dear Mr. President: Washington July 9, 1918.

As I surmised Lord Reading was responsible for the interview which I had this afternoon with him and the French and Italian Ambassadors (you see they asked Jusserand to come with them). This was evident because Jusserand requested Reading to do the talking and he did it all though Jusserand, being the doyen of the corps, was natural spokesman.

Lord Reading stated that they wished to know whether the Allied Governments were not to take part in the initial landing of troops at Vladivostok or whether it was our purpose to confine the enterprise to Japanese and American troops.

I replied that I had never discussed the question with you and I could see no object in doing so until the Japanese had agreed to the principle of joint equal military action; that our view had been that it was useless to consider details until the Japanese had approved the general plan; and that it had been always our purpose to lay the matter before the Allied Governments and to advise with them provided the Japanese accepted our program.

Lord Reading said that he was not complaining of the course which we had pursued but that he thought that the Allies should have a chance to land available troops in this initial movement in order to impress the Russians with the idea that we were a unit and that the United States and Japan were not acting independently without the sanction of the other powers.

To this I answered that this seemed to me rather a matter of national pride and sentiment than a practical question; that I could not understand why this subject should be raised and that it showed to me the wisdom of the course which we had taken in not consulting all the Allied Governments before we had acted as apparently there would have been delay in discussing the details which would have been very unfortunate in view of the necessity of prompt action.

Lord Reading said that I should not hold that point of view as he only intended to suggest that it would be wise to have unity of action in this important step and that he felt that we should impress the Russian people with the united purpose of all the Governments to resist the attacks upon the Czecho-Slovaks.

I answered to this that I unfortunately could not agree with him; that the whole question was one of expediency which involved the advisability of participation by other powers in the proposed enterprise; and that I was not disposed to consider the sentimental phase but only the expedient side of the question. I went on to say that after Japan had agreed to the proposed program of 7,000 American and 7,000 Japanese being landed this Government would consider the question of British troops being incorporated in the landing force, but until Japan had so agreed the details seemed to me to be needless.

To this Lord Reading answered that while I might be right, he was sure that his Government would not understand action which did not include all parties. I said in reply that I was sorry to have him express this opinion, because I was sure that you had no intention of submitting the questions to the Allied Governments until Japan had declared that she was favorable to the general plan. I repeated that I thought expediency should control and that if expediency was opposed to British participation that, to my mind, ended it, although it possibly might be advisable for all the powers to declare in favor of preserving unimpaired Russian political and territorial sovereignty.

The British Ambassador was manifestly disturbed but did not pursue the subject further.

The French Ambassador asked if we had made any suggestion about superior military command. I replied that the subject had not been raised; that I could see no value in raising it at the present time; that the principal question was as to Japan's military cooperation; and that inviting controversy at a time when the Czecho-Slovaks needed our assistance immediately was most unwise.

Throughout this conference I felt that the French Ambassador and in a measure the Italian approved of our program, but that the British Ambassador was not entirely favorable because he felt Great Britain had been ignored.

Faithfully yours,   Robert Lansing[1]

TLS (WP, DLC).
[1] Lord Reading to D. Lloyd George and A. J. Balfour, July 9, 1918, No. 3112, T telegram (W. Wiseman Papers, CtY), and J. J. Jusserand to the Foreign Ministry, received July 10, 1918, T telegram (État-Major de l'Armée de Terre, 4 N 46, Service Historique, FMD-Ar) substantially repeat Lansing's report on this conference.

From William Phillips

Dear Mr. President: Washington July 9, 1918.

The French Ambassador tells me that the University of Paris is anxious to confer upon you an honorary degree, and that no French University has ever conferred honorary degrees either in or out of France so that this degree, if accepted by you, will actually be the first honorary degree conferred by any French University.

Before taking any further steps, however, the University desires to be informed whether you would be willing to receive the degree. Will you kindly let me know what reply I may make to the Ambassador?

I am, my dear Mr. President,

Faithfully yours,   William Phillips

TLS (WP, DLC).

From Scott Ferris

Washington, D. C., July 9, 1918.

Am so distressed about the contemplated veto of wheat amendment[1] members from West think it ruinous to them, they ask me to make this last appeal to you to spare us the veto.

Scott Ferris.

T telegram (WP, DLC).
[1] About this matter, see HCH to WW, July 10, 1918, and Wilson's veto message, printed at July 12, 1918.

From Lincoln Ross Colcord

Dear Mr. President: Washington, D. C. July 9, 1918.

In looking over my letter of July 7, I find that, almost unaccountably, I neglected to mention in it the treaty of Brest-Litovsk. This brings me fully to realize how unimportant I have always held the actual matter of the Brest-Litovsk treaty to be as a diplomatic event. I have never for a moment suspected it of being a pro-German manifestation, or sought to explain it by any but the most natural and candid of arguments; and I have never been able to find a fact, either in the history of the transaction itself or in the complex of resultant events, which did not fall in line with this simple explanation.

My whole letter, of course, was based on the assumption that it would be possible to shift the circumstances which brought on the Brest-Litovsk treaty and to change the state of mind which subscribed to it; and on the further assumption that the Soviets have always represented the only dependable anti-German sentiment in Russia. The circumstances which brought on the Brest-Litovsk treaty already have shifted of themselves; the Soviets have tasted the integrity of the Imperial German Government. This, too, has partially changed the state of mind. All its negative elements have been righted. The righting of its positive and controlling elements lies in our hands.

If America subscribes now to the decision of the Versailles Council, I can see no other explanation of it than that we have passed under the shadow of that same militarism which we are fighting. It will mean that Foch is now dictating the foreign policies of the Allies and America. German militarism means to me chiefly that: the subordination of the civil arm of government, and primarily of the foreign office, to the military arm.

I am, my dear Mr. President,

Faithfully and respectfully yours,   Lincoln Colcord

TLS (WP, DLC).

Newton Diehl Baker to Tasker Howard Bliss

[Washington] July 9, 1918.

Number 68 Confidential

General March and I have been in conference with the President about the Murman expedition. As we understand it, the permanent military representatives are unanimous in recommending that the expedition as now proposed be duly undertaken. None of us can see the military value of the proposal and assume that other considerations moved in favor of it. Please cable us for the President fully your personal views, military and otherwise, on the subject. Baker.   McCain.

TC telegram (WDR, RG 407, World War I Cablegrams, DNA).

Sir William Wiseman to Sir Eric Drummond

[New York] July 9, 1918.

VERY SECRET: *No. 110*. VISCOUNT ISHII, Japanese Ambassador, went to Magnolia Saturday to visit COLONEL HOUSE.

The following is the substance of long conversation:

ISHII hoped the PRESIDENT's declaration with regard to justice for all nations would apply to JAPAN as she had not received justice from other nations in the past. The Japanese want the same rights to trade throughout the world and have their share in developing new countries as other nations have. Hitherto they had not been allowed these rights. Even in British Colonies such as South Africa and Australia there are restrictions against Japanese immigration. In SIBERIA before the war the Imperial Russian Government had begun to restrict Japanese subjects from trading in Siberia. This was particularly resented by the Japanese in view of the fact that

Russia, a European power, was trying to prevent them from having a share in the development of an Asiatic country. The Californian legislation had hurt their national pride. HOUSE assured him that the Administration was most friendly towards Japan and recognised that she was destined to be the dominating power in the Far East. ISHII was at first not very enthusiastic about intervention in SIBERIA but rather altered his tone when he learned that HOUSE was thoroughly in favor of it providing it was accompanied by an Economic Commission. The idea of an economic commission appealed to ISHII as opening up trade possibilities in the future for the Japanese in Siberia. ISHII said that Japanese would go beyond Eastern Siberia providing there were not found to be insurmountable military difficulties. HOUSE asked whether the Japanese would give arms and munitions at once to the CZECHS at Vladivostock. ISHII said he could promise on behalf of the Japanese Government that they would. HOUSE wrote a full report of the conversation to the President, and suggested he should send for ISHII as soon as he returned to Washington.[1] The PRESIDENT did so yesterday.

I asked HOUSE to write to MR. BALFOUR regarding his interview, and he has promised to do so.

T telegram (W. Wiseman Papers, CtY).
[1] EMH to WW, July 6, 1918 (first letter of that date).

From the Diary of Josephus Daniels

July Tuesday 9 1918

WW—My father thought all sin came from Ego. Some men make themselves the centre of the universe instead of making God the centre & that [gives] them a wrong outlook upon the world Everything was for self & that makes sin

Speaking of War Councils advice on Russia, he said they proposed such impractical things to be done immediately that he often wondered whether he was crazy or whether they were. Once, after reading a page of examination paper & could make no sense he turned to Mrs W— & asked her to read it. Is there any sense in it? He asked after she had read it & was overjoyed when she said "No" for he then was convinced that he was not crazy

To Joseph Patrick Tumulty

Dear Tumulty: [The White House, c. July 10, 1918]

I think it would be worth while to explain to this gentleman that the angelus is in this case merely a name, not the adoption of a ceremony or anything historically connected with that ceremony.[1] It was a convenient term by which to indicate the wish of the Senate that the citizens of the country might pause every day at noon for a moment of prayer.   The President.

TL (WP, DLC).
[1] Wilson was responding to C. M. Spaulding to WW, July 9, 1918, T telegram (WP, DLC). Claude M. Spaulding, a Christian Scientist from New York, protested against a resolution (S.J. Res. 164) adopted by the Senate on July 5, which asked Wilson to commend by proclamation to the American people the observance of one minute of prayer at noon each day for victory in the war. During the debate in the Senate, the term "angelus" had been used to describe the prayer. Spaulding told Wilson that he and other loyal and religious people would object to the observance of the Angelus, which, he stated, was a distinctive form of daily prayer of the Roman Catholic Church. For the adoption of the resolution, see *Cong. Record*, 65th Cong., 2d sess., pp. 8672-75.

To William Phillips

My dear Mr. Phillips: [The White House] 10 July, 1918

I have your letter of yesterday informing me that the French Ambassador has told you that the University of Paris is anxious to confer an honorary degree upon me. I hope that you will say to the French Ambassador how very much honored I should feel by such an action on the part of the University. I particularly appreciate this honor in view of its extraordinary character, inasmuch as no French University has ever conferred an honorary degree of any kind before. I am very much touched by this evidence of their friendship.

Cordially and sincerely yours,   Woodrow Wilson

TLS (Letterpress Books, WP, DLC).

From Robert Lansing

My dear Mr. President: Washington July 10, 1918.

The Japanese Ambassador called this afternoon. He said that he had not heard from his Government, but that it might possibly expedite a decision if some arrangement could be made as to the chief commander of the combined forces.

I told him that I had not discussed the subject with you because it did not seem of prime importance but that in view of his raising the question I would lay it before you. While making light of the matter to Ishii I think that it is really a serious subject which will have to be settled very soon. It presents considerable embarrassment, and, to tell the truth, I am at a loss what to say as I am sure the Japanese will expect to be in high command. Will you please be good enough to give me your judgment as to how I should treat the subject with the Ambassador?

Faithfully yours,   Robert Lansing.

TLS (WP, DLC).

From Herbert Clark Hoover

Dear Mr. President: Washington 10 *July, 1918*

I am informed that the contention has been raised that the $2.40 wheat means a rise of only about twenty cents a bushel to the farmer and a similar cost to the consumer. This argument is based on the contention that our present price basis is, say, $2. Salt Lake, $2.26 Chicago, $2.39½ New York. It neglects the fact that the new Congressional price is based on No. 2 wheat instead of No. 1, in which there is a difference of three cents, but of much more importance than this, it is based on the assumption that it is possible, commercially, to make a universal price for wheat.

I have now consulted the men in the Food Administration Grain Corporation and they have earnestly considered every possible method by which this might be accomplished and the final conclusion is that while it could be accomplished, it would necessitate an immediate working capital of $500,000,000 and would necessitate not only that we buy all the wheat in the country for the Government, instead of 15% or 20%, as under the present scheme, but would necessitate a proportionate expansion in organization. Furthermore, it could not be accomplished unless at the same time we took over the operation, direction and distribution of all the flour mills in the country because the differences in conditions in freight would maintain in flour the same as in wheat. As showing how quickly a rise in wheat may affect other food products with which there is no real relation, many exchanges reported yesterday increased prices of corn on the possibility that the Bill might not be vetoed.

Should you be considering the approval of this legislation I earnestly hope that you would first hear Mr. Barnes, the head of our Cereal Division, on its whole bearings. Any consideration of the problem with all its complexities will come to only one result, that if this legislation is confirmed, it will be necessary to increase the price of wheat at every terminal in the United States by 43 cents a bushel.   Yours faithfully,   Herbert Hoover

TLS (WP, DLC).

From James Francis Abbott, with Enclosure

Sir: Saint Louis July 10, 1918.

I have the honor to submit the attached memorandum in response to a telegram from Mr. Charles R. Crane, stating that you desired me to do so. It has reference to certain features attending the proposed military intervention in East Siberia. I returned a fortnight ago from a five months' sojourn in the Far East where I spent my whole time in a study of political and economic conditions in Japan, Manchuria and North China.

I have the honor to be, Sir,

Your most obedient servant,   J. F. Abbott

TLS (WP, DLC).

E N C L O S U R E

Memorandum on Japanese Intervention in Siberia. July 10, 1918
1. Present-Day Conditions in Japan.

Japan is governed at present by an oligarchy that parallels the Prussian one to an extraordinary degree. Both are essentially feudal. Both present a combination of "Big Business" with Government to the end that the foreign policy of the country may be largely determined by the possibility of private profit for privileged individuals. Both utilize the state-directed educational system for the purpose of developing a national mind, responsive to the appeals of imperialistic ambition.

The events of the past two or three years have wrought tremendous changes in Japanese society. Certain groups of manufacturers and the owners and builders of ships have become very wealthy on account of war-conditions, and the laborers in those industries have shared in the unparalleled bounty. All the laboring classes, in fact, find themselves with increased wages but with a greatly enhanced cost of living, a disturbing factor in itself, particularly if the boom conditions should suddenly disappear with the close of the war. The middle and salaried classes are finding it almost impossible to make ends meet on account of the universal rise of the cost of living; at the same time the newly-rich are throwing money about right and left. There is growing up a large student class whose heads are filled with half-baked theories and grievances. Industrial unrest is rapidly increasing in spite of the fictitious prosperity. Strikes are becoming constantly more frequent and more extensive; (there were over 80 significant industrial strikes in 1915 over 100 in 1916, nearly 400 in 1917 and even a larger number in the first half of 1918) Corruption and bribery scandals are becoming more and more frequent. In short, below the surface of things in Japan there is a fierce social ferment at work.

At the same time, the governing group, keenly sensitive to all this and alive also to the possibility of socialist infection from Russia, and in particular from America (witness the Hepburn foundation controversy)[1] represses the slightest manifestation of resistance to the established order or the growth of democracy among the people, by a vigorous and watchful exercise of the police power and censorship. It is screwing down the steam valve on the boiler without drawing the fires. The ruling classes are much worried by the situation. They have everything to lose and nothing to gain by an extension of democratic ideas and institutions in Japan. I know of a conference held only a few weeks ago at instance of Premier Terauchi at the residence of the president of one of the largest spinning companies, in which politicians and capitalists were brought together to discuss the situation. At this conference some were fearful of the future others calmly secure in the belief in their own strength to meet any crisis but no one had any solution for a problem that all realized to be imminent and dangerous.

Democratic sentiment is undoubtedly growing among the masses of the Japanese people. The word "kiken-shiso" (dangerous thoughts), employed when it becomes necessary to squelch a publication or a public man, has been used until it has become a byword. The struggle for representative government, year before last, between the Japanese people backed by a united press, on the one hand, and Premier Terauchi and the Genro on the other, which ended in the dissolution of parliament twenty-four hours after its organization, to for[e]stall a vote of lack of confidence, and the apparent victory of the reactionaries, is a struggle that will inevitibly be renewed in the near future, and the ruling group are very fearful of it.

I was shown confidentially a short time ago the censored films of the Universal Film Co. in Tokyo which included sections of the "Universal Weekly." These included the following excerpt from a speech of President Wilson:

"This is the last decisive issue between old principles of power and new principles of freedom."

and the following from an address by President Poincaré:

---

[1] Alonzo Barton Hepburn, a financier and philanthropist of New York, had given $60,000 to the Imperial University of Tokyo in February 1918 to endow a professorship in American constitutional history and diplomacy. Neither the newspaper accounts nor Hepburn's biographer mention anything about a "controversy." See the *New York Times*, Feb. 2, 1918, and Joseph B. Bishop, *A. Barton Hepburn: His Life and Service to His Time* (New York, 1923), pp. 295-316.

"*We shall fight on and on until the cause of liberty shall triumph.*"
These were eliminated by the police before permission to show the
film could be obtained, on the ground that they were "dangerous
thoughts." I could give any amount of similar evidence to the effect
that however much the exigencies of the diplomatic and political
situation may compel us officially to ignore it, the fact remains that
the Japanese Government (not necessarily the Japanese people) are
not only not in sympathy with the *political* aims of the United States
Government in the present war even though our military aims may
coincide, but are in such a domestic situation that they cannot
afford to permit the discussion of such aims in public.
2. *Relation of the Siberian problem to Japan.*

It is an old and accepted solution of such a difficulty as has just
been outlined, to provoke trouble abroad in order to divert pressure
at home. China and East Siberia offer open fields and Japan has
entered both in different ways. With regard to the Chinese situation
which is highly complicated, I shall submit a second memorandum
in the near future.[2] In Siberia, from the Japanese point of view, the
matter is much simpler. It is acknowledged on all sides that should
the Japanese enter East Siberia they could establish complete authority with great ease. It would be far easier and less complicated
than the occupation of Chinese territory but the wave of patriotic
fervor and of emotional imperialism that would follow such a course
(compare our occupation of the Philippines) would successfully
divert all attention from domestic problems in Japan, that are rapidly
approaching a crisis. This of course is but a personal opinion, for
I have no means of knowing other than by inference the real motives
that actuate Japanese foreign policy. I do know, however, that ever
since it has been known that the United States was in opposition
to Siberian intervention, the Japanese vernacular papers (which I
read) have been full of the most inflammable news-stories regarding
American activities in Siberia, stories of the investment of great
sums of American capital, the purchase by Americans of all the
Amur and Sungari shipping, the acquisition of timber areas etc.,
etc. Knowing the positive control of the Japanese papers by the
authorities, through police censorship, the only explanation of such
propaganda would seem to be the preparation of the public mind
for a conflict of interest between the United States and Japan in
the near future. In other words, the difficulties of the Japanese
"junkers" at home are likely to tempt them to risk a possible con-
flagration that would involve the whole Far East in order to save
their own position.

---

[2] If Abbott ever submitted the memorandum, it is missing in WP, DLC.

The danger from German and Austrian prisoners in Siberia has been and is illusory, as the data in the possession of our State Department shows. Siberia, to be sure, is in a state of chaos at present and a reorganization cannot be anticipated until famine has wiped out an enormous fraction of the Russian population, both in Europe and in Asia. In my opinion, nothing can prevent this progressive dissolution of the social structure of the Empire during the next few months. Now it seems almost self-evident, that without the active and effective cooperation of all the Russians from the Pacific to the western frontier it would be practically impossible for Japan to produce the slightest impression upon the German or Austrian front, and the almost complete disorganization of transportation, to say nothing of the reduction of civil government to the unit of the soviet would make such cooperation physically impossible even if the Russian people really desire to reopen hostilities with the Central Powers,—an assumption which is problematical to say the least.

The problem is of course a military one. But my purpose in the present memorandum is to oppose a purely Japanese intervention or a joint-intervention in which the other Allies should play a subordinate part. Under no circumstances should the proposed army of occupation contain more Japanese than American soldiers. Things are too fluid and chaotic in the Far East to permit Japan to establish "interests" that will certainly become potent nuclei of trouble in the future. Japan's interests may not always be our own. Yet if I understand Japanese public opinion which of course is an echo of official opinion, it is determined on two points: first,—Japan will not endure the loss of face that would be consequent upon a cooperative intervention; she will go either alone or with the Chinese or not at all; and second,—she cannot hope to go far enough to the west to produce the slightest effect upon the European front and has no idea of doing so.

Under such circumstances, the real purposes that will determine Japanese action must be kept constantly in mind. As I have pointed out briefly, the Japanese ruling classes are opposed to the fundamental war-aims of the United States, at least so far as they involve the extension of democratic principles and they are lik[e]ly to profit by the occasion of a Siberian intervention to reduce further the possibility of the development of such ideas in the Far East.

In fact, it is a matter of universal comment at the present time in Japan that the Germans are expected to win the war or at any rate to bring it to a profitible draw, and despite the fact that in word and deed, the Government officials have refrained scrupulously from anything that might invite criticism, (with the exception noted below), nevertheless a large and influential element of the Japanese people, including many officials, are either coldly neutral or passively pro-German. The American press sometimes fails to keep this in mind. I was in Tokyo when the famous interview with Premier Terauchi, published in the "Outlook" of May 1st by Gregory Mason, was made public.[3] It of course created a storm of excited comment and was referred to in general, as a "blazing indiscretion." The standing of Mason (whom I know well) as well as the circumstances of the interview, which was conducted through Mr. Tsurumi,[4] Terauchi's son-in-law and a high official in the Imp. Railways Bureau are such as to remove all question of its authenticity. It will be recalled that Mason's question was "What are the chances for an alliance between Japan and Germany," and Premier Terauchi's answer was "That will depend entirely on how the present war may end. It is impossible to predict the changes which the conclusion of the war may bring. If the exigencies of international relationships demand it, Japan being unable to maintain a position of total isolation may be induced to seek an ally in Germany, but as far as I can judge from the existing condition of affairs, I see no such danger." (Mar 8, published May 1st). The interview was translated into Japanese, corrected and approved by Terauchi and by the Foreign and Home ministers before publication. Far from being an indiscretion, it was in my opinion, a covert threat, almost an official one. And in all the storm and criticism in Tokyo it was neither retracted nor explained.

My point is that a power whose official policy is advertised to the world to be primarily opportunist and self-seeking, should not be permitted to gain a preponderance of power in a situation so complicated and delicate as that of Russia, in which our concern, as Americans is that even in beating the Germans we are not to lose sight of the fundamental principles at stake. It would be a calamity if in our endeavors to crush a militant oligarchy in central Europe we should connive at the formation of a similar one in East Asia.

J. F. Abbott

TS MS (WP, DLC).
    [3] Gregory Mason, "Japan, Germany, Russia, and the Allies," *The Outlook*, CXIX (May 1, 1918), 18-22.
    [4] That is, Yūsuke Tsurumi. He was, in fact, the son-in-law of Baron Shimpei Gotō, the Japanese Foreign Minister.

From Abbott Lawrence Lowell

Dear President Wilson: Cambridge July 10, 1918.

As Chairman of the Executive Committee of the League to Enforce Peace, it is my duty to send to you the following:

"RESOLVED, that the Chairman of the Executive Committee be asked to lay before the Government at Washington the advisability of the appointment of a committee in connection with similar committees of our Allies to consider the establishment of a League of Nations now."

Perhaps there is no objection in suggesting that if, as I suppose, you desire to maintain the leading part in directing the movement for a League of Nations, to which you gave the first great international impulse, it is important that you should take the initiative, now that other nations are, through official committees, formulating plans. You could do so either by an official committee appointed to communicate with those abroad, or by conferences of informal committees on this side which kept in close, though unofficial, touch with you.   Very truly yours,   A. Lawrence Lowell.

TLS (WP, DLC).

Lord Reading to David Lloyd George and Arthur James Balfour

Washington. July 10, 1918.

Following for Prime Minister and Mr. Balfour. Very Urgent Personal and Secret.

My telegram No. 3112.[1]

Secretary Lansing has assured me today that the only object of consulting the Japanese Ambassador immediately and on the lines indicated was to save time and avoid preliminary discussions with the five Governments. The President sent me a message through Lansing to similar effect and emphasized the opportunities for consultation that will be given to the Allied Governments immediately the answer is received from Japan.

These assurances and explanations have resulted from my stating to Mr. Lansing that I feared that the Allied Governments would be surprised at the course taken by the U. S. Government. I expressed a personal opinion that it was a pity a course had been pursued which was capable of being misunderstood and which I felt sure was more a matter of form than substance.

I am now satisfied that the U. S. Government will upon receipt of the Japanese answer confer with us freely and with an open mind as to the composition of the expedition.

Immediate action is contemplated for the purpose of the protection of the Czecho Slovaks, the U. S. Government intending to send regiments from the Phillipines and Hawaii. There are however still the difficulties as to command of the expedition. As I have frequently said to you the Japanese are most anxious to do everything they possibly can to please the U.S.G. and will make every effort to fall in with their views.

I hope I have managed to convey to you that I regard the step, very partial as it is, as a real progress and attributable largely to the method of approach to the U.S.G. by means of the resolution of the Supreme War Council and General Foch's views.

In conversation Lansing said this expedition may well be the means eventually of creating a Russian front.

The President basing himself upon the opinion of his military advisers and other experts is not willing to cooperate in the recreation of an Eastern front in the sense of sending an army large enough for this task. He is however willing to take the first step and by way of a military expedition.

It is so complete a change of his policy and I suggest must mean so much for the future that I hope you will see it in the same light as I am representing it to you and will agree with my view.

T telegram (W. Wiseman Papers, CtY).
¹ See RL to WW, July 9, 1918, n. 1.

David Lloyd George to Lord Reading

[London, July 10, 1918]

Following from Prime Minister.

Private and Secret.

Although I am glad that President has come down on side of intervention I am very disappointed with action which he proposes to take. 14,000 men is better than nothing but there is no military opinion that could be cited in favour of its sufficiency to attain objects Allies have in mind. If we are to act in Siberia at all surely what matters is that we should send a force which can make sure that Czecho-Slovaks will not have their throats cut by German and Austrian prisoners and will definitely secure Siberia to Urals against German-Bolshevist attack.

It is more urgent that we should act in sufficient force because it is daily becoming clearer that Bolshevists are going over to Ger-

mans and Germans will shortly be in practical control of Russia
either through Bolshevist or reactionary Allies. It is now really a
race between Germans and ourselves. Unless we act at once and
act effectively Germans will establish themselves not only in Russia
but in Western Siberia as well. In present circumstances therefore
a proposal to send an expedition confined arbitrarily to 14,000 without reference to military need is really preposterous. It is repeating
fatal error of Khartoum expedition to relieve Gordon and unless it
is modified it might end in exactly the same tragic results.

Moreover I am very anxious as to possible effect on Japanese of
this proposal. Although they have men on the spot, have accepted
conditions in regard to non-interference and evacuation and are
ready to move at once so as to link up the Czecho-Slovaks if they
are assured of support of U. S. they are told that Allies will only
agree to their entering Siberia if an American Police Force equivalent in numbers is sent with them. This is proposal which is made
to them after months of hesitation and doubt on the part of U. S.
Seeing that Far East is Japan's special sphere of interest, to insist
on conditions now proposed may have effect of deeply injuring their
national pride and driving them into a resentfull neutrality which
would inevitably produce disastrous results on the whole Far Eastern situation. I am sure that the proper way to deal with Japanese
is to ask them to undertake same obligations towards Russia as rest
of Allies and to make expedition part and parcel of Allied plan of
campaign against Germany and ? in future to agree to trust them
completely. It is of course of the greatest importance that character
of the expedition as an Allied expedition sent to help and not to
harm Russia should be scrupulously maintained. Hence our proposal that French Italian and British contingents should also be
included. Value of which for this purpose U.S.G. does not seem to
appreciate. I also recognise difficulties connected with relations
between American and Japanese troops where latter are more numerous. But it is surely possible to do something more effective in
a military sense which is both consonant with legitimate feelings
of Japan and not inconsistent with Russia's distrust of a purely
Japanese intervention seeing that large Czecho-Slovak forces are
already on the spot than to send a force of 14,000 men of which
half are American and half Japanese.

I hope that this private expression of my views may help you to
prove to President total inadequacy of his present proposals and
induce him to amend them in the sense of Supreme War Council's
resolution. Of course if we can get this expedition and cannot get
more we must accept it and press on with it as fast as we can for
essential thing is that we should get movement started without

delay. We have only a few months before Russian Harbours freeze and if we are to save Russia from becoming a German Province we must have firmly established ourselves in Siberia before the winter arrives.

T telegram (W. Wiseman Papers, CtY).

A Veto Message

The White House, *July 11, 1918.*

To the Senate: I regret to be obliged to return without my signature Senate joint resolution 159, "To extend the time within which the President may relinquish control of any railroad or system of transportation, as provided in section fourteen of an act entitled 'An act to provide for the operation of transportation systems while under Federal control, for the just compensation of their owners, and for other purposes,' approved March twenty-first, nineteen hundred and eighteen, to January first, nineteen hundred and nineteen." I do so because I very respectfully but very earnestly dissent from the policy which it embodies. Under its terms the Government would be obliged to assume the control and administration of all short-line railroads without discrimination. I respectfully submit that this is not in the public interest. There are terminal short lines at many centers of freight shipment and some seventeen hundred short lines which were built and are controlled by manufacturing, mining, lumbering, and other companies and which are operated merely for the convenience of those companies, which would be included under the language of this resolution, very few of which, it seems to me, if any, ought to be taken over and administered by the Government.

The remaining short roads are feeders to the main trunk lines, and more than mere feeders, most of them, for they have in most instances played a very important part in building up the industries of the communities through which they run and have become essential to the prosperity of hundreds of towns and neighborhoods all over the Union. I quite agree that practically all of these should be retained and that they should not only be retained, but that they should be accorded a fair division of joint rates—a fairer division than some of them have been accorded hitherto—an equitable allotment of cars and motive power, and fair routing arrangements. Some of them constitute connecting links between two or more trunk-line systems. Those which play this part in the system of railways ought to be accorded as full a share in through shipments as is consistent with the general interests of the shipper and the public.

This is the policy which the Railroad Administration will pursue toward these roads. They will not be put at an unfair or ruinous disadvantage. The Government owes a recognized obligation to the communities which they serve, but it is not, in my judgment, wise to oblige the Government to deal in the same way with all of them regardless of the very great variety of circumstances which affect their facilities and their administration. I beg that the Congress will leave the Government free to enter into arrangements with them which will in each case be to the interest alike of the road dealt with and of the local public.   Woodrow Wilson.

Printed in *Message of the President of the United States Vetoing Senate Joint Resolution 159 . . .* (Washington, 1918).

To Charles Richard Crane

My dear Friend: [The White House] 11 July, 1918

Thank you warmly for sending me Professor Ross's paper. I shall read it at once and incorporate it into my thinking about the perplexing Russian problem.

With warmest regard, in necessary haste,
                    Faithfully yours,   Woodrow Wilson

TLS (Letterpress Books, WP, DLC).

To Abbott Lawrence Lowell

My dear President Lowell: The White House 11 July, 1918

I have your letter of July tenth quoting the resolution of the League to Enforce Peace with regard to the appointment of a committee to act in connection with similar committees in the nations with whom we are associated in the war "to consider the establishment of a league of nations now."

The only committees in the countries with whom we are associated of which I have heard were committees appointed by the governments. I should consider it very embarrassing to have a private organization like the League to Enforce Peace take this matter up, since the immediate establishment of a league of nations is a question of government policy not only, but constitutes part of the intricate web of counsel now being woven between the associated governments. I am having this matter studied myself and hope very sincerely that if the League to Enforce Peace undertakes its study, it will not in addition undertake to establish international connections with committees of a different origin abroad.

Very sincerely yours, Woodrow Wilson

TLS (A. L. Lowell Papers, MH-Ar).

To Gilbert Monell Hitchcock

My dear Senator: [The White House] 11 July, 1918

After your call the other day, I made a point of having a talk with the Secretary of State about the bill[1] you were kind enough to submit for my opinion with regard to the recognition of the independence of Poland. I found that the Secretary had the same judgment that I had about the matter, namely, that while the passage of such a bill would have this very substantial advantage, that it would take all Poles out of the alien enemy class under our existing statutes, it would involve this very serious embarrassment:

The Czecho-Slovaks and the Jugo-Slavs have recently effected, as you know, an organization very similar to and quite as influential as the organization which the Poles have effected, and we are dealing with both. The Poles may be said to represent a definable territory, but the Czecho-Slovaks and the Jugo-Slavs do not. It is not likely that if they followed their own preferences, they would unite in a single state. I should not like in the present circumstances of unrest in the Austrian Empire to throw the least cold water upon the Bohemians and the Slavs to the south of them, and I fear separate action with regard to Poland would have that effect.

Thanking you for seeking my judgment,

Sincerely yours, Woodrow Wilson

TLS (Letterpress Books, WP, DLC).
[1] Unnumbered bill, filed with G. M. Hitchcock to RL, July 5, 1918, TLS (SDR, RG 59, 860c.01/111, DNA).

From Joseph Patrick Tumulty

Memorandum for the President: The White House July 11, 1918.

Senator Curtis, of Kansas, has just telephoned to say, speaking as a friend, though not belonging to the President's party, that there were quite a number of Republican Senators and quite a number of Democratic Senators who were opposed to the adoption of the telegraph and telephone control bill, but that if these Senators were assured that the President thought the passage of this bill was necessary as a war measure, they would vote for its passage without hesitation. When astonishment was expressed to the Senator that there should be any question of this kind in the minds of any Senators, he stated that the President's letter to Representative Pou[1] was not broad enough; that Senator Martin had never read his letter[2] to the Senate, and that Senator Pomerene had never shown his letter[3] to anyone. Senator Curtis stated that he did not feel that it was necessary for him to appear in the matter at all, but thought it was important that the President should, through some Democratic Senator, or in some way, let the Senate know that he regarded the passage of this bill as necessary as a war measure.

Shall a copy of the President's letter to Senator Martin be read to Senator Curtis, with the added statement that the President does regard the passage of this bill as necessary as a war measure?

TL (WP, DLC).
    [1] It is missing.
    [2] WW to T. S. Martin, July 6, 1918.
    [3] WW to A. Pomerene, July 6, 1918.

From Edward Mandell House

Dear Governor: Magnolia, Massachusetts. July 11, 1918.

Thank you for giving me the pleasure of reading Herron's letter. While he overstates the case still there is no denying that there has recently been a great acceleration of the thought and desire for a League of Nations. This thought has crystalized around your name, and I believe you are wise in giving it immediate and thorough consideration.

It is an exceedingly difficult problem to solve in a way to satisfy the hopes of the peoples, and yet satisfy a practical mind. Yet it can be done, because the world will be so weary of war and the thought of it, that it will seize upon any intelligent way out.

I hope to see you solve this difficulty as you did our banking and financial problems. They are not without analogy. In spite of the scepticism of the financial world, panics have been made impossible, and the shadow of impending disaster has been lifted. Now if war can be made impossible, what a glorious culmination of your other accomplishments.

I shall get at the matter immediately, and will send you something for consideration early next week. One of the difficulties to be encountered is the desire of the French not only to have a League of Nations started by the Entente before the war ends, but to exclude the Central Powers afterwards. Lord Grey's recent assertion that a League of Nations would be incomplete without them,[1] has raised a storm in France and only a few socialist papers have commended the idea.   Affectionately yours,   E. M. House

TLS (WP, DLC).
  [1] Grey made this assertion in his pamphlet *The League of Nations* (New York, 1918), p. 8. The work appeared about June 19. *New York Times* and London *Times*, June 20, 1918.

From Russell Cornell Leffingwell,[1] with Enclosure

Dear Mr. President: Washington July 11, 1918.

I have the honor to hand you herewith a letter which the Secretary of the Treasury has today received from the British Ambassador.

Lord Reading states that his attention has been called to the bill now before you in which it is proposed to fix the price of wheat in the United States at $2.40 on the farms as against the present price of $2.20 at the terminals, and makes certain comments upon this bill, which comments he asks the Secretary to lay before you.

I am, my dear Mr. President, with great respect,
                        Faithfully yours,   R C Leffingwell.

  [1] At this time Acting Secretary of the Teasury.

ENCLOSURE

Lord Reading to William Gibbs McAdoo

My dear Mr. Secretary,   Washington 11th July 1918.

My attention has been called to the Bill now before the President in which it is proposed to fix the price of Wheat in the United States at $2.40 on the farms as against the present price of $2.20 at the terminals. I would point out that one effect of this proposal would inevitably be to force the Canadian Government to raise the price in Canada to correspond with the United States price. From the standpoint of finance I am informed that the addition to the price will involve an additional expenditure by the Wheat Export Company of approximately $100,000,000 for purchases from the North American Wheat crop of 1918.

This will involve an addition to the burden of its expenditures in North America which must necessarily involve an increase in the demands to be made on the United States Treasury for financial assistance to my own Government and the other Allied Governments to an aggregate amount equal to the additional cost of all wheat purchased for export to the Allied countries.

Will you be good enough to represent at once to the President the views of my Government with regard to this proposal?

Believe me, my dear Mr. Secretary,

Very sincerely yours,   Reading

TLS (WP, DLC).

From William Bauchop Wilson

My dear Mr. President: Washington July 11, 1918.

I have come to the conclusion that it is not only advisable but necessary to create a corporation to carry out the housing program. I have authorized the creation of such a corporation under the laws of the State of New York, with one thousand shares, no par value. Nine hundred and ninety-eight shares will be registered in my name, one share in the name of Mr. Eidlitz,[1] and one share in the name of Mr. Box,[2] who is the Disbursing Officer, formerly the Disbursing Officer of the Department. The resignations of the Directors will be placed in my hands immediately upon their selection so that absolute control will be maintained over the corporation at all times. Mr. Eidlitz will be made its President.

The two important reasons that have brought me to this conclusion are (1st) the difficulty of management under the direct control of the Government, such as the taking in and paying out of moneys in the dormitories when erected, and the necessity of providing our own fire and police protection, sometimes in units that will not be sufficiently large to warrant such organization, and (2d) at the end of the fiscal year all of the working capital necessary for management purposes would have to be turned back into the Treasury, leaving us entirely dependent upon new appropriations for working capital for the succeeding fiscal year. With a corporation the working capital would be continuous.

I am bringing this to your attention before any of the funds have been transferred to the corporation so that if your judgment is against using a corporation agency, no money need be transferred to it and it can be allowed to die.

Faithfully yours,   W B Wilson

TLS (WP, DLC).

[1] Otto Marc Eidlitz, head of a building construction firm of New York, at this time Director of the Bureau of Industrial Housing and Transportation of the Department of Labor.

[2] George G. Box.

Arthur James Balfour to Lord Reading

[London, July 11, 1918]

No. 4321 From your recent telegrams with regard to intervention in Siberia and military measures at Murmansk it is clear that there is some misunderstanding in the President's mind as to the new position of General Foch.

General Foch is General in Chief of the allied forces other than those of Belgium in France and is entrusted with the strategical direction of military operations and the coordination of action of the Allied armies on the Western Front. His powers of coordination are also extended to the Italian Front. He only becomes General in Chief on the Italian Front if circumstances bring about the presence of allied armies fighting together in the same conditions as in France.

He has not supreme control in other theatres of the war and is only consulted by the Allied Governments in order to ascertain how military measures taken in those theatres would affect the Western Front. Military advisers in these cases are Generals in Command and Chiefs of Staff of the various Governments together with Versailles experts. When therefore General Foch sends his views on intervention in Russia they are confined to Western Front aspect to which constitutionally his opinion is limited. He is not concerned with the broader aspects of matter. In the circumstances his views may be very differently expressed to what they would be had he to deal with the allied military situation in all theatres.

I do not suggest that you should formally communicate these facts to the President indeed to do so might weaken the effect of General Foch's advocacy of Siberian intervention but I think that you ought to be aware of them so that you may be able to dispel any misunderstanding should occasion arise.

I am content however to leave this to your discretion.

T telegram (W. Wiseman Papers, CtY).

A Veto Message

The White House, *12 July, 1918.*

To the House of Representatives: I regret to return without my signature so important a measure as H.R. 9054, entitled "An Act making appropriations for the Department of Agriculture for the fiscal year ending June thirtieth, nineteen hundred and nineteen," but I feel constrained to do so because of my very earnest dissent, from the point of view of principle as well as of wise expediency, from the provision of that part of section 14 which prescribes a uniform minimum price for No. 2 Northern spring wheat of $2.40 per bushel.

I dissent upon principle because I believe that such inelastic legislative price provisions are insusceptible of being administered in a way that will be advantageous either to the producer or to the consumer, establishing as they do arbitrary levels which are quite independent of the normal market conditions, and because I believe that the present method of regulation by conference with all concerned has resulted in the most satisfactory manner, considering the complexity and variety of the subject matter dealt with.

It is evident that the present method of determining the price to be paid for wheat has had the most stimulating effect upon production, the estimated crop of spring wheat for this year exceeding all high records in a very remarkable and gratifying way. By an overwhelming majority of the farmers of the United States the price administratively fixed has been regarded as fair and liberal, and objections to it have come only from those sections of the country where, unfortunately, it has in recent years proved impossible to rely upon climatic conditions to produce a full crop of wheat and where, therefore, many disappointments to the farmer have proved to be unavoidable. Personally, I do not believe that the farmers of the country depend upon the stimulation of price to do their utmost to serve the Nation and the world at this time of crisis by exerting themselves to an extraordinary degree to produce the largest and best crops possible. Their patriotic spirit in this matter has been worthy of all praise and has shown them playing a most admirable and gratifying part in the full mobilization of the resources of the country. To a very greatly increased production of wheat they have added an increased production of almost every other important grain, so that our granaries are likely to overflow, and the anxiety of the nations arrayed against Germany with regard to their food supplies has been relieved.

The administrative method of agreeing upon a fair price has this very great advantage which any element of rigidity would in large part destroy, namely, the advantage of flexibility, of rendering possible at every stage and in the view of every change of experience a readjustment which will be fair alike to producer and consumer.

A fixed minimum price of $2.40 per bushel would, it is estimated, add $2 per barrel to the price of flour; in other words, raise the price of flour from the present price of $10.50 at the mill to $12.50 at the mill, and inasmuch as we are anticipating a crop of approximately 900,000,000 bushels of wheat, this increase would be equivalent to the immense sum of $387,000,000.

Such an increase of the price of wheat in the United States would force a corresponding increase in the price of Canadian wheat. The allied Governments would, of course, be obliged to make all of their purchases at the increased figure, and the whole scale of their financial operations in this country, in which the Government of the United States is directly assisting, would be thereby correspondingly enlarged. The increase would also add very materially to the cost of living, and there would inevitably ensue an increase in the wages paid in practically every industry in the country. These added financial and economic difficulties, affecting practically the whole world, can not, I assume, have been in contemplation by the Congress in passing this legislation.   Woodrow Wilson.

Printed in *Message from the President of the United States Vetoing H.R. 9054* . . . (Washington, 1918).

To Joseph Patrick Tumulty

Dear Tumulty: [The White House, c. July 12, 1918]

You know John Dwyer more intimately than I do and will know how to explain to him how impossible it is for me to do what he asks in this letter.[1] I utterly despise John Wanamaker and could not with any sort of sincerity send such a letter as Dwyer desires, much as I should like to do it for Dwyer's sake.

The President.

TL (WP, DLC).
    [1] Wilson was responding to John P. Dwyer to WW, July 9, 1918, TLS (WP, DLC). Dwyer, editor of the *Philadelphia Record*, had asked that Wilson write Wanamaker "a little note of congratulation" on the occasion of his eightieth birthday on July 11.

From William Procter Gould Harding

Dear Mr. President: Washington July 12, 1918.

Ever since the organization of the War Finance Corporation, the time of the directors has been employed to a large extent, in the consideration of applications from public utility companies for relief. The situation of many of these companies is nothing short of desperate, and the public utility industry as a whole is in a perilous position. No[t] only are bonds issued twenty or thirty years ago approaching maturity, but in many cases short time notes are due which issuing companies have been unable to renew on any terms. The utility companies are operating under rates which were fixed by commissions or prescribed in franchises years ago and which are now entirely inadequate. Some of the stronger concerns have been able to obtain renewals of their obligations by paying ruinous rates of interest, but conditions are daily becoming more acute.

The directors of the War Finance Corporation are advised that about one hundred towns and cities have permitted an increase of rates sufficient to cover the advance in wages, but in a majority of cases no action has been taken by local authorities. In the opinion of the directors of the War Finance Corporation, the only adequate means of relief lies in a centralized authority to advance rates wherever and whenever necessary, for while the Corporation might postpone impending receiverships for the time being by taking over obligations now held by the public, the position of the utility companies would be unchanged as to revenue and solvency, and there would merely be a transfer of obligations from one set of creditors to another. There does not appear to be any reasonable prospect of securing general advances from the various municipalities, and it is not clear that an advance sufficient for the requirements of today would be adequate for the rising costs of the future.

Consequently, the directors of the Corporation have, as a rule, felt obliged to decline applications for assistance on account of the provision in the War Finance Corporation Act requiring adequate security. The Railroad Administration can make advances to the steam lines with more confidence for the reason that it is empowered to advance rates in order to meet rising costs of operation.

In the present circumstances the directors of the War Finance Corporation do not feel that they can relieve the situation in the manner anticipated by the public when the War Finance Corporation Act was passed, and have reached the conclusion that Federal control over utility rates will be necessary to save the utility companies. It may be argued that the public could be served by the operation of these companies under receivers, but fixed charges and operating costs would still have to be provided for, and a large number of receiverships and financing by receivers' certificates would unquestionably be detrimental to the financial situation.

I enclose herewith for your consideration, argument of P. H. Gadsden, Esq., and brief of the War Board of the American Electric Railway Association, relating to the power of the President to fix rates of fare for electric railways;[1] and also an editorial by Honorable William Howard Taft which appeared in the Public Ledger of Philadelphia yesterday.[2]

We respectfully request that you take this matter under advisement, and that in case you should reach the conclusion that you have no power in the premises, that you consider asking Congress to give you the necessary authority. I am informed that the investment in public utilities in the United States aggregates about ten billion dollars, and in view of the extreme urgency of the situation and of the important relation that many of these utilities bear to war industries and to the comfort and welfare of the public, we respectfully request that you give this matter your earnest and immediate consideration.   Respectfully,   W P G Harding

TLS (WP, DLC).
¹ *Argument of P[hilip] H[enry] Gadsden, Esq. and Brief of the War Board of the American Electric Railway Association in the Matter of the Power of the President to Fix Rates of Fare for Electric Railways*, printed pamphlet (WP, DLC).
² It is missing, but it was William H. Taft, "Wages of Street-Car Men and the Rate of Fare," Philadelphia *Public Ledger*, July 11, 1918. Taft said that it was the responsibility of the National War Labor Board to establish fair and just wage scales for street railway employees, regardless of the financial condition of the companies involved. However, he believed that the federal government had to have the power to increase fares for these lines during the war emergency in order to keep them solvent. If President Wilson's legal advisers determined that he did not possess the power to do so under existing law, then Congress should grant him that power at once.

Tasker Howard Bliss to Newton Diehl Baker and Peyton Conway March

Versailles, July 12th [1918]

FOR THE SECRETARY OF WAR AND CHIEF OF STAFF:
Number 148 Confidential.

Paragraph 1. Reference Secretary of War's cable number 68¹ I report as follows. The whole question is a delicate one. Entering upon military plan *mainly* is necessarily a *compromise*. If one of us knows that his Government will not approve he refuses to give his assent. But if we believe that the Allies in general desire us to suggest a plan each of us surrender such of his objections as not radical in order to reach an agreement and we leave the respective governments to indicate modifications of it. Otherwise any allied action here would be impossible.

Paragraph 2. The Murmansk and Archangel plan was such a *compromise*. Prior to July 2d when Sir Eric Geddes presented to the Supreme War Council the view of the British General Poole commanding at Murmansk my attitude toward this plan was as follows. My colleagues have steadily held to the view that sooner or later there would be intervention in Siberia. They have believed that at any moment the attitude of Germany towards Russia might become such that the United States would approve of this intervention. I agreed with them that should such intervention come it was most desirable that the Allies possess a point of support and access to Western Russia that would embarrass the Germans in their effort to check intervention in Siberia and that would eventually permit military supplies to be carried into Russia directly from the West as well as from the East.

Paragraph 3. But I have not taken part in any plan based on the assumption of intervention. The only official information given me from Washington is directly opposed to it. The occupation of the Northern Russian ports as part of a general plan of intervention would require a force large enough to move South and control or threaten railroad communications between West and East. I did not believe this force could be sent in from the outside and kept supplied but would have to be raised in the country from friendly Russians. I and my colleagues therefore agreed upon a small force of at most six and possibly only four battalions distributed among the four Allies, which, with the land and sea forces already there, we believed sufficient to hold the Northern ports during the coming winter. This plan was strongly supported by General Foch and the naval authorities.

Paragraph 4. Under that plan the United States would send one or at most two battalions probably Marines. With this small contribution we would, first, get possession of the large amount of military stores still held at Archangel and which would be of great value to Germans. Second, we would retain access to Russia by the way of Murmansk. From humanitarian view I think this very important. All reports indicate severe famine in Northern Russia this and next year. It may be necessary to send food, medicine, Red Cross assistance generally. This would give opportunity for peaceful American intervention of greatest value to Russia and to Allies. Third, there is incidental advantage that would result from holding the Northern ports *in case* for any reason intervention should be agreed upon. It is assumed that this small force can hold the port until after opening of campaign next year. By that time question of general intervention will certainly have been decided. Should intervention come it will have been a grave mistake to have surrendered the Northern ports if we can possibly hold them.

Paragraph 5. After above plan was submitted General Poole commanding at Murmansk submitted his plan calling for the same total force of between five and six thousand men but including two batteries of artillery and three companies of engineers. He expected this force to be entirely British. British decided they could not send it whereupon Lord Milner cabled Lord Reading his request for the large American contribution indicated in his cable of June 11th. This caused matter to be held up till session of Supreme War Council July 2-4 inclusive. The Prime Minister held that General Poole's plan was in substantial agreement with Joint Note Number 31. My military colleagues did the same. My view was that in any event, since the total force remained the same, General Poole's view as to its composition should be accepted. Without asking the opinion of the military representatives the Prime Ministers agreed upon the resolution asking the United States to contribute three battalions, two batteries of artillery and three companies of engineers. In my cable 143[2] I recommended approval. I did this for the following reasons. Paragraph 4 of your cable 60 dated May 31st[3] indicated that our Government contemplated without expression of disapproval the possibility of military operations from Murmansk Archangel. The last clause of paragraph one of your cablegram 59 dated May 28th[4] says that President is heartily in sympathy with any practical military efforts that can be made at and from Murmansk or Archangel, provided they proceed on the sure sympathy of the Russian people and do not interfere with their political liberty. Murmansk is already in the possession of Allied [Allies] and Archangel partially so. I assume that no military movement from these places to the South can be made if Russians are not sympathetic. I believe that the occupation of the Northern ports would be "practically military effort" which justify the small expedition proposed and the risks involved. If we went into the expedition at all I thought that we might contribute the force asked of us provided my government was satisfied with British declaration that it could contribute nothing further.

Paragraph 6. Your 68 asks for a full expression of my "personal view, military and otherwise, on the subject." My military view is above. My personal view is that there will be growing friction over the question of these expeditions large and small unless our government makes known to its allies a definite policy to which it will adhere in our military efforts. It seems to me that there are evidences that our Allies want the United States to commit itself to expeditions to various places where after the war they alone will have any special interests. It is very possible that you may have requests to participate in the Macedonian adventure, although I have communicated to my colleagues the decision of my government on this subject as given in second paragraph of your 66 dated July 1st.[5] I often hear it said by political men that they look to the United States to settle the Balkan question after the war. General Radcliffe,[6] Chief of British Mission with the Italian Army, called on me yesterday representing urgent request of Italian General Staff that we send to *Italy* at least three complete divisions. I told him I had nothing to say on that subject. We must fight somewhere and we originally selected France and at the latters request. My view is that, looking to the future, we ought to keep our army as intact as possible on lines we originally took. It would then be obvious that our sole object is to defeat Germany and we are not tying ourselves up with Allies who have many and different objects in view after defeat of Germany. I think it would be well for our Government to announce to its allies some such *military policy* as the following. First that we are sending our army to France because that is the only place where we can feed and clothe and supply it as we wish with any certainty. Second, that in case our allies find it desirable to send expeditions to various places and which are expeditions that we would not send on our own volition, they should take their own troops and allow ours to replace them in France. In the case of any expedition to Russia I have assumed that our Government desire it to be really an inter-allied one and that therefore it would take its part. But in view of the loan we are now making of troops to England we are warranted in demanding that a British force at least equal to our own should go on any expedition to Murmansk and Archangel. French battalion is ready to sail and Italian battalion is preparing. There will be undercurrents of resentment if we take no part. Moreover refusal on our part will decidedly add to chances of failure of expedition. On the whole I think that we should be represented but only by our fair part.

Bliss

TC telegram (WDR, RG 407, World War I Cablegrams, DNA).
  [1] That is, NDB to T. H. Bliss, July 9, 1918.
  [2] Printed as an Enclosure with NDB to WW, July 6, 1918.
  [3] That is, NDB to T. H. Bliss, May 31, 1918.
  [4] Printed as Enclosure II with NDB to WW, May 28, 1918.
  [5] That is, NDB to T. H. Bliss, July 1, 1918.
  [6] Brig. Gen. Charles Delme-Radcliffe.

Lord Reading to David Lloyd George

[New York] July 12, 1918.

Please deliver following message from LORD READING to KERR for PRIME MINISTER only: It is personal and most secret. (Begins):

(A). F. O. Cable No. 4287 announcing that GENERAL KNOX[1] may visit Washington en route for Vladivostock prompts me to make a few further observations for your personal information on the attitude of the PRESIDENT and the public here generally regarding RUSSIA.

(B). The overthrow of the CZAR and establishment of a republic was welcomed with the utmost enthusiasm in America. The sympathy and hope for the new republic was, I believe, far stronger and more genuine here than in Europe. Ever since the question of intervention was first discussed Americans have feared that the interventionist movement would be controlled by friends of the old Imperial regime and, however disguised, intervention would eventually prove to be a reactionary weapon and an anti-republican influence. Further, the President is apprehensive lest any intervention should be converted into an anti-Soviet movement and an interference with the right of Russians to choose their own form of government.

Americans have observed that some of the strongest supporters of intervention have been men with conservative views and some of its strongest opponents the more advanced liberals.

I do not know what military advantage there may be in sending GENERAL KNOX to SIBERIA, but there is an impression here that he has always been against the revolution, and if this is so he would be likely to gather round him in Russia ex-imperial officers and supporters, and this would give the British part of the expedition a reactionary appearance.

I would suggest that, in addition to any military officers, you should also send a labour or socialist delegation headed by some prominent labour leader. I think this would have a good effect in Russia, but I am quite certain it would have a most excellent effect here and be in itself an answer to much of the present doubt and criticism. We should take care to reassure opinion here in order to carry the President with us in any further movement that may become necessary. At present his intention is to help the CZECHO-SLOVAKS, but, nevertheless, as I read his mind it is still opposed to intervention and somewhat apprehensive lest the step he is now willing to take should lead him into a much more extended policy. It is for this reason I think it is important to give a liberal turn to our assistance to Russia. Of course, we should inform and consult him before sending such a delegation. The very proposal would, I believe, be helpful.   R.

T telegram (W. Wiseman Papers, CtY).
¹ Maj. Gen. Alfred William Fortescue Knox, Military Attaché in Petrograd, 1911-1918; chief of the British Military Mission to Siberia, 1918-1920.

To James Hamilton Lewis

My dear Senator: [The White House] 13 July, 1918

I have heard with concern that you thought of not accepting a renomination for the Senate and undertaking a campaign. I hope sincerely that if that has been your inclination, you will reconsider your judgment in the matter and undertake the race. We are counting upon you to put your usual spirit and energy into a campaign which I am sure will assist to make the issues clear in Illinois.

Cordially and sincerely yours,   Woodrow Wilson

TLS (Letterpress Books, WP, DLC).

From William Sowden Sims

My dear Mr. President: London, S.W.1 13 July 1918

I beg to acknowledge receipt of your letter of 31 May, introducing Mr. Samuel G. Blythe.[1]

As you say, Mr. Blythe needs no introduction at all, as I know him for the delightful writer he is. I have read many of his articles on various subjects, and I am very glad indeed that a man of his prominence in this respect has consented to come over here and give the American people something of our atmosphere and activities.

We have until recently rather felt that the American people did not receive sufficient information as to the Navy's various activities in Europe.

This was having its effect upon the personnel of the forces, as all letters were carefully censored and both officers and men were debarred from mentioning anything but purely personal matters. This left the impression that their strenuous work was not appreciated as it should be. The recent excellent accounts in the press have removed this impression.

The trouble was largely due to the reticence of the British naval authorities, whose practice has been not to allow anything to be published about what is popularly called over here "The Silent Service." There was no logic behind it.

In fact it was, in my opinion, entirely mistaken psychology, and it was only after patient explanation of the difference in the conditions over here and at home that the British Censors were finally induced to allow a certain amount of information about our activities to be sent over to America and published in our press.

This has been successfully done by a number of capable writers. One of the most successful of these was Mr. Ralph Payne, who has written a number of articles for the "Saturday Evening Post" and other publications. He has recently published a book which is a summary of his recent articles,[2] and this gives a very good picture, not so much as to what the Navy is actually doing, as of the spirit which actuates all of our naval forces.

We realize of course that there is no real naval war going on on this side. The enemy's fleet remains "contained" and his activities are confined to the submarine, and to certain mining and counter-mining operations. The submarine is not making war on our military vessels, but, on the contrary, avoids them and devotes his attention to the destruction of commerce. This places the Navy in the position of defenders of the lines of communication of the Army. This is completely understood between General Pershing and myself, and we are working together, not only in the most complete co-operation but in the most complete harmony and sympathy.

I have appointed a naval officer from my force as a member of General Pershing's Staff so as to keep us intimately in touch with each other. By this and other means we have been able to establish the best possible relations between all branches of the Army and the Navy on this side. While it might naturally be supposed that this was a foregone conclusion, I can assure you that the experience is pretty nearly unique in combined warfare. It is really astonishing how much antagonism, not to say bitterness, has arisen from time to time between the naval and military forces of the same countries, during this distressing War.

As for the differences that have arisen between Allies, you doubtless know much more about that than I do. As an indication of this, one of the most distinguished of the Allied Generals made the facetious remark to me the other day, in answer to the usual enquiry as to when the war will end: "I don't know when this particular war will end, but after it is finished, it is quite likely that the Allies will have to fight each other." Though the remark was a facetious one, still it is an indication of the frictions that have arisen.

Insofar as our Navy is concerned, I am glad to be able to state that there has not at any time been the slightest difficulty of any kind in co-operating with the principal Allied navies. This is due to the fact that we recognized, and established as an inflexible policy from the first, that there should be in all of the various areas absolute unity of command, similar to that which was established on the Western Front when the necessity became imperative.

I am also glad to say that we now believe that we have the submarine campaign well in hand. It will doubtless be continued to the end, and we will doubtless suffer further more or less serious losses, but it is perfectly apparent that the means of offence are gradually being improved, and the number of anti-submarine vessels increased, while the submarines are decreasing in number and in efficiency, so that there would appear no possibility of the enemy ever succeeding in destroying enough commerce to bring the Allies to terms.

Within the last few weeks the morale of all of our forces over here and the morale of all the Allies has been tremendously "bucked up." This happy result was brought about by the success of the Italians against the Austrians, and later by the demonstration on the Western Front that the American soldiers are just as good as those of any of the Allies.

This is not only true of the soldiers, but also of our splendid body of American marines. It would be impossible to exaggerate the enthusiasm of French military men over the fighting qualities of our marines. Major Bacon[3] confirms this opinion. They have always been some of the very best American troops; and, in fact, marines of all countries are usually the best troops a country has, on account of the peculiar advantages to the soldier of a certain amount of a sailor's training.

Another, and very important reason for the improvement in the morale of the people and armies of our Allies is the authoritative announcement you have made of the number of troops that has been sent over each month during the past year. This has had an effect upon the French which could hardly be exaggerated. The importance of this was not only the fact that there are a million American troops in France, but the equally, if not more, important fact that they are now coming over at the rate of about a quarter of a million a month.

So impressive has this been, that I have heard competent military men state already that they do not believe that Germany will persist in the drive on the Western Front, knowing that such a further drive would cost at least 200,000 men, and that success would be very doubtful; and that the enemy will "dig in" and attempt to arrange a peace. At all events, it would appear that the spirit of the forces engaged on our side is such that the enemy cannot win.

I am, Sir,   Very respectfully,   Wm S Sims

TLS (WP, DLC).
[1] WW to W. S. Sims, May 31, 1918, TLS (Letterpress Books, WP, DLC).
[2] Ralph Delahaye Paine, *The Fighting Fleets: Five Months of Active Service with the American Destroyers and Their Allies in the War Zone* (Boston and New York, 1918).
[3] That is, Robert Bacon, at this time chief of the American Military Mission at British General Headquarters in France.

From Bernard Mannes Baruch

My dear Mr. President: Washington July 13, 1918.

As Russia's greatest enemy, in my opinion, is going to be hunger and privation, might I suggest (and I do so most hesitatingly) that Mr. Hoover should head the mission. If anything at all has trickled into their minds from the outside world, the Russians will realize in sending him you are sending someone to help, not to conquer.

May I ask if you have come to any decision regarding Mr. Jesse Jones whom I am very anxious to have placed on the Price Fixing Committee, which needs strengthening?

Very sincerely yours,   Bernard M Baruch

TLS (WP, DLC).

Two Letters from Newton Diehl Baker

Dear Mr. President: Washington. July 14, 1918.

The following extract from a recent cable from General Pershing gives the formal report of a German Intelligence Officer at the headquarters of the Seventh German Army, under date of June 17, 1918. The document was recently captured by us in France. You may be interested to read the estimate of this German officer of the American forces.[1]   Respectfully yours,   Newton D. Baker

TLS (N. D. Baker Papers, DLC).

[1] J. J. Pershing to H. P. McCain, July 12, 1918, T telegram (N. D. Baker Papers, DLC). The report of the German intelligence officer, a Lt. von Berg, was based largely on interviews with American prisoners of war. While noting that the American soldiers had little interest in, or knowledge of, the details of military lore, he praised highly their physical condition, courage, and high morale. They had fought well and seemed to take it for granted that they had come to Europe to defend their country.

Dear Mr. President: Washington. July 14, 1918.

Emmett Scott (former secretary to Booker Washington) who is assisting me at the War Department in dealing with questions affecting negroes in the military service, sent you some days ago a report on the meeting of negro editors,[1] and I think is anxious to have an acknowledgment of the report from you, in order that it may appear in the colored press and show the colored people of the country that this important conference did actually come to your attention.

I venture to submit a note of acknowledgment for your signature, if it meets with your approval.[2]

Respectfully yours,   Newton D. Baker

TLS (WP, DLC).

[1] It is printed as an Enclosure with G. Creel to WW, July 5, 1918.

[2] Baker's draft is missing; however, see WW to E. J. Scott, July 31, 1918.

From Edward Mandell House

Dear Governor: Magnolia, Massachusetts. July 14, 1918.

I have spent yesterday and today in formulating a draft of a Convention for a League of Nations.

I will not send it to you until Monday or Tuesday for I would like a day or two to lapse before reading it over and making any corrections which seem pertinent. A memorandum will also be attached explaining the reason for each article where it is not obvious.

The draft was written without reference to the British Covenant which you sent. When finished the two were compared and several of the Articles of the British were incorporated as a whole. In my opinion the British document would not at all meet the requirements of the situation. The reason I wrote the draft without reference to the British was to keep from getting entangled with their plan.

If you approve of the draft I believe it would be wise for you to take some means of giving it to the world and as quickly as possible in order to let thought crystalize around your plan instead of some other. It would be better, I think, to do this without consulatation [consultation] with any foreign government and so state in your announcement. If you take it up with the British or French there will be heart-burnings if the others are not brought into it.

It is written with a view of not hurting the sensibilities of any nation either in the Entente or the Central Powers. It is also written with a view that the League might be confined to the Great Powers, giving the smaller powers every benefit that may be derived therefrom. If the smaller nations are taken in, the question of equal voting power is an almost insurmountable obstacle. Several of the smaller nations have indicated a willingness to come into a League of Nations only upon condition that the voting power of each country shall be the same—notably Switzerland.

If this were agreed upon, Mexico and the Central American States could out-vote Germany, England, France, Italy, Japan and the United States and yet in the enforcement of peace, or of any of the decrees of the League of Nations, they would not only be impotent but unwilling to share the responsibilities.

These smaller nations might become neutralized as Belgium and Switzerland were, with representation without voting power, just as our Territories have had representation in Congress without votes.

I believe you will find the draft a basis of a practical working arrangement.   Affectionately yours,   E. M. House

TLS (WP, DLC).

Two Letters to Frank Lyon Polk

My dear Mr. Counselor,   The White House. 15 July, 1918.

Please remind me what the matter was which Mr. Stovell mentioned in his 3884, July fifth.[1] Herron has been so fine that I should like to give him all the guidance or advice he asks for.

Faithfully Yours,   W.W.

WWTLI (WP, DLC).
[1] Printed as an Enclosure with WW to RL, July 8, 1918 (third letter of that date).

My dear Mr. Counselor,   The White House. 15 July, 1918.

I do not understand or like the way in which the governments mentioned are acting independently of us in this matter,[1] but I think that perhaps it would be all right to advise Reinsch not to object, while not cooperating where his cooperation is apparently not asked. It is my clear judgment, however, that the Chinesh [Chinese] Government should be much more than "informed" about this business. Their acquiescence and approval should be sought. Do you not think so?   Faithfully Yours,   W.W.

WWTLI (SDR, RG 59, 861.00/2241, DNA).
[1] Wilson was responding to RL to WW, July 11, 1918, TLS, enclosing J. V. A. MacMurray to RL, July 9, 1918, T telegram, both in SDR, RG 59, 861.00/2241, DNA. MacMurray reported that the French, British, and Japanese Ministers, considering it imperative to transfer Czech forces from Vladivostok to assist Czechs in western Siberia, were requesting the Russian legation in Peking to arrange with the Russian railway authorities at Harbin for the transportation of these troops by the Chinese Eastern Railway. Upon receiving the expected favorable reply, they proposed "simply to inform the Chinese Government" that these forces were to pass through Manchuria. In the absence of instructions, MacMurray continued, he had not felt warranted in associating himself with these "demarches which contemplate the probability of conflict with Bolshevik forces near Chita and which might therefore be considered as an act of intervention." He requested instructions as to the attitude he should take in regard to this and other movements of the Czech forces in Siberia. Lansing's covering letter commented as follows: "This seems an opportunity to bring the Chinese Government into participation in aiding the Czecho-Slovaks, if it seems advisable. Should we send instructions to our Chargé at Peking to renew the request already made upon the Chinese Government?"

To Newton Diehl Baker, with Enclosure

My dear Baker: [The White House] 15 July, 1918

I don't need to tell you who Upton Sinclair is, and I am handing on this letter of his which is summarized in the attached slip of paper, in order to ask whether you think his idea is a practicable one or not.

Cordially and faithfully yours,   [Woodrow Wilson]

CCL (WP, DLC).

ENCLOSURE

From Upton Beall Sinclair

My Dear President Wilson: [Pasadena, Cal.] July 9, 1918.

You have recently put a white mark to your credit by certain humane regulations in the matter of conscientious objectors. I take the liberty of suggesting another practicable measure which would strengthen the regard in which you are held by liberals.

A few days ago I visited in prison a clergyman who is serving a long term for utterances in opposition to war. I do not share this gentleman's views, but his whole life proves his sincerity. He is a scholar, a man of fine sensibility, who will be valuable in the time of reconstruction which is coming. He is now confined in a miserable city jail, without adequate ventilation, without opportunity for exercise, and under the control of men who obtained their appointment through political "pull." I presume you know our American prison system, and will agree that it is not a credit to the country.

We have not been accustomed in America to recognize political prisoners. But this man is truly a political prisoner, and we should not be behind the nations of Western Europe in recognizing the status of such. Let me say that I am not referring to those who have committed acts of violence, or who have plotted with the enemy; I am referring to those who, whether because of Religion or Socialism, have felt it their duty to speak against war. These men are invariably men of honor, whose word could be taken, and so it is not necessary to shut them up behind stone and steel as if they were animals.

What I suggest is that you should order these prisoners sent to a separate place of confinement, constructed on the plan of a modern prison farm colony. No such place exists at present, but it could be constructed by the prisoners' own labor in some locality where the materials are at hand. My idea is that each prisoner should be invited to give his word that he would make no attempt to escape, or to engage in propaganda; having given this pledge, he should be taken to the site of the colony, and put to work at building his own home and raising his own food.

The advantage to the prisoner would be that he would have healthful work in the open and under decent conditions. The advantages to the government would be many. First and foremost, its moral prestige would be increased, and the bitterness of those radicals and opponents of the war who are not yet in jail would be reduced. Second, the bitterness of the prisoners themselves would be lessened; and the case of Russia at present should teach our propertied classes that this is a desirable thing. Third, the prisoners would become self-sustaining, instead of being, as they are at present, a charge upon county, state or nation. There must be several thousand of them at the present time, and many are kept in entire idleness, with able-bodied men withheld from war-work to guard and feed them. Finally, the government would accomplish its purpose of keeping the prisoners from engaging in propaganda. At present they are carrying on propaganda among their fellow-prisoners, and also they are occasionally smuggling it outside, as I positively know. For these many reasons I venture to hope that you will give consideration to this plan.

With sincere esteem,   Upton Sinclair.

Printed circular (U. Sinclair Papers, InU).

To Bernard Mannes Baruch

Dear Baruch: The White House 15 July, 1918

I agree with you in your estimate of Hoover, but I cannot without dislocating some of the most important things we are handling spare him from his present functions.

I am sorry to say that I can't come to a definite conclusion about Jones yet, because my list in the other matter isn't made up and I am not sure that I shall not need him.

Cordially and sincerely yours,   Woodrow Wilson

TLS (B. M. Baruch Papers, NjP).

To William Procter Gould Harding

My dear Governor Harding: [The White House] 15 July, 1918

I am deeply concerned about the financing of the public utility concerns and am taking pleasure today in complying with your request[1] that I ask the Attorney General for an opinion with regard to the assistance the War Finance Corporation could render the proposed public utilities.

Cordially and sincerely yours,   Woodrow Wilson

TLS (Letterpress Books, WP, DLC).
[1] See W. P. G. Harding to WW, July 12, 1918.

To Thomas Watt Gregory

My dear Gregory: [The White House] 15 July, 1918

Here is a matter which has caused all of us the greatest concern and I would be very much obliged if you would read carefully the enclosed letter of Governor Harding of the Federal Reserve Board and let me know what your opinion is with regard to the question which he raises as to what the War Finance Corporation is legally able to do in assisting the public utilities financing company which is here, I think very sensibly, proposed.

Cordially and faithfully yours,   Woodrow Wilson[1]

TLS (Letterpress Books, WP, DLC).
    [1] The reply to this letter is G. Carroll Todd to WW, July 27, 1918, TLS (WP, DLC). Todd, then the Acting Attorney General, restricted his opinion solely to the question of whether the limitations imposed by Section 10 of the War Finance Corporation Act of April 5, 1918 (40 *Statutes at Large* 506), applied to advances made by the War Finance Corporation to banks, bankers, or trust companies under the authority of Section 7 of that act. Todd concluded that the limitation of aggregate advances to any corporation to 10 per cent of the capital stock of the corporation did apply to banks, bankers, and trust companies. There was no direct mention in his opinion of how this ruling might apply to the financing of public utilities. Wilson forwarded a copy of this opinion to Harding without comment in WW to W. P. G. Harding, July 29, 1918, TLS (Letterpress Books, WP, DLC).

To George Creel

My dear Creel: [The White House] 15 July, 1918

I would like to express to the gentlemen who signed this telegram[1] my warm appreciation of their message, but I don't know where to get at them. If you do know, will you not be kind enough to tell them how sincerely I appreciated it and how happy I am to have been able to express to them my sincere friendship for Mexico and to help win their friendship for this great country which desires nothing more than to be the best possible neighbor.

Cordially and sincerely yours,   Woodrow Wilson

TLS (Letterpress Books, WP, DLC).
    [1] It is missing in both WP, DLC, and the G. Creel Papers, DLC.

To Harry Augustus Garfield

My dear Garfield: The White House 15 July, 1918

I suppose, of course, the enclosed is not true,[1] but I thought perhaps it would be useful to tell you that I have not the least confidence in George W. Perkins and would think it a mistake for him to be associated with the administration in any way. I dare say you have the same instinct about him.

Cordially and sincerely yours,   Woodrow Wilson

TLS (H. A. Garfield Papers, DLC).
[1] "Perkins Urged for Fuel Administrator," undated clipping from New York *Sun* (H. A. Garfield Papers, DLC). This news report stated that Perkins would become the New York State Fuel Administrator to succeed Albert Henry Wiggin, who had resigned.

From George Creel, with Enclosure

My dear Mr. President: Washington, D. C. July 15, 1918.

The attached article, from Norman Angell, may or may not be interesting to you.

Leaving aside the accepted generalities concerned in his paper the logic of it seems to be the putting into effect at once of the League of Nations, starting with those nations now combined against the Central Powers.

This is my interpretation of the various phrases, which he uses about making "unification effective," "coming to peace table a united and cohesive league," "political reality at the settlement," etc.

This idea has been suggested within the past two weeks, if I recall correctly, by Lord Curzon, in England, and by Bourgeouis[1] in France. The immediate criticism was that it was only another way of stating the fact that two groups of nations would stand for different purposes and would come to the peace table much the same as they now are, as warring organizations. The attempt to create the League of Nations before the end of the war in any concrete way and have it different in membership and evidently different in spirit would depend upon bringing in the smaller nations now neutral, such as Holland, the Scandinavian countries and Spain. The ability to do that would depend wholly upon their faith primarily in your leadership, as would the participation of these now associated with us in the war.

The whole line of Mr. Angell's argumentation is to bring such a policy in as an integral part of "the attainment of our military ends." In my opinion that would be the difficulty of the matter from the standpoint of a neutral nation, who would immediately see it from that angle.

The thing may not be impossible if one accepts his psychology of success in these matters, i.e., belief in them is to half accomplish them. It is good psychology but our believing in them is not equivalent to the very vital point which is having the neutrals and associated powers believe in them.

It seems to me that certain things must be accomplished before we pass as readily as Mr. Angell has from existing conditions to the desirable state where "the combined strength of a society is behind the rule of law, which insured the production of each," etc.

Taking it into consideration, I have not deemed it wise to touch the matter at all, and shall not do so unless you think my refusal unwise.   Respectfully,   George Creel

TLS (WP, DLC).
¹ Léon-Victor-Auguste Bourgeois.

E   N   C   L   O   S   U   R   E

THE POLITICAL CONDITION OF MILITARY SUCCESS
The Obligations of intellectual leadership during the war.¹

America is fighting for a new international condition, or policy, the outlines of which have been indicated by the President: one that will make the world safe for democracy. Perhaps the feelings of most Americans towards that policy is that an understanding of its nature, and the respects in which it differs from policies that have governed international relations in the past, can well be left until after the war; that it has nothing to do with the actual waging of the war or the attainment of our military ends.

But that is a profound error.

The President's international policy is not only our ultimate aim in the war; its application during the war to our relations with our Allies, is a condition of our military success. And no policy can be successfully carried out by a democracy, if it is likely at any moment to encounter misunderstanding and opposition.

In what way does the President's policy affect the actual waging of the war? Is not our military success just a matter of efficient military force—men, munitions, ships, well-planned battles? And in what way can public opinion affect foreign policy? Is not the public fully prepared to trust the President; and stand behind him in any policy that he may announce?

Those questions can be answered very simply.

In the case of a war fought by a large alliance, made up of a number of nations, different in character and outlook, success does not depend merely upon the material factors of men and munitions,

¹ N. Angell to G. Creel, March 3 [1918], TCL (WP, DLC), indicates that this "memorandum," as Angell called it, was written just prior to that date at Creel's request. The article or memorandum was apparently not published in the form printed here. However, Angell soon published a book, *The Political Conditions of Allied Success: A Plea for the Protective Union of the Democracies* (New York and London, 1918), which greatly expanded on many of the ideas contained herein. The preface of the book is dated "May, 1918."

upon the individual strength of each state, but also upon the capacity of these states to act together for a common purpose. If one member of the Alliance has one object, and another a different one, so that they do not create a "single front," or so that disagreement sets in, it is obvious that an enemy group, with inferior forces, but united purpose, may well have the military advantage. It is, in other words, obvious that the policies and ultimate aims of the members of an alliance have everything to do with its unity and permanence. If the aims of the members are at variance, it will go to pieces. And where public opinion is ill-informed, there is always a danger that political parties or persons within one nation may, with the very best intentions, make demands or set up movements that will bring it into conflict with other members of the Alliance.

It is clear therefore that bad civilian politics can add enormously to the soldier's burden; may indeed, make his task impossible.

The propositions here indicated might be summarised thus:

The military success of the Allies depends upon certain political factors—as, for instance, upon the Unity of the Alliance, the absence of such misunderstanding or internal disintegration as that which has put Russia out of the war—as well as upon the more material elements, such as men and munitions to which attention is more readily give[n].

Those non-military factors, which are indispensable to military success, depend upon good management by the civilian rulers, the politicians.

Effective civilian rule depends upon civilian public opinion. It is civilian opinion alone which, for instance, in Europe deposes one government, like that of Mr. Asquith, in favor of another, like that of Mr. Lloyd George. If that change was wise it must greatly have facilitated the task of the soldier, if unwise greatly have hindered it.

Now, stated in that form those propositions are almost truisms. Yet they run directly counter to the position that the public can have nothing to do with policy, or that policy has nothing to do with military success.

The grave fact in the history of the war is that public opinion in some of the Allied countries, has at some junctures, with the best intentions in the world, been largely responsible for errors of policy which have added enormously to the military difficulties. Internal upheavals, changes of policies and cabinets, sudden losses of confidence, errors in relations with Allies, have occurred, sometimes because sincerely patriotic people have overlooked the fact that intensity of feeling and emotion—however good of themselves— cannot stand for sound political judgement. There are situations in life in which sheer emotional fervour is the one thing necessary to carry one through to safety; but there are others—as when someone cries "fire" in a crowded theatre—when our emotional instinct not only will not furnish any sure guide as to the right thing to do, but will beyond doubt destroy us if we obey it. The great need in such circumstances is to "keep our heads"; there must be a certain moral discipline. Without a certain atmosphere of public opinion, a capacity for sane and sound judgement sufficient to enable us to judge between good and bad policy, the soldier cannot bring us victory, whatever his efficiency and sacrifice.

The President hinted the other day[2] that if the policy of the Allies towards Russia on the morrow of the Revolution had been somewhat different, if they had made a clear declaration of revised aims, as Kerensky desired, Bolshevik and German forces would not have been able to trade on Russian suspicion as they did, Kerensky might still be in power, and Russia still a part of the Alliance, if not fighting, at least not directly under enemy influence. Suppose this implication of the President is sound. The case furnishes a striking illustration of the fashion in which civilian policy may have vast military consequences, consequences measured in terms of whole armies and years of war; of the way in which civilian policy may add enormously to the soldier's burden, or lighten it. No increase of merely military preparedness would have prevented this disaster; it might have made it worse. If the material now ready for shipment had reached Russia, we might be faced by the possibility of its actually being used against us. For victory depends not alone upon guns and munitions, but upon the direction in which the guns shoot. And that depends upon policy, which depends mainly upon civilians. We have only to make a few more mistakes like those which may have marked the relations with Russia to find the Alliance going to pieces, during or after the war, and that would give the victory, ultimately, to Germany, however well our soldiers may have done their work.

Why did the Alliance fail to make that statement of aims which, it is reasonable to suppose, might have aided the more moderate Russian element? We now know that, among other causes, certain Italian claims, which not only might have been regareded [regarded] by Russia as "Imperialistic," but which came into conflict with the claims of certain other allies, made such a statement difficult. This is no reflection whatever upon Italy, for she made those

---

[2] The Editors have found no written comment of this nature by Wilson. There is no record of a meeting between Wilson and Angell at this time. Wilson's comment was probably repeated to Angell by some mutual acquaintance. Angell was clearly convinced of its authenticity, for he repeated it in somewhat altered wording in *ibid.*, p. 148.

claims from motives which must come first with every nation—motives of national self-preservation. In a world in which nations can only depend upon their own strength for security, a world of shifting alliances, and armament competition, and unstable balance of power, she had to look to her future strength, and so had to command the Adriatic, and so needed the Dalmatian Coast, Islands in the Aegean, stations in Asia Minor, even though all that did collide with the aspirations of Greece and Serbia.

But suppose the alliance had been able to say to Italy: "The old Europe of shifting alliances and international anarchy, of struggle for power one against the other, is not going to be re-established after this war. We really are going to create this League of Nations that President Wilson talks about. You do not need to command the Adriatic because our whole naval force will be available for your defense." If they had been able to say that, Italy would not have made, and Italian public opinion sanctioned, claims that threatened the solidity of the Alliance, and have actually resulted in making a great breach in it.

Why could not the Allies make that proposal in terns [terms] of the League of Nations? Because there was no assurance in 1915 that the policy of the League of Nations would become a reality. Nobody had any particular belief in it. The general attitude was: "We hope of course that it may come one day. We would welcome it. But there is no certainty of it, and so we cannot trust our future security to it. We must meantime trust to the more material things—territory and strategic position. We are sorry if our claims collide with others, or do violence to the principle of nationality, but our own safety must come first." Such an attitude at critical junctures has been typical in the past in some degree of all European states. It has marked in some degree the policy of Japan. And the divergent claims, or conflicts of policy usually thus set up, create an atmosphere of rivalry and suspicion, which undermines any real belief in the future likelihood of a League of Nation[s.] And that lack of belief in turn causes states to resort to the scramble for individual power, which again, stands in the way of the creation of the League. Thus is the fatal vicious circle established and maintained.

Unless it can be broken, we shall come to the Peace Table with the seeds of disintegration deeply embedded in the Alliance, even if there should be no further disintegration during the war.

We see by this also why the territorial settlements cannot be made satisfactorily until we have won general faith in a League of Nations, until that policy has become a political reality. If its future is uncertain, every state in the position of Italy or Japan will say: "Since we cannot depend on the Society of Nations we must assure our safety and economic opportunity by our own strength: strategic frontiers, access to the sea, possession of sources of raw material." So long as that is the position aspirations are bound to come into conflict. The respective policies of Czarist Russia, France, Italy, Serbia, Roumania and Japan have all been twisted in varying degrees by the hard necessities of the difficult choice of this dilemma. The political and economic security of one creates the insecurity of another.

Perhaps we shall realise how nearly the question of policy touches our success if we put the foregoing truths into an extended proposition thus:

The survival of the Western democracies through the effective use of their force, depends upon their being able to act as a unit, and remain a unit after the war; upon, that is, a degree of workable internationalism. That unity we have not attained completely, even for the purposes of the war, because we have refused to recognise its necessary conditions.

If we scattered democracies, a heterogenious group of five, or ten or fifteen different nations, are to use our power effectively against a group of states geographically contiguous, and unified politically and militarily by the predominant power of one member, we must achieve a unification equally effective. In our case that can only come through the voluntary co-operation of equals—a democratic internationalism. That unity is impossible on the basis of the old policies, the European statecraft of the past. For that assumes a condition of the world in which each state must look for its national security to its own isolated strength; and such assumption compels each member, as a measure of national self-preservation, and so justifiably, to take precautions against drifting into a position of inferior power, compels it that is, to enter into a competition for the sources of strength—territory and strategic position. Such a condition will inevitably, in the case of any considerable alliance, produce a situation in which some of its members will be brought into conflict by claims for the same territory. In the end, that will inevitably disrupt the Alliance. Just that thing has already occurred, even during the war, within our own Alliance. The process is the story of Europe since the establishment of the sovereign state.

For this relation between internationalism and democracy on the one side, and autocracy and territorial consolidation in disregard of nationality on the other, is organic, not accidental. The great experiment of political freedom, the "self-determination of peoples," the independence of separate national groups implies necessarily the growth of separated tendencies which, if unchecked by a voluntary and self-imposed discipline of an international order, will make co-operation, or a common centralised direction even for self-protection, impossible. Contrarywise, autocracy grows by the strength of a central power, and is able to impose common action and centralised direction upon the different national units over which it has succe[e]ded in asserting dominion (sometimes historically just because the smaller units were incapable of self-directing co-operation and were split by irreconcilable differences). The enemy, by reason of the very circumstances of his historical development and the philosophy which his experiment (as against ours) involves, has less need than ourselves of a policy which will unify many states widely separated in character (and, incidentally, in geographical distance) and ensure their free co-operation to a common end. As already noted, the special position, geographical, economical, historical, and political of one state in the enemy alliance, ensures a centralised direction by virtue of power and authority, and enables the group to dispense with that voluntary, democratic internationalism which alone will enable the western group to hold its own.

The price of the preservation of nationality is a workable internationalism. If this latter is not possible then the smaller nationalities are doomed. Thus, though internationalism may not be in the case of every member of the Alliance, the object of the war, it is the condition of its success.

This alternative to the older statecraft, the alternative for which President Wilson stands, is based upon what is, in fact, the first law of life for any Society—whether of persons within a state, or of States within an Alliance, or League—namely, that the security of each is assured by the strength of the whole. To put the combined strength of a Society behind the rule or law which ensures the orotection [protection] of each (which Mr. Wilson has called the Community of Power) is the only method of preventing a condition which compels the units to enter into competition one with another for individual power—efforts which could only give security if each unit could be stronger than any of the others—a mathematical absurdity.

But Mr. Wilson's policy can only become operative as the result of an "act of faith"—the conviction, that is, on the part of statesmen and public that the risks involved in the newer policy are less than those involved in the old. So long as nations do not believe in the possibility or reliability of a new system, they will fall back upon covert or overt competition for preponderant power, territory and strategic position which of itself creates that disruptive rivalry, anarchy, and suspicion which destroys reliance upon agreement. Each by his own act in such a case, creates the very conditions which he urges as justification for his conduct. The one thing which alone will enable us to break the vicious circle is the general conviction that, though the proposed system may fail, the old certainly will. Upon the moral courage to act on that faith depends the survival of the Western Democracies.

The ultimate fact in our problem therefore is a moral one. The chief obstacles to the abolition of the old disintegrating policy and the success of the new, are not mainly physical, like difficulty of communication over wide distance, (which mechanical develop- ment has in large measure met) but moral and intellectual diffi- culties, the mental habits, opinions and impulses of men, which have not kept pace with the changes wrought by our progress in mechanical contrivance. Our management of matter has altogether outstripped our management of human relationships, of our own minds and natures.

William James, in his essay on "The Will to Believe"[3] has an illustration to enforce the truth here indicated, namely, that very often in political, as in certain other affairs, the one factor necessary to make a policy or method practical, is just the general decision that it is practical. So long as men believe that a thing is impossible, that belief of itself renders the belief true; just as the contrary belief would render the contrary true.

"I am climbing in the Alps," says James, "and have worked myself into such a position that I cannot get back. If I am to save my life I must jump a chasm that confronts me. I engage in a calculation as to whether it can be done, and decide that it can, attempt it with courage and energy and save my life. The fact of saving my life is proof that I was right. But I should have been just as right if I had decided that I could *not* do it. For by virtue of that decision I should either not have made the attempt, or making it, launched myself in a moment of indecision and despair, and have destroyed myself. The fact of my destruction would have been proof positive that my pessimism was justified."

And that is the moral for the Western World at this moment. It may decide that new policies, "new and unprecedented things," cannot be done. In that case the decision will be justified by the event. But the contrary decision, that better policies can be made to produce better results than in the past—that decision too, would be justified by the event.

T MS (WP, DLC).
    [3] William James, "The Will to Believe," *New World*, V (June 1896), 327-47, reprinted in *The Will to Believe, and Other Essays in Popular Philosophy* (New York and London, 1897), pp. 1-31.

From Frank Lyon Polk, with Enclosure

My dear Mr. President: Washington July 15, 1918.

The matter referred to in Mr. Stovall's 3884, July fifth, was of such importance that I thought it wiser not to attempt to make a digest, and I therefore enclose a copy[1] attached to Mr. Stovall's telegram of the eleventh. I suppose there is no harm in keeping the door open, as Herron suggests, but it does not seem probable that any move of any importance could come from Bavaria at this time. Yours faithfully, Frank L Polk

TLS (WP, DLC).
[1] Printed as an Enclosure with WW to RL, July 8, 1918 (third letter of that date).

ENCLOSURE

Pontarlier (Berne) July 11th, 1918

3932. I have received written statement from Herron on matter reported orally, mentioned in my 3884, July fifth. Statement is being forwarded by me.

Herron writes as follows: "May I suggest that you intimate to Washington that if there is anything to say, if the President or the State Department cares to express any wish as to what I, individually and unofficially, may say or may not say, this would need to be done as quickly as possible. I think that Washington might well let me know, for my own personal guidance, whether it is thought wise to keep this Bavarian door open, even though a negative answer or no direct answer at all be given to Bavaria."

While I am not clear what answer, if any, the Department may care to make I consider it advisable to transmit this request.

Stovall

T telegram (WP, DLC).

From Frank Lyon Polk, with Enclosure

My dear Mr. President: Washington July 15, 1918.

In connection with the Siberian situation, I beg to report the French Ambassador called on Saturday afternoon to tell me that he had heard from his Government; that it was quite willing to accept the plan proposed for sending troops to Vladivostok, and would be glad to cooperate with us in every way.

The Japanese Ambassador came in to see me also on Saturday and told me that he had not yet heard from his Government in regard to the proposal of sending troops into Vladivostok. He was very apologetic, explaining that it was a very serious question for his Government and that it would probably take them some little time to consider it. Before leaving, he brought up the subject of [the] high command and intimated that this might be one of the questions his Government was considering. I think if we were disposed to tell him that we had no objection to a Japanese officer being the senior military officer, and therefore in command of the troops, we would hear very shortly that the Japanese Government were willing to cooperate. He mentioned, in the course of the conversation, that he had just heard that the British were sending troops from Hongkong to Vladivostok. He wanted to know whether this in any way affected the situation, and when I told him I did not think so he seemed to be very much relieved.

In connection with the sending of these British troops, I attach a copy of a telegram from Mr. Balfour, which the British Ambassador left with me. You will notice that it was sent on the tenth from London, and is possibly evidence of the fact that the sending of these troops was ordered before they heard of our proposal.

Yours faithfully,   Frank L Polk

TLS (WP, DLC).

E N C L O S U R E

PARAPHRASE OF TELEGRAM FROM MR. BALFOUR TO LORD READING
July 10, 1918.

Czechs at Valdivostok.   BRITISH EMBASSY, WASHINGTON,
July 11, 1918.

Please inform the United States Government of the steps taken by His Majesty's Government and explain that our action has not been adopted with any intention to start intervention but for the sole purposes of ensuring order in Vladivostok, securing the communications of the Czech forces and safeguarding the Allied stores in the City. At the present crisis the greatest importance is attached to all of these objects.

T MS (WP, DLC).

From David John Lewis

My dear Mr. President: Washington July 15, 1918.

May I express the most earnest felicitations upon the prompt passage by Congress of the legislation empowering you to assume control of the electrical communicating systems of the country.[1]

A review of the entire situation suggests to me strongly the wisdom of prompt action in employing the powers thus granted. The telegraph wires have apparently proved inadequate; but by coordinating them with the toll and long distance wires telegraph facilities will be increased nearly 200%, these telephone wires being susceptible of simultaneous use for both dispatches and conversation. There are near to 1000 villages, towns and cities in the United States where competing exchanges exist, and the patron has to subscribe for two telephones, or if for only one be content with half a service.

If I were to say that Secretary McAdoo by merely raising the flag over the railways could double the tons of freight and the number of passengers carried without additional employees or equipment, I should be making a gross *over*statement of the fact. But when I make the same statement with regard to the communicating wires I am making an understatement of the fact. The mere connection of the telegraph wires along with our postal system will insure a reduction in telegraph operating expenses of not less than 20%, not to speak of very substantial economies to result from such connection in telephone operation.

I trust you will pardon this intrusion upon your counsels. It involves the deepest public interests of my life. With much appreciation of the very kindly consideration always extended me by you, I am,   Very sincerely yours,   David J. Lewis

TLS (WP, DLC).
[1] The Senate had debated H.J. Res. 309 on July 11, 12, and 13, 1918, and had adopted it by a vote of forty-six to sixteen on the latter date. *Cong. Record*, 65th Cong., 2d sess., pp. 8964-66, 8968-85, 8986-9010, 9062-94.

From Francis Patrick Walsh

Dear Mr. President: Washington July 15, 1918.

Your letter of the 9th inst., with regard to the electric urban and suburban railway systems in connection with federal relief, was duly received and forthwith forwarded to my colleague, Hon. William H. Taft, who is endeavoring to take a short vacation at Murray Bay, Canada.

It will give me pleasure to follow the course so wisely and logically suggested in your letter, and feel that I may almost assume to make the same answer for Mr. Taft. He will, however, resume his duties on the Board upon next Monday, and very shortly thereafter I hope that our joint action may be taken in the matter.

My reason for addressing you at this time is that in today's mail I received a communication upon the same subject from Mr. Charles E. Elmquist, Secretary of the National Association of Railway and Utilities Commissioners, enclosing his letter of the 12th inst. addressed to you,[1] and that you may be advised that the entire matter is receiving prompt attention.

Respectfully and sincerely,   Frank P. Walsh

TLS (WP, DLC).
   [1] Charles E. Elmquist to WW, July 12, 1918, TLS (WP, DLC).

A Draft of An Aide-Mémoire

[July 16, 1918]

The whole heart of the United States is in the winning of this war. The controlling purpose of the Government of the United States is to do everything that is necessary and effective to win it. It wishes to cooperate in every practicable way with the allied governments, and to cooperate ungrudgingly; for it has no ends of its own to serve and believes that the war can be won only by common counsel and intimate concert. It has sought to study every proposed policy or action in which its cooperation has been asked in this spirit, and states the following conclusions in the confidence that, if it finds itself obliged to decline participation in any undertaking or course of action, it will be understood that it does so only because it deems itself precluded from participating by imperative considerations either of policy or of fact.

In full agreement with the allied governments and upon the unanimous advice of the Supreme War Council, the Government of the United States adopted, upon its entrance into the war, a plan for taking part in the fighting on the western front into which all its resources of men and material were to be put and put as rapidly as possible, and it has carried out that plan with energy and success, pressing its execution more and more rapidly forward and literally putting into it the full energy and executive force of the nation. This was its reponse, its very willing and hearty response, to what was the unhesitating judgment alike of its own military advisers and of the advisers of the allied governments. It has concentrated all its plans and all its resources upon this single absolutely necessary object.

It feels it to be its duty to say, in such circumstances, that it cannot, so long as the military situation on the western front remains critical, consent to break or slacken the force of its present effort by diverting any part of its military force to other points or objectives. The United States is at a great distance from the field of action on the western front; it is at a much greater distance from any other field of action. The instrumentalities by which it is to handle its armies and its stores have at great cost and with great difficulty been created in France. They do not exist elsewhere. It is practicable for her to do a great deal in France; it is not practicable for her to do anything of importance or on a large scale upon any other field. The American Government, therefore, very respectfully requests its Associates to accept its deliberate judgment that it should not dissipate its force by attempting operations elsewhere.

It regards the Italian front as closely coordinated with the western front, however, and is willing to divert a portion of its military forces from France to Italy if it is the judgment and wish of the Supreme Command that it should do so. It wishes to defer to the decision of the Commander-in-chief in this matter, as it would wish to defer in all others, particularly because it considers these two fronts so closely related as to be practically but separated parts of a single line and because it would be necessary that any American troops sent to Italy should be subtracted from the number used in France and be actually transported across French territory from the ports now used by the armies of the United States.

It is the clear and fixed judgment of the Government of the United States, arrived at after repeated and very searching reconsiderations of the whole situation in Russia, that military intervention there would add to the present sad confusion in Russia rather than cure it, injure her rather than help her, and that it would be of no advantage whatever in the prosecution of our main design, to win the war against Germany. It cannot, therefore, take part in such intervention or sanction it in principle. Military intervention would, in its judgment, even supposing it to be efficacious in its immediate avowed object of delivering at [an] attack upon Germany from the east, be merely a method of making use of Russia, not a method of serving her. Her people could not profit by it, if they profitted by it at all, in time to save them from their present distresses, and their substance would be used to maintain foreign armies, not to reconstitute their own. Military action is admissible in Russia now, as the Government of the United States sees the circumstances, only to help the Checho-Slovaks consolidate their forces and get into successful cooperation with their Slavic kinsmen and to steady any efforts at self-government or self-defence in which the Russians themselves may be willing to accept assistance. Whether from Vladivostock or from Murmansk and Archangel, the only legitimate object for which American or allied troops can be employed, it submits, is to guard military stores which may subsequently be needed by Russian forces and to render such aid as may be acceptable to the Russians in the organization of their own self-defence. For helping the Checho-Slovaks there is immediate necessity and sufficient justification. Recent developments have made it evident that that is in the interest of what the Russian people themselves desire, and the Government of the United States is glad to contribute the small force at her disposal for that purpose. It yields, also, to the judgment of the Supreme Command in the matter of establishing a small force at Murmansk, to guard the military stores at Kola and to make it safe for Russian forces to come together in organized bodies in the north. But it owes it to frank counsel to say that it can go no further than these modest and experimental plans. It is not in a position, and has no expectation of being in a position, to take part in organized intervention in adequate force from either Vladivostock or Murmansk and Archangel.

It hopes to carry out the plans for safeguarding the rear of the Checho-Slovaks operating from Vladivostock in a way that will place it and keep it in close cooperation with a small military force like its own from Japan and that will assure it of the cordial accord of all the allied powers; and it proposes to ask all associated in this course of action to unite in assuring the people of Russia in the most public and solemn manner that none of the governments uniting in action either in Siberia or in northern Russia contemplates any interference of any kind with the political sovereignty of Russia, any intervention in her internal affairs, or any impairment of her territorial integrity either now or hereafter, but that each of the associated powers has the single object of affording such aid as shall be acceptable, and only such aid as shall be acceptable, to the Russian people in their endeavour to regain control of their own affairs, their own territory, and their own destiny.

It is the hope and purpose of the Government of the United States to take advantage of the earliest opportunity to send to Siberia a commission of merchants, agricultural experts, labour advisers, Red Cross representatives, and agents of the Young Men's Christian Association accustomed to organizing the best methods of spreading useful information and rendering educational help of a modest sort, in order in some systematic way to relieve the immediate economic necessities of the people there in every way for which opportunity may open. The execution of this plan will follow and will not be permitted to embarrass the military assistance rendered in the rear of the westward-moving forces of the Checho-Slovaks.

WWT MS (F. L. Polk Papers, CtY).

To Joseph Patrick Tumulty, with Enclosure

Dear Tumulty: [The White House, c. July 16, 1918]

When Mr. Holt turns up, will you not be kind enough to have it explained to him that I haven't been feeling very well the last day or two and have been obliged to cut my appointments down to a minimum?   The President.

TL (WP, DLC).

E N C L O S U R E

From Hamilton Holt

To the President: New York July 12 1918

I have just returned from a three months trip to Europe where I have visited the Belgian, British, French, American and Italian fronts. I have seen America in France from the ports of disembarkation up to the front line trenches, as probably very few Americans have. I was the first civilian to arrive at our front lines after the Battles of Seicheprey and Catigny, the first real battles America took part in in the war. I have lunched with Generals Pershing and Bliss and a dozen other Generals. I feel I have got in the closest touch with those in England France and Italy who are advocating the League of Nations idea. I have had long interviews with Mr. Balfour and Lord Robert Cecil of the Foreign Office, Lord Bryce and President Poincare, Premier Clemenceau and Leon Bourgeois, head of the French Official Commission studying the League idea, King Victor Emmanuel, Premier Orlando, and Foreign Minister Sonnino, as well as some of the leading intellectuals, literary men, and labor heads and socialists in the Allied countries.

I found everywhere a desire to establish a League of Nations now but a feeling that in this sphere of action it was the United States that must take the lead. Mr. Bourgeois and Mr. Balfour gave me some especially significant information on this question.

I am to be in Washington all day Tuesday the 16th and if there is anything that I have learned that would be of service to you I should be glad to call upon you and put my information at your disposal. Should you care to see me, but not on Tuesday, of course

I shall be more than glad to come any time that will best suit your convenience.   Yours very respectfully   Hamilton Holt

TLS (WP, DLC).

To Joseph Patrick Tumulty

Dear Tumulty: [The White House, c. July 16, 1918]
    I realize the hardship to the North Dakota farmers but I did not feel that we ought to fine the rest of the country to support them.[1]
                                        The President.

TL (WP, DLC).
    [1] Wilson was responding to John Burke to JPT, July 13, 1918, TLS, enclosing G. S. Wooledge to J. Burke, July 12, 1918, T telegram, both in WP, DLC. Wooledge, a "prominent Democrat" of Minot, North Dakota, declared that the minimum price for wheat, which Wilson had recently vetoed, was an absolute necessity to North Dakota farmers. Burke, the Treasurer of the United States and a former three-term Governor of North Dakota, supported Wooledge's position with a more detailed discussion of the problems which North Dakota wheat farmers faced. He hoped that Wilson would reconsider his stand if the question came up again.

To William Lacy Kenly

My dear General Kenly: [The White House] 16 July, 1918
    Mr. Charles L. Swem, who for quite six years has been associated with me as a stenographer and confidential secretary, is about to take the physical examinations with the hope of qualifying for service in the Aviation Corps. I am very sorry indeed to part with Mr. Swem, but I can commend him very sincerely to your interest. He is thoroughly qualified in my judgment by intelligence and energy for the service he seeks and if he proves to be physically qualified, it will be my hope that he can be promptly inducted into the Aviation Corps in the usual manner. I can testify to his entire trustworthiness.   Cordially and sincerely yours,   Woodrow Wilson

TLS (Letterpress Books, WP, DLC).

To David John Lewis

My dear Mr. Lewis: The White House 16 July, 1918
    No apology was needed for your interesting letter of yesterday, which I have read with the greatest interest. I am expecting to act upon the authority conferred upon me by Congress in the matter

of the wire control at a very early date, and your letter still further stimulates my interest.

Cordially and sincerely yours,   Woodrow Wilson

TLS (D. J. Lewis Papers, NcD).

To Edgar Rickard[1]

My dear Mr. Rickard: The White House 16 July, 1918

I would very much like your advice about the matter referred to in the enclosed letter from the Honorable Jouett Shouse of Kansas.[2] It occurs to me to ask these questions:

How much money would be needed for this?

And, if it were judged permissible for me to advance the sum out of the fund at my disposal for national security and defense, would the Grain Corporation be legally qualified to handle the loan?[3]

Sincerely yours,   Woodrow Wilson

TLS (Hoover Archives, CSt-H).
  [1] Acting Food Administrator.
  [2] J. Shouse to WW, July 11, 1918, TLS (WP, DLC). Shouse was concerned with the urgent need for money to enable farmers of Kansas, Nebraska, Oklahoma, and other adjacent states who had suffered two successive crop failures to buy seed wheat for the ensuing autumn and spring plantings. Rickard had already informed Shouse that officials of the Food Administration Grain Corporation lacked the legal authority to advance funds for this purpose from the corporation's financial surplus. Shouse, at Rickard's suggestion, suggested to Wilson that the powers of the Grain Corporation should be extended to allow it to make such loans. He noted that there was pending in the Senate an amendment to the Emergency Agricultural Appropriation bill which would provide some money for seed wheat through the Department of Agriculture. However, the fight over the prohibition amendment to this bill would delay its passage for many weeks, if indeed it did not prevent its passage altogether. Shouse said that the concerned farmers had to know very soon whether they could expect federal assistance in order that they might have the time required to prepare the ground for fall planting.
  [3] Rickard replied in E. Rickard to WW, July 18, 1918, TLS (WP, DLC). He stated that $15,000,000 would be needed adequately to assist the wheat farmers of Kansas, Nebraska, and Oklahoma. If officials of other states afflicted by crop failures made similar requests for funds, at least $15,000,000 more would be required. If the needed money came from Wilson's discretionary funds, the Grain Corporation could legally make the loans as Wilson's agent. However, in view of the fact that the Grain Corporation had no bureau to administer loans to individual farmers, Rickard suggested that the Federal Farm Loan Board could best carry out the loan program as Wilson's agent.

Two Letters to George Creel

My dear Creel: The White House 16 July, 1918

Thank you for your letter of yesterday enclosing Norman Angell's article. Your letter certainly assists to interpret it and it concerns a matter about which I have been thinking a great deal recently.

Cordially and faithfully yours,   Woodrow Wilson

TLS (G. Creel Papers, DLC).

My dear Creel: [The White House] 16 July, 1918

   I would hardly venture to write such a letter as you suggest here without a further study of the Lithuanian question.¹ I was quite ready to express my sympathy with the aspirations of the Lithuanians,² but to make these specific pledges with regard to the settlements at the peace conference I think would be a little rash, though it is my intention, barring the disclosure of facts that I do not now know, to pursue that very course.

Cordially and faithfully yours,   Woodrow Wilson

TLS (Letterpress Books, WP, DLC).
   ¹ G. Creel to WW, July 12, 1918, TLS, enclosing a draft of a letter to the Lithuanian National Council of Washington, T MS, both in WP, DLC. Creel suggested that Wilson send this letter upon the occasion of a trip by three members of the American branch of the Lithuanian National Council to Switzerland "to throw out the pro-German influences in control of the Council there." Creel's draft letter concluded: "It is my hope that your brothers in the Old Country will attain at the end of this war to that right of self-government which is the higher end of the great struggle. The question of Lithuania will have a hearing at the peace conference, and in her case, as in that of all other small nations, the United States will adhere to the principle of the rights of peoples to determine their own future."
   ² About Wilson's meeting with representatives of the Lithuanian National Council, see G. Creel to WW, May 2, 1918, n. 1, Vol. 47.

From Edward Mandell House, with Enclosure

Dear Governor: Magnolia, Massachusetts. July 16, 1918.

   I am enclosing you the draft for a League of Nations. The Preamble and Articles 1, 2, & 3 are the keystone of the arch.

   It is absolutely essential for the peoples of the world to realize that they can never have international peace and order if they permit their representatives to sanction the unmoral practices of the past. Every large nation, as you know, has been guilty. Bismark's forgery of a telegram in order to force a war on France is a notable modern instance. Roosevelt's rape at Panama brings it closely home. If these things had been done by private individuals they would have been classed as criminals

   Articles 1, 2 and 3 might well come under the Preamble. The reason they are segregated is that it gives them emphasis and makes the pledge binding.

   No. 4. was written with the intention of satisfying those who would be distrustful of Germany in the event she became a signatory power.

   It is necessary I think to do away with the abominable custom of espionage, but to abolish it and leave some dishonorable nation free to surreptitiously prepare for war would be a mistake. It is to be remembered that nations are even more suspicious of one another than individuals, and such suspicions, as in the case of individuals, is nine times out of ten unfounded. Instead of letting this condition grow there should be some way by which the truth could be openly arrived at.

No. 6. is taken largely from Article 5 of the British Draft. Two alternatives are named for the seat of meetings because it is conceivable that there might be trouble between Holland and Belgium, and if either of them represented X or Y it might be necessary to move the conference to Z.

No. 9. The first and last sentences in this are taken verbatim from Article 7 of the British Draft. I interlarded a sentence providing for a Secretariat and for the funds to maintain it.

To all intents and purposes the representatives of the contracting powers become automatically an International Parliament, and I am sure it will be necessary for them to be in almost continuous session. I believe that it will be a place of such power and consequence that the contracting parties will send their leading statesmen to represent them. It will be a greater honor to become a member of this body than to hold any other appointive position in the world, and it is probable that ex-Presidents, ex-Prime Ministers and ex-Chancellors will be chosen.

No. 10 provides for an International Court to have jurisdiction to determine certain questions which are now determined in many countries in courts of last resort. This court should be smaller than fifteen members.

In the past I have been opposed to a court, but in working the matter out it has seemed to me a necessary part of the machinery. In time the court might well prove the strongest part of it.

No. 11, was written largely to conform with the laws and practices of certain nations, particularly the Latin American Republics.

No. 12, has in mind the possibility of using, if desired, courts of last resort, now in being, as a medium for the settlement of disputes in the event other methods prescribed do not appeal to certain nations. I also had in mind that if such a provision were a part of the Covenant, it would have a tendency to make all courts of last appeal broader and less biased in passing upon international questions.

Nos. 16, 17, 18 and 19 are obvious and, in the event that it is desirable to have a League limited to the Great Powers, these articles would force every nation not a member of the League to submit their disputes to the League, or use the forms of settlement prescribed by it.

Articles 13, 14, 15 and 16 of the British Draft seek in a measure to accomplish the same purpose, but in an entirely different way.

No. 20 was written with the thought that it would not do to have territorial guarantees inflexible. It is quite conceivable that conditions might so change in the course of time as to make it a serious hardship for certain portions of one nation to continue under the government of that nation. For instance, it is conceivable that Canada might sometime wish to become a part of the United States. It is also a possibility that Chihuahua, Coahuila or Lower California might desire to become a part of this country and with the consent in each instance of the mother country.

No. 22. The first sentence of this article is taken verbatim from the British Article 17. I did not use their second sentence for the reason that it seemed to point to Germany, and I have worded the second sentence of No. 22 differently to avoid this.

No. 23 is almost a verbatim copy of Article 18 of the British.

Affectionately yours,   E. M. House

TLS (WP, DLC).

ENCLOSURE

Suggestion For
A COVENANT OF A LEAGUE OF NATIONS.
Preamble.

International civilization having proved a failure because there has not been constructed a fabric of law to which nations have yielded with the same obedience and deference as individuals submit to intra-national laws, and because public opinion has sanctioned unmoral acts relating to international affairs, it is the purpose of the States signatory to this Convention to form a League of Nations having for its purpose the maintenance throughout the world of peace, security, progress and orderly government. Therefore it is agreed as follows:

Article 1.

The same standards of honor and of ethics shall pervail [prevail] internationally and in affairs of nations as in other matters. The agreement or promise of a power shall be inviolate.

Article 2.

No official of a Power shall either directly or by indirection, on behalf of his Government, be expected or permitted to act or communicate other than consistently with the truth, the honor and the obligation of the power which he represents.

Article 3.

Any attempt by a Power, either openly or in secret, whether by propaganda or otherwise, to influence one Power or nation against another shall be deemed dishonorable.

Article 4.

Any open or direct inquiry regarding the acts or purposes of a Power may be made by another Power as of course, and shall be regarded as an act of friendship tending to promote frankness in international relations, but any secret inquiry to such end shall be deemed dishonorable.

Article 5.

Any war or threat of war is a matter of concern to the League of Nations, and to the Powers, members thereof.

Article 6.

The Ambassadors and Ministers of the Contracting Powers to X and the Minister for Foreign Affairs of X shall act as the respective delegates of the Powers in the League of Nations. The meetings of the delegates shall be held at the seat of government of X, and the Minister for Foreign Affairs of X shall be the presiding officer.

If the delegates deem it necessary or advisable, they may meet temporarily at the seat of government of Y or Z, in which case the Ambassador or Minister to X of the country in which the meeting is held, shall be the presiding officer pro tempore.

Article 7.

The Delegates shall meet in the interests of peace whenever war is rumored or threatened, and also whenever a Delegate of any Power shall inform the Delegates that a meeting in the interests of peace is advisable.

Article 8.

The Delegates shall also meet at such other times as they shall from time to time determine.

Article 9.

The Delegates shall regulate their own procedure and may appoint committees to inquire and report. The Delegates shall constitute a Secretariat and fix the duties thereof and all expenses of the Secretariat shall be paid by the Contracting Powers as the Delegates may determine. In all matters covered by this article the Delegates may decide by the votes of a majority of the Contracted Powers represented.

Article 10.

An International Court composed of not more than fifteen members shall be constituted, which shall have jurisdiction to determine any difference between nations which has not been settled by diplomacy, arbitration, or otherwise, and which relates to the existence, interpretation, or effect of a treaty, or which may be submitted by consent, or which relates to matters of commerce, including in such matter, the validity or effect internationally of a statute regulation or practice. The Delegates may at their discretion submit to the Court such other questions as may seem to them advisable.

The judges of the International Court shall, both originally and from time to time as vacancies may occur, be chosen by the Delegates. A judge of the International Court shall retire from office when he shall have reached the age of seventy-two years, and may be so retired at any time by a vote of two thirds of the Delegates, but in case of retirement of a judge from office, the salary paid to him shall be continued to be so paid during his natural life.

A judge may be removed by a vote of two-thirds of the Delegates.

The International Court shall formulate its own rules of procedure.

Article 11.

Any difference between nations relating to matters of commerce and which involves the validity or effect internationally of a statute regulation or practice, shall, if the Power having adopted such statute regulation or practice so request, be submitted to its highest national court for decision, before submission to the International Court.

Article 12.

The highest national court of each Contracting Power shall have jurisdiction to hear and finally determine any international dispute which may be submitted by consent for its decision.

Article 13.

The Contracting Powers agree that all disputes between or among them or any of them of every nature whatsoever, which shall not be settled by diplomacy and which are not within the provisions of Article 10 shall be referred for arbitration before three arbitrators, one to be selected by each party to the dispute and one to be chosen by two arbitrators so selected, or in the event of their failure to agree in such choice, the third arbitrator shall be selected by the Delegates.

The decision of the arbitrators may be set aside on the appeal of a party to the dispute, by a vote of three-fourths of the Delegates, if the decision of the arbitrators was unanimous, and by a vote of two-thirds of the Delegates if the decision of the arbitrators was not unanimous, but shall otherwise be finally binding and conclusive.

When any decision of the arbitrators shall have been set aside by the Delegates, the dispute shall again be submitted to arbitration before three arbitrators, chosen as heretofore provided, but none of whom shall have previously acted as such and the decision of the arbitrators upon the second arbitration shall be finally binding and conclusive without right of appeal.

Article 14.

Any Power which the Delegates determine shall have failed to submit to the International Court any dispute of which that Court has jurisdiction as of course, or failed or neglected to carry out any decision of that Court, or of a national court to which a dispute has been submitted by consent for decision, or failed to submit to arbitration any dispute pursuant to Article 13 hereof, or failed to carry out any decision of the arbitrators, shall thereupon lose and be deprived of all rights of commerce and intercourse with the Contracting Powers.

Article 15.

If any Power shall declare war or begin hostilities before submitting a dispute with another Power, as the case may be, either to the International Court or to arbitrators, as herein provided, or shall declare war or begin hostilities in regard to any dispute which has been decided arversely [adversely] to it by said Court or by Arbitrators or pursuant to Article 12 hereof, as the case may be, the Contracting Powers shall not only cease all commerce and intercourse with that Power as in Article 14 provided, but shall also arrange to blockade and close the frontiers of that power to Commerce and intercourse with the world.

Article 16.

As regards disputes between one of the Contracting Powers and a Power not a party to this Convention, the Contracting Power shall endeavor to obtain submission of the dispute to judicial decision or to arbitration. If the other state will not agree to submit the dispute to judicial decision or to arbitration the Contracting Power shall bring it before the Delegates. In the latter event the Delegates shall in the name of the League of Nations invite the state, not a party to this Convention to become *ad hoc* a party and to submit its case to judicial decision or to arbitration and in such case the provisions hereinbefore contained shall be applicable to the dispute both against and in favor of such state in all respects as if it were a party to this Convention.

Article 17.

If the state not a party to this convention will not accept the invitation to become *ad hoc* a party, the Delegates shall inquire into the dispute and shall make a recommendation in respect thereof.

Article 18.

If hostilities shall be commenced against the Contracting Power by the other state before a decision of the dispute, or before the recommendation made by the Delegates in respect thereof, or contrary to such recommendations, the Contracting Powers will thereupon cease all commerce and intercourse with the other state and will also arrange to blockade and close the frontiers of that state to commerce and intercourse with the world and any of the Contracting Powers may come to the assistance of the Contracting Power against which hostilities have been commenced.

Article 19.

In the case of a dispute between states not parties to this Convention, any Power may bring the matter before the Delegates, who shall tender the good offices of the League of Nations with a view to the peaceable settlement of the dispute.

If one of the Powers, party to the dispute, shall offer and agree to submit its interests and cause of action in regard thereto wholly to the control and decision of the League of Nations, that Power shall *ad hoc* be deemed a Contracting Power. If no one of the Powers, parties to such dispute shall so offer and agree, the Delegates shall take such action and make such recommendations to their Governments as will preserve peace and prevent hostilities and result in the settlement of the dispute.

Article 20.

The Contracting Powers unite in several guarnatees [guarantees] to each other of their territorial integrity and political independence, subject however, to such territorial modifications, if any, as may become necessary in the future by reason of changes in present racial conditions and aspirations, pursuant to the principle of self-determination and as shall also be regarded by three-fourths of the Delegates as necessary and proper for the welfare of the peoples concerned; recognizing also that all territorial changes involve equitable compensation and that the peace of the world is superior in importance and interest to questions of boundary.

Article 21.

The Contracting Powers recognize the principle that permanent peace will require that national armaments shall be reduced to the lowest point consistent with safety, and the Delegates are directed to formulate at once a plan by which such a reduction may be brought about. The plan so formulated shall not be binding until and unless unanimously approved by the Governments signatory to this Covenant.

The Contracting Powers agree that munitions and implements of war shall not be manufactured by private enterprise and that publicity as to all national armaments and programs is essential.

Article 22.

Any Power not a party to this Convention may apply to the Delegates for leave to become a party. The Delegates may act favorably on the application if they shall regard the granting thereof as tending to promote the peace and security of the world.

Article 23.

A. The Contracting Powers severally agree that the present Convention abrogates all treaty obligations *inter se* inconsistent with the terms hereof, and that they will not enter into any engagements inconsistent with the terms hereof.

B. Where any of the Contracting Powers, before becoming party to this Convention, shall have entered into any treaty imposing upon it obligations inconsistent with the terms of this Convention, it shall be the duty of such Power to take immediate steps to procure its release from such obligations.

T MS (WP, DLC).

From Frank Lyon Polk

My dear Mr. President: Washington July 16, 1918.

The Italian Ambassador has informed us that his Government is prepared to participate in an Interallied expedition in Siberia with a force of about two thousand men. These men are for the most part ex-Austrian soldiers of Italian nationality, made prisoners by the Russians, and are now at Tientsin.

Yours fiathfully [faithfully],   Frank L. Polk

TLS (SDR, RG 59, 861.00/2837, DNA).

From Newton Diehl Baker

My dear Mr. President: Washington. July 16, 1918.

Shortly after the receipt of the charges presented through Mr. Gompers against the Governor of Porto Rico,[1] I conferred with Mr. Gompers and Mr. Iglesias[2] and had the Chief of the Bureau of Insular Affairs[3] with me.

Mr. Gompers presented briefly his views of the situation in Porto Rico, and Mr. Iglesias made a short statement of his views. In order, however, that Mr. Iglesias could be given all the time necessary for a full presentation of his views, I had him go over the case with the Chief of the Bureau of Insular Affairs. As a result of their discussion there were prepared for my signature two letters to the Governor of Porto Rico, copies of which I enclose. I have transmitted these two letters to the Governor.

The letter marked "A"[4] disposes of the charges. The letter marked "B"[5] explains itself, and while it contemplates, in large part, what Mr. Gompers and Mr. Iglesias have asked for, it is not the result of the charges against Governor Yager, nor is it desired that the investigation in Porto Rico contemplated should have anything to do with these charges. Before transmittal and, in fact, before they were submitted to me, copies of these two letters were given Mr. Iglesias and by him shown to Mr. Gompers. As a result of this, Mr. Gompers wrote to me a letter, copy of which is hereto attached marked "C."[6]

In this letter Mr. Gompers recommends in outline the scope of the suggested investigation. I am hopeful that the commission to be appointed by you will not enter on their duties in a spirit of controversy. The commission and each member thereof should go to Porto Rico having in mind the benefit of the laborers of Porto Rico. I am afraid that any effort to designate members of the commission by class or as representing a class will create a controversy which it is desirable to avoid.

Respectfully yours,   Newton D. Baker

TLS (WP, DLC).
    [1] S. Gompers to WW, May 6, 1918, and n. 1 thereto, Vol. 47.
    [2] That is, Santiago Iglesias.
    [3] That is, Maj. Gen. Frank McIntyre.
    [4] NDB to A. Yager, July 8, 1918, TCL (WP, DLC). Baker's conclusion was as follows: "In view of evidence at hand, it is unnecessary to make further investigation. The charges, in so far as they reflect on you personally or on the conduct of your office, have no foundation. To go through the forms of an investigation in view of available evidence would at such a time as this be a severe reflection on this Department."
    [5] NDB to A. Yager, July 8, 1918 (second letter of that date), TCL (WP, DLC). Baker informed Yager that he intended to take up with Wilson "the question of having a general study of labor conditions in Porto Rico, industrial and agricultural, made by persons whose views and recommendations would command the respect of all in Porto Rico." Baker declared that this was the best way to secure reforms which both he and Yager had at heart. He hoped that the persons making the study could visit the island "about next September."
    [6] S. Gompers to NDB, July 11, 1918, TCL (WP, DLC). Gompers recommended that the proposed investigation be conducted under the direction of the National War Labor Board and by the same principles and methods formulated for that agency by the National War Labor Conference Board; that the President of the United States appoint the commission to make the investigation; that the commission be made up of four or six persons, half representing employers and half representing employees, each group to select one of its members to preside alternately at meetings; and that the commission have the power "to summon witnesses, to scrutinize books and documents, to undertake mediation and conciliation and to make complete investigation and report its findings and recommendations to the President of the United States and to the National War Labor Board."

From Harry Augustus Garfield

Dear Mr. President: Washington, D. C. July 16, 1918

I entirely share your opinion concerning Mr. George W. Perkins and have several times told New York people that his name was not under consideration and would not be considered by me.

Cordially and faithfully yours,   H. A. Garfield.

TLS (WP, DLC).

From the Diary of Frank Lyon Polk[1]

July 16, 1918.

CABINET:

President authorized me to telegraph to Herron not to cut off any avenue of approach or not to encourage them. Read me statement in reply to questions of the Supreme War Council as to our going into Russia. Opposed to any military intervention. In favor of helping Czechs at Vladivostok. Agreed to let the Japanese have the supreme command when they landed in Vladivostok. (Saw the Japanese Ambassador at my house at 7:15 and gave him this information.)

T MS (F. L. Polk Papers, CtY).
  [1] In this extract, Polk records his conversation with Wilson after a meeting of the cabinet late in the afternoon of July 16.

To Frank Lyon Polk, with Enclosure

My dear Mr. Counselor,   The White House. 17 July, 1918

Here is the paper I read to you yesterday, corrected as suggested in our little conference with the Secretary of War.[1] I think it will be wise to communicate it to the governments we spoke of as soon as possible. If you could hand it to them severally in person (not together, because their points of view are so different) with a few words to the effect that the memorandum embodies our most conscientious consideration of questions which we felt obliged to test by every practical consideration, I think they will be the more likely to convey it to their governments in a right atmosphere of comment. We can now proceed to business!

The memorandum is of so confidential a nature that I have, as you will see, written it myself on my own typewriter.

Faithfully Yours,   Woodrow Wilson

Delivered to French British Italian and then copies to Japanese & Chinese. FLP

WWTLS (F. L. Polk Papers, CtY).
  [1] Wilson added the new text of this document first in shorthand on the versos of the pages of the draft of the aide-mémoire printed at July 16, 1918.

E N C L O S U R E

The White House.

MEMORANDUM to be communicated to the Governments of Great Britain, France, and Italy, associated in the Supreme War Council.

Also to be communicated, for information, to the Government of Japan.

The whole heart of the people of the United States is in the winning of this war. The controlling purpose of the Government of the United States is to do everything that is necessary and effective to win it. It wishes to cooperate in every practicable way with the allied governments, and to cooperate ungrudgingly; for it has no ends of its own to serve and believes that the war can be won only by common counsel and intimate concert of action. It has sought to study every proposed policy or action in which its cooperation has been asked in this spirit, and states the following conclusions in the confidence that, if it finds itself obliged to decline participation in any undertaking or course of action, it will be understood that it does so only because it deems itself precluded from participating by imperative considerations either of policy or of fact.

In full agreement with the allied governments and upon the unanimous advice of the Supreme War Council, the Government of the United States adopted, upon its entrance into the war, a plan for taking part in the fighting on the western front into which all its resources of men and material were to be put, and put as rapidly as possible, and it has carried out that plan with energy and success, pressing its execution more and more rapidly forward and literally putting into it the entire energy and executive force of the nation. This was its response, its very willing and hearty response, to what was the unhesitating judgment alike of its own military advisers and of the advisers of the allied governments. It is now considering, at the suggestion of the Supreme War Council, the possibility of making very considerable additions even to this immense programme which, if they should prove feasible at all, will tax the industrial processes of the United States and the shipping facilities of the whole group of associated nations to the utmost. It has thus concentrated all its plans and all its resources upon this single absolutely necessary object.

In such circumstances it feels it to be its duty to say that it cannot, so long as the military situation on the western front remains critical, consent to break or slacken the force of its present effort by diverting any part of its military force to other points or objectives. The United States is at a great distance from the field of action on the western front; it is at a much greater distance from any other field of action. The instrumentalities by which it is to handle its armies and its stores have at great cost and with great difficulty been created in France. They do not exist elsewhere. It is practicable for her to do a great deal in France; it is not practicable for her to do anything of importance or on a large scale upon any other field. The American Government, therefore, very respectfully requests its Associates to accept its deliberate judgment that it should not dissipate its force by attempting important operations elsewhere.

It regards the Italian front as closely coordinated with the western front, however, and is willing to divert a portion of its military forces from France to Italy if it is the judgment and wish of the Supreme Command that it should do so. It wishes to defer to the decision of the Commander-in-chief in this matter, as it would wish to defer in all others, particularly because it considers these two fronts so closely related as to be practically but separate parts of a single line and because it would be necessary that any American troops sent to Italy should be subtracted from the number used in France and be actually transported across French territory from the ports now used by the armies of the United States.

It is the clear and fixed judgment of the Government of the United States, arrived at after repeated and very searching reconsiderations of the whole situation in Russia, that military intervention there would add to the present sad confusion in Russia rather than cure it, injure her rather than help her, and that it would be of no advantage in the prosecution of our main design, to win the war against Germany. It cannot, therefore, take part in such intervention or sanction it in principle. Military intervention would, in its judgment, even supposing it to be efficacious in its immediate avowed object of delivering an attack upon Germany from the east, be merely a method of making use of Russia, not a method of serving her. Her people could not profit by it, if they profitted by it at all, in time to save them from their present distresses, and their substance would be used to maintain foreigy [foreign] armies, not to reconstitute their own. Military action is admissible in Russia, as the Government of the United States sees the circumstances, only to help the Czecho-Slovaks consolidate their forces and get into successful cooperation with their Slavic kinsmen and to steady any efforts at self-government or self-defence in which the Russians themselves may be willing to accept assistance. Whether from Vladivostock or from Murmansk and Archangel, the only legitimate object for which American or allied troops can be employed, it submits, is to guard military stores which may subsequently be needed by Russian forces and to render such aid as may be acceptable to the Russians in the organization of their own self-defence. For helping the Czecho-Slovaks there is immediate necessity and sufficient justification. Recent developments have made it evident that that is in the interest of what the Russian people themselves desire, and the Government of the United States is glad to contribute the small force at its disposal for that purpose. It yields, also, to the judgment of the Supreme Command in the matter of establishing a small force at Murmansk, to guard the military stores at Kola and to make it safe for Russian forces to come together in organized bodies in the north. But it owes it to frank counsel to say that it can go not further than these modest and experimental plans. It is not in a position, and has no expectation of being in a position, to take part in organized intervention in adequate force from either Vladivostock or Murmansk and Archangel. It feels that it ought to add, also, that it will feel at liberty to use the few troops it can spare only for the purposes here stated and shall feel obliged to withdraw those forces, in order to add them to the forces at the western front, if the plans in whose execution it is now intended that they should cooperate should develop into others inconsistent with the policy to which the Government of the United States feels constrained to restrict itself.

At the same time the Government of the United States wishes to say with the utmost cordiality and good will that none of the conclusions here stated is meant to wear the least colour of criticism of what the other governments associated against Germany may think it wise to undertake. It wishes in no way to embarrass their choices of policy. All that is intended here is a perfectly frank and definite statement of the policy which the United States feels obliged to adopt for herself and in the use of her own military forces. The Government of the United States does not wish it to be understood that in so restricting its own activities it is seeking, even by implication, to set limits to the action or to define the policies of its Associates.

It hopes to carry out the plans for safeguarding the rear of the Czecho-Slovaks operating from Vladivostock in a way that will place it and keep it in close cooperation with a small military force like its own from Japan, and if necessary from the other Allies, and that will assure it of the cordial accord of all the allied powers; and it proposes to ask all associated in this course of action to unite in assuring the people of Russia in the most public and solemn manner that none of the governments uniting in action either in Siberia or in northern Russia contemplates any interference of any kind with the political sovereignty of Russia, any intervention in her internal affairs, or any impairment of her territorial integrity either now or hereafter, but that each of the associated powers has the single object of affording such aid as shall be acceptable, and only such aid as shall be acceptable, to the Russian people in their endeavour to regain control of their own affairs, their own territory, and their own destiny.

It is the hope and purpose of the Government of the United States to take advantage of the earliest opportunity to send to Siberia a commission of merchants, agricultural experts, labour advisers, Red Cross representatives, and agents of the Young Men's Christian Association accustomed to organizing the best methods of spreading useful information and rendering educational help of a modest sort, in order in some systematic manner to relieve the immediate economic necessities of the people there in every way for which opportunity may open. The execution of this plan will follow and will not be permitted to embarrass the military assistance rendered in the rear of the westward-moving forces of the Czecho-Slovaks.

W.W.

WWTI MS (SDR, RG 59, 861.00/3130a, DNA).

To the White House Staff

[The White House, July 17, 1918]

Please say to Doctor Garfield that I would not for anything have him make any exception with regard to the country clubs at which I play golf during winter.[1] I would not consent in any case, but as a matter of fact, I never make use of the club houses.

The President.

TL (WP, DLC).
[1] Wilson was responding to the White House Staff to WW, July 13, 1918, TL (WP, DLC). This memorandum stated that Garfield had telephoned to say that he was issuing an order prohibiting the use of fuel by country clubs during the coming winter, but that he would be pleased to grant exemptions from this order to any country club at which Wilson might play during the winter months.

To Joseph Patrick Tumulty, with Enclosure

Dear Tumulty: [The White House, c. July 17, 1918]

This is certainly a courteous and considerate letter and I think you would be entirely justified in conveying to Mr. Burton the information that I am wholly and unalterably opposed to any such proposition as the one numbered "2" in this letter. It would not only embarrass the administration but would, I am sure, lead to a great deal of adverse comment throughout the country.

The President.

TL (WP, DLC).

ENCLOSURE

Theodore Elijah Burton[1] to Joseph Patrick Tumulty

My dear Mr. Tumulty: New York July 13, 1918.

Once when I was in Washington, you very kindly suggested that I call upon you for any suggestions or aid in any proposition pending.

A situation has arisen of importance, which might embarrass the administration, about which I thought best to write.

A meeting is to occur at Washington next Wednesday, outlined in the enclosed clipping from the "Journal of Commerce" this morning.[2] Two proposals will come before this meeting:

1. To establish a chain of cotton warehouses for the deposit of raw cotton upon which advances could be made by banks more readily than now. It is probable that the Government will be asked to guarantee bonds to the amount of $20,000,000. for the acquisition and construction of these warehouses.

2. A proposition which has been favored by resolutions of bankers and cotton growers; that the Government purchase cotton on a very large scale, the cost of which would amount to hundreds of millions.

General[ly] speaking the former is advocated by the cotton manufacturers; the latter by cotton growers and many bankers in the south.

I fear this latter proposition especially might embarrass the administration and should like to be placed in touch with someone who would be able to express the opinion of the President or other authority in regard to it. The information, of course, will be absolutely confidential.

I might be able to prevent any radical or injudicious action.

The situation as regards the cotton crop is about as follows:

Amount left over from the crop of 1917	3,000,000 bales
Probable cotton crop of 1918	15,000,000 bales
	18,000,000 bales
Probable domestic demand	6,000,000 bales
Probable foreign demand	3,000,000 bales
	9,000,000 bales

These figures, which are, of course, an approximation would leave a balance of 9,000,000 bales of cotton crop undisposed of, and will create a serious situation. I am quite sure that a strenuous effort will be made to commit the Government to the purchase of a large share of this surplus crop.

I repeat that I should be glad if you could present this situation to the President or other person who could act for him, for suggestions.

I expect to go to Washington by the Congressional Limited Tuesday afternoon, stopping at the Hotel Lafayette, and should be pleased to have some information from you here before going or after arrival in Washington.

With kind regards,   Sincerely yours,   Theo. E. Burton

TLS (WP, DLC).
    [1] Former Republican congressman and senator from Ohio; at this time president of the Merchants National Bank of New York.
    [2] "Favor U. S. Chain of Cotton Warehouses," New York *Journal of Commerce*, July 13, 1918.

From the White House Staff

The White House.
Memorandum for the President: July 17, 1918

Hon. William Jennings Bryan, who is at the LaFayette, asks if he may see the President for a few minutes today.

I am exceedingly sorry, but no days that I remember since I came to Washington have been so crowded with duties that needed immediate and careful attention. I am bound, therefore, in conscience to refrain from making any engagement that is not imperative. Please explain to Mr. Bryan, with an expression of my sincere regret. I am sure he will understand and pardon.   W. W.

TL and WWTLI (WP, DLC).

From William Jennings Bryan

My dear Mr President   [Washington] July 17 1918

I am sorry your engagements prevent my seeing you today or this week, but no one knows better than I the burden you are carrying & I would not ask for time but for the fact that I feel that the matter which I desire to lay before you is of great importance. The government of Costa Rica has asked me to represent it & I shall await your convenience. I go to Asheville N. C. (our summer home) tonight to attend a war work meeting of the Y.M.C.A. at our house, but I shall be pleased to return on next Monday the 22nd if you can give me a hearing. Please have Mr Fo[r]ster wire your answer to Asheville. *After* the 22nd meetings—at each of which I make an appeal for support of the government along every line of its work—will occupy my time until some time in August.

With assurances of esteem I am, my dear Mr President,
                              Very truly yours   W. J. Bryan

ALS (WP, DLC).

From William Procter Gould Harding

My dear Mr. President: Washington, July 17, 1918.

I have some information regarding cotton conditions in the South which I think may perhaps be of interest to you at this time, and if you can spare the time I would like very much to discuss the subject with you for fifteen or twenty minutes whenever it may be convenient to you. If you prefer, I could send a written memorandum, but I think perhaps I can express myself a little more clearly orally than I can in writing.

My feeling is that the South ought to be willing to make a decided concession in price immediately, before the market yields under the weight of the new crop, rather than to ask for assistance after a slump has taken place. I am inclined to think that there should also be a minimum and a maximum price provided for, in order to make it to the interest of the producers to withhold cotton from the market.

The situation as regards cotton is, as I understand it, quite different from that which relates to wheat. There is not sufficient warehouse capacity in the South to admit of the concentration of cotton in the larger towns, and the problems of transportation and financing would be greatly intensified should there be a rapid movement of cotton away from the initial points. In case a price for cotton should be fixed, I would suggest that a minimum price be provided for at which purchases would be made by the Government, but that a maximum price be also permitted, which would encourage producers to market as small a portion of their crop as might be necessary and would insure a large part of the crop being held back at the farms.

I see no insuperable obstacles in the way of financing the coming cotton crop except the uncertainty which prevails as to the price. There must be some well defined sentiment as to values upon which to base loans. In the absence of such a sentiment, I fear that a crop of the magnitude indicated by the Department of Agriculture would result in complete demoralization throughout the cotton states.

Respectfully yours,   W P G Harding

TLS (WP, DLC).

From Harry Augustus Garfield

Dear Mr. President: [Washington] July 17, 1918

While it is true that we have produced more coal during the past week than ever before, the total reaching 13,000,000 tons, the increasing demand makes me extremely apprehensive of midwinter results.

I still hope that you will think it wise to issue a proclamation inaugurating an industrial army as proposed in Mr. Neale's memorandum left with you last week.[1] It is important that whatever is done be done quickly. I am, therefore, offering an alternative suggestion, but only in the event of a decision against the creation of an industrial army, namely, that you issue a proclamation to those engaged in coal mining along the lines indicated by the enclosed. This also was prepared by Mr. Neale, and he tells me has the hearty approval of Mr. McCormick.

Cordially and faithfully yours, [H. A. Garfield]

CCL (H. A. Garfield Papers, DLC).
[1] H. A. Garfield to WW, July 3, 1918, TLS, enclosing James Brown Neale to H. A. Garfield, July 3, 1918, TCL, both in WP, DLC. Neale, chief of the Bureau of Production of the Fuel Administration, set forth a plan to organize the coal-mine workers of the nation into a "Service Army" with the President as commander in chief, in order to encourage the maximum production of coal.

Sir William Wiseman to Lord Robert Cecil

[New York] July 17, 1918.

In reply to your F. O. Cable No. 4392 of the 15th:[1]

I gave COL. HOUSE a copy of PHILLIMORE's report on June 20th, and at his request wrote a memorandum[2] on which he partly based his letter to you.[3] His letter, however, is not intended to be so much a reply to the Phillimore report as an expression of his views on the subject generally.

When the PRESIDENT received a copy of the report from LORD READING he sent it to COL. HOUSE (Col. House did not inform him that I had already given him a copy) with a letter, which I have seen, asking COL. HOUSE to prepare a reply for him to send to H.M.G. Col. House is now considering the views of various prominent people here who have interested themselves in the subject, and tells me he will keep you fully informed of his progress.

I have discussed the subject generally with the President. He recognises the practical difficulties far better than most people suppose.

I am writing you fully by mail leaving Friday.[4]

T telegram (W. Wiseman Papers, CtY).
[1] A. J. Balfour to Lord Reading, No. 4392, July 15, 1918, T telegram (W. Wiseman Papers, CtY): "Following for Sir W. Wiseman. Following from Lord R. Cecil. Has Colonel House been given a copy of Phillimore's report and if so when? He has written me a letter dated June 24th and I should be glad to know if I am to take it as a reply to that report."
[2] Printed as Enclosure II with W. Wiseman to R. Cecil, July 18, 1918.
[3] That is, EMH to R. Cecil, June 25, 1918, printed as an Enclosure with EMH to WW, June 25, 1918.
[4] That is, W. Wiseman to R. Cecil, July 18, 1918.

INDEX

NOTE ON THE INDEX

THE alphabetically arranged analytical table of contents at the front of the volume eliminates duplication, in both contents and index, of references to certain documents, such as letters. Letters are listed in the contents alphabetically by name, and chronologically within each name by page. The subject matter of all letters is, of course, indexed. The Editorial Notes and Wilson's writings are listed in the contents chronologically by page. In addition, the subject matter of both categories is indexed. The index covers all references to books and articles mentioned in text or notes. Footnotes are indexed. Page references to footnotes which place a comma between the page number and "n" cite both text and footnote, thus: "418,n1." On the other hand, absence of the comma indicates reference to the footnote only, thus: "59n1"—the page number denoting where the footnote appears.

The index supplies the fullest known form of names and, for the Wilson and Axson families, relationships as far down as cousins. Persons referred to by nicknames or shortened forms of names can be identified by reference to entries for these forms of the names.

All entries consisting of page numbers only and which refer to concepts, issues, and opinions (such as democracy, the tariff, the money trust, leadership, and labor problems), are references to Wilson's speeches and writings. Page references that follow the symbol Δ in such entries refer to the opinions and comments of others who are identified.

Two cumulative contents-index volumes are now in print: Volume 13, which covers Volumes 1-12, and Volume 26, which covers Volumes 14-25. Volume 39, covering Volumes 27-38, is scheduled for publication in May 1985.

INDEX

Abancourt, France, 389

A. Barton Hepburn: His Life and Service to His Time (Bishop), 582n1

Abbeville, France: Supreme War Council's meeting at, 32,n3, 34, 386; German attacks on, 389

Abbott, James Francis, 450,n2, 451,n3, 457, 485, 581-85

Abbott, John Jay, 518,n1

Académie des Sciences Morales et Politiques of the Institut de France, 27n1

Address of President Wilson . . . May 18, 1918, 57n

Africa, 27

agricultural appropriations bills: and Gore amendment on wheat prices, 42,n1, 74; and Randall's prohibition amendment, 161,n2, 166; WW on, 260; and Jones amendment, 428n2; WW vetoes because of wheat section, 595-97

agriculture: Lever and House of Representatives Committee on, 259-60; and Indiana Democratic platform, 319; breakup of Washington State Grange meeting in Walla Walla, 291-94; *see also* farmers and farming

Agriculture, Committee on (House of Representatives): Lever and, 259-60, 272

Agriculture, Department of, 8, 219-20,n1, 298, 344

Agriculture and Forestry, Committee on (Senate), 428n1

aircraft production: C. E. Hughes agrees to assist in investigation of, 3, 15, 45-46, 50,n1; and Senate Military Affairs Committee, 10n1; military production separated from Signal Corps, 73-74

Alabama, 553

Albert, King of the Belgians, 151

Albert, France, 332

alcohol: *see* prohibition

Alien Property Custodian, 228n1

Allied Maritime Transport Council, 233n1

Allied Naval Council: *see* Inter-Allied Naval Council

Allied Purchasing Commission, 145n3

Allies: and war declaration against Turkey and Bulgaria, 79-80; and intervention in Russia, 99-102, 103-104, 430-31, 441n1; joint request for more U.S. troops, 226; and proposed Russian Relief Commission, 315-16; House on building morale of, 400; and aid to Czech troops, 428-29, 496-97; and U.S. policy toward minorities in Austria-Hungary, 447-48; Hoover on food and, 466-68; issue of Japan and intervention plan, 495-96, 560-61, 574-75, 586-87; urge WW to accept Supreme War Council's resolution on intervention in Russia, 496-501; troop plan for proposed intervention in Murmansk and Archangel, 536-38; Sims on

friction between, 605; *see also* under the names of the individual countries

All Russian Union of Cooperative Societies, 359

Alsace-Lorraine, 153, 214, 215, 553, 554

Alte, Viscount of (José Francisco da Horta Machada da Franca), 173,n1

Amateur Diplomacy Abroad (Dell), 482n3

Ambassador Morgenthau's Story (Morgenthau), 284n1

America and the Fight for Irish Freedom, 1866-1922 (Tansill), 118n1

American Alliance for Labor and Democracy, 275-76

American Economic Cooperation with Russia (Robins), 489,n1

American Fair Trade League, 17n1

American Federation of Labor: WW's message to, 275, 309; on government takeover of telegraph companies, 313, 349; and Mooney case, 404; and resolution on detective agencies, 438-39,n1

American Group (proposed), 371-74, 519-20, 522

American Group of the Six-Power Consortium (1913): *see* Six-Power Consortium

American International Corporation, 372-73

American-Jewish Joint Distribution Committee, 98n6

American News Company, 187n4

American Newspaper Publishers' Association, 148n1, 149

American Opinion and the Irish Question, 1910-23: A Study in Opinion and Policy (Carroll), 118n1

American Radiator Company, 484n1

American Red Cross, 221; and WW's participation in war fund drive, 6, 16, 53-57, 59, 94, 116, 119n1, 199,n1,2, 231; and Porto Rico, 35-36; Mrs. Lansing asks WW for contribution, 45; WW's address in New York on behalf of, 53-57; WW's speech mentioned, 66, 120, 256-57; WW makes personal contribution to, 78; WW refuses to appear at a Sunday meeting, 119,n1; WW on aid to Belgium and, 151; and "White House wool," 191,n3, 475; success of war fund drive, 199,n1; and Blue Devils, 307n1

American Red Cross Commission to Switzerland, 250-51,n2

American Red Cross Mission to Russia, 142n4, 234

American Red Cross Mission to Rumania, 303n1, 477

Amiens, France, 332

Amur Railway, 105

Anderson, Henry Watkins, 303,n1

Angell, Norman, 629; on league of nations, 613, 617-18; on political condition of military success, 614-21

662 INDEX

Lever Food and Fuel Control Act (1917), 161n2, 168
Le Verrier, Marie Louise, 26
Lewis, David John: and telegraph legislation, 556,n1, 623, 628-29
Lewis, Fred W., 294
Lewis, James Hamilton, 307, 435n1; WW urges to seek reelection in 1920, 603-604
Liberator, The, 93,n1
Liberty Loans: first, 123, 125-26; third, 126, 307n1
Lister, Ernest, 293,n4
Lithuania, 97-98, 630,n1
Lithuanian National Council, 630n1
Litvinov, Maksim Maksimovich, 265, 276
Livermore, Seward W., 50n1, 260n2
Lloyd George, David, 33, 47, 153, 245, 381, 395, 546, 586, 602-603, 615; and German plot in Ireland, 65, 68; wishes to have House at Supreme War Council meeting, 79, 94-95, 135; and Belgian relief, 80; and joint Allied request for more U.S. troops, 226-27, 243, 246, 252; and Irish conscription, 300n2; and intervention in Russia, 448,n1, 587-88
Lockhart, Robert Hamilton Bruce, 99, 100, 101, 102-104, 274, 378, 431; views on Russian intervention, 39-40, 112, 380-81, 398, 398-99
London *Times*, 66, 67,n1,3, 187
Long, Breckinridge: and Chinese loan, 517, 518-19, 519-20
Long, Walter Hume, 228,n1
Lorraine, 33, 245; *see also* Alsace-Lorraine
Louisiana: and woman suffrage, 237,n2, 352
Lowell, Abbott Lawrence (incorrectly named Amos Lawrence Lowell on p. 513, Vol. 43, and p. 12, Vol. 44), 152, 153,n1; on league of nations, 561-62, 586, 590-91; and Red Cross, 250-51,n2
Ludendorff, Erich Friedrich Wilhelm, 552, 554-55,n6
Ludwig III (of Bavaria), 553,n3
lynchings, 160-61, 463,n3; Walton on, 302; Moton on, 323-24, 416; WW urged to make statement against, 323-24, 476; WW promises to make statement, 346; Baker on, 476

McAdoo, Eleanor Randolph Wilson (Mrs. William Gibbs), daughter of EAW and WW, 70, 313n1
McAdoo, William Gibbs, 219-20,n1, 313n1, 570, 593-94; on conscription of railroad workers, 12, 151-52,n1; and railroad fuel question, 31, 51-52, 62, 80-93, 98; talk of resignation, 52, 69, 70, 95; talk of the presidency and, 70; House and WW discuss, 70-71; on need for revenue legislation, 119n2, 121-27, 128; issues joint statement with Garfield on fuel issue, 148,n1; on revolving fund for federal operation of coal mines, 168; and Chinese loan, 371
Macauley, Charles Raymond, 29-30
McCain, Henry Pinckney, 219, 331, 386, 418, 481, 577

McCarthy, Thomas D., 146,n2
McCormick, Vance Criswell, 69, 233, 247, 647; suggested as permanent representative in Paris, 267, 331; memorandum on coordination of Allied nonmilitary activities, 324-29
McCosh, James, 532,n5
Macedonia, 481,n1
Macfarland, Grenville Stanley, 449-50, 474
McGarrity, Joseph, 63n1
Macgowan, David Bell, 429,n1
Machado da Franca, José Francisco de Horta: *see* Alte, Viscount of
McIntyre, Frank, 35, 35-37, 75, 130, 637,n3
Mackay, Clarence Hungerford, 281,n5, 282-83, 298, 301
McKellar, Kenneth Douglas, 395, 444
MacMurray, John, 155-61
MacMurray, John Van Antwerp, 609n1
Magennis, Peter Elias, 118n1
Maginnis, Marguerite, 118n1
Magnes, Judah Leon, 98,n6
Mahany, Rowland B., 43
Making of a State: Memories and Observations, 1914-1918 (Masaryk), 358n1
Mamatey, Victor Samuel, 358n1
Manjiro, the Man Who Discovered America (Kaneko), 569n1
March, Peyton Conway, 73, 74, 243, 353, 357, 401-403, 418, 484,n1, 503, 542, 544, 577, 599; appointed Chief of Staff, 181,n6; on intervention in Russia, 182, 418-21, 479-80; on importance of all-American army divisions, 244; Jusserand meets with, 253-54
Marshall, Josephine Banks (Mrs. Charles Henry), 63,n2
Martin, Edward Sandford, 152n1
Martin, Gertrude S., 345n1
Martin, Hugh Street, 142n8, 288,n1
Martin, Thomas Staples, 10, 14, 51, 119,n2, 129, 154, 405, 592; and wire-control bill, 526, 534, 535,n1
Maryland: compulsory work laws in, 248-49,n1, 270
Masaryk, Thomas (Tomás) Garrigue, 106, 202,n1, 273, 274, 335n1, 353, 353-54, 354, 355, 398; WW meets with, 283, 358,n1; photograph, *illustration section*
Mason, Gregory, 585,n3
Masses, The: comments on trial of editors, 59n1,2, 93n1, 146,n1, 197-98, 208-209, 220, 251n2
May, Arthur James, 114n2
Mayflower, U.S.S., 440
meat industry, 308
meat-packing industry, 487n1; and Federal Trade Commission's investigation and reports, 7-9, 44, 75-77, 107-10, 178,n1, 507-11, 562,n1, 564n1
Mee-Mee, *see* Brown, Mary Celestine Mitchell
Memoranda and Letters of Dr. Muehlon (Smith, trans.), 213n8
Memorandum on Power of President to Raise Street Railway Rates, 526,n1
Merchants' Association of New York, 472n1

WOODROW WILSON

on not delivering speeches in large auditoriums, 6; elected to Académie des Sciences Morales et Politiques of the Institut de France, 27n1; presented with Baker's inscribed Frontiers of Freedom, 30,n2; address in New York on behalf of Red Cross, 53-57, 120; parades on behalf of Red Cross, 53n1, 59; makes contribution to Red Cross, 78; message to various ethnic societies, 117; approves of a mourning badge, 117; waives royalties on History of the American People on behalf of Italian-American Union, 120; on use of his discretionary war fund, 137-39, 168, 335n1, 463n1; address to joint session of Congress on new revenue legislation, 162-65, 173, 233; receives map from Foch, 178,n1; contributes proceeds from "White House wool" to Red Cross, 191,n3,